CONTENTS

THE BALANCE SHEET:
CAPITAL EMPLOYED

ASSETS:
FIXED ASSETS

CURRENT ASSETS

CURRENT LIABILITIES

THE PROFIT AND LOSS ACCOUNT

CASH FLOW

THE GROUP

OTHER TOPICS

PREFACE

'He could read a balance sheet like a book'

Obituary of the senior partner of a Big Eight firm of accountants

He was, indeed, brilliant, a leader of his profession. But he couldn't read a balance sheet like a book. We can't. No one can. And you must not expect to. A balance sheet is not a book and it cannot be read like a book.

What the writer we quote above probably meant was: 'He was really on the ball. You couldn't put one over on *him*. He knew just what questions to ask.'

Two things we emphasise: firstly, the need to study a report and accounts 'with one's mind engaged'; and, secondly, to question what one reads. We use a marker pen to highlight anything that at first reading seems significant, interesting or inconsistent. And we keep handy a note pad to jot down questions (see Chapter 31).

But to know what is significant or inconsistent and to ask the right questions it is necessary to know something about accounting, about accounts and how they are prepared, what they tell you and what they don't.

The history of investment and of the City is not merely a fascinating one, but it is a story full of the greed and incompetence on the part of banks and other institutions, of management and of investors. We seek to explain not just the way things are, the background to reports and accounts, the legislation, the Stock Exchange requirements and, above all, the accounting standards, but *why* things are the way they are – and that is a story all about horses, and stable doors that were bolted too late. Unfortunately, that is how the rules have tended to develop.

People have always tried to outwit the system. Over the years, in earlier editions, we have pointed the finger at countless individuals, companies, abuses and loopholes. Although they may not come this way again, others will follow. What we, in this book, are trying to do, is not just to provide a guide on where to look but to inculcate more than a touch of scepticism: 'If it looks too good to be true, it probably is.'

At the same time, we try to provide the reader with the confidence he needs to ask questions. Whether he is a small investor, a professional investor, an analyst working for a major institution, a lender, a journalist or someone in a trading relationship, he is entitled to ask. Admittedly, some are in a stronger position than others to insist on an answer.

But before you can ask, before you are prepared to stand up at an annual meeting, or to go up to the chairman after the meeting, with your questions, you need to be confident that you know what you are talking about. That ability, and that confidence, are what this book seeks to develop.

The book has long been used by a number of universities and colleges, and is recommended reading for several professional examinations. To assist both lecturers and the courses they teach, and readers working alone, there is a problem at the end of each Chapter to encourage readers to put our ideas into practice.

The law and references to accounting standards are as at 31 May 1999.

G.H.

A.S.

Chapter 1

COMPANY REPORTS AND ACCOUNTS – AN INTRODUCTION

This book is designed to be a practical guide to the interpretation of reports and accounts. Although frequent reference is made to the legal, accounting and Stock Exchange requirements that accounts have to meet, this is done in order to show just what information the reader should expect to find, where to look for it, and how then to use it, rather than as an explanation of how to prepare a set of accounts.

The report and accounts

The report and accounts, normally produced annually, is the principal way in which shareholders and others keep themselves informed on the activities, progress and future plans of a company. Its style and content vary somewhat in line with the directors' views on its use as a public relations vehicle. As is permitted by law, a growing number of larger companies, e.g. NATWEST GROUP, produce an annual review and summary financial statement as an alternative to their annual report and accounts, and shareholders may choose which they receive. NatWest include an interesting note in their Review:

NATWEST GROUP *Extract from annual review*

Important notice to shareholders
The Annual Review and Summary Financial Statement does not give you all the information you need to gain as full an understanding of the results of the Group and the state of affairs of the Bank or of the Group as our full Annual Report and Accounts. You can receive a free copy of our full Annual Report and Accounts by writing to ...

To keep employees informed, some companies distribute a summary of their report and accounts to all employees, or include extracts in their house newspaper. Some produce and distribute to share- holders and/or employees a separate 'company pro- file'. But others argue that any unnecessary disclo- sure is risky in case the information may be of use to competitors.

Nevertheless, there is a minimum of informa- tion that must be disclosed to comply with the law. For example, the annual report and accounts must by law contain four basic components:

1. a directors' report;
2. a profit and loss account;
3. a balance sheet; and
4. an auditors' report.

The form and content of accounts are also subject to Financial Reporting Standards, about which we will have more to say in Chapter 2, and which add to the list of required contents.

In addition, when a company's shares are listed on The Stock Exchange, the report and accounts have to contain further information prescribed by The Stock Exchange. For instance, companies listed on The Stock Exchange have to produce a half-yearly (or 'interim') report. Details are to be found in The Stock Exchange's book *The Listing Rules*, known in the City as 'The Yellow Book'. We say more about the Listing Rules in Chapter 4.

The directors' report

Under the Companies Acts, a directors' report must give a mass of information, some of which is obvious from the accounts anyway, some of which is of comparatively little interest either to shareholders or analysts, and appears to have been motivated by political considerations, e.g. contributions for political purposes, but some of which may be of vital interest and importance to anyone interpreting the accounts, e.g. the review of the year and likely future developments.

The directors' report must also state the names of the directors and provide details of their shareholdings; provide particulars of significant changes in fixed assets and provide information on important events affecting the company which have occurred since the end of the year. A very mixed bag.

Although it is not a legal requirement, most listed companies include a chairman's statement and also a chief executive's review and some a financial review (see Chapter 25).

The profit and loss account

The profit and loss account is a record of the activities of a company for a stated period of time. This period, which is called the accounting period, is normally a year. Example 1.1 shows a typical profit and loss account; and the Terminology box alongside explains the main terms used.

Accounts are required to include the figures for two periods, normally those for the year being reported on and corresponding figures ('comparatives') for the preceding year. For simplicity, at this stage we show only figures for the year.

Example 1.1 A typical profit and loss account

Profit and loss account for the year ended 31 December 2000

	£000	£000
Turnover		7,200
Cost of sales		3,600
Gross profit		3,600
Distribution costs	1,100	
Administrative expenses	1,300	
		2,400
		1,200
Other operating income		95
Trading or operating profit		1,295
Interest receivable		20
		1,315
Interest payable		100
Pre-tax profit on ordinary activities		1,215
Taxation		415
Profit on ordinary activities after taxation		800
Dividends		560
Profits retained		240

TERMINOLOGY

Profit and loss account

The **profit and loss account** is a record in monetary terms of the activities of a business during a stated period of time. This period, usually referred to as the accounting period, is normally a year. A balance sheet is drawn up on the last day of the company's accounting period.

Turnover (also called sales) represents money received, or to be received, by the business from goods or services sold during the year.

Expenses represent costs incurred in producing those goods and services. They are normally divided into:

(i) **Cost of sales** i.e. the cost of the goods themselves, e.g. raw materials and wages

(ii) **Distribution costs** i.e. the cost of getting the goods to the customer

(iii) **Administrative expenses** i.e. other expenses which cannot be or are not allocated to particular products, i.e. which do not form part of cost of sales, or under other headings.

(iv) **Interest paid** on borrowed money (**interest received** represents income from interest on money lent e.g. deposits at the bank)

Gross profit = Turnover − Cost of sales.

Operating profit or **trading profit** = Turnover − Expenses (i.e. (i) to (iii) above).

Where expenses (i) to (iii) above exceed turnover, the difference is an **operating loss**.

Other operating income is a catch-all heading for income and expenses which fall outside the above headings, e.g. found under this head might be property income of a trading company or patent income. Provision is made for the depreciation of fixed assets (see page 52). The cost of each fixed asset is written off over its expected life. Using the most common method of depreciation, **the straight line method**:

$$\text{Depreciation for the year} = \frac{\text{Cost of asset} - \text{Residual value}}{\text{Expected useful life}}$$

Depreciation is an expense appearing as part of (i) .. (iii) above, as appropriate.

Dividends are distributions to shareholders, i.e. the owners of the company, paid out of profits after tax.

Corresponding figures or 'comparatives', are those for the same item for the preceding accounting period.

The balance sheet

The balance sheet is a statement of the assets and liabilities of a company at the close of business on a given day, i.e. on the balance sheet date. The balance sheet is always drawn up on the last day of the company's accounting period.

Example 1.2 shows a typical balance sheet; and the Terminology box alongside explains the main terms used in balance sheets.

Example 1.2 A typical balance sheet

Balance Sheet as at 31 December 2000

	£000	£000	£000
Fixed assets			
Freehold land and buildings		950	
Fixtures and fittings		175	
Motor vehicles		535	
		———	1,660
Current assets			
Stock (of goods)		500	
Debtors		1,040	
Cash		5	
		———	
		1,545	
Less: Current liabilities:			
Creditors due within 1 year:			
Trade creditors	300		
Taxation payable	415		
Dividends payable	560		
Overdraft	90		
	———	1,365	
		———	
Net current assets			180
			———
Net assets			1,840
			———
Capital and reserves			
Ordinary share capital			1,000
Reserves:			
Retained profits: b/f		600	
for the year		240	
		———	
			840
			———
Ordinary shareholders' funds			1,840
			———

Double entry bookkeeping

Traditionally, companies employ what is termed double entry bookkeeping, which sees each transaction as having two aspects (rather like a coin has two sides), a 'receiver' and a 'giver'.

TERMINOLOGY
Balance sheet

A **balance sheet** is a statement of the assets and liabilities and ownership interest of an enterprise at the close of business on a stated day, i.e. on the balance sheet date.

Assets are things which a business owns and on which a book value can be placed.

Book value is cost less accumulated depreciation or, if the asset has been revalued, it is the valuation figure less any subsequent depreciation.

Liabilities are amounts owed by a business.

Net assets = all assets – all liabilities.

Fixed assets are assets (like land and buildings, plant and machinery) not held for resale but for use by the business.

Current assets are cash and other assets that the company expects to turn into cash (e.g. stock).

Assets can also be described as **tangible**, from the Latin *tango*, I touch, (e.g. motor vehicles, land and buildings) or **intangible** i.e. not susceptible to touch (e.g. patent rights and trade marks).

Current liabilities, which are usually described as 'Creditors due within 1 year', are the liabilities that the company expects to have to meet within twelve months.

As illustrated in Example 1.2, the modern accounting practice is to show the current liabilities below the current assets and to deduct them from the current assets to produce **net current assets**.

The **members** (shareholders) of a company provide some or all of the finance in the form of **share capital** (that is, they subscribe for shares) in the expectation that the company will make profits, and pay dividends.

Ordinary shareholders' funds (sometimes called ownership interest) is made up of ordinary share capital and all accumulated reserves.

Financial statements is the term which covers the annual accounts as a whole, i.e. the profit and loss account, balance sheet, cash flow statement and statements forming part of the statutory accounts, as against internal **management reports**, or published quarterly or half-yearly figures, often termed **interim statements**.

These two aspects give rise to what are termed debits and credits, respectively. The simplest way of visualising this is to imagine a traditional **cash book**. This is a record of cash received on the left hand side, and cash paid out on the right.

Transactions on the left hand side are termed **debits**, and those on the right, **credits.**

Every receipt (which produces a debit entry in the cash book) is reflected by a credit entry somewhere else in the system. For example, a receipt from a customer results in a debit entry in the cash book and a credit entry in the account of the customer. Every payment (which produces a credit entry in the cash book) is reflected by a debit entry somewhere else in the system.

An advantage of double-entry is that if one added the balance of each account, the total of the debit balances should equal that of the credit balances (i.e. the 'trial balance' should agree). Modern computer systems use control totals for a similar purpose. In this book we are not concerned with the mechanics of double-entry, but rather with the way transactions are reflected in published accounts.

HOW THE FIGURES FIT TOGETHER

One does not need to be a bookkeeper to understand accounts, but it does help to be able to envisage how the figures come together. In the case study which follows, we have kept things simple, and have worked one stage at a time, but the principles apply to companies large and small.

Basic example of a company's accounts

Arthur, Bill, Freda, and Thomas, are friends and neighbours. They live in a small village in West Sussex, and drink together in the village pub, the 'Golden Goose'. This, and the fact that, with four others, they enter the National Lottery each week as a syndicate, is really all they have in common apart, that is, from disgust at the way the village shop (owned by William Last), has 'gone to pot' – largely because of the owner's ill-health.

The week they won the Lottery was not a particularly 'good' week (47 people shared first prize). Two or three syndicate members had a grand holiday, one went on a trip to visit his daughter in Australia, ... but once the first excitement was over, they all continued to work.

At that stage the shop-owner's health deteriorated further, and there was talk of his selling up. It was Arthur who suggested that they form a company and buy the shop. Not only would it benefit the community, it would provide an investment.

Forming a company

To cut a long story short: Bill was equally enthusiastic; Freda offered to manage the shop; each member of the syndicate (eight of them) agreed to put up £5,000 to buy 5,000 shares of £1 each. Arthur became chairman, Freda, managing director, and Bill, a director. The others did not want an active role. Arthur found from a company formations specialist that it would cost £1,050 to form a company, to be called Golden Goose (1998) Ltd., with authorised capital (the maximum the directors can raise without shareholders' approval), £50,000.

If they did that, the balance sheet would be that shown below. The figures in accounts are normally supplemented by, and explained in, a series of notes, often covering many pages which, in law, form part of the accounts. In this example, we have used the notes to explain how figures are built up, not least because it is important to get into the habit of looking in the notes for further information.

 Key point

To study a set of accounts without reference to the notes is most unwise: all sorts of nasty things may be lurking in them.

GOLDEN GOOSE (1998) LTD *Balance sheet on formation:*

	Note	£	£	£
Fixed assets				
Freehold land and buildings			–	
Fixtures and fittings			–	
Motor vehicles			–	
				–
Current assets				
Stock (of goods)			–	
Debtors			–	
Cash at Bank	1		38,950	
				38,950
Less: Current liabilities:				
Creditors: due within 1 year		–		
Overdraft		–		
			–	
Net current assets				38,950
Net assets				38,950
Ordinary share capital (Authorised £50,000)				40,000
Reserves:				
Loss to date	2			(1,050)
				38,950

NOTES:

1. *Bank balance*:

Received from 8 investors at £5,000	£40,000
Less: Formation expenses	(1,050)
	38,950

2. *Profit/(Loss) to date*:

Formation expenses	(£1,050)

At one time formation expenses (termed preliminary expenses) were carried forward as an asset (an intangible asset) in the balance sheet, but it is normal today to write them off immediately.

Buying the business

Willie Last, the shopkeeper, was willing to sell to them. The premises proved to be rented (at £12,000 per annum); and the landlord agreed to transfer the lease to the new company (on their paying legal expenses of £800).

It was agreed that:

(i) on 31 December 1998 the assets of the shop were valued (for a fee of £500) at:

	£
Fixtures and fittings	8,000
Motor van	6,800
Stock, at cost	5,900
	20,700

(ii) the former owner would accept this amount for them; and
(iii) the new company would adopt these valuations in its books.
(iv) Legal expenses and valuer's fees totalled £1,300.

At this point the balance sheet would look like that shown alongside.

But we are getting a little ahead of ourselves.

What purchasers of a business should look for

No one in their right mind would buy a business without making:

(i) a detailed examination of its track record (studying copies of recent accounts and, if possible, management reports and accounts);
(ii) an estimate of its trading prospects; and
(iii) their own business plan.

And, as we shall see, our group did all those things.

GOLDEN GOOSE (1998) LTD *Balance sheet as at 31 December 1998 (immediately after acquisition of the business)*

	Note	£	£	£
Fixed assets				
Freehold land and buildings			–	
Fixtures and fittings			8,000	
Motor vehicles			6,800	
				14,800
Current assets				
Stock (of goods)			5,900	
Debtors			–	
Cash at Bank	1		16,950	
			22,850	
Less: Current liabilities:				
Creditors: due within 1 year		–		
Overdraft		–		
			–	
Net current assets				22,850
Net assets				37,650
Ordinary share capital (Authorised £50,000)				40,000
Reserves:				
Loss to date	2			(2,350)
				37,650

NOTES:

	£	£
1. *Bank balance*		
Received from 8 investors at £5,000		£40,000
Less: Formation expenses	(1,050)	
Purchase price	(20,700)	
Legal expenses and valuer's fees	(1,300)	
		(23,050)
		£16,950

	£	£
2. *Profit/Loss to date*:		
Formation expenses	(1,050)	
Legal expenses and valuer's fees	(1,300)	
		2,350

What the previous year's accounts showed

Once he saw they were serious, Willie Last provided Arthur and Freda with a copy of his previous year's accounts and auditors' report. The profit and loss account looked like this:

WILLIE LAST ESQ. *Profit and loss account for the year ended 31 December 1997*

	£	£	£
Turnover			157,200
Cost of sales			115,000
Gross profit			42,200
Distribution costs:			
Depreciation of van	2,000		
Petrol, insurance and maintenance	1,800		
		3,800	
Administrative expenses:			
Rent and rates	15,300		
Wages	3,600		
Insurance	500		
Printing etc.	450		
		19,850	
			23,650
Other operating income			–
Trading or operating profit			18,550
Interest receivable			–
			18,550
Interest payable			50
Pre-tax profit on ordinary activities			18,500

At first sight, the business was a bargain (profits of £18,500 per annum for a stake of £20,700).

But, as Arthur pointed out:

1. The accounts were for the previous completed accounting year; and Willie Last's illness only began in the current year. The figures were thus a year out of date; and related to an entirely different trading situation (when Willie was a fit man) – a mistake sometimes made even by financial journalists.
2. There was a very low charge for wages. In the accounts of a sole trader there is normally no charge for the proprietor's services. Similarly, if he owns the premises, there is no charge for rent.

Indeed, to estimate the likely profits under new ownership, whether the business is large or small, a sole trader, company or group of companies, it is normally necessary to make a number of adjustments.

Enquiries elicited that, because of Willie's illness:

1. Turnover in the immediate past year was 25% down on that in 1997.
2. It had been necessary to employ an assistant for 20 hours a week at a total cost for the year of £5,500.

A more realistic view of profitability in 1998 thus might be:

WILLIE LAST ESQ. *Estimated profit and loss account for year ended 31 December 1998*

	£	£	£
Turnover			117,900
Cost of sales			86,250
Gross profit			31,650
Distribution costs:			
Depreciation of van	2,000		
Petrol, insurance and maintenance	1,800		
		3,800	
Administrative expenses:			
Rent and rates	15,300		
Wages	9,100		
Insurance	500		
Printing etc.	450		
		25,350	
			29,150
Other operating income			–
Trading or operating profit			2,500
Interest receivable			–
			2,500
Interest payable			50
Pre-tax profit on ordinary activities			2,450

… always assuming there was no change in distribution costs or interest.

A business plan

Freda was prepared to open the shop from 9 a.m. to 6 p.m. six days a week (i.e. to work for 54 hours) but was looking for £14,000 a year; making a payroll of, say, £18,000 with the wages of a part-time van driver.

Arthur, Freda and Bill developed a simple business plan:

1. To set up a frozen foods section in the shop, and to promote it aggressively, focusing in particular on ready-prepared meals.
2. To re-equip the delivery van to provide a travelling shop specialising in frozen foods.

This would require: (i) Expenditure on fixed assets, i.e. refrigerated display cabinets and re-equipping the van, £9,800; (ii) Depreciation of fixtures and fittings of £2,450; (iii) Maintenance of additional stocks: £4,650.

Turnover they believed would return to its level prior to Willie's illness. But, in addition, they would sell frozen foods to the value of £3,500 a month; the profit margin on which would be $33\frac{1}{3}\%$. For the sake of simplicity: interest would be zero and other costs would not change. They expected to have to pay corporation tax of (for simplicity) 30% of the profit before tax.

'But', said Freda, 'one of the new frozen food customers will be the Golden Dragon. They expect a month's credit. Assuming they buy £12,000 a year, that means debtors at the end of the year of £1,000.' 'And £1,000 less cash coming in', chipped in John. 'The cash and carry won't give us any credit, but the frozen food people will allow us a month', Arthur added. 'That's creditors of £3,500.'

They projected the accounts for their first year on the basis that all changes occurred immediately.

GOLDEN GOOSE (1998) LTD. *Profit and loss account for the year 1999 (estimated)*

	£	£	£
Turnover (£157,200 + £42,000)			199,200
Cost of sales (£115,000 + £28,000)			143,000
Gross profit			56,200
Distribution costs:			
Depreciation of van	2,000		
Petrol, insurance and maintenance	1,800		
		3,800	
Administrative expenses:			
Rent and rates	15,300		
Wages	18,000		
Insurance	500		
Depreciation	2,450		
Printing etc.	450		
Formation expenses	1,050		
Legal expenses and valuer's fees	1,300		
		39,050	
			42,850
Other operating income			–
Trading or operating profit			13,350
Interest payable (receivable)			–
Pre-tax profit on ordinary activities			13,350
Corporation tax			4,005
Profit after tax			9,345

GOLDEN GOOSE (1998) LTD *Balance sheet as at 31 December 1999 (estimated)*

	Note	£	£	£
Fixed assets				
Freehold land and buildings				–
Fixtures and fittings (£8,000 + 9,800 − 2,450)			15,350	
Motor vehicles (£6,800 − 2,000)			4,800	
				20,150
Current assets				
Stock (of goods) (£5,900 + 4,650)			10,550	
Debtors			1,000	
Cash at Bank	1		25,150	
			36,700	
Less: Current liabilities:				
Creditors: due within 1 year				
Trade creditors		3,500		
Corporation Tax payable		4,005		
Overdraft		–		
			7,505	
Net current assets				29,195
Net assets				49,345
Ordinary share capital (Authorised £50,000)				40,000
Reserves:				
Profit to date				9,345
				49,345

NOTES:

1. *Bank balance*:

	£	£
Received from 8 investors at £5,000		40,000
Receipts from sales (£199,200 − 1,000)		198,200
		238,200
Less:		
Formation expenses	(1,050)	
Purchase price	(20,700)	
Legal expenses and valuer's fees	(1,300)	
Refrigerated display cabinets and re-equipping the van	(9,800)	
Goods purchased (£143,000 − 5,900 + 10,550 − 3,500)	(144,150)	
Petrol, insurance and maintenance	(1,800)	
Rent and rates	(15,300)	
Wages	(18,000)	
Insurance	(500)	
Printing etc.	(450)	
		213,050
Closing balance		25,150

But that cannot be right …

John simply did not believe the figures. 'We have £16,950 in the bank now. You say we should spend:

1. £9,800 on fixed assets (refrigerated display cabinets) and re-equipping the van.
2. £4,650 on buying additional stocks.

That would surely leave £2,500. If we make a profit of £9,345 after tax, like you say, that comes to £11,845. Yet according to the balance sheet we should have £25,150. Where has the extra £13,305 come from?'

John is not alone in seeking to explain the closing cash balance in this way. In times gone by investment analysts tried to do much the same thing, using the concept of *net cash flow*. But it is not as easy as he suggested.

Cash flow

The profit and loss account is drawn up on what is termed an 'income and expenditure basis', rather than on a 'cash basis'. That is to say, it shows as income all the revenue earned in the period whether or not it has actually been received in cash; and it shows as expenditure all the expenses incurred in the period whether or not they have actually been paid.

Perhaps the most obvious difference lies in the treatment of fixed assets and their depreciation. In accounts drawn up on a normal, 'income and expenditure', basis, fixed assets appear in the balance sheet, but a charge is made in the profit and loss account each year for their depreciation. We have more to say about depreciation in Chapter 8, but very often the provision for depreciation represents the cost of the asset less the expected net proceeds (its estimated residual value), spread evenly over the asset's estimated useful life; each year's provision being charged in the profit and loss account, and the cumulative depreciation being offset against the cost of the asset in the balance sheet.

In cash terms, however, money is paid out for the asset at the time it is purchased; and nothing is paid out by way of 'depreciation' in later years. Realising this, analysts devised the term 'net cash flow':

Net cash flow = Retained profits + Depreciation.

Net cash flow was a broad indicator of what a company would have had available to replace or expand its fixed assets, or to expand its net current assets, if it had made no issues of shares etc., and had not changed its level of borrowings.

Working in this way, analysts reasoned:

GOLDEN GOOSE (1998) LTD *Funds flow statement for the year ended 31 December 1999 (estimated)*

	£	£
Profit before tax		13,350
Add: Deprecation:		
Motor van		2,000
Refrigerated display cabinets etc.		2,450
Net cash flow		17,800
Fixed assets acquired:		
Fixtures and fittings	8,000	
Motor vehicles	6,800	
Refrigerated display cabinets	9,800	
Corporation tax paid	–	
		24,600
		(6,800)
Working capital:		
Decrease (increase) in trade creditors	(3,500)	
Increase (decrease) in trade debtors	1,000	
Increase (decrease) in stocks	10,550	
	8,050	
Increase (decrease) in cash	(14,850)	
		(6,800)

In other words:

Cash balance at the beginning of the year	£40,000
Increase (decrease) during the year	(14,850)
Cash balance at the end of the year	£25,150

which is exactly what the balance sheet showed.

It was clearly wrong to leave users to work out the cash flow situation for themselves. Accountants therefore incorporated a statement along similar lines in the accounts. After much debate, a standard form was agreed, termed a 'cash flow statement'.

Annual accounts now consist essentially of:

1. A profit and loss account;
2. A statement of total recognised gains and losses;
3. A balance sheet; and
4. A cash flow statement;

though there are a number of other supplementary statements (see Chapters 18 and 19).

The cash flow statement for GOLDEN GOOSE is at the top of page 9.

GOLDEN GOOSE (1998) LTD *Cash flow statement for the year ended 31 December 1999 (estimated)*

	£	£
Net cash flow from operating activities		9,750
Returns on investment and servicing finance:		
Dividends paid		–
Taxation:		
Corporation tax paid		–
Investment activities:		
Fixed assets acquired:		
Fixtures and fittings	8,000	
Motor vehicles	6,800	
Refrigerated display cabinets	9,800	
		(24,600)
Financing:		
Ordinary shares issued		40,000
Increase (decrease) in cash and cash equivalents		25,150

Reconciliation of Operating Profit (Loss) to Net Cash Inflow from Operating Activities	£
Operating profit	13,350
Depreciation	4,450
(Increase) in stocks	(10,550)
(Increase) in debtors	(1,000)
Increase in creditors	3,500
Net cash flow from operating activities	9,750

As we shall see in Chapter 19, because cash flow statements cover not only cash but cash at bank and overdrafts, a number of other reconciliation statements are required.

Problem 1.1

Elcho (Mossdale) Ltd is a small company manufacturing a simple safety device. Chairman and managing director, Mr Charles Farnesbarn, is offered a two year contract by JQB, a do-it-yourself chain, which would double the current production and turnover of the company. It would be necessary to acquire additional plant and machinery costing £60,000. To do this, Farnesbarn seeks overdraft facilities from the company's bankers. Currently, the company has an overdraft limit of £50,000 and Farnesbarn is seeking to increase this to £110,000.

Profit after tax to turnover is running at 2.6%, so Farnesbarn is looking for profits to increase by, perhaps, £25,000 per annum. He presents his bank manager with accounts for the last trading year – see alongside. Although such facilities would earn the bank 3% or 4% over base rate on the amount outstanding, the bank manager is of a mind to reject Farnesbarn's request. Suggest three reasons why that might be so.

For solutions to problems, see Appendix 5, page 297.

ELCHO (MOSSDALE) LTD
Profit and loss account for last year

	£	£
Turnover		600,000
Cost of sales (including depreciation £10,000)		460,000
Gross profit		140,000
Distribution costs:		
Depreciation of motor vehicles	5,000	
Petrol, insurance and maintenance	11,900	
		16,900

Administrative expenses:	£		
Rent and rates	43,300		
Wages	50,000		
Insurance	2,500		
Printing etc.	1,450		
Legal expenses etc.	1,300		
		98,550	
			115,450

		£
Trading or operating profit		24,550
Interest payable		2,000
Pre-tax profit on ordinary activities		22,550
Corporation tax		6,765
Net profit after tax		15,785

Balance sheet at end of last year

Fixed assets		£
Plant and machinery	40,000	
Motor vehicles	20,000	
		60,000
Current assets		
Stock (raw materials, work in progress and finished goods)	100,000	
Debtors	65,000	
Cash	650	
	165,650	
Less: Current liabilities:		
Trade creditors	45,000	
Corporation tax	6,765	
Overdraft	41,385	
	93,150	
		72,500
Net assets		132,500

		£
Ordinary share capital		100,000
Reserves:		
Profit and loss account:		
Balance b/f	16,715	
Profit for the year retained	15,785	
		32,500
Ordinary shareholders' funds		132,500

Chapter 2

FINANCIAL REPORTING STANDARDS AND PRINCIPLES

FINANCIAL REPORTING STANDARDS

Introduction

Until 1990 the Accounting Standards Committee (ASC) was the authority on the treatment and presentation of company accounts.

It was made up of representatives from the main accounting Institutes and Associations in the UK and Ireland, and exercised its authority by issuing Statements of Standard Accounting Practice (SSAPs).

The system had three serious drawbacks:

1. As the unanimous agreement of all members was required before an SSAP was issued, there was often compromise.

   The worst example was on the treatment of goodwill in an acquisition. Two fundamentally different treatments were allowed and, of course, companies chose whichever treatment suited them.
2. Although the ASB's work supplemented the requirements of the Companies Acts, there were no legal sanctions to compel companies to comply with SSAPs.
3. Standards did not always command wholehearted acceptance by either the accounting or the business community. See, for instance, Chapter 29 regarding attempts to impose systems of inflation accounting.

Competition for business was rife between the leading firms of accountants, who became prepared to take a very flexible view of the rules in order to retain their existing clients and acquire new ones.

Barry Riley summed up the situation pretty succinctly in the *Financial Times* in December 1990:

FINANCIAL TIMES *Extract from article on accountants December 1990*

Essentially the external auditor has ceased to devote himself primarily to presenting the users of accounts with the truth, but instead has come to help the financial director of his client company to show his results in the best possible light, taking due advantage of all the loopholes.

The Dearing Report

On the recommendations of a committee chaired by Sir Ron Dearing the Government set up a new structure for setting and enforcing accounting standards, headed by the Financial Reporting Council (FRC). It also included a definition of 'accounting standards' in the Companies Act and, where a company's accounts do not comply with the requirements of the Act, the court is given the power to order the preparation of revised accounts at the expense of the directors (CA 1985 s. 254B). It is this that gives accounting standards their teeth.

The present structure

The FRC is constituted as a company limited by guarantee, and its constitution provides for a council whose function is to determine general policy.

The chairman and three deputy chairmen of the council are appointed jointly by the Secretary of State for Trade and Industry and the Governor of the Bank of England. The aim is that the Council should include a wide and balanced representation at the most senior level of preparers, auditors and users of accounts and others interested in them.

Reporting to the FRC are two bodies:

1. The *Financial Reporting Review Panel* (FRRP), which enquires into financial statements where it appears that the requirements of the Companies Act, principally that the financial statements show a true and fair view, might have been breached. The FRRP is autonomous in carrying out its function.

    The role of the Panel is to examine departures from the accounting requirements of the Companies Acts and, if necessary, to seek an order from the court to remedy them.

    It does not scrutinise on a routine basis all company accounts falling within its ambit; it acts upon matters drawn to its attention, either directly or indirectly. Experience shows that it is both able and willing to take on Britain's larger groups and professional firms, and is able to make them toe the line. Companies publicly examined include BRITISH GAS (now BG), FOREIGN & COLONIAL the UK's biggest investment trust, ROYAL BANK OF SCOTLAND and SECURICOR.

    Where a company has to revise its accounts, its reputation can be severely damaged. For example ASSOCIATED NURSING SERVICES, which had been in trouble with the Review Panel in 1992, was in serious trouble five years later, as the *Investors Chronicle* reported in February 1997:

    ASSOCIATED NURSING SERVICES *Extract from Investors Chronicle 21 February 1997*

    OFF BALANCE
    An accounting watchdog this week fired a warning shot at the property industry when it told Associated Nursing Services (ANS), a nursing home operator, to revise its accounts for 1995 and 1996.

    After an 18-month investigation the Financial Reporting Review Panel said the way ANS had treated the sale and leaseback of its nursing homes did not comply with accepted accounting standards. For the year ending March 1997, ANS's earnings per share will be reduced by 45 per cent.

    The *Investors Chronicle* followed this up in July 1998 with a piece entitled 'Accounting policies still not care-free' and gave a Sell recommendation. As shown in the adjoining column, the share price movement was a clear indicator of the loss of confidence.

2. The *Accounting Standards Board* (ASB), which develops, issues and keeps accounting standards up to date.

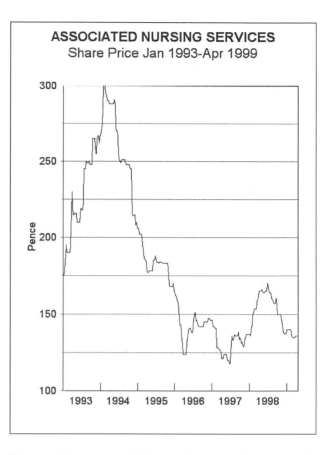

Figure 2.1 Associated Nursing Services: loss of confidence

In addition, the ASB has set up an *Urgent Issues Task Force* (UITF). Its main role is to assist the ASB in areas where an accounting problem exists by providing an interim solution (i.e. a pronouncement on the subject) pending the development and issue of an accounting standard.

Financial Reporting Standards

The Companies Act 1989 not only introduced into the Companies Act 1985 a definition of 'accounting standards', it required that directors of companies (other than most small or medium sized companies) disclose in the accounts:

(a) whether the accounts have been prepared in accordance with applicable accounting standards;
(b) particulars of any material departure from those standards; and
(c) the reasons for the departure.

Accounting standards issued by the ASB are known as Financial Reporting Standards (FRSs) and Exposure Drafts as Financial Reporting Exposure Drafts (FREDs).

Where an area is particularly important or controversial, ASB's practice is to issue a Discussion Paper which, after taking account of comment by interested parties, leads to a FRED.

11

Fifteen FRSs have so far been published, including FRS 1, which requires the annual report and accounts to contain a cash flow statement, and FRS 3, which requires a statement of total recognised gains and losses.

In addition, at its first meeting, the ASB unanimously agreed to adopt all the extant SSAPs published by its predecessor, the ASC, thereby giving them statutory clout. The financial reporting standards currently in force are listed in Appendix 1.

Statements of Recommended Practice

Statements of Recommended Practice (SORPs) are developed by bodies recognised by the ASB to provide guidance on the application of accounting standards to specific industries, e.g. the British Bankers' Association's SORP on the treatment of securities. Companies are encouraged to comply with SORPs, but they are not mandatory.

International accounting standards

Certain aspects of the traditional body of UK accounting principles are, in the words of the ASB, 'becoming increasingly out of step with developments internationally.' To help facilitate international co-operation and harmonisation, the Board is working with other leading national standard-setting bodies, as well as the International Accounting Standards Committee (IASC). But 'if the Board is to participate meaningfully and credibly in international debates about financial reporting, it must move closer to the conceptual frameworks of other leading standard-setters.'

PRINCIPLES OF FINANCIAL REPORTING

Need for a conceptual framework

One criticism that had for a long time been levelled at UK accounting standards was the absence of agreement on the fundamental principles of accounting and reporting. This made it difficult to produce a consistent and coherent standards framework.

Fundamental accounting concepts

Prior to the formation of the ASB, four fundamental accounting concepts had been laid down by the ASC in SSAP2, *Disclosure of accounting policies*:

1. The *going concern concept*: the accounts are compiled on the assumption that there is no intention or need to go into liquidation or to curtail the current level of operations significantly.
2. The *accruals (or matching) concept*: revenue and costs are accrued (accounted for) as they are earned or incurred, not as the money is received or paid, and revenue and profits are matched with associated costs and expenses by including them in the same accounting period.
3. The *consistency concept:* accounting treatment of like items is consistent from one period to the next.
4. The *concept of prudence*, which is the overriding concept, demands that:

    (a) revenue and profits are not anticipated;
    (b) provision is made for all known liabilities (expenses and losses), whether the amount is known with certainty or has to be estimated.

The ASB has retained these concepts, which it regards as 'bedrock' and is incorporating them in its *Statement of Principles for Financial Reporting*.

Statement of Principles for Financial Reporting

The *Statement of Principles for Financial Reporting*, which was published as an Exposure Draft (ED) in 1995, set out to meet these criticisms. But progress is slow. The ED received so much comment that it had to be reissued in March 1999 as a Revised ED (RED), together with a Technical Summary and an Introductory Booklet.

As Shakespeare might have put it: 'Me thinks they do explain too much'.

Both the ED and the RED have been based on the International Accounting Standards Committee's (IASC's) *Framework for the Preparation and Presentation of Financial Statements*, with the hope and belief that if standard setters work with a common set of principles it will be easier to achieve harmonisation of accounting practice with other countries.

As well as several fairly obvious truisms – the need for reliability, relevance, consistency, completeness, neutrality and understandability to the user – the ED also spells out a number of important accounting concepts in addition to those in SSAP 2:

*   *'Substance over form'*: This concept was introduced by FRS 3. It requires items to be accounted for so as to reflect their commercial substance rather than their legal form, if these differ. For example, where a company is for all practical purposes the owner of an asset, but is not technically the *legal* owner, the asset should

be included in the company's balance sheet. This could occur where a company was already deriving virtually all the commercial benefit from an asset, and had an indefinite option to buy it from its owner for a nominal sum.

- *Materiality:* If any information is not material it does not have to be included in financial statements. Although the ED doesn't give a definition of materiality, SSAP3 *Earnings per share* did so in the context of disclosure of fully diluted earnings per share (f.d. eps – see Chapter 18), which did not need to be given if the dilution was not material. Dilution of 5% or more was regarded as material.

- *Comparability:* Users need to be able to compare an entity's financial information over time in order to identify trends in its financial performance and financial position.

   They also need to be able to compare the financial information of different entities in order to evaluate their relative financial performance and financial position. (RED para. 3. 19).

In practice comparability over time is distorted unless figures are adjusted to allow for the effects of general inflation. This is demonstrated in Chapter 29 where JOHN LAING'S earnings over five years are adjusted by the movement of the Retail price index (RPI) during the period.

Comparability over time can also be distorted if a company changes its accounting policies. For example the videotape hire company CITYVISION, before it was taken over by BLOCKBUSTER, a US company in the same business, revised the estimated useful life of its tape libraries, depreciating them over 30 months instead of 15 months. This increased reported profits by nearly 60%.

Comparability between companies can be distorted if their accounting policies are different; for example CABLE & WIRELESS and BRITISH TELECOM depreciate similar equipment over different useful lives.

Comparability between companies can also be distorted by differences in the way assets are financed. For example, a retailer which owns all its outlets cannot be fairly compared with a similar retailer that rents all its outlets, unless the analyst adjusts the figures to allow for the difference. Adjustments are also needed if the companies' financial years are not coterminous.

What financial statements comprise

The annual report of the auditors to the company's shareholders often begins 'We have audited the financial statements on pages xx to yy', i.e. the pages containing the financial statements (but nothing else unless specifically stated).

These include all the primary statements we

described in Chapter 1:

- Profit and loss account
- Statement of recognised gains and losses
- Balance sheet
- Cash flow statement.

Financial statements also include:

- The notes to the financial statements
- The statement of accounting policies

The notes and the primary financial statements form an integrated whole, and should be read as such to obtain a complete picture.

The need to read the notes

The role of the notes is to amplify and explain the primary financial statements, and it can be very misleading to read the primary financial statements in isolation.

Although the 1995 ED says 'disclosure of information in the notes to the financial statements does not correct or justify a misrepresentation or omission in the primary financial statements' (ED para. 6.13), some companies have certainly tried it on in the past, and will probably do so in the future. Let us give you two examples from the accounts of now defunct companies:

1. A year or so before its demise the Southampton-based golfing and tennis hotel company LEADING LEISURE's P&L account showed a pre-tax profit of £6.7m. Note 1 to the accounts reported that trading profit generated by the disposal of properties to joint ventures amounted to £10m. Note 12 revealed additions to loans to related companies of £35.8m.

   A sceptical analyst might suspect that Leading Leisure had loaned its joint venture partner the money to buy a 50% stake in the properties, and that the price of the 50% stake had been pitched to give Leading Leisure a £10m trading profit.

   Amongst other little gems in the notes, note 6 showed an extraordinary item of £1.3m 'Reorganisation and aborted fund raising costs.' There was obviously more than one Doubting Thomas about. In the next twelve months or so the share price fell from 96p to 2p, at which point the shares were suspended. A week later the banks called in administrative receivers.

2. RESORT HOTELS provides our second cautionary tale about the dangers of not reading the notes. As well as running its own hotels, Resort had management contracts to run a number of hotels financed by Business Expansion Schemes (a tax break to encourage investment in young and expanding companies).

Resort charged these BES financed hotels management fees. The hotels weren't profitable enough to be able to pay the fees. But the unpaid fees were counted as income by Resort, thus bolstering Resort's profits and, at the same time, producing an ever increasing debtor item of management fees due in Resort's balance sheet. Eventually the bubble burst.

In the last report and accounts before its demise, Resort's balance sheet did give a warning clue: an alarming rise in 'Amounts due from managed companies' from £8.646m to £12.987m, an increase of £4.341m.

But you had to read the notes to find out what was actually going on. Note 1 showed a breakdown of turnover between Hotel operations £11.874m and Hotel management fees £4.219m, almost exactly the increase in the amounts due from managed companies.

The objective of financial statements

The objective of financial statements is to provide information about the financial position and performance of an enterprise that is useful to a wide range of users for assessing the stewardship of management and for making economic decisions (ED para. 1.1).

Users and their information needs

Financial information about the activities and resources of an entity is typically of interest to many people. Although some of these people are able to command the preparation of special purpose financial reports in order to obtain the information they need, the rest – usually the vast majority – will need to rely on general purpose financial reports (RED para. 1.1). As the RED points out, Annual Reports and Accounts and Interim Reports are of interest not only to Investors, but to:

- Lenders (although banks demand and get a lot more timely and detailed information than is generally available);
- Suppliers and other trade creditors (to decide how much credit to allow a company);
- Customers (a retailer to assess the financial strength of a potential supplier);
- Employees (whether to buy some shares, or to start looking for another job);
- Governments and their agencies (who are a nosey lot at the best of times), and
- the General Public (for example where a company makes a substantial contribution to a local economy by providing employment and using local suppliers).

What users look for

Economic decisions often require *an evaluation of the enterprise's ability to generate cash* and the timing and certainty of its generation. To do this users focus on the enterprise's (i) financial position, (ii) performance and (iii) cash flows; and use these in predicting expected cash flows.

The *financial position* of an enterprise encompasses the economic resources it controls, its financial structure, its liquidity and solvency, and its capacity to adapt to changes in the environment in which it operates. Much, but not all, the information on financial position needed is *provided by the balance sheet*.

The *performance* of an enterprise comprises the return obtained by the enterprise on the resources it controls, including the cost of its financing. Information on performance is *provided by the profit and loss account* and *the statement of total recognised gains and losses*.

Controversial areas

At the heart of any statement of principles lie questions of recognition:

- When exactly *is* something (i) an asset; (ii) a liability?
  and
- Just when *does* one recognise (i) a gain; (ii) a loss?

For example, a well known construction and housebuilding company used to have an accounting policy which said that the profit on building houses should only be recognised when all the houses in a development had been sold. This gave the directors wonderful flexibility: they could (and did) build an estate of say 200 houses, sell 199 of them, and keep one unsold until they wanted to bring the profit on the whole estate into their accounts. This may have been extremely *prudent*, but it was hardly *true and fair*.

The Draft Statement is controversial, so we will not spell out its proposals, some of which are certain to change. Instead, in coming chapters we seek to explain, as we consider individual parts of the financial statements, what we perceive to be UK GAAP (Generally Accepted Accounting Principles) as they stand currently.

Accounting policies

SSAP 2 requires the accounting policies (the various bases on which the accounts have been prepared) to be disclosed. They are usually shown after the accounts proper and either immediately before the notes to the accounts or as the first note. But some companies like BRITISH TELECOM and CADBURY SCHWEPPES show them at the beginning of their accounts, immediately before their P & L account.

Typically, statements of accounting policies include the basis of accounting for: sales (treatment of VAT and duties); deferred taxation; depreciation of fixed assets; investment grants; research and development; stocks and work in progress; extraordinary items; translation of currencies; plus any items specially related to the company's business, such as the treatment of long-term contracts, hire-purchase transactions or growing timber.

As an illustration of accounting policies we have chosen THE BODY SHOP, firstly because it's a well-known name in the high street, and secondly it's a very interesting company to study. We will look at the report and accounts in detail in Chapter 31. In this illustration we have made some comments in square brackets:

THE BODY SHOP *Accounting policies 1998*
The financial statements have been prepared under the historical cost convention and in accordance with applicable accounting standards ...

The principal accounting policies, which have not changed in the year, are:

BASIS OF CONSOLIDATION The Group uses the acquisition method of accounting to consolidate the results of subsidiary undertakings and the results of subsidiary undertakings are included from the date of acquisition to the date of disposal.

[The other method, the merger method, takes in the acquired company's results for the whole year in which the acquisition is made.]

GOODWILL Goodwill arising on the acquisition of a subsidiary or business is the difference between the consideration paid and the fair value of the assets and liabilities acquired. Goodwill is written off immediately to reserves.

VALUATION OF INVESTMENTS Investments held as fixed assets are stated at cost less any provision for a permanent diminution in value.

DEPRECIATION Depreciation is provided to write off the cost, less estimated residual values, of all tangible fixed assets, except for freehold land, over their expected useful lives.

It is calculated using the following rates:

Freehold buildings –	Over 50 years
Leasehold property –	Over the period of the respective leases
Plant and equipment –	Over 3 to 20 years

[3 to 20 years is rather vague. Most companies show more detail, e.g. the rates for motor vehicles, computer equipment.]

STOCKS Stocks are valued at the lower of cost and net realisable value. Cost is calculated as follows:

Raw materials	Cost of purchase on first in first-out basis.
Work in progress and finished goods	Cost of raw materials and labour together with attributable overheads.

Net realisable value is based on estimated selling price less further costs to completion and disposal.

THE BODY SHOP INTERNATIONAL EMPLOYEE SHARE TRUST The company is deemed to have control of the assets, liabilities, income and cost of the Body Shop International Employee Share Trust (EST). It has therefore been included in the financial statements of the Group and the Company in accordance with the Urgent Issues Task Force (UITF) 13.

FOREIGN CURRENCY Profit and loss accounts and assets and liabilities of foreign subsidiary undertakings are translated into sterling at the rates of exchange ruling on the balance sheet date ...

RESEARCH AND DEVELOPMENT Research and development expenditure is charged to the profit and loss account in the year in which it is incurred.

DEFERRED TAXATION Provision is made for timing differences between the treatment of certain items for taxation and accounting purposes to the extent that it is probable that a liability or asset will crystallise. [This is at present the standard practice in the UK. But it allows too much discretion to individual companies. It is out of line with International Accounting Standards, where full provision is made for deferred tax, whether or not the company thinks it will probably crystallise.]

LEASED ASSETS Assets held under finance leases are capitalised at amounts approximating to the present value of the minimum lease payments payable over the term of the lease. The corresponding leasing commitments are shown as amounts payable to the lessor. ...

PENSION COSTS Contributions to the Group's defined contribution pension scheme are charged to the profit and loss account in the year in which they become payable.

Do not expect to understand fully the significance of the company's accounting policies at this stage. Just what each of THE BODY SHOP's policies means will become clear in subsequent chapters.

Problem 2.1
State the four fundamental accounting concepts. Explain why each is important to users of accounts.

Chapter 3

FORMING A COMPANY

References: Tables A and B of the Schedule to the Companies (Tables A to F) Regulations 1985.

Incorporation of a company

When a company is formed by incorporation under the Companies Acts a Certificate of Incorporation is issued and the company assumes a legal identity separate from its shareholders.

Before incorporation can take place, a Memorandum of Association and Articles of Association have to be drawn up and filed with the Registrar of Companies in England and Wales or with the Registrar of Companies in Scotland.

Memorandum of Association

The Memorandum lays down the rules which govern the company in its relations with the outside world. It states the name of the company; the country in which the Registered Office will be situated; the objects of the company (i.e. activities the company may pursue); the authorised share capital; the nominal value of the shares; a list of initial subscribers and whether the liability of members (shareholders) is limited. An example is given in Table B of the First Schedule to the Companies (Tables A to F) Regulations 1985.

Articles of Association

The Articles lay down the internal rules within which the directors run the company. The main items covered are:

(a) the issue of shares, the rights attaching to each class of share, the consent required for the alteration of the rights of any class of shareholders, and any restrictions on the transfer of shares;
(b) the procedure for board and general meetings

and for altering the authorised share capital;
(c) the election and retirement of directors, their duties and their powers, including borrowing powers;
(d) the declaration of dividends;
(e) the procedure for winding up the company.

A model set of Articles is given in Table A of the Schedule to the Companies (Tables A to F) Regulations 1985.

Members' (shareholders') liability

The liability of members (shareholders) of a company can either be limited by shares or by guarantee, or the liability can be unlimited.

Limited by shares

This is the method normally used for a company engaged in business activities. If the shares are fully paid, the members' liability is limited to the money they have put up: the maximum risk a shareholder runs is to lose all the money he has paid for his shares, and no further claim can be made on him for liabilities incurred by the company. If the shares are only partly paid, shareholders (and to a limited extent former shareholders) can be called upon to subscribe some or all of the unpaid part, but no more than that.

Limited by guarantee

This method is used for charitable and similar organisations, where funds are raised by donations and no shares are issued. The liability is limited to the amount each member personally guarantees, which is the maximum each member may be called upon to pay in the event of liquidation. This form of incorporation is not normally used for a business.

Unlimited

This method is used by professional firms that want the tax advantages of being a company; the members have joint and several liability in the same way as a partnership (each member can individually be held entirely responsible).

Public company

Reference: Companies Act 1985, Sections 1 (3), 11 and 25.

A public company is defined as one:

(a) which is limited by shares or guarantee, with a minimum issued share capital of £50,000, or such other sum specified by statutory instrument (the shares must be at least 25% paid up, with any share premium fully paid up); and

(b) whose Memorandum states that it is a public company; and

(c) which has been correctly registered as a public company.

All other companies are private companies.

A public company registered as such on incorporation cannot do business until the Registrar of Companies has issued a certificate that he is satisfied that the share capital requirements have been met.

The name of a public company must in all cases end either with the words 'Public Limited Company' or with the abbreviation 'PLC', neither of which may be preceded by the word 'Limited'.

A public company does not automatically have its shares listed on The Stock Exchange, but the process of obtaining a listing (see Chapter 4) is often referred to as 'going public', as a private company cannot obtain a listing on The Stock Exchange.

Private company

A 'private company' is a company that is not a public company (CA 1985, s. 1 (3)).

A company limited by shares or by guarantee (not being a public company) must have 'Limited' as the last word in its name (CA 1985, s. 25). Thus all companies whose names end with 'Limited' are private companies.

Chartered company

Companies may also be established by Royal Charter, the method used before any Companies Acts existed; for example, the PENINSULAR & ORIENTAL STEAM NAVIGATION COMPANY was incorporated by Royal Charter in 1840. The legal position of a chartered company is similar to an incorporated company, except that any change to the Articles involves a petition to the Privy Council.

Close company

Reference: Income and Corporation Taxes Act 1988, Section 414.

Broadly speaking, a close company is one which is under the control of five or fewer persons together with their associates or is under the control of its directors.

The original rules on close companies, introduced in 1922, were designed to prevent individuals avoiding high rates of personal tax by not making distributions from companies they controlled. With the highest rate of personal tax now no longer a great deal higher than Corporation Tax, these rules, the 'apportionment' provisions, were abolished in the Finance Act 1989. However, a number of fairly obscure tax provisions are still in force for close companies, including special rules on loans to controlling shareholders/directors.

A listed company is not a close company if shares carrying not less than 35% of the voting power are unconditionally and beneficially held by the public.

The Stock Exchange requires a listed company to include, in its annual report, a statement showing whether or not, as far as the directors are aware, the company is a close company.

Small and medium-sized companies

Small and medium-sized companies are defined by the Companies Act 1989 as companies meeting two or more of the following criteria:

	Small company	Medium-sized company
Turnover not exceeding	£2.8m*	£11.2m*
Balance sheet total not exceeding	£1.4m*	£5.6m*
Number of employees not exceeding	50	250

* Updated periodically to take account of inflation.

Small and medium-sized private companies are permitted to file abbreviated accounts but they are still required to send full accounts to their members.

Problem 3.1

1. How would you tell whether a company was (a) a public or (b) a private limited company; or (c) was one limited by guarantee; or (d) was an unlimited company?

2. XY plc is a close company. How would you tell? Why might it concern an investor?

Chapter 4

ADMISSION TO LISTING

Stock Exchange listing – 'quoted companies'

Reference: The London Stock Exchange's book *The Listing Rules*, known as 'The Yellow Book'.

Provided that it meets certain criteria, a public company may have its shares and/or debentures, unsecured loan stocks and warrants 'listed', i.e. included in The Stock Exchange Official List, so that a market is 'made' in the securities. Although it is usual for all the securities of a company to be listed, it is possible for this not to be the case. For example, SAINSBURY's preference shares were listed for many years before its ordinary shares were offered to the public.

Companies which have securities that are listed are often referred to as 'quoted companies', 'having a quotation' or 'being listed', although it is the company's securities that are listed, not the company itself. 'Having a quotation' is simply the old term for being 'listed', and the department which deals with applications for listing, the Stock Exchange's Listing Department, used to be called the Quotations Department.

Requirements for listing

The minimum legal requirements that a company has to meet before any of its securities can be listed are contained in Part 4 of the Financial Services Act 1986, which implements in the United Kingdom four EEC directives, known as the Admission directive, the Listing Particulars directive, the Interim Reports directive, and the Mutual Recognition directive on the UK listing of EEC companies listed elsewhere in the EEC.

These requirements are incorporated in The Stock Exchange's *The Listing Rules* (The Yellow Book), together with The Stock Exchange's own requirements.

Listing Particulars (prospectus)

Chapter 6 of The Yellow Book contains details of the contents of Listing Particulars, which have to be supplied to The Stock Exchange for approval prior to listing, and which have to be included in any prospectus inviting initial public subscription for the company's shares.

The Listing Particulars are designed to ensure that the company makes available sufficient information on its history, current position and future prospects to enable the general public to assess the value of the company's shares as an investment, and they are very comprehensive. The prospectus issued by a company when it goes public is therefore a most valuable source of information.

Minimum size of issue

The Stock Exchange has to satisfy itself that sufficient dealings are likely to take place in the class of security for which application is being made to make a realistic market, and thus justify a listing. The Yellow Book lays down two minimum criteria for listing – the expected market value of the securities for which listing is sought (the expected market price multiplied by the number of shares issued and to be issued: currently a minimum of £700,000 for shares and £200,000 for debt securities), and the proportion of shares to be held by the public (currently 25% of any class of share).

Keeping the public informed

The Stock Exchange also has to ensure that the general public will be kept satisfactorily informed of the company's activities and progress in the future, and that the shareholders' interests will be adequately protected: this is done by requiring an applicant for listing to accept 'Continuing

Obligations' as a condition of admission to and subsequent maintenance of listing.

Continuing Obligations

Chapter 9 of The Yellow Book deals with the Continuing Obligations of listed companies, designed to protect shareholders and to keep them properly informed. Additional continuing obligations are contained in Chapters 10 to 16.

Companies are required to submit to The Stock Exchange through the company's official sponsors, normally brokers, drafts for approval of all circulars to holders of securities, notices of meetings, forms of proxy and notices by advertisement to holders of bearer securities.

Companies are also required to notify The Stock Exchange of profit announcements; dividend declarations; material acquisitions; changes of directors; proposed changes in the nature of the business and any other information necessary to enable holders of the company's listed securities and the public to appraise the position of the company and to avoid the establishment of a false market in its listed securities.

In particular a company must notify the Company Announcements Office, by way of a warning announcement, of information which is likely to lead to substantial movements in the price of its securities if at any time the necessary degree of confidentiality cannot be maintained, or that confidentiality has or may have been breached.

In addition, amongst various requirements on interim reports, proxy voting, registration of securities and several other topics, The Yellow Book requires companies to include in the annual report and accounts:

(a) if the results for the period under review differ by 10% or more from any published forecast or estimate by the company for that period, an explanation of the difference;

(b) the amount of interest capitalised;

(c) particulars of the waiving of emoluments by any director, and of the waiving of dividends by any shareholder;

(d) the name of the principal country in which each subsidiary operates;

(e) particulars of each associated undertaking;

(f) the identity of independent non-executive directors with a short biographical note on each;

(g) in the case of a company incorporated in the UK, a statement as to whether or not it has complied with with 'The Combined Code' on corporate governance (see Chapter 26), which must be reviewed by the auditors.

(h) details of each director's beneficial and non-beneficial interests in the company's shares and options;

(i) information on holdings, other than by directors, of 3% or more of any class of voting capital;

(j) details of any authority for the purchase by the company of its own shares, and details of any purchases made otherwise than through the market;

(k) details of shares issued for cash other than pro rata to existing shareholders;

(l) where a company has listed shares in issue and is a subsidiary of another company, particulars of the participation by the parent in any placing;

(m) particulars of significant contracts during the year in which any director is or was materially interested;

(n) a statement by the directors that the company is a going concern;

(o) a report to shareholders by the Remuneration Committee.

Listed companies are also expected to issue their report and accounts within six months of their year end, but may apply for the six-month period to be extended if they have significant overseas interests.

Methods of obtaining a listing

Chapter 4 of The Yellow Book describes the ways in which a company can obtain a listing. Briefly, they are as follows:

1. *Offer for sale*

   An offer for sale is the most common method of obtaining a listing. Both new and/or existing securities can be offered to the public. The issuing house or the sponsoring broker purchases the securities from existing securities holders and/or from the company, and offers them on to the public at a slightly higher price.

2. *Offer for subscription*

   An invitation is made to the public by, or on behalf of, an issuer to subscribe for new shares or other securities.

3. *Offer for sale by tender*

   This is a variation of methods 1 or 2, in which applicants are invited to bid for securities at or above a minimum issue price. The securities are then all sold at one price, the 'striking price', which may be the highest price at which all the securities can be sold, or a little lower, if this is necessary to ensure a good spread of holders.

4. *Placing*

   Securities are placed with specified persons or clients of the sponsor or any securities house assisting in the placing. There is no offer to the public and no general offer to existing holders.

5. *Intermediaries offer*

Securities are offered by, or on behalf of, the issuer to intermediaries for them to allocate to their own clients.

6. *Introduction*

An introduction is used where the company's securities are already widely held and/or are already listed outside the United Kingdom, or where a new holding company issues its securities in exchange for those of one or more listed companies; there is no formal offer of securities, but a listing is obtained for existing securities.

Methods 1 to 5 are referred to broadly as 'new issues', because the company's securities are new to the stock market, although only method 2 necessarily involves the issue of any new securities.

Alternative Investment Market

Reference: The Stock Exchange Rules, Chapter 16 – AIM Admission Rules

The Alternative Investment Market, AIM, was set up in 1995 to provide an alternative source of capital and a trading platform for companies unable or unwilling to join the Official List.

The entry requirements are less demanding than for a full listing:

- no requirement for a minimum trading record;
- no minimum levels of capitalisation;
- no requirement for any given percentage of the share capital of the company to be in public hands.

Although entry documentation has been kept as simple as possible, entrants to AIM must provide a prospectus or similar document which meets European Union directives, and audited accounts set out under company law. Companies must arrange for a member firm to support trading. They must also meet certain ongoing obligations including publication of unaudited interim figures and of all directors' dealings.

Price sensitive information must be published promptly; and trading on the new market is subject to the same level of surveillance and supervision as the Official List. The new market has proved extremely popular; a huge variety of companies have joined, with market capitalisations ranging from about £1m to more than £100m.

By the end of 1998 more than 300 companies were trading on AIM.

Tradepoint

This is an entirely independent market which began trading in September 1995, dealing in 400 already listed equities. By March 1999 this had been increased to over 2,000 equities. It is *order driven*, i.e. it matches buy and sell orders, in contrast to the London Stock Exchange, which was entirely *quote driven,* i.e., market makers make bid and offer prices in shares. Almost all overseas markets are order driven.

The Stock Exchange Trading System (SETS)

In response to Tradepoint the London Stock Exchange, deeply embedded in the traditions of the quote driven market and the vested interests of the market makers, finally launched its own order driven system, SETS, which was opened by the Chancellor, Gordon Brown, in October 1997. Initially SETS only covered the 100 largest quoted companies, although stocks that drop out of the FTSE 100 Index will continue to be traded on the system. By April 1999 more than half the business in shares of FTSE 100 companies was being done on SETS.

The plan is, in time, to extend coverage to include companies in the FTSE 250 Index of mid-cap stocks.

Reuters intervenes

The competition from SETS restricted Tradepoint's market share to around 1%. This prevented it from becoming profitable, and it looked as though it might go under until it was rescued by a consortium led by REUTERS.

Backed by the consortium, Tradepoint should be able to mount a formidable challenge to the dominance of the London Stock Exchange in the UK equity market.

Problem 4.1

From an investor's point of view, what are the advantages and disadvantages of a quote driven market, compared with an order driven market?

Chapter 5

SHARE CAPITAL AND RESERVES

SHARE CAPITAL

A key point to check is whether shares in a company are widely held or whether the company is under the control of one person, or of a number of people, e.g. family controlled.

The normal means of control is to have at least 50% of the votes. Simple if there is only one class of share, and each share carries one vote.

But there are complications when there is more than one class, with different voting rights, or there is a 'golden share' which carries an all powerful vote in certain circumstances.

 Control

If a company is under the control of one person or group of persons, the other investors can be on a hiding to nothing. Check Directors holdings and look out for any note on Substantial shareholdings, e.g.:

MAXWELL COMMUNICATION CORPORATION *Paragraph in the 1990 Report of the Directors*

Substantial shareholdings
As at the date of this report, pursuant to Section 198 of the Companies Act 1985, the Company had been advised of the following interests of 3% or more in the ordinary share capital of the company:

Name	Number of shares	% of issued share capital
Maxwell Foundation and its subsidiaries	202.558,076	31.34%
Robert Maxwell, his family and companies controlled by him and his family	155,912,928	24.14%

In 1990 Maxwell Communication Corporation was one of the world's top ten publishers, capitalised at about £1.4 billion. But the tyrannical management style of the controlling shareholder drove the company into administrative receivership less than two years later.

Authorised and issued share capital
When a company is formed, the authorised share capital and the nominal value of the shares are established and written into the company's Memorandum of Association, and the procedure for increasing the authorised share capital is included in the company's Articles of Association. This usually requires the approval of the shareholders.

Thereafter the directors of the company cannot issue new shares in excess of the authorised number, nor can they issue securities carrying rights to new shares that would exceed that number (e.g. convertibles and warrants: see below).

Both the authorised and the issued share capital are shown in the company's accounts, divided into equity and non-equity shares, e.g.

BELLWAY *Extract from 1998 Group balance sheet*

	1998 £000	1997 £000
Capital and reserves		
Equity share capital		
Ordinary shares	13,549	13,071
Non-equity capital		
Preference shares	20,000	20,000
Called up share capital	33,549	33,071
...		

Details of the authorised share capital are normally shown in a note to the accounts.

Types of share capital

Although all shares are referred to generally as 'risk capital', as the shareholders are the first investors to lose if the company fails, the degree of risk can vary within the same company from hardly any more than that of an unsecured lender to highly speculative, with prospects of reward usually varying accordingly.

The main types of share, in increasing order of risk, the order in which they would rank for distribution in the event of liquidation, are:

(a) preference shares
(b) ordinary shares
(c) deferred shares
(d) warrants to subscribe for shares.

Unlike interest paid on loan capital, distributions of profits to shareholders are not an 'allowable expense' for company taxation purposes; i.e. dividends have to be paid out of profits *after* Corporation Tax has been deducted.

Preference shares

Preference shares carry a fixed rate of dividend, normally payable half-yearly, but unlike the holders of loan capital, who can take action against a company in default of interest payments, preference shareholders have no legal redress if the board of directors decides to recommend that no preference dividends should be paid. However, if no preference dividend is declared for an accounting period, no dividend can be declared on any other type of share for the period concerned, and the preference shareholders usually become entitled to vote at shareholders' general meetings. (Provided their dividends are paid, preference shares do not normally carry a vote.)

Varieties of preference shares can include one or a combination of the following features:

- *Cumulative*. If the dividend on a cumulative preference share is not paid on time, payment is postponed rather than omitted. When this happens, the preference dividend is said to be 'in arrears', and these arrears have to be paid by the company before any other dividend can be declared. Arrears of cumulative preference dividends must be shown in a note to the accounts.
- *Redeemable*. The shares are repayable, normally at their nominal (par) value, in a given year, e.g. 2001, or when the company chooses within a given period, e.g. 2001/04.
- *Participating*. In addition to receiving a fixed dividend, shareholders participate in an additional dividend, usually a proportion of any ordinary dividend declared.
- *Convertible*. Shareholders have the option of converting their preference shares into ordinary shares within a given period of time, the conversion period.

Where a company has a large proportion of non-equity shares, it is important to check whether a significant number are due for redemption in the near future.

Golden shares

Where nationalised industries have been privatised, the Government has, in some cases, retained a 'golden share' to prevent takeover and/or has placed limits on the maximum size of any one holding or on the percentage that can be held by foreigners, e.g. the Secretary of State for Transport holds a Special Rights redeemable preference share of £1 in BAA, and BAA's articles of association limit the holding of any one shareholder to 15% of the ordinary shares.

Another example of control by a single share is REUTERS, where there is a single Founders £1 share designed to preserve Reuters' independence. The share is held by a Trust, and may be used to outvote all ordinary shares if other safeguards fail and there is an attempt to seize control of the company.

Ordinary shares

Ordinary shares usually form the bulk of the share capital of a company. Ordinary shareholders are normally entitled to all the profits remaining after tax and preference dividends have been deducted although, as explained later, not all these attributable profits are likely to be distributed. Ordinary shareholders are entitled to vote at general meetings, giving them control over the election of directors.

However some companies, e.g. STOREHOUSE, put a clause in their articles of association to allow them to disenfranchise a shareholder where the shares are held in a nominee name and the nominee holder fails to respond to a request for information on the underlying holder (CA 1985, s. 216). This protects the company against the building up of anonymous holdings prior to a possible bid.

Under Section 159 of the Companies Act 1985 companies are now allowed to issue redeemable ordinary shares, provided they also have shares in issue which are not redeemable; i.e. the share capital of a company cannot consist solely of redeemable shares. A company may now also purchase its own shares, subject to a large number of conditions, including the prior approval of its shareholders (see page 31).

Ordinary stock

Ordinary stock is a historical legacy from the days when every share in issue had to be numbered; some companies used to convert their shares into stock when they became fully paid (as this avoided the bother of numbers), and a few companies continue to use the term.

Ordinary stock can, in theory, be transferred in any monetary amount, while shares can only be bought and sold individually; in practice ordinary stock is normally traded in multiples of £1, so the terms 'ordinary share' and 'ordinary stock' are effectively synonymous.

Non-voting shares

A number of companies have more than one class of share (other than preference shares), with differing rights on voting and/or dividends and/or on liquidation. The most common variation is in voting rights, where a second class of share, identical in all other respects to the ordinary class, either carries no voting rights (usually called N/V or A shares), or carries restricted voting rights (R/V shares).

The trend over the last few years has, however, been towards the abolition of non-voting shares, and it is becoming increasingly difficult (if not actually impossible) to raise new money by the issue of non-voting shares. Several companies, led by MARKS & SPENCER in 1966, and including most recently, in 1996, the Parker Knoll furniture group CORNWELL PARKER have enfranchised their non-voting shares, giving scrip (free) issues to voting shareholders by way of compensation, but there are still a few exceptions. For example GLENMORANGIE the scotch whisky company (formerly MACDONALD MARTIN) has a two tier structure in which the founding family retain the majority of the B shares:

GLENMORANGIE *Extract from 1998 accounts*

Called up share capital

	£000
A Ordinary Shares (one vote per share) of 10p each	1,165
B Ordinary Shares (5 votes per share) of 5p each	200

Investing in shares that have fewer votes than another class of share, or have no votes at all, is very much a case of *caveat emptor* (buyer beware).

You may find yourself invested in a company like C. H. BAILEY, where the B ordinary shares, largely family owned, carry 100 times the votes of the more widely held ordinary shares.

The chairman, Mr C.H. Bailey, has taken full advantage of his controlling position by paying himself over £1.4m in the last 10 years, while shareholders have had only one dividend in the same period.

The company discourages them from complaining by holding the AGM. at Alexandra Docks in Newport, Gwent, in the middle of winter, inconveniently close to Christmas. In 1998 it was held on 22 December.

Another company with non-voting shares is the electro-components and power supplies company BULGIN, which also illustrates another key point:

The jigsaw

Like doing a jigsaw (or in any intelligence gathering organisation), the analyst often needs to put together several pieces of information to get the picture.

A.F. BULGIN *Note 23 to the 1997 accounts*

	1997
Called up share capital	£000
Authorised …	
Allotted, called up and fully paid	
2,000,000 Ordinary shares of 5p each	100
26,340,000 A Non-Voting shares of 5p each	1,317
	1,417

Extract from Report of the Directors

Directors and their interests

Beneficial interests	Ordinary	A Ordinary
R. A. Bulgin [Chairman/MD*]	307,200	645,087
R. E. Bulgin	201,800	96,059
G.A. Stone [Company Sec.*]	2,000	5,387
R. A. R. Bulgin	86,200	259,201
C. S. Bulgin (Resigned 29 April 1997)	6,002	21,000
C. M. Leigh [FD*]	2,000	1,000

Non-beneficial interests …

* As shown in the list of Directors and Advisers

The Bulgin family directors have a shade over 30% of the voting shares. Are there any other substantial shareholdings? Yes, and very interesting they are too (as we show at the top of the next page).

A.F. BULGIN *Extract from report of the directors 1997*

Substantial shareholdings
The Company is advised of the following interests in the issued voting ordinary shares of 5p each at 23 May 1997:

	Ordinary	%
National Westminster Bank Plc (mainly as managing trustees of certain settlements executed by the late Mr A. F. Bulgin)	658,500	32.9
Mars UK Pension Fund	65,000	3.3
Specialist Holdings Limited	260,000	13.0
G. M. Barber	74,500	3.7

Bulgin directors' holdings and the late Mr A. F. Bulgin's settlements together give voting control.

A.F. BULGIN *Note 9 to the 1997 accounts*

Directors' emoluments

	Salary £000	Benefits £000	Pension contrib. £000	Total £000
R. A. Bulgin	125	25	50	200
R. E. Bulgin	70	20	57	147
G. A. Stone	66	10	52	128
R. A. R. Bulgin	55	24	10	89
C. S. Bulgin	55	12	6	73
C. M. Leigh	55	20	8	83
	426	111	183	720

The Bulgin share of the total remuneration of the directors was £509,000, more than 70% of the total. Set this against a pre-tax profit for the year of £238,000 and one is led to ask: 'Are the shareholders happy?' and 'What do the non-executive directors think?'

'Has the Company any non-executive directors?' At the 1997 year end the answer was 'No'.

Two were appointed after the year end:

A.F. BULGIN *Extract from Report of the Directors*

On 17 February 1997 the following non-executive directors were appointed:
J. A. D. Skailes (59) – until he retired, a stockbroker at Vivian Gray ... taken over by Gerrard & National.
A. S. Winter (50) – a management consultant specialising in corporate finance. Previously a Vice President of investment bankers Bear Stearns and before that of Chase Manhatten Bank.

So something was happening.
The company's stockbrokers are Gerrard Vivian Gray. Stockbrokers largely earn their living by telling clients what they want to hear, not necessarily what they ought to hear. That is rather different from the role of an effective non-executive director, which in four words is to provide 'independent and objective counsel'.

We continued our intelligence gathering:

A.F. BULGIN *Extract from report of the directors 1997*

Results and dividends
The profit for the year after taxation was £151,000 (1996: £691,000). The Directors recommend a final dividend of 0.50 pence per share amounting to £142,000 (1996: £127,000) and that £9,000 (1996: £564,000) be transferred to reserves.

No interim dividend had been paid for some years, so the total dividend increased by 11.1% in a year in which profits fell by 78.1%. What would the City make of that? The 1997 accounts were published in May 1998 – see the graph on page 25.

Another substantial shareholder
Turning back to the list of Substantial shareholders, we asked ourselves: 'Who are Specialist Holdings Limited? Where do they come into the picture?' There is a clue in a note to the accounts:

A.F. BULGIN *Note 4 to the 1997 accounts*

Net operating expenses	£000
Exceptional administrative expenses comprise:	
Redundancy costs	71
Requisitioned extraordinary meetings costs	55
Defalcation	89
	215

So dissident shareholders have been requisitioning EGMs. 'What is the betting', we asked ourselves, 'that they included Specialist Holdings Limited – whose 13.0% holding would go a long way to mustering enough votes to requisition an EGM.' We could not find any amplification in the report and accounts, so we checked elsewhere:

INVESTORS CHRONICLE *17 Jan 1997 'Smaller Companies'*

Dyson tactics at Bulgin
Electronic components maker A. F. Bulgin will be expected to appoint an independent consultant to examine enfranchising its non-voting shares if, as expected, a seemingly anodyne resolution put forward by dissident shareholder Specialist Holdings is passed at next week's EGM.

SPECIALIST HOLDINGS are, in fact, renowned for stirring things up in companies, not so much in an altruistic crusade for the fair treatment of non-voting shareholders, but to make money.

We sympathise to some extent with the long term non-voting shareholders, but they really have only themselves to blame for buying N/V shares in the first place: you do so at your own peril.

But before we leave this little saga, let's see what disparity in price there is between Voting and Non-Voting shares. It's no good looking in the FT, which typically only shows the N/V price (companies have to pay the FT an annual fee to have their share price listed each day, and Bulgin wouldn't be over keen to publicise the disparity between the two classes of share). The *IC* is more informative:

INVESTORS CHRONICLE *24 Oct 1997 'Smaller Companies'*

BULGIN
Electronic Components, power supplies

A N/V Ord price:	13½p	Market value:	£3.56m
Ord price:	77½p	Market value:	£1.77m

But that did not necessarily rule out the non-voting shares as an investment. Something was changing and if one is in on a change before everyone else, it *can* be profitable.

A year later, we read:

A. F. BULGIN *Extract from the statement of Mr A. S. Winter* [recognise the name?] *in the 1998 accounts*

Chairman's Statement
Introduction
I wish to start this, my first statement, by saying how proud I am to have become Chairman. I am only the third Chairman in the Group's 75 year history and the first who is not a member of the founding family.

My association with the Group dates back over four years: initially, as an external adviser and then as a member of the Main Board ...

Accordingly, I wish to pay tribute to all past and current members of the Bulgin team whose efforts have made it possible to celebrate our 75th birthday.

...

Management changes
During the course of the year four members of the Main Board either resigned or retired. A substantial element of the resulting cost savings has been reinvested in the recruitment of new sales and marketing staff at each of the operating companies

...

In December 1997 we paid our first interim dividend for some years; 0.25p per share. Your new Board is confident that cash generation will continue allowing new investment to take place this year, and still enabling it to recommend a final dividend of 1.0p per share [double the previous year].

...

We are also actively studying the effect of our current capital structure on our share price. Moreover, the current capital structure, by limiting our ability to raise fresh funds on the Stock Market, is likely to prevent us from making a major strategic acquisition. This will become a more pressing matter over the next twelve to twenty four months.

So it comes as no surprise to find:

A. F. BULGIN *Extract from the report of the directors 1998*

Directors and their interests ...
The changes in the interests of Directors between the year end and 30 April 1998 were:

A S Winter
bought 57,000 A Non-Voting Ordinary shares on 26 February 1998 – beneficial
R A R Bulgin
acquired (by exercise of options on 26 February 1998) 100,000 A Non-Voting Ordinary shares – beneficial
bought 50,000 A Non-Voting Ordinary shares on 28 April 1998 – beneficial
J A D Skailes
bought 100,000 A Non-Voting Ordinary shares on 16 February 1998 – beneficial
bought 50,000 A Non-Voting Ordinary shares on 29 April 1998 – non-beneficial
bought 50,000 A Non-Voting Ordinary shares on 30 April 1998 – non-beneficial.
.·.

But the market does not place the same value on an A Non-Voting share as it does on an Ordinary.

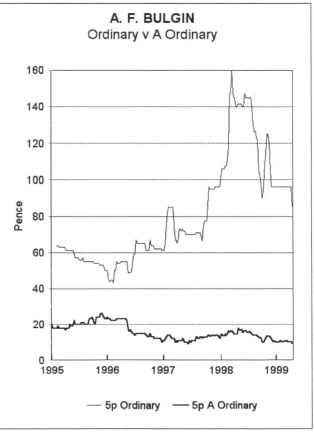

Example 5.1 An obvious disparity in share prices

As we said at the beginning: it is a case of *caveat emptor*. The same warning applies to companies where all shares (other than preference shares) carry equal voting rights, and one person effectively controls more than 50% of the votes; other shareholders are relying very heavily on that one person, but at least the controlling shareholder doesn't enjoy power that is disproportionate to his stake in the company.

Deferred shares

Another, but now quite rare, class is the deferred share, where no dividend is payable either:

(a) until ordinary shareholders' dividends have reached a certain level; or
(b) until conversion into ordinary shares.

For example in 1989 LONDON MERCHANT SECURITIES made a 3 for 1 scrip issue of Deferred Ordinary giving details in a five page circular to a shareholders:

LONDON MERCHANT SECURITIES *Extract from Circular to shareholders dated 29 September 1989*

It was announced today that your directors were proposing a capitalisation issue on the basis of one new Deferred Ordinary share for every three Ordinary shares held by shareholders. ...

Reason for the Proposed Capitalisation Issue
Record growth in asset value was achieved in the year ended 31 March 1989. Shareholders funds now stand at £356m, compared with the issued share capital of £60m
...

Effect of proposed issue
We recognise that shareholders have differing financial objectives. The existence of both Ordinary and Deferred Ordinary shares will enable present and future investors to adjust their shareholdings to their particular investment objectives.

Rights of the New Deferred Ordinary shares
The Deferred Ordinary shares will rank pari passu [equal in every respect] with the existing Ordinary shares save that they will not rank for any dividend until after the AGM held in 2004, when they will be converted automatically into Ordinary shares.

In 1989 the marginal rate of income tax was 60%, and had been as high as 70% in the 1970s, with an Investment Income surcharge of 15% when LMS made its first issue of Deferred Ordinary shares. Now that the marginal rate of Income Tax has come down to the same level as Capital Gains Tax (40%), there is much less advantage to holding deferred shares.

Warrants

Warrants are transferable options granted by the company to purchase new shares from the company at a given price, called the 'exercise price'. The warrant is normally exercisable only during a given time period, the exercise period, although one or two perpetual warrants have been issued.

Warrants can be issued on their own, for example HANSON used warrants plus cash in its acquisition of Kidde Inc. in 1987, of Consolidated Goldfields in 1989 and of Beazer in 1991.

They can also be issued attached to new issues of loan stock or bonds to give the holder an opportunity of subsequently participating in the equity of the company; the warrant element makes the issue more attractive and is sometimes referred to as the 'sweetener' (see Chapter 6).

Warrants provide a high risk/high reward form of equity investment. For example, if the ordinary shares of a company stood at 100p, warrants with an exercise price of 75p would then be worth a minimum of 25p. If the ordinary shares doubled to 200p then the warrants would be worth a minimum of 125p, a fivefold increase. In practice warrants command a premium over the ordinary price minus exercise price, although this premium tends to fall over the life of the warrant, reaching zero at the end of the exercise period.

Warrants are comparatively rare in the United Kingdom. Most recent issues have been made by investment trusts, which have attached them to issues of ordinary shares.

Exercise rights

Details of a warrant's exercise rights should be shown in the report and accounts. For example:

SCHRODER ASIA PACIFIC FUND *Note to 1998 accounts*

Share capital

There ware 27,999,400 warrants remaining in issue at 30 September 1998. Each warrant entitles the holder to subscribe for one ordinary share of 10p at a price of 100p, on 31 January in any of the years from 1999 to 2006 inclusive.

Accounting for warrants

Until FRS 4 *Capital instruments* came into force in 1994, there was no requirement to account separately for the value of warrants issued. Now the net proceeds from the issue of warrants has to be credited to shareholders' funds (FRS 4 para. 45). See, for example, SCHRODER ASIA PACIFIC FUND on the next page.

SCHRODER ASIA PACIFIC FUND *Note to 1998 accounts*

Warrant Reserve	1998	1997
	£000	£000
Warrant reserve at 30 September	8,704	8,704

In accordance with the accounting standard on Capital Instruments (FRS 4) the premium arising on the issue of shares where there are warrants attached has been apportioned between the shares and the warrants as part of shareholders' funds on the basis of the market value of the shares and warrants as on the first day of dealing. The warrant element is referred to as the 'warrant reserve'.

Perpetual warrants

A UK property company, DELANCEY ESTATES, also used a warrant package in a spectacular issue in 1998, taking net assets from £22 million to £150 million. Units of 5 shares and one warrant were issued at £5.00 per unit:

DELANCEY ESTATES *Note to the 1998 accounts*

Post Balance Sheet events

Details of a subscription, open offer and acquisition were announced on 29 May 1998 ... a total of 26,020,000 warrants have been issued.

Each warrant entitles the holder to subscribe for one new ordinary share at a subscription price of £1 per share exercisable, at the earliest, within 28 days following the publication of the financial statements of the company for the year ending 31 March 2001.

In other words they are perpetual warrants which, in the past, have had rather speculative connotations.

The main subscriber to this issue was a wholly owned subsidiary of Quantum Realty Fund, who are supervised by Soros Fund Management.

Warrant price behaviour

Although one or two hefty and rather expensive books have been compiled about warrants, the clearest and most concise explanation we have found of the behaviour of warrant prices in practice is given in Chapter 16 of R.A. Brealey's book *Security Prices in a Competitive Market.*

The book was published by The M.I.T. Press in 1971, following Dick Brealey's statistical work on the behaviour of common stock prices on Wall Street. The chapter on warrants describes the empirical method, based on the graph of Warrant price divided by Exercise price plotted against Share price divided by Exercise price; i.e. WP/EP against SP/EP.

ADRs

ADRs (American Depositary Receipts) are used in America to simplify the holding of securities in non-United States companies. The securities purchased on behalf of the American investor are deposited abroad in a custodian bank, and the corresponding ADR certificates are issued by a US depository bank. The ADR bank then acts both as depositary and stock transfer agent, dealing with the payment of dividends and the handling of proxies and rights issues for the American investor. ADRs can be unsponsored, normally traded on the Over-The-Counter (OTC) market, or sponsored by the non-US company. Sponsored ADRs can be traded on the New York and American stock exchanges, but the non-US company must register with the Securities and Exchange Commission (SEC) and meet the specific requirements of the exchange, including the filing of an annual report (usually Form 20-F).

Share schemes for directors and employees

A number of companies have encouraged share ownership amongst their staff for many years (ICI, for example, introduced a profit-sharing scheme as long ago as 1954, under which employees received a salary-related allocation of shares each year, according to the profitability of the company), but it is only since the 1970s that governments have actively encouraged wider share participation by the introduction of substantial tax concessions. These concessions now apply to three types of scheme: savings related share option schemes (SAYE schemes), profit-sharing schemes and, most recently, company share option plans, which replaced executive share option schemes in July 1995.

Savings related share option schemes

In a SAYE scheme, 'approved' under the Finance Act 1980, an employee enters into a 'save as you earn' contract for a maximum of £250 per month for a minimum of five years and at the same time is given an option to subscribe for shares with the sum saved at a given price, which must be not be less than 80% of their market value on the date the option is granted.

At the end of the SAYE contract period the employee can either use the lump sum from the SAYE contract to exercise the option, if the shares have done well in the mean time, or he can keep the cash. In either case he will not be charged income tax, but any profit on disposal is subject to assessment for capital gains tax. Details of options outstanding under the scheme will be shown in the annual report and accounts, e.g. the brewery group GREENALLS (shown on the next page).

GREENALLS *Note to the 1998 accounts*

The Greenalls Sharesave Schemes 1981 and 1995
At 25 September 1998 options outstanding in respect of grants made under the Sharesave Schemes were as follows:

Exercise period	*Shares*	*Option price*
Up to 31 October 2004	2,712,338	271p – 469p

Profit-sharing schemes
In this type of scheme, introduced by Labour under pressure from the Liberals, companies have, since 1978, been allowed to allocate up to a maximum sum per employee (currently £3,000 p.a. or 10% of earnings if more, up to a maximum of £8,000 p.a.) to be used to purchase shares at full market value through specially created trusts.

The shares have to be held in trust for at least two years; income tax has to be paid only if the shares are sold within five years, and then only on a reducing scale according to how long they have been held, but normal capital gains tax rules apply.

Company share option plans
Companies may grant options to employees up to a limit of £30,000 each on the value of shares under option at any one time (based on the value of shares at the time options are granted).

Providing the plan is approved by the Inland Revenue and the exercise price of the options is not less than the share price at the time of issue, no income tax is payable either when the options are granted or when they are exercised.

Performance share plans
In this type of plan, also known as LTIPS (Long Term Incentive Plans), selected executives are granted the right to receive a fixed number of shares in the company at some future date, subject to one or more criteria.

For example, SCHRODERS has a plan in which the number of shares issued at the end of a five year period depends on where the Total Shareholder Return (TSR) of Schroders' shares rank in the FT-SE 100 Index:

Below 50th place	no shares issued
41st to 50th	40% of the shares issued
31st to 40th	60%
21st to 30th	80%
20th or above	100%.

The issue is also subject to a minimum average post-tax real return on equity of 7.5% per annum.

The Chancellor of the Exchequer, in his November 1996 budget, ruled that CGT would be payable on the issue of these shares, not on their subsequent disposal.

Options granted to directors and employees under incentive schemes produce potential dilution of equity earnings in the same way as warrants (see Chapter 18).

Shares purchased with loans
Section 153 (4)(c) of the Companies Act 1985 allows loans to employees, but not to directors, for the purpose of purchasing fully paid shares in the company; the aggregate amount of any outstanding loans must be shown in the company's balance sheet. Because of the tax advantages of other schemes, loans for the purchase of shares are likely to become increasingly rare.

The investor's viewpoint
Companies that encourage employee share participation on favourable terms are generally regarded as more likely to prosper than those which do not. In particular, companies that grant options to executive directors and key senior staff, on whose efforts the success of a company largely depends, can expect better than average performance. In short, giving the directors and employees a 'slice of the action' should be regarded as a plus point for investing in a company, providing the directors aren't being too greedy. Avoid companies where the boardrooms' total rewards are high in comparison with pre-tax profits.

Effect of inflation
At times of high inflation there is a serious flaw in share schemes for directors and employees:

SHARE SCHEMES *Effect of high inflation*

Options are granted at the current share price of 100p, exercisable in between 3 and 7 years.

After 7 years the value of money has halved, and the share price has gone up to 200p. The real value to the shareholder is unchanged, but the option holders have doubled their money.

The fair thing would be to index the exercise price by the RPI.

Limitations on the issue of further equity
There are three limitations to the issue of further equity:

1. As already mentioned, there must be sufficient share capital authorised.
2. The Stock Exchange, in its Continuing Obligations for listed companies, forbids the issue of equity, convertibles, warrants or options for cash, other than to the equity shareholders of the company, except with the prior approval of ordinary shareholders in general meeting, and the approval of The Stock Exchange. The

Stock Exchange normally restricts issues of equity capital by way of placings to protect the interests of existing shareholders (see The Yellow Book, Chapter 9, para. 18), but these restrictions can be relaxed when market conditions or the individual circumstances of a company justify doing so.

3. Section 100 of the Companies Act 1985 prohibits the issue of shares at a discount, i.e. for less than their nominal value.

Rights issues

A rights issue is an issue of new shares offered to shareholders in proportion to their existing holdings at a discount to the current market price. Shareholders who do not wish to subscribe can sell their rights 'nil paid'. The discount varies according to the 'weight' of the rights issue; 1 new share offered for every 8 or 10 shares already held would be regarded as a 'light' issue, probably requiring a discount of not more than 15%, while more than 1-for-4 would be 'heavy' and likely to need nearer 20% discount, or more if the company is in poor health. At these discounts underwriting would be arranged to ensure buyers for any shares not taken up by shareholders, but companies occasionally choose to make a rights issue at very much below the market price, the lowest price normally permitted being the par value of the shares.

The effect on the balance sheet of an issue at par is to add the total nominal value of the shares being issued to the issued share capital, and to show the cash received on the assets side. The expenses of the issue would normally be written off against the share premium account.

If the new shares are issued above par, the nominal value of the shares issued is added to the issued share capital and the difference between the issue price and the nominal price of each new share, i.e. the premium at which the shares were issued, is added to the share premium account.

For example, in March 1999, WASTE RECYCLING GROUP made a 7-for-20 rights issue of 30,308,859 ordinary 25p shares at 406p. The issue added £7.6m to the ordinary share capital (30.308m × 25p nominal value) and £111.5m (30.308m × 381p premium), less expenses, to the share premium account, as illustrated by WASTE RECYCLING GROUP at the top of the next column.

There are two methods of dealing with convertible stock in a rights issue. Either the holders are offered new shares on the basis of the number of ordinary shares they would hold on full conversion, or the stock has its conversion terms adjusted to allow for the rights issue, whichever method is laid down in the convertible's trust deed (see Chapter 6). Similarly, either warrant holders are

offered new shares or the warrant's terms are adjusted.

WASTE RECYCLING GROUP *Rights issue*

	Pre-rights £m	Post-rights £m
Issued share capital		
Ordinary share capital	11.7	19.3
Share premium		
Pre-rights	27.7	27.7
Premium on shares issued		115.5
Expenses of rights issue		(2.6)
	39.4	159.9

Placing and open offer

This method, colloquially known as a placing with clawback, is an alternative to a rights issue, and is usually done in conjunction with an acquisition. For example, in January 1999 the lossmaking steel wire manufacturer ASW HOLDINGS raised £17m by an Open Offer to fund the acquisition of its main UK competitor CO-STEEL SHEERNESS.

Shareholders were invited to subscribe for the new ordinary 10p shares at 14p, on the basis of 73 new ordinary shares for every 50 ordinary shares held, and the issue was underpinned by the Birmingham stockbrokers Albert E Sharp and Candover Investments. There was a 53.8% take-up.

The main advantage of a placing with open offer is either that it is done at a much tighter discount than a rights issue, under 10%, or can be done, as in ASW's case, when a rights issue would have been difficult if not impossible to underwrite.

The disadvantage is that shareholders who do not want to subscribe cannot sell their rights nil paid.

Scrip issues

A scrip issue, also known as a bonus or capitalisation issue, is a free issue of additional new shares to existing shareholders, made by capitalising reserves. For example, HALMA made a 1-for-3 scrip issue in August 1997. The effect on the balance sheet is shown at the top of the next page.

As a scrip issue is basically a bookkeeping transaction, the share price would normally be expected to adjust accordingly (e.g. would fall from 240p to 180p with a 1-for-3), and it is open to debate as to whether scrip issues serve any useful purpose.

HALMA *Effect of 1-for-3 scrip issue*

	Pre-scrip £000	Post-scrip £000
Ordinary share capital	26,919	35,905
Share premium account	2,479	614
Profit and loss account	52,283	45,136
Shareholders' funds	81,681	81,655*

* Fall in shareholders' funds due to £26,000 scrip issue costs, which were charged to the share premium account.

The main arguments in favour of scrip issues are the following:

(a) scrip issues are popular with the investing public, and therefore enhance share prices. Research shows that shares tend to outperform the market after the announcement of a scrip issue, but that companies make scrip issues only when they are doing well, i.e. when their share price would be expected to outperform just as much without the scrip issue;

(b) a 'heavy' share price in the market, say over £2, tends to make the shares harder to trade and artificially depresses the price. Scrip issues can be used to scale the price down;

(c) a scrip issue, being 'paid for' out of reserves, enables retained profits and / or the increased value of assets to be reflected by an increased share capital;

(d) the rate of dividends, expressed as a percentage of an unrealistically small share capital, can look excessive;

(e) an issued share capital of at least £1m is needed for Trustee status.

The last argument appears to be the only factual one in favour of scrip issues; the remainder are psychological, although only a sound and flourishing company is likely to be able to make substantial scrip issues every few years. HALMA's record illustrates this well: the company also made a 1-for-3 scrip issue in 1985, a 1-for-2 scrip issue in 1987 and 1989, and 1-for-3 scrip issues in 1991, 1993 and 1995. Thus an investor who purchased 1,000 Halma shares in 1984 would now have a holding of 9,473 ordinary shares.

The arguments against scrip issues are firstly the administrative costs incurred and secondly the increased risk of the share price subsequently falling close to or below par, thus precluding a rights issue. The cost is small, but reducing the market price can cause serious embarrassment if the company wants, at a later date, to make a rights issue only to find that its share price is too low to do so.

Share splits

Where a company feels its share price is 'heavy' but does not want to capitalise reserves – i.e. it does not want to make a scrip issue – it can split its shares into shares with a smaller par value. For example, in 1996 REGENT INNS split its 25p shares, which were standing at around 1200p at the time, into 5p shares, and the share price adjusted to around 240p.

Scrip (stock) dividends

There are two types of scrip or stock dividends:

(a) where the company issues shares instead of paying cash dividends – shareholders have no choice (as ULTRAMAR did in the 1970s);

(b) where each shareholder can choose whether he or she wishes to receive a cash dividend or a stock dividend.

Stock or scrip dividends can only avoid tax if they are not an alternative to cash dividends, i.e. type (a) above, which is in effect a scrip issue with no dividends!

In type (b) shareholders are sent a form of election in advance of each dividend payment, giving them the opportunity to opt for a scrip dividend, although some companies also pay a nominal cash dividend at least once each year in order to preserve 'wider range' investment status under the Trustee Investment Act 1961. The number of shares is calculated to give the same value as the net dividend payable, and counts as income, so there is no tax advantage, and a positive disadvantage for 'gross' funds (pension funds and charities, which pay no tax).

Scrip dividends are popular with private shareholders, because they can add to their holding at middle market price without paying stockbrokers' commission.

From the company's point of view, it is able to raise additional equity capital from its existing shareholders without the expense of a rights issue.

Further information on shares

Details of shares and debentures issued during the year should be given in a note to the balance sheet (CA 1985, Sch. 4, paras. 39 and 41). The terms for redemption of all redeemable shares and the details of all outstanding rights to acquire shares either by subscription or conversion should also be given (CA 1985, Sch. 4, paras. 38 (2) and 40).

In addition, FRS 4 requires a brief summary of the rights of each class of share, other than ordinary shares, to be given, including: (i) the rights to dividends; (ii) date at which redeemable, and amount payable on redemption; (iii) priority and amount receivable on a winding up; (iv) voting rights.

LILLESHALL *Note to the 1997 accounts*

Share capital	Note	1997 £000
Allotted and fully paid		
210,000 3.5% cumulative preference shares of £1 each	1	210
3,000,000 8% cumulative redeemable preference shares of £1 each	2	3,000
6,436,933 9% cumulative convertible redeemable preference shares of £1 each	3	6,437
28,409,324 ordinary shares of 10p each		2,841
		12,488

Notes

1. The 3.5% cumulative preference shares are irredeemable.

2. The 8% cumulative redeemable preference shares are redeemable at par as follows:

   (a) at the Company's option, a max. of 750,000 shares in the period 2 July 1999 to 1 July 2000;
   (b) at the Company's option, a max. of 1,500,000 shares, less the number redeemed under (a) above, in the period 2 July 2000 to 1 July 2001; and
   (c) the balance on 2 July 2001.

3. Convertible into ordinary shares at the holders' option on the basis of one ordinary share for each £1.30 nominal value of preference shares in May 1998. If not converted, they will be redeemed at par on 1 January 1999.

The preference shares carry no voting rights and, in a winding up of the Company, the net assets shall be applied first in repaying (a), secondly (b) and thirdly (c).

This information will usually make it clear why a class of share has been classified an equity or non-equity, but additional information should be given, if necessary. Where rights vary according to circumstances, these circumstances and the variation should be described (FRS 4, paras. 56–57).

Company purchasing its own shares

Under Sections 162 to 169 of the Companies Act 1985, a company may purchase its own shares, providing it doesn't buy in all its non-redeemable shares. General authority may be given for market purchases up to a maximum number of shares, within a given price range and within a maximum of 18 months from the date the resolution is passed.

Most companies pass a resolution each year at their AGM giving the directors authority, until the next AGM, to purchase the company's shares, normally up to a maximum of 10% of the shares issued at up to 5% above the middle market price.

Where a company wishes to purchase shares outside the market, the transaction must be authorised in advance by a special resolution. For example in December 1992 FROGMORE ESTATES called an EGM (Extraordinary General Meeting) to authorise the purchase of 13.1% of its issued share capital from another property company at a discount of around 7% to the market price. The EGM was required firstly because the purchase was by private treaty, i.e. 'off-market', and secondly because the purchase was of more than 10% of its issued share capital, the maximum of the general authority approved at the previous AGM.

To protect investors, Chapter 15 of The Stock Exchange's *'Yellow Book'* lays down various rules about the purchase of own securities. One of these is that companies are normally not allowed to purchase their own shares within two months before the announcement of half-yearly or full-year results or when price-sensitive information has become known to the company but has not been released to the public; i.e. the same rules that apply to the directors (Yellow Book, Chapter 15, para. 5).

Several property companies, including FROGMORE, took advantage of the 1985 Act to purchase their ordinary shares at a price below asset value, thus increasing the asset value of the remaining shares. More recently, in the last two or three years, there has been a spate of companies falling over themselves to return 'spare cash' to their shareholders. This can be done:

(a) by a company buying its own shares. Shares bought in have, by law, to be cancelled, or

(b) by, in effect, giving cash back to shareholders. In order to avoid the returned cash being treated as a distribution for tax purposes, the return is achieved by a bonus issue of B shares, which are then redeemed by the company, or

(c) by a combination of (a) and (b), which is what W.H. SMITH did:

W.H. SMITH GROUP *Circular to shareholders April 1998*

Proposed Return of Capital to Shareholders

On 30 March 1998 the Company announced that it had successfully completed the sale of Waterstone's [a chain of bookshops] for £300m and that it proposed to return approximately £250m of capital to shareholders.

Approximately £153m will be returned by way of a bonus issue of one B share for each Existing Ordinary Share. The Company will subsequently offer to redeem the B shares. The balance of the £250m is intended to be returned to Shareholders by way of a rolling programme of on-market purchases.

Reduction of share capital

Under Section 135 of the Companies Act 1985 a company may, with court approval, reduce its share capital in any way and, in particular, may:

(a) reduce or extinguish liability on share capital not fully paid up;

(b) cancel any paid-up share capital which is lost or unrepresented by available assets; and

(c) repay any paid-up share capital in excess of its requirements.

Where the net assets no longer exceed the paid-up value of the issued share capital, the reserves will appear negative in the balance sheet.

Take, for example, a company which has 1 million £1 ordinary shares in issue and negative reserves of £831,000. It might, with court approval, reduce its capital to 1½ million 25p shares and eliminate share premium account to remove the accumulated losses (see Example 5.1).

Example 5.1 Effect of share capital reduction on the balance sheet

	Before reduction	After reduction
	£000	£000
Issued share capital	1,000	375
Share premium account	206	–
Other reserves	(831)	–
Shareholders' funds	375	375

Arrangements and reconstructions

A company may make an arrangement with its creditors or shareholders. One possibility is a reorganisation of the company's share capital by consolidation of different classes and/or division into different classes, under Section 425 of the Companies Act 1985.

A meeting has to be called for each class of creditor or shareholder concerned, at which a resolution to make the arrangement requires at least three-fourths by value of those present and voting to vote in favour; after subsequent sanction by the court, the arrangement is then registered with the Registrar of Companies and becomes binding on all creditors and shareholders concerned.

Documentation in connection with arrangements and reconstructions is generally both lengthy and complex but it often provides 'new' material, i.e. information which was never reported in the accounts. But most shareholders are so disappointed by the outcome of their original investment that they devote neither the time nor the trouble to study the information and so, possibly, to learn by the mistake.

RESERVES

Where reserves come from

Reserves can arise in several ways:

(a) by the accumulation of profits, either by retained profits from the profit and loss account or from the sale of assets;

(b) by the issue of shares at a premium, i.e. at more than their nominal value: the issue can be either for cash or as consideration (payment) in an acquisition;

(c) by the issue of warrants;

(d) by upward revaluation of assets (see page 58);

(e) by the acquisition of assets at below their balance sheet value.

They can be reduced by losses, share issue and share redemption expenses, revaluation deficits and the writing off of goodwill. In addition, foreign currency translation differences are taken direct to reserves (see Chapter 23).

The balance sheet formats in Schedule 4 of the Companies Act 1985 require reserves to be shown in three main subdivisions:

> Share premium account,
> Revaluation reserve, and
> Other reserves.

Reserves should not include provision for deferred taxation, or any other provision.

Capital and revenue reserves

Under Section 264 (2) of the Companies Act 1985, a company's *undistributable reserves* are:

(a) the share premium account;

(b) the capital redemption reserve;

(c) unrealised profits (i.e. the revaluation reserve);

(d) any other reserve that a company is prohibited from distributing by its memorandum or articles.

Share premium account
Reference: Companies Act 1985, s. 130.

When shares are issued at a premium over their nominal value, the premium element must, by law, be credited to the share premium account, unless the rules of merger accounting apply (see page 187).

The share premium account has to be shown separately on the balance sheet and no part may be paid out to shareholders except on liquidation or under a capital reduction scheme authorised by the court.

It is permissible, however:

(a) to capitalise the share premium account to pay up unissued shares for distribution to shareholders as a scrip issue (otherwise known as a bonus or capitalisation issue), for instance:

	£
Ordinary share capital	100,000
Share premium account	85,000
Company makes 1-for-2 scrip issue:	
Ordinary share capital	150,000
Share premium account	35,000

(b) to charge to the share premium account:
   (i) the preliminary expenses of forming a company,
   (ii) the expenses and commissions incurred in any issue of shares.

Revaluation reserve
The surplus (or shortfall) on the revaluation of assets should be credited (or debited) to a separate reserve, the revaluation reserve. The amount of the revaluation reserve shall be shown 'under a separate sub-heading in the position given for the item "revaluation reserve" in the balance sheet formats, *but need not be shown under that name*'. (Our italics. CA 1985, Sch. 4, para. 34.)

Reserve funds
Where a reserve is represented by earmarked assets (e.g. quoted securities, an endowment policy and/or cash specifically set aside), it is called a reserve fund. For example, if a company issues a £250,000 debenture repayable in 20 years and decides to set aside £8,000 each year towards the cost of eventual redemption (the old-fashioned type of sinking fund as described in Chapter 6), it will treat it as a separate fund, investing the money in earmarked assets, usually risk-free gilt-edged securities, to earn interest between now and the redemption date.

Debenture redemption reserve funds are comparatively rare these days as almost all debenture issues now either have no sinking fund at all or provide for a small proportion of the debenture to be redeemed by drawings or repurchase each year, rather than setting the money aside in a fund.

Capital redemption reserve
Shares may only be redeemed or purchased by the company out of distributable profits or out of the proceeds of a new issue of shares. Where redemption or purchase is out of distributable profits, an amount equal to the amount by which the company's issued share capital is diminished must, by law, be transferred to a reserve, called the capital redemption reserve (CA 1985, s. 170). This reserve is shown separately under Other reserves. The idea behind the law is to prevent a company's overall share capital plus non-distributable reserves from being reduced when share capital is repaid: the reserve can never be distributed except upon liquidation or in a capital reduction scheme, but it can be capitalised by a bonus issue, as in Example 5.2.

Example 5.2 Capital redemption reserve

1. Initial position:

Issued share capital	£
30,000 £1 Redeemable preference shares	30,000
100,000 £1 Ordinary shares	100,000
	130,000
Reserves	
Revenue reserve (retained profits)	75,000

2. Company then uses retained profits to redeem all the preference shares:

Issued share capital	£
100,000 £1 Ordinary shares	100,000
	100,000
Reserves	
Capital redemption reserve	30,000
Revenue reserve (retained profits)	45,000

3. Company then decides to make a 3-for-10 scrip issue, which brings the issued share capital back to £130,000.

Issued share capital	£
130,000 £1 Ordinary shares	130,000
	130,000
Reserves	
Revenue reserve (retained profits)	45,000

Problem 5.1
Q is the wholly owned subsidiary of X Group, a listed company. Q's share capital includes 100m £1 3.5% cumulative preference shares. You hold 10,000 £1 cumulative preference shares. Is X bound to pay the dividend on your shares?

Chapter 6

LOAN CAPITAL

The advantages of borrowing

If a company confidently expects that its return on capital (i.e. the trading profit expressed as a percentage of the capital the company employs) will exceed the cost of borrowing, then borrowing will increase the profit attributable to the ordinary shareholders. There are, however, various limitations on the amount a company can borrow, which we will discuss later in this chapter, and borrowing also increases risk.

The risk of borrowing

The risk of borrowing is twofold: firstly the interest on most borrowings has to be paid promptly when due (unlike dividends on shares, which can be deferred or omitted altogether) and secondly most borrowings have to be repaid by a certain date (unlike most share capital, which is only repayable on liquidation).

In a poor year, interest charges can drastically reduce the pre-tax profits of a heavily borrowed company. Take, for example, two companies that are identical except that one, Company A, is financed entirely by shareholders while the other, Company B, is financed half by shareholders and half by borrowing, which bears a rate of interest of 10% per annum.

The table in Example 6.1 on the next page shows the profitability of the two companies with varying rates of return on capital employed: in an average year Company B earns 15% on money borrowed at 10%, and so gains 5% on £2,000,000, adding £100,000 to pre-tax profits. This extra profit, after tax, adds 3.5p to the earnings attributable to each of the 2,000,000 shares that Company B has issued, making the earnings per share 14.0p compared with 10.5p for Company A.

In a good year the advantage of borrowing will enhance Company B's earnings per share even more (28p compared with 17.5p for Company A) but in a poor year, as our table shows, all the trading profit is used servicing the borrowings of Company B, while Company A still manages to earn £140,000 after tax for its shareholders.

The point at which the two companies do equally well as far as their shareholders are concerned is shown in the graph below. Their earnings per share are both 6.7p when the return on capital employed is 10% per annum; as one would expect, borrowing at 10% to earn 10% neither adds to nor detracts from Company B's profits. As the graph also shows, borrowing makes a company's profits more volatile and the risk of borrowing is further increased when money is borrowed at a variable rate of interest (e.g. on overdraft). If interest rates had risen above 10% in our example's 'poor year', Company B would have actually made a loss.

We will come back to the effects of borrowing later in this chapter, but let us now look in detail at various types of borrowing.

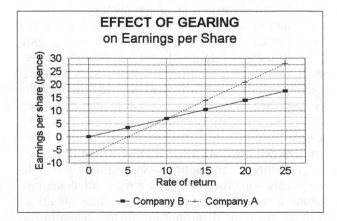

Example 6.1 Financing by share capital and by borrowing

	Company A				Company B		
Issued equity (£1 shares)		£4,000,000				£2,000,000	
Borrowings (10% interest)		Nil				£2,000,000	
	Good year	*Average year*	*Poor year*		*Good year*	*Average year*	*Poor year*
Rate of return	25%	15%	5%		25%	15%	5%
	£000	£000	£000		£000	£000	£000
Trading profit	1,000	600	200		1,000	600	200
Interest	–	–	–		200	200	200
Pre-tax profit	1,000	600	200		800	400	0
Taxation (30%)	300	180	60		240	120	0
Profit after tax	700	420	140		560	280	0
Earnings per share	17.5p	10.5p	3.5p		28.0p	14.0p	0p

Types of borrowing

There are many ways in which a company can borrow money, the main characteristics of different types of debt being:

(a) the length of time for which the money is borrowed;

(b) the rate of interest paid;

(c) the security offered to the lender by way of charges on the assets of the company;

(d) the negotiability of the debt instrument (i.e. does the lender receive a piece of paper which he can sell if he wishes to disinvest before the date of repayment?);

(e) the flexibility to the company and to the lender in the timing of borrowing and repayment;

(f) any deferred equity option given to the lender.

A company's borrowings fall broadly into three categories:

1. Debentures and unsecured loan stock, issued on the UK market, and bonds, issued on the Eurobond and other markets (see alongside). These can be held by the general public, and can be bought and sold in the same way as shares.

2. Loans from banks and other financial institutions.

3. Bank overdrafts (described in Chapter 13).

Categories 1 and 2 are shown separately in the balance sheet, with a note describing the terms on which each loan is repayable and the rate of interest, dividing them into secured and unsecured loans.

An analysis of the maturity of debt should be given, showing amounts falling due:

(a) in one year or less, or on demand;

(b) between one and two years;

(c) between two and five years; and

(d) in five years or more (FRS 4 *Capital instruments*, para. 33).

This is an important point to watch, because a loan coming up for repayment may significantly weaken the company's liquidity position, and can be a very serious threat to a company that is already short of funds if it is likely to have any difficulty refinancing the loan.

Security given to the lender

When a company wishes to issue loan capital it can offer the lender some specific security on the loan. If it does so, the loan is called a debenture (£100 units) or debenture stock (usually units of £1); if not it is an unsecured loan stock (ULS), and these are the two main types of loan capital raised in the UK from the general public.

Debentures

Debentures can be secured by fixed and/or floating charges described below, the most common type of debenture being one that is secured on specific land or buildings, sometimes called a mortgage debenture.

Fixed charge

A fixed charge is similar to a mortgage on a house. The company enters into a debenture deed which places a charge on specific identifiable assets. This gives the debenture holder a legal interest in the assets concerned as security for the loan, and the company cannot then dispose of them unless the debenture holder releases the charge (which he is unlikely to do unless offered some equally good alternative security). If the company defaults or falls into arrears on interest payments or capital repayments, the debenture holder can either:

(a) appoint a receiver to receive any income from the assets (e.g. rents) or

(b) foreclose, i.e. take possession and sell the assets, using the proceeds of the sale to repay the debenture holders in full; any surplus remaining is then paid to the company, but if the proceeds of selling the assets charged are insufficient to repay the debenture holders in full, the debenture holders then rank equally with unsecured creditors for the shortfall.

Floating charge
This is a general charge on the assets of a company. But the debenture holder has no legal interest in the assets unless and until an event specified in the debenture deed occurs; for example, if the company goes into liquidation or ceases trading, or falls behind with interest payments or capital repayments, or exceeds specified borrowing limits. In the event of default the debenture holder can then appoint a Receiver, who takes physical possession of the assets of the company. The Receiver can also be appointed as the Manager or a separate Manager can be appointed to continue running the company, or the Receiver can sell off the assets; the former course is adopted if possible, because a company can normally be sold as a going concern for more than the break-up value.

The ranking of ULS
In a liquidation the holders of unsecured loan stock rank equally with other unsecured creditors, that is after debenture holders and preferential creditors (tax, rates and certain obligations to employees). In practice trade creditors often restrict a company to 'cash with order' terms if they see it running into difficulties, and to that extent a ULS tends to rank behind suppliers.

Typical characteristics of debentures and ULS

Interest
Most debentures and ULS carry a fixed annual rate of interest (known loosely as the 'coupon') which is payable (normally half-yearly) regardless of the company's profitability. Interest is deductible before the company is assessed for tax, i.e. it is an allowable expense for tax purposes, and therefore costs the company less than the same amount paid out in dividends on shares.

Redemption
Each issue is normally for a given term, and is repayable at the end of the term (at the redemption date) or, where there is a redemption period (e.g.

2002/04), it is repayable when the company chooses within that period. A few irredeemable stocks do exist, but they are rare, except in the case of water companies.

Liquidation
In the event of liquidation, debenture holders are entitled to repayment in full from the proceeds of disposal of the charged assets. Then the ULS holders and other unsecured creditors, and the fixed charge debenture holders if not already fully satisfied, rank equally after preferential creditors, and have to be repaid before the shareholders are entitled to anything.

The trust deed
Where a debenture or loan stock is to be issued to more than a very small number of holders, and particularly when it is going to be listed on The Stock Exchange, a trustee or trustees are appointed to represent the holders collectively, and the company enters into a trust deed rather than a debenture deed.

For listing, The Stock Exchange also requires that at least one trustee must be a trust corporation which has no interest in or relation to the company which might conflict with the position of the trustee. A large insurance company or the specialist LAW DEBENTURE CORPORATION is often appointed as trustee.

The deed contains all the details of the issue, except the issue price, including:

(a) details of fixed and floating charges, together with provision for substitution (securing further assets to replace secured assets which the company may subsequently wish to dispose of during the term of the loan). Provision may also be made for topping up (securing further assets if the value of secured assets falls below a given limit);

(b) redemption price and redemption date or period, and details of any sinking fund;

(c) conditions under which the company may repurchase in the market, by tender and from individual holders;

(d) redemption price in the event of liquidation;

(e) conditions for further pari passu (equal ranking) issues, restrictions on prior borrowings and, for ULS, overall borrowing limits;

(f) minimum transferable unit;

(g) powers to approve modifications to the terms and conditions.

The trust deed may also include restrictive clauses:

(h) to prevent the nature of the company's business being changed; this is known as a 'Tickler' clause, after the celebrated case of the jam manufacturer who was taken to court by the holders of an unsecured loan stock;

(i) to prevent major disposals of the company's assets – a 'disposals' clause;

(j) to restrict the transfer of assets between charging subsidiaries (those within the charging group, i.e. included in the charge on assets) and other subsidiaries – sometimes known as a 'ring fence' clause.

Accounting for finance costs

There are three elements to finance costs. The first is the interest payable each year. The second and third are the issue expenses and the difference between the issue price and the amount payable on redemption, i.e. the premium or discount on issue if redeemable at par. These two are amortised and charged against profits at a constant rate over the life of the debt instrument.

So the carrying amount, the amount at which the debt instrument is shown in the balance sheet at any time, starts off as the net proceeds of the issue and ends up at the redemption date as the amount payable on redemption (FRS 4, paras 27 to 29).

Repurchase of debt

Where the cost of repurchase or early settlement of debt differs from the carrying amount in the balance sheet, the difference is taken to the profit and loss account in the accounting period of repurchase or early settlement (FRS 4, para. 32).

Deep discount issues

Some companies issue loan capital at a substantial discount to par value in order to reduce the coupon, i.e. to reduce the amount of interest they have to pay during the life of the security concerned. The investor is compensated for receiving less interest by getting back appreciably more than he or she paid when the security is redeemed.

For tax purposes, a *deep discount security* is one:

(a) where the discount on issue represents more than 15% of the capital amount payable on redemption, or

(b) where the discount is 15% or less but exceeds half the number of complete years between issue and redemption.

The income element is calculated as the percentage rate at which the issue price would have to grow on a compound basis over each income period to equal the redemption price at the date of redemption. The income element is treated as income of the holder and as a deductible expense of the issuer, as CGU shows in its accounting policies.

CGU *Extract from accounting policies*

Debenture loans

Borrowings issued at a discount are included in the balance sheets at their proceeds, net of expenses, together with amortised discount to the balance sheet date. The discount, amortised on a compound basis, and expenses are charged to loan interest in the profit and loss account over the term of the borrowing.

An extreme example of a deep discount issue is BRITISH TELECOMMUNICATIONS issue of £200m zero coupon bonds 2000. The accounts to 31 March 1998 showed an increase in the book cost of £17m, and explained the accounting policy being adopted:

BRITISH TELECOMMUNICATIONS *Notes to the 1998 accounts*

Loans and other borrowings

	1998 £m	1997 £m
Zero coupon bonds 2000 (less unamortised discount £38m)	162	145

Interest

Discounts or premiums and expenses on the issue of debt securities are amortised over the term of the related security and included within interest payable.

Sinking funds

Some debenture and loan stock issues make provision for part or all of the stock to be redeemed gradually over a period of time by means of a sinking fund, e.g. LAND SECURITIES' mortgage debentures.

The normal method for a sinking fund to redeem stock is by annual or six-monthly drawings (lotteries of stock certificate numbers), with the company in some cases having the option of purchasing stock in the market if it can do so at or below the drawing price. The company may also be allowed to invite holders to tender stock for redemption.

There are three types of sinking fund:

1. Original concept – no early redemptions

The sinking fund or redemption reserve fund, as originally conceived, was a fund into which a company put a given sum each year, the money being invested in government or other safe fixed interest securities rather than being used to make early redemptions. The sums, together with interest earned, went on accumulating in the balance sheet year by year until the redemption date. This method is now rarely used.

2. Non-cumulative

Each year in which the sinking fund is in operation the company normally sets aside enough cash to redeem a fixed amount of stock, expressed as a given percentage of the total issue, and uses it to redeem stock on or by the date of the second interest payment (Example 6.2).

Example 6.2 Non-cumulative sinking fund

A 25-year stock with a 2% sinking fund starting at the end of the 5th year would be redeemed at the rate of 2% per annum at the end of years 5 to 24, leaving 60% of the stock to be redeemed at redemption date.

Provided redemptions each year are by drawings at par, the average life of a stock can be calculated by working out the average life of the stock redeemed by the sinking fund, in this case 14½ years, and then weighting it by the percentage redeemed by the sinking fund, in this case 40%:

$$\text{Average life} = \frac{(14.5 \times 40\%) + (25 \times 60\%)}{100\%}$$

---

3. Cumulative

In a cumulative sinking fund the cash used for redemption each year is variable and normally consists of a fixed amount of cash plus the amount of interest saved by prior redemption (Example 6.3 below).

Yields

The yield on an irredeemable security is the gross amount of income received per annum divided by the market price of the security. Redeemable securities have two yields, their running yield and their gross redemption yield.

Running yield

The running yield is the same as the yield on an irredeemable security: it measures income and is concerned purely with the annual gross interest and the price of the stock; for instance, an 8% unsecured loan stock issued at £98% will yield 8% ÷ 0.98 = 8.16% at the issue price, or a 4½% debenture purchased at £50% will give the purchaser a yield of 9%, ignoring purchase expenses.

Redemption yield

The gross redemption yield is rather more complicated, as it measures 'total return'; i.e. it takes into account both the stream of income and any capital gain (or loss) on redemption. It is not just the sum of the running yield and the capital gain per annum, but is obtained by discounting the future interest payments and the redemption value at a rate that makes their combined *present value* equal to the current price of the stock. (The concept of discounting to obtain present value is explained in Appendix 2.) The rate required to do this is the gross redemption yield (see Example 6.4 opposite).

Typical gross redemption yields for a well secured debenture are ¾% to 1½% above the yield on the equivalent gilt-edged security (i.e. a UK Government stock of similar life and coupon), and 1% up to 5% or more for ULS, depending very much on the quality of the company and the amount of prior borrowings (borrowings that would rank ahead in a liquidation).

Example 6.3 Cumulative sinking fund

If our previous example had been a £10m issue of a 25-year stock with a 10% coupon and a cumulative sinking fund starting at the end of year 5, and with all redemptions made by drawings at par, the annual redemptions would be:

End of year	Fixed amount of cash	Variable amount (interest saved)	Stock redeemed in year	Total stock redeemed	Stock remaining
	£	£	£	£	£
4	Nil	Nil	Nil	Nil	10,000,000
5	200,000	Nil	200,000	200,000	9,800,000
6	200,000	20,000	220,000	420,000	9,580,000
7	200,000	42,000	242,000	662,000	9,338,000
8	200,000	66,200	266,200	928,200	9,071,800

and so on. The average life can be calculated by time-weighting each year's redemption, e.g. 200,000 × 5 years plus 220,000 × 6 years, etc. ÷ 10,000,000. However, if redemptions are made by purchases in the market or by tender at below the redemption price, the amount redeemed will be greater, the amount of interest subsequently saved will be larger and the whole process of redemption will accelerate.

Example 6.4 Gross redemption yield

A 6% debenture due for redemption at £105% in four years' time is standing in the market at £90. Interest is payable in the normal manner, half-yearly in arrears (at the end of each six months). The present value of the stock is the sum of the present values of the eight future six-monthly interest payments discounted at $(1 + i)$ per half-year (where i expressed as a decimal = gross redemption yield).

$$\frac{3}{(1+i)^{0.5}} + \frac{3}{(1+i)^{1.0}} + ... + \frac{3}{(1+i)^{4.0}}$$

plus the present value of the sum received on redemption in four years' time:

$$\frac{105}{(1+i)}$$

Solving for i by trial and error:

Value of i	Present value of income	Present value of redemption		Total
10% =	19.48	+	71.72	= £91.20
11% =	19.09	+	69.15	= £88.24

Inspection suggests that the gross redemption yield on a market price of £90 is about 10½%, and a more accurate figure can be obtained by further manual calculation or by computer. Alternatively, the yield can be obtained from Bond Tables.

Net redemption yields (i.e. the yields after tax) vary with the individual holder's rate of income tax payable on the stream of interest payments and the rate of tax on any capital gain on redemption.

Redemption date

When a stock has a final redemption period, e.g. 1999/2004, it is assumed in computing redemption yields that the company will choose the earliest date for redemption, 1999, if the stock is currently standing above par, otherwise the latest date, 2004. When there is a sinking fund which allows redemptions only by drawings, the average life can be calculated accurately and should therefore be used as the number of years to redemption in calculating redemption yields. However, if the company is allowed to redeem by purchase in the market or by inviting tenders, the stockholder can no longer be sure that early drawings at par will take place, and the average life is therefore ignored.

Bonds

A bond is the generic name given to loan capital raised in the Eurobond market and in the US and other domestic markets. Issues in the Eurobond market may be denominated in sterling or in a foreign currency, and are normally of between 7 and 10 years' duration.

The Eurobond market began with the issue of Eurodollar bonds – US$ denominated securities issued outside the United States. It now encompasses offshore issues in a variety of currencies, but it is still mainly a US$ market. An increasing number of UK companies make use of this market, e.g. PEARSON:

PEARSON *Note on borrowings by instrument*

	1998
Secured	£m
...	
Unsecured	
10.5% Euro-sterling Bonds 2008	100
9.5% Euro-sterling Bonds 2004	117
10.75% Euro-sterling Bonds 2002	100
Unsecured bank loans and overdrafts, commercial paper ...	

Notes and loan notes

These are promissory notes issued to one or a small number of other companies or individuals, and are normally of between 1 and 10 years' maturity on issue. They are often issued to individuals in an acquisition in lieu of cash to defer the individuals' liability to Capital Gains Tax.

Commercial paper (CP)

This is a short-term loan vehicle between the borrower (the issuer) and the purchaser (the investor); the issuer can sell direct to the investor or use banks as intermediaries.

Commercial paper takes the form of negotiable unsecured promissory notes. In the sterling CP market notes have a maximum maturity on issue of 1 year and a minimum of 7 days; they are usually for £½m or £1m. Although short term, CP is often bought as part of a company's medium term borrowing programme, backed by medium term banking facilities. e.g. RIO TINTO:

RIO TINTO *Note on medium and long term borrowings*

	1997
	US$m
Commercial paper	
US commercial paper	1,866
Canadian commercial paper	267
Australian commercial paper	133
	2,266

In accordance with FRS4 commercial paper of US$1,333m is classified as short term borrowings though backed by medium term facilities. Under US and Australian GAAP these amounts would be classified as medium term borrowings.

We agree with the US and Australian view. The notes are bearer securities issued at a discount to allow for interest, i.e. there is no separate payment of interest.

Rates are very competitive for companies with good credit ratings; commercial paper is easy to administer and costs are low.

By far the largest CP market is in the United States, where about $550 billion is outstanding.

The amount a company can borrow

The amount a company can borrow may be limited by the following:

(a) *its borrowing powers*. The directors' borrowing powers are normally limited by a company's Articles of Association, and cannot be altered except with the approval of shareholders at a general meeting. Borrowing powers are usually expressed as a multiple of shareholders' funds (issued share capital plus reserves, excluding intangible assets such as goodwill, although some companies, e.g. CADBURY SCHWEPPES, now include purchased goodwill in defining the directors' borrowing powers);

(b) *restrictions imposed by existing borrowings.* The terms of the trust deeds of existing loan capital may restrict or preclude the company from further borrowing. In particular the terms of an unsecured loan stock may include a clause preventing the company from issuing loans that rank ahead of the stock concerned, and unduly restrictive clauses are often the reasons for companies redeeming loan capital in advance of the normal redemption date;

(c) the lender's requirement for *capital and income covers*;

(d) *the lender's general opinion* of the company and its overall borrowing position.

Capital and income covers

These are two standard measures that the intending purchaser of a debenture or loan stock may use to assess the security of his investment.

The *capital* or asset cover can be calculated in two ways, on a simple basis or on a 'rolled-up' basis.

Using the simple basis, the cover is the total capital less all prior-ranking stocks, divided by the issued amount of the stock in question. Using the 'rolled-up' basis, the cover is the total capital divided by the stock in question plus all prior-ranking stocks.

As Example 6.5, below, shows, the two equal-ranking ULS issues are three times covered on a simple basis (£60m total capital less £15m prior-ranking debenture, divided by the total of £15m ULS), but only twice covered on a rolled-up basis. The more conservative rolled-up basis is normally used for assessing capital covers.

For a floating charge debenture a rolled-up capital cover of at least 3 or 4 is expected by the lender, and 2½ times is the normal minimum for an unsecured loan stock, but both depend on the quality of the assets, i.e. the likely realisable value of the assets on the open market in the event of a liquidation.

Example 6.5 Capital cover

Capital	Amount	Cumulative total	Simple cover	Rolled-up cover
	£000	£000		
6% Debenture	15,000	15,000	4.0	4.0
8% ULS	10,000			
10% ULS	5,000	30,000	3.0	2.0
Ordinary shares	12,000			
Reserves (less goodwill)	18,000	60,000		
Total capital		60,000		

Example 6.6 Income cover

A company has £5.76m of earnings before interest and tax, and the following loan capital, with the ULS and the CULS ranking equally:

Nominal value of issue	Annual interest	Cumulative interest	Times covered	Priority percentage
£12m of 6% Debenture	£0.72m	£0.72m	8.0	0–12½%
£10m of 8% ULS	£0.80m			
£8m of 5% CULS	£0.40m	£1.92m	3.0	12½–33⅓%

The *income cover* is normally worked out on a rolled-up rather than a simple basis: i.e. it is the number of times the interest on a stock plus the interest on any prior-ranking stocks could be paid out of profits before interest and tax. This cover can also be expressed as a priority percentage, showing the percentile ranking of a stock's interest, with earnings before interest and tax representing 100% (see Example 6.6 above).

Convertible loan capital

Convertible loan capital, which is usually convertible unsecured loan stock (CULS) or convertible bonds rather than convertible debentures, entitles the holder to convert into ordinary shares of the company if he or she so wishes (see also convertible preference shares, Chapter 5).

The coupon on a convertible is usually much lower than the coupon needed for the issue of a straight unsecured loan stock with no conversion rights. This is because a convertible is normally regarded by the market as deferred equity, valued on the basis of the market value of the shares received on conversion plus the additional income enjoyed before conversion (the coupon on issue being higher than the yield on the ordinary shares).

Because convertibles are a form of deferred equity, listed companies can issue them without shareholders' prior approval only as a rights issue or as part or all of the consideration in an acquisition. In a takeover situation the bidder can use a suitably pitched convertible to provide the shareholders of the company being acquired with a higher initial income than they would receive from an equivalent offer of the bidder's ordinary shares. This is particularly useful when a bidder with low-yielding shares wants to avoid the shareholders of the company he or she wishes to acquire suffering a fall in income if they accept his offer.

CULS is attractive to investors seeking higher income, for example to an income unit trust, and it also provides greater security than ordinary shares for both income and capital. From a company's point of view, CULS is cheaper to service than convertible preference shares, as the interest on the former is deducted in the assessment of Corporation Tax, but this advantage has been considerably eroded by the reduction in the rate of Corporation Tax. Most companies now prefer to issue convertible preference shares rather than CULS in order to reduce rather than increase their gearing.

Terms of a convertible loan

The holder has the option of converting into ordinary shares during a given period in the life of the loan stock or bond (the conversion period), at a given conversion price per share, expressed as so many shares per £100 of stock, or as so much nominal stock per ordinary share (Example 6.7).

Example 6.7 Convertible loan: GREAT PORTLAND ESTATES

In January 1988 GREAT PORTLAND ESTATES made a rights issue of a 9½% convertible loan stock 2002 at par, on the basis of £1 nominal of CULS for every 4 ordinary 50p shares held. The stock, when issued, was convertible into 30.303 ordinary shares per £100 stock (equivalent to a price of 330p per share when issued at par) in the August of any year between 1992 and 2002 inclusive; these conversion terms will be adjusted for any scrip issues to the ordinary shareholders in the meantime. The terms were subsequently adjusted twice, to give a conversion price of 273p.

Any rights issues to ordinary shareholders will *either* be made to the holders of the convertible as if they had been converted, *or* an adjustment will be made to the conversion terms (most CULSs specify only one method).

In the event of a bid the company will endeavour to ensure that a like offer is made to the CULS holders as if they had converted; they would, however, lose any income advantage they enjoyed over the ordinary shareholders. This is a risk you have to take if you buy the CULS rather than the ordinary shares.

If more than 75% of the stock is converted, GREAT PORTLAND has the right to force remaining stockholders to convert or redeem straight away; this is a fairly standard condition, enabling the company to clear a convertible off its balance sheet once most of it has been converted. Stock that remains unconverted at the end of the conversion period will be redeemed by GREAT PORTLAND at par on 1 December 2002.

41

The period between issue and the first date for conversion is sometimes called the 'rest period', and the period from the last date for conversion and the final redemption date the 'stub'. Diagrammatically the GREAT PORTLAND convertible can be shown as:

		Stub
Rest period	Conversion period	
1988	1992	2002

A rest period of two or three years is normal, and most conversion periods run for at least four or five years. Some convertibles have a stub of several years, which is more prudent because if convertible holders decide not to exercise their conversion rights the company concerned is probably not doing very well and would not want to be faced with having to redeem the stock almost as soon as the conversion rights lapsed.

To protect investors the terms of some convertible debt (and some convertible preference shares) include what is known as *bid protection*, a fairly recent innovation. This protection can be either an enhancement of the conversion terms, or compensation based on the average premium over the preceding year, in the event of a takeover.

Another piece of convertible jargon is the *conversion premium*. This is the premium one pays by buying the ordinary shares via the convertible rather than buying them direct. For example, if the GREAT PORTLAND convertible in Example 6.7 was standing at 120% (per £100 nominal) and the ordinary shares were standing at 300p, the cost of getting into the ordinary shares through the convertible would be £120 ÷ 36.63 (£30.303 adjusted for subsequent scrip issues) = 327.6p, a conversion premium of just over 9%.

A good indication of the likely market price of a convertible can be obtained by discounting the future income advantage to present value and adding it to the market value of the underlying equity. One caveat to this method is that if the price of the ordinary shares is very depressed, the price of the convertible in the market can become mainly dependent on its value as a fixed-interest security, particularly if the conversion period has not long to run.

Convertibles with 'put' options

In the euphoria before the market fall in October 1987, several companies were so confident that their share price was going on up for ever that they agreed to the innovation suggested by fee-hungry US investment banks to include a 'put' option in the terms of their convertibles. This 'put' option gave the convertible bond holders the option to redeem after four or five years at a substantial premium, which was calculated to give a specified gross redemption yield.

From an investor's point of view, an early 'put' option is a 'heads I win, tails I can't lose' situation (unless the company goes bust). But from a company's point of view it is asking for trouble: if the ordinary share price is depressed when the date for exercising the 'put' option approaches, it is unlikely to be a good time for the company to have to redeem the convertible.

In addition, the market may become worried about whether the company has the financial resources to meet the repayment; this may further depress the share price, increasing the likelihood of investors exercising their 'put' options, e.g. the fashion retailer NEXT.

Next had one £50m and one £100m convertible with conversion prices of 286p and 430p respectively, and 'put' options to redeem in 1992. Next's share price peaked in 1987 at 378p, but fell to under 100p in 1989 as the company was hit by the recession and moved into loss. By this time the market became anxious about whether Next could fund redemption, and the share price tumbled to 6½p at one point.

Next did survive, but only by selling off its mail order subsidiary Grattan in 1991 to pay for the 'put' options which were, of course, exercised. As the result of Next and several other companies burning their fingers badly, the drawbacks of 'put' options are now well appreciated, and companies issuing convertibles have stopped giving them. However, they may appear again in the euphoria of the next roaring bull market; if they do – beware.

Warrants

A warrant gives the holder the right to subscribe at a fixed price for shares in a company at some future date. Where a company is reluctant to raise loan capital, e.g. when very high long-term interest rates prevail, or investors are reluctant to commit themselves to purely fixed-interest securities, loan capital can be raised with a lower coupon by attaching warrants to issues of stock.

Warrants issued in this way are normally detachable and exercisable as soon as the stock to which they are attached is fully paid, and in some issues stock can be surrendered at its nominal value as an alternative to cash payment when the warrants are exercised.

For accounting purposes, when a debt instrument is issued with warrants attached, the proceeds of the issue should be allocated between the debt and the warrants (FRS 4, para. 22).

In a takeover situation, warrants can provide a more flexible way for the bidder to give loan stock an equity interest than convertibles, because the number of warrants, sometimes called the equity 'kicker', can be varied as the company wishes, while the quantity of ordinary shares to which convertible holders are entitled is defined within a narrow range by the limit the market will accept on the conversion premium.

On the other hand, a drawback to warrants is that they will seldom be exercised until close to the final exercise date, because they are bought by investors who want the gearing they provide, so the future flow of money into the company's equity is more chancy than with a convertible.

Mezzanine finance

Mezzanine finance is the term used to describe a form of finance that lies between straight debt and share capital. It is used in situations, e.g. management buy-outs (MBOs) and institutional purchases, where the amount of debt that can be raised is limited, and the amount of cash available to subscribe for shares is insufficient to make up the total required.

It is usually in the form of a loan that ranks after the normal debt (the 'senior' debt) and, because of the higher risk, bears a higher rate of interest and either carries an option to convert part of the loan into equity or has a warrant to subscribe for equity.

For example BBA's sale of its automotive products businesses in the spring of 1995; the purchase by the new company AUTOMOTIVE PRODUCTS GROUP LTD. was arranged by leading venture capital company CINVEN, financed as follows:

AUTOMOTIVE PRODUCTS GROUP *Financing of institutional purchase* £000

Senior debt	90,000	(Note 1)
Mezzanine finance	20,000	(Note 2)
Senior management investment	1,244	
Cinven investment	62,956	(Note 3)
Opening revolving credit	4,435	
	£178,635	

Notes:
1. Medium term loan at 2% over LIBOR, reducing to 1.5% providing certain profit targets are met. Final repayment date December 2001.
2. 8 year term loan at 3.5% over LIBOR. Carries warrants to subscribe for an additional 9% of the ordinary share capital.
3. Equity underwritten by Cinven's clients, who also underwrote a further £1.5m share offer to the remaining employees.

Highly geared (leveraged) deals are high risk; hence the need for the mezzanine debt to have an equity 'sweetener'.

Complex capital issues

There is almost no limit to the ingenuity of companies and their financial advisers in devising innovative terms for the issue of loan capital. In addition to the deep discount bonds and convertibles with 'put' options that we have described, complex capital issues include:

(a) *Stepped interest bonds*, where the interest payable increases by fixed steps over the life of the bond e.g. GREYCOAT's £150m secured deep discount bonds 6.25%/12.5% 2002, where the coupon increased from 6.25% to 12.5% in 1996. The bonds were subsequently redeemed early. In these cases the profit and loss account should be charged at a constant rate computed over the anticipated life of the bond, irrespective of the amount of interest paid each year (FRS 4, para. 28).

(b) *Bonds with variable payments*, where the interest payments and the amount payable on redemption are adjusted by the Retail Price Index or some other index. An annual charge should be made against profits to reflect the variations caused by the movement in the relevant index during the year (FRS 4, para. 31), e.g. ANGLIAN WATER's 5.125% Index Linked Loan Stock 2008, where the value of the capital and interest elements are linked to movements in the Retail Price Index.

Off balance sheet financing

The problem of what became known as 'off balance sheet financing' became evident in the 1980s. In that period a number of complex arrangements were developed which, if accounted for in accordance with their legal form, resulted in accounts that did not report the commercial effect of the arrangement; In particular did not show the finance as a liability on the balance sheet.

This was, of course, precisely what the devisors of these schemes intended. These developments raised fundamental questions about the nature of assets and liabilities and when they should be included in the balance sheet – questions which, lacking a fundamental theory of accounts, the accountancy profession found it difficult to answer. Although generally termed 'off balance sheet' some of the transactions also affected the profit and loss account and/or the cash flow statement.

Substance over form

In response to the problem, the concept of 'substance over form' was developed. Freely translated this means 'ignore the legal position. Accounts should reflect the reality of the situation.' This led to the publication of FRS 5.

FRS 5 *Reporting the substance of transactions*

We cover FRS 5 in this chapter, on the ground that it is largely concerned with borrowing, but it applies to all transactions or arrangements of a reporting entity whose financial statements are intended to give a true and fair view except:

1. Forward contracts and futures (such as the use of foreign currencies or commodities).
2. Foreign exchange and interest rate swaps.
3. Contracts where a net amount will be paid or received based on the movement in a price or an index (called 'contracts for differences').
4. Expenditure commitments (such as purchase commitments) and orders placed, until the earlier of delivery or payment.
5. Employment contracts.

Essentially the Standard is very simple: 'A reporting entity's financial statements should report the substance of the transactions into which it has entered. In determining the substance of a transaction, all its aspects and implications should be identified and greater weight given to those more likely to have commercial effect in practice.'

The effect of FRS 5 can be considerable in individual companies: GREAT UNIVERSAL STORES used to include finance advances and related unearned service charges in their sales figures. When, in 1995, in compliance with FRS 5, it excluded them, the reported figure for turnover was reduced by £700m. The accounting policy is now:

GREAT UNIVERSAL STORES *Accounting policies 1998*

Instalment and hire purchase debtors

The gross margin from sales on extended credit terms is recognised at the time of sale. The finance charges relating to such sales are brought into profit as and when instalments are received. The income from finance companies under instalment agreements is credited to profit in proportion to the reducing balances outstanding.

Quasi-subsidiaries

Under FRS 5 a quasi-subsidiary is 'a company, trust, partnership or other vehicle that, though not fulfilling the definition of a subsidiary, is directly or indirectly controlled by the reporting entity and gives benefits for that entity that are in substance no different from those that would arise were the vehicle a subsidiary.'

'Where the entity has a quasi-subsidiary, the substance of the transactions entered into by the quasi-subsidiary should be reported in the consolidated financial statements.'

BRITISH AIRWAYS accounts explain in a note:

BRITISH AIRWAYS *Note on Accounting Policies*

Quasi-subsidiaries

When an entity, though not fulfilling the legal definition of a subsidiary, gives rise to benefits for the Group that are, in substance, no different than those that would arise were the entity a subsidiary, that entity is classified as a quasi-subsidiary.

In determining whether the Group has the ability to enjoy the benefits arising ... regard is given as to which party is exposed to the risks inherent in the benefits and which party, in practice, carries substantially all the risks and rewards of ownership.

Linked presentation

The FRS employs a new 'linked presentation' to deal with a limited class of non-recourse finance arrangements (including most securitisations) which shows, on the face of the balance sheet, the finance deducted from the gross amount of the asset it finances. Strict conditions attaching to its use require, inter alia, that the finance is repaid from the asset it finances and that there is no provision for the asset to be kept on repayment.

It will be seen that FRS 5 is very broadly drawn and should bring disclosure or put an end to most if not all existing forms of off balance sheet finance. But merchant banks and other financial advisors have long earned substantial fees from devising this sort of scheme and will not give up easily.

GEARING RATIOS

Financial ratios fall into two broad groups, gearing ratios and liquidity ratios.

Gearing is concerned with the proportion of capital employed that is borrowed, the proportion provided by shareholders' funds and the relationship between the two, while liquidity ratios (see page 101) are concerned with the company's cash position.

Financial gearing

Financial gearing can be defined in a multiplicity of ways, the two most common being:

(a) the Debt/Equity ratio, shown as Borrowings/Shareholders' Funds in the *Investors Chronicle*, and called 'leverage' in the United States and elsewhere; and

(b) the percentage of capital employed represented by borrowings.

Whatever method is used to compute gearing, a company with 'low gearing' is one financed predominantly by equity, whereas a 'highly geared' company is one which relies on borrowings for a significant proportion of its capital.

To illustrate (see Example 6.8 in the next column), let us take the bottom half of three different companies' balance sheets, adjusting them to include bank overdraft and any other borrowings falling due within one year (these are normally netted off against current assets in a company's balance sheet, but are just as much a part of capital employed as long-term borrowings are). As you can see, Debt/Equity ratio is a more sensitive measurement of gearing than Debt/Capital Employed, and it also gives a better indication of the effect of gearing on equity income, known across the Atlantic as the 'leverage effect'. But it can be distorted by the treatment of deferred tax under provisions varying from company to company, or varying within a company from year to year.

Leverage effect

The effect of leverage can be expressed as a ratio: percentage change in earnings available to ordinary shareholders brought about by a 1% change in earnings before interest and tax (EBIT).

Suppose each of the three companies in Example 6.9 has a return on capital employed (ROCE) of 10%, and that the rate of Corporation Tax is 30%; then earnings before interest and tax (EBIT) will be as shown in Example 6.9 on the next page.

Example 6.8 Calculation of gearing and Debt/Equity ratios

		Company		
		A	B	C
		£000	£000	£000
Ordinary share capital		600	500	250
Reserves		850	550	300
Ordinary shareholders' funds [A]		1,450	1,050	550
Redeemable preference share capital (3.5%) [B]		–	100	–
Minorities [C]		150	150	150
Provisions		400	400	400
Loan stock (10%) [D]		–	150	400
Overdraft (currently 12%) [E]		–	150	500
Capital employed [F]		2,000	2,000	2,000

	A	B	C
Debt/Equity (Leverage) = $\left(\dfrac{B + D + E}{A + C}\right)$	0%	32%	128%
Debt/Capital employed = $\left(\dfrac{B + D + E}{F}\right)$	0%	20%	45%
Gearing	None	Low	High

[B] The treatment of preference shares is a problem: although they are not debt they do carry a *fixed* rate of dividend that is payable ahead of ordinary dividends. On balance we favour treating them as debt if redeemable in the reasonably near future, say in less than 10 years, but otherwise as equity when looking at capital (because it would be misleading to ascribe the same Debt/Equity ratio to a company with, say, 60 debt/40 equity as one with 60 pref./40 equity).

[C] Minorities have been included as equity in the calculation of Debt/Equity ratios, on the assumption that minority interests in subsidiaries are all pure (non-redeemable) equity.

Example 6.9 Calculation of leverage effect

	Company		
	A	B	C
	£000	£000	£000
EBIT	200.00	200.00	200.00
Less			
Loan stock interest	–	(15.00)	(40.00)
Interest on overdraft	–	(18.00)	(60.00)
Pre-tax profits	200.00	167.00	100.00
Tax at 30%	(60.00)	(50.10)	(30.00)
Profits after tax	140.00	116.90	70.00
Preference dividends	–	3.50	–
Available for minorities and ordinary shareholders [G]	140.00	113.40	70.00
1% change in EBIT	2.00	2.00	2.00
Tax	0.60	0.60	0.60
Available for minorities and ordinary shareholders [H]	+ 1.40	+ 1.40	+ 1.40
Leverage ratio			
$\dfrac{H}{G} \times 100$	1.00	1.23	2.00

Leverage, of course, works both ways; if EBIT fell by 50% then earnings available to ordinary shareholders would fall to £70,000 (Company A); £43,400 (Company B); and Company C would be on the point of making a loss.

Interest rate sensitivity

A simple calculation can be made to see the sensitivity of a company's profits to interest rates: if, in Example 6.9, the rate charged on overdrafts rose to 16% (or fell to 8%), Company C's pre-tax profit would be reduced (or increased) by 20%.

Operational gearing

In assessing what level of financial gearing might be reasonable for a company, we must first look at the volatility of profits. This depends to a large extent on the sensitivity of profits to turnover, which we will call operational gearing (although the term 'operational gearing' is sometimes used in the sense of overall gearing to include the effects of financial gearing as well).

The operational gearing of a company can be described as the ratio of the percentage change of trading profit which results from 1% change in turnover, and depends on the relationship between fixed costs, variable costs and net profit, where

fixed costs are costs that are incurred regardless of turnover, and variable costs are directly proportional to turnover:

Operational gearing =

(Turnover - Variable costs) ÷ Trading profit

or

(Trading profit + Fixed costs) ÷ Trading profit

Example 6.10 demonstrates this.

Example 6.10 Effects of operational gearing

	Turn-over	Fixed costs	Vari-able costs	Trad-ing profit	Operational gearing
	£m	£m	£m	£m	
Company D	100	20	70	10	3:1 (100 – 70:10)
Company E	100	70	20	10	8:1 (100 – 20:10)

If turnover increases by 10%:

	£m	£m	£m	£m	Change in Profits
Company D	110	20	77	13	+ 30%
Company E	110	70	22	18	+ 80%

This is fine for both D and E, especially for E, which is much more highly geared operationally than D. But, as with high financial gearing, high operational gearing works against a company when turnover falls. Assume a 10% fall in turnover:

	£m	£m	£m	£m	Change in Profits
Company D	90	20	63	7	– 30%
Company E	90	70	18	2	– 80%

Profit/volume chart

The effect of gearing can also be illustrated graphically on a 'profit/volume chart', as shown in Example 6.11. A profit/volume chart is constructed by plotting two points:

(a) trading profit against actual turnover;
(b) fixed costs against zero turnover;

and joining the two points together. The point where this line crosses the horizontal 'zero profit' line represents the level of turnover at which the company 'breaks even', i.e. makes neither a profit nor a loss. The steeper the gradient of the line the higher the operational gearing of the company.

The break-even point can also be calculated:

Break - even turnover

$$= \text{Fixed costs} = \frac{\text{Turnover}}{\text{Turnover - Variable costs}}$$

e.g. Company D $= 20 \times \dfrac{100}{100 - 70} = £66.67\text{m}$

e.g. Company E $= 70 \times \dfrac{100}{100 - 80} = £87.50\text{m}$

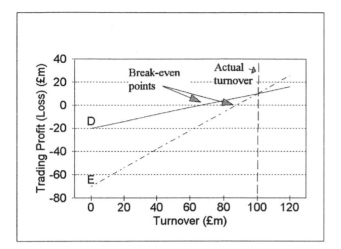

Example 6.11 Profit/Volume chart

Aggravating the problem

It is fairly obvious that a company with high operational gearing aggravates the problem by gearing up financially. Suppose, for instance, that Company E has borrowings that incurred interest charges of £3m p.a.; Example 6.12 shows the effect on profits.

Example 6.12 Effect of high financial gearing coupled with high operational gearing

Turnover	Net trading profit	Interest charges	Pre-tax profits
£m	£m	£m	£m
100	10	3	7
110	18	3	15
90	2	3	− 1

But the directors of a property company with mainly completed developments let to substantial clients will know that they have an assured rental income coming in each quarter, and they would not be considered imprudent to borrow heavily (i.e. gear up) provided the level of interest payments plus running expenses could not exceed the stream of rental income. We say 'could not exceed', because one of the ways property companies get into trouble is by borrowing short term with a variable interest rate (e.g. on bank overdraft), rather than at a fixed rate; they then get caught out when interest rates go up faster than rental income.

Problem 6.1

Grouch Group is seeking to dispose of one of its less profitable subsidiaries to management (as a management buy-out). The asking price is £10m. The management team plans to form a company, Hopeful plc, and is prepared to invest £2m in the form of ordinary share capital; and a venture capital company has offered to put up either (i) £8m as a medium term loan at 10% fixed; or (ii) £6m as a medium term loan at 9% fixed and £2m in the form of ordinary share capital.

A business plan suggests that Hopeful will produce profits before interest of from £750,000 to £1,500,000. Ignoring tax, (a) calculate the profits available to management on their investment under scenarios (i) and (ii) for the range of profits projected; (b) depict this in a chart; (c) calculate the return earned (i) by management; and (ii) by the venture capital company on the same bases.

Chapter 7

INTANGIBLE FIXED ASSETS

Schedule 4 to the Companies Act 1985 requires fixed assets to be presented in the balance sheet under three headings: intangible assets, tangible assets and investments. We deal with the intangible assets in this chapter, with tangible fixed assets in Chapter 8 and with investments in Chapter 9.

Intangible fixed assets
Intangible fixed assets comprise:

(a) capitalised development costs;
(b) what we will call 'rights' (e.g. licences, concessions, patents and trademarks); and
(c) purchased goodwill.

Capitalised development costs
Under SSAP 13 *Research and development* all expenditure on R & D should normally be written off in the year in which it is incurred.

However, where development is for clearly defined projects on which expenditure is separately identifiable and for which commercial success is reasonably certain, companies may if they wish defer charging development expenditure 'to the extent that its recovery can reasonably be regarded as assured'. Capitalised development expenditure should be separately disclosed. However the trend amongst companies which capitalise development is to change to the more prudent policy of immediate write-off. For example ML LABORATORIES:

ML LABORATORIES *Extracts from 1998 Directors' report and accounts*

Research & Development
The Group is engaged in the research into, and the development of, a diverse portfolio of pharmaceutical, medical and other novel products.

During the year the Group has changed its accounting policy of capitalisation and subsequent amortisation to one of immediate write-off. Full details of this change are in notes 1 and …

The loss for the year [£8,442,697] is stated after charging research and development expenditure of £7,719,642.

Note 1. Change in accounting policy
The comparative results for the year to 30 September 1997 have been adjusted as follows:

	£
Profit as originally reported	683,810
Change in treatment of R & D	(5,671,095)
Restatement of minority interest	437,427
Loss as restated	(4,549,848)

Rights

Intangible assets purchased separately from a business, i.e. not part of an acquisition, should be capitalised at cost (FRS 10 para. 9). They include:

(a) copyright and similar publishing rights;

(b) know-how;

(c) licences;

(d) patents and trademarks.

Copyright and similar publishing rights

Copyrights provide the holder with the exclusive right to produce copies of, and control over, an original musical, artistic or literary work. From 1 January 1996, a statutory instrument, the Duration of Copyright and Rights in Performances Regulations 1995 (SI 1996/3297), enacting an EC Directive to harmonise the term of protection of copyright and related rights, governs the period of copyright in the UK. For literary (including compilations and computer programs), dramatic, musical and artistic works, copyright expires 70 years from the end of the calendar year in which the author died. The sums involved can be considerable. For example EMI GROUP's balance sheet at the year end 31 March 1998 showed copyrights of £372.2m after a £27.0m amortisation charge for the period.

Know-how

Some companies capitalise know-how (i.e. technical knowledge or skill). This may be people-dependent or process-dependent; purchased by acquisition of, say, a specialist service. For example RACAL:

RACAL *Extract statement of accounting policies 1998*

Know how

Payments made to acquire manufacturing licences for specific products are amortised against profits over a period of 3 to 5 years being the period of utilisation of such manufacturing knowledge.

Licences

Licences are agreements that a company enters into with government or with a third party which enables it to carry out certain trading functions. Examples are brewers which operate licensed prem4ises, or bookmakers, who are required to obtain a licence for each bookmaking shop.

Companies may also purchase licences which allow them to use software or technology developed by third parties, and licences from government authorities e.g. VODAFONE:

VODAFONE GROUP *Extracts from 1998 accounts*

Statement of accounting policies
INTANGIBLE FIXED ASSETS
Purchased intangible fixed assets, including licence fees, are capitalised at cost except for subscriber contracts, which are written off to reserves in the year in which they are acquired. [Cost of subscriber contracts is the difference between the amount a new subscriber pays for his mobile phone and the actual, and much higher, cost of the phone.]

Network licence costs are amortised over the periods of the licences. Amortisation is charged from commencement of service of the network. The annual charge is calculated in proportion to the expected usage of the network during the start up period and on a straight line basis thereafter.

Note 8 Intangible fixed assets

	Licence and spectrum fees £m
Cost	
1 April 1997	151.5
Exchange movements	(29.2)
Additions	24.9
31 March 1998	147.2
Amortisation	
1 April 1997	4.1
Exchange movements	(1.6)
Charge for the year	7.1
31 March 1998	9.6
Net book value	
31 March 1998	137.6
31 March 1997	147.4

Patents and trademarks

A patent is in effect a document granted by the government assuring an inventor of the sole right to make, use and sell his invention for a determined period, e.g. a pharmaceutical company patenting a drug it has developed.

Registering a trademark provides legal protection to the name or symbol used to differentiate the products supplied by a manufacturer or authorised distributor from those of competing manufacturers and dealers. Given their identifiable cost and their value to businesses over long periods in terms of income stream generation, it is not unreasonable to capitalise those costs and amortise them over their useful lives; but that decision is one for the directors. BASS does not capitalise costs of this nature. On the other hand

LATCHWAYS, a small producer and distributor of industrial safety products, is heavily dependent on world wide patents to protect its inventions. The 1998 balance sheet showed intangible assets of £180,000, and details were contained in a note to the accounts:

LATCHWAYS *Note to the 1998 accounts*

Intangible fixed assets
Patents, trade marks and registered designs

	£000
Cost	
At 1 April 1997	252
Additions in the year	32
At 31 March 1998	284
Depreciation	
At 1 April 1997	82
Charge for the year	22
At 31 March 1998	104
Net book value	
At 31 March 1998	180
At 31 March 1997	170

Purchased goodwill

The difference between the fair value of the consideration paid for an acquired entity and the aggregate of the fair values of that entity's identifiable assets and liabilities is termed purchased goodwill.

GOLDEN GOOSE (1998) LTD *Continuing the illustration on page 5.*

The purchasers agreed that the tangible assets at the time of acquisition were:

	£
Fixtures and fittings	8,000
Motor van	6,800
Stock, at cost	5,900
	20,700

Imagine that the previous owner asked £25,000 for the business; and that the new company paid that:
Purchased goodwill = £25,000 − £20,700 = £4,300.

Purchased goodwill - old rules

Until recently the normal way of dealing with purchased goodwill had been to write it off immediately against reserves.

This was thoroughly unsatisfactory for two main reasons:

1. Millions and millions of pounds of shareholders' money disappeared from the balance sheet without trace. Well, almost without trace: the Companies Act required the cumulative amount of goodwill written off against reserves to be shown in the accounts.

    But it was usually put in some obscure note, and very few analysts paid any attention to it, except when an acquisition was subsequently disposed of, where the goodwill written off in the acquisition had to be reinstated. This often turned a handsome profit on disposal into a thumping loss.
2. Reducing the size of shareholders' funds played merry hell with some ratios. Two key ones that most investors still clung to with touching, almost childlike, faith were Return On Capital Employed (ROCE), and Gearing (Debt to Equity ratio). Due to 'immediate write-off', both were often grossly misleading.

Hardly surprising, when some companies actually reported negative shareholders' funds.

Purchased goodwill - new rules

Under FRS 10 *Goodwill and intangible assets* and *FRS 11 Impairment of fixed assets and goodwill*, purchased goodwill and intangible assets must be capitalised and either:

(a) amortised over their useful economic lives; or
(b) where their useful economic lives exceed 20 years, or they are not amortised, their value must be reviewed annually for impairment.

CADBURY SCHWEPPES *Extract from accounting policies 1998*

(o) Intangibles
Intangibles represent significant owned brands acquired since 1985 valued at historical cost. No amortisation is charged as the annual results reflect significant expenditure in support of these brands. For the 1998 financial statements, the Group has adopted FRS 10 *Goodwill and Intangible Assets* and FRS 11 *Impairment of Fixed Assets and Goodwill*. As permitted by FRS 10 and FRS 11, the Group will continue its policy of capitalising acquired intangible assets (brands) and reviewing the carrying values on an annual basis for any impairment in value.

Under transitional arrangements, any goodwill which had previously been written off to reserves could remain there, until such time as the related business is disposed of.

Companies have, however, the option to rein-state as an asset old goodwill previously written off to reserves. If they do this, either all old goodwill or all post-FRS 7 goodwill should be reinstated.

Impairment

FRS 11 *Impairment of Fixed Assets and Goodwill* came into force for periods ending on or after 23 December 1998. Companies Act requirements already call for the writing down of fixed assets if they are judged to have become permanently impaired. What is new about FRS 11 is the methodology imposed. Impairment is to be assessed by reference to discounted cash flows. The standard introduces the implication that assets must be stated in the balance sheet at amounts that are expected to earn at least a satisfactory rate of return. Companies earning a poor rate of return, even though profitable, will have to write down their assets.

An impairment review has to be conducted:

1. When goodwill or intangibles appear in the balance sheet and are not amortised over 20 years or less.
2. Where there are indicators of impairment that suggest that the company's assets may not be fully recoverable, e.g. persistent operating losses; negative operating cash flows; a signifi-cant fall in an asset's market value; an asset being physically damaged, or becoming obso-lete; a significant adverse change in the com-petitive or regulatory environment; a reorgani-sation; or even loss of key employees.

Past impairment losses can only be reversed subse-quently if the recovery in value is due to the rever-sal of the reason which gave rise to the impairment in the first place. So previous impairment losses will rarely be reversed.

The standard applies not only to any goodwill that is recognised as an asset but to most fixed as-sets, except derivatives and oil exploration expen-diture.

Problem 7.1

ML Laboratories (see example on page 48). By changing its policy on R & D from capitalisation and amortisation to immediate write-off, ML in-creased a loss of £0.72m in 1998 into one of £8.44m, and restated 1997 as a £4.55m loss rather than a £0.68m profit.

Immediate write-off is undoubtedly more pru-dent, but do you think it gives a more realistic view of a company's performance? ML's share price doubled in 12 months after two years of apparently heavy losses. What can the private shareholder do to understand why?

TERMINOLOGY

Intangible fixed assets

Intangible fixed assets are non-monetary fixed assets that have no physical substance but are iden-tifiable and are controlled by the entity (company) through legal rights or physical custody.

They include:

- purchased goodwill
- capitalised development costs
- concessions, patents, licences, trade marks and similar rights and assets.

Purchased goodwill represents the difference be-tween the consideration paid for an acquisition and the aggregate of the fair values of that acquisition's net assets.

Fair value is the amount at which an asset could be exchanged in an arm's length transaction between informed and willing parties, other than in a forced or liquidation sale (FRS 7 para.2).

Positive goodwill arises when the consideration exceeds the aggregate fair values of the identifiable assets and liabilities. **Negative goodwill** arises when the aggregate fair values exceed the consid-eration paid.

Carrying value is simply another term for book value (which avoids suggesting that the balance sheet is a valuation statement).

Impairment is a reduction in the recoverable amount of an asset below its carrying value.

Recoverable amount is the higher of net realisable value of an asset and its value in use.

The **useful economic life** of an intangible asset is the period over which the entity expects to derive economic benefit from it. The useful economic life of purchased goodwill is the period over which the value of the underlying business is expected to ex-ceed the values of its identifiable net assets.

Value in use is the present value of the future cash flows obtainable as a result of an asset's continued use, including those resulting from its ultimate dis-posal (FRS 10 para.2).

Chapter 8

TANGIBLE FIXED ASSETS

Reference: FRS 15, *Tangible fixed assets.*

Tangible fixed assets are those long-lived assets not held for resale in the ordinary course of business but for the purpose, directly or indirectly, of earning revenue. Thus they include not only things like plant and machinery which are actually used to provide the product, but assets used to house or support operations, such as land, buildings, furniture, vehicles, ships and aircraft. Also included are leased assets (see page 108).

Depreciation is a measure of the loss of value of an asset due to use, the passage of time and obsolescence, including the amortisation of fixed assets whose useful economic life is predetermined (e.g. leases) and depletion of wasting assets, e.g. BLUE CIRCLE:

BLUE CIRCLE INDUSTRIES *Accounting policies 1998*

Depreciation

...

Depreciation on freehold and leasehold mineral lands is provided on the basis of tonnage extracted.

Traditionally fixed assets are shown in the balance sheet at cost less accumulated depreciation to date (i.e. at net book value). This book value is not, and does not purport to be in any sense, a valuation, though fixed assets, particularly land and buildings, are often revalued. In UK practice, sometimes, but by no means always, the valuation is taken into the books.

Companies Act requirements

The requirements of the Companies Act 1985 with regard to fixed assets are complex. In summary:

(a) fixed assets may be shown on a historical cost basis, or at valuation, or at current cost (see Chapter 29), and should be classified under headings appropriate to the business;

(b) land must be analysed into freehold, long leaseholds (over 50 years unexpired) and short leaseholds;

(c) where fixed assets are included on a historical cost basis, the aggregate figure for the following amounts must be shown under each heading:

  (i) cost;
  (ii) provision for depreciation since acquisition;
  (iii) the book value (i minus ii);

(d) where fixed assets are included at a valuation, the amount so included must be shown, together with the years and amounts of the valuations and, for assets valued during the year, the names of the valuers and the basis of valuation (see page 59, QUEENS MOAT HOUSES);

TERMINOLOGY

Accounting bases

Two accounting bases are permitted by the Companies Acts:

Historical cost under which assets are stated in the balance sheet at depreciated actual cost.

In practice, UK companies frequently adopt what may be termed the **modified historical cost** convention under which historical cost is employed but certain assets are revalued.

Current cost (termed 'alternative accounting rules') under which assets are stated at their value to the business.

(e) where fixed assets are included at valuation or at current cost, historical cost details must also be disclosed;

(f) particulars must be given of additions and disposals during the period.

Disclosure requirements on depreciation

Schedule 9 of the Companies Act 1985 requires companies to disclose:

(a) the amount of depreciation charged to revenue;
(b) if depreciation has been calculated on other than book value;
(c) any amounts, additional to depreciation, charged by way of provision for renewal of fixed assets;
(d) if no provision has been made for depreciation or replacement; or the method used if other than by depreciation charge or provision for renewals.

SSAP 12 requires companies to disclose the method of depreciation used for each category of asset, together with the effective useful lives assumed.

Rates of depreciation

The following are typical rates (using the straight line method of depreciation, described below):

Freehold land	Nil
Freehold buildings	2% = 50 year life
Leasehold property:	
Long leases (over 50 years)	2% = 50 years
Short leases	Over life of the lease
Tenants' improvements	Over life of the lease
Plant and machinery	10% = 10 years
Vehicles	20% = 5 years
Ships, according to type	4–10% = 10–25 years
Furniture and equipment	10% = 10 years

Subnormal depreciation charges

Where a company charges a subnormal rate of depreciation, or does not charge depreciation on assets (other than freehold land), it will report higher pre-tax profits than it would otherwise have done.

For example, a number of companies in the retail sector, including KINGFISHER, MARKS & SPENCER and BOOTS, no longer provide depreciation on their freehold and long leasehold properties, and explain why in their accounts, e.g., KINGFISHER.

KINGFISHER *Note on accounting policies 1998*

Depreciation

Depreciation of fixed assets is provided where it is necessary to reflect a reduction from book value to estimated residual value over the useful life of the asset to the Group. It is the Group's policy to maintain its properties in a state of good repair to prolong their useful lives. The directors consider that, in the case of freehold and long leasehold properties occupied by the group, the estimated residual values at the end of their useful economic lives, based on the prices prevailing at the time of acquisition or subsequent valuation, are not materially different from their current carrying values. The lives of these properties and their residual values are such that no provision for depreciation is considered necessary. Depreciation of other fixed assets is calculated by the straight line method and the annual rates applicable to the principal categories are:

...

SAINSBURY and TESCO, which at one time took this view, both now depreciate properties.

BASS, WHITBREAD and ALLIED DOMECQ are among companies which do not depreciate licensed premises that are freehold or long leasehold.

Analysts sometimes make allowances for differing depreciation policies when making comparisons between companies.

Nevertheless, determination of useful economic life (the period over which the present owner expects to derive economic benefit from the asset's use) is a matter for management and depends on business circumstances. For example, in the Chairman's Statement of THE JERSEY ELECTRICITY COMPANY, he refers to a site redevelopment that will allow relocation of the company's head office and provision of commercial retail and other office space. A note to the accounts discloses that the site has been examined in relation to FRS 11 *Impairment of fixed assets and goodwill*. As a result of this examination, depreciation has been accelerated to ensure that the assets will be written off during the development period. As a consequence, additional depreciation of £0.7m has been charged in 1998. It seems that this charge relates principally to buildings which will be demolished to allow completion of the development.

Where depreciation is shown in the accounts

Depreciation appears in several places; HALMA provides (see the top of the next page) an example of what a good set of accounts shows:

1. In the note on accounting policies.
2. In a note to the profit and loss account: the charge for the year.
3. In a note on the 'Consolidated Cash Flow Statement'.
4. In a note to the balance sheet item 'Fixed assets – Tangible assets': the charge for the year and the cumulative amount to date.

HALMA *Extracts from the 1998 accounts*

♦ *Accounting policies:*

Depreciation

With the exception of freehold land, depreciation is provided on all tangible fixed assets on the straight line method, each item being written off over its estimated life.

The principal annual rates used for this purpose are:

Freehold buildings	2%
Leasehold properties	
more than 50 years unexpired	2%
less than 50 years unexpired	Period of lease
Plant, machinery and equipment	8% to 20%
Motor vehicles	20%
Short-life tooling	33⅓%.

♦ *Note 10:*

Fixed Assets – Tangible Fixed Assets

Group	Freehold Properties	Long Leases	Short Leases	Plant Equipment Vehicles etc.	Total
					£000
At 29 March 1997	1,615	160	650	23,545	25,970
Charge for the year	304	28	123	4,873	5,328
Disposals	–	–	(135)	(3,602)	(3,737)
Exchange adjustments	(49)	–	(16)	(319)	(384)
At 28 March 1998	1,870	188	622	24,497	27,177

♦ *Note 3 to the profit and loss account:*

	1998 £000	1997 £000
Operating Profit is arrived at after charging:		
Depreciation	5,328	4,993

♦ *Reconciliation of operating profit to net cash inflow from operating activities:*

Operating profit	42,270	37,157
...		
Depreciation	5,328	4,993

Methods of depreciation

The most common method or basis of depreciation, used by over 80% of major companies, is the straight line (or fixed instalment) method.

Other methods include:

(a) the declining (or reducing) balance method;
(b) the sum of the years' digits method;
(c) the renewals method;
(d) the production unit method;
(e) the annuity method;
(f) the sinking fund method.

As will be seen, the different methods of depreciation affect:

(i) net asset values
(ii) net profit
(iii) return on capital employed.

The straight line or fixed instalment method

Depreciation under the fixed instalment method is computed as follows (see also Example 8.1 at the top of the next page):

$$\text{Annual depreciation} = \frac{\text{Cost - Residual value}}{\text{Useful economic life}}$$

TERMINOLOGY

Tangible fixed assets

Tangible fixed assets include:
- land and buildings
- plant and machinery
- fixtures, fittings, tools and equipment
- payments on account of tangible fixed assets

Depreciation is the measure of the wearing out, consumption or other reduction in the useful economic life of a fixed asset whether arising from use, effluxion of time or obsolescence through technological or market changes.

The **useful economic life** (or expected useful life) of an asset is the period over which the present owner expects to derive economic benefits from its use.

Residual value is the realisable value of the asset at the end of its useful economic life, based on prices prevailing at the date of acquisition or revaluation, where this has taken place. Realisation costs should be deducted in arriving at the residual value.

Recoverable amount is the greater of the net realisable value of an asset and, where appropriate, the amount recoverable from its further use.

Example 8.1 Straight line depreciation

If a machine having a useful economic life of five years is purchased for £10,000, and is expected to have a residual value of £1,000 at the end of that life, depreciation will be:

$$\frac{£10,000 - £1,000}{5} = \frac{£9,000}{5} = £1,800 \text{ per annum}$$

and the accounts will show:

End of year	Depreciation for the year shown in the P & L account	Cost	Provision for depreciation to date	Net book value
			←—— shown in the balance sheet ——→	
	£	£	£	£
1	1,800	10,000	1,800	8,200
2	1,800	10,000	3,600	6,400
3	1,800	10,000	5,400	4,600
4	1,800	10,000	7,200	2,800
5	1,800	10,000	9,000	1,000

The straight line method is ideal where the service provided by the asset continues unabated throughout its useful economic life, as might be the case with a 21 year lease of a building. It is the method generally used wherever the equal allocation of cost provides a reasonably fair measure of the asset's service, for example, for buildings, plant, machinery, equipment, vehicles and patents. A key advantage is that it is easy to calculate, and conceptually simple to understand.

The declining balance method

The declining balance (or reducing balance) method used to be the most popular method of depreciation; but, except for tax purposes, it has largely been supplanted in recent years by the straight line method.

Under the declining balance method, the annual depreciation charge represents a fixed percentage of the net book value brought forward (i.e. cost less accumulated depreciation). The calculation of the annual charge is simple enough once the appropriate percentage has been determined, but this requires the use of tables or a calculator:

$$\text{Depreciation rate} = 1 - (\text{Residual value} \div \text{Cost})^{1/n}$$

where n = useful economic life in years and depreciation rate is a decimal.

Example 8.2 illustrates the calculation.

Example 8.2 Declining balance depreciation

The rate for the machine in Example 8.1 would be computed as follows:

$$\text{Depreciation rate} = 1 - (£10,000 \div £1,000)^{1/5} = 1 - 0.631 = 0.369 = 36.9\%$$

Thus the rate to apply is 36.9%.

End of year	Depreciation for the year (shown in the P & L account)	Cost	Provision for depreciation to date	Net book value
			←—— shown in the balance sheet ——→	
	£	£	£	£
1	3,690	10,000	3,690	6,310
2	2,328	10,000	6,018	3,982
3	1,470	10,000	7,488	2,512
4	927	10,000	8,415	1,585
5	585	10,000	9,000	1,000

Among the disadvantages of the declining balance method are these:

(a) most users do not calculate the rate appropriate to each particular item of plant, but use standard percentages, which tend to be too low rather than too high;

(b) unless notional adjustments are made to cost and residual value, it is impossible to calculate satisfactorily a declining balance rate if the residual value is nil: the net book value can never get to nil, as it can only be reduced by a proportion each year;

(c) even if the asset is assigned a nominal scrap value (say £1 so that it is not overlooked in the books) or if there is some residual value but it is small in relation to cost, the method is unlikely to be satisfactory without notional adjustments, because it leads to such high charges in the early years, as Example 8.3 shows.

Example 8.3 Declining balance depreciation, small residual value

Taking our previous example of plant costing £10,000, but with a residual value of £200 instead of £1,000, we get:

Year	*Depreciation with residual value*	
	£200	*£1,000*
	£	£
1	5,425	3,690
2	2,482	2,328
3	1,135	1,470
4	520	927
5	238	585
Accumulated depreciation at the end of year 5	9,800	9,000
Residual value	200	1,000

The sum of the years' digits method

The sum of the (years') digits method is not commonly found in the United Kingdom, though it is used a good deal as a method of allowing accelerated depreciation in the United States (where accounting depreciation, provided it is computed by an acceptable method, is used for tax purposes too). It is occasionally found in the United Kingdom in connection with activities like leasing which involve heavy outlays in early years.

In this method, the cost less any residual value is divided by the sum of the years' digits to give what, for the purpose of this explanation, may be termed a unit of depreciation. In the last year of expected life, one unit of depreciation is provided; in the next to last, two; in the one before that, three; and so on.

The sum of the years' digits is simply the sum of the series: $(1 + 2 + 3 + 4 \ldots + n)$, where n represents the expected life of the asset.

The formula for computing the sum of the digits is $n(n + 1) / 2$, where n is the number of years. Thus, to apply the sum of the digits to an asset having a life of 5 years, the divisor (i.e. the sum of the years' digits) is $5(5 + 1) / 2 = 15$, and the first year's depreciation is 5/15ths of (cost minus residual value), the second year's 4/15ths, and so on.

Comparison of methods

It is interesting to compare the balance sheet value of this asset year by year under sum of the digits (SD) with the value under the straight line (SL) and the declining balance methods (DB£1000 for a residual value of £1,000 and DB£200 for one of £200), as shown in Example 8.5 on the next page.

Example 8.4 Sum of the years' digits method of depreciation

Taking our example of a machine costing £10,000, with an estimated life of five years and a residual value estimated at £1,000: the sum of the year's digits is 15, and a unit of depreciation is thus $(£10,000 - £1,000) \div 15 = £600$, so:

End of year	*Depreciation for the year* (shown in the P & L account)	*Cost*	*Provisions for depreciation to date*	*Net book value*
		<———— shown in the balance sheet ————>		
	£	£	£	£
1	3,000	10,000	3,000	7,000
2	2,400	10,000	5,400	4,600
3	1,800	10,000	7,200	2,800
4	1,200	10,000	8,400	1,600
5	600	10,000	9,000	1,000

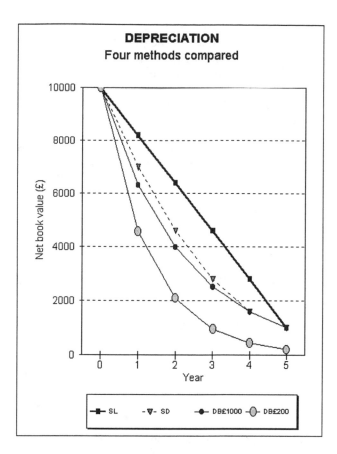

Example 8.5 Balance sheet values compared for four methods of depreciation.

The value under the sum of the digits method, on the other hand, is reduced in decreasing steps, year by year, reaching residual value at the end of the asset's expected life, regardless of the size of the residual value, if any.

There is a similarity in the charges produced by the two methods, but the sum of the digits method does not need the notional adjustments of the declining balance method to cope with small or nil residual values.

The renewals method

Definable major assets or components within an infrastructure or network with determinable finite lives should be treated separately and depreciated over their useful economic lives.

For the remaining tangible fixed assets within the system or network, renewals accounting may be used as a method of estimating depreciation (FRS 15 para. 97).

Where renewals accounting is adopted, the level of annual expenditure required to maintain the operating capacity of the infrastructure asset is treated as the depreciation charged for the period (FRS 15 para. 98).

Change in expected useful life

The useful economic life of a tangible fixed asset is reviewed as part of the normal end of period reporting procedures. If it is revised, the carrying amount of the tangible fixed asset at the date of revision should be depreciated over the revised life (FRS 15 para. 93).

Changes in useful life can have a significant effect on profits. For example STORM, the cartoon character licensing group, changed its accounting policy on film costs in its 1992 accounts to reflect a change in group strategy, as the chairman explained.

STORM GROUP *Extract from Chairman's statement*

It was decided that Storm would no longer utilise its own funds to invest in animated cartoon film productions ... all production work would be funded from commissions, external funding or pre-sales revenue.

As a result of this change in strategic focus, the Board elected to adopt a revised accounting policy in respect of film costs and to write them off to the profit and loss account as incurred. The total sum involved was £2.289m, of which £1.538m was charged in 1992 and the balance treated as a prior year item.

The effect of the change in accounting policy was the major cause of the group reporting a pre-tax loss of £2.1m. But the chairman's statement went on to say:

STORM GROUP *Second extract from Chairman's statement*

It is, however, vitally important to emphasise that the write-off of film production costs should not be seen to detract from the inherent value of the animation programmes to which they relate. Animated cartoons have traditionally generated revenues over a long period ...

Storm claimed that the revised policy had been adopted on the grounds of prudence, but does it necessarily provide 'a true and fair view'? Future profits will be enhanced by hundreds of thousands of pounds per annum for several years, because animation programmes will no longer have to be depreciated.

Writing down of asset values

As explained in Chapter 7, FRS 11 *Impairment of Fixed Assets and Goodwill*, which came into force for periods ending on or after 23 December 1998, calls for the writing down of fixed assets if they are judged to have become permanently impaired. The standard introduces the implication that assets must be stated in the balance sheet at amounts that are expected to earn at least a satisfactory rate of return. Companies earning a poor rate of return, even though profitable, will have to write down their assets (see page 51 regarding impairment reviews).

The useful economic life of a tangible fixed asset should be reviewed at the end of each reporting period and revised if expectations are significantly different from previous estimates. If a useful economic life is revised, the carrying amount of the tangible fixed asset at the date of revision should be depreciated over the revised remaining useful economic life (FRS 15 para. 93).

What is more, where the residual value is material that review has to take account of reasonably expected technological changes based on prices prevailing at the date of acquisition (or revaluation). A change in its estimated residual value should be accounted for prospectively over the asset's remaining useful economic life, except to the extent that the asset has been impaired at the balance sheet date (FRS 15 para. 95).

Changing method

A change from one method of providing depreciation to another is permissible only on the grounds that the new method will give a fairer presentation of the results and of the financial position. Such a change does not, however, constitute a change of accounting policy; it does not give rise to an exceptional item: the carrying amount of the tangible fixed asset is depreciated using the revised method over the remaining useful economic life, beginning in the period in which the change is made (FRS 15 para. 82).

Freehold land and buildings

Traditionally, neither freehold land nor buildings were depreciated, though the majority of companies had been depreciating freehold buildings in years before accounting standards were introduced.

Under FRS 15 companies are normally required to depreciate freehold and long leasehold buildings.

If, however, no depreciation charge is made on the grounds that it would be immaterial, or on the grounds that the estimated remaining useful life of the asset is over 50 years, tangible fixed assets should be reviewed for impairment at the end of each reporting period.

The revaluation of assets

Under historical cost accounting, assets appear at cost less depreciation, and they are not revalued to show their current worth to the company. But because of the effects of inflation, the practice grew up in the United Kingdom of revaluing assets, particularly freehold land and buildings, from time to time.

Indeed, Schedule 7 para. 1 of the Companies Act 1985 requires the difference between the market value of property assets and the balance sheet amount to be disclosed in the directors' report if, in the opinion of the directors, it is significant. UK companies thus face the choice; they must either:

(a) incorporate any revaluation in the accounts, or

(b) disclose it in the directors' report.

Where assets are revalued and the revaluation is incorporated in the accounts, both 'sides' of the balance sheet are affected, and depreciation from then on is based on the revalued amounts, as Example 8.8 illustrates.

Example 8.8 Effects of revaluation

A company has freehold land which cost £10m and buildings which cost £4.2m, have a useful life of 50 years and were 10 years old on 31 December 1999. Depreciation to that date would therefore be 2% p.a. for 10 years on £4.2m = £840,000, so the balance sheet would show:

	£m
Freehold land and buildings at cost	5.200
less depreciation to date	0.840
Book value at 31 December 1999	4.360

On 1 January 2000 the land was revalued at £3.800m and the buildings at £8.100m. After the revaluation the accounts would show freehold land and buildings at the valuation figure of £11.900m, an increase of £7.540m. On the other side of the balance sheet the reserves would normally be increased by £7.540m. (If, however, the company has decided in principle to dispose of the buildings, SSAP 15, para. 12 requires a provision to be made out of the revaluation surplus for the tax which would be payable on disposal, and this would be credited to deferred tax, the remainder of the surplus being credited to reserves.)

The 2000 accounts would be required to disclose the basis of valuation used and the name or qualification of the valuer (CA 1985, Sch. 4, para. 43 (b)).

The revaluation will affect the company in several ways:

1. The annual depreciation charge on the buildings, based on the new value and the current estimate of the remaining useful life (40 years), will increase from £84,000 to £202,500 (2½% p.a. on £8.100m), thus directly reducing the pre-tax profits by £118,500 in each future year.
2. The overall profitability of the company, as measured by the ratio Return on Capital Employed (ROCE, described in Chapter 16), will also appear to deteriorate because the capital employed will have increased by £7.540m. For instance, if the company in our example went on to make £3.000m before interest and tax in 2000, and had £20.000m

capital employed before the revaluation, the 2000 return on capital employed would be:

No revaluation	*Revaluation*
$\dfrac{3,118,500}{20,000,000} = 15.9\%$	$\dfrac{3,000,000}{27,540,000} = 10.9\%$

3. The borrowing powers of most companies are expressed as a multiple of share capital and reserves, so the increase in reserves will raise the borrowing limits, and improve the capital cover of existing lenders.
4. The higher property value may give more scope for borrowing on mortgage.
5. The increase in reserves will also increase the n.a.v., the net asset value per share, described in Chapter 24.

For example, for 1992 the hotel group QUEENS MOAT HOUSES reported a pre-tax loss of over £1 billion, due mainly to a net deficit on revaluation of tangible fixed assets below historical cost.

The *new* chairman explained the background:

QUEENS MOAT HOUSES *Extract from Chairman's statement*

At 31 December 1991, the group's properties were valued by Weatherall Green & Smith (WGS) at £2.0 billion, a valuation which was incorporated in the 1991 audited balance sheet ...

In June the previous board appointed Jones Lang Wootton (JLW) to value the group's hotel portfolio in place of WGS. They have valued the portfolio of properties as at 31 December 1992 at £861 million ...

After careful consideration the board accepted the JLW valuation and it has been incorporated into the group's balance sheet at 31 December 1992. In the UK and Continental Europe there was considerable hotel expansion in the late 1980's fuelled by the abundant availability of capital. Circumstances have changed materially over the past few years and the recent market place for hotels in the UK has been dominated by distressed sale values. On the continent, the declining profitability has lagged the UK but the market place has shown similar adverse developments. It is this adverse context of declining profitability and limited purchasers' interest in hotels in which the valuation has been prepared ...

Valuations of tangible fixed assets

This is a dodgy area: people have been dodging it ever since the Great CCA (Current Cost Accounting) Fiasco, proposals for 'inflation accounting' which went down like a lead balloon in the 1980s. The ill-fated SSAP 16, which tried to impose a system riddled with subjective judgment on an unwilling world of business and commerce, was suspended in June 1985, and formally withdrawn in April 1988 (see Chapter 29).

The arguments for and against valuations

On the one hand, valuations can produce figures that fluctuate wildly – e.g. Queens Moat House – and a lot may depend on the valuer, and whether he thinks his client wants a 'very full' valuation, or a parsimonious one. The tendency is for new management to opt for the latter.

On the other hand, as the chairman of the ASB, Sir David Tweedie, has pointed out, it is nonsense to have a property shown in the balance sheet at £10m if the bank, valuing it at £50m, has accepted it as security for a £40m loan.

We rather agree with Sir Adrian Cadbury, who said at his last AGM as chairman of CADBURY SCHWEPPES that the only time the real value of a brand [or any other asset] is known is when it changes hands.

FRS 15 *Tangible fixed assets*

The ASB has now grasped the nettle somewhat cautiously. Under FRS 15, in force for financial periods ending on or after 23 March 2000, revaluing tangible fixed assets remains optional.

But, where a policy of revaluation is adopted, it must be applied to a whole class of assets and the valuations kept up-to-date. This will generally be achieved by a five-yearly full valuation of an asset with a qualified external valuer, and an interim valuation in year 3. Valuations in the intervening years are only required where there is likely to have been a material change in value.

Revaluation gains should be recognised in the profit and loss account only to the extent that they reverse valuation losses on the same asset that were previously recognized in the profit and loss account. All other revaluation gains should be recognised in the statement of total recognised gains and losses (FRS 15 para. 63).

Revaluation losses caused by a clear loss of economic benefit should be recognised in the profit and loss account. Other revaluation losses should normally be recognized in the statement of total recognised gains and losses until the carrying amount reaches its depreciated historical cost (FRS 15 para. 65).

Sales and other disposals of fixed assets

Where fixed assets are disposed of for an amount which is greater (or less) than their book value, the profit or loss on disposal should be shown separately on the face of the profit and loss account after operating profit and before interest, and attributed to continuing or discontinued operations (FRS 3 paras 19 and 20), e.g. TESCO at the top of the next page.

TESCO *Extract from profit and loss account 1999*

	£m	£m
Operating profit	934	849
Loss on disposal of discontinued operations	–	(8)
Net loss on disposal of fixed assets	(8)	(1)
Share of operating profit/ (loss) of joint ventures	6	(6)
Profit on ordinary activities before interest	932	834
Net interest payable	(90)	(74)
Profit on ordinary activities before taxation	842	760

Where assets which have been revalued are subsequently disposed of, the gains or losses are to be calculated against the carrying value (valuation amount less any subsequent depreciation).

Investment properties

Currently, while FRS 15 requires annual depreciation charges to be made on fixed assets, and makes it clear that an increase in the value of a fixed asset does not remove the necessity to charge depreciation, a different treatment is applied to fixed assets held as disposable investments.

Under SSAP 19, 'investment properties' (i.e. properties held as disposable investments rather than for use in a manufacturing or commercial process) are not depreciated, but are revalued each year at their open market value, and the valuation is reflected in the balance sheet. Changes in the value of investment properties should be treated as a movement on an 'investment property revaluation reserve'. The cumulative amounts credited to reserve can be very large; see leading property company LAND SECURITIES below. If, however, there is a fall in value that exceeds the balance in the investment property revaluation reserve, the excess should be charged to the profit and loss account; i.e. the reserve cannot 'go negative'.

LAND SECURITIES *Extracts from notes to 1998 financial statements*

1. Accounting policies

(e) DEPRECIATION AND AMORTISATION In accordance with SSAP 19, no depreciation or amortisation is provided in respect of freehold or leasehold properties held on leases having more than 20 years unexpired. This departure from the requirements of the Companies Act 1985, for all properties to be depreciated, is, in the opinion of the Directors, necessary for the financial statements to give a true and fair view in accordance with applicable accounting standards, as properties are included in the financial statements at their open market value.

11. Properties

	Leasehold		Freehold	Total
	Over 50 years to run	Under 50 years to run		
GROUP	£m	£m	£m	£m
At 1 April 1997; at valuation	4,459.6	1,267.4	33.0	5,760.0
Additions	146.2	42.6	0.8	189.6
Sales	(182.4)	(64.5)	–	(249.6)
	4,423.4	1,245.5	33.8	5,702.7
Unrealised surplus on valuation	558.4	166.0	8.6	733.0
At 31 March 1998; at valuation	4,981.8	1,411.5	42.4	6,435.7

22. Reserves

	Share premium account	Revaluation reserve	Other reserves	Profit and loss account	Total
GROUP	£m	£m	£m	£m	£m
At 1 April 1997	53.2	2,349.0	503.6	515.9	3,521.7
Premium arising on issues of shares	160.0	–	–	–	160.6
Unrealised surplus on valuation of properties	–	733.0	–	–	733.0
Realised on sale of properties	–	(53.3)	53.3	–	–
Retained profit for the year	–	–	–	45.1	45.1
Transfer to amortised discount of bonds	(0.7)	–	–	0.7	–
At 31 March 1998	213.1	3,028.7	556.9	661.7	4,460.4

Government grants

Reference: SSAP 4 *Accounting for government grants*

Capital-based grants

Capital-based grants are grants made as a contribution towards specific expenditure on fixed assets. SSAP 4 requires capital-based grants to be credited to revenue (i.e. to the profit and loss account) over the expected useful life of the asset concerned.

Revenue-based grants

These include grants to finance the general activities of an enterprise over a specific period, which SSAP 4 requires to be credited to the profit and loss account in the period in which they are paid.

RMC GROUP *Extract from accounting policies 1998*

Grants

Grants received from government and similar agencies, where they relate to expenditure on fixed assets or are to finance the activities of the group over a number of years, are recognised in the profit and loss account over the expected useful economic lives of the related assets or over that number of years, and to the extent not so recognised are treated as deferred income. Grants which are intended to give immediate financial support or assistance or which are made to reimburse costs incurred are included in the profit and loss account so as to match with those costs in the period in which they become receivable.

Where the amounts involved are material, grants will appear:

(i) separately in the profit and loss account or notes as a contribution to profit and

(ii) in the balance note on creditors and deferred income.

Hybrid grants

With some grants, e.g. Regional Selective Investment Grants, which are made to help generate jobs in Assisted Areas, it is debatable whether they should be treated as capital grants or as revenue grants.

Ratios: Fixed assets

In considering fixed assets it is useful to monitor:

$$\frac{\text{Sales}}{\text{Tangible fixed assets}} \text{ expressed as a percentage}$$

Significant variation from year to year, or a marked difference from the ratio found in similar companies, deserves further investigation. Among the causes which one might pin-point are sales growth unmatched by a similar growth in fixed assets,

brought about, for example, by:

(a) better capacity utilisation with improved sales;

(b) failure to replace plant (allowing it to run down and hence presaging future problems).

A related ratio is:

$$\frac{\text{Tangible fixed assets}}{\text{Equity shareholders' funds}} \text{ expressed as a percentage}$$

Significant change from year to year, a marked difference from the ratio found in similar companies, or an extreme ratio, certainly deserve further consideration.

BLUEBIRD TOYS *Extract from group balance sheet 31 December 1995*

	1995 £m	1994 £m
Fixed assets:		
Tangible assets	8.046	8.675
...		
Equity shareholders' funds	32.362	23.046
$\dfrac{\text{Tangible fixed assets}}{\text{Equity shareholders' funds}} =$	$\dfrac{8.046}{32.362}$	$\dfrac{8.675}{23.046}$
=	24.86%	37.64%

Further study elicits:

1. Bluebird returned to profitability in 1992 after a period of loss-making.

2. Dividend payout continues to be low (9.00p on earnings per share of 24.2p in 1995). As a result £7.412m was retained in 1995.

3. But that did not account for the entire increase in equity shareholders' funds. Two tranches of Unsecured Loan Stock were compulsorily converted to Ordinary Shares.

4. After four years of expanding sales (during which turnover grew from £42.595m to £99.416m, i.e. by 133.4%), it fell in 1995 to £87.261m.

5. Cash at bank and in hand grew during 1995 from £30.492m to £34.150m; and at 31 December 1995 represented 105.5% of equity shareholders' funds.

6. Bluebird Toys operates in a very fickle market. A toy which hits the headlines and is a market leader one year may fail to come up to expectations and be discontinued the next.

A cash pile of this sort is worth watching.

It may represent a planned build-up of funds for, say, a massive re-equipment; or an acquisition. It may lead management to spend, possibly foolishly, rather than to be seen to be sitting on a cash mountain and either:

(i) look inefficient; or
(ii) be gobbled up by a predator.

Alternatively, management, seeing no better use for the funds, may simply reduce its capital base, as Bluebird did. On 15 March 1996 a share purchase programme was initiated and 3.289m of its own shares were purchased for £10.070m. The market was not impressed. The share price fell from a 1996 high of 363p to a 1997 low of 78p. The following Spring the company was rescued from a hostile bid by US toy giant MATTEL, with whom it already had close business ties.

The ratio:

$$\frac{\text{Depreciation}}{\text{Tangible fixed assets}} \quad \text{expressed as a percentage}$$

provides a broad indication of the way in which the fixed asset base is wearing out (and thus likely to need replacing). For example, a production line with an expected life of 5 years and zero net residual value at the end of that life might cost £120m. Straight line depreciation would be £24m per annum, and if this was the only tangible fixed asset, the ratio Depreciation/Tangible fixed assets would be £24m/£96m = 25% in year 1; and £24m/£48m = 50% two years later.

But a sharp change in the ratio may point to other factors. The ratio:

$$\frac{\text{Additions to plant and machinery}}{\text{Depreciation on plant and machinery}} \quad \text{as a percentage}$$

often provides an indication of whether a manufacturer is keeping his plant and machinery up to date.

Problem 8.1

Fleetwood has a fleet of 20 identical Ajax 1.6 litre motor cars purchased as follows:

1 January 1996	5 at	£10,000
1 January 1997	5 at	£11,000
1 January 1998	5 at	£12,000
1 January 1999	5 at	£12,500

Useful economic life is four years at the end of which sales proceeds are expected to be 40% of cost. These are the only motor vehicles.

Show the balance sheet item 'Motor vehicles' and its make up as at 31 December 1999.

Chapter 9

FIXED ASSET INVESTMENTS

Types of investment

Investments may be fixed assets or current assets. This chapter considers only investments which are fixed assets, i.e. held long-term, rather than for resale or as a temporary store of value.

Fixed asset investments fall into four categories:

(a) investment in subsidiaries;
(b) investment in associated undertakings (which includes joint ventures);
(c) other participating interests;
(d) other investments.

Investment in subsidiaries

In simple terms, a subsidiary undertaking is a company, partnership, or unincorporated association, where the company owning the investment (the holding company) is able to control the board of directors, either by virtue of its voting power or in some other way. A holding company is required by law to produce group accounts, in which the profits, assets and liabilities of the subsidiary are combined with those of the holding company, as described in detail in Chapters 20–21.

A company which is a holding company thus publishes two balance sheets: one for the company itself and a group balance sheet. This is demonstrated in the extract from the accounts of HIGHLAND DISTILLERIES shown below. The figures in the section headed COMPANY are for investments owned directly by Highland Distilleries itself.

The composition of GROUP figures, which are clearly quite different, is explained in Chapters 20 to 22.

HIGHLAND DISTILLERIES *Extract from notes to the accounts 1998*

	Subsidiary undertakings £m	Joint ventures £m	Associates £m	Participating interests £m	Other investments £m	Total £m
GROUP						
At 31 August 1997	–	1.9	74.6	123.7	0.2	200.4
Share of retained (losses)/profits	–	(0.3)	5.9	–	–	5.6
At 31 August 1998	–	1.6	80.5	123.7	0.2	206.0
COMPANY						
At 31 August 1997	253.4	0.6	0.2	85.9	0.2	340.3
Disposals	(0.1)	(0.1)	–	–	–	(0.2)
At 31 August 1998	253.3	0.5	0.2	85.9	0.2	340.1

Investment in associated undertakings

For accounting purposes, an associated undertaking is a non-subsidiary undertaking in which the investing group or company's position in it is:

(a) effectively that of a partner in a joint venture or consortium; or

(b) long-term and substantial (i.e. not less than 20% of the equity voting rights) and can include partnerships and unincorporated associations as well as companies. In each case the investing group must be in a position to exercise a significant influence over the operating and financial policy of the undertaking; this is usually by representation on the board of directors.

The investing group's share of the associated company's turnover, profits before tax, taxation, extraordinary items and net profit retained are shown separately in the group's consolidated accounts, as described more fully in Chapter 22.

Participating interests

A participating interest is an interest held by the investing group or company on a long-term basis to secure a contribution to its activities by the exercise of control or influence. A holding of 20% or more of the shares of an undertaking is presumed to be a participating interest unless the contrary is shown. An interest includes convertible securities and options as well as shares (CA 1989, s. 22). A participating interest is only an interest in an associated undertaking where a significant influence is exercised over its operating and financial policy.

Investments in associated undertakings and in other participating interests, i.e. participating interests that are not associates (see Chapter 22), are reported separately (CA 1989, Sch. 2, para. 21 (2)).

Other fixed asset investments

Whereas at first sight it may seem that these will consist entirely of investments of less than 20% this is not always the case. However, where a company has a holding of 20% or more in another undertaking, but does not treat it as an associated undertaking or as a participating interest, it should explain why. For example:

TT GROUP *Extract from note to 1998 accounts*

Fixed asset investments

The UK listed Investments of the Group ... include a 26.39% holding in the ordinary shares of Prestwick Holdings plc which has not been treated as an associated undertaking because the Group did not participate in the direction of its investment during the year and had no board representative.

Other investments may include works of art (e.g. CORDIANT, formerly SAATCHI & SAATCHI). Investments in works of art, other than by art dealers, should be viewed with distinct suspicion; directors should not indulge their artistic tastes with shareholders' money. In the past it has often been a warning sign of an arrogant top management.

They may also include life assurance policies (GIBBON GROUP) and the company's own shares held for employee share option schemes:

DIAGEO *Extracts from the notes to the 1998 accounts*

14. Fixed assets – investments

Investment in associates of £1,092m comprises the cost of shares, less goodwill written off on acquisition, of £900m plus the group's share of post-acquisition reserves of £192m. Investment in associates includes £825m in respect of Moet Hennessy.

The investment in Inntrepreneur Pub Company Ltd was sold during the period.

Other investments include £7m investments in own shares (see note 33).

The net book value of investments listed on UK stock exchanges was £32m. At 30 June 1998, these investments had a market value of £37m.

33. Fixed assets

Investment in own shares comprise £7m in respect of 1,640,509 ordinary shares ... The shares are held by employee trusts for the sole purpose of satisfying obligations under employee share schemes operated by the group.

A company is allowed to buy in its own shares for cancellation, but not for purposes of its own investment or for resale.

Listed investments should be shown at cost, divided into those listed on a recognised stock exchange in the United Kingdom and those listed overseas:

KINGFISHER *Extract from note to 1998 accounts*

Fixed asset investments

Other Investments	Listed in the UK	Listed Overseas	Unlisted
	£m	£m	£m
At 2 February 1997	0.4	4.8	18.2
Additions	–	–	0.1
Disposals	–	–	(17.6)
Effect of foreign exchange rate changes		(0.6)	
At 31 January 1998	0.4	4.2	0.6

The aggregate market value should also be shown where it differs from cost (CA 1985, Sch. 4, para. 45). Unlisted investments should be shown at cost or valuation.

Disclosures on significant holdings

Schedule 3 of the Companies Act 1989, para. 24, requires that where a company:

(i) holds 10% or more of the nominal value of any class of share in an undertaking, or

(ii) the holding exceeds one-tenth of the company's assets the accounts must state:

- the name of the undertaking;
- the country in which it is incorporated (if other than Great Britain); or (if incorporated in Great Britain) whether it is registered in England & Wales or in Scotland; or, if unincorporated, its address;
- the identity of each class held, and
- the proportion held.

This information need not be disclosed in respect of undertakings established or carrying on business outside the United Kingdom if the directors of the investing company consider disclosure would be harmful and the Department of Trade and Industry agrees (CA 1989, s. 6).

Holdings of 20% or more in another undertaking

Where a company has a significant holding of 20% or more, the aggregate amount of the capital and reserves and the profit or loss for the most recent year must also be given (CA 1989, Sch. 3, para. 25).

In addition, The London Stock Exchange's Listing Rules, Chapter 12, para. 12.43 requires disclosure of:

(i) the principal country of operation;

(ii) its issued capital and debt securities; and

(iii) the percentage interest in each class of security.

Balance sheet presentation

Schedule 4 of the Companies Act 1985 (amended by CA 1989) requires that where investments are shown as fixed assets, a further breakdown should be given, if individual amounts are material, either in the balance sheet itself or in notes:

(a) shares in group undertakings;

(b) loans to group undertakings;

(c) interests in associated undertakings;

(d) other participating interests;

(e) loans to undertakings at (c) and (d);

(f) other investments other than loans;

(g) other loans;

(h) own shares.

Points to watch

A holding may indicate:

- the possibility of an eventual bid, particularly if the holder is predatory by nature;
- a blocking position taken by the holder to protect his trade interests from the risk of the company concerned being taken over by some (larger) competitor.

There is no hard and fast rule about which is which, and a holding could indicate a blocking position pending a possible bid in the distant future.

In this context it is worth checking whether directors have substantial holdings and, if so, whether any are nearing retirement age.

If the holding is of *20% or more* and the company is not treated as an associate, the chances are probably more in favour of a bid than a blocking position – the unwelcome holder of a substantial stake being unlikely to be given a seat on the board.

If the holding is of *25% or more* the holder is in the strong position of being able to block any arrangements and reconstructions that the company might wish to make with creditors and members under Section 425 of the Companies Act 1985, which require three-fourths to vote in favour.

Interlocking holdings

Where a number of companies under the same management have substantial holdings in each other or in another company, the holdings may be entirely innocent; but interlocking holdings can give scope for manipulation to the detriment of outside shareholders and should be viewed with caution.

A classic illustration of the dangers of interlocking holdings was provided by the affairs of several companies in the LOWSON GROUP, which came under investigation by the Department of Trade in 1973.

The appointed inspectors found that a number of defaults in the management 'were knowingly committed by Sir Denys [Lowson] and constituted grave mismanagement of the affairs of the companies concerned' and that in some transactions 'his motive was to obtain a very substantial gain for himself and his family'.

Care should also be exercised where a director's private interests seem difficult to distinguish from those of the group he manages.

As Robert Maxwell showed in connection with PERGAMON and MAXWELL COMMUNICATION CORPORATION, danger lies in wait for shareholders, employees, pensioners, and for the reputations and profits of city institutions and auditors alike,

TERMINOLOGY

Fixed asset investments

Fixed asset investments fall into four categories:

- investment in subsidiaries;
- investment in associated undertakings (which include joint ventures);
- other participating interests;
- other investments.

A **subsidiary undertaking** is a company, partnership, or unincorporated association, where the company owning the investment (the **holding company**) is able to control the board of directors, either by virtue of its voting power or in some other way.

A holding company and its subsidiaries are termed a **group.**

An **associated undertaking** is a non-subsidiary undertaking in which the investing group or company's position in it is:

(a) effectively that of a partner in a joint venture or consortium; or

(b) long-term and substantial (i.e. not less than 20% of the equity voting rights) and can include partnerships and unincorporated associations as well as companies.

For it to be an associated company, the investing group must be in a position to exercise a significant influence over the operating and financial policy of the undertaking; usually by representation on the board of directors.

A **participating interest** is an interest held by the investing group or company on a long-term basis to secure a contribution to its activities by the exercise of control or influence. A holding of 20% or more of the shares of an undertaking is presumed to be a participating interest unless the contrary is shown.

once private and public interests become intertwined.

We have more to say about related party transactions in Chapter 22.

Problem 9.1

Companies hold fixed asset investments for a variety of reasons.

(i) Suggest five possible reasons; and

(ii) Explain why it is important for the reader of accounts to have as clear an idea as possible of the reasons for any significant holding.

Chapter 10

STOCKS AND WORK IN PROGRESS

Reference: SSAP 9 *Stocks and work in progress*.

Different classes of stock

Most manufacturing companies have traditionally shown stocks as a single figure under current assets, described either as 'stocks', as 'inventories' or as 'stocks and work in progress', but these terms cover three very different classes of asset:

(a) items in the state in which they were purchased; these include raw materials to be used in manufacture, components to be incorporated in the product and consumable stores (like paint and oil) which will be used in making it;

(b) items in an intermediate stage of completion ('work in progress', or in the United States 'work in process');

(c) finished goods.

For wholesalers and retailers, stocks are almost entirely goods purchased for resale.

Subclassification

The balance sheet formats in Schedule 4 of the Companies Act 1985 require stocks to be analysed under the following subheadings:

(a) raw materials and consumables;

(b) work in progress;

(c) finished goods and goods for resale;

(d) payments on account (for items of stock not yet received).

SSAP 9 calls for the accounts to show the subclassification of stocks and work in progress 'in a manner which is appropriate to the business and so as to indicate the amounts held in each of the main categories'. For example DIAGEO, which was formed by the merger of Grand Metropolitan and Guinness, gives a subclassification of stocks that includes whisky:

DIAGEO *Note to the 1998 accounts*

Stocks	£m
Raw material and consumables	265
Work in progress	18
Maturing whisky	1,372
Finished goods and goods for resale	581
	2,236

The matching principle

Expenditure on stocks which remain unsold or unconsumed at the balance sheet date (or upon work in progress which is incomplete) is carried forward into the following period and set against the revenue from the stocks when it arises. This is an application of what accountants term the matching principle, i.e. matching cost and revenue in the year in which the revenue arises rather than charging the cost in the year it is incurred.

Dead stock

Stocks and work in progress should be valued at the lower of cost and net realisable value (SSAP9 para. 26), and any irrecoverable cost (e.g. due to deterioration or obsolescence) should be charged to revenue.

Allowing 'dead' stock to be carried forward at cost is a classic way of boosting profits.

Consistency

The method of valuing stock should be consistent, and most sets of accounts include a brief statement in the notes on how stocks have been valued:

THE BODY SHOP *Extract from accounting policies 1998*
Stocks are valued at the lower of cost and net realisable value. Cost is calculated as follows:

Raw materials	Cost of purchase on a first-in first-out basis.
Work in progress	Cost of raw materials and finished goods and labour together with attributable overheads.

Net realisable value is based on estimated selling price less further costs to completion and disposal.

DIAGEO *Extract from accounting policies 1998*
Stocks are stated at the lower of cost and net realisable value. Cost includes raw materials, direct labour and expenses, and an appropriate proportion of production and other overheads.

It is interesting that DIAGEO adopted Grand Metropolitan's more prudent policy on stocks. Guinness used to include in costs 'the financing costs in respect of whisky and other spirit stocks during their normal maturation period', i.e. it rolled up the interest on its stock of spirits.

A particular point to look for is any statement of a change in the basis between year ends and, when one is made, why, and whether any indication is given of how much difference the change has made to the year-end stock figure and, hence, to profits.

The importance of stock valuation

The accurate valuation of stock on a consistent basis is important, because quite small percentage variations can very significantly affect profits:

Example 10.1 Stock valuation

	£000	£000
Sales		2,000
Cost of goods sold:		
Opening stock	600	
Purchases in period	1,500	
	2,100	
Closing stock	400	
		1,700
		300
Wages, overheads, etc.		200
Operating profit		100

Had the opening stock been overstated by 10% (at £660,000) and the closing stock undervalued by 10% (at £360,000), the cost of goods sold would appear £100,000 higher and the operating profit would have been wiped out.

Problems in valuing stock

Three main problems arise in valuing stock:

(a) the price to be used if an item has been supplied at varying prices;
(b) the value added in manufacture both to incomplete items (work in progress) and to completed items (finished goods);
(c) the assessment of net realisable value.

Stocks in a large retail business

Having defined the main principles and problems, let us now look at stocks in practice, beginning with the control of stocks in a large retail business, where virtually all stocks are goods purchased for resale and the complications of work in progress (WIP) and finished goods do not arise.

The central management of most supermarkets controls the efficiency and honesty of local stores by charging goods out to those stores at selling price, and by maintaining overall stock control accounts in terms of selling price by broad product groups. By suitably analysing takings it will then be possible, for each of these product groups, to compare theoretical stock with actual stock:

Opening stock at selling price	+	Deliveries at selling price	− Takings =	Theoretical closing stock at selling price

With this sort of operation, it is usual for the purpose of monthly, quarterly, half-yearly and annual accounts to deduct from the value of stock at selling price the normal gross profit margin:

TESCO *Extract from accounting policies 1999*
Stocks comprise goods held for resale and development properties, and are valued at the lower of cost and net realisable value. Stocks in stores are calculated at retail prices and reduced by appropriate margins to the lower of cost and net realisable value.

SSAP 9 requires that before such a figure is used for the purposes of the annual accounts, it be tested to ensure that it gives a 'reasonable approximation of the actual cost'.

Stocks in the manufacturing business

Most manufacturing businesses employ a system of cost accounting. They do so:

(a) as an aid to price fixing, so that they can charge the customer with the materials used and the time actually taken to complete his job – as is the case with a motor repair garage, or jobbing builder;
(b) in order to provide the estimating department with information on which to base future estimates or tenders; and/or

(c) as a means of controlling operating efficiency.

The type of record employed varies widely, from a few scribblings on the back of an envelope, to a cost system parallel to the normal financial system, reconciled with it but not part of it, right up to a completely integral cost and financial accounting system. In all but the first of these there is normally some form of stock record.

A problem often arises in the case of the manufacturing business over the pricing of issues from stock. When there are relatively few items, and where they are easily identifiable and can each be kept separate, each stock issue can be priced at its specific price, and no problem arises. But in many cases it is not possible, or not convenient, to keep identical items from different purchase consignments separate.

Several different methods of pricing issues from stock are commonly employed, and the value of the stock remaining depends to some extent on the pricing method used:

First in, first out (FIFO)
Good storekeeping demands that goods should, so far as is possible, be used in the order in which they are received; it merely assumes for accounting purposes that the normal rules of good storekeeping have been followed.

Average or weighted average price
When an organisation receives a number of deliveries during an accounting period at a series of different prices, it is reasonable to take the average price or, for more accuracy, the weighted average price.

Standard price
Many businesses employ a standard cost system, that is to say, they predetermine for each type of unit manufactured the price which ought to be paid for material, the material usage, the wage rate of the personnel employed to produce it, the time they should take, and so on. In such a system materials issued from store are priced at standard cost, as are work in progress at all stages and any finished goods in stock. Any variances from standard are written off as operating losses (or profits) at the time they occur. In certain circumstances the standard price may be employed for financial accounting purposes.

Base stock
Under the base stock method, a fixed unit value is ascribed to a predetermined number of units of stock, any excess over this number being valued on the basis of some other method.

These different methods of pricing issues each give rise to a slightly different closing stock value and thus to a slightly different profit for the year.

But this is not important provided that a company adopts the same method consistently in each accounting period. It is not permissible to chop and change.

Replacement cost and NIFO
In the past, items in stock were occasionally stated in the accounts at replacement cost when this was lower than both cost and net realisable value. The effect of this was to increase the cost of goods sold for the period, and thus reduce reported profits. The statement of stocks at the lowest of cost, net realisable value and replacement cost is no longer (under SSAP 9) an acceptable basis of stock valuation.

LIFO
Another method of valuation, permitted by the Companies Acts and commonplace in the United States but unacceptable under SSAP 9, is the last in, first out (LIFO) basis in which issues are charged at the latest price at which they could conceivably have come. This has the advantage of charging the customer with the most recent price; but in the balance sheet stocks appear at the price of the earliest delivery from which they could have arisen. The basic rule of good storekeeping is (in theory only) reversed, and goods received latest are assumed to be used first.

Thus, in a time of rising prices LIFO has the effect of:

(a) showing stocks in the balance sheet at a cost appropriate not to recent purchases but to those many months or even years earlier; and, consequently,

(b) reducing profit made on holding stock.

Taxation of stock profits
Suppose that a company has an opening stock of raw materials of £10m at the beginning of the year. At the end of the year the closing stock comprises exactly the same material quantities as the opening stock but, because of inflation and/or rising commodity prices, the value under FIFO has risen to £11m:

Opening stock of raw materials	£10,000,000
Closing stock of raw materials	11,000,000
Increase in value of stock	1,000,000

This increase in value of £1m reduces the cost of goods sold by £1m, which adds £1m to pre-tax profit. This stock profit, although unrealised, bears Corporation Tax at 30% = £300,000 tax, which has to be paid even though the physical amount of stock is unchanged.

In the early 1970s, when almost all prices were rising rapidly with inflation, companies that needed to carry large stocks were very hard hit: they were taxed on their stock profits and had to find more working capital each year just to maintain the same volume of stock. Their plight was eventually recognised by the government, which introduced stock relief in the Finance Act 1975, but it discontinued it in 1984 once inflation eased (see Chapter 29).

The problems of stocks in an inflationary situation will be discussed further in Chapter 29.

Requirements of the Companies Act 1985 and of SSAP 9 on stocks and WIP

The Companies Act 1985 allows the use of FIFO, LIFO, weighted average price or any other similar method to be used for fungible assets (assets substantially indistinguishable from one another) but, where the amount shown differs materially from the replacement cost (or the most recent purchase price or production cost), the amount of that difference must be disclosed (Sch. 4, para. 27).

The inclusion of overheads in cost
It was at one time accepted that companies should be free to choose whether to value work in progress and finished goods:

(a) at prime cost: that is to say, to exclude all overheads; or

(b) at variable (or marginal) cost: that is to say to exclude all fixed overheads, but include prime cost plus variable overheads; or

(c) at the full cost of purchase plus the cost of conversion (including fixed overheads too).

The Companies Act 1985 and SSAP 9 both regard (c) as the only proper method. The classification of overheads between fixed and variable is regarded as an unsuitable one for determining whether or not they should be included in the cost of conversion: the dividing line is too imprecise.

Costs of general management, as distinct from functional management, are excluded unless directly related to current production (as they may be to some extent in smaller companies), but the Companies Act 1985 does allow a reasonable proportion of interest on capital borrowed to finance production costs to be included in the value of stock; however, if this is done the amount must be disclosed (Sch. 4, para. 26).

Net realisable value
Net realisable value is 'the actual or estimated selling price (net of trade but before settlement discounts) less:

(a) all further costs to completion; and

(b) all costs to be incurred in marketing, selling and distributing'.

TERMINOLOGY

Stocks

Cost, in relation to stocks, is expenditure which is incurred in the normal course of business in bringing the product or service to its present location and condition. It includes, in addition to cost of purchase, costs of conversion that are appropriate to that location and condition.

Cost of purchase comprises purchase price including import duties, transport and handling costs and any other directly attributable costs, less trade discounts, rebates and subsidies.

Cost of conversion comprises:

(a) costs which are specifically attributable to units of production, e.g., direct labour, direct expenses and sub-contracted work;

(b) production overheads;

(c) other overheads, if any, attributable in the particular circumstances of the business to bringing the product or service to its present location and condition.

Production overheads are overheads incurred in respect of materials, labour or services for production, based on the normal level of activity, taking one year with another.

Net realisable value is the actual or estimated selling price (net of trade but before settlement discounts) less:

(a) all further costs to completion; and

(b) all costs to be incurred in marketing, selling and distributing.

Unit cost is the cost of purchasing or manufacturing identifiable units of stock:.

Average price is the price computed by dividing the total cost of the item by the total number of units. This average price may be arrived at by means of continuous calculation, a periodic calculation or a moving periodic calculation.

FIFO (first in, first out) represents the calculation of the cost of stocks on the basis that quantities in hand represent the latest purchases or production.

LIFO (last in, first out) represents the calculation of the cost of stocks on the basis that quantities in hand represent the earliest purchases or production.

Replacement cost is the cost at which an identical asset could be purchased or manufactured.

Standard cost represents the calculation of the cost of stocks on the basis of periodically predetermined costs calculated from management's estimates of expected levels of costs and of operations and operational efficiency and the related expenditure.

The danger of rising stocks

Although SSAP 9's requirement to include production overheads in arriving at the cost of finished goods gives a fair picture when stocks are being maintained at prudent levels in relation to demand, when a manufacturer leaves production unchanged in periods of lower demand their inclusion can produce unduly optimistic profits, see example 10.2 alongside. In practice, the profit from full production would be likely to be reduced by interest charges to finance carrying increased stock, but even so management may try to bolster profits in the short term by continuing high production in the face of falling demand. Rising stocks unmatched by rising turnover may give some warning here, and this can be monitored by the ratio stocks/turnover.

Here is an example of a rising stocks/turnover ratio giving warning of trouble. It illustrates two key points. See if you can spot them:

SPRING RAM *Extract from chairman's statement 1991*
'A most satisfying result was achieved for the year under review, despite a generally very difficult economic climate. Group profits before tax advanced to a record £37.6m (1990 £30.1m), an increase of 25% on the previous year. Consolidated turnover of £194.2m (1990 £145.3m) ... Earnings per share were 7.1p (1990 5.4p)'.

But in market conditions described by the chief executive of one housebuilder, BELLWINCH, as 'certainly the worst in post-war years', Spring Ram's results seemed too good to be true. The sharp rise in the ratio 'finished goods and goods for resale/turnover', to the unprecedented level of 13.5%, was a warning signal.

The 1992 interim results showed further growth in turnover, profits and earnings per share. It wasn't until the week before the 1992 final figures were due to be announced that Spring Ram issued a profit warning and asked for its shares to be suspended.

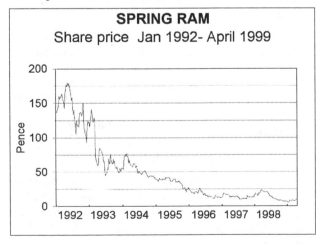

SPRING RAM
Share price Jan 1992- April 1999

Example 10.2 Rising stocks
A company with a single-product factory faces a year in which demand is forecast to fall by 30% due to an economic recession:

    Production overheads (rent of factory, etc.) = £1m
    Production capacity = 100,000 units per annum
    Variable costs = £10 per unit
    Selling price = £25 per unit
    Sales last year = 100,000 units

The management is faced with the decision of whether:

(a) to continue at full production, hoping that demand will pick up sharply the following year if not sooner, and that it possibly won't fall quite as sharply as forecast; or

(b) to cut production by up to 30%.

Under SSAP 9, assuming demand does fall by 30%, the figures that will be reported at the end of the year under these two choices will be:

	(a) Full production	(b) Production cut by 30%
	Units	Units
Opening stock	20,000	20,000
Units manufactured	100,000	70,000
	120,000	90,000
Units sold	70,000	70,000
Closing stock	50,000	20,000
Fixed costs	1,000,000	1,000,000
Variable costs (£10 per unit)	1,000,000	700,000
Total costs	2,000,000	1,700,000
Costs per unit manufactured	£20	£24.285

Profit and loss account

	£	£
Sales (£25 per unit)	1,750,000	1,750,000
Cost of goods sold:		
Opening stock (£20 per unit)	400,000	400,000
Cost of units manufactured	2,000,000	1,700,000
less Closing stock by FIFO method	1,000,000 (£20)	485,700 (£24.285)
Cost of goods sold	1,400,000	1,614,300
Gross (or Trading) profit	350,000	135,700

NOTE: A watchful auditor would require to be satisfied (i) as to the net realisable value of the closing stock under (a); and (ii) that the requirements of SSAP 9 regarding spreading of overheads on the basis of 'normal production' were met.

SPRING RAM *Extract from 1987–1991 accounts*

	1987 £000	1988 £000	1989 £000	1990 £000	1991 £000
Turnover	60,785	85,173	121,017	145,285	194,173
Stocks					
Raw materials	3,296	6,386	8,035	8,813	12,984
Work in progress	297	927	1,160	1,277	1,787
Finished goods and goods for resale	4,508	10,041	10,984	15,019	26,255
Total stocks	8,101	17,354	20,179	25,109	41,026
Ratios (%)					
Raw materials /turnover	5.4	7.5	6.6	6.1	6.7
WIP/turnover	0.5	1.1	1.0	0.9	0.9
Finished goods and goods for resale/turnover	7.4	11.8	9.1	10.3	13.5
Total stocks /turnover	13.3	20.4	16.7	17.3	21.1

Profits at a bathroom manufacturing subsidiary had been overstated by £5.6m, mainly through the inflation of stock values and sales.

Key point 1

When a sector of the market is going through hard times, and the management of a company in that sector tells you 'we are going to buck the trend', be highly sceptical. Our experience is that they are about to run into very serious trouble.

Key point 2

If a company's results seem too good to be true, don't believe them.

Long-term contracts

A long-term contract is defined by SSAP 9 as 'a contract entered into for manufacture or building of a single substantial entity or the provision of a service where the time taken to manufacture, build or provide is such that a substantial proportion of all such contract work will extend for a period exceeding one year'.

Shipbuilders, constructional engineers and the like frequently engage in long-term contracts. Because of the length of time such contracts take to complete, to defer taking profit into account until completion would result in the profit and loss account reflecting not a true and fair view of the activity of the company during the year, but rather the results of those contracts which, by the accident of time, were completed by the year end.

It is normal with long-term contracts to have an arrangement under which the contractor receives payment on account on the basis of the 'work certified' by an architect or surveyor. Traditionally, there are two ways of computing the profit to be taken. The 'work certified' is an essential piece of information whichever of the two ways of arriving at the profit to date is adopted.

Under the first method, profit to date is computed as follows:

$$\text{Work certified at balance sheet date} - \text{Costs incurred on contract to date} = \text{Profit to date}$$

The second method takes the overall profit expected:

$$\text{Total contract price} - \text{Total costs incurred on contract to date} - \text{Total estimated further costs to completion}$$

and multiplies it by: $\dfrac{\text{Work certified to date}}{\text{Total contract price}}$

to arrive at the Profit to date.

If the first formula is used it is still necessary to have regard to the costs likely to be incurred in completing the job, for it is clearly wrong to take a profit on the first stage of a contract if the profit is likely to be lost at a later stage. In either case, in considering future costs, it is necessary to allow for likely increases in wages and salaries, in the price of raw materials and in general overheads, in so far as these items are not recoverable from the customer under the terms of the contract: inflation can play havoc with the profitability of fixed-price or inadequately protected contracts, as many companies have learned to their cost.

In neither case is it usual to take up the entire profit to date. Some companies take only two-thirds, others only three-quarters.

Many multiply by a further fraction:

$$\frac{\text{Amount received to date}}{\text{Work certified to date}}$$

Where the customer is entitled (as is usually the case) to retain, say, 10% of the amount certified as 'retention monies', so as to ensure satisfactory rectification of any defects, the use of this further fraction of, in this case, 9/10ths, has the effect of disregarding that part of the profit appropriate to the amount retained.

The amount reflected in the year's profit and loss account will be the appropriate proportion of the total profit by reference to the work done to date, less any profit already taken up in prior years on the contracts still on hand. The aim of using a multiplying factor of two-thirds or three-quarters is to ensure that unless the remaining work on a contract is disastrous, some profit remains to be taken when the contract is finally completed.

The second formula relies on an estimate of future costs and is therefore open to subjective judgement. Results should be viewed with caution if the overall profitability margin is estimated to be higher than the margin to date; i.e. if the second formula allows a higher profit to be taken now than the first formula would allow.

Example 10.3 Long-term contracts: COMMERCIAL CONTRACTS LTD

COMMERCIAL CONTRACTS LTD is engaged in a long-term bridge-building contract.

		£000
Work certified to 31 December 1999	W	1,250
Total contract price	P	2,000
Costs incurred on contract to 31 December 1999	C	1,025
Estimated further costs to completion	E	575
Amount received from customer by 31 December 1999	R	1,125
Profit taken on the contract in 1998	T	45

The company takes up three-quarters of the profit earned to date, reduced by the fraction:
amount received to date ÷ work certified to date.
What profit will be taken up on the contract in 1999?

Using the first formula:
Profit to date = W – C = £1,250,000
Of which ¾ × R ÷ W = ¾ × 1,125,000 ÷ 1,250,000 = 67½% (£151,875) will be taken as profit by 31 December 1999.
But £45,000 of this was taken up in 1998, so only £106,875 remains to be taken in 1999.

Using the second formula:
Profit to date = (P – C – E) × W ÷ P
= (£2,000,000 – £1,025,000 – £575,000) × 1,250,000 ÷ 2,000,000 = £250,000.
Of this £250,000 profit, 67½% will be taken up (as before), i.e. £168,750, less the £45,000 already taken up in 1998 = £123,750.

The difference between the two figures for profit to date is due to the difference between the profit margin on that part of the contract completed to date (£225,000 on £1,250,000 in the first formula = 18%) and that estimated on the contract as a whole (£400,000 on £2 million in the second formula = 20%).

SSAP 9 requirements on long-term contracts

In the past, accounting treatment of long-term contracts has varied enormously from company to company. BOVIS, for example, in its 1972 accounts noted that 'no provision is made for anticipated future losses' and a year later had to be rescued by P. & O. At the other end of the scale companies like JOHN LAING pursued policies of extreme prudence: all losses were taken when they were foreseen, but no account was taken of profits on contracts unfinished at the end of the year.

SSAP 9 requires that 'The amount at which long-term contract work in progress is stated in periodic financial statements should be cost plus any attributable profit, less any foreseeable losses and progress payments received and receivable', and the amount of attributable profit included should be disclosed. Attributable profits on contracts are, however, only required to be taken up when 'it is considered that their outcome can be assessed with reasonable certainty before their conclusion'; if the outcome cannot be reasonably assessed, 'it is prudent not to take up any profit', so management is still left with a certain latitude, and the key point to watch for is undue anticipation of profits.

SSAP 9 also requires balance sheets to show how the amount included for long-term contracts is reached by stating:

(i) the amount of work in progress at cost plus attributable profit (i.e. profit or loss taken to date), less foreseeable losses;
(ii) cash received and receivable at the accounting date as progress payments on account of contracts in progress.

Example 10.4 Long-term contracts: COMMERCIAL CONTRACTS LTD (continued)

If the bridge contract we discussed in Example 10.3 was the only contract of Commercial Contracts Ltd to appear in the balance sheet at 31 December 1997, and if the first formula was used, it would appear in the balance sheet as follows:

	£	£
Work in progress, at cost plus Profit taken to date	1,176,875	
Less Cash received from customer	1,125,000	
		51,875

Reclassification of assets – a loophole closed

In 1991 TRAFALGAR HOUSE, a property and shipping company that was subsequently taken over, decided that some properties held for resale (and therefore classified as current assets) were no longer for sale because of the acutely depressed state of the property market – property development companies were going down like ninepins.

The board therefore decided to transfer these properties to tangible fixed assets, and did so at cost, rather than at the lower of cost and net realisable value, thus avoiding having to take a £68 million hit on the profit and loss account. The properties were then revalued and the £68m deficit was taken to revaluation reserve.

This was drawn to the attention of the Urgent Issues Task Force (UITF), who ruled in Abstract No. 5 that the properties should have been transferred at the lower of cost and net realisable value, and that the £68m should have been taken to the profit and loss account.

In view of UITF 5, and concerns expressed by the Financial Reporting Review Panel, Trafalgar House adopted the requirements of the abstract in its 1992 accounts and restated the 1991 comparatives.

Stock ratios

As we have seen, stocks comprise stocks of raw materials and consumables, purchased components, work in progress (net of progress payments), finished goods, goods for resale, and payments on account (shown under stocks). Except when stocks are built up in anticipation of sharp price rises, well-run companies usually try to carry the minimum stock needed for the satisfactory running of their business: they do so:

(a) to minimise interest charges on the money tied up in stocks;

(b) to save unnecessary storage costs (including pilferage); and

(c) to reduce the risk of being left with goods that can't be sold due to deterioration, becoming obsolete or going out of fashion.

Although some distortion can occur with accelerating growth, because stock is a year-end figure while sales occur throughout the year (on average several months earlier), a rising stock ratio without any special reason is regarded as bad news, reflecting lack of demand for goods and/or poor stock control.

Stocks/Turnover

The most generally used stock ratio (as shown in our Spring Ram example on page 71) is:

$$\frac{\text{Stocks}}{\text{Turnover}} \text{ expressed as a \%}$$

Stocks/Turnover ratios vary enormously with the nature of a business. At one end of the scale, and apart from advertising agencies and other service industries, ready-mixed concrete companies probably have one of the lowest Stocks/Turnover figures of any industry: aggregates are extracted from the ground when required and the product is delivered the same day, so all that is needed in stock is a supply of fresh cement and fuel, giving a typical Stocks/Turnover figure of 5%. At the other end of the scale a company which maintains depots of finished goods and replacement parts world-wide, like a power transmission and mechanical handling systems manufacturer, can reasonably be expected to have a ratio as high as 35% in order to maintain a first-class service to its customers all over the world. Nevertheless, a high ratio in comparison to similar companies is undesirable.

For an average manufacturing company a Stocks/Turnover ratio of around 15–20% would be reasonable, increasing the larger and more complex the goods made; for instance, an aircraft manufacturer might have stocks and WIP representing 30–35% of turnover and this level could be subject to sharp fluctuations, depending on whether completed aircraft had been delivered to clients just before or just after the end of the year; in contrast, a company making a limited range of nuts and bolts could probably run on a few weeks' stock, though if supplies were subject to interruption and/or shortages it might be prudent to carry more raw materials, and if orders tended to be erratic a higher stock of finished goods would be needed.

Stocks/Cost of sales ratio

P & L accounts using Format 1 (see page 99) show the *cost of sales*. Where this is available it can be used to compute the average amount of stock held during the year, which can be expressed as so many months stock, or so many days stock. Many analysts take the average of the opening and closing stocks, which has a smoothing effect, and dampens the effect of a major change in stocks over the period.

$$\text{Stock (months)} = \frac{(\text{Opening stock} + \text{Closing stock}) \div 2}{\text{Cost of sales}} \times 12$$

$$\text{Stock (days)} = \frac{(\text{Opening stock} + \text{Closing stock}) \div 2}{\text{Cost of sales}} \times 365$$

Cost of sales/Stock ratio

The previous ratio can be inverted, Cost of sales/Stock, to give the number of times the stock has been turned over in the year, the **stockturn**:

$$\text{Stockturn} = \frac{\text{Cost of sales}}{(\text{Opening stock} + \text{Closing stock}) \div 2}$$

Example 10.5 Calculation of Stock ratios

Extracted from accounts:

	1998 £m	1999 £m	2000 £m
Year-end stock	2.10	2.20	3.00
Sales		10.00	12.00
Cost of sales		7.50	8.00

Ratios:

	1999	2000
Stocks/Sales	22.0%	25.0%
Stock (days)	104.6 days	118.6 days
Stockturn	3.49 ×	3.08 ×

Problem 10.1

You are given the following extract from a group's accounts:

16. Stocks

	1998 £m	1997 £m
Raw materials and consumables	1.8	1.8
Finished goods and goods for resale	19.7	15.7
Residential developments		
Land	176.7	154.4
Development and construction costs	170.6	126.2
Commercial, industrial and mixed		
development properties	57.7	57.3
	426.5	355.4

(i) Provide a brief description of the group.

(ii) What do the figures suggest? Where would you look for confirmation (or otherwise) of your hypothesis?

(iii) Imagine that Land included an estate which cost £56m, which, six months later, the group no longer plans to develop, but which it proposes to hold as a fixed asset investment. Suitably sized parcels of the estate will be offered to other developers subject to long leases. The estate is included above at cost; but its realisable value is now estimated to be only £27.6m. How should the proposed change be handled in next year's accounts; and why?

Chapter 11

DEBTORS

TRADE DEBTORS AND OTHER DEBTORS

Reference: FRS 5, *Reporting the substance of transactions*.

Debtors (also known as 'receivables') are a current asset, representing amounts owing to the business.

The balance sheet formats in Schedule 4 of the Companies Act 1985 require debtors to be subdivided into:

- trade debtors – those arising from the sale of goods on credit;
- amounts owed by group undertakings – see Chapter 20;
- amounts owed by undertakings in which the company has a participating interest – see Chapter 22;
- other debtors – for example debts due from the sale of fixed assets or investments; and
- prepayments and accrued income – for example rent or rates paid in advance.

The amount falling due after more than one year should be shown separately for each item included under debtors (CA 1985, Sch. 4, note (5) to the balance sheet formats). Other items which may be found shown separately under debtors (and which are not trade debtors for the purpose of computing collection ratios) include:

(a) ACT recoverable (see Chapter 17);
(b) Corporation tax recoverable (in respect of loss relief etc. – see Chapter 17);
(c) Deferred taxation (see Chapter 17);
(d) Pension prepayments (see Chapter 16);
(e) Amounts receivable under finance leases (see Chapter 16);
(f) Loan notes (see Chapter 6).

Most companies show a single figure for debtors in their balance sheet, and give the required details in a note, as illustrated here.

THE BODY SHOP *Extract from note to the 1998 accounts*

Debtors	1998 £m	1997 £m
Amounts falling due within one year		
Trade debtors	31.3	31.7
Assets held for resale	1.6	–
Other debtors	7.0	7.9
Prepayments	5.2	3.1
	45.1	42.7
Amounts falling due after more than one year		
Other debtors	1.9	2.3
	47.0	45.0

Other debtors falling due after more than one year include variable rate loan notes of £0.4m (1997: £0.6m) which formed part of the consideration for the disposal of Eastwick Trading BV in 1994, and £nil (1997: £0.2m) which formed part of the consideration for the disposal of The Body Shop Norway A/S in 1995.

Bad debts and doubtful debtors

The granting of credit inevitably involves some risk that the debtor will fail to pay, that is, will become a bad debt. When a business recognises that a debt is bad, the debt is written off to profit and loss account. That is to say, the balance appearing as 'debtors' falls by the amount of the debt, and 'bad debts' appears as an expense. But this expense is shown separately in the published accounts only if the amount is material.

In addition, it is normal to set up a 'provision for doubtful debtors'. To do so a charge is made to profit and loss account and, in the balance sheet, the cumulative provision for doubtful debtors is deducted from the total debtors. Once again, the provision for doubtful debtors is disclosed separately in the published accounts only if it is material. A provision for doubtful debtors may be specific, that is to say where management estimate the probable loss, studying each debt in turn; for instance, there is a 10% probability that Tin Pott plc will fail to pay its debt of £121,000, they must therefore provide £12,100; or it may be general, e.g. 2½% of total debtors; or a combination of the two.

The importance of debtors

Companies such as supermarket chains, whose turnover is almost entirely for cash, will have very few debtors; the figure appearing in the balance sheet is likely to be largely prepayments and non-trade debtors. Trade debtors may have little significance. SAINSBURY, for example, with sales excluding VAT of £14,500m, showed trade debtors of a mere £50m in its 1998 accounts. At the other extreme are companies whose entire turnover is on credit terms, in which case very large amounts of working capital may be tied up in debtors. Here the efficiency with which credit accounts are handled, and the timing of the taking of profit where payments are by instalment, are of considerable interest to the analyst.

Debt collection period

The ratio Trade debtors/Sales can be used to monitor a company's credit control. Logically it should be sales including VAT, because the debtors include VAT, but the VAT inclusive figure is not usually available.

Analysts often feel that a more meaningful measure is that expressed in terms of time, as the debt collection period (or, simply, the collection period) in days or months:

$$\text{Debt collection period (days)} = \frac{\text{Trade debtors}}{\text{Sales}} \times 365$$

$$\text{Debt collection period (months)} = \frac{\text{Trade debtors}}{\text{Sales}} \times 12$$

But it may be expressed simply as a percentage of sales:

$$\frac{\text{Trade debtors}}{\text{Sales}} \times 100$$

For example, given Trade debtors of £8.219m and Sales of £50m:

$$\text{Collection period} = \frac{£8.219m}{£50m} \times 365 = 60 \text{ days}$$

$$\text{Collection period} = \frac{£8.219m}{£50m} \times 12 = 1.97 \text{ months}$$

$$\frac{\text{Trade debtors}}{\text{Sales}} = \frac{£8.219m}{£50m} \times 100 = 16.4\%$$

Trade debtors/Sales has the advantage of stating the percentage of the year's sales which were outstanding at the balance sheet date (which is correct) rather than suggesting that the business' debtors represent 60 days' sales (which we cannot say).

Apart from 'strictly cash' businesses like supermarkets, with virtually zero debtors, normal terms tend to be payment at the end of the month following delivery, so with 100% prompt payment the average credit given would be between 6 and 7 weeks, making debtors about 12% of turnover. In practice, a figure of 15–20% is quite normal although some companies may, as a matter of policy, give more generous credit in order to give themselves a competitive edge, while others may factor their debts (see page 82) and thus possibly show abnormally low debtors.

A falling collection period is generally a good sign – an indication of effective financial control – but it could reflect a desperate need for cash, involving extra discounts for cash and undue pressure on customers.

It is interesting to compare ratios for companies in the same sector, and to look at a five year period to see if there is any significant trend. In doing so, acquisitions and disposals may make the figures erratic. Example 11.1 (on the next page) compares three companies in the food manufacturing sector.

Huge multinational UNILEVER has some excellent brands and sufficient financial muscle to withstand pressure from the supermarkets for longer credit. It is well able to drive its Trade creditors/Sales ratio down to single figures.

HAZLEWOOD FOODS is a medium sized company with operations in the UK and the Netherlands. Over the last five years it has managed to get its ratio down below 10%. A new FD, formerly the FC, was appointed in 1994. From his photo in the annual report, he looks pretty tough.

PERKINS FOODS also operates in the UK and Northern Europe, but appears to have trade debtors less tightly controlled than Hazlewood. There may, of course, be good commercial reasons for allowing their customers more credit.

Example 11.1 Trade Debtors/Sales ratio: Food manufacturers

Company	Note	Year	Sales	Trade debtors	Ratio
UNILEVER		1993	27,863	3,104	11.1%
		1994	29,666	3,357	11.3%
		1995	31,516	3,107	10.5%
	U1	1996	33,522	3,107	9.3%
		1997	28,473	2,545	8.9%
		1998	27,094	2,628	9.7%
HAZLEWOOD		1993	761.8	96.3	12.6%
FOODS	H1	1994	662.4	91.4	14.2%
		1995	722.3	74,4	10.3%
		1996	766.0	72.2	9.4%
		1997	790.0	64.0	9.3%
		1998	758.7	62.2	8.2%
PERKINS		1993	373.4	42.2	11.4%
FOODS		1994	358.2	50.4	14.1%
		1995	430.7	54.0	12.5%
		1996	466.2	64.8	13.9%
		1997	626.8	70.6	11.3%
	P1	1998	261.2	37.6	14.4%

Notes

U1 Disposal of specialty chemicals business; turnover of which in 1996 = £2,663m.

H1 Rationalisation in Europe. £11.3m cash paid for acquisitions. Disposals raised £15.5m cash.

P1 Disposal of Fresh produce division; turnover of which in 1997 = £400.2m

What we would like to know

In a seasonal business it is more accurate to compute the collection period on a month-by-month basis, but this is not possible without inside knowledge. Indeed, the analyst can tell comparatively little about debtors unless a significant proportion of debtors are due after more than one year or unless the company discloses more than the minimum information required by law. Among the things which one would like to find out (and should be on the look out for any hint about in the chairman's statement or financial review) are the following:

1. Is an undue proportion due from one major customer, or from customers in one industry?
2. Would failure of one or two customers have a material effect upon the company's future?
3. What is the age pattern of debtors? Are some unduly old?
4. Is there adequate provision for bad and doubtful debts?
5. Are any of the debts which fall due after more than one year very longterm in nature? In the United Kingdom debtors appear at their face value regardless of when they are due. In the United States, if a debt is not due within one year, it is usually necessary to discount it, i.e.

to take account of imputed interest. Thus, a debt of $1m due three years hence might appear, taking interest into account at 10%, as $751,300.

Factors affecting the debt collection period

A short debt collection period is, other things being equal, preferable to a longer one; but as with many ratios one has to qualify this general principle. For by restricting credit and selling entirely for cash, a business can have a zero debt collection period; but if this drives its customers into the arms of competitors it is scarcely an improvement so far as the business as a whole is concerned. Subject to that qualification, any improvement in collection period, since it represents a reduction in overall debtors, means that more capital is available for other purposes, or that there is less need to borrow money from the bank.

At first sight it may seem that an increase in collection period represents a fall in the efficiency of the debt collection section. This is likely to be the case, but it is not necessarily so. The debt collection period may increase (decrease) between one period and another for a number of reasons:

- If there is a policy change with regard to:

  (a) credit terms to existing customers; if, for example, the board of directors, to obtain a valuable order from a major customer, offers two months' credit instead of one;

  (b) the granting of credit; for instance, if potential customers whose credit ratings were formerly insufficient for them to be granted credit, are granted credit – for such customers are unlikely to be among the fastest payers.

- Where there is poor credit management or accounts administration, e.g.:

  (a) if credit is given to unsatisfactory customers;

  (b) if the invoicing section falls behind; customers will not pay until they receive an invoice and, in general, pay at a fixed time determined by the date on which they receive it, e.g. at the end of the month in which they receive the invoice;

  (c) if statements are late – while some businesses ignore statements, others wait until they receive one;

  (d) if there is no consistent follow-up of overdue debts, by letter and/or telephone, or as a last resort in person.

- if a subsidiary with an atypical debt collection period is disposed of or acquired, e.g. BASS's sale of the CORAL betting business and over 300 managed pubs in 1998 increased the group's debt collection period by several days.
- if factoring or invoice discounting is introduced or discontinued (see page 82).

Although it is necessary for most businesses to offer some credit, any unnecessary credit is bad management because it ties up money which (normally) earns no return, and which is subject to increased risk. The customer who is short of money, and who finds he can order things from a company without having to pay for them at the end of the month, tends to place more and more of his orders with that company; if he later goes into liquidation, he may do so owing a hefty amount.

Debtors due after more than one year
Traditionally, liabilities were regarded as current if they were expected to fall due within one year. Similarly, assets were treated as current if it was expected that they would be turned into cash within one year. An EC Directive, incorporated into the Companies Act 1985, changed that. Debtors are now shown under current assets whenever they fall due, though the amount falling due after more than one year is required to be shown separately for each item (CA 1985, Sch. 4, note (5) to the balance sheet formats). The inconsistency is clearly evident in the accounts of the leisure management group KUNICK (see next column), where the figure for net current assets of £172,000 in 1998 included as a current asset the item 'Debtors; falling due after more than one year' of £4.495m. The Act does not require companies to show the split on the face of the balance sheet (like KUNICK does), but UITF Abstract 4, para 3, requires this where the amount is material in the context of net current assets. But the misdescription 'net current assets' usually remains, leading the unwary to compute a false current ratio (see page 102).

Where long-term debtors seem an important factor in assessing a group's future, considerable research may be necessary. Companies are sometimes so keen to get rid of an unprofitable activity (perhaps an unwanted part of an acquisition) that they will sell to anybody who is willing to take the activity off their hands, regardless of their financial weakness, and give them extended credit.

And it's not unknown for companies to guarantee borrowings the acquirer has made to help finance the deal, which is simply asking for trouble (see Contingent liabilities on page 106). Debts which persist long after a subsidiary is sold, should raise suspicions.

Similarly, advances to a company which later becomes a subsidiary, raise the question of whether the acquisition itself was in some way forced (to maintain supplies, or custom), and whether the advance has become in the nature of capital.

It would also be worth asking about the £2.772 of properties that KUNICK was holding for resale. Were the properties surplus in a reorganization after acquisitions or disposals? How much is a carry forward from 1997's figure of £3.176m? Has it not been possible to find buyers?

KUNICK *Extract from 1998 consolidated balance sheet*

	Notes	1998 £000	1997 £000
Current assets			
Assets held for resale	17	2,772	3,176
Stocks	18	8,541	8,768
Debtors:			
Falling due after one year	19	4,495	5,452
Falling due within one year	19	27,779	25,277
Cash at bank and in hand		4,188	3,517
		47,775	46,208
Creditors			
Amount falling due within one year		47,603	41,161
Net Current Assets		172	5,047

Note 17. Assets held for resale

Properties		2,772	3,176

Note 19. Debtors: Amounts falling due after more than 1 year

Prepayments and accrued income		4,495	5,452

HIRE-PURCHASE AND CREDIT SALE TRANSACTIONS

Reference: SSAP 21 *Accounting for leases and hire purchase contracts.*

Definitions

A *hire-purchase transaction* is a transaction in which the hirer agrees to hire goods from their owner in return for which he pays (usually) a deposit and a series of weekly, monthly, quarterly or yearly payments. The intention is that when the hiring period comes to an end, the ownership of the goods will pass to the hirer, sometimes on the payment of a nominal sum, sometimes with the final instalment; ownership, therefore, does not pass to the hirer until all payments have been made.

A *credit sale* is an outright sale (usually by a retailer) where payment by instalments is agreed in writing as a condition of the sale. Under a credit sale arrangement the property in the goods passes immediately to the purchaser, who becomes the owner of the goods, but payment is required to be made over a period.

Interest is normally charged by the seller both in credit sale and hire-purchase arrangements; the great difference between them is that in a credit sale the 'purchaser' owns the goods from the outset, whereas in the case of a hire-purchase sale, they do not become his until the final payment is made. Thus the seller cannot reclaim the goods in the case of a credit sale if the purchaser defaults, whereas, subject to the terms of the agreement and the law on hire purchase, he can in the case of a hire-purchase transaction.

Amounts due under credit sale transactions are debtors, and normally appear with other trade debtors, though they may be shown separately. In the case of a hire-purchase transaction, there has, strictly speaking, been no sale, and the goods involved are still an asset of the seller; but, adopting the principle of 'substance over form', most companies refer to 'hire-purchase debtors' or 'instalments due under hire-purchase agreements'.

Timing of profit taking

Whether the sale is a credit sale or on hire purchase, there are two elements of profit: the profit on the sale of the goods themselves and interest upon the amounts outstanding. There are a number of ways in which these two forms of profit can be spread over the accounting periods involved; but essentially these break down into two methods:

1. Take all the profit on the sale immediately, and spread only the interest element.
2. Spread both the profit on the sale and the interest over the life of the agreement.

Although method 1 is permissible for credit sales, method 2 is the more prudent. Method 1 is not recommended for hire purchase, as the goods have not actually been sold.

Where a credit sale is made on truly 'interest free' terms, there is no interest to spread, though logically there is an interest cost so far as the selling company is concerned. This is not normally taken into account, though it could be, by taking into account imputed interest. But it is always necessary to make provision for collection costs. Such a provision might, for instance, be 10% of the credit sale account debtors outstanding on balance sheet date.

The rule of 78

Finance companies frequently apply the 'rule of 78' in spreading either the interest alone, or the whole profit and interest, over the life of the agreement. This is simply a form of the 'sum of the years' digits method' already discussed in connection with depreciation in Chapter 8. What happens is this: the period of the agreement is set down in months (or it could be weeks in the case of a weekly agreement, or years where payments were on an annual basis), and the sum of the digits represents the sum of $1 + 2 + 3 + 4 \ldots$ to n, where n is that number of months (or weeks or years). It is called the rule of 78 because for a year's agreement, the sum of $1 + 2 + 3 + \ldots + 12$ is 78. Any interest charge is then spread as follows (in this case a year's agreement):

First month 12/78ths of total interest

Second month 11/78ths

Third month 10/78ths

... Twelfth month 1/78th

Many companies take the profit immediately and spread the interest in respect of hire-purchase transactions, though it was at one time considered more prudent to spread both profit and interest over the life of the transaction (Example 11.2 on the next page), rather than to take profit at the outset. This could be said to be an example of 'substance over form' (see page 44).

The rule of 78 is a simple, though not totally accurate, way of spreading interest or profit over the period of an agreement. Some companies use more sophisticated techniques, spreading interest or profit by what is termed the 'actuarial method', taking into account interest (at the true effective rate payable) on the balance outstanding period by period.

Example 11.2 Taking of profit on hire purchase transactions

The hire-purchase trading account of DEFERRALS LTD for 1999 is as follows:

Hire-purchase sales		£120,000
less Cost of goods sold		80,000
Gross profit on HP sales (33⅓%)		£40,000

Receipts from 1999 HP sales =	£36,000	
Profit to be taken in 1999		
£36,000 × 33⅓% profit margin =	£12,000	
Provision for unearned profit		
carried forward on 1999 HP sales		
= £40,000 – £12,000 =	£28,000	
HP sales in 1999		£120,000
less Cash received		36,000
		84,000
less Provision for unearned profit		28,000
Hire-purchase debtors		
(from 1999 sales)		£56,000

If, say, £63,000 is received in 1999 in respect of transactions from 1998 and £42,000 from 1997, when the profit margins were 30% and 35% respectively, the total profit from HP sales to be taken in 1999 would be:

From 1999	£12,000
From 1998 (30% of £63,000)	18,900
From 1997 (35% of £42,000)	14,700
Total profit	£45,600

Hire-purchase information given in accounts

A good set of accounts will gives quite a lot of information on hire-purchase and credit sale business, e.g. how profit is taken and how interest is brought in. See GREAT UNIVERSAL STORES below.

Some companies (like Great Universal Stores) arrange for some or all of their credit sales and hire-purchase transactions to be handled by a separate finance company, so that they receive payment for goods at once and thus reduce their requirements for working capital.

In the absence of any provision for recourse by the finance company, the amounts outstanding are then of no concern to the selling company and do not appear in its accounts. Transactions which potentially involve recourse to the seller are required by FRS 5 *Reporting the substance of transactions* to be accounted for (a) as a debtor; and (b) as a corresponding liability.

GREAT UNIVERSAL STORES *Information on hire purchase*

Note on debtors

The Group	1998 Due within one year £m	Due in more than one year £m	1997 Due within one year £m	Due in more than one year £m
Trade debtors:				
Instalment and hire purchase debtors	1,425.2	748.6	1,401.7	765.2
Deduct: Provision for unearned finance charges	(122.6)	(75.1) (116.5)	(74.8)	
	1,302.6	673.5	1,285.2	690.4
Add: Other trade debtors	211.1	–	121.5	–
Total trade debtors	1,513.7	673.5	1,406.7	690.4

...

Accounting policies

Instalment and hire purchase debtors

The gross margin from sales on extended credit terms is recognised at the time of sale. The finance charges relating to such sales are brought into profit as and when instalments are received. The income from finance companies under instalment agreements is credited to profit in proportion to the reducing balances outstanding.

FACTORING

Factoring involves the sale of a company's trade debtors to a factoring house. Factoring houses offer three facilities:

1. The provision of finance for working capital.
2. A credit management and sales accounting service.
3. Bad debt protection.

The provision of finance

This is the main reason why companies use factoring. The factor assesses the client's trade debtors and agrees the level of 'prepayment' that he will provide; this is normally between 70% and 80% of the value of the invoices. The client may then sell his existing trade debts to the factor and receive prepayment immediately; the debtors are informed that the debts have been factored, and are asked to make payment direct to the factor.

All new invoices then carry an assignment notice, asking the debtors to make payment direct to the factor. Copies of all invoices are sent to the factor, who will make the agreed prepayment. If the agreed level of finance is 75%, the client will receive the balance of 25%, less the factor's charges, as his debtors settle each invoice. The factor provides credit advice and runs the sales ledger, sending statements and reminders.

Service charge

A service charge is made, usually between 1% and 3%, depending on the number of customers and invoices involved. The factor also makes a finance charge on any funds drawn under the prepayment arrangement, usually at rates similar to bank overdraft rates of interest. Because factoring finance is based on the trade debtors, it fluctuates automatically with the level of business, and is thus more flexible than an overdraft.

Bad debt protection

There are two types of factoring agreement: 'with recourse' and 'without recourse' to the client. Under a with recourse agreement, the client takes the risk of bad debts, and the factor will pass the debt back to his client if the debtor has not paid within 90 or 120 days.

Most factors offer bad debt protection as an optional extra, providing cover on all *approved* invoices. The cover is for 100%, which compares favourably with the 80% offered by most credit insurance companies. Factors usually add between ¼% and ¾% to their service charge for bad debt protection, depending on the industry involved.

International factoring

An increasing proportion of British goods go to Western Europe, North America and other markets. Many exporters use factors primarily to obtain credit advice and bad debt protection, although prepayment finance is available.

Factors handling exports send correspondence and make telephone calls in the language of overseas customers, and know the local business practices; this usually enables them to obtain faster collection of export debts.

Invoice discounting

This is similar to factoring except that, under an invoice discounting arrangement, the client continues to run his sales ledger and collect the payments, which he banks to the account of the discounting company. When each debtor's payment is banked, the discounter deducts the prepayment already made to the client, plus charges, and pays the balance into the client's bank account.

Most invoice discounting agreements are with recourse, i.e. the client takes the risk of bad debts. Because the client goes on running the ledger and collecting payments, it is sometimes called *confidential invoice discounting*.

Factoring in the accounts

In the past it has not always been possible to tell from the accounts whether a company was using factoring or invoice discounting. However, under FRS 5 *Reporting the substance of transactions*, companies are normally required to disclose factoring and invoice discounting and the degree of debt protection.

Debt factoring is considered in Application Note C of FRS 5, which also covers invoice discounting. Accounting treatment depends upon the precise terms of the contract. If the debts are sold at a fixed price, with no recourse, the seller has no further interest in the debts which no longer appear in the balance sheet; but an interest charge will normally appear in the profit and loss account. See, for instance, PIC INTERNATIONAL (formerly DALGETY) at the top of the next page.

PIC INTERNATIONAL *Extract from 1998 accounts*

Note 4 Interest

	1998	1997
	£m	£m
Interest payable and similar charges:		
On bank loans and overdrafts	15.2	20.6
Non recourse finance	1.4	2.0

In respect of the prior year non recourse finance, the Group was not obliged to support any losses and did not intend to do so. The providers of this finance ... confirmed that they would not seek recourse from the Group.

However, when the factor or invoice discounter has full recourse in the event of bad debts, the substance of the transaction is that the company is taking all the risk, and the factor or invoice discounter is merely providing finance. The company's accounts would therefore show (where £80m was advanced by a factor, with full recourse, on debtors of £100m):

	£m
Current assets:	
Debtors	100
Current liabilities:	
Finance from factor	80

rather than debtors of £20m, as was long the case.

Linked presentation

What is termed a linked presentation may be adopted where there is limited recourse by the factor (FRS 5 paras. 26–28). The accounts of engineering company BRUNEL HOLDINGS provide an illustration:

BRUNEL HOLDINGS *Extract from the notes to the 1997 and 1998 accounts*

Note 15. Debtors	1998	1997
	£000	£000
Amounts falling due within one year:		
Trade debtors	17,458	24,794
Debts factored with limited recourse	–	602
...		
Debts factored with limited recourse		
Gross debts		7,484
less non-recourse proceeds		(6,882)
		602

Problem 11.1

THE BODY SHOP

	1998	1997
	£m	£m
Turnover	293.1	270.8

Use this fact together with the information on page 76 to calculate, for each year:

(i) the collection period in months;
(ii) the ratio Trade debtors/Sales as a percentage.

Comment briefly.

Chapter 12

CURRENT ASSET INVESTMENTS, CASH AT BANK AND IN HAND

Reference: FRS 5 *Reporting the substance of transactions*.

Types of investment

As explained in Chapter 9, investments may be held as fixed assets or as current assets. This chapter considers only investments which are current assets, i.e. held short term, either for resale or as a temporary store of value; and not intended for use on a continuing basis in the company's activities.

Treatment of current asset investments

A current asset investment is initially recorded at its purchase cost, including expenses, and is normally included in the balance sheet at the lower of cost and net realisable value. It must be written down to its net realisable value at the balance sheet date if that is less than its cost, and the loss taken to the P & L account. If at a subsequent balance sheet date the net realisable value has increased again, that higher value (up to the purchase cost) must be taken as the balance sheet value and any increase credited to the P & L account.

Under the Companies Act 1985 Sch 4 para. 31, historical cost principles can be replaced by alternative accounting rules to allow for revaluations and current cost accounting (see Chapter 29). The provisions allow investments of any description to be shown either at market value determined at the date of their last valuation or at a value ('fair value') determined on any basis which appears to the directors to be appropriate in the circumstances of the company. The method of valuation and the reasons for adopting it must be shown in the notes to the accounts.

This makes possible a variety of treatments (including the writing up of investments to market value and the taking of the profit so disclosed to P & L account); so it is necessary to read the accounting policies with care.

Disclosure requirements

Disclosure requirements are the same whether an investment is a fixed or a current asset:

(i) the amount relating to listed investments must be shown, distinguishing it between those listed on the Stock Exchange, London, and those listed on other exchanges;

(ii) the aggregate market value of listed investments must be shown if different from the book value, and the stock exchange value if it is less than the market value;

(iii) various details must be provided where the investment is 'significant', i.e. where it is either 10% or more of the nominal value of the shares of that class in the investee, or it represents more than 10% of the investor's own assets. The details to be disclosed are: (i) the name of the investee; (ii) its country of incorporation (if outside Great Britain) or registration (i.e. England and Wales or Scotland), if different from that of the investor; and (iii) a description and the proportion of each class of shares held;

(iv) the overall income from listed investments must be stated but there is no requirement to show the income from listed investments held as fixed assets and the income from listed investments held as current assets separately.

Types of current asset investment

Current asset investments include:

1. Short-term government and other listed securities:

    (a) intended to be held to maturity;
    (b) not intended to be held to maturity (but for trading).

2. Certificates of deposit.
3. Certificates of tax deposit.
4. Commercial paper.
5. Short-term deposits, e.g. money market deposits.
6. Short-term local authority bonds.
7. Options.
8. Other unlisted investments.

Current asset investments in practice

Many listed companies only have cash and short term deposits. Some, like THE BODY SHOP, seem to prefer to hold cash. But there are groups which do have very large amounts of current asset investments. e.g.:

GLAXOWELLCOME *Extracts from notes to 1998 accounts*

17. Net debt

Liquid investments	Market value		Book value	
	1998	1997	1998	1997
	£m	£m	£m	£m
Government and equiv-				
alent investments	340	270	332	263
Other investments	884	801	882	801
Deposits at banks	403	344	403	344
	1,627	1,415	1,617	1,408

At the balance sheet date the Group's liquid investments included listed investments of £218m (1997 – £130m), with an aggregate market value of £228m (1997 – £133m).

2. Accounting policies

Current asset investments are stated at the lower of cost and net realisable value. In the case of securities acquired at a significant premium or discount to maturity value, and intended to be held to redemption, cost is adjusted to amortise the premium or discount over the life to maturity of the security. Floating rate bonds are stated at cost. Equity investments are included as current assets when regarded as available for sale.

Some companies, like REUTERS, draw a distinction between Government securities and other listed investments and, within unlisted securities, between CDs (certificates of deposit), Term deposits and Other investments:

REUTERS GROUP *Extract from the notes to the 1998 accounts*

21. Short-term investments

		1998	1997
		£m	£m
Listed			
Government securities:	UK	2	2
	Overseas	115	83
Other investments:	Overseas	–	265
		117	350
Unlisted			
Certificates of deposit		127	144
Term deposits:	UK	511	647
	Overseas	103	73
Other investments:	UK	3	–
	Overseas	101	61
		845	925

Significance of short-term investments

Cash rich companies like GLAXOWELLCOME and REUTERS have a significant part of their assets in short-term investments, they are not central to the operation of the company.

But in a few companies they are. For example C.H. BAILEY, a company we have mentioned before in the context of Voting and Non-voting shares (see page 23):

C.H. BAILEY *Extracts from 1998 accounts*

Consolidated balance sheet	1998	1997
	£	£
Fixed assets …		
Current assets:		
Stocks and WIP	277,979	151,411
Debtors	1,120,815	1,035,455
Current investments	8,156,187	8,768,862
Cash at bank and in hand	953,790	1,054,023
	10,508,771	11,009,751
…		
Net assets	15,369,561	15,750,322

In 1998 the Group made a pre-tax loss of £303,767, while income from current asset investments was reported as £202,887, and profit from sale of investments £616,063.

As we pointed out earlier, the controlling shareholder of a company can do very much what he likes within his own personal feifdom. Many do, though some less patently than others.

Availability of short-term investments

Do not assume that current asset investments are necessarily available to meet current liabilities; read the small print, e.g. TATE & LYLE:

TATE & LYLE *Note from 1998 accounts*

Current asset investments	1998	1997
	£m	£m
Listed on overseas exchanges	73.1	82.3
Unlisted investments	1.3	5.3
Loans, short-term deposits and unlisted fixed interest securities	110.9	77.5
	185.3	165.1

included in the above are deposits of £15.0m (1997 – £14.5m) pledged as security for loans to joint ventures and associates. In addition deposits of £19.9m (1997 – £24.4m) are pledged as security for loans to other subsidiaries.

Cash at bank and in hand

The last item among current assets in the standard formats is Cash at bank and in hand. Apart from this, the Companies Acts contain no specific requirements on cash balances; and while the sums involved can be considerable, most companies do not explain the amount shown either by way of note or in their accounting policies:

DIAGEO *Extract from the consolidated balance sheet as at 30 June 1998*

	1998	1997
	£m	£m
...		
Cash at bank and in hand	1,244	1,522
...		

Cash at bank and in hand forms part of Cash as defined in FRS 1 (revised); but only part (see Chapter 19). It is closely related to Current asset investments; indeed while many companies previously treated deposits as Current asset investments, others treated them as bank balances.

Cash at bank and in hand is shown on the face of the balance sheet, but the formats are inconsistent: loans and overdrafts, as we shall see in Chapter 13, are relegated to a note.

Where a group has both credit balances and overdrafts with the same bank, the question arises as to the extent to which one can be set off against the other (and how this should be reflected in the accounts). Many groups have banking arrangements similar to those of ARJO WIGGINS APPLETON:

ARJO WIGGINS APPLETON *Extract from note 25 to the 1998 accounts*

Contingent liabilities

The Company is a participant in a cash-pooling arrangement operated by its UK clearing bank. The Company has guaranteed the overdraft balances of the participating companies, all of which are subsidiaries of the Company, subject to a maximum amount equal to the aggregate of the Company's own cash balances with the bank.

We discuss contingent liabilities in Chapter 15. Meanwhile, guidance on offsetting is provided by FRS 5 *Reporting the substance of transactions*.

Problem 12.1

Companies hold current asset investments for a variety of reasons. You are asked: (a) to suggest five possible reasons; and (b) to explain why it is important for the reader of accounts to have a clear idea of the reasons for any significant holding.

Chapter 13

BANK LOANS AND OVERDRAFTS

Bank facilities

There are three main methods by which a company can borrow money from a bank:

(a) by overdrawing on its current account;
(b) by loans; and
(c) by the use of acceptance credits.

The bank normally agrees with a company the maximum amount that can be borrowed under each method, and this is called granting a facility. For example, a company that has the bank's permission to run an overdraft of up to £1m has overdraft facilities for that amount.

What is shown in the balance sheet is, however, only the amount actually borrowed from the bank at the balance sheet date, although the average amount overdrawn during the year can be estimated from the interest charged to the profit and loss account.

The bank facilities available to a company do not have to be disclosed, but broad statements may be made about the company having 'ample overdraft facilities', and the trend is towards being more specific, e.g. BLUE CIRCLE:

BLUE CIRCLE *Extract from note to 1998 accounts*

20. Financial instruments: Liquidity risk profile
The group had undrawn committed facilities available at 31 December 1998 in respect of which all conditions precedent had been met as follows: £m

	£m
Expiry in one year or less	77.9
Expiry in more than one year but not more than two years	–
Expiry in more than two years	97.3
	175.2

Bank loans and overdrafts fall in the formats under the headings Creditors: amounts falling due within one year and Creditors: amounts falling due after more than one year, and are often grouped with finance leases.

Where security has been given (see page 35), the amounts secured and a general indication of the security must be stated (Companies Act 1985 Sch. 4 para. 48 (4)). For example, ICI:

ICI *Extract from note to 1998 accounts*

21. Loans	Repayment dates	1998 £m	1997 £m
Secured loans:			
US dollars	1999/2016	25	31
Taiwanese dollars	1999/2001	5	9
Other currencies	1999/2004	89	61
Total secured		119	101
Secured by fixed charge – bank loans		85	75
– other		27	16
Secured by floating charge – bank loans		7	10

For each item the following amounts must under Sch. 4 para. 48 (1) be shown separately:

(a) amounts payable otherwise than by instalments five years hence;
(b) those payable by instalment, any of which are due more than five years hence;
(c) the total of such instalments.

In addition listed companies must disclose amounts which are payable between one and two years, and those payable between two and five years. ICI more than meet this requirement, disclosing year by year up to 5 years:

ICI *Extract from note to 1998 accounts*

Loan maturities	1998	1997
...	£m	£m
Total loans		
Loans or instalments repayable:		
After 5 years	1,181	1,313
From 4 to 5 years	164	641
From 3 to 4 years	667	219
From 2 to 3 years	228	261
From 1 to 2 years	714	541
Total due after more than one year	2,954	2,975
Total due within one year	585	950
Total loans	3,539	3,925

Where any part of the debt is repayable after more than five years, the terms of repayment and rates of interest payable should be shown. If the information is excessive, a general indication of terms and rates of interest is permitted (Sch. 4 para. 48 (2) and (3)).

Overdrafts

The traditional method of clearing bank lending is to allow the customer to overdraw on his current account. It was originally designed to cover fluctuations in the company's cash during the year and gives the company complete flexibility of drawing within a given limit, which is normally reviewed annually.

Bank advances on overdraft are technically repayable on demand and, although this is seldom enforced, the bank when granting overdraft facilities may expect the customer to produce budgets and cash flow forecasts to show the purposes for which the facilities are intended and the plans for eventual repayment. Bank lending on overdraft is traditionally short term in character, designed to cover fluctuations in working capital requirements rather than to provide permanent capital for the company.

When long-term interest rates were driven high by inflation, few finance directors were willing to commit their companies to long-term fixed interest rate debt, especially if they expected interest rates to fall in due course. Instead they resorted more and more to borrowing from their banks, where interest on an overdraft is charged at an agreed percentage over the clearing bank's base rate (see below), which they hoped would average less than the long-term rate at the time, and where the company is free to reduce its borrowing whenever it wishes. Although it is now quite common for companies to finance a large part of their working capital in this way, clearing banks are usually reluctant to let companies increase their overdraft ad lib, even against a floating charge, preferring their clients to convert any 'hard-core' borrowing that has built up on overdraft into loans (see Bank facilities on page 87).

The cost of borrowing on overdraft

The interest a company has to pay on its overdraft is usually set at a given percentage above its bank's base rate, depending on the standing of the customer; a financially stable, medium-sized company might pay a fixed 1½% above base.

The base rate, the datum on which the rates of interest are based, is adjusted up and down to reflect fluctuations in short-term interest rates. Each bank sets its own base rate, though in practice the clearing banks' base rates keep very much in line with each other.

Fluctuations in amount

As we have said, the overdraft figure given in the balance sheet is the amount the overdraft facility is being used at the year end. Companies normally choose their year end to fall when business is at its slackest, and the balance sheet figure is most unlikely to be the maximum amount the company has overdrawn during the year.

For example, a company in a seasonal business, with peak sales in the summer, could be expected to build up stocks from early spring and to carry high debtors across the summer. With an annual turnover of say £15m, £200,000 in the bank at its year end (31 December) and £120,000 bank interest paid (reflecting an average overdraft of £1.5m during the year, bearing interest on average at 8%), the amount the company was actually overdrawn during the year would be likely to fluctuate with the sales cycle as shown in Example 13.1.

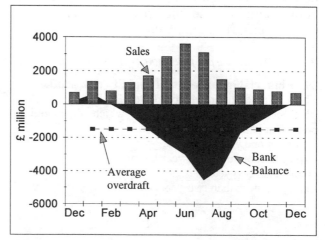

Example 13.1 Annual fluctuation in sales and overdraft

In practice, profit on sales and depreciation on assets would accumulate during the year, steadily improving the overdraft position, but sharp increases would be expected with the payment of dividends and Corporation Tax, and capital expenditure would also have an immediate effect on the overdraft position.

Vulnerability

Companies which rely heavily on borrowing on overdraft and on floating-rate loans (see below) are vulnerable to rising interest rates, particularly if their profit margins are small, and those which let their overdrafts steadily increase year by year without raising further equity or fixed-interest capital are steadily increasing their interest rate risk. Another hazard of financing on overdraft is that the amount a bank can lend has in the past been subject to Bank of England controls, which were tightened from time to time without much warning.

Banks are also liable to restrict credit on their own account when they find themselves up against their own overall lending limits or too heavily lent in the particular sector in which the company operates. As credit restrictions often come when conditions are unfavourable for capital raising, a company which is financed extensively by overdraft can all too easily find its operations severely constrained by its immediate cash position.

Bank loans

The simplest type of bank loan is one where the full amount is drawn by the borrower at the outset and is repaid in one lump sum at the end of the period. The duration (or 'term') of the loan is seldom more than seven years but, unlike an overdraft, a bank loan cannot be called in before the end of the term unless the borrower defaults on any condition attached to the loan.

Interest is charged either at a fixed rate or, more frequently, at a floating rate: an agreed percentage over base rate, or over London Inter-Bank Offer Rate (LIBOR). Where LIBOR is used, an interest period is agreed between the borrower and the bank, and the bank then, on the first day of each interest period, determines the rate at which deposits are being offered in the inter-bank market for the relevant period.

For example, if a rate of ½% over LIBOR and a three-month interest period have been agreed and the three-month LIBOR rate is 5.7% at the start of the period, the borrower will pay 6.2% for the next three months, and the rate will then be redetermined. Banks frequently allow borrowers to vary their choice of interest period – one month, three months or six months – during the life of a loan.

Where the borrower doesn't need all the money at once, the bank may allow the loan to be drawn down in tranches (specified instalments). Repayments may also be arranged in instalments, which may often be a stipulation of the lender; banks like to see money coming back gradually to make repayment easier for the borrower and to give early warning of a borrower getting into difficulties over repayment. Details of drawing down and repayment are agreed in advance, together with the rate of interest payable and the security to be given, although any of these features can be altered subsequently by mutual agreement.

Security

Bank loans are sometimes secured on assets acquired by the loan or on other assets of the company, but a floating charge is more usual. If the loan is not secured at all, the company may be required to give a *negative pledge*, i.e. to undertake not to give security to any new or existing creditor or to borrow further amounts under existing security without the bank's prior agreement in writing.

Flexible loan facilities

There is an increasing trend, particularly in European banking, to provide companies with more flexible financing than term loans by granting loan facilities, usually for periods of between 3 and 5 years. Drawing down (usually with a minimum limit on any one drawing) can be allowed at any time given a little notice, repayment is flexible, and subsequent redrawing is often allowed, but the borrower will be charged for this flexibility by a commitment commission payable on any unused portion of the facility for as long as the facility is left open. Facilities giving this flexibility are called revolving, and can be single- or multi-currency.

Some companies, like UNIGATE, give details:

UNIGATE *Extract from note to 1998 accounts*

16. Borrowings and Finance Leases

...

At 31 March 1998, the Group had revolving credit facilities of £160m (1997: £230m) under which it may repay amounts borrowed at its option while retaining the flexibility to re-borrow under the facilities. No amount was outstanding under the facilities at 31 March 1998 and 31 March 1997.

BILLS OF EXCHANGE

Definition

A bill of exchange is, briefly, an order in writing from one person (the *drawer*) to another (the *drawee*) requiring the drawee to pay a specified sum of money on a given date. When the drawee signs the bill he becomes the *acceptor* of the bill, and the person to whom the money is to be paid is the *payee*. The main legislation on bills is contained in the Bills of Exchange Act 1882, and their use in practice is clearly and concisely described in a book, *The Bill on London*, produced by Gillett Brothers, one of the discount houses.

Primary purpose

The primary purpose of a bill of exchange is to finance the sale of goods when the seller or exporter wishes to obtain payment at the time the goods are despatched and the buyer or importer wants to defer payment until the goods reach him, or later.

In these circumstances A, the supplier of goods to B, would draw a bill of exchange for the goods, which B 'accepts', acknowledging the debt and promising payment at some future date, often three months ahead. Bills of this type are called trade bills.

A can then sell the bill to a third party, C, at a discount to the face value of the bill; and C in turn can endorse it and sell it on to D. In this case if B subsequently defaults, D can claim payment from A, and if A also defaults D can then claim on C.

Alternatively A can retain the bill, which gives a legal right to payment at a given date in the future (the date of maturity), or the bill can be deposited at a bank as a security against borrowings.

Balance sheet presentation

If Company A's year ends before the bill has reached maturity, then:

(a) if A still holds the bill, it would be shown separately under current assets as Bills receivable or included in debtors; or

(b) if A discounted the bill, traditionally it would not appear in the balance sheet, but would be shown as a contingent liability recognising the possibility that B may subsequently default. FRS 5 *Reporting the substance of transactions* has changed that. Most companies now show bills of exchange discounted as a liability until the time for payment has passed (i.e. there has been no recourse).

In Company B's balance sheet the outstanding bill would be shown under creditors as a bill of exchange payable.

The engineering group BRUNEL makes extensive use of discounting:

BRUNEL HOLDINGS *Extract from note to 1998 accounts*

18. Creditors	1998
	£000
Amounts falling due within one year:	
Bank loans and overdrafts	4,957
Payments received on account	3,807
Trade creditors	13,789
Bills of exchange discounted with recourse	2,794
Proposed dividends	1,302
...	

Discounting

When a bill of exchange is discounted, i.e. sold to a third party at a discount to its face value, this is usually done through one of the discount houses, which will trade it in the money market. The discount on a trade bill depends on prevailing interest rates, on the creditworthiness of the drawer, the acceptor and any subsequent endorsers, and on the nature of the underlying transaction. In the case of a bank bill, that is one where a bank is the acceptor of the bill, or has endorsed it, the discount rate will be less than on a trade bill. The finest rates are obtained in discounting bills drawn against exports or imports and accepted by 'eligible banks' (i.e. those banks whose acceptances are eligible for rediscount at the Bank of England).

Acceptance credits

Many eligible banks specialise in accepting bills for customers. They provide this type of short term finance by granting the client an acceptance credit facility up to a given limit for an agreed period, and the client can then draw bills of exchange on the bank as he wishes, provided the running total of bills outstanding does not exceed the prescribed limit (in other words, it is a revolving credit facility). The bank 'accepts' the bills, which can then be discounted in the money market at the finest rate, and the customer receives the proceeds of the sale, less the acceptance commission he has to pay to the accepting house (normally between 3/8% and 1/2% p.a. for good-quality borrowers). When the bill falls due for payment (usually three months later), the customer pays the bank the full face value of the bill and the bank in turn honours the bill when it is presented by the eventual purchaser. The bank has to honour the bill even if the customer defaults, because it had 'accepted' responsibility for meeting the bill when it fell due.

The acceptance of bills by banks is related to commercial transactions, either specifically matched or linked to the general volume of business, so that the bills are self-liquidating.

Unlike an overdraft, the interest on discounted bills is paid in advance by the deduction of discount charges from the face value of the bill and, in addition, if the bills have been accepted by a bank, the company will also have to pay the acceptance commission in advance. In spite of these extra costs, variations of interest rates often make the use of acceptance credit facilities cheaper than an overdraft or a bank loan.

The future obligation of a company to provide cash cover to meet bills that have yet to mature under an acceptance credit facility must, if material, be shown separately in a company's balance sheet under creditors as 'Bills of exchange payable' (CA 1985, Sch. 4 formats), as illustrated by BRUNEL HOLDINGS on 92.

The big picture

Chapter 12 considered, amongst other things, cash at bank; and explained that under the Companies Acts formats it appears separately on the face of the balance sheet as part of the current assets.

As we have seen in this chapter, amounts borrowed from the bank do not normally appear on the face of the balance sheet but fall within Creditors as amounts due within one year or amounts due after more than one year; and are detailed in the notes to the balance sheet.

There is thus no netting of amounts owed by banks and amounts owing to banks; but while this might be important to an economist, as such it is not particularly significant either to the company or to analysts and investors.

What matters are:

- How much is available to meet the debts and obligations of the business?
- Is it in a position to meet its debts as they fall due?

The balance sheet and the notes to it do not answer either of these questions.

This is largely due to the British system of operating with an overdraft. Although theoretically an overdraft is repayable on demand, in practice a limit is agreed for a specific time and normally adhered to by the bank. But as we have seen, that limit does not have to be disclosed. If it is not disclosed, one has no way of assessing how much is available.

Imagine two companies, A and B, much the same size. Each owes wages and other creditors due tomorrow of £1.5m. A has an overdraft of £27m, B has £1m in the bank. At first sight, B looks more solvent than A. But if A has an

overdraft limit of £50m, £23m of which remains unused, and B, having a poor reputation for past dealings and a low credit rating, cannot raise an overdraft or borrow elsewhere, we would not normally be able to tell from the balance sheet.

'Going concern' assurances required in the directors' report (see pages 233–4), and the auditors' report upon them, offer a safeguard, though a somewhat limited one.

Chapter 19 is devoted to FRS 1 *Cash flow statements*. Nevertheless, because of its close relationship to the content of this Chapter, it is perhaps right to say a few words here.

Cash is defined in FRS 1 to be:

(a) cash in hand and deposits repayable on demand with any qualifying financial institution (i.e. an entity that as part of its business receives deposits or other repayable funds and grants credits for its own account); less
(b) overdrafts from any qualifying financial institution repayable on demand.

To qualify as 'cash' the deposits must be capable of being withdrawn at any time without notice and without penalty. They count as 'on demand' if a maturity or period of notice of not more than 24 hours or one working day has been agreed. Cash includes cash in hand and deposits denominated in foreign currencies.

It will be seen that the definition of 'cash' for the purposes of FRS 1 is extremely narrow.

This chapter has looked at something quite different: at all forms of bank borrowing not just those that count as negative 'cash' for purposes of FRS 1.

Nevertheless, FRS 1 does also take in the big picture. It requires (para. 33) a note reconciling the movement of cash in the period with the movement in net debt (i.e. all capital instruments which are classified as liabilities under FRS 4 *Capital instruments* plus related derivatives and obligations under finance leases). And this reconciliation provides another place to look for information on bank borrowings and debt more generally. That of BRUNEL HOLDINGS for 1998 is shown on the next page.

BRUNEL HOLDINGS *Notes to the 1998 group cash flow statement*

A. Reconciliation of operating profit to net cash (outflow)/inflow from operating activities

...

B. Reconciliation of net cash flow to movement in net debt

	1998 £000	1997 £000
Increase in cash in period	18,117	2,208
Reduction in lease finance	372	767
Increase in bills of exchange discounted	(1,193)	(613)
Change in net debt from cashflows	17,296	2,362
Finance leases disposed of with subsidiaries	1,454	1,079
New finance leases	(465)	(972)
Translation difference	(2)	(5)
Movement in net debt in period	18,283	2,464
Net debt at 1 July	(26,310)	(28,774)
Net debt at 30 June	(8,027)	(26,310)

C. Analysis of net debt

...

Note A shows 'Net cash outflow from operating activities (465)'. Note B, the reconciliation of net cash flow starts with the bottom line of the cash flow statement: 'Increase in cash 18,117', and ends with 'Net debt (8,027)'.

The change in net debt from (26,310), the closing figure in 1997, to (8,027) is then analysed in Note C, which shows a reduction in overdraft of more then £20m.

Problem 13.1

Consider the example of BRUNEL HOLDINGS above. Apart from finance leases, there was no new financing during the year.

1. What was the net change in finance leases in 1998?
2. How did Brunel Holdings improve its debt position so dramatically in 1998?
3. What was the figure for Bills of Exchange discounted in the 1996 and 1997 balance sheet? – see Note on Brunel's creditors on page 90.

Chapter 14

DERIVATIVES AND OTHER FINANCIAL INSTRUMENTS

Reference: FRS 13 *Derivatives and other financial instruments*.

Introduction

The complexity of this subject is reflected by the length of this FRS. Complete with its Summary and its Appendices, FRS 13 runs to 165 pages.

Disclosure requirements depend on whether you are a Bank (Part B), an Other financial institution (Part C), or neither (Part A). Parts B and C are, appropriately, printed on pink paper.

In this chapter we will concentrate on non-financial institutions, and the disclosures required of them, which fall broadly into:

- *Narrative Disclosures*, usually contained in the Operating and Financial Review (OFR) or the Directors' report; and
- *Numerical Disclosures* in the notes to the accounts.

Derivatives can seriously damage your wealth

Although much of the business done by companies in this market is for the prudent reduction of risk – primarily interest rate risk, currency risk and commodity risk – much is sheer speculation: the unacceptable face of capitalism, doubled and redoubled.

Let us be quite clear about two things:

1. In business school parlance, derivatives are a 'zero sum game'. If anybody is going to 'make a bomb', somebody else is going to 'lose a bomb'. The overall outcome is zero.
2. This is cowboy country. As the *Daily Telegraph* reported on 6 October 1995:

DAILY TELEGRAPH *Extracts from article by Banking correspondent*

P & G accuses Bankers Trust of racketeering

Proctor & Gamble ... alleges that 'a culture of greed and duplicity', permeated through Bankers Trust. 'Fraud was so pervasive Bankers Trust employees used the acronym ROF – short for rip-off factor – to describe one method of fleecing clients'.

...

Proctor and Gamble highlights one taped conversation in which a Bankers Trust employee describes a deal he has just concluded with the company as 'a massive gravy train'...

Another tape related to massive profits made by Bankers Trust on a leveraged derivatives transaction sold to Proctor & Gamble. 'They would never know.' said one saleswoman. 'They would never be able to know how much money was taken out of that.' A colleague replied 'Never, no way. That's the beauty of Bankers Trust.'

'Funny business, you know,' said one salesman in a taped conversation. 'Lure people into that calm and then just totally f*** them.'

Definition of a derivative

A derivative financial instrument is a financial instrument that derives its value from the price or rate of some underlying item.

Underlying items include equities, bonds, commodities, interest rates, exchange rates and stock market and other indices.

They include futures, options, forward contracts, interest rate and currency swaps, interest rate caps, collars and floors, forward interest rate agreements, commitments to purchase shares or bonds ... (FRS 13 para. 2)

Risk management, and derivative trading

Most large companies, and particularly multinationals, use derivatives to reduce exposure to various types of risk. This is a perfectly normal and usually fairly safe activity, providing you choose your counterparties carefully; i.e. don't deal with cowboys.

Other companies also *trade* in derivatives; this can be a very dangerous activity unless it is:

- run by experienced and responsible staff; and
- tightly controlled.

Disclosure requirements

FRS 13 requires both narrative and numerical disclosures on the use of financial instruments.

Narrative disclosures

GLAXOWELLCOME makes it clear that it wouldn't touch derivatives trading with a bargepole:

GLAXOWELLCOME *1998 accounting policies*

Derivative financial instruments

- The group does not hold or issue derivative financial instruments for trading purposes.
- Derivative financial instruments are used to manage the currency profile of Group assets and liabilities, and are treated from inception as an economic hedge ...
- Currency swaps and forward exchange contracts are used to fix the value of the related asset or liability in the contract currency ...
- Interest differentials under interest swap and cap agreements are recognised ... by adjustment of interest expense over the life of the agreement.

SHELL, on the other hand, has always been in the business of trading in oil, as its full name, Shell Transport & Trading implies, and has a huge depth of experience in the management of trading:

SHELL TRANSPORT AND TRADING *Extract from 1998 Operational and financial review*

Risk management

... Apart from forward foreign exchange contracts to meet known commitments, the use of derivative financial instruments by most Group companies is not permitted by their treasury policy.

Some Group companies operate as *traders* in crude oil, natural gas and oil products and use commodity swaps and options as a means of managing price and timing risks ... the use of derivatives is generally confined to specialist oil trading and central treasury organisations which have appropriate skills, experience, supervision, and control and reporting systems.

Numerical disclosures

Numerical disclosures show how the company's objectives and policies were implemented in the period and provide supplementary information for evaluating significant or potentially significant exposures. See page 97.

Common types of derivative

The most common types of derivative that the ordinary investor is likely to come across are:

(a) options;
(b) futures and forward contracts; and
(c) currency and interest rate swaps.

An *options contract* is a contract giving the holder the right, but not the obligation, to buy ('call'), or sell ('put'), a specified underlying asset at a pre-agreed price, at either a fixed point in the future (European-style), or a time chosen by the holder up to maturity (American-style). Options are available in exchange-traded (e.g. on LIFFE, the London International Financial Futures Exchange), and over-the-counter (OTC) markets (shorthand for anywhere else, between any two parties).

A *futures contract* on the other hand is an agreement (obligation) to buy or sell a given quantity of a particular asset, at a specified future date, at a pre-agreed price. Futures contracts have standard delivery dates, trading units, terms and conditions.

In a *forward contract* the purchaser and its counterparty are obligated to trade a security or other asset at a specified date in the future. The price paid for the security or asset is either agreed upon at the time the contract is entered into, or determined at delivery. Forward contracts are generally traded over-the-counter.

In a *currency swap* a company borrows foreign currency for a given period, and lends the equivalent sterling for the same period. In an *interest rate swap* the company swaps a fixed rate of interest with a bank for a floating rate, or vice versa.

While these are the most common types of derivative that ordinary investors are likely to come across, the range of derivatives possible is limited only by the imagination of investment banks. New types of derivative are being created all the time.

It is convenient to classify derivatives as either:

(a) commodity related; or
(b) financial.

Commodity related derivatives

Manufacturers whose business depends upon a particular key commodity (like sugar or cocoa) may well 'hedge', i.e. buy or sell options or futures contracts or employ forward contracts to fix the price of the underlying raw material, or the sales proceeds of a product.

TATE & LYLE discloses its policy on commodity derivatives in its OFR:

TATE & LYLE *Extract from 1998 Operating and financial review*

Commodities

Derivatives are used to hedge movements in the future prices of commodities in those domestic and international markets where the Group buys and sells sugar and maize.

Commodity futures and options are used to hedge inventories and the costs of raw materials for unpriced and prospective contracts not covered by forward product sales.

The options and futures hedging contracts generally mature within one year and are all with organised exchanges.

Tate & Lyle added in a note to the accounts that: 'Changes in the fair value of instruments used as hedges are not recognised in the financial statements until the hedged position matures.' This is known as *hedge accounting* (FRS 13 para. 58).

In other words, whatever the total cost of acquiring the raw material this way, then that is its 'cost'; and whatever the net sales proceeds are as a result of the future, those are the sales proceeds.

Providing the management lays down limits to the amount of hedging, and has control systems in place to ensure that these limits are not exceeded without permission, then hedging is a perfectly normal and reasonable business activity.

Where things go wrong is when you get a *rogue trader*. This happened some years ago in a chocolate manufacturer, where a commodity dealer started to gamble on cocoa futures and went way beyond the company's requirement for cocoa, thinking he could make a lot of money for the company.

When it was noticed that he was over the limits set for him, management stood over him while he closed all his positions. The moment they were out of the room, he opened them all up again.

When he was finally rumbled, a very substantial loss was incurred covering all his positions. In the aftermath of this débâcle the company's share price fell by more than 80%.

Reducing the risks of trading in derivatives

One secret of good management with any trading or dealing in derivatives is to ensure that the functions of confirmation and of settlement are kept entirely separate from the dealing department. In the celebrated case of currency swaps that brought down BARINGS, all these functions in Barings' Singapore office came under one person: Leeson.

Investors should also be wary when a company's dealers are 'earning' huge bonuses. Greed comes before a fall.

Financial derivatives

Companies have traditionally borrowed in foreign currencies to help finance overseas investment and reduce exposure to currency risk. In this modern day and age the mobility of capital in most of the developed countries of the world – exchange controls are still prevalent in LDCs – and the increasing sophistication of the financial markets, has led to the development of a wide range of financial instruments to hedge against both currency and interest rate risk.

It no longer follows that you borrow French francs long term at fixed rates of interest to finance long-term investment in France; it may be advantageous to borrow variable rate in sterling and do a currency swap and an interest rate swap.

Currency swaps

A currency swap is, in effect, the same as a reciprocating or back-to-back loan: the company borrows foreign currency for a given period and, in the same transaction, lends an equivalent amount of sterling for the same period.

For example, a UK company wants to borrow US dollars, but also wants to avoid the currency risk on the principal amount borrowed, i.e. it wants to hedge the currency risk. So it raises, say, £100m by a 7-year 10% Eurobond issue and swaps it for 7 years with a bank for say $160m at 7½%. During the 7 years the company pays interest to the bank in dollars at 7½% per annum on the $160m and the bank pays interest to the company in sterling at 10% per annum on the £100m. At the end of the 7 years the swap is reversed, so the company gets its £100m back regardless of the sterling/US$ exchange rate and in time to redeem the Eurobond issue.

Currency swaps normally appear either in a note to the accounts or in the financial review, e.g. BP AMOCO.

BP AMOCO *Extract from financial review 1998*

Financial risk management

...

Our foreign exchange management policy is to minimise economic and material transactional exposures from currency movements against the US dollar ... most of the group's borrowings are in US dollars, are hedged with respect to the US dollar. or are swapped into dollars where this achieves a lower cost of financing.

Interest rate swaps

An interest rate swap can be used by a company to protect itself against the impact of adverse fluctuations in interest rates on the interest charge it has to pay on its floating rate debt. The company agrees a fixed rate with bank on a nominal sum for a given period; the company then pays the bank the fixed rate and the bank pays the company the floating rate; as, for example, GLAXOWELLCOME.

GLAXOWELLCOME *Extract from note to the 1998 accounts*

26. Financial instruments and related disclosures
Interest rate risk management
INTEREST RATE SWAP The Group has agreed with a commercial bank to exchange, at specified intervals, the difference between the fixed and floating rate interest amounts calculated by reference to a total principal amount of £500m, exchanging sterling floating interest rate for a fixed rate of 8.61 per cent.

When used in conjunction with a currency swap, an interest rate swap enables a company to lock in at a fixed rate of interest in one currency to cover floating-rate interest charges in another currency.

Companies may also use interest rate swaps in the reverse direction to reduce the proportion of their fixed-rate interest charges if they take the view that interest rates will fall. In neither case is there any transfer of principal.

The swap market has grown in recent years for another reason: to exploit the differences that exist between the fixed rate and the extremely competitive floating-rate credit markets in order to reduce the cost of borrowing, as illustrated in Example 14.1 at the bottom of the page.

Interest rate caps

Another way for a company with floating-rate debt to hedge against increases in interest rates is to buy a *cap*. A cap is a contract in which a counterparty, in exchange for a one-time premium, agrees to pay the bond issuer if an interest rate index rises above a certain percentage rate, known as the cap or *strike rate*. It is also called a *ceiling*.

The advantage of a cap over an interest rate swap from floating to fixed is that a cap not only protects the company from the effect of rising interest rates, but allows it to benefit from any fall in interest rates.

A *collar* is the simultaneous purchase of a cap and sale of a floor by the issuer, in which it trades any benefits from a potential fall in the interest rate index for protection against an excessive rise. Under a collar agreement, the issuer defines a specific range for its interest rate payments.

Caps and collars protect issuers from having to pay higher interest rates on variable rate debt if market rates increase beyond the cap rate.

A *floor* is the mirror image of a ceiling. With a floor contract, the bond issuer receives an up-front fee from a counterparty. If the interest rate index falls below the floor or strike level, the issuer makes payments to the counterparty. Similar to a cap agreement, if the floating index rate does not fall below the strike level, the issuer pays nothing.

Example 14.1 Use of swaps to reduce the cost of borrowing

Two companies both want to borrow money for five years. One has a AAA Standard & Poor's credit rating and wants to borrow floating rate, while the other, rated BBB, wants to borrow fixed. Market conditions are:

Company rating	AAA	BBB
Cost of 5-year fixed rate bond	10%	11½%
Cost of 5-year bank loan	LIBOR + $^1/_8$%	LIBOR + $^5/_8$%
Cost of a swap:		
Company pays	LIBOR	10½%
Company receives	10$^3/_8$%	LIBOR

The AAA company, wanting to borrow floating, would issue 5-year bonds at 10% and swap; cost of borrowing floating = 10% + LIBOR − 10$^3/_8$% = LIBOR − $^3/_8$% compared with the 5-year bank loan's cost of LIBOR + $^1/_8$%.

Similarly the BBB company, wanting to borrow at a fixed rate, would take out a bank loan at LIBOR + $^5/_8$% and swap; cost of borrowing fixed = LIBOR + $^5/_8$% − LIBOR + 10$^1/_2$% = 11$^1/_8$ %, which is cheaper than issuing bonds at 11½ %.

One company that uses a mixture of caps, swaps and forward agreements is SHELL (shown in the right hand column):

Numerical disclosures

These give an overall picture of a company's currency and interest rate exposure, as TATE & LYLE'S accounts illustrate at the bottom of the page.

Counterparty risk

Companies which use derivatives are subject to *counterparty risk*, i.e. the risk that the counterparty defaults. The counterparty is simply the party with whom one does the transaction.

Some companies with large exposure to derivatives, like REUTERS, describe the risk:

REUTERS *Note to the 1998 accounts*
All derivative instruments are unsecured. However, Reuters does not anticipate non-performance by the counterparties who are all banks with recognised credit ratings of 'A' or higher.

SHELL *Note to the 1998 accounts*
26. Financial instruments

(b) Interest rate risk
Some Group companies, primarily those with specialist treasury operations, use derivatives to manage their exposure to movements in interest rates

The total contract/notional amounts and estimated fair values of Group companies interest rate swaps/forward rate agreements and interest rate caps at 31 December were:

	$m 1998	
	Contract/ notional amount	Estimated fair value
Interest rate swaps/ forward rate agreements and interest rate caps	6,376	(5)

The amount of hedging gains or losses on these instruments which had been deferred at 31 December 1998 in respect of firm commitments was not significant.

TATE & LYLE *Note to the 1998 accounts*
30. Currency and interest rate exposure of financial assets and liabilities

After taking into account the various interest rate and cross currency interest rate swaps entered into by the Group, the currency and interest rate exposure of the financial liabilities of the Group as at 26 September 1998 was:

Currency	Total £m	Fixed rate £m	Floating rate £m	Non-interest bearing £m
Sterling	171.2	165.5	3.3	2.4
United States Dollars	718.4	332.6	381.4	4.4
Canadian Dollars	49.5	–	49.5	–
Australian Dollars	17.0	–	17.0	–
EU currencies (excl. Sterling)	240.1	62.2	175.9	1.6
Others	8.6	0.7	7.9	–
Total	1,204.8	561.4	635.0	8.4
of which – gross borrowings	1,198.0	561.4	635.0	1.6
– working capital	4.4	–	–	4.4
– non-equity shares	2.4	–	–	2.4
Total	1,204.8	561.4	635.0	8.4

Interest rates	Average interest rate (%) of fixed rate liabilities	Average years to maturity of fixed rate liabilities	Average years to maturity of non-interest bearing liabilities
Sterling	10.8	2.6	–
United States Dollars	6.6	3.2	0.5
Canadian Dollars	–	–	–
Australian Dollars	–	–	–
EU currencies (excl. Sterling)	5.3	0.9	4.5
Others	7.6	3.2	–
Average	6.6	2.8	1.6

Concern about derivatives

What is disturbing about derivatives is that:

1. It is likely that anyone who today has funds invested will, usually unwittingly, be indirectly exposed to derivatives. Many major companies use them in one way or another; investment trusts, unit trusts and pension funds employ them in an effort either to protect themselves or to boost returns; as do some local authorities.

2. The sums involved are astronomical. For instance, BARCLAYS alone reported that at the end of 1998 it held or had issued:

	Contract or underlying principal amount £m
Foreign exchange derivatives	434,452
Interest rate derivatives	1,111,858
Equity and stock index derivatives	38,303
Commodity derivatives	12,941

3. Dealings are international and controls have yet to be agreed internationally.

There has been a series of derivative based disasters in various countries – BARINGS was no isolated case – which have alerted management to the risks, but there is still plenty of ignorance around.

How can you blame the ignorant when a team of 'big hitters', as they call them in the United States, including the winner of a Nobel Prize for his research work on derivatives, set up an outfit called LTCM, Long Term Credit Management, got backing to the tune of $600 billion, turned out in practice to be Short term Catastrophic Asset Mismanagement (SCAM), but a scam of such gigantic proportions that it had to be rescued by the Fed (The U.S. Federal Reserve Bank).

But why bother with derivatives?

You may well ask 'Why do companies go to all this trouble to complicate matters, when they would probably do just as well in the long run to carry the risk themselves?' Good question. Plenty of companies would agree with you, e.g.:

RIO TINTO *Extract from 1998 financial review*

Exchange rates, reporting currencies and currency exposure

... the Group does not generally believe currency hedging would provide long term benefits to shareholders ...

Rio Tinto's business is mining, not commodity trading. The Group does not undertake transactions in products other than those it produces itself ... the Group does not believe a commodity price hedging programme would provide long term benefit to shareholders.

We can think of three reasons why companies and others use derivatives:

1. The real professionals, like SHELL and TATE & LYLE, have an enormous amount of in-house expertise and long experience of making profits on trading.

2. Although year on year currency risk and interest rate risk would probably be a case of swings and roundabouts, companies prefer to minimise the risk of a big hiccough in their reported profits. Investors don't like them, and in a bad year a sharp drop in profits due to adverse movements in currencies and/or interest rates could leave a company open to predators.

3. There is much international competition in banking these days and the traditional business of taking deposits and lending is much less profitable than it used to be. So bankers turn to other means of earning a crust and *some* aren't too particular how they do it.

Benefits of disclosure

There is a great deal of work involved in collecting and disclosing the information required by FRS 13; information which is likely to be beyond the average investor. But the very process of collecting and reviewing the required information brings to the attention of directors and managers the nature and amount of risk which the company is running, and helps them meet their responsibilities. And most of the problems we have seen over derivatives, whether financial or commodity based, have been due to weakness of controls and lack of higher management attention.

Problem 14.1

Just before Christmas, a fund manager decides that he would like to purchase £10m of UK stocks, but the funds will not be available until February.

The FT-SE 100 Index stands at 4,000 at the end of December and he is looking for it to rise 5% over the next month. The fund manager wants to limit the price he has to pay in the future to a value of 4,100.

The fund manager decides to purchase 250 (£10m ÷ (4,000 × (£10)) March 4,000 calls for 100. Each contract represents £10 per index point movement.

1. What is his initial outlay?
2. What is the maximum amount risked by the manager?
3. If on 15 February it becomes clear that the £10m will not after all be available but the market has risen to 4,155, what can the investment manager do?

Chapter 15

CREDITORS, PROVISIONS, CONTINGENT LIABILITIES AND CONTINGENT ASSETS

CREDITORS

Presentation

The two balance sheet formats in Schedule 4 of the Companies Act 1985 present creditors in different ways:

1. Format 1 shows them under two headings, *Creditors: amounts falling due within one year* and *Creditors: amounts falling due after more than one year.*
2. Format 2 shows them under a single heading, *Creditors*, in which case the amounts falling due within one year must be shown separately for each item and in aggregate.

Most companies use Format 1, which nets out *Creditors falling due within one year* (also known as Current liabilities), against *Current assets* to produce Net current assets (liabilities). Amounts falling due after one year are then deducted from Total assets less current liabilities, to give Net assets; see THE BODY SHOP in the next column.

Types of creditor

The following items are required to be shown, if material:

(a) debenture loans (see Chapter 6);
(b) bank loans and overdrafts (see Chapter 13);
(c) payments received on account;
(d) trade creditors;
(e) bills of exchange payable (see Chapter 13);
(f) amounts owed to group undertakings (see Chapter 20);
(g) amounts owed to undertakings in which the company has a participating interest (see Chapter 22);

THE BODY SHOP *Extract from 1998 Group balance sheet*

	Note	1998 £m	1997 £m
Fixed assets			
Tangible assets		78.4	74.9
Investments		2.0	0.5
		80.4	75.4
Current assets			
Stocks		47.7	34.8
Debtors		47.0	45.0
Cash at bank and in hand		29.6	47.1
		124.3	126.9
Creditors: amounts falling due within one year	16	70.4	59.0
Net current assets		53.9	67.9
Total assets less current liabilities		134.3	143.3
Creditors, amounts falling due after more than one year	17	2.9	13.0
Provisions for liabilities			
Deferred tax		1.1	0.2
[Net assets]		130.3	130.1

(h) other creditors, including taxation and social security;
(i) accruals and deferred income.

Details of creditors are usually given in the notes rather than in the balance sheet itself.

THE BODY SHOP *Extract from 1998 accounts*

13. Creditors: Amounts falling due within one year

	1998	1997
	£m	£m
Bank loan	18.6	–
Bank overdraft	0.4	–
Variable rate loan stock - unsecured	–	2.8
USA loan notes - unsecured	–	5.5
USA variable rate loan stock	0.9	0.6
Trade creditors	11.0	10.2
Corporation tax	12.2	15.8
Other taxes, social security costs	3.4	2.7
Proposed dividend	7.3	6.2
Other creditors	4.0	3.3
Accruals	12.6	11.9
	70.4	59.0

Note 17 (not shown) is mainly concerned with bank and other loans falling due after more than one year.

Trade creditors represent money owed for goods supplied. The size of trade creditors shows the extent to which suppliers are financing a company's business. For example, TESCO's suppliers finance not only its stock and debtors, but also its money market investments and deposits, earning interest for Tesco not for its suppliers:

TESCO *Extracts from 1998 accounts*

	1998	1997
Current assets	£m	£m
Stocks	584	550
Debtors	133	78
Investments	196	80
Cash at bank and in hand	29	65
	942	773

Creditors: Amounts falling due within one year

...

Trade creditors	972	826

Taxation and social security are each shown separately. Taxation due within 12 months will normally include one year's mainstream Corporation Tax (but see Chapter 17 re large companies), and any foreign tax due.

An *accrual* is an apportionment of a known or determinable future liability in respect of a service already partly received. Thus, a business paying rent of £60,000 half-yearly in arrears on 30 June and 31 December would, if it had an accounting year ending 30 November, show an accrual of £50,000 (the five months' rent from 1 July to 30 November unpaid at the end of its accounting year).

Dividends proposed: under Section 8 of the Companies Act 1989, the directors' report must state any amount which the directors recommend be paid by way of dividend. Although the company cannot, in law, pay these proposed dividends until they have been approved at the annual general meeting, companies always show them as a liability.

Also under Creditors may appear, various items that are not in THE BODY SHOP example:

Deferred income is money received by or due to the company but not yet earned. Companies like VODAFONE (shown below) which take a month's rental in advance may well have greater accruals and deferred income than trade creditors.

VODAFONE *Note to the 1998 accounts*

13. Creditors:

Amounts falling due within one year

	1998	1997
	£m	£m
Bank loans and overdrafts	156.7	75.8
Commercial paper	332.4	123.7
Trade creditors	198.2	169.5
Amounts owed to associated undertakings	0.3	–
Taxation	205.3	176.2
Other taxes and social security costs	27.2	24.0
Other creditors	80.5	84.8
Proposed dividend	86.9	75.3
Accruals and deferred income	394.8	283.9
	1,432.3	1,013.2

Other types of borrowing which include bonds, loan notes and commercial paper (see Chapter 6).

Deposits in addition to deposits in respect of a contemplated purchase (included under payments received on account), deposits may have been charged where goods have been despatched in containers, drums, barrels or boxes, to ensure their return. The container, etc., remains part of the stock of the despatching company, until it becomes apparent that it will not be returned, e.g. when the return period has elapsed, when it is treated as having been sold.

In financial companies, where deposits are a major item, representing money deposited to earn interest, they are shown as a separate heading.

Payments received on account arise where a customer is asked as a sign of good faith to deposit money in respect of a contemplated purchase. If the purchase goes through, the deposit becomes a part payment and ceases to be a creditor. Should the sale not be consummated, the deposit would normally be returned, though it could conceivably be forfeited in certain circumstances.

WORKING CAPITAL AND LIQUIDITY RATIOS

Now that we have described Stocks, Debtors and Creditors, this may be a good place to deal with Working Capital, the Working Capital Ratio, and Liquidity Ratios.

Watch the working capital ratio
The working capital ratio is important for two reasons:

- Firstly, if it is high, expansion of the business, especially rapid expansion. is going to gobble up cash like crazy.
- Secondly, if it is not kept under control, the business will eat up more cash than it should.

Some types of business are well placed with working capital. Supermarkets do particularly well, as illustrated by the TESCO example we showed on the previous page. In contrast, in a sector like Distributors you may find the company *has* to keep large stocks in order to provide a really good service to its customers world wide. For example specialist paper manufacturer and distributor ARJO WIGGINS APPLETON:

ARJO WIGGINS APPLETON *Extract from 1998 accounts*

	1998 £m	1997 £m
Stocks	443.0	444.5
plus: Trade debtors	654.9	664.4
minus: Trade creditors	379.9	401.6
Working capital	718.0	707.3
Turnover (Sales)	3,181.8	3,266.6
Working capital ratio	22.6%	21.7%

Even a quite small deterioration (i.e. increase) in the working capital ratio can make a surprisingly large impact an borrowings:

- 22.6% – 21.7% = 0.9% of turnover = £28.6m increase in borrowings, putting around £2m on the interest charge.

Let's see how well THE BODY SHOP has controlled its figure over the last five years:

THE BODY SHOP *Working capital 1993 to 1998*

Year end	1993 £m	1994 £m	1995 £m	1996 £m	1997 £m	1998 £m
Stocks	35.3	34.6	38.6	37.6	34.8	47.7
+ Trade debtors	22.6	24.7	29.3	27.5	31.7	31.3
− Trade creditors	8.9	8.2	9.8	7.7	10.2	11.0
Working capital	49.0	51.1	58.1	57.4	56.3	68.0
Turnover (Sales)	168.3	195.4	219.7	256.5	270.8	293.1
RATIOS						
Stocks/Sales	21.0%	17.7%	17.6%	14.7%	12.9%	16.3%
Trade debtors/Sales	13.4%	12.6%	13.3%	10.7%	12.9%	10.7%
Trade creditors/Sales	5.3%	4.2%	4.5%	3.0%	3.8%	3.8%
Working capital/Sales	29.1%	26.1%	26.4%	22.4%	20.8%	23.2%

Comment on The Body Shop's ratios

Stocks and trade debtors

Control of both ratios has improved over the period, apart from the sharp jump in stocks in 1998. If stocks had increased in 1998 in line with the increase in sales, they would have been £37.7m at the year end, instead of £47.7m.

The company had plenty of cash at the year end, so the £10m extra stock wasn't increasing the overdraft. But even so it could have earned a useful £0.5m on deposit.

What is much more important is that a sharp increase in stocks is like a small cloud on the horizon, perhaps no bigger than a man's fist, but often the first sign of stormy weather ahead.

Trade creditors

This ratio is surprisingly small. This could be for either of two reasons, or a combination of both: firstly that the raw material and packaging costs are only a small proportion of the selling price, and/or that The Body Shop pays its suppliers very much quicker than most.

Liquidity ratios

The two ratios most commonly used in assessing a company's liquidity are concerned with current assets (stocks and WIP, debtors and cash) and current liabilities (creditors, bank overdraft and any debts due to be settled within the next 12 months):

1. **Current ratio**

$$= \frac{\text{Current assets}}{\text{Current liabilities}}$$

2. **Quick ratio**

$$= \frac{\text{Current assets - Stock}}{\text{Current liabilities}}$$

The Companies Act 1985 requires all amounts owing by the company to be included under creditors, with amounts due within one year and after one year being shown separately. When they can be identified, provisions for amounts due within one year should be included in current liabilities.

Current ratio

The current ratio is a broad indicator of a company's short-term financial position: a ratio of more than 1 indicates a surplus of current assets over current liabilities. A current ratio of 2 or more used to be regarded as prudent in order to maintain credit worthiness, but in recent years a figure of about 1.5 has become quite normal, and a higher figure isn't necessarily a good sign: it may be due to excessive stocks or debtors, or it may mean that the directors are sitting on an unduly large amount of cash which could be more profitably invested.

When looking at an individual company's current ratio, there is no simple rule of thumb on what the company's ratio 'ought' to be, because it so much depends on a number of different factors, including the following:

1. *The nature of the company's business*. If large stocks and the giving of generous credit terms are normal to the business, the current ratio needs to be higher than the general average, whereas a retail business with only cash sales, no work in progress and with stocks financed mainly by suppliers (i.e. creditors a large item) may be expected to have a lower than average current ratio.

2. *The quality of the current assets*. Stocks, for example, may be readily saleable, e.g. gold, or virtually unsaleable, e.g. half-completed houses in a property slump.

3. *The imminence of current liabilities*. A large loan due for repayment very soon could be embarrassing. It would be acutely embarrassing if gearing was already very high, there was no scope for an equity issue and neither cash nor further overdraft facilities were available. Even that is not perhaps as embarrassing as being unable to pay the wages next week, and next week's wages do not, of course, appear in the balance sheet.

    The key factor is whether a company has scope for further borrowings or is right up against its limits, but facilities available (as opposed to facilities being used) are not necessarily revealed in annual reports.

4. *The volatility of working capital requirements*. A company with a highly seasonal business pattern, for instance a Christmas card manufacturer or a UK holiday camp operator, may well make use of a much higher average level of borrowings during the year than the balance sheet shows, particularly as companies usually arrange their year end to coincide with low stocks and/or a low level of activity. When the interest charge in the P & L account is disproportionately large in comparison to the borrowings shown in the balance sheet, this is a clear indication that borrowings during the year have been significantly higher than at the year end.

Because of these individual factors, the most informative feature of a current ratio is its normal level and any trend from year to year. A drop below normal levels is worth investigating, and a continuing decline is a warning signal that should not be ignored.

Quick ratio or acid test

As we have said, not all current assets are readily convertible into cash to meet debts; in particular stocks and work in progress may be able to be run down a certain amount, but not eliminated if the business is to continue. The quick ratio recognises this by excluding stocks from current assets and applies the 'acid test' of what would happen if the company had to settle up with all its creditors and debtors straight away: if the quick ratio is less than 1 it would be unable to do so.

Some companies whose normal terms of trade allow them to sell goods for cash before paying for them habitually operate with a quick ratio of well under 1 (0.2 is typical for a supermarket); so it is a poorer than average figure compared with other companies in the same industry, coupled with a de-clining trend, that signals possible trouble ahead. A feature that a low and declining ratio often highlights is a rising overdraft: the question then is, 'Are their bankers happy?' Fears in this direction may be allayed by a statement in the annual report about operating well within the facilities available, or by a statement at the time that new money is raised confirming that working capital will be adequate.

A large difference between the current ratio and the quick ratio is an indication of large stocks:

$$\text{Current ratio - Quick ratio} = \frac{\text{Stocks}}{\text{Turnover}}$$

Bathroom and kitchen unit manufacturer SPRING RAM, which has had a very chequered time in the last 10 years, provides an interesting example:

THE SPRING RAM CORPORATION *Current ratio and Quick ratio*

	1990 £m	1991 £m	1992 £m	1993 £m	1994 £m	1995 £m	1996 £m	1997 £m
Current assets	91.1	128.8	128.0	91.3	109.5	130.1	83.8	72.1
Current liabilities	54.9	79.4	95.1	90.5	65.7	105.1	70.6	72.2
Current ratio	1.66	1.62	1.35	1.01	1.67	1.24	1.20	1.29
Stocks	25.1	41.0	52.4	45.4	47.7	64.7	38.8	33.1
Current assets - Stock	66.0	87.8	75.6	45.9	61.8	65.4	45.0	37.0
Quick ratio	1.20	1.11	0.79	0.51	0.94	0.62	0.64	0.51
See Note	1	2	3	4				

NOTES:

1. *Chairman's statement:*
   Bonus issue The strength of the Group's balance sheet is such that, on 26 April 1991, shareholders approved a one for one bonus issue, the fifth since flotation in 1983 ...
   Management The number and quality of the Corporation's management teams continues to grow. There are now 47 directors managing 16 autonomous operating companies.
2. Stock increased by more than 60%, although Turnover was marginally down from £194m to £191m. Invested £37.1m in buildings and plant. Spent £12.8m on Stag furniture acquisition.
3. *New chairman's statement:* The five months of 1993 since the new team was installed have been used to stabilise the financial position of the company ... severe recession in the UK housing market. Prompt action was necessary to eliminate the excessive decentralization which had led both to the Group's businesses competing with each other and to the duplication of overheads and stockholdings ... the number of businesses operated by the company was reduced from 22 to 11.
4. Rescue rights issue; 2 for 9 to raise £42.1m net.

We would like to tell you that, after the rescue rights issue, the company was soon restored to good health. Sadly not. As the ratios continue to indicate, this company is still a sick chick. Its share price bottomed at 4p, down from 188p in the heyday of the first chairman. They now languish at around 10p, far too low, at present, for a second rescue rights issue.

The wounds were deep. Due to the unbounded optimism of the first chairman in the face of a recession, the company had gone from cash at bank of £45.8m at the beginning of 1992 into net bank borrowings of £37.8m by the end of August 1993.

But worse still was the damage done to the integrity of the company by some serious creative accounting. As the *Investors Chronicle* wisely warned its readers:

INVESTORS CHRONICLE *Extract from 26 March 1993*

Battered Ram

Cautious investors would be right to avoid Spring Ram shares until credibility is restored.

Investors have good reason to be angry with the former market darling Spring Ram ...

First there was last November's debacle at Balterley Bathrooms. The problem is believed to have been the result of huge pressure on the divisional finance director to perform. He apparently overvalued stocks to produce the figures that head office wanted to see.

Although the group sought to reassure shareholders that this was an isolated incident this week's shocks have undermined its attempt.

Last week, trading in its shares was suspended ahead of a profit warning. Management blamed more stringent accounting policies.

PROVISIONS

Reference: FRS 12 *Provisions, contingent liabilities and contingent assets.*

Background

Before FRS 12 the making of provisions gave imaginative companies enormous scope for enhancing profits. All you had to do was this:

- Year 1 make a huge provision, so large that analysts would ignore it in their calculation of that year's earning per share, and forget about it in subsequent years.

- Year 2 and in subsequent years, offset against the provision costs that you would prefer not to hit the profit and loss account, until such times as the 'kitty' is used up.

- Then scratch around for another suitable provision.

The two classics were ICI's provision of several hundred million for 'Restructuring' and Unilever's £800m for 'Entry into Europe'.

We are sure that both these companies were scrupulous in choosing what costs to offset against these Jumbo provisions, but the scope for creative accountancy was enormous. FRS 12 severely curtails the scope for this particular dodge.

Definition

A *provision* is a liability that is of uncertain timing or amount. A provision should be recognised when a company has an obligation which it will probably be required to settle, and a reliable estimate can be made of the amount of the obligation. Unless these conditions can be met, no provision should be recognised.

A 'provision' (as defined by CA 1985, Sch. 4, paras 88 and 89) is either:

(a) any amount written off by way of providing for depreciation or diminution in the value of assets (in which case it is deducted from the fixed asset); or

(b) any amount retained to provide for any liability or loss which is either likely to be incurred, or certain to be incurred but uncertain as to the amount or as to the date on which it will arise (it then appears among provisions for liabilities and charges).

Provisions for liabilities and charges are frequently made for:

(a) pensions and similar obligations (see page 119);

(b) taxation, including deferred taxation (see Chapter 17); and

(c) other provisions.

Pension schemes can be either funded, i.e. contributions paid away to separate funds (see page 119), or unfunded. In an unfunded scheme, which is the norm in some foreign countries, the company makes a provision for future liabilities in its accounts.

Particulars should also be given of any pension commitments for which no provision has been made (CA 1985, Sch. 4, para. 50 (4) (b)).

The item taxation will normally only include deferred taxation (see Chapter 17), as other taxation will be shown under Creditors, unless the amount is uncertain.

When to make provisions

Under FRS 12 a provision – a liability that is of uncertain timing or amount – should *only* be recognised when:

- a company has an *obligation* which it will probably be required to settle; and

- a *reliable estimate* can be made of the amount of the obligation.

Unless these conditions can be met, no provision should be recognised.

Use of provisions

A provision should be used only for expenditure for which the provision was originally recognised (FRS 12 para. 64).

Annual review and disclosure

Provisions should be reviewed at each balance sheet date and adjusted to reflect the current best estimate.

If it is no longer probable that a transfer of economic benefits will be required to settle the obligation, i.e. if it looks as though the company is no longer likely to have to cough up, the provision should be reversed.

The company's annual report should disclose:

- the carrying amount at the beginning and end of the period;
- additional provisions made in the period, including increases to existing provisions;
- amounts used (i.e. incurred and charged against the provision) during the period; and unused amounts reversed during the period.

See ICI at the bottom of the column.

Comment on ICI's provisions

In its 1999 accounts, ICI will have to comply with FRS 12, which came into force for accounting periods ending on or after 23 March 1999. As its plans for divesting most of its Industrial Chemicals business have been publicly announced, it will be able to take the view that it is now committed to carrying out its programme, and make provisions accordingly.

But the 'do as you please' regime will no longer apply. ICI may be somewhat constrained by the new rules:

- A restructuring provision should include only the direct expenditures arising from the restructuring, which are those that are both: (a) necessarily entailed by the restructuring and (b) not associated with the ongoing activities.

- A restructuring provision does not include such costs as: (a) retraining or relocating continuing staff; (b) marketing; or (c) investment in new systems and new distribution networks.
- No obligation arises for the sale of an operation until the company is committed to the sale i.e. there is a binding sale agreement.

Provisioning – the main areas

Provisions can involve huge sums of money. The main areas are:

Disposals and restructuring, e.g. ICI below; Environment, e.g. SHELL below; and Litigation, e.g. GKN below.

SHELL *Operational and Financial Review 1998*

Environmental and decommissioning costs

At the end of 1998, the total liabilities being carried for environmental clean-up were $515m (1997: $683m), whilst additions to provisions in 1998 amounted to $53m. Provisions being carried for expenditures on decommissioning and site restoration, including oil and gas platforms, amounted to $2,601m (1997: $2,324m).

GKN *Note to the 1997 accounts*

Provisions for liabilities and charges

	1997 £m	1996 £m
Deferred taxation	2	7
Post-retirement and other provisions	174	173
Meineke litigation	266	270
	442	450

[continued at the top of the next page.]

ICI *Note to the 1998 accounts*
23. Disposal and restructuring provisions

	Disposal provisions 1998 £m	Disposal provisions 1997 £m	Restructuring provisions 1998 £m	Restructuring provisions 1997 £m
At beginning of year	263	–	130	106
Exceptional items before tax Rationalisation of operations	–	–	164	202
Profit and loss account	305	346	–	–
Amounts paid	(156)	(25)	(58)	(72)
Asset write-offs	–	(49)	(36)	(105)
Exchange and other adjustments	9	(9)	(9)	(1)
At end of year	421	263	191	130

Disposal provisions
ICI commenced reshaping its portfolio of businesses in 1997 consistent with its plans to focus its resources on specialty chemicals. In pursuit of this strategy the Group has announced that it intends to divest most of its Industrial Chemicals business.

Meineke litigation

In the interests of prudence. an exceptional litigation provision of $270m was made in the 1996 accounts following a judgment of the US District Court, Charlotte, North Carolina in respect of claims brought by certain of its franchisees against Meineke Discount Muffler Shops Inc. (owned by one of GKN's subsidiaries) alleging breach of contract and fiduciary duty ... by Meineke. ... appeal with the US Court of Appeal ...

The movement on the provision represents legal costs incurred in the year.

So GKN's lawyers took a cool $4m off the company in 1998. Litigation is a serious hazard in doing business in the United States. (Rumour has it that US pharmaceutical and cosmetic companies are using lawyers rather than rats for testing new products. This is for two reasons: firstly there are more of them – and secondly you are less likely to get attached to them).

Other Accounting Standards on provisions

Where another FRS or an SSAP deals with a more specific type of provision, that standard applies, rather than FRS 12. These include:

- long-term contracts (SSAP 9, see page 72);
- deferred tax (SSAP 15, see page 135);
- leases (SSAP 21, see page 108);
- pension costs (SSAP 24, see page 119).

Other uses of the term 'provision'

The term 'provision' may also be used in the context of items such as depreciation, impairment of assets and doubtful debts: these are adjustments to the carrying amounts of assets, and are not covered by FRS 12.

What does all this mean to the investor?

Prior to FRS 12 the recognition (making) of a provision was based on management's intention, or possible intention, of making expenditures, rather than on any legal or moral obligation to do so.

In particular, as we have mentioned, was the use of what Sir David Tweedie, chairman of the ASC, called *'big bath' accounting*. Several years of future expenditure, including items related to continuing operations, and possibly a sum to cover unforeseen costs, would be heaped together into one large provision, which would be reported as an exceptional item.

This gave enormous scope for earnings to be *'smoothed'*: large fluctuations in reported earnings being avoided by provisions being released in lean years.

The new rules should make management much more accountable. The hope is that companies will keep shareholders more closely informed about provisions and exceptional expenditure. Companies which haven't already adopted the recently introduced Operational and Financial Review should do so to help achieve this better communication.

The danger is that management will become less inclined to 'grasp nettles' in continuing operations, for fear of causing a 'blip' in reported profits.

CONTINGENT LIABILITIES AND CONTINGENT ASSETS

Definition

A contingent liability is a potential liability which had not materialised by the date of the balance sheet. By their nature, contingent liabilities are insufficiently concrete to warrant specific provision being made for them in the accounts, and none is in fact made.

However, under the Fourth Schedule of the Companies Act 1985 a company must show by way of note or otherwise:

(a) any arrears of cumulative dividends (para. 49);

(b) particulars of any charge on the assets of the company to secure the liabilities of any other person, including, where practicable, the amount secured (para. 50 (1));

(c) the legal nature of any other contingent liabilities not provided for, the estimated amount of those liabilities, and any security given (para. 50 (2)).

Examples of contingent liabilities

Typical contingent liabilities include:

(a) bills of exchange discounted with bankers (where an FRS 5 linked presentation is not used (see page 44));

(b) guarantees given to banks and other parties;

(c) potential liabilities on claims (whether by court action or otherwise);

(d) goods sold under warranty or guarantee;

(e) any uncalled liability on shares held as investments (i.e. the unpaid portion of partly paid shares held).

Contingencies frequently arise in respect of an acquisition as the result of an 'earn-out', where part of the consideration is based on future profits.

Litigation, impending litigation and threatened litigation are popular breeding grounds for contingent liabilities. See, for example, BP AMOCO on the next page.

BP AMOCO *Note to the 1998 accounts*

39. Contingent liabilities
Approximately 200 lawsuits were filed ... arising out of the Exxon Valdez oil spill in Prince William Sound in March 1989.

Most of these suits named Exxon, Alyeska Pipeline Service Company (Alyeska), which operates the oil terminal at Valdez, and the seven oil companies which own Alyeska ... BP Amoco owns a 50% interest in Alyeska ...

Exxon has indicated that it may file a claim for contribution against Alyeska for a portion of the costs and damages which it has incurred.

How an oil terminal operator can be held responsible for a tanker running aground is way beyond our comprehension (unless Alyeska provided the pilot), but in the US it seems they'll try anything.

As explained below, companies are also required to disclose 'commitments'. It is often quite difficult to decide just what is a commitment and what a contingent liability; and many groups, like ICI, treat them in a single note.

ICI *Extract from note to the 1998 accounts*

42. Commitments and contingent liabilities
In 1995 ICI Explosives USA Inc and a former employee each admitted to a single offence in breach of US antitrust laws relating to the sale of certain commercial explosives between 1988–1992 and as a result ICI Explosives USA Inc paid a fine of US$10m. Subsequently, ICI Explosives USA Inc was named as a defendant in a number of lawsuits by parties claiming unquantified damages from a number of explosives companies in the United States ... Actions arising from the violation of US antitrust laws, if established, can result in the payment of substantial penalties and damages.
...

The significance of contingent liabilities
In many cases notes on contingent liabilities are of no real significance, for no liability is expected to arise, and none does. Occasionally, however, they are very important indeed, and points to watch for are a sharp rise in the total sums involved, and liabilities that may arise outside the normal course of business.

Key point
To guarantee the liabilities of someone, or some company, over which one has no control entails undue risk, and calls into question the management's judgment if the sums involved are significant.

In particular, experience suggests that any contingent liability in respect of a subsidiary that has been disposed of can be extremely dangerous.

For example, when COLOROLL took over JOHN CROWTHER it accepted more than £20m of contingent liabilities in order to help the MBO of Crowther's clothing interests, which it wanted to get rid of quickly.

COLOROLL *Note to the accounts*

Contingent liabilities
At 31 March 1989 the group had contingent liabilities in connection with the following matters:

(a) the sale with recourse of £7,500,000 of redeemable preference shares and £14,250,000 senior and subordinated loan notes in RESPONSE GROUP LTD which were received as part consideration for the sale of the clothing interests of JOHN CROWTHER GROUP PLC;
(b) the guarantee of borrowings and other bank facilities of . . .

In February 1990 the Response Group called in the receivers, and Coloroll followed four months later!

Guaranteeing the borrowings of associated undertakings or joint ventures may also be dangerous.

Capital commitments
Schedule 4, para. 50 (3) of the Companies Act 1985 requires that, where practicable, the aggregate amounts or estimated amounts, if they are material, of:

* contracts for capital expenditure (not already provided for) and
* capital expenditure authorised by the directors, which has not been contracted for,

be shown by way of note, as the extract below from ICI shows.

ICI *Extract from note to the 1998 accounts*

42. Commitments and contingent liabilities

	1998	1997
Commitment for capital expenditure not provided for in these accounts (including acquisitions)		
Contracts placed for future expenditure	157	138
Expenditure authorised but not [yet] contracted	120	173
	277	311

Such a note provides some indication of the extent to which the directors plan to expand (or replace) the facilities of the group, and thus of the potential call upon its cash resources. It should be read in conjunction with the directors' report and chairman's statement and any press announcements by the company, but it is not a particularly helpful guide to future cash flows unless it gives some information on timing. Although the sums involved are material, it is impossible to tell from the note below how long the various facilities to which ICI is committed will take to build or deliver, and when payments will fall due.

Other financial commitments

The Companies Act 1985 requires particulars to be given of any other financial commitments which have not been provided for and which are relevant to assessing the company's state of affairs (Sch. 4, para. 50 (5)). This requirement covers such things as leasing commitments and long-term contracts, where the sums involved can be very large indeed, as illustrated by SHELL TRANSPORT AND TRADING's note on commitments, shown here:

SHELL TRANSPORT AND TRADING *Note to the 1998 accounts*

16. Commitments

(a) Leasing arrangements
The future minimum lease payments under operating leases and capital leases, and the present value of net minimum capital lease payments at 31 December 1998 were as follows:

	Operating leases	$ million Capital leases
1999	1,644	65
2000	1,255	51
2001	1,024	80
2002	737	41
2003	626	48
2004 and after	2,123	156
	7,409	441

The figures represent minimum commitments existing at December 31, 1998 and are not forecasts of future total rental expense.
(b) Long term purchase obligations ...

The distinction between operating leases and capital (finance) leases is explained below.

Leases

SSAP 21 *Accounting for leases and hire purchase contracts* divides leases into two types, finance leases and operating leases, and requires quite different accounting treatment for each type.

A *finance lease* is defined as a lease which transfers substantially all the risks and rewards of ownership of an asset to the lessee. All other leases are *operating leases*.

Finance leases: the lessee
Prior to SSAP 21 a company could enter into a finance lease instead of borrowing the money to purchase an asset, and neither the asset nor the commitment to pay leasing charges would appear in the balance sheet. This was an example of what was known as 'off balance sheet financing', which produced 'hidden gearing', as the company had effectively geared itself up just as much as if it had borrowed the money to purchase the asset, except that it had to pay leasing charges rather than paying interest and bearing depreciation charges.

SSAP 21 requires a finance lease to be recorded in the balance sheet of the lessee as an asset and as an obligation to pay future rentals. The initial sum to be recorded both as an asset and as a liability is the present value of the minimum lease payments, which is derived by discounting them at the interest rate implicit in the lease. The method of accounting is illustrated in Example 15.1.

Example 15.1 Accounting for a finance lease
A company acquires a small computer system on a finance lease. Lease payments are £10,000 p.a. for five years, with an option to continue the lease for a further five years at £1,000 p.a. Payments are made annually in advance, i.e. the first payment is made on taking delivery of the computer. The interest rate implicit in the lease is 10%, and the estimated useful life of the system is five years.

The present value of the minimum lease payments discounted at 10% p.a. can be calculated using the table Present value of 1 in *n* years' time in Appendix 2:

Payment date	Present value of 1 (from table)	Present value of £10,000 payment £
On delivery	1.000	10,000
In 1 year	0.909	9,090
In 2 years	0.826	8,260
In 3 years	0.751	7,510
In 4 years	0.683	6,830
Present value of minimum lease payments		£41,690

The computer system will thus be recorded as an asset of £41,690 and the liability for future rental payments will also be recorded as £41,690. After the first year:

(a) the asset will be depreciated over the shorter of the lease term (the initial period plus any further option period, i.e. a total of ten years in this case), and its expected useful life (five years). Annual depreciation charge on a straight line basis is therefore one-fifth of £41,690 = £8,338, reducing the asset value to £33,352.

(b) the present value of the remaining minimum lease payments is recomputed. There is no longer a payment due in four years' time (£6,830 in our table above), so the present value of future payments is now £41,690 – 6,830 = £34,860. £6,830 is deducted from the future liability and the remaining £3,170 of the £10,000 payment made on delivery is shown as interest paid.

These calculations would then be repeated each subsequent year as shown in Example 15.2.

Example 15.2 Accounting for a finance lease – subsequent years

End of year	Balance sheet		P & L account	
	Asset value	Remaining payments	Interest charge	Depreciation charge
	£	£	£	£
1	33,352	34,860	3,170	8,338
2	25,014	27,350	2,490	8,338
3	16,676	19,090	1,740	8,338
4	8,338	10,000	910	8,338
5	Nil	Nil	Nil	8,338

Finance leases: the lessor

In the past the practice of 'front-ending', taking a high proportion of the profits on a lease in the first year, has got a number of companies into serious difficulties, e.g. SOUND DIFFUSION, which went into liquidation primarily as a result of taking 60% of profits on leasing electrical equipment – telephone switchboards, fire-alarm and public-address systems – in the first year.

Under SSAP 21, front-ending is not allowed. The amount due under a finance lease should be recorded as a debtor at the net investment after provisions for bad and doubtful rentals, etc., and the earnings in each period should be allocated to give a constant rate of return on the lessor's net investment (SSAP 21, paras. 38 and 39).

Operating leases

An operating lease is normally for a period substantially shorter than the expected useful life of an asset; i.e. the lessor retains most of the risks and rewards of ownership.

Under an operating lease the lease rentals are simply charged in the profit and loss account of the lessee as they arise. Leased assets and the liability for future payments do not appear in the balance sheet, even though companies can enter into operating leases of several years' length, as the extract from SHELL TRANSPORT AND TRADING's accounts illustrated on page 108.

While SSAP 21 sets out the distinction between an operating lease and a finance lease, FRS 5, *Reporting the substance of transactions*, looks behind the lease at the nature of the underlying transaction. But this application of 'substance over form' does not meet with universal approval.

Problem 15.1

(a) Distinguish clearly between:

   (i) an accrual and a provision;
   (ii) income in advance and a deposit;
   (iii) a commitment and a contingent liability.

(b) Provide examples of each.

(c) Explain the significance of each to an analyst seeking: (i) to estimate a group's future cash flows/liquidity; (ii) to consider its viability medium term.

Chapter 16

PROFIT AND LOSS ACCOUNT

INTRODUCTION

As described briefly in Chapter 1, the profit and loss account is a score-card of how the company did in the period reported on, normally the last year. The Companies Act 1985 offers companies the choice of four profit and loss account formats:

- Formats 1 and 2 are 'modern' single-page vertical formats;

- Formats 3 and 4 are 'traditional' two-sided formats, common in the UK until 50 years ago, still used in Europe and elsewhere, but rarely found among listed UK companies. They will not be considered further.

Formats 1 and 2, the upper parts of which are shown in Examples 16.1 and 16.2 respectively:

take turnover (i.e. sales invoiced); and
deduct operating costs, to produce trading profit;.
add to this other income; and
deduct other charges, to reach pre-tax profit.

The difference between Formats 1 and 2 is the way they show operating costs:

- Format 1 breaks down operating costs by function:

  Cost of sales (which will include all costs of production, such as factory wages, materials and manufacturing overheads, including depreciation of machinery);

  Distribution costs (costs incurred in getting the goods to the customer);

  Administrative expenses (e.g. office expenses, directors' and auditors' fees).

Example 16.1 Profit and loss account: Format 1

	£000	£000
Turnover		7,200
Cost of sales		3,600
Gross profit		3,600
Distribution costs	1,100	
Administrative expenses	900	
		2,000
		1,600
Other operating income		50
[Trading or operating profit]		1,650
Income from interests in associated undertakings		30
Income from other participating interests		10
Income from other fixed asset investments		5
Other interest receivable		120
		1,815
Amounts written off investments	15	
Interest payable	600	
		615
[Pre-tax profit on ordinary activities]		1,200

- Format 2 breaks down operating costs into:
  Raw materials and consumables
  Staff costs Wages and salaries; Social security costs; Other pension costs
  Depreciation and other amounts written off fixed assets
  Other external charges
  Change in stock of finished goods and work in progress

Example 16.2 Profit and loss account: Format 2

	£000	£000	£000
Turnover			7,200
Changes in stocks of finished goods and work in progress		160	
Other operating income		50	
			7,410
Raw materials and consumables		1,700	
Other external charges		1,120	
Staff costs			
Wages and salaries	2,050		
Social security costs	300		
Other pension costs	120		
		2,470	
Depreciation and other amounts written off tangible and intangible fixed assets		400	
Other operating charges		70	
			5,760
[Trading or operating profit]			1,650
Income from interests in associated undertakings			30
Income from other participating interests			10
Income from other fixed asset investments			5
Other interest receivable			120
			1,815
Amounts written off investments		15	
Interest payable		600	
			615
[Pre-tax profit on ordinary activities]			1,200

The formats reflect the disclosure requirements of the EEC Fourth Directive as incorporated in Schedule 4 of the Companies Act 1985. Items in square brackets, 'Trading profit' and 'Pre-tax profit', have been included because they are important to the analyst, although they do not actually appear in the formats in Schedule 4. Most companies now adopt Format 1, though some use a combination of Formats 1 and 2. For example, UNILEVER gives a single figure for 'Operating costs' in its profit and loss account and, in a note, shows cost of sales, distribution, selling and administration costs (i.e. Format 1). The note also gives a detailed breakdown of staff costs, raw materials and packaging, depreciation, etc. (i.e. Format 2).

Very few companies adopt Format 2. One which does, but puts most of the detail in the notes to its accounts (see page 112), is PIC INTERNATIONAL, the profit and loss account of which shown below. We look at PIC International again later in this chapter in connection with audit fees and, later, fundamental restructuring.

Profit before taxation

As shown in Examples 16.1 and 16.2:
- trading profit, *plus*
- income from interests in associated undertakings and from other participating interests (see Chapter 22), *plus*
- income from other investments and other interest receivable, *less*
- interest payable and any amounts written off investments,
- leaves the profit before tax, or 'pre-tax profit'.

PIC INTERNATIONAL *Extract from group profit and loss account for the year ended 30 June 1998*

	Note	Operations before fundamental restructuring £m	Fundamental restructuring £m	1998 £m	1997 £m
Turnover					
Continuing operations					
Group and share of joint ventures		246.2	–	246.2	246.1
less: share of joint ventures		(26.3)	–	(26.3)	(34.2)
Group turnover		219.9	–	219.9	211.9
Discontinued operations		3,040.4	–	3,040.4	3,935.8
		3,260.3	–	3,260.3	4,147.7
Operating profit/(loss)					
Continuing operations		17.7	–	17.7	(6.1)
Discontinued operations		55.0	–	55.0	(51.0)
Group operating profit/(loss)	2	72.7	–	72.7	(57.1)
Share of operating profit in joint ventures		1.7	–	1.7	4.7
Share of operating loss in associates		–	–	–	(1.4)
Profit/(loss) before interest, tax and fundamental restructuring		74.4	–	74.4	(53.8)

PIC INTERNATIONAL *Extract from note 2 to the accounts for the year ended 30 June 1998*

2. Operating profit/(loss)

Operating profit/(loss) is calculated as follows:

	1998 £m	1997 £m
Turnover	3,260.3	4,147.7
Charges		
Change in stocks of finished goods and work in progress	1.7	10.4
Raw materials and consumables	2,593.1	3,315.3
Other external charges	281.0	382.5
Staff costs (note ...)	255.9	349 8
Depreciation of tangible fixed assets	40.0	75.0
Hire of plant and machinery	3.5	4.3
Other operating lease rentals	26.0	29.1
Goodwill on businesses for disposal	–	46.3
Provision for surplus properties	–	15.9
Total charges	3,201.2	4,228.6
Income		
Own work capitalised	0.9	2.3
Net rental income	0.5	0.9
Gain on currency contracts	–	5.4
Income from other fixed asset investments	–	0.8
Other operating income	12.2	14.4
Total income	13.6	23.8
Operating profit/(loss)	72.7	(57.1)

...

Included above are the following amounts relating to continuing operations (excluding acquisitions), acquisitions and discontinued operations ...

PIC INTERNATIONAL is one of a growing number of companies which show the information required by one or other of the formats laid down not on the face of the profit and loss account but in the notes.

The three parts

Whatever format is used, the profit and loss account (sometimes referred to as the revenue account or statement of income) can conveniently be divided into three parts which show:

- How the profit (or loss) was earned.
- How much was taken by taxation.
- What happened to the profit (or loss) that was left after taxation.

This chapter covers the first part. Chapter 17 is devoted to taxation and Chapter 18 considers profits after tax, dividends and earnings per share.

Additional disclosures

Profit and loss accounts of listed companies are rarely quite as simple as those shown in Examples 16.1 and 16.2.

The formats do not cover everything. Additional disclosures are required by:

(a) the Companies Act itself;
(b) Accounting Standards; and
(c) The Stock Exchange.

We focus separately on each of these in the sections which follow. Examples later in this chapter and in the chapters which follow illustrate:

(a) how accounting standards and the requirements of The Stock Exchange affect the profit and loss account; and
(b) the use which the investor and analyst can make of that information.

DISCLOSURES REQUIRED BY THE COMPANIES ACT

Turnover

Turnover is the amount derived from the provision of goods and services falling within the company's ordinary activities (after deduction of trade discounts and before adding VAT and other sales-based taxes). Companies are required by the standard formats of the Companies Act 1985 to disclose turnover (i.e. total sales) in their profit and loss account. The following must also be given:

(a) Under Sch. 4, para. 55 (1)), if a company carried on two or more classes of business during the year which in the directors' opinion differ substantially from each other, it should de-

scribe the classes and show each one's turnover and pre-tax profit.

(b) If in the year a company supplied geographical markets which in the directors' opinion differ substantially, the turnover attributable to each should be stated (Sch. 4 para. 55(2)).

However this information need not be disclosed if, in the opinion of the directors, it would be seriously prejudicial to the interests of the company to do so, but the fact that it has not been disclosed must be stated (Sch. 4 para. 55 (5)).

Segmental reporting (SSAP 25), is considered later in this chapter (see page 129).

Other items in the profit and loss account

Schedule 4 of the Companies Act 1989 requires that the following be shown separately in the profit and loss account or in the notes:

1. ***Chairman's emoluments*** for each person acting as chairman during the year, unless the duties were wholly or mainly discharged outside the United Kingdom (para. 3).

2. ***Directors' emoluments*** the aggregate amount of emoluments including pension contributions, other benefits, and sums paid for accepting office as a director, i.e. 'golden hellos' (para. 1); the number of directors who fall into each band of £5,000, i.e., up to £5,000, between £5,001 and £10,000 and so on, and the emoluments of the highest-paid director if more than the chairman, but excluding directors whose duties were wholly or mainly discharged outside the UK (para. 4); the number of directors who have waived rights to receive emoluments and the aggregate amount waived (para. 6).

3. ***Particulars of staff***: the average number employed during the year, and the aggregate amounts of their (a) wages and salaries, (b) social security costs, (c) other pension costs (CA 1985, Sch. 4, para. 56), see page 119.

4. ***Auditors' remuneration*** in their capacity as such, including expenses. Remuneration for services other than those of auditors should be shown separately (CA 1989 s. 121).

   A sharp increase in the auditors' remuneration (i.e. more than merely keeping pace with inflation) may be an indication of difficulties; for example SOCK SHOP paid their auditors £60,000 for the 17 months ended 28 February 1989 compared with £10,000 for the previous year, and went into receivership in 1990. Or to take a recent example:

PIC INTERNATIONAL *Extract from note 2 to the accounts for the year ended 30 June 1998*

	1998 £m	1997 £m
Audit fees: Group	0.8	1.2
...		
Non-audit fees: Group		
UK	4.2	0.3
Non-UK	0.7	0.4
	—	—
	4.9	0.7

...

Non-audit fees mainly related to work in respect of accounting, tax, due diligence and other financial advice in relation to the fundamental restructuring of the Group.

5. ***Hire of plant and machinery***: to be shown if material (CA 1985, Sch. 4, para. 53(6)).

   There are basically two types of hiring or leasing: the first is where equipment is hired on a temporary basis and can be returned when no longer required (an operating lease); the second type is where equipment is leased for its useful life (a finance lease, which has to be capitalised in the balance sheet, see Chapter 15). Some companies incur substantial hire charges on finance leases as part of a deliberate policy to reduce the amount of capital tied up in fixed assets and to take advantage of the favourable terms a lessor offers. The lessor is able to offer favourable terms on finance leases because he receives the benefit of the capital allowances on the assets leased, which help to defer his Corporation Tax liability (see Chapter 17).

   However, extensive finance leasing may also reflect a shortage of cash – the company having resorted to leasing to avoid the immediate capital outlay. A useful yardstick, for purposes of comparison year by year, is the ratio of interest on finance leases to depreciation.

6. ***Depreciation*** and diminution in value of fixed assets (see Chapter 8). In Format 1 depreciation is not shown as a separate item, but in all formats the amount provided during the year will be found in the note on fixed assets.

7. ***Investment income***: Companies must distinguish in their profit and loss account (or in the notes) between income from listed investments and that from unlisted investments (CA 1985, Sch. 4, para. 53(4)). Until 1967 it was necessary to distinguish between income from trade investments and other investments, and some companies continue to do this. A trade investment is an investment made for a trade reason, rather than as a means of earning income. It might, for example, be an investment in a supplier (to help the supplier, to obtain information, or to act as a lever in dealing with him), in a competitor, or customer.

8. ***Interest paid***: The Companies Act 1985 (Sch. 4, para. 53(2)) requires the disclosure of the interest paid on bank loans and overdrafts, on loans repayable within five years and on other loans. Most companies show a single figure in their profit and loss account, giving details in a note which may include: (i) some netting out of interest received; (ii) discount amortisation of deep discount bonds; (iii) interest capitalised and other adjustments; as, for example the note explaining 'net interest payable' in PIC INTERNATIONAL's 1998 accounts shown on page 114.

PIC INTERNATIONAL *Extract from note 4 to the accounts for the year ended 30 June 1998*

Interest

	1998 £m	1997 £m
Interest payable and similar charges:		
On bank loans and overdrafts	15.2	20.6
Finance leases	–	0.1
Non recourse finance	1.4	2.0
Interest capitalised	–	(2.0)
Interest receivable	(12.1)	(2.9)
Net interest payable	4.5	17.8

Tax relief on interest capitalised of £nil (£0.6m) has been credited in the profit and loss account.

In respect of the prior year non recourse finance, the Group was not obliged to support any losses and did not intend to do so. The providers of this finance had no recourse under the relevant agreements and confirmed that they would not seek recourse from the Group.

Although all this information may be shown on the face of the profit and loss account, it rarely is. In general one finds it early in the notes to the accounts, in a note entitled something like 'Profit on ordinary activities before tax', though there is then usually a separate note on employment costs and/or directors' emoluments.

Parent company profit and loss account

If, at the end of a financial year, a company is a parent company, group accounts have to be prepared as well as individual accounts for the parent company (CA 1985, s. 227), although small and medium-sized private groups are exempt from this (CA 1985, s. 248).

As will be explained in Chapter 20, group accounts comprise a consolidated balance sheet and profit and loss account dealing with the parent company and its subsidiary undertakings.

Under Section 230 (3) of the Companies Act 1985, the parent company's profit and loss account may be omitted from the consolidated accounts providing the parent company's balance sheet shows the parent company's profit or loss for the year. Since most listed companies are holding companies, i.e. have subsidiaries, in practice one seldom if ever sees the parent company's own profit and loss account; one sees only the profit and loss account of the group.

DISCLOSURES REQUIRED BY STANDARDS

A large number of Accounting and Financial Reporting Standards require the disclosure of information in the profit and loss account or the notes:

1. Segmental reporting

SSAP 25 *Segmental reporting* requires companies which have two or more classes of business or which operate in two or more geographical segments to report turnover (differentiating between external sales and sales to other segments), pre-tax profits and net assets for each class of business and for each geographical segment. A separate section of this chapter beginning on page 129 is devoted to the requirements of SSAP 25.

2. Research and development

SSAP 13 *Research and development* requires that all expenditure on research and development should normally be written off in the year in which it is incurred (see also page 116).

PIC INTERNATIONAL *Extract from note 2 to the accounts for the year ended 30 June 1998*

Research and development expenditure

This amounted to £17.6m (£20.6m), including £5.1m (£4.1m) which related to enabling and development research in continuing operations.

3. Pension costs

Until the introduction of SSAP 24 *Accounting for pension costs,* accounts simply showed the contributions paid during the year in a note to the accounts. This practice of 'cash accounting', i.e. showing what the company had paid into its pension funds rather than accounting for the increase in pension liabilities that had accrued during the year, enabled companies by increasing or reducing their contributions during a year to reduce or increase their reported profits at will.

A separate section of this chapter beginning on page 119 is devoted to the requirements of SSAP 24.

4. Investment income

Under SSAP 8, incoming dividends from UK resident companies were included before tax in the profit and loss account at the amount of cash received or receivable plus a tax credit. Since 6 April 1999 there is no tax credit (see Chapter 17), and such dividends appear at the amount received or receivable.

Dividends paid by another UK company out of profits which have already borne UK Corporation Tax are said to be 'franked' and no further corporation tax is payable upon them by the receiving company. Investment income received from a source that has not borne UK Corporation Tax, which includes almost all types of interest received and any dividends from overseas companies are unfranked and subject to corporation tax in the hands of the receiving company. This is considered further in Chapter 17.

5. Hire purchase and credit sale transactions

SSAP 21 *Accounting for leases and hire purchase contracts*, which is concerned with the taking of profit on hire purchase and credit sale transactions, is considered in Chapter 11.

6. Substance over form

The influence of FRS 5 *Reporting the substance of transactions* has been considered in Chapters 6, 11, 12 and 13.

7. Foreign exchange

Under SSAP 20 *Foreign currency translation* the treatment of foreign currencies differs somewhat between an individual company itself trading abroad and a group with overseas subsidiaries. In the latter case, profit and loss account items should be translated using either the average rate for the accounting period or the closing rate and the method chosen should be applied consistently. Any difference between translation at the average rate and the closing rate should be taken to reserves.

As explained in Chapter 23, whether the average rate or the closing rate is used can make a considerable difference to the reported profit.

8. Subsidiaries and groups

FRS 2 *Accounting for subsidiary undertakings*, FRS 6 *Acquisitions and mergers*, FRS 7 *Fair values in acquisition accounting*, FRS 10 *Goodwill and intangible assets*, and FRS 11 *Impairment of fixed assets and goodwill* all affect the profit and loss account in one way or another. They are considered in Chapters 20–21.

9. Associated undertakings

'Income from interests in associated undertakings' and 'Income from other participating interests' both appear in the formats but FRS 9 *Associates and joint ventures* calls for additional disclosures as explained in Chapter 22.

10. Provisions

The making of provisions and utilisation of provisions made in earlier years both affect profits. This is covered by FRS 12 *Provisions, contingent liabilities and contingent assets* which is considered in Chapter 15.

11. Exceptional and prior year items

FRS 3 *Reporting financial performance* is concerned, amongst other things, with items disclosed as exceptional or prior year. It will be considered later in this chapter.

DISCLOSURES REQUIRED BY THE STOCK EXCHANGE

Greenbury

Following public uproar about huge increases in the remuneration and benefits of directors of nationalised industries after privatisation, a study group was appointed under the chairmanship of Sir Richard Greenbury, the chairman of Marks & Spencer, to study directors' remuneration. The *Greenbury Report*, published in July 1995 (see Chapter 26), made a number of recommendations including Remuneration committees and greater disclosure. The recommendations were implemented by amendments to the Listing Rules, effective for accounting periods ending on or after 31 December 1995. Since then, details of salaries, benefits, compensation for loss of office and other payments have to be disclosed for *each director by name* (Listing Rules para 12.43 (x)).

Yellow Book requirements and the profit and loss account

Several Yellow Book requirements (see Chapter 4) concern the profit and loss account:

(a) if the results for the period under review differ by 10% or more from any published forecast or estimate by the company for that period, an explanation of the difference must be given;

(b) a statement is required of the amount of interest capitalised;

(c) particulars must be given of the waiving of emoluments by any director, and of the waiving of dividends by any shareholder;

(d) certain particulars must be provided for each associated undertaking.

EFFECT OF ACCOUNTING POLICIES ON PROFITABILITY

Accounting policies

The company's accounting policies, which usually appear either as 'Note 1' to the accounts, or as a separate statement, should be read carefully to see if there are any unusual features that might affect the company's reported profits.

Abnormal accounting policies which can materially alter the reported profits include:

1. *Valuation of stock.* The higher the value of stocks at the end of the period, the lower the cost of goods sold and the higher the profits. Stock valuation is to an extent subjective, so that when times are hard there is a temptation for management at the worst to inflate figures or at best simply to look through rose coloured spectacles at items which may prove to be unsaleable. To do this is to improve current results at the expense of the future.

2. *Depreciation.* The lower the charge for depreciation in a particular year, the higher the book value of fixed assets carried forward and the higher the profits. For example in 1992 SPRING RAM changed its policy on depreciation, and showed the effect of the change in a note.

SPRING RAM *Note to the 1992 accounts*

Consistency of Accounting Policies

The financial statements for the year ended 3 January 1993 have been prepared under the same accounting policies as in prior years, except as described below:

	Reduction in profit on ordinary activities before taxation	
	Effect on 1992 £000	Effect on 1991 £000
In prior years, no depreciation was provided on freehold buildings. Freehold buildings are now depreciated at a rate of 2% per annum on the revalued amounts	660	362

In other words, profits of earlier years (almost certainly not just the last two) had had the benefit of there having been no depreciation charge in respect of freehold buildings.

Selection of an appropriate method of depreciation, the estimation of the useful economic life of an asset and its residual value at the end of that life are all under FRS 15 a matter for management; the accounts reflect their judgement in this regard, which may or may not coincide with that of the auditors or that of the management of other companies engaged in a similar business.

3. *Capitalising expenditure.* All expenditure incurred by a company must either add to the value of the assets in the balance sheet or be charged in the profit and loss account. In the sense that it would otherwise be a charge against profits, any amount that can be capitalised will increase profits directly by the amount capitalised at the expense of the profits in future years, when increased capital values will require increased depreciation.

What is it reasonable to capitalise?

Items which are sometimes capitalised include:

- research and development;
- finance costs;
- starting-up costs.

Research and development

As explained earlier, under SSAP 13 *Research and development* all expenditure on research and development should normally be written off in the year in which it is incurred. However, where development is for clearly defined projects on which expenditure is separately identifiable and for which commercial success is reasonably certain, companies may if they wish defer charging development expenditure 'to the extent that its recovery can reasonably be regarded as assured'. Capitalised development expenditure should be separately disclosed.

Finance costs

Capitalising interest on a project during construction is a normal and reasonable practice provided interest is not capitalised outside the planned timescale of the project. There are, indeed, strong arguments in favour of capitalisation:

(i) finance costs are not intrinsically different from other directly attributable costs of constructing a tangible fixed asset;

(ii) capitalising finance costs results in a tangible fixed asset cost that more closely matches the market price of completed assets;

(iii) treating the finance costs as an expense distorts the choice between purchasing and constructing a tangible fixed asset. the accounts are more likely to reflect the true success or failure of the project.

The ASB would like to make it mandatory but was influenced by the argument that 'if capitalisation is to become mandatory, in theory notional interest should also be capitalised.' Otherwise, capitalisation of finance costs results in the same type of asset having a different book value, depending on the method of financing adopted by the enterprise. It is inconsistent to allow debt-funded entities to include interest costs in the cost of an asset, whilst prohibiting equity-funded entities from reflecting similarly the cost of capital in the cost of an asset.

But 'notional interest' would certainly be contentious. In the absence of international agreement, the ASB has maintained the optional capitalisation of finance costs (Appendix IV to FRS 15 *Tangible fixed assets*).

But FRS 15 tightens the rules. If a policy of capitalisation is adopted:

1. It must be consistently applied to all finance costs directly attributable to the construction of tangible assets.
2. The amount capitalised in any period may not exceed finance costs incurred in that period, so notional interest may not be capitalised.
3. Capitalised finance costs must be 'directly attributable', i.e. they must be incremental, avoidable if there had been no expenditure on the asset.
4. Finance costs are to be capitalised gross, i.e. before the deduction of any tax relief attributed.
5. All finance costs, as defined by FRS 4 *Capital instruments,* have to be capitalised, not just the interest on the debt. This means that issue costs that are deducted in arriving at the net proceeds of the debt instrument will be capitalised to the extent that they form part of the finance charge.
6. If a company borrows funds specifically to construct an asset, the costs to be capitalised are the actual finance costs during the period.
7. If the project has been financed from the company's general borrowings, a detailed calculation method is laid down.
8. Capitalisation should begin when:

   (a) finance costs are being incurred;
   (b) expenditures for the asset are being incurred; and
   (c) activities that are necessary to get the asset ready for use are in progress. Necessary activities can, in fact, start before the physical construction of the asset, for example technical and administrative costs such as obtaining permits.

9. Capitalisation must cease when the asset's physical construction is complete and ready for use, even if it has not yet been brought into use.

In the past few groups have been specific about finance costs capitalised and few companies disclosed their method of calculating interest to be capitalised. One exception, which suggests the sort of accounting policies we may see more generally in future, is MEPC:

MEPC *Extract from the 1998 accounts*

Accounting policies

Properties ...

An amount equivalent to interest and other outgoings less rental income attributable to properties in course of development is transferred to the cost of properties. For this purpose the interest rate applied to funds provided for property development is arrived at by reference, where appropriate, to the actual rate payable on borrowings for development purposes and, in regard to that part of the development cost financed out of general funds, to the average rate paid on funding the assets employed by the Group.

In property construction, companies have in the past often continued to capitalise costs (e.g. interest and letting costs) on properties which have been built but which are not yet fully let. The argument has been that the asset being constructed is not just the physical structure of the building but a fully tenanted investment property, so the 'production period' should include not simply the construction period but also the letting period.

MEPC *Extract from note to the 1998 accounts*

1. Accounting policies

Properties

A property ceases to be treated as being in the course of development at the earliest of: (1) the date when the development becomes fully let and income producing (2) the date when income exceeds outgoings (3) a date up to three years after completion to allow for letting.

Under FRS 15, capitalisation has to cease when the building is physically complete, not at some later dates when the development is deemed to be complete. A property in the course of construction is not an investment property in the terms of SSAP 19, which specifically excludes properties in respect of which construction work and development are continuing.

The new rules will require a change in accounting policy for many non-construction companies, e.g. SAINSBURY:

SAINSBURY *Accounting policies 1998*

Capitalisation of interest

Interest incurred on borrowings financing specific property developments is capitalised net of tax relief.

Starting-up costs

FRS 15 does not permit capitalisation of start-up costs unless 'the asset is available for use but incapable of operating at normal levels without such a start-up or commissioning period'. The costs of a commissioning period, necessary for running in of machinery or testing equipment, may be capitalised as part of the cost of the asset. But costs incurred when demand is low in, for example, a new hotel or bookstore, do not meet the definition of being 'directly attributable': they have been incurred after physical completion and they are not necessary in order to use the asset.

In the past companies have sometimes capitalised starting-up costs when (or because) they were expanding faster than prudent. When the new project failed to live up to expectations the company ran into serious trouble. SOCK SHOP provides a good example.

SOCK SHOP *Extracts from the 1988–89 accounts*

Accounting policies

Overseas subsidiary set-up costs

Costs incurred in establishing overseas operations in the first year are capitalised as intangible assets and amortised over 4 years on a straight-line basis commencing at the end of the first year.

Intangible assets	£000
Overseas subsidiary set-up costs:	
At beginning of period	–
Additions	354
At end of period	354

The capitalising of £354,000 was not, in itself, significant; it only represented 8% of reported pre-tax profits of £4.32m, but the overseas expansion proved disastrous: less than a year later the company:

- reported an interim loss of £3.97m;
- announced heavy write-offs on the closure of 17 loss-making US outlets;
- went into receivership.

Changes of accounting policy

The statement of accounting policies should point out any changes to policies, and companies are required to report 'any material respects in which any items shown in the profit and loss account are affected by any change in the basis of accounting' (CA 1985, Sch. 9, para. 18 (6) (b)). Changes in accounting policies can have a dramatic effect on reported profits or losses, and result in a prior period adjustment (see page 159) as we showed in relation to ML LABORATORIES on page 48.

Often there will be no choice: the change of accounting policy is required by financial reporting standards. But it does help if exactly what is happening is spelled out:

BP AMOCO *Extract from accounting policies 1998*

Accounting standards

These accounts are prepared in accordance with applicable UK accounting standards. The group has adopted the following Financial Reporting Standards (FRSs) during 1998: FRS 9 *Associates and Joint Ventures*; FRS10 *Goodwill and Intangible Assets*; FRS 11 *Impairment of Fixed Assets and Goodwill* and FRS 14 *Earnings per Share*.

The financial information for 1997 has been restated to comply with the requirements of FRS 9 See Note … for further information. The restatement has had no effect on the profit for the year and net assets.

In the past it was not unknown for a company to change its accounting policies for cosmetic reasons – if this is spotted it is a danger signal.

Changes of presentation

Companies also change their minds upon how certain transactions should be treated and there is nothing sinister or unusual about that. They may not even tell you provided they consider the change is not 'material' and the auditors agree. BARCLAYS are specific:

BARCLAYS *Extract from accounting policies 1998*

Accounting presentation

Changes in accounting presentation

Within the classification other operating income, income from the long-term assurance business now includes amounts previously reported within other income (1997 £14m, 1996 £15m).

Following a reassessment, certain BGI managed funds, previously reported within life-fund assets attributable to policyholders, are now more appropriately classified as funds under management. Accordingly these funds, and their related liabilities, have been excluded from the consolidated balance sheet (1997 £2,228m).

Comparative numbers have been restated for the impact of these changes. Total operating income and operating profit are not affected.

PENSION COSTS

SSAP 24 *Accounting for pension costs* requires the employer to 'recognise the expected cost of providing pensions on a systematic and rational basis' over the period of employment. Cash accounting is not permitted, and companies are required to disclose detailed information on their pension arrangements.

Types of pension scheme

Pension schemes can be either funded or unfunded:

- In a *funded* scheme, the company's contributions (and the employees' contributions if it is a 'contributory' rather than a 'non-contributory' scheme) are paid away to be invested externally to meet future pension liabilities, and the assets of the scheme are held in trust outside the company.
- In an *unfunded* scheme, which is the norm in some foreign countries, the company makes a provision for future liabilities in its accounts.

There are three types of pension scheme in the UK:

1. SERPS, the State Earnings-Related Pension Scheme. Companies pay the employer contribution and have no further liability.
2. Defined contribution schemes.
3. Defined benefit schemes.

Defined contribution schemes and defined benefit schemes are invariably funded.

Defined contribution schemes

In a defined contribution or 'money purchase' scheme, the employer has no obligation beyond payment of the contributions he has agreed to make. The benefits may vary with the performance of the investments purchased by the contributions, but this risk is borne by the employees.

The cost of providing pensions is thus straight-forward: it is the amount of contribution due for the period, and will be charged against profits, e.g. TESCO.

TESCO *Note on pension commitments 1999*

26. Pension commitments

...

The group also operates a defined contribution pension scheme for part-time employees which was introduced on 6 April 1988. The assets of the scheme are held separately from those of the group, being invested with an insurance company. The pension cost represents contributions payable by the group to the insurance company and amounted to £17m (1998 – £15m). There were no material amounts outstanding to the insurance company at the year end.

The group also operates defined contribution schemes in the Republic of Ireland and Hungary. The contributions payable under these schemes of £1m (1995 – £3m) have been fully expensed against profits in the current year.

Smaller companies tend to run this type of scheme, or to contribute to SERPS or to employees' own Personal Pension Plans, in order to avoid taking on any open-ended future commitment. Indeed, a number of larger companies have in recent years closed defined benefit schemes and moved to defined contribution schemes to avoid this liability.

Defined benefit schemes

In a defined benefit or 'final salary' scheme, the pensions to be paid depend on the employees' pay, normally the pay in the final year of employment, so the employer's liability is open-ended.

Because of the complexities of estimating the contributions needed to provide for pensions based on wages or salaries often many years hence, consulting actuaries are used to carry out periodic valuations, usually every three years, and to determine the contribution rate required.

Where an actuarial valuation reveals a material deficiency or surplus in a defined benefit scheme, SSAP 24 requires that it should normally be taken into account by adjusting the current and future costs in the accounts over the remaining service lives of the current employees, or over the average life. See SSAP 24, paras 81 to 83 for exceptions.

Actuaries use a number of techniques and assumptions in arriving at a valuation, and they do not all use the same. SSAP 24 explains the terminology, e.g. 'attained age' or 'projected unit' method. Where there are changes to the actuarial assumptions, or to the valuation method or to the benefits of the scheme, their effect on pension costs should also be spread over the remaining service lives or average life.

The disclosure requirements of SSAP 24 are very extensive. Items of particular interest to the analyst are:

- the accounting policy and, if different, the funding policy and any resulting provisions or prepayments;
- the pension cost charge and the reasons for any significant change from the previous year;
- details of the expected effects on future costs of any material changes in pension arrangements.

Because several schemes are often involved, sometimes in several countries, notes on pensions can be exceedingly long and complex. Most tend to be in narrative form, e.g. TESCO.

TESCO *Note on pension commitments 1998*

25. Pension commitments

The group operates a funded defined benefit pension scheme for full-time employees, the assets of which are held as a segregated fund, administered by trustees.

The pension cost relating to the scheme is assessed in accordance with the advice of an independent qualified actuary using the projected unit method. The latest actuarial assessment of this scheme was at 5 April 1996. The assumptions which have the most significant effects on the results of the valuation are those relating to the rate of return on investments and the rate of increase in salaries and pensions. It was assumed that the investment return would be 8½% per annum with dividend growth of 4% per annum, that salary increases would average 5½% per annum and that pensions would increase at the rate of 3½% per annum.

At the date of the latest actuarial valuation, the market value of the scheme's assets was £792m and the actuarial value of the scheme's assets represented 108% of the benefits that had accrued to members, after allowing for expected future increases in earnings.

Benefit improvements to members have been agreed with the trustees which have resulted in an increased company cost. This increasing ongoing cost has been offset by the amortisation of the surplus as a level percentage of pay over nine years.

The pension cost of this scheme to the group was £44m (1997 – £39m).

...

TESCO is among a growing number of companies that operate a scheme offering post-retirement healthcare benefits. The cost of providing for these benefits is usually accounted for on a basis similar to that used for defined benefit pension schemes. Companies listed in the US are required to disclose the provision for such schemes, which can be massive, e.g. SHELL in its 1997 accounts provided £776m in respect of unfunded post-retirement benefits other than pensions.

What to look for

What is important to the analyst is:

- The regular cost of pensions, which represents a very long-term obligation.
- Variations from regular cost, the reasons for them, and the time over which they are likely to persist.
- Changes in actuarial assumptions, and the reasons for them.
- Changes in benefits and their probable future cost.
- Any very substantial increase in salary (often

to a departing chief executive subject to a final salary scheme).
- Any unfunded liability.
- Any significant unexplained prepayment to the pension fund (e.g. BRUNEL had prepaid £20.4m at 30 June 1998).
- Investment of the pension fund in assets used by the company (e.g. see BRUNEL, page 125).

A tabular presentation like that provided by ARJO WIGGINS APPLETON (see below) often makes funding assumptions easier to understand and interpret and goes some way to bring out that:

- Pension funding is a very long-term business.
- It is necessary to make assumptions about matters which are very difficult to predict (e.g. the rate of inflation over, say, the next 30–40 years, mortality over that period, and the performance of the stock market as a whole, and that of the fund's investment managers in particular).
- Benefits payable tend to improve over time.

ARJO WIGGINS APPLETON *Extract from note 3 to 1997 accounts*

3. Employee information

...

	Main UK scheme	Main US schemes
Method of valuation	'Projected unit credit'	'Projected unit credit'
Date of most recent actuarial valuation	31 December 1996	31 December 1996
Actuarial value of assets	£269.0m	£90.1m
Percentage of accrued benefits covered by assets	117%	97%
Market value of scheme assets at date of valuation	£340.3m	£120.7m
Date of next valuation	31 December 1999	31 December 1999
Assumed annual rate of:		
• inflation	5.0%	3.50%
• return on investments	9.0%	7.75%
• increase in pensionable remuneration	6.5%	4.75%*/3.096%**
• increase in dividends	4.5%	Not applicable
increase in pensions in payment	4.5%	Nil
Discount rate	9.0%	7.75%
Long-term funding rate	11.4%	Not applicable

*salaried employees ** hourly paid employees

Under US regulations and standards, the actuarial value of the assets of the US schemes, both for accounting and funding purposes, is £104.5m and the levels of funding range from 88% to 111%.

Problems faced by actuaries and pension funds

The playing field is not level: the Government changes the rules from time to time. The Finance Act 1993 changed the amount of tax credit attaching to UK dividends received after 5 April 1993 from 25% to 20%, and began a downward process. On 2 July 1997 the Chancellor announced that 'payment of tax credits will be abolished for pension schemes and UK companies (other than charitable companies) on dividends paid on or after today'. This completely invalidated one key long-term assumption made by all funds: the assumed return on investments.

The abolition of dividend credits was condemned by the National Association of Pension Funds (NAPF) as 'the biggest attack on pension provision since the war'. NAPF's chairman, Mr Peter Murray, estimated that the Chancellor's move would require public and private sector employers to contribute an extra £50bn over the next 10years'. He went on: 'Even Robert Maxwell only took £400m.'

The changes in the tax system could not have come at a more unfortunate time. Pension schemes are still relatively new. For the last 20–30 years, as funds built up, contributions, in general, exceeded outgoings. Only recently have we begun to see mature funds in which pensions and other benefits being paid exceed the contributions coming in; increasing the fund's dependence on income and making it necessary in some cases to sell investments to meet benefits.

To add to the difficulties of pension administrators face a new Pensions Regulator, and minimum funding requirements came into force in April 1997; and recent case law suggests that companies may not possess the freedom they have in the past believed they had to use pension fund surpluses to fund redundancies or reorganisations.

Wide awake companies like DIAGEO have asked their actuaries what effect all this is likely to have. They seem undismayed.

DIAGEO *Extract from Note 11 to the 1998 accounts*

(i) Pension plans

...

Valuations of the GrandMet plans were carried out in 1997 and draft valuations of the Guinness plans are currently being finalised. All valuations were done by independent actuaries using the projected unit method to determine pension costs. The principal assumptions were: real rate of return on assets 4.25% to 4.8% (1996 – 4.5% to 4.8%); real annual increase in wages and salaries 1.9% to 2.4% (1996 – 1.9% to 2.4%); real rate of future dividend growth for UK equities 0% to 0.5% (1996 – 0% to 0.5%) and pension increases to increase approximately in line with inflation...

Following the removal during the period of the ability of pension schemes to reclaim UK tax credits on dividend income, an informal actuarial review of the impact of this change on the defined benefit pension plans was commissioned. The impact is not material and has been taken into account in the above valuations.

Disclosure of information

The provisions of the Occupational Pension Schemes (Disclosure of Information) Regulations 1996 and The Occupational Pension Schemes (Requirement to obtain Audited Accounts and a Statement from the Auditor) Regulations 1996, made under the Pensions Act 1995 to replace the 1986 Disclosure of Information regulations, became mandatory for accounting periods ending on or after 6 April 1997. Most types of pension scheme must, within not more than seven months after the end of the scheme year, make available an annual report, including audited accounts. Trustees who fail to do this are guilty of a criminal offence, and liable to a fine.

The auditor must report both on the accounts and on whether or not contributions have been paid in accordance with the schedule of contributions or payment schedule. A SORP *Financial reports of pension schemes*, applicable for scheme years ending on or after 6 April 1997, reflects the accounting requirements of the new Regulations. Scheme. Accounts now contain two primary statements: (i) a fund account, combining the existing income and expenditure and net asset movements statements, and (ii) a net asset statement.

Discussion Papers

In July 1998 the ASB published a discussion paper *Aspects of accounting for pension costs* which deals with key aspects of pension cost accounting. An earlier discussion paper, issued by the ASB in June 1995, set out two alternative approaches:

- an actuarial approach, retaining the basic principles of SSAP 24 with some reductions in options and improved disclosure; and
- a market value approach.

Although responses to the 1995 discussion paper showed almost unanimous support for retaining the SSAP 24 approach, the new discussion paper opts for a market value approach, justifying this on the basis of international harmonisation – IAS 19, the international accounting standard on pension costs issued in March 1998, adopts such an approach. The discussion paper focuses on three other main issues: the basis of valuation of the assets; the rate at which pension liabilities are discounted; and the method of dealing in the accounts with actuarial gains and losses.

EXCEPTIONAL ITEMS

Basic purpose of the profit and loss account

There are two conflicting views of the basic purpose of the profit and loss account:

(a) the current operating performance concept;
(b) the all-inclusive concept.

(a) Current operating performance concept

Advocates of the current operating performance concept believe that the profit and loss account should be designed to disclose the earnings of the business which arise from the normal operating activities during the period being reported upon.

If this were followed to the extreme, the profit and loss account would include only the ordinary activities of the business during the reporting period; anything exceptional, extraordinary or relating to prior years, and the effects of accounting changes, would be excluded.

A profit and loss account prepared in this way facilitates comparison both with those of the same business for earlier periods and with those of other companies for the current period.

(b) All-inclusive concept

Advocates of the all-inclusive concept, on the other hand, believe that the profit and loss account should include all transactions which bring about a net increase or decrease in net tangible assets during the current period, apart from dividend distributions and transactions such as the issue of shares. The aggregate income shown by such income statements over the life of an enterprise then constitutes a complete historical summary of net income.

Advocates of the all-inclusive concept warn that if extraordinary items, the effect of accounting changes and prior period adjustments are charged or credited directly to retained earnings, as they are under the current operating performance concept, there is a danger that they will be overlooked in a review of operating results of several periods.

There has been a shift of opinion towards the all-inclusive concept during the past few years, not only in the United Kingdom but also in the United States and Canada, although none of these countries adopts a pure all-inclusive basis.

Is it extraordinary or exceptional?

Prior to FRS 3 *Reporting financial performance*, published in 1993, companies were allowed to show *Extraordinary items* 'below the line' in their profit and loss account, i.e. below the figure for profit attributable to ordinary shareholders, on which earnings per share were calculated, while Exceptional items came 'above the line'.

Exceptional items are items which fall within the ordinary activities, but which are required to be disclosed separately or which the directors choose to disclose separately.

Prior to FRS 3, *Extraordinary items* were defined as 'material items which derive from events or transactions that fall outside the ordinary activities of the company and which are therefore not expected to recur frequently or regularly.'

That definition of extraordinary items was open to a variety of interpretations, and led to widespread abuse: companies tended to classify unusual losses as extraordinary and unusual profits as exceptional, in order to enhance their reported earnings per share. For example, redundancy and reorganisation costs in continuing businesses were frequently treated as extraordinary items, while profits on disposals were treated as exceptional. In some cases the questionable classifications of items more than doubled reported profits, e.g. in 1990 the hotel group STAKIS reported a pre-tax profit of £30.6m which included gains on the sale of properties of £18.5m. (Management was replaced in 1991.)

In order to stop what had probably become the most widespread form of creative accounting, FRS 3 not only produced a much tighter definition of an extraordinary item, so as to make them extremely rare, but also requires extraordinary (as well as exceptional) items to be included in the calculation of earnings per share.

Under FRS 3 *Extraordinary items* are:

'Material items possessing a high degree of abnormality which arise from events or transactions that fall outside the ordinary activities of the reporting entity and which are not expected to recur. They do not include exceptional items nor do they include prior period items merely because they relate to a prior period.'

One consequence of FRS 3 is that profits before taxation now have to include large 'one-off' items. This has led to much increased volatility, in some cases even turning a profit into a loss.

FRS 3 has not met with universal approval either among companies or analysts. Although the computation of earnings per share is explained in Chapter 18, this is nevertheless an appropriate point to consider the adjustments which analysts make. In order to focus on the profitability of the normal trading operations of a company (i.e. to move nearer to a current operating performance basis as described above), the Institute of Investment Management and Research (IIMR) has developed a standard approach to reported profits, which eliminates capital transactions and abnormal items. This produces what are called the *Headline earnings*.

'Headline' or 'Normalised' earnings

Headline earnings exclude the following items:

1. Profits or losses on the sale or termination of an operation.
2. Profits or losses on the disposal of fixed assets.
3. Expropriation of assets.
4. Amortisation of goodwill.
5. Bid defence costs.
6. Diminution in the value of fixed assets.
7. Profit or loss on the capital reorganisation of long-term debt.
8. Profits or losses on the disposal of trade investments.

The IIMR approach, focusing on the trading activities of a company, has been followed by most leading stockbrokers, to produce what are termed *Normalised earnings*, but with some variations.

The main variation between brokers is that some follow the IIMR recommendation to include 'costs of a fundamental reorganisation or restructuring having a material effect on the nature and focus of the reporting entity's operations' (one of the items shown separately below operating profit), while others exclude it on the grounds of abnormality and of being unlikely to recur.

The trouble with excluding it is that doing so encourages companies to classify relatively minor reorganisations as 'fundamental' in order to avoid the costs reducing 'normalised' profits and earnings per share.

The other problems with adjusting or 'normalising' earnings are taxation and minority interests. With the three items that have to be disclosed separately after operating profit (sale or termination of an operation, fundamental reorganisation and restructuring, and disposal of fixed assets), FRS 3 requires relevant information on the effect of these items on the tax charge and on any minority interests (see Chapters 20–1) to be shown.

With the other items listed by the IIMR for stripping out, e.g. expropriation of assets, the effect on the tax charge may have to be estimated by the analysts. And the effect on minorities will not be known unless disclosed by the company.

FRS 3 *Reporting financial performance*

Besides greatly increasing the number and amount of items appearing on the face of the profit and loss account as exceptional, FRS 3 introduced two new and valuable features to the profit and loss account:

1. *Subdivision of results* down to operating profit level into Continuing operations; Acquisitions (considered in Chapters 20–1); and Discontinued operations.
2. *Separate disclosure*, after operating profit and before interest, of three important items:

   (a) profits or losses on the sale or termination of an operation;
   (b) costs of a fundamental reorganisation or restructuring having a material effect on the nature and focus of the reporting entity's operations (see PIC INTERNATIONAL on page 111 and page 124 to see just how material some restructurings can be); and
   (c) profits or losses on the disposal of fixed assets.

Items (a), (b) and (c) are sometimes referred to as 'the paragraph 20 items', because they are contained in para. 20 of FRS 3.

The way exceptional items might be handled is illustrated in two examples in FRS 3:

- a single column format; and
- a multi-columnar format.

In practice, in simple cases, companies simply show the exceptional item separately, without even labelling it 'exceptional'. For example, SURREY GROUP 1998 accounts showed after the operating loss 'Property losses £252,000', explaining in a note that this represented 'Loss/(profit) on disposal of betting offices £188,000; Diminution in value of betting office licences £114,000 and Profit on sale of land £(50,000).'

At the other extreme, HOGG ROBINSON in its 1998 accounts (not illustrated) takes the multi-column format to the limit with nine columns of current year figures:

Continuing:	Before exceptional items
	Operating exceptional items
	Total
Discontinued:	Before exceptional items
	Non-operating exceptional items
	Total
Total:	
	Before exceptional items
	Total exceptional items
	Total

and seven more columns of preceding year figures – something of an overkill.

PIC INTERNATIONAL *Extract from group profit and loss account for the year ended 30 June 1998*

		Operations before fundamental restructuring	Fundamental restructuring	1998	1997
	Note	£m	£m	£m	£m
Profit/(loss) before interest, tax and fundamental restructuring		74.4	–	74.4	(53.8)
Fundamental restructuring	3				
– Sale of businesses			183.7	183.7	
– Other consequential costs		–	(27.7)	(27.7)	
Net interest payable and similar charges	...	(4.5)	–	(4.5)	(17.8)
Profit/(loss) on ordinary activities before tax		69.9	156.0	225.9	(71.6)

...

PIC INTERNATIONAL *Extracts from Note 3*

3. Exceptional items

1998: Fundamental restructuring

The Group has undergone a fundamental restructuring during the year precipitated by the disposal of the following businesses:

Date	Business	Purchaser
24 Jan 1998	Cereal Derived Functional Ingredients	E I DuPont de Nemours & Co.
20 Mar 1998	Food Ingredients	Kerry Group PLC
24 Apr 1998	Food Distribution	Reyes Holdings Inc.
1 May 1998	Petfoods	Nestle S.A.
22 May 1998	Agricultural Supplies	Management

...

The financial impact of the fundamental restructuring may be summarised as follows:

	Profit/(loss) before tax £m	Tax (charge)/ relief £m	Profit/ (loss) after tax £m
Sale of businesses:			
Food ingredients	161.7	(29.5)	132.2
Food distribution	94.7	(36.8)	57.9
Petfoods	343.7	(31.7)	312.0
Agricultural supplies	(105.9)	4.5	(101.4)
Goodwill on businesses sold	(310.5)	–	(310.5)
	183.7	(93.5)	90.2
Other consequential costs:			
– staff costs	(10.1)	–	(10.1)
– other operating lease rentals	(6.9)	–	(6.9)
– other amounts written off tangible fixed assets	(1.4)	–	(1.4)
– other external charges	(9.3)	–	(9.3)
– tax relief	–	6.9	6.9
	(27.7)	6.9	(20.8)
	156.0	(86.6)	69.4

The other consequential costs of the fundamental restructuring include the closure of the Group's London Head Office, the relocation of the Head Office to California, additional surplus property provisions and professional fees associated with the return of cash to shareholders and the introduction of the new parent company under the Scheme of Arrangement.

BRUNEL HOLDINGS employs a simple multicolumn format (not shown) but supports it with a note (see page 125) giving further detail. Most companies seem to use this format where there are both discontinued operations and/or acquisitions and/or disposals, and exceptional items. We reproduce (on page 125) note 3 from the BRUNEL HOLDINGS accounts in full as it provides an indication of the variety of items likely to be reported as exceptional; and the cause of significant difference between that company's earnings before and after exceptional items: according to accountants BRUNEL'S earnings fell in 1998 by 0.6p (from 1.8p to 1.2p). Analysts would tell you that they rose by 10.2p (from –6.0p to +4.2p). Few companies are as forthcoming.

Comparative figures

The analysis of comparative figures between continuing and discontinued operations is not required on the face of the profit and loss account. Nevertheless, experience suggests that most companies do show it there.

Whichever method is employed, the composition of the comparative figures needs to be understood. As para. 64 of the Explanations to FRS 3 explains:

'To aid comparison, the comparative figures in respect of the profit and loss account should be based on the status of an operation in the financial statements of the period under review and should, therefore, include in the continuing category only the results of those operations included in the current period's continuing operations. ... the

BRUNEL HOLDINGS *Extract from the notes to the 1998 accounts*

3. **Exceptional items**	Notes	1998 £000	1997 £000
Exceptional items within operating profit:			
Redundancy costs	(i)	(408)	–
Provision for termination costs of Mr T.C. Walker	(ii)	(320)	–
Provision for onerous property contract	(iii)	(1,400)	–
		(2,128)	–
Profit/(loss) on disposal of discontinued operations:			
Profit on disposal of Brunel America		5,800	–
Loss on termination of Cameron Equipment's belt press operation	(iv)	(571)	–
Further loss on disposal of Yonder Hill	(v)	(250)	–
Loss on disposal of other businesses		–	(9,580)
		4,979	(9,580)
Profit on sale of property in continuing operation	(vi)	750	–
Total exceptional items		3,601	(9,580)

(i) As part of the restructuring of the Group significant personnel cut backs were made during the year at Dickinson Engineering, Cameron Equipment, Spooner Industries and at the Group's head office. The cost of these redundancies was £408,000. The cost of terminating Mr T.C. Walker's two year service contract was provided for as at 30th June 1998.

(ii) The Company has a contract with the Brunel Holdings Pension Scheme to purchase its head office premises in Chippenham by September 1999 for £2.7m. The directors have assessed the value of this property to be £1.3m and hence have made a provision of £1.4m against this contract.

(iii) Cameron Equipment's belt press operation ceased trading in the year. The loss of £571,000 comprises a £351,000 write down of intangible assets and a £220,000 provision against stocks.

(iv) The net assets of Yonder Hill Limited were sold in March 1997. The new owner however failed to meet its obligations under the sale contract and consequently the Group had to incur additional costs of £250,000. These costs related to the payment of certain creditors and legal costs.

(v) Wincanton Engineering sold its freehold factory site during the year and a net profit of £750,000 was realised on this disposal. The proceeds are being reinvested in a purpose built new site.

comparative figures for discontinued operations will include both amounts relating to operations discontinued in the previous period and amounts relating to operations discontinued in the period under review, which in the previous period would have been included as part of continuing operations.'

RATIOS

Most well-run companies of any size make extensive use of ratios internally, to monitor and ensure the efficient running of each division or activity.

In addition to the published report and accounts of a group, resort can be made to Companies House for accounts filed by subsidiaries, although these can be misleading:

- if goods and services have been transferred within the group at unrealistic prices; or
- if major adjustments have been made on consolidation.

In any case, the accounts of subsidiaries are often not filed at Companies House until some time after the group accounts have been published.

Comparison with the previous year

The simplest method of comparing one year's figures with another involves working out the percentage change from the previous year of each main component of the accounts, e.g. QUEENSBOROUGH (page 126), a company which employs the single column format to display the effects of acquisitions in its profit and loss account.

Percentage changes in themselves may reveal a certain amount about a company's performance, but, like many ratios, they are of most value in prompting further enquiry. For example: Why did turnover of the continuing operations rise so much faster than the operating profit from them?

QUEENSBOROUGH *Extracts from the accounts for the year ended 31 January 1998*

	Notes	1998 £000	1997 £000
Turnover	...		
Continuing operations		35,056	30,328
Acquisitions		1,514	–
Total turnover		36,570	30,328
Cost of sales	...	(15,256)	(13,000)
Gross profit	2	21,314	17,328
Operating profit			
Continuing operations	2	5,540	5,363
Acquisitions		187	–
Total operating profit	...	5,727	5,363
...			
Capital employed (i.e. Total Assets less Current Liabilities) (which represents Shareholders' funds + Creditors: amounts falling due after one year + Provision for liabilities and charges)		51,138	45,748

Year-on-year growth:

Continuing operations only:	
Turnover	15.59%
Operating profit	3.30%
With the acquisitions:	
Turnover	20.58%
Operating profit	6.79%
Capital employed	11.78%

Vertical analysis

Year on year comparisons can be thought of as working across the page, comparing each item with the previous year to get the percentage change, or looking at several years to see the trend of an item.

If we work vertically, calling the total 100, we can construct what are termed 'common size' statements giving a percentage breakdown of an account item.

The advantages of this method are, firstly, that the items are reduced to a common scale for inter-company comparisons and, secondly, that changes in the financial structure of a company stand out more clearly.

Vertical analysis can be used over several years to show how the sales/profitability pattern or financial structure of a company is changing.

Operating ratios

The three main operating ratios are:

1. Profit margin.
2. Return on capital employed.
3. Sales to capital employed.

1. **Profit margin** $= \dfrac{\text{Trading profit}}{\text{Sales}}$ **as a %**

where:

Trading profit = profit before interest charges and tax. Investment income and the company's share of the profits of associated undertakings are not included.

Sales (Turnover) = Sales (excluding VAT and excluding transactions within the group).

This ratio gives what analysts term the profit margin on sales; a normal figure for a manufacturing industry would be between 8% and 10%, while high volume/low margin activities like food retailing can run satisfactorily at around 3%. This profit margin is not the same thing as the gross profit margin (the difference between selling price and the cost of sales, expressed as a percentage of selling price), which can be obtained only if the company reports cost of sales (like QUEENSBOROUGH does).

Unusually low margins can be set deliberately by management to increase market share or can be caused by expansion costs, e.g. new product launching, but in general depressed margins suggest poor performance.

Somewhat better than average margins are normally a sign of good management, but unusually high margins may mean that the company is 'making a packet' and will attract competition unless there are barriers to entry (e.g. huge initial capital costs, high technology, patents or other special advantages enjoyed by the company).

The converse also applies: if a company has lower margins than others in the same sector, there is scope for improvement. For example, in the past few years TESCO has managed to more than double its margins as it shifted away from the 'pile it high and sell it cheap' philosophy of its founder, the late Sir Jack Cohen, towards SAINSBURY's quality image and better margins. Neither is now finding it easy to maintain margins, let alone to continue to increase them.

Example 16.3 Comparison of margins

Year ended	1985	1993	1997	1998
TESCO	2.7%	6.5%	5.6%	5.5%
SAINSBURY	5.1%	8.1%	5.2%	5.8%

Trading profit margins are also important in that both management and investment analysts usually base their forecasts of future profitability on projected turnover figures multiplied by estimated future margins.

An alternative definition of trading profit, used by Datastream and some analysts, is before deducting depreciation, the argument being that different depreciation policies distort inter-company comparisons. If this approach is used, then trading profit should also be before deducting hire charges, to bring a company that leases rather than owns plant and machinery on to a comparable basis. Our view is that depreciation is a cost and should be deducted in any calculation of profit; we therefore prefer to deal with cases where a company's depreciation charge seems unduly low (or high) by making an adjustment, rather than by adding back every company's depreciation charge. Datastream also excludes exceptional items.

2. **Return on capital employed** $= \dfrac{\textbf{Trading profit}}{\textbf{Capital employed}}$

Return on Capital Employed (ROCE), expressed as a percentage, is an important measure of profitability for several reasons:

- a low return on capital employed can easily be wiped out in a downturn;
- if the figure is lower than the cost of borrowing, increased borrowings will reduce earnings per share (e.p.s.) unless the extra money can be used in areas where the ROCE is higher than the cost of borrowing;
- it serves as a guide to the company in assessing possible acquisitions and in starting up new activities – if their *potential* ROCE isn't attractive, they should be avoided;
- similarly, a persistently low ROCE for any part of the business suggests it could be a candidate for disposal if it isn't an integral part of the business.

ROCE can be calculated either for the company overall or for its trading activities:

Capital employed (in trading) = Share capital + reserves + all borrowing including obligations under finance leases, bank overdraft + minority interests + provisions – associates and investments. Government grants are not included.

Capital employed (overall) Associates and investments are not deducted, while the overall profit figure includes income from investments and the company's share of the profits of associated companies, in addition to trading profit.

However, ROCE can be seriously distorted by intangible fixed assets and by purchased goodwill that has been written off directly to reserves (immediate write-off). Ideally, purchased goodwill that was written off direct to reserves should be added back in calculating ROCE but FRS 10 does not require this in the accounts; and information which would allow the analyst to do this for himself is not always available.

We suggest that Intangible items shown in the balance sheet should be included in capital employed at their cost less any subsequent amortisation; e.g. patents, newspaper titles and brand names that have been purchased, but not newspaper titles and brand names that have been built up internally. As Sir Adrian Cadbury said, after RHM had put £678m of brands at valuation in its balance sheet: 'The market value of a company's brands can only be established objectively when their ownership is transferred. Any other form of valuation is by definition subjective.'

The figure for capital employed should, strictly speaking, be the average capital employed during the year, but for simplicity's sake it is normally satisfactory to use the capital employed at the end of the year unless there have been major changes. Some companies label the total at the bottom of their balance sheet as 'capital employed' (QUEENSBOROUGH – opposite – doesn't, it terms it Equity shareholders' funds). But using the balance sheet total can be deceptive, in that bank overdrafts and loans repayable within 12 months are netted out against current assets, giving a company that has perhaps an embarrassingly large short-term debt a better ROCE than a company whose debt is more prudently funded long term.

Another variation used by some analysts is to deduct any cash from the overdraft or, where a company has a net cash position, to deduct net cash in calculating capital employed. Netting out cash against overdraft can be justified where cash and overdraft are both with the same bank and the bank is known to calculate interest on the net figure (overdraft – cash), but in general we accept the figures used for the purposes of FRS 5 (see Chapters 5, 6, 12 and 13) and FRS 1 (see Chapter 19).

If a company feels it prudent to operate with a large cash margin it should be measured accordingly, and if the company's cash is locked up somewhere (for example, if it has arisen from retaining profits overseas to avoid UK taxation) the situation should be reflected in the ratio.

Any upward revaluation of property is likely to reduce ROCE in two ways:

(a) it will increase capital employed (the surplus on revaluation being credited to capital reserve), and

(b) it will probably increase the depreciation charge, and thus reduce profits.

See Chapter 8 regarding valuations under FRS 15 *Tangible fixed assets*.

3. $$\frac{\text{Sales}}{\text{Capital employed in trading}}$$

expressed as a multiple.

Improving the return on capital employed

A rising ratio Sales/Capital employed ratio usually indicates an improvement in performance, i.e. the amount of business being done is increasing in relation to the capital base, but beware of an improvement in the ratio achieved when a company fails to keep its plant and machinery up to date; depreciation will steadily reduce the capital base and improve the ratio without any improvement in sales. Beware, too, of any rapid increase in the ratio, which may well be a warning signal of overtrading, i.e. trying to do too much business with too little capital.

In inter-company comparisons care should be taken to compare like with like: the ratio can be misleading unless the operations of the companies concerned are similar in their activities as well as in their products. For example, a television manufacturing group which is vertically integrated (makes the tubes, electronic circuits and the cabinets and then puts them together) will have much more capital employed than a company which merely assembles bought-in components.

A better measure of performance might be that of value added compared with capital employed, but value added is rarely included in published information.

The three ratios are, of course, interrelated:

$$\frac{\text{Trading profit}}{\text{Sales}} \times \frac{\text{Sales}}{\text{Capital employed}}$$
$$= \frac{\text{Trading profit}}{\text{Capital employed}}$$

as seen from QUEENSBOROUGH at the top of the next column.

QUEENSBOROUGH *Extracts from the accounts for the year ended 31 January 1998*

	Notes	1998 £000	1997 £000
Total turnover		36,570	30,328
Total operating profit	...	5,727	5,363
Capital employed (i.e. Total Assets less Current Liabilities)		51,138	45,748
(which represents Shareholders' funds + Creditors: amounts falling due after one year + Provision for liabilities and charges)			
Profit margin		15.66%	17.68%
Return on capital employed		11.20%	11.72%
Sales/Capital employed		0.72	0.66

Not a happy picture. Nevertheless the equation helps to illustrate the four ways in which management can increase trading profit in relation to capital employed:

1. by increasing the first factor by:

   (a) reducing costs or
   (b) raising prices

   to produce higher profit margins

2. by increasing the second factor by:

   (a) increasing sales or
   (b) reducing capital employed

   so raising volume of output per £1 of capital.

A healthy way of improving profitability is to dispose of low profitability/high capital parts of the business, provided this can be done without adversely affecting the remainder.

Massaging the figures

There was another way of producing the same optical effect other than by running down capital investment: by leasing rather than buying plant and machinery (or by selling and leasing back fixed assets already owned), but this loophole has largely been closed by SSAP 21 *Accounting for leases and hire purchase contracts*, which requires companies to capitalise financial leases in their balance sheet (see Chapter 15).

Two other ways in which companies used to be able to reduce their apparent capital employed were by factoring their debtors and by off balance sheet financing of stock. FRS 5, *Reporting the substance of transactions*, requires both the debtors and the stock to remain on the balance sheet unless the risks and rewards have been transferred to the other party; i.e. unless the factor has no recourse to the company on bad debts, and the company has no obligation to repurchase the stock.

SEGMENTAL REPORTING

Accounting standard

SSAP 25 *Segmental reporting* requires companies which have two or more classes of business or which operate in two or more geographical segments to report turnover (differentiating between external sales and sales to other segments), pre-tax profits and net assets for each class of business and for each geographical segment.

Where there are acquisitions or disposals, segmental analyses generally reflect this, as do those of QUEENSBOROUGH:

QUEENSBOROUGH *Extracts from the accounts for the year ended 31 January 1998*

3. Segmental analysis by class of business

The analysis by class of business of the group's turnover, profit before taxation and net assets is set out below.

The group's turnover and profit before taxation principally arise in the United Kingdom. All sales are external and turnover by geographical destination is not materially different to turnover by origin.

Class of business	1998 £000 Turnover	1997 £000 Turnover	1998 £000 Profit before taxation	1997 £000 Profit before taxation
Day visitor attractions – UK	8,071	7,524	1,748	1,761
Caravan parks – UK	20,997	16,393	3,403	2,460
Caravan parks – France	1,358	616	38	101
Hotel – UK	6,073	5,795	1,510	1,304
Restaurants – UK	71	–	(174)	–
	36,570	30,328	6,525	5,626
Associated undertaking			–	15
Net interest payable			(2,138)	(1,792)
Central costs			(792)	(626)
Profit on sale of surplus properties			–	363
Profit before taxation			3,595	3,586

Net assets by class of business

	1998 £000	1997 £000
Day visitor attractions – UK	12,122	11,206
Caravan parks – UK	27,366	25,407
Caravan parks – France	5,985	1,844
Hotel – UK	10,290	10,258
Restaurants – UK	817	–
Net operating assets	56,580	48,715

Unallocated net assets/(liabilities)

Fixed asset investments	33	144
Head office fixed assets	90	78
Head office debtors	1,241	404
Head office creditors	(1,816)	(855)
Cash and deposits	579	697
Borrowings	(24,557)	(22,335)
Net assets	32,150	26,848

Included in the figures alongside are the following amounts in respect of acquisitions during the financial year:

	£000 Turnover	£000 Profit/(loss) before tax
Caravan parks – UK	764	268
Caravan parks – France	679	48
Restaurants – UK	79	(174)
Total since date of acquisitions	1,514	142

Analysis of profitability

The analyst can work on a segmental analysis, calculating various ratios and using them to compare performance between classes of business and between geographical areas. He can also gain some idea of the profitability of acquisitions and of the possible effect of disposals and closures. Note should be taken of the chairman's statement, the chief executive's report or review of operations and/or financial review as, in a good set of accounts, these will contain comment on the reasons for marked changes in profitability, and may indicate trends.

Four problems with segmental analysis are:

1. The different ways in which companies define capital employed.
2. The huge amounts of purchased goodwill that companies wrote off under earlier accounting rules (see Chapter 20).
3. Where an analysis by geographical segment is provided the same breakdown is not always used for the analysis of profit and capital employed.
4. The differing, and not always scientific, ways companies allocate central overheads and finance costs. LONRHO, for example, used to say:

LONRHO *Extract from note on pre-tax profits*

Central finance charges have been allocated over the various activities and geographical areas in proportion to profit contribution from continuing operations before exceptional items.

For these reasons many analysts no longer use ROCE, focusing instead on margins and earnings per share. Nevertheless, it needs to be remembered that most management decisions are based on, or take account of, return on capital employed.

Problem 16.1

Study note 3 to the accounts of QUEENSBOROUGH for the year 1998 (on page 129).

(a) Compute as a percentage the year-on-year change overall and for each segment of QUEENSBOROUGH's turnover, profit before tax and capital employed.
(b) Using vertical analysis, compare segmentally, that company's turnover, profit before tax and net assets in 1997 and 1998.
(c) Use the information provided to produce a brief summary describing the company's activities, and the changes which occurred in 1998.
(d) Compute the return on the net assets employed for 1997 and 1998. To what extent do you consider this company's ROCE to be a valid indicator of its progress?

Chapter 17

TAXATION

INTRODUCTION

A UK resident company is liable to Corporation Tax (CT) on its income and capital gains, and until 5 April 1999 had to pay Advance Corporation Tax (ACT) when it distributed dividends. If it has income taxable abroad, it will also suffer overseas tax. All this appears in the profit and loss account under the heading 'Taxation'.

VAT, Excise Duty, employee PAYE and other forms of taxation that the company may bear or be involved in are not normally shown (e.g. POWERGEN showed only by way of note that its figures for tax charge 'exclude the exceptional Windfall tax of £266m, of which the first instalment of £133m was paid in December 1997').

In the profit and loss account

Schedule 4 of the Companies Act 1985 requires taxation to be shown in the profit and loss account under three headings:

1. Tax on profit or loss on ordinary activities.
2. Tax on extraordinary profit or loss.
3. Other taxes not shown under the above.

The notes to the accounts should give details of the basis of computation, any special circumstances affecting the tax liability, and under para. 54 (3):

(a) the amount of UK corporation tax;
(b) the extent of double taxation relief;
(c) the amount of UK income tax; and
(d) the amount of foreign tax charged to revenue.

The notes may also include details of:

(e) irrecoverable ACT;
(f) over/under-provision for prior years' taxation;
(g) deferred taxation;

(h) prior to 6 April 1999, tax credit on UK dividends received;
(i) taxation on share of profit of associated undertakings (see Chapter 22).

Items (e), (g) and (h) are required by SSAP 8.

HOGG ROBINSON's profit and loss account illustrates a typical presentation of a fairly complex tax charge, where there are discontinued activities.

HOGG ROBINSON *Note 8 to the 1998 accounts*

8. Taxation

	1998 £000	1997 £000
Current:		
UK corporation tax at 31% (1997 33%)	5,589	8,491
Double tax relief	(216)	(811)
Net UK corporation tax	5,373	7,680
Overseas tax	1,265	1,235
Deferred tax	(2,801)	848
Adjustments in respect of prior years:		
UK corporation tax	(2)	(745)
Overseas tax	19	(3)
Deferred tax	55	539
Share of associate companies	561	191
	4,470	9,745
Continuing businesses	4,089	8,735
Discontinued businesses	381	1,010
	4,470	9,745

The effective 1998 Group rate of tax on profits for continuing businesses, before exceptional items, was 28.6% (1997 34.4%). The effective rate of tax is lower than the standard rate because of the impact of shares issued to QUEST less disallowable items and timing differences. Excluding the tax benefit of £945,000 (1997 £nil) arising from the issue of shares to QUEST the effective 1998 Group rate of tax on profits for continuing businesses, before exceptional items, would have been 31.8% (1997 34.4%).

Extract from financial review 1998
Taxation
The effective rate of tax for Continuing Businesses has reduced to 31.8% (34.4%) although with the benefit of a tax credit from the Employee Share Trust more than off-setting a high (55.9%) charge on Transport's profits, the overall rate for 1997/98, before exceptional items, was reduced to 29.2% (34.6%).

Adjustments due to changes in tax rates and tax allowances should normally be disclosed separately as part of the tax charge and the effects of changes in the basis of taxation shown separately on the face of the profit and loss account (FRS 3, para. 23).

In the balance sheet

In the balance sheet taxation will appear:

1. *Under creditors falling due within one year*: the amount falling due within one year has typically included one year's mainstream Corporation Tax, any foreign tax due, ACT on any dividends recently paid, and ACT on any proposed dividends. But this is in the process of changing:

    (a) ACT is not payable after 5 April 1999;
    (b) Large companies (i.e. those with taxable profits of £1.5m or more) are required in respect of accounting periods ending on or after 1 July 1999 to make quarterly payments (due on the 14th of months 7, 10, 13 and 16 following the start of the accounting period). Transitional rules apply for three years.

2. *Under provisions*: any provision for deferred taxation (see page 134) and any provision for other taxation, shown separately (CA 1985, Sch. 4, para. 47).

3. *Under assets*: ACT paid and payable which has not yet been offset against the company's CT liability (unrelieved ACT is normally off-set against deferred tax, and only occasionally appears separately as an asset).

In the cash flow statement

FRS 1 *Cash flow statements* lays down that the cash flow statement should list cash flows for the period classified under eight standard headings, the third of which is 'Taxation'. In the past this item has normally represented one year's payment of

corporation tax (that for the previous tax year) and, in the case of a group with foreign activities, one year's overseas tax (usually shown separately). From 1999, as explained in the previous section, large companies pay corporation tax quarterly. The effect of the change is that large companies will pay five years' mainstream corporation tax in the next four years, i.e. their cash flow will be adversely affected.

Tax years and rates of tax

The fiscal (or Income Tax) *year* runs from 6 April of one year to 5 April the following year and is referred to by stating both years, e.g. Income Tax year 1999/2000 is the year from 6 April 1999 to 5 April 2000.

For Corporation Tax purposes, *the financial year* (FY) runs from 1 April to 31 March and is referred to by the year in which it *starts*, e.g. financial year 1999 is the year from 1 April 1999 to 31 March 2000. The rate of Corporation Tax for each financial year is normally set in the Budget in the November before the start of the financial year. Tax rates since 1988 appear below:

Financial year	*Corporation Tax rate*	*Basic rate of Income Tax (6 Apr)*	*ACT as fraction of dividend*
1988 to 1989	35%	25%	1/3rd
1990	34%	25%	1/3rd
1991 to 1993	33%	25%	1/3rd
1994	33%	25%	9/31sts
1995	33%	25%	1/4th
1996	33%	24%	1/4th
1997	33%	23%	1/4th
1998	31%	23%	1/4th
1999	30%	23%	nil

If a company's accounting year falls partly in one financial year and partly in the next, the profits are divided between the two financial years on a time basis and bear Corporation Tax at the appropriate rate for each financial year. The rate of ACT, however, was always the rate of ACT at the date of dividend payment (not the rate at the date the dividend was declared nor the rate in force in the period in respect of which the dividend was being paid).

If a trading company's taxable profits (income and capital gains) do not exceed £300,000 in a year, its income is subject to a lower rate of Corporation Tax, the *small companies' rate* (20 per cent from 1 April 1999). There is marginal relief for companies with profits of between £300,000 and £1,500,000.

Corporation Tax – the imputation system

Corporation Tax was introduced by the Finance Act 1965 and was subsequently modified from 1 April 1973 by the introduction of the imputation system. Under the imputation system, when a company paid dividends to shareholders, it was required to hand over to the Inland Revenue what was termed *Advance Corporation Tax* (ACT) and the shareholder received a *tax credit.*

The rate of ACT payable was determined by the fraction, $I \div (1.00 - I)$, set each year by the Finance Act. Until 1992/93, $I\%$ was equal to the basic rate of Income Tax. For example, the basic rate of Income Tax (25% in that year) gave a fraction 25/75ths, i.e. $33\frac{1}{3}\%$ of the actual dividend paid. That relationship ceased to exist in 1993/94.

ACT served two purposes (i.e. it was counted twice):

1. It was a part payment of the company's Corporation Tax liability for the period in which the dividend was paid. (The remaining Corporation Tax payable was known as *mainstream Corporation Tax.)*
2. In addition, it was 'imputed' to the shareholder as a *tax credit.* Until 1992/93 that tax credit exactly discharged the basic rate UK Income Tax liability on the dividend (leaving the higher rate taxpayer to account for the difference between the basic rate and higher rate on the gross equivalent). From 1993/94 the position has been more complex, but the higher rate taxpayer always had to pay further tax.

From 6 April 1999 private shareholders receive on their dividend a 10% tax credit. A non taxpayer cannot reclaim anything. A basic rate taxpayer has no further tax to pay; and a higher rate taxpayer is required to pay additional tax equivalent to 25% of the net dividend (that's 20% of the 'gross' dividend payout i.e. the 'net' dividend actually received plus the 10% tax credit.).

Is the tax charge 'normal'?

The tax charge shown in the profit and loss account is unlikely to be 'normal', i.e. what the layman might expect, namely, pre-tax profits × average rate of Corporation Tax during the company's accounting year. It is important to understand why this is the case.

The amount of Corporation Tax payable does not depend purely on the company's pre-tax profit figure. The tax charge varies not only because of: (i) differences that arise between the taxable profit and the profit shown in the company's accounts (the 'book profit'), but because of (ii) differences in the rate charged on particular types of income.

The differences fall into three categories:

1. *Timing difference,* where the company may be liable to pay the full rate of tax at some time, but not in the year being reported upon (see the next page).
2. *Previous years* where the effect of losses and/or unrelieved ACT brought forward can materially reduce the tax charge for the year (see pages 137 and 139).
3. *Permanent differences* where expenses are disallowed or income is tax-free or is taxed at a rate other than that of UK Corporation Tax (see page 136).

One of the most important differences in most companies is the timing difference caused by depreciation (in the company's accounts) not being the same as the capital allowances available.

Depreciation and capital allowances

Different classes of asset have long been treated quite differently for tax and accounting purposes. For some, like office buildings, there is no allowance at all for tax purposes for depreciation, or in Revenue terms: no 'capital allowances' are available, except in Enterprise Zones. Others have been treated generously (e.g. plant and machinery), and some more harshly than similar assets (e.g. expensive or high capacity private motor cars. From 1 April 1986 allowances have been:

Asset category	*Allowance*
Plant and machinery	Writing down
Patent rights	25% a year on
Know-how	reducing balance
Industrial buildings	Writing down
Hotels	4% a year
Agricultural works	on cost
Scientific research	Initial
Commercial buildings in Enterprise Zones	100% on cost
New ships	'Free depreciation'

- From 1 November 1992 to 31 October 1993 there was an initial allowance of 40% (20% for hotels).
- In 1997, capital allowances on machinery and plant were reduced from 25% to 6% for assets with a working life of 25 years or more but only as regards businesses spending more than £100,000 a year on such assets.
- In 1996 a first year allowance at 40 per cent was introduced for expenditure by small and medium sized businesses on machinery or plant on or after 25 November 1996. This is to continue until 1 July 2000.

Example of a timing difference

A company pays less Corporation Tax than normal if the capital allowances received for the year are greater than the amount the company provides for depreciation, as Example 17.1 shows.

Example 17.1 Depreciation and capital allowances

If a large company invested £1m in plant and machinery in 1999 and used straight line depreciation spread over an expected ten-year life, the capital allowances and depreciation would be:

	Capital allowances £	Depreciation £
1999	250,000	100,000
2000	187,500	100,000
2001	140,625	100,000
2002	105,469	100,000
2003	79,102	100,000
2004	59,326	100,000
2005	44,495	100,000
2006	33,371	100,000
2007	25,028	100,000
2008	75,084	100,000
	1,000,000	1,000,000

Note: This assumes that trading ceased in 2008 and that the plant and machinery had no residual value. If the company continued trading, the allowances would continue ad infinitum at 25% a year on the declining balance, i.e. £18,771 in 2008, £14,078 in 2009 ... £334 in the year 2022, and so on.

The advantage of the declining balance method is that it simplifies calculations.

If the company made taxable trading profits before capital allowances of £2m in each of the ten years and we ignore all other allowances for the purpose of illustration, the Corporation Tax payable, assuming a 30% rate throughout, would be:

	Taxable profit £		Corporation Tax liability £
1999	1,750,000		525,000
2000	1,812,500		543,750
2001	1,859,375		557,813
2002	1,894,531		568,359
2003	1,920,898		576,269
2004	1,940,674		582,202
2005	1,955,505		586,651
2006	1,966,629		589,989
2007	1,974,972		592,492
2008	1,924,916	(Note 1)	577,475
	19,000,000	(Note 2)	5,700,000

Notes:
1. Assuming trading ceases in 2008 and the plant and machinery has no residual value, to give capital allowances of £75,084 that year.
2. The reported profit before tax each year would be £1,900,000 (£2m less £100,000 depreciation), so the total taxable profit over the ten years would be the same as the total reported profit, and the total tax payable would be the same as a tax charge of 30% each year on reported profit.

DEFERRED TAXATION

In order to remove the effect of timing differences from the profit and loss account, i.e. to allow for deferred tax liability, companies transfer to a Deferred Tax Account a sum equal to the difference between the Corporation Tax actually payable on taxable trading profits and the tax that would have been payable if the taxable trading profits had been the same as the accounting profit (e.g. as if capital allowances had equalled the depreciation shown in the company's accounts).

Accounting for deferred taxation

In 1975 the Accounting Standards Committee proposed to make it obligatory for all companies to account for deferred taxation on *all* material timing differences. This is clearly the prudent thing to do:

(a) the system of capital allowances might change adversely (as it did in 1984);
(b) a company falling on hard times, which had to cut back heavily on capital expenditure, could find itself with an onerous tax charge.

Example 17.2 How deferred tax works in the accounts
In Example 17.1, between 1999 and 2002, the taxable profit each year is less than the reported profit of £1,900,000 a year. This would be shown in 1999 as:

Profit and loss account	£000
Pre-tax profits	1,900
Taxation (see Note)	570
Profit after tax	1,330

Note:	Corporation Tax payable	525
	Transfer to provision for deferred tax	45
	Total tax charge (£1.9m at 30%)	570

The deferred tax thus *originated* is then added to the accumulated figure for 'deferred tax' in the balance sheet in respect of any other transactions. In the years 2003 to 2007 the effect of the timing difference would be *reversed* in that more tax would be payable than the tax charge shown in the profit and loss account; the transfer would be from the deferred tax account.

However, the proposal met with considerable opposition and, as the result of representations from the CBI and others, it was decided to allow partial provision. This is currently the requirement: tax deferred by timing differences should *not* be accounted for if it is probable that it will not crystallise (SSAP 15, para. 26), but the amount of tax not provided for in the period should be disclosed in a note (SSAP 15, para. 35). See HOGG ROBINSON on page 131 for an example showing net transfers to deferred taxation in 1997 and net transfers from it in 1998. At one time companies tended to refer in their accounting policies to provision 'except where it is unlikely to become payable'. Most now refer to provision 'to the extent that it is probable that a liability will arise.'

The SSAP goes on to say that the assessment of whether deferred tax will or will not crystallise should be based on reasonable assumptions, taking into account all relevant information available. But what is a reasonable assumption? The scope for differences of treatment from company to company is enormous.

Arguably, by allowing only partial provision SSAP 15 ignores the normal concept of prudence. This caught up with companies when, in the 1984 Budget, the timing of capital allowances was radically altered with the phasing out of previously generous first-year allowances. As a result most companies had to make a substantial extra provision for deferred tax. In some cases these provisions were very large indeed:

ROYAL BANK OF SCOTLAND GROUP *Effect of 1984 Budget on deferred tax provisions*

Consolidated profit and loss account

	1984 £m	1983 £m
Profit before extraordinary items	72.4	95.1
Extraordinary items:		
Profits less losses on disposals	25.1	(1.6)
Provisions required for corporation tax changes	(177.7)	–
Transfer from reserves	177.7	–
Profit attributable to ordinary shareholders	97.5	93.5

These provisions were treated as extraordinary items (as SSAP 15 then required), leaving earnings per share (e.p.s.) unscathed, although providing less than fully for deferred tax had, in previous years, boosted e.p.s. Under FRS 14 such increased provisions would hit e.p.s.

A discussion paper *Accounting for tax* was published by ASB in March 1995. Much of this was devoted to deferred tax which some saw as an income smoothing device. SSAP 15 remains the standard, but the ASB is continuing to develop proposals. These, it has announced, will reflect the impact of a recent International Standard (IAS 12) which requires entities applying IASs to provide for deferred tax on a full provision basis. The ASB takes the view that, whilst provisions should be made for reversing timing differences such as accelerated capital allowances, they should not necessarily be made *automatically* for deferred tax on gains, such as unrealised revaluation gains, where the tax might never be paid. The Board is consulting further on whether long-term deferred tax balances should be discounted. Meanwhile: (i) analysts should be sceptical where after-tax profits are increased by reducing or omitting provision for deferred taxation; and (ii) UK GAAP are out of step with US.

Other timing differences

In addition to differences between capital allowances and depreciation, timing differences requiring deferred tax treatment also arise over the following items:

1. Accruals

Certain items of expenditure or income are accrued in the accounts but are not included for tax purposes until paid or received. SSAP 15 calls for the provision of deferred taxation on these.

2. Prepayments

A payment in advance which is allowable as an expense for tax purposes, e.g. a prepayment to the pension fund, may not give rise to one in the period for accounting purposes.

3. Revaluation of assets

If a surplus on revaluation is written into the accounts, SSAP 15 requires that a provision for taxation should be made out of the revaluation surplus as soon as a liability is foreseen, usually at the time a company decides in principle to dispose of the asset; but not before that. If a company's year end falls after the decision in principle but before the actual disposal, the provision for taxation would be included in deferred tax.

4. Asset sales: balancing allowances and charges

Where an industrial building is sold, the proceeds of sale are compared with the tax written-down value; if the proceeds exceed the tax written-down value a balancing charge is made, or if they are less a balancing allowance is given. Balancing charges increase taxable profits, and balancing allowances reduce taxable profits. The balancing charge (or balancing allowance) represents the difference between the sale proceeds (or cost if that is less) and the tax written-down value.

Example 17.3 Computation of balancing charge

If an industrial building which cost £5m was sold for £15m when it had a written-down value for tax purposes of £3m, the balancing charge would be:

(Proceeds of sale or cost, whichever is the less) – Tax written-down value = £5m – £3m = £2m

and the company's taxable profits would be increased by £2m.

Example 17.4 Sale proceeds exceed original cost

An industrial building which cost £5m in October 1986 (when the RPI was 98.5, as shown in Appendix 3) was sold in December 1998 (when the RPI was 164.4) for £15m:

Indexation factor = (164.4 – 98.5) ÷ 98.5 = 0.669
Indexation allowance = £5m × 0.669 = £3.345m
Chargeable gain = £15m – £5m – £3.345m = £6.655m.
Tax on this £6.655m would be in addition to the tax on the balancing charge in Example 17.3.

In the case of plant and machinery (but not cars), a 'pool' is maintained of plant available for writing-down allowances. Where such assets are sold, the proceeds of sale (or their cost if less) are simply deducted from the pool; there is normally no balancing allowance or balancing charge.

5. Asset sales – capital gains and losses

When an asset is sold and the proceeds exceed the original cost, Corporation Tax may be payable on the capital gain, but that part of the gain arising before 31 March 1982 is not taxable, and relief is given against gains (but not losses) to allow for the fall in the value of money since that date.

This relief, called indexation allowance, is calculated using the Retail Prices Index (RPI) in the months of purchase and sale:

The chargeable capital gain is the proceeds of the sale minus the original cost, minus the indexation allowance.

When an asset was bought before 31 March 1982, the value at that date is used instead of the original cost and the RPI for March 1982 is used instead of the RPI in the month of purchase.

6. Asset sales – rollover relief

If a company disposes of a building (or other qualifying assets, e.g. a ship or an aircraft) at a profit and purchases another, it can obtain what is known as 'rollover relief' by electing to have the gain arising on the disposal deducted from the cost of the new building rather than paying tax on it:

Example 17.5 Rollover relief

If freehold premises costing £5m were sold for £15m, producing a chargeable capital gain of £6.655m (as it did in Example 17.3) and new freehold premises were bought for £18m, the company could defer payment of tax on the £6.655m by electing to deduct the gain from the cost of the new premises.

However, if the new premises were subsequently sold for, say, £26m, tax would be assessed on the gain of £26m less (£18m – £6.655m = £11.345m), i.e. on £14.655m less indexation allowance based on £11.345m (not £18m).

SSAP 15 does not normally require provision for deferred tax where advantage has been taken of rollover relief.

REASONS FOR 'ABNORMAL' TAX CHARGES

Even if full provision were made for deferred taxation, differences would remain between the tax charge and what might be expected bearing in mind the pre-tax profits and the normal rate of Corporation Tax. For instance, small companies pay Corporation Tax on income at a lower rate, see page 132.

Adjustments to previous years

Where tax on profits of an earlier period proves to be more or less than previously provided, FRS 3 requires that this should be included in the profit and loss account, and the effect stated if material (most companies show it by way of note; see HOGG ROBINSON on page 131 for example).

Permanent differences

Permanent 'differences' in tax charge, the effects of which are not offset by provisions for deferred tax, include the following items.

1. Disallowed expenses

Some items, such as the cost of entertaining customers, are charged by companies to their profit and loss account properly reducing pre-tax profits, but are not allowed as expenses by the Taxes Act in calculating taxable profits. This causes the tax charge to appear higher than 'normal'.

Provisions for expenditure are often not allowable as SAFEWAY (on the next page) shows.

SAFEWAY *Extract from Note 8.0 to the 1998 accounts*

8.0 Tax on profit on ordinary activities

In the year ended 28 March 1998, no taxation relief has been assumed on the net property losses of £5.0m nor on the fixed asset losses and reverse premia provisions totalling £13.5m which form part of the store portfolio review and redundancy programme. Tax relief of £4.8m has been assumed on the operating items charge totalling £16.5m included within the store portfolio review and redundancy programme.

2. Franked income

This is income that has already borne Corporation Tax, i.e. dividends received from other UK companies. Franked income is not subject to Corporation Tax a second time which means that companies receiving dividends incur no further tax. Thus the gross value of franked income to a *company* is now normally the dividend received grossed up at the Corporation Tax rate. But this is not how it is shown. SSAP 8 requires the total of dividends plus tax credits to be brought in at the pre-tax level and an amount equal to the tax credits to be included in the taxation charge. For example, if in financial year 1996 taxable income was £800,000 in dividends from other companies, together with associated tax credits of £200,000, the profit and loss account would have shown:

	£000
Pre-tax profits	1,000
Taxation	200
Profits after tax	800

the apparent tax rate would have been 20%; and there would be no further liability on the income. There are no longer any tax credits so far as companies are concerned. So, if in financial year 1999 a company has taxable income of £800,000 in dividends from other companies, the profit and loss account will show:

	£000
Pre-tax profits	800
Taxation	–
Profits after tax	800

the apparent tax rate will be 0%; and, again, there will be no further liability on the income.

3. Capital gains

Tax payable on capital gains, is included in the Corporation Tax charge. For example, if a company's sole taxable profit for the year arose from the £4m sale of freehold land costing £3m, and the indexation allowance was £400,000, the chargeable gain would be only £600,000.

The profit and loss account would show:

	£000
Pre-tax profit	1,000
Taxation (30% on £600,000)	180
Profit after tax	820

and the apparent rate of tax would be 18%.

4. Loans

Gains on loans are not normally subject to Corporation Tax, and losses on loans are not deductible as expenses. For example, if a company issued a loan stock at £99% and subsequently bought it in for cancellation at £95%, neither the £1% loss on issue nor the £5% gain on repurchase would be included in the calculation of the company's Corporation Tax charge. However, in 'deep discount' issues (see page 37), the 'income element' is an allowable expense.

5. Losses

Where a company makes a loss, it may carry that loss back for a limited period to recover Corporation Tax previously paid or, failing that, can carry the loss forward indefinitely to offset against future profits. However:

(a) Capital losses, for example the loss on sale of fixed assets, cannot normally be offset against trading profits.

(b) Losses by UK-resident subsidiaries cannot be offset against profits elsewhere in the group unless the subsidiary is at least 75% owned by the parent company (but the provisions are complex). If the loss-making subsidiary is less than 75% owned (so that group relief is unavailable), the group's tax charge will appear abnormally high, but the losses can be carried forward within the subsidiary and, if and when it returns to profitability, subsequently matched against future profits of that subsidiary. The effect on the group's tax charge will then be reversed.

(c) The losses of a subsidiary in one country cannot be offset against the profits of subsidiaries in other countries, and this can result in an abnormally high tax charge, as THE BODY SHOP (see next page) illustrated in 1998:

137

THE BODY SHOP 1998 accounts
Consolidated profit and loss account 1998

	£m
Profit on ordinary activities before tax	38.0
Taxation (Note 7)	(15.2)
Profit for the financial year after tax	22.8

Note 7 Taxation	1998
	£m
The charge consists of:	
UK corporation tax	12.4
Deferred tax	2.3
Overseas tax	0.5
	15.2

The effective tax rate is higher than the standard UK corporation tax of 31% as a result of the losses of the US subsidiary in the year of approximately £11.5m which are not available for relief in the year.

An indication of available losses should be given by either the note on taxation or that on deferred taxation and there may be comment on probable future tax charges, as BOC for example:

BOC GROUP *Extract from the accounts to 30 September 1997*

d) Unused tax credits

...

On a consolidated basis, the Group has net operating loss carryforwards of £119.9m, of which £112.6m are provided for by a valuation allowance. A valuation allowance is provided when it is more likely than not that some or all of the losses will not be realised. If not offset against taxable income, these losses will expire as follows:

	Net operating loss
Year	*£m*
1998	19.5
1999	4.1
2000	3.4
2001	2.0
2002	4.1
Thereafter, or no expiry date	86.8

Tax reliefs brought forward eventually get used up (see BENSONS CRISPS on page 142), so many analysts, in comparing companies, apply the standard rate of Corporation Tax to UK profits.

6. Overseas income

Overseas income presents special problems:

1. Overseas income of non-resident subsidiaries is not generally liable to UK taxation; it bears only foreign tax. The foreign tax may be at a higher or lower rate than UK Corporation Tax. In particular some countries, such as Ireland, give foreign companies several years of tax holidays to encourage them to set up subsidiaries there.
2. Dividends, interest or royalties remitted to the UK from certain countries, including the USA, may bear a further 'withholding tax'.
3. Overseas income of a UK-resident company is liable to UK tax whether remitted or not.
4. Double taxation relief (DTR) is given for overseas tax on income liable to UK tax, so dividends paid to the UK by overseas subsidiaries normally bear no UK tax if the foreign tax has already been borne at a rate equal to or greater than UK Corporation Tax. If the foreign tax is lower, only the difference is payable in the UK, but in both cases this is only true for foreign taxes of an income nature (taxes of a capital nature do not qualify for relief). Example 17.6 illustrates the way in which double taxation relief is applied and HOGG ROBINSON on page 131 provides an example.

Example 17.6 Double taxation relief

A UK holding company does not trade, but has one overseas subsidiary whose profit and loss account is:

	£000
Pre-tax profits	10,000
Tax paid at 25%	2,500
	7,500
Dividends	3,000
Retentions	4,500

The UK holding company's £3,000,000 dividends are subject to 10% withholding tax (£300,000) on remittance, so the UK company actually receives £2,700,000. For UK tax purposes the dividend received by the holding company is grossed up:

	£000
Dividend from subsidiary	3,000
Associated foreign tax at 25%	1,000
Gross income from subsidiary	4,000

UK tax is: Corporation Tax 30% on £4,000,000	1,200
less DTR, which is the lesser of	
(a) Tax paid on £2,700,000 net £1,000,000 + £300,000 = £1,300,000	
(b) UK CT liability of £1,200,000	1,200
Tax payable in the UK	0

The UK holding company's profit and loss account would show:

	£000	£000
Pre-tax profits		10,000
Taxation		
UK Corporation Tax	1,200	
less Double tax relief	1,200	
		–
Overseas tax	2,500	
Withholding tax	300	2,800
Profit after tax		7,200

7. *Exceptional items*

Under FRS 3, exceptional items should, as explained in Chapter 16, be credited or charged in arriving at the profit or loss on ordinary activities under the statutory format headings to which they relate, and attributed to continuing or discontinued operations as appropriate.

Certain items, including provisions in respect of them, have under para. 20 of FRS 3 to be shown separately on the face of the profit and loss account after operating profit and before interest, again under the appropriate heading of continuing or discontinued operations, namely:

(a) profits or losses on the sale or termination of an operation;
(b) costs of a fundamental reorganisation or restructuring having a material effect on the nature and focus of the reporting entity's operations; and
(c) profits or losses on the disposal of fixed assets.

Relevant information regarding the effect of these items on the taxation charge and, in the case of consolidated financial statements, any minority interests should both be shown in a note to the profit and loss account. As a minimum the related tax and the minority interest should both be shown in aggregate, but if the effect of the tax and minority interests differs for the various categories of items further information should be given, where practicable, to assist users in assessing the impact of the different items on the net profit or loss attributable to shareholders.

Many companies show the tax effect of all significant exceptional items, as for example GREAT UNIVERSAL STORES:

GREAT UNIVERSAL STORES *Extract from notes to the 1998 accounts*

6. Exceptional items
Profit before taxation for the year to 31 March 1998 includes an exceptional credit of £68.6m. This relates to two items: a credit of £70.3m from VAT refunds in the UK Home Shopping division; and the loss of £1.7m on the termination of Canadian businesses. The loss of £1.7m in Canada comprises a gain of £17.1m on the sale of Superior Acceptance Corporation and a loss of £18.8m on the closure of the Group's Canadian retail company. The comparative figure includes an exceptional credit of £21.5m, largely in respect of previously overpaid VAT in the UK Home Shopping division.

9. Tax on profit on ordinary activities

	1998	1997 (restated)
	£m	£m
United Kingdom Corporation tax at 31% (1997 33%)	159.7	157.1
...		
The tax charge includes the following amounts attributable to exceptional items:		
Tax on refund of VAT	21.8	6.1
Tax on sale of Superior Acceptance Corporation Limited	7.5	
Tax relief on closure of the Canadian retail company	(5.3)	
Tax on profit on sale of investment property portfolio		1.0
	24.0	7.1

The deferred tax charge is reduced by £0.2m as a result of the reduction in the UK Corporation tax rate. The prior years' adjustments for deferred tax in the year to 31 March 1997 arose as a result of a reassessment of the recoverability of deferred tax assets.

DISTRIBUTIONS AND ADVANCE CORPORATION TAX

Advance Corporation Tax (ACT)

Advance corporation tax ceased to be payable as regards dividends paid on or after 6 April 1999. Prior to that the payment of dividends affected the company's overall tax liability if:

(a) the dividends were very high; or
(b) a large proportion of the company's earnings came from overseas and bore foreign tax at anything more than a modest rate.

In either case some of the ACT paid on the distribution of dividends was likely to be *unrelieved*, i.e. the company was not be able to offset it against the company's corporation tax liability. We provide details of this because, as explained below, relief is still available for unrelieved ACT from earlier years (and the effect of this could be substantial).

Limitations on the use of ACT

ACT could, and this is still the case, only be set off against the Corporation Tax liability for an accounting period on profits (income and chargeable gains), and on unfranked investment income, subject to a *maximum set-off* (from 1994/95) of 20% of the profits chargeable to Corporation Tax. The balance is termed the mainstream Corporation Tax (referred to from now on as 'mainstream tax'), as illustrated in Example 17.7.

Example 17.7 Unrelieved ACT due to high dividend distribution

In the financial year 1996 tax rates were as follows:

Corporation Tax rate	33.0%
Rate of ACT (1/4 of the net distribution)	20.0%
Minimum rate of mainstream tax	13.0%
i.e. Maximum set-off	20.0%

In that year, if a company operating solely in the United Kingdom made £10m pre-tax and distributed £9m, i.e. considerably more than its profits after tax of £6,700,000 (perhaps to maintain its dividend in a poor year) it would suffer unrelieved ACT as follows:

	£000
Pre-tax profit	10,000
Corporation Tax (33%)	3,300
	6,700
Dividends paid	9,000
ACT paid (1/4 of £9m)	2,250
Maximum ACT set-off (20% of £10m)	2,000
Unrelieved ACT	250

ACT was set off against the Corporation Tax liability for the year in which the related dividend was distributed, but any *surplus ACT* that could not be used in that year (i.e. was 'unrelieved') could be carried back for up to six years, or carried forward indefinitely. But as explained above the total amount which could be set off in a year was limited to the 'maximum set-off'. When ACT was carried back it had to be relieved in later years first (sometimes called 'on a LIFO basis').

Alternatively, it could, subject to certain restrictions, be surrendered to other companies in a group and offset against their tax liability.

Irrecoverable ACT

Although ACT could be carried forward indefinitely, SSAP 8 regarded it as *irrecoverable* if its recoverability was not 'reasonably certain and foreseeable'. The carry-forward 'should normally not extend beyond the next accounting period' (see OCTROI GROUP below).

Alternatively, unrelieved ACT could be deducted from that proportion of the balance of deferred tax against which ACT could be set off in the future (not deferred tax representing future mainstream tax or tax on deferred chargeable gains). If unrelieved ACT was set off against deferred tax it would be deducted from deferred tax in the balance sheet rather than being charged to the profit and loss account, and so would not increase the profit and loss account figure for tax.

Irrecoverable ACT, on the other hand, was to be included as part of the tax charge, and the amount separately disclosed if material – as shown by OCTROI GROUP (formerly OCEONICS) in 1998:

OCTROI GROUP *Extract from notes to the 1998 accounts*

8. Tax charge on profit on ordinary activities

	1998 £000	1997 £000
ACT written off	(72)	(69)
Other UK taxation	(12)	(36)
Overseas taxation	37	(182)
Group relief surrendered to former subsidiary	100	–
Share of tax attributable to associated company	(368)	(206)
	(235)	(493)

ACT and relief for foreign tax

Relief for foreign tax, which is called Double Taxation Relief (DTR), was offset against a company's UK Corporation Tax liability before ACT offset. If DTR plus ACT exceeded the corporation tax liability, the ACT was unrelieved. Like other unrelieved ACT, this could be carried back for up to six years and carried forward indefinitely.

Timing of ACT payments and offset

Advance Corporation Tax was payable within fourteen days of the end of the quarter in which the distribution was made, and offset against the Corporation Tax liability for the company's accounting period in which the dividend was distributed. This liability was due nine months after the end of the company's accounting period (it no longer is as regards large companies).

The present position

ACT has been abolished as regards dividends paid on or after 6 April 1999. But s. 32 Finance Act 1998 and a very complex statutory instrument, Corporation Tax (Treatment of Surplus Advanced Corporation Tax) Regulations 1999, enable unrelieved ACT that a company has at 6 April 1999 to be set off against its liability to corporation tax on profits charged to corporation tax for an accounting period beginning on or after that date. This 'shadow ACT' is subject to the existing 20% maximum set-off (see page 140).

As explained earlier, although ACT could be carried forward indefinitely, SSAP 8 regarded it as *irrecoverable* if its recoverability is not 'reasonably certain and foreseeable'; and the carry-forward then should normally not extend beyond the next accounting period. Because of this it may be difficult to discover from the accounts just how much shadow ACT will be available to a company. A few companies actually disclose this, e.g. ELECO HOLDINGS (in the next column); and others refer to the matter in their operating and financial review, as BENSONS CRISPS does (page 142)..

ELECO HOLDINGS *Extract from note 11 to the 1998 accounts*

...

The Group has tax losses to carry forward against future profits of certain continuing operations of approximately £3,300,000. The total amount of surplus ACT carried forward is £441,000 (1997: £417,000).

Once the ACT in respect of dividends paid in the accounting period spanning 6 April 1999 has been recovered (normally against Corporation Tax due in respect of the first period post 5 April 1999, most companies are likely to have little surplus ACT.

Those that will have surplus ACT are those which, like ELECO HOLDINGS. have made losses over recent periods, have relied unduly upon overseas earnings to pay dividends, or have simply paid 'excessive' dividends. Such companies will display an abnormally low effective rate of Corporation Tax, possibly for a number of years.

EFFECTIVE RATE OF TAX

It is instructive to compute the ratio of Taxation/Profits before tax. Because tax has such a major influence on earnings (and hence earnings per share) be on the look out for (a) anomalies and (b) significant changes from year to year.

Para. 23 of FRS 3 requires that where any special circumstances affect the overall tax charge or credit for the period, or may affect those of future periods, they should be disclosed by way of note to the profit and loss account and their individual effects quantified. Such disclosures should include any special circumstances affecting the tax attributable to exceptional items.

Where a group prepares a financial review, the rate of tax is often one item focused on. As will be seen, the rate may be very high, and suggest that worse is to come (e.g. AMERSHAM INTERNATIONAL):

AMERSHAM INTERNATIONAL *Extract from finance director's review 1997*

Effective rate of taxation

The effective rate of taxation is 40.6 per cent of profit before tax compared with 35.6 per cent in the previous year. The increase reflects a higher proportion of profits coming from high tax territories, notably Japan, offset by benefits of £1.8m from adjustments in respect of prior years. The effective rate in the second half following completion of the NMP transaction is 40.9 per cent compared with 40.1 per cent in the first half of the year.

In the absence of any major changes in the tax regimes or tax rates applicable to the Group's operations we expect the effective rate of tax to increase to 43 per cent in the year ending 31 March 1998.

Or the effective tax rate may be very low, include exceptional items and refer to FIDs (since abolished) as is the case with BRENT INTERNATIONAL:

BRENT INTERNATIONAL *Extract from operating and financial review 1997*

The effective tax rate for 1997 was 24% of pre-tax profits. This low level resulted from the UK tax effect of an exchange loss on inter-group loans used to finance subsidiaries. This reduced the 1997 tax charge by £0.8m.

The tax rate for 1997 is made up as follows:

Underlying corporation tax	32.2
Exchange losses	(9.1)
Other	0.1
	24.2

For the medium term we expect our tax charge to be in the region of 30–33%, provided the Group structure and corporation tax rates remain unchanged.

In the past the Group has had to write off significant amounts of advance corporation tax. With the abolition of advance corporation tax in 1999, in future years it may be possible to reduce the tax charge as these amounts become recoverable.

The final dividend for 1997 will be paid as a foreign income dividend. This will enhance shareholder value by accelerating the recovery of advance corporation tax previously written off by the Group, with consequent cost savings and cash flow benefits. However, shareholders who are exempt from UK tax on their investment income, or who hold shares in a personal equity plan, will not be able to reclaim a tax credit. Notes on the tax treatment of a foreign income dividend are given for shareholders' guidance on page ...

It may be different from the previous year and give an indication of future tax levels as is the case with BENSONS CRISPS:

BENSONS CRISPS *Extract from operating and financial review 1997*

The Group will now recommence taxation payments following the utilisation of tax losses brought forward, leading to an effective tax rate of 7% for the year. The Group is now also able to start to recover ACT arising from the return to the dividend list last year. Despite the substantial lift in dividend payments this year, the Group has retained a prudent dividend cover of 3 times earnings.

An indication may be given in the operating and/or financial review of areas of dispute and hence of *potential* tax problems.

GLAXO WELLCOME *Extract from half-year financial review 1998*

Taxation

...

The Group has significant open taxation issues relating to inter-company transfer pricing in the UK and the USA. Despite protracted negotiations, there continues to be a wide variation between the claims of the revenue authorities and the Group's estimation of its taxation liabilities. The Group continues to believe it has made adequate provision for all liabilities likely to arise from open taxation assessments.

Warning had in fact been sounded by the press releases issued as background to the 1997 Budget:. 'Transfer prices' are the prices at which associated enterprises transfer goods, services and other assets between one another. The UK's transfer pricing legislation was, by current international standards, very unusual in that it only applied when the Board of Inland Revenue directed that it should.

The effect of this was that taxpayers were not obliged to apply an arm's length standard to pricing when submitting their tax returns. The system depended upon the Inland Revenue detecting inap-

propriate transfer pricing and intervening to set things right. In the increasingly global economy, this left the UK tax base vulnerable to unacceptable risks. It also created potential unfairness as between taxpayers who took care to set their prices on the arm's length basis and those who did not.

A new requirement to apply the arm's length principle in calculating taxable profits is in line with best business practice and consistent with transfer pricing guidelines published by the Organisation for Economic Co-operation and Development (OECD).

Introduced by the Finance Act 1998, the changes form part of a wider reform of the Corporation Tax regime which included the introduction of self assessment for companies (CTSA). For accounting periods ending on or after 1 July 1999 and years of assessment 1999/2000 onwards self assessment is the rule; and penalties apply in respect of 'transgressions', including improper transfer pricing. It seems likely therefore that GLAXO WELLCOME will not be alone in facing transfer pricing problems.

Where there is no financial review, some light may be thrown on an unusually low or high rate of tax by the note on taxation itself (see, for example, HOGG ROBINSON on page 131).

To sum up: whatever the cause of abnormality in the tax charge, it should be of interest to the analyst, because the effective rate of tax has a direct effect on profit after tax, and hence upon earnings per share, cover and the price earnings ratio – matters which we discuss in Chapter 18.

Problem 17.1

Examining the report and accounts of a group, you find that the effective rate of tax (i.e. taxation as a percentage of pre-tax profits) is:

(a) much less, or
(b) much greater,

than the normal rate of UK corporation tax.

Suggest in each case why this might be so. Where would you look for further information? Why is this important?

Chapter 18

PROFIT ATTRIBUTABLE TO ORDINARY SHAREHOLDERS, DIVIDENDS AND EARNINGS PER SHARE

 Profit attributable to ordinary shareholders

In general, it is the ordinary shareholders who take the ultimate risk and who, after others (like preference shareholders) have taken their share of the profits after tax, depend upon the balance, termed the profit attributable to ordinary shareholders:

- for payment of their dividend; and
- for the future 'growth' of the company.

Profit attributable to ordinary shareholders (sometimes called 'profit attributable to the company' or 'earnings after exceptional items') is a thus a vitally important figure both to ordinary shareholders and to analysts. Surprisingly, it does not usually appear in the profit and loss account; but it can always be found in the note on earnings per share; of which, as we explain later, it forms one vital component.

Profit attributable to the ordinary shareholders is the profit after tax and all other charges (including exceptional items, any preference dividends and, in the case of a company with subsidiaries, any minority interests) have been deducted.

Minority interests: As explained in detail in Chapter 20, minority interests occur when a group has one or more subsidiaries, the shares in which are only partially owned by the group. Where the other ('minority') shareholders in the 'partially owned' subsidiary are equity shareholders they are entitled to a share in the profit or loss of that subsidiary; their share, called 'equity minority interests', has to be deducted in arriving at the profit attributable to the group's shareholders; so have the dividends attaching to any 'non-equity minority interests'.

Preference dividends, like ordinary dividends, are paid net and, in the case of individual shareholders, carry an associated tax credit (see page 133). When the imputation system of taxation was introduced the basic rate of Income Tax was set at 30% and the coupons (the rates of dividend) on all UK preference shares were adjusted by statute to 70% of their former value on a once-and-for-all basis.

Thus, for example, a 5% £1 preference share became a 3½% £1 preference share, receiving a dividend fixed at 3½p, plus an associated tax credit originally dependent on the rate of ACT at the time of payment of the dividend. In 1999, as a result of the Finance Act 1998, they reverted to 5%.

Preference dividends and any arrears of cumulative preference dividends have to be met before any ordinary dividends can be declared.

Where there are preference shares, it is necessary in computing the profits attributable to ordinary shareholders to deduct:

(a) the amount of any preference dividends on noncumulative preference shares declared in respect of the period; and

(b) the full amount of the required preference dividends for cumulative preference shares for the period, whether or not the dividends have been declared. The amount of preference dividends for the period does not include the amount of any preference dividends for cumulative preference shares paid or declared during the current period in respect of previous periods.

See page 145 for more about preference dividends.

DIVIDENDS

Distribution of dividends

In deciding what profits to distribute the directors of a company should have in mind:

(a) the company's cash position (considered in Chapter 19);
(b) what is prudent;
(c) what is legally permissible.

Ideally, directors should choose the lowest of these three figures.

What is prudent

In deciding what would be prudent, directors should weigh up the cost of raising capital in various ways. Is it, for instance, better to borrow (i.e. increase the gearing) rather than ask equity shareholders to contribute more towards the net assets of the company? And, if equity shareholders are to be called upon to provide more, should they be asked to do so by means of a rights issue, in which case each shareholder has the choice of whether to take up, or sell, his rights; or should profits be 're-tained', in which case the individual shareholder has no choice?

Unfortunately, the picture is confused by inflation and the present, historical cost, method of accounting. With no inflation (or an inflation accounting system recognised for tax purposes) a company would, in theory, be able to distribute its earnings and still maintain its assets in real terms. With inflation most companies need to retain a proportion of their earnings as calculated by historical cost accounting in order to maintain their assets in real terms (but more of that in Chapter 29).

Having decided how much it is necessary to retain in order to continue the existing scale of operations, and how much should be retained out of profits in order to expand the scale of operations, the directors should look at what remains.

Ideally, a company should pay a regular, but somewhat increasing, dividend. For example, from a market point of view, it is preferable to pay: 8.0p; 9.0p; 9.0p; 9.0p; 9.5p; 10.0p; rather than 8.0p; 12.0p; 10.5p; 4.0p; 10.0p; 10.0p – though both represent the same total sum in dividends over the six years – because investors who need steady income will avoid companies which are erratic dividend payers, and because a cut in dividend undermines confidence in the company's future. In other words, the directors of a company should think twice before paying a dividend this year which they may not be able to maintain, or setting a pattern of growth in the rate of dividend which could not reasonably be continued for the foreseeable future. For if they do either of these things, they are liable to disappoint shareholder expectations, to damage their market rating and to see their share price slashed if their dividend has to be cut or the rate of dividend growth cannot be sustained.

What is legally permissible

Prior to the Companies Act 1980 companies could, in general, distribute profits arising in an accounting period without making good previous revenue or capital losses, and could also distribute unrealised surpluses on asset revaluations.

Companies are now allowed to distribute only the aggregate of accumulated realised profits not previously distributed or capitalised less accumulated realised losses not previously written off in a reduction or reorganisation of capital (CA 1985, s. 263). The word 'realised' is not defined in the Act, but SSAP 2 says that profits should be included in the profit and loss account 'only when realised in the form of cash or of other assets the ultimate cash realisation of which can be assessed with reasonable certainty'.

In addition, a public company may pay a dividend only if the net assets of the company after payment of the dividend are not less than the aggregate of its called-up share capital and undistributable reserves (s. 264 (1)). Undistributable reserves are defined in Section 264 (3) as:

(a) share premium account;
(b) capital redemption reserve;
(c) accumulated unrealised profits not capitalised less accumulated unrealised losses not previously written off in a capital reduction or reorganisation;
(d) any reserve which the company's Memorandum or Articles prohibit being distributed.

This requirement reflects the 'capital maintenance' principle of the EEC Second Directive and means that public companies now have to cover net losses (whether realised or not) from realised profits before paying a dividend.

Where the company's audit report has been qualified, the auditor must provide a statement in writing as to whether the qualification is material in deciding whether the distribution would be a breach of the Act, before any distribution can be made.

Investment companies (a class of company created by the Companies Act 1980 and defined in Section 266 of the Companies Act 1985 as a UK listed company investing mainly in securities with the aim of spreading investment risk and obtaining the benefit of specialist management and which has given notice to the Registrar of Companies) have the option of paying dividends either on the basis of the capital maintenance section (s. 264) or on an asset ratio test (s. 265). This test requires the investment company's assets after the distribution to equal not less than one and a half times its aggregate liabilities.

Preference dividends

As explained on page 143:

- preference shares carry a fixed rate of dividend, normally payable half-yearly;
- preference shareholders have no legal redress if the board of directors decides to recommend that no preference dividends should be paid;
- if no preference dividend is declared for an accounting period, no dividend can be declared on any other type of share for the period concerned, and the preference shareholders usually become entitled to vote at shareholders' general meetings;
- if the dividend on a cumulative preference share is not paid on time, payment is postponed rather than omitted and the preference dividend is said to be 'in arrears', and these arrears have to be paid before any other dividend can be declared. Arrears of cumulative preference dividends must be shown in a note to the accounts.

Company articles on dividend distribution

Most companies lay down their own rules for dividend distribution in their Articles by adopting Articles 114 to 116 of Table A (the model set of Company Articles given in the First Schedule to the Companies Act 1948). These Articles say:

114. The company in general meeting may declare dividends, but no dividend shall exceed the amount recommended by the directors.
115. The directors may from time to time pay to the members such interim dividends as appear to the directors to be justified by the profits of the company.
116. No dividend shall be paid otherwise than out of profits.

Accounting treatment

Under UK practice, any dividends the directors *recommend* should be shown:

(a) in the profit and loss account, together with any interim dividend already paid (CA 1985, Sch. 4, para. 51 (3));
(b) in the balance sheet as a liability.

In many other countries, including the USA, dividends only appear in the accounts when *approved* by the shareholders.

Dividends *paid* during the accounting period appear in a separate section of the cash flow statement.

Interim dividends

Interim dividends can be declared by the directors without reference to the shareholders, but by convention they do not normally exceed half the anticipated total for the year.

However, if the latest audited accounts disclose a 'non-distributable' position or if the level of accumulated profits has fallen significantly, interim accounts must be prepared to justify the payment of an interim dividend (CA 1985, s. 272).

Interim dividends appear in the profit and loss account as a distribution, and either in the balance sheet as a liability if the company has not paid the interim dividend by the end of the accounting period or in the cash flow statement as a payment.

Foreign income dividends

Foreign income dividends (FIDs) were introduced in the Finance Act 1994 to help companies with Advance Corporation Tax (ACT) problems due to a high proportion of their profits arising overseas. Under the Finance Act 1994, companies could pay FIDs out of foreign earnings that had borne foreign tax. ACT was still payable, but could be reclaimed by the company. Although FIDs did not carry a tax credit, there was no tax liability for standard and lower rate taxpayers, but nil taxpayers, e.g. pension funds, could not claim any refund.

Since 6 April 1999, FIDs are no longer permitted. A number of companies brought their 1998 dividend forward to take advantage of a FID.

GROWTH

⚿ Growth sustains equity prices

Prior to the Second World War, the prudent investor tended to choose gilt edged or other fixed interest securities. Equities were seen as risk investments. That changed shortly after the war with the coming of inflation. It became apparent that the income from, and the capital value of, fixed interest stocks tended to fall in terms of purchasing power as time went by.

Equities, because they were asset-backed, and because profits (and dividends) tended to be sustained in real terms, were seen as 'a hedge against inflation'. As a consequence a 'reverse yield gap' developed. Instead of equities yielding more than gilt edged (to recognise the increased risk) they began to yield less (in anticipation that they would protect against the effect of inflation).

Leading equities tend to be on a low yield because they are expected to show growth *in real terms*. When they fail to live up to expectations, their share price crashes. The remainder of this chapter, and much of the rest of the book, is concerned with how one measures growth.

Wonder growth by acquisition

There is nothing fundamentally wrong with improving a company's earnings per share by acquisition, and it can be beneficial all round if there is some industrial or commercial logic involved, i.e. if the acquired company's business fits in with the acquiring company's existing activities or employs common skills and technology, or if the acquirer can provide improved management and financial resources. However, the practice was open to abuse, especially in bull markets.

Enter the 'whiz-kid' (known as a 'gunslinger' on the other side of the Atlantic), who might proceed as follows:

1. Acquire control of a company that has a listing on The Stock Exchange, but little else, e.g. the DEMISED TEA COMPANY, known in the jargon as a 'shell'.
2. Reverse the shell into an unlisted company, thus giving his victim the benefit of a ready market for his shares and himself the benefit of a company with real assets.
3. Sell off some of the assets, particularly property that is ripe for development. He doesn't lose any sleep over the fact that closing a factory throws 200 people out of work, as the office block that will replace it will house twice that number of civil servants in the department recently set up to encourage investment in industry; this 'asset-stripping' process is essential to provide the cash to gain control of his next victim.
4. By now the earnings per share of the Demised Tea Company, since renamed ANGLO-TRIUMPH ASSETS, have shown remarkable growth, albeit from a very low base (it's very easy to double profits of next-to-nothing), the bull market has conveniently started and the Press has noticed him.

He projects a suitable image of dynamic young management, talking to them earnestly about the need for British industry to obtain a fair return on assets, and his photograph appears in the financial sections of the Sunday papers. The 'whiz-kid' has arrived.
5. His share price responds to Press comment, putting his 'go-go' company on a PER of 15 or 20; he continues to acquire companies, but now uses shares rather than cash, thus continually boosting his e.p.s., as we have shown.
6. Following Press adulation, he broadens out into TV financial panels, seminar platforms, and after-dinner speeches; the bull market is now raging. Anglo-Triumph features regularly as an 'up stock' in the price changes table in the FT as the PER climbs towards 30. Deals follow apace, and Anglo-Triumph thrusts ahead, acquiring a huge conglomeration of businesses in an ever-widening range of mainly unrelated activities – it may be shoes, or ships or sealing-wax, but it's certainly Alice in Wonderland.
7. The moment of truth. The bull market, after a final glorious wave of euphoria, tops out. Profits in Anglo-Triumph's businesses turn down as little or nothing has been done to improve their management. Asset-stripping becomes politically unacceptable, and the word 'conglomerate' is coined to describe hotch potch outfits like Anglo-Triumph.

Down goes Anglo-Triumph's share price, and with it the market rating; without a high price earnings ratio the company can no longer boost profits by acquisition, and the game is up.

Whether the whole edifice of Anglo-Triumph collapses completely or it becomes just another lowly rated ex-glamour stock depends on the financial structure of the company. If it has geared up (i.e. has built up debt, on which interest has to be paid), and hasn't the cash to service the debt, the company will probably be forced into liquidation unless some sympathetic banker (possibly embarrassed by the prospect of disclosing a huge loss if the company goes under) decides to tide things over until 'hopefully' better times.

Two things, both of which are required by FRS 3, do much to prevent this happening today.

They are:

(i) the publication of earnings per share; and
(ii) the subdivision of results down to operating profit level into continuing operations, acquisitions and discontinued operations (see page 123, and Chapter 19), both of which have made this sort of behaviour much more transparent.

EARNINGS PER SHARE (E.P.S.)

 Earnings per share (e.p.s.)

Earnings per share (e.p.s.) are a key measure of a company's profitability; they are one measure of its ability to pay dividends; and probably the best single measure of 'growth'.

SSAP 3 *Earnings per share*, issued in February 1972, called for companies to show in their profit and loss account their earnings per share (e.p.s.). It laid down detailed rules for the computation of e.p.s., particularly as regards changes in capital structure, and the way earnings per share for previous periods were to be adjusted when shown as comparative figures or in a historical summary. We explain these rules on pages 124–5.

Basic earnings per share are a much better indicator of a company's actual past performance than profits, which as we have seen can be boosted by acquisitions paid for by an issue of shares or out of the proceeds of a rights issue.

Basic earnings per share =

$$\frac{\text{Profit attributable to ordinary shareholders}}{\text{Weighted average number of ordinary shares in issue}}$$

In addition to basic earnings per share, SSAP 3 required companies in certain circumstances to publish also what were termed *fully diluted earnings per share*. In October 1998 the ASB published FRS 14 *Earnings per share* which supersedes SSAP 3 and is standard as regards periods ending on or after 23 December 1998. Amongst other things: the word 'fully' has been dropped and reference is now to 'diluted earnings per share'; and the rules, to cater for instruments developed in recent years, have become somewhat more complex.

Earnings per share in practice

Companies are free, as we explain later, subject to rules laid down in FRS 3 *Reporting financial performance*, to show their own figures for earnings and earnings per share as well as the basic earnings per share required by FRS 3.

As we said earlier, the profit attributable to ordinary shareholders often is not shown on the face of the profit and loss account, but it can always be identified, though as we shall see sometimes with a certain amount of difficulty, in the note on earnings per share. And companies do not always clearly distinguish basic, FRS 3, earnings per share from their own preferred version. Take, for instance, THE RANK GROUP (on page 148). The profit and loss account shows three figures of earnings per share 1998: 26.5p marked [C], (5.3)p marked [D] and 21.2p marked [E]. The basic earnings per share were 21.2p [E]. They represent actual performance, i.e. how much per share was actually available from 1998 earnings to pay ordinary dividends and provide ploughed back profits. Had the group not incurred exceptional items of (5.3)p per share [D] it would have had 26.5p [C] to pay ordinary dividends and provide ploughed back profits. Note 8 explains the calculations.

THE RANK GROUP *How the calculations work using note 8 (see page 148)*	1997 £m	1996 £m
Net profit for the year before exceptional items	236	222
is termed in the profit and loss account:		
Profit (loss) for the financial year [B]		
This is the profit after tax and after minority interests [A] shown in note 23. The second line of note 8:		
Less: Preference dividends [H]	(20)	(21)
[H] consists not simply of the dividends [F] but also provision for the redemption premium [G].		
Earnings before exceptional items	216	201
is the sub-total from which are deducted:		
Exceptional items after tax	(43)	(256)
column [I] in the profit and loss account to leave:		
Earnings (loss) after exceptional items [J]	173	(55)
which is the profit attributable to ordinary shareholders; and it is this which is divided by: Weighted average number of		
Ordinary shares [K]	814.3m	834.9m
to give the basic earnings per share on an FRS 3 basis,		
Earnings (loss) per share [C]	21.2p	(6.6)p

THE RANK GROUP *Group profit and loss account 1997*

Group Profit and Loss Account for the year ended 31 December 1997

		1997			1996		
		Before exceptional items	Exceptional items	Total	Before exceptional items	Exceptional items	Total
	Note	£m	£m	£m	£m	£m	£m
Profit on ordinary activities before tax		303	(43)	260	297	(232)	65
Tax on profit on ordinary activities	...	(64)	–	(64)	(72)	(24)	(96)
Profit (loss) on ordinary activities after tax		239	(43) [I]	196	225	(256)	(31)
Minority interests (including non-equity interests) [A]	23	(3)	–	(3)	(3)	–	(3)
Profit (loss) for the financial year [B]		236	(43)	193	222	(256)	(34)
Dividends and other appropriations							
Preference	7	(20)	–	(20)	(21)	–	(21)
Ordinary	7	(137)	–	(137)	(142)	–	(142)
Transfer to (from) reserves	22	79	(43)	36	59	(256)	(197)
Earnings (loss) per Ordinary share	8	26.5p [C]	(5.3)p [D]	21.2p [E]	24.1 p	(30.7)p	(6.6)p

---

THE RANK GROUP *Extracts from notes to the 1997 accounts*

7. Dividends

	1997 £m	1996 £m
Convertible Redeemable Preference shares		
Dividends payable for the period [F]	18	19
Provision for redemption premium [G]	2	2
	[H]20	21

...

8. Earnings per Ordinary share

	1997	1996
Net profit for the year before exceptional items [B]	236	222
Less: Preference dividends [H]	(20)	(21)
Earnings before exceptional items	216	201
Exceptional items after tax	(43)	(256)
Earnings (loss) after exceptional items [J]	173	(55)
Weighted average number of Ordinary shares [K]	814.3m	834.9m
Earnings per share before exceptional items [E]	26.5p	24. 1p
Earnings (loss) per share [C]	21.2p	(6.6)p

(a) Earnings per share before exceptional items has been calculated to show the impact of exceptional items as these can have a distorting effect on earnings and therefore warrant separate consideration [D].

(b) The earnings per share would not be materially lower if calculated on a fully diluted basis.

23 Analysis of minority interests [A]

	Equity £m	Non-equity £m	Total £m
Balances at 31 December 1996	1	25	26
Minority interest in the profit on ordinary activities after tax	1	2	3
Dividends payable to minority shareholders	–	(2)	(2)
Balances at 31 December 1997	2	25	27

The non-equity minority shareholders have no rights against Group companies other than the issuing entity, except in the event that the issuer defaults. In such circumstances, a put option exists to require the Company to purchase the shares at par.

Going for growth ...

In the 4th edition of this book we gave an interesting example of a company whose pre-tax profits had *grown* by 41.9% p.a. between 1984 and 1988, but whose e.p.s. had *fallen* by 8.3% p.a. The company was MAXWELL COMMUNICATION CORPORATION, and we said: 'chairman Robert Maxwell's stated goal was to become "a global information and communications corporation before the end of the decade with annual revenues of £3–5 billion, with profits growth to match." Maxwell's sales in the period had grown from £266.5m to over £1bn, at an annual rate of 42.9% with profits growth almost to match, but this was achieved by the profligate use of paper, and earnings per share suffered accordingly.'

As subsequent events confirmed, companies which go for growth regardless of e.p.s. are best avoided. But the fact that an acquisition for paper makes e.p.s. grow at a slower rate than profits does not necessarily mean that acquisitions for paper are bad for e.p.s. It all depends on whether the e.p.s. are higher with the acquisition than they would have been without it (as they are in Example 18.1).

The effect of acquisitions on earnings per share

Buying earnings cheaply enables a company to boost its e.p.s. when its own earnings are static, or even falling. Suppose in Example 18.1 that the attributable profits of the company were expected to fall the following year to £912,000, despite the recently acquired business performing satisfactorily. The company finds another victim (Example 18.2).

'But,' you may say, 'how did the company in Example 18.2 manage to get the shareholders of the second acquisition to accept 2.4 million shares for attributable earnings of £468,000, which is 19.5p per share, far higher than the e.p.s. of the acquiring company?' And well may you ask – the secret is in 'market rating'.

Example 18.1 Acquisition for paper

	Existing company	*Acquisition*	*Company post-acquisition*
Attributable profit	800,000	200,000	1,000,000
Issued equity (shares)	8,000,000		
Vendor consideration (shares)		1,600,000	
Resulting equity (shares)			9,600,000
e.p.s.	10.0p		10.4p

In this case 1.6m shares are issued for a company bringing in £200,000 at the attributable profit level, or 12.5p for each new share, which is higher than the e.p.s. of the existing company, so the e.p.s. of the company, post-acquisition, are improved. Had the acquiring company paid more than 2m shares for the acquisition, its earnings per share would have fallen.

Example 18.2 Further acquisition

	Present company	*Second acquisition*	*Resulting company*
Attributable profits (£)	912,000	468,000	1,380,000
Issued equity (shares)	9,600,000		
Vendor consideration (shares)		2,400,000	
Resulting equity (shares)			12,000,000
e.p.s.	9.5p		11.5p

Market rating – the PER

The measure of a company's market rating is its Price earnings ratio (P/E ratio, PE ratio or PER):

$$\text{Price earnings ratio} = \frac{\text{Market price per ordinary share}}{\text{Basic earnings per share}}$$

It is normal to take the previous day's middle market price of the ordinary share divided by the earnings per share. Analysts and newspapers often take not the basic earnings per share but normalised e.p.s. (see below), so watch with care.

The PER one can expect depends mainly on four things:

- the overall level of the stock market;
- the industry in which the company operates;
- the company's record; and
- the markets' view of the company's prospects.

In an average market the PER of the average company in an average sector might be around 12, with high-quality 'blue chips' like BOOTS or MARKS & SPENCER standing on a PER of around 15 and small glamour growth stocks on 20 or more, while companies in an unfashionable sector might be on a multiple of only 8.

We say more about PERs in the section 'Investment ratios' on page 161.

Other measure of earnings

Before ACT was abolished in 1999 it was common to see other earnings figures:

1. **Nil earnings** were the after-tax earnings that a company would have reported, assuming it paid no dividends.
2. **Net earnings** were the same as nil earnings unless the dividend distribution the company made increased the company's overall tax liability.
3. **Full distribution earnings** were the earnings that would be attributable to ordinary shareholders if all earnings were distributed as dividends; they were expressed at the gross level, i.e. including tax credit.

Under the present tax regime none of these is relevant.

Normalised and company earnings

FRS 3 *Reporting financial performance,* as explained in Chapter 16, requires companies to include all exceptional items, and any extraordinary items, in their reported earnings. But FRS 3 allows companies to show their own figures for earnings and earnings per share as well as the FRS 3 figures, providing any additional earnings per share figures are calculated and presented on a consistent basis over time and reconciled to the amount required by the FRS. The reconciliation must list the

items for which an adjustment is being made and disclose their individual effect on the calculation. The earnings per share required by the FRS should be at least as prominent as any additional version presented and the reason for calculating the additional version should be explained.

Many companies do provide additional e.p.s. numbers; though there is no universal view as to the basis of such a number.

A few companies do show on the face of the P & L account basic e.p.s. and diluted e.p.s. (see page 154) computed on an FRS 3 and FRS 14 basis and on an IIMR basis; as SEC GROUP does:

SEC GROUP *Extract from consolidated profit and loss account to 30 September 1998*

		1998	1997
(Loss)/earnings per share		(4.41)p	12.79p
Fully diluted (loss)/earnings per share	11	(2.41)p	12.72p
Earnings per share (IIMR basis)		4.08p	12.79p
Fully diluted earnings per share (IIMR basis)		4.98p	12.72p

Note 11 is shown in another context on page 158.

Most, like THE RANK GROUP on pages 147-8, seem to ignore the IIMR, and to prefer their own version.

As FRS 3 makes clear, basic earnings per share are only a starting point. No one number can encapsulate everything about a company's performance. It is up to the analyst to decide which, if any, of these bases provides the best view of normal earnings; or whether to make his own adjustments in calculating 'normalised' earnings. But the current position in which the scorer (accountant/auditor) adopts one set of rules (basic earnings), the commentator (analyst) another (IIMR or normalised), and the players (management) choose for themselves (company's own figures), is scarcely satisfactory.

Investigating trends

It is frequently a worthwhile exercise to set alongside one another, growth in:

(a) turnover;
(b) profit before tax;
(c) earnings per share;
(d) dividend per share.

If they are wildly different, the cause should be investigated. In the sixth edition we looked at MITIE GROUP, a relatively small cleaning and maintenance contractor, saying that it was 'taking advantage of the trend towards out-sourcing such services' while at the same time expanding by making a series of small acquisitions.

MITIE GROUP *Group statistical record 1995 and 1998 (extracts)*

	1998 £000	1997 £000	1996 £000	1995 £000	1994 £000	1993 £000	1992 £000	1991 £000	1990 £000
Turnover	236,293	209,425	161,149	125,183	101,732	72,994	52,276	32,699	15,594
Profit on ordinary activities before taxation	11,100	8,210	6,302	4,571	3,361	2,402	1,808	1,231	649
Earnings per share	10.3p	8.1p	6.5p	4.9p	3.4p	3.4p	3.0p	2.8p	2.37p
Dividend per share	2.5p	2.0p	1.6p	1.2p	0.9p	0.9p	0.7p	0.5p	0.25p

Earnings and Dividend per share figures have been re-stated to reflect the sub-division of shares in 1994 and 1997. The results of merger accounted acquisitions are reflected in full in the year of acquisition and subsequent years but only the year prior to acquisition has been re-stated on a comparable basis.

We have adjusted the figures for 1990–1995 so that all are on the same basis – which has no effect on the ratios which are shown in Example 18.3.

As we said in the sixth edition, growth in 1990–1995 had been spectacular:

- turnover was up almost 703% in 5 years;
- profits had almost, but not quite, kept pace (up 604%); but
- because of acquisitions for paper, e.p.s had grown only 165%;
- from a very low base (and covered nine times) dividends had increased 500%;

so shareholders certainly did not complain.

We decided to follow up the story in 1998, looking at 1995–98. As will be seen from Example 18.3, the very rapid growth in turnover has been replaced by more moderate growth (up 89% in 3 years). But there has been a consolidation: profitability before tax up 143%.

Changes in the tax system had meant that the effective rate of tax fell from 33.49% (tax of £1.531m in 1995 on profits before interest and tax (PBIT) of £4.571m) to 30.80% (tax of £3.419m in 1998 on PBIT of £11.100m) i.e. by 8.7%, not shown above. There was a much greater dependence on partly owned subsidiaries: minorities as a percentage of equity shareholders' funds increased from 5.4% in 1995 to 22.0%, not shown above.

Earnings rose 110% (not quite as fast as profits before tax) and dividends kept pace (up 108%). Cover (see page 162) remained high (at about 4 times) enabling most acquisitions to be for cash. For the ninth year in succession growth in profits exceeded 30%.

The point we are making is that, however spectacular a company's growth is, the pattern (the ratios) tend to change as it matures:

Example 18.3 MITIE GROUP *Growth statistics*

	Increase 1990–95	Increase 1995–98
Turnover	7.03	0.89
Profit on ordinary activities before taxation	6.04	1.43
Earnings per share	1.65	1.10
Dividend per share	5.00	1.08

ADJUSTMENTS TO BASIC EARNINGS PER SHARE

When the number of shares in issue changes

If a company issues new ordinary shares (or redeems ordinary shares) during the year, the basic e.p.s. for that year have to be calculated using the time-weighted average number of shares in issue during the year, and those of previous years have to be adjusted to allow for any bonus element in the share issue.

FRS 14 *Earnings per share* (which superseded SSAP 3) describes in detail the method of adjustment to be used by companies for each type of issue:

1. Share split

Use the year-end figure for number of shares, and apply a factor to previous years' e.p.s. to put them on a comparable basis. For a split of 1 old share into z new shares it is $1/z$.

Example 18.4 Effect of share split on e.p.s.

On 31 March 1999 MITIE GROUP had an issued share capital of 66,428,155 ordinary shares of 10p each. If each 10p share is split into two ordinary shares of 5p each, making the issued share capital 132,856,310 shares of 5p, the factor to be applied to previous years' earnings will be ½.

2. Scrip (Bonus or Capitalisation) issue

Use the year-end figure for number of shares, and apply a factor to previous years' e.p.s. to put them on a comparable basis. For a scrip issue of y shares for every x shares held, the factor is $x \div (x + y)$.

Example 18.5 Effect of scrip issue on e.p.s.

Let us suppose that UNIVERSAL plc is a company whose year ends on 31 December. At the end of 1999 the issued share capital was £4.0m, of which £1m was in 3½% preference shares and £3m was the equity share capital of 12m ordinary shares of 25p each. No new shares were issued in 2000. Profits after tax and minority interests were £995,000. So the attributable profits reported in 2000 would be:

£995,000 – £35,000 = £960,000 and the e.p.s.: £960,000 ÷ 12m = 8.00p. No adjustments would be required to previous years' e.p.s.

In 2001 the company made a 1-for-3 scrip issue and profits after tax and minority interests increased from £0.995m to £1.235m.

Attributable to ordinary would be:

£1.235m – £35,000 = £1.200m and

earnings per share for 2001 would £1.200m ÷ 16m = 7.5p which, at first sight, appear to be down on the previous year, but 2000's figure of 8p has to be adjusted by a factor of $3 \div (3 + 1)$ to make it comparable with 2001: ¾ of 8p = 6p.

---

3. Shares issued in an acquisition

Shares issued in an acquisition are assumed to have been issued at market price (even if the shares issued, the 'vendor consideration', were placed at a discount at that time). The weighted average number of shares in issue during the year is calculated and used for working out the e.p.s.:

Example 18.6 Effect of acquisition issue on e.p.s.

On 1 April 2002 Universal had in issue 16m ordinary shares of 25p each. That day it acquired another company and issued 2m new fully paid 25p ordinary shares in payment (an acquisition 'for paper').

At the year end, the profits of the new subsidiary for the period 1 April to 31 December 2002 were included in Universal's consolidated profit and loss account and the weighted average number of shares in issue during the year was calculated:

$$\frac{(16m \times 3) + (18m \times 9)}{12} = 17.5m$$

If profits at the attributable level were £1.4m that would give earnings per share for 2002 of:

£1.4m ÷ 17.5m = 8.0p.

There would be no adjustment to the e.p.s. of earlier periods.

---

4. Rights issue

A rights issue is regarded as being partly an issue at the market price and partly a scrip issue (the bonus element); the e.p.s. of previous years are adjusted by the factor appropriate to the bonus element in the same way as a scrip issue (Example 18.7).

Example 18.7 Effect of rights issue on first day of company's year on e.p.s.

Let us suppose Universal, which had in issue 18m ordinary shares of 25p each on 1 January 2003, made a rights issue on the basis of one new share for every 4 shares held at a price of 80p per share, against a market price of 100p on the last day the old shares were quoted cum-rights. The number of shares in issue would become 22.5m and the issue would have the same effect as a 1-for-5 at 100p, followed by a 1-for-24 scrip issue. The factor for adjusting the e.p.s. for previous years is thus $24/(1 + 24)$, which can be calculated in more complicated cases using the formula:

Theoretical ex-rights (xr) price ÷ actual cum-rights price on the last day of quotation cum-rights

where the Theoretical xr price is, in this case, 1 share at 80p plus 4 old shares at 100p each = 5 shares for 480p = 96p, and 96/100 = 24/25.

On the basis that the e.p.s. reported previously were:

2000	6.0p
2001	7.5p
2002	8.0p

comparative figures for earnings for earlier years would be:

2000	5.76p
2001	7.20p
2002	7.68p

If the profits attributable to ordinary were £1.710m in 2003, the e.p.s. for that year would be: £1.710 ÷ 22.5m = 7.6p.

If, instead of being made on the first day of the company's year (as in Example 18.7), a rights issue is made during the company's year, the calculation of the bonus element and the factor for adjusting previous years' e.p.s. is just the same but, in addition, the weighted average number of shares in issue during the year has to be calculated (see Example 18.8).

Example 18.8 Rights issue (during company's year)

If Universal (see Example 18.7) had made its 1-for-4 rights issue on 1 September 2003, then the number of shares at the beginning of the year would be adjusted by the reciprocal of the e.p.s. factor and the calculation to find the weighted average is:

$$\left[18m \times \frac{25}{24} \times \frac{8}{12}\right] + \left[22.5m \times \frac{4}{12}\right] = 20m \text{ shares}$$

which would give e.p.s. of 8.55p for the year 2003, rather than 7.6p.

Adjusting the number of shares in issue during the first 8 months of 2003 by 25/24 allows for the bonus element of the rights issue, i.e. it puts the shares in issue at the beginning of the year on the same basis as the shares in issue at the end of the year.

6. Share consolidations

A consolidation of shares reduces the number of ordinary shares outstanding without a reduction in resources. The number of ordinary shares outstanding before the event is adjusted for the proportionate change in the number of ordinary shares outstanding as if the event had occurred at the beginning of the earliest period reported.

But no adjustment is made to the number of ordinary shares outstanding before the event where a share consolidation is combined with a special dividend and the overall commercial effect in terms of net assets, earnings and number of shares is of a repurchase at fair value.

Example 18.9 Share consolidation

At 31 December 2003 Universal (see Example 18.8) had in issue 22.5m ordinary shares of 25p each.

It reported basic earnings per share of:

2000	5.76p
2001	7.20p
2002	7.68p
2003	8.55p

If on 1 July 2004 it performed a share consolidation, consolidating each four ordinary shares of 25p each into one ordinary share of £1 (leaving it with 5,625,000 shares of £1 each); and if profits attributable to ordinary for the 2004 were £1,968,750; earnings per share for 2004 would be £1,968,750 ÷ 5,625,000 = 35.00p and the earnings for earlier years would be adjusted to 4 times their earlier amount:

	As originally reported	*As reported in 2004*
2000	5.76p	23.04p
2001	7.20p	28.80p
2002	7.68p	30.72p
2003	8.55p	34.20p

7. Purchase of shares for cash

Where a company repurchases its own shares during the period this affects the weighted average number of shares outstanding, i.e. its works exactly like an issue in respect of an acquisition but in reverse.

Example 18.10 Purchase of shares for cash

If on 30 June 2005 Universal (in Example 18.9) repurchased 4,625,000 ordinary shares out of its issued capital of 5,625,000 ordinary shares of £1 each leaving it with 1m ordinary shares of £1 each; and if profits attributable to ordinary in that year were £993,750; the weighted average number of shares in issue would be (working in months):
$$((6 \times 5{,}625{,}000) + (6 \times 1{,}000{,}000)) \div 12 = 3{,}312{,}500$$
and the e.p.s for 2005 would be £993,750 ÷ 3,312,500 = 30.0p.

Earnings of past years would not be recomputed.

Shares held by a group member

Company shares in issue that are held by a group member and are not cancelled are treated as if they were cancelled for earnings per share purposes and excluded from the calculation. Shares that are held by an employee share ownership plan (ESOP) trust and reflected in the company balance sheet as assets of the company are similarly to be treated as if they were cancelled for this purpose until such time as they vest unconditionally in the employees.

DILUTED EARNINGS PER SHARE

FRS 14 requirement

Where a company has in issue any form of security that does not, at the time the accounts are published, rank for ordinary dividends but may do so in the future FRS 14 requires it to publish in addition to the basic earnings per share what are termed diluted earnings per share.

SSAP 3 required companies to show fully diluted earnings per share if dilution reduced the basic e.p.s. by 5% or more. FRS 14 *requires* publication wherever the effect is dilutive, and *not* where it is antidilutive.

The calculation of diluted earnings per share follows the same rules as for basic earnings per share but gives effect to all dilutive potential ordinary shares that were outstanding during the period. That is to say the net profit attributable to ordinary shareholders and the weighted average number of shares outstanding are adjusted for the effects of all dilutive potential ordinary shares.

For this purpose the number of ordinary shares should be the weighted average number of ordinary shares calculated as before, plus the weighted average number of ordinary shares that would be issued on the conversion of all the dilutive potential ordinary shares into ordinary shares. Potential ordinary shares should be deemed to have been converted into ordinary shares at the beginning of the period or, if not in existence at the beginning of the period, the date of the issue of the financial instrument or the granting of the rights by which they are generated.

Where does dilution arise?

What sort of things give rise to dilution, the reader may ask. Such financial instruments or rights include (but they are not restricted to):

(a) convertible debt or equity instruments;
(b) share warrants and options;
(c) rights granted under employee or other share purchase plans; and
(d) rights to ordinary shares that are contingent upon the satisfaction of certain conditions resulting from contractual arrangements, such as the purchase of a business or other assets, i.e. contingently issuable shares.

Only those potential shares whose issue would have a dilutive effect on e.p.s. are brought into the calculation. Specifically, potential ordinary shares are only to be treated as dilutive if their conversion to ordinary shares would decrease net profit per share *from continuing operations*.

1. Convertible debt or equity instruments

As might be expected, the number of ordinary shares that would be issued on the conversion of dilutive potential ordinary shares is determined from the terms of the financial instrument or rights through which they are generated, but the computation is required to assume the most advantageous conversion rate or exercise price from the standpoint of the holder of the potential ordinary shares.

Example 18.11 Convertible bonds bringing dilution

Throughout year 2000 Dilute plc had this capital structure:

> 5m ordinary shares of 10p each
> £5m 5% convertible bonds.

Each £1 nominal of convertible bonds is convertible into 3 ordinary shares of 10p.

Profit attributable to ordinary shareholders for the year ended 31 December 2000 was £100,000, comprising £400,000 from continuing operations and a loss of £300,000 from discontinued activities.

Corporation tax is 30%.

Net profit per share from continuing activities is:
£400,000 ÷ 5m = 8.0p.

If the convertible bonds were redeemed, the company would save interest of 5% on £5m = £250,000 which, allowing for tax relief lost of 30% of £250,000 = £75,000, means there would be a saving of £175,000 a year. On the other hand, the number of equity shares would increase by 15m to 20m. This gives diluted e.p.s. from continuing operations of:
(£400,000 + £175,000) ÷ 20m = 2.875p; so there is dilution (when compared with 8.0p).

Reported earnings however, will be:
Basic e.p.s. = £100,000 ÷ 5m = 2.0p
Diluted e.p.s. = (£100,000 + £175,000) ÷ 20m = 1.375p.

Example 18.12 Convertible preference shares not bringing dilution

Throughout year 2000 Nonplussed plc had this capital structure:

> 5m ordinary shares of 10p each
> 5m 5% convertible preference shares of £1 each.

Each 2 convertible preference shares are convertible into 1 ordinary share of 10p.

Profit attributable to ordinary shareholders for the year ended 31 December 2000 was £100,000, comprising £400,000 from continuing operations and a loss of £300,000 from discontinued activities.

Preference Dividends are not an allowable expense for Corporation tax purposes.

Net profit per share from continuing activities is:
£400,000 ÷ 5m = 8.0p.

If the convertible preference shares were converted, the company would save preference dividends of 5% on £5m = £250,000. On the other hand, the number of equity shares would increase by 2.5m to 7.5m.

This gives diluted e.p.s. from continuing operations of: (£400,000 + £250,000) ÷ 7.5m = 8.667p; so there is no dilution.

Reported earnings will be:
Basic e.p.s. = £100,000 ÷ 5m = 2.0p
Diluted e.p.s. which would be (£100,000 + £250,000) ÷ 7.5m = 4.667p will not be shown.

Where a company has a number of different potential ordinary shares, in deciding whether they are dilutive (and hence reflected in the calculation), each type is to be considered in sequence from the most to the least dilutive. Only those potential shares which produce a cumulative dilution are to be included. This means that some potential shares which would dilute basic e.p.s. if viewed on their own may need to be excluded but this results in a diluted e.p.s. showing the maximum overall dilution of basic e.p.s.

It is not uncommon for a subsidiary, joint venture or associate to issue potential ordinary shares that are exchangeable for either ordinary shares of the subsidiary, joint venture or associate, *or* ordinary shares of the reporting entity (the group). If these potential ordinary shares of the subsidiary, associate or joint venture would, on conversion, have a dilutive effect on the consolidated basic earnings per share of the reporting entity (i.e. of the group), they are included in the calculation of diluted earnings per share.

2.   Share warrants and options
In considering whether share warrants and options are dilutive, FRS 14 uses the term 'fair value' to mean the average price of the ordinary shares during the reporting period.

Options and other share purchase arrangements are dilutive when they would result in the issue of ordinary shares for less than fair value. The amount of the dilution is fair value less the issue price.

Such arrangements are treated as consisting of:

(a) a contract to issue a certain number of ordinary shares at their average fair value during the period. The shares so to be issued are fairly priced and are assumed to be neither dilutive nor anti-dilutive. They are ignored in the computation of diluted earnings per share; and

(b) a contract to issue the remaining ordinary shares for no consideration. Such ordinary shares generate no proceeds and have no effect on the net profit attributable to ordinary shares outstanding. Therefore such shares are dilutive and they are added to the number of ordinary shares outstanding in the calculation of diluted earnings per share.

Example 18.13 Share options bringing dilution
For the calendar year 2000 Beefup plc showed profits attributable to ordinary shareholders of £1.2m.

The weighted average number of ordinary shares in issue was 5m and the average fair value of an ordinary share during 2000 was £4.

The weighted average number of shares under option in the year was 1m and the exercise price for shares under option was £3.

Computation of basic e.p.s.
The basic earnings per share for the year would be £1.2m ÷ 5m = 24p.

Computation of diluted e.p.s.
The number of shares under option is 1m.

The number of shares that would have to have been issued at fair value is: (1m × £3) ÷ £4 = 750,000.

The diluted earnings per share £1.2m ÷ (5m + (1m − 750,000) = 22.9p:

---

3.   Employee share and incentive plans
For the purpose of diluted earnings per share a distinction is made between incentive schemes in which awards are based on performance criteria, and other schemes. Performance-based awards are treated as contingently issuable shares, since their issue or exercise is contingent upon factors other than the passing of time, such as the level of future earnings (see 4 below).

All other awards made under an employee share or other incentive scheme are regarded as options for the purpose of calculating diluted earnings per share. They are to be regarded as outstanding as of the grant date even though their exercise may be contingent upon vesting. They are to be included in the computation even if the employee may not receive (or be able to sell) the shares until some future date. Accordingly, all shares to be issued are included in calculating diluted earnings per share if the effect is dilutive. Where the awards are granted during the period, the shares to be issued are weighted to reflect that fact.

UITF 17 *Employee share schemes* is concerned with how companies should recognise and measure the cost of new shares issued as part of an employee share scheme. UITF 17 does not apply to Inland Revenue approved Save-As-You-Earn schemes and similar arrangements.

UITF 17 states that the total amount charged to the profit and loss account in such instances should be the fair value of the shares at the time the right to the shares is granted to the employee (less any amount payable by him or her).

Shares are therefore regarded as issued at whatever the market value was at date of grant, and this holds true whether the market value at the date turns out to be higher or lower.

For the purposes of the rules on share premium account, however, the consideration for the issue of the shares is the amount subscribed for the shares, which means that the difference (the excess of market value at the date of grant over the cash subscribed) can be credited to another reserve, including profit and loss account reserve, on issue of the shares.

The cost is to be recognised in the profit and loss account over the period to which the employee's performance relates, usually on a straight line basis unless some other basis better matches the services received. This may be in one year, in the case of an annual bonus, or a longer period for a long-term incentive scheme. The period will not normally extend to include any secondary 'loyalty' period (for which the employee must remain in employment after meeting the performance conditions) 'unless it is clear that the effect of the scheme is to reward services over the longer period'. The amount charged to the profit and loss account will continue to be adjusted during this period as estimates of the total cost are refined – this will reflect changes in assumptions such as the likelihood of the performance conditions being met, the number of employees leaving the company before qualifying for the awards, and so on.

This accounting treatment also applies to the grant of share options. So any options granted at a discount to the then ruling market price of the shares will require the discount to be charged to the profit and loss account. The Stock Exchange requires shareholder approval before listed companies can grant options to directors at a discount.

Example 18.14 Share option scheme not related to performance

Donor plc has in place an employee share option scheme that awards share options to employees and their dependants on the basis of period of service.

The provisions of the scheme are as follows at 31 December 2000:

Date of grant	1 January 2000
Market price at grant date	£4.00
Exercise price of option	£2.50
Date of vesting	31 December 2002
Number of shares under option	1m

Applying UITF 17, the profit and loss account is charged with 50p per option in each of the three years 2000–2002.

Net profit for year 2000	£1,200,000
Weighted average number of ordinary shares outstanding	5m
Average fair value of an ordinary share during the year	£5.00
Assumed proceeds per option	£3.50

(exercise price of £2.50 and compensation cost attributable to future service, not yet recognised, of £1.00). Next year £3.00 (i.e. £2.50 plus 50p).

Computation of earnings per share

	per share	earnings	shares
Net profit for year 2000		£1,200,000	
Weighted average shares outstanding for 2000			5m
Basic earnings per share	24p		
Number of shares under option			1m
Number of shares that would have been issued at fair value: (1m × £3.50) / £5.00			(0.7m)
Diluted e.p.s.	22.6p	£1,200,000	5.3m

Contingently issuable shares are included in the calculation of diluted earnings per share as of the beginning of the period (or, if not in existence at the beginning of the period, from the date of the relevant financial instrument or the granting of the rights).

4. Contingent rights

The number of contingently issuable shares to include in the calculation is based on the number of shares that would be issuable if the end of the reporting period was the end of the contingency period. The diluted earnings per share computation includes those shares that would be issued under the terms of the contingency on the assumption that the current amount of earnings or status of the condition, as appropriate, were to remain unchanged until the end of the agreement, if the effect is dilutive.

Where a condition is expressed as an average over a period it has the same effect as if it were expressed as a cumulative amount over the period – the performance achieved to date is deemed to be that achieved over the whole of the contingency period. For example, if the number of shares to be issued depends on whether profits average £100,000 over a three-year period, the condition is expressed in terms of a cumulative target of £300,000 over the three-year period. If, at the end of the first year, profits are £150,000, no additional shares are brought into the calculation.

Where the number of shares that may be issued in the future depends upon the market price of the shares of the issuing company, the number of shares to be included in the calculation of diluted earnings per share, if dilutive, is based on the number that would be issued, based on the current market price at the end of the current reporting period or the average over a specified period, depending on the terms of the underlying contract.

For deferred consideration agreements, in which the consideration is fixed but the number of shares issuable is not known, the number of shares to be included in the calculation is based on the market price at the balance sheet date as if it were the end of the contingency period.

If the contingency is based on a condition other than earnings or market price, the contingently issuable shares are included on the assumption that the status of the condition at the end of the reporting period will remain unchanged until the end of the contingency period. For example, if a further issue of shares is generated on the opening of the tenth new retail outlet and at the year-end only five have been opened, no contingently issuable shares are included in the diluted earnings per share computation.

Where the number of shares that may be issued depends upon any combination of future events, the number to be included is based on the status of all relevant conditions at the end of the reporting period. No shares are included where one of the conditions is not met.

Example 18.15 Performance related scheme

Growbig plc has 1m ordinary shares outstanding at 1 January 2000. The terms of a deferred consideration agreement, related to a recent business acquisition, provide for the following contingently issuable shares:

- 2,000 additional ordinary shares for each £1,000 of total net income in excess of £700,000 over the three years ending 2002.
- 20,000 additional ordinary shares for every new retail outlet opened in each of the three years 2000–2002.

Any additional shares will issued on 1 January in the accounting period following that in which a condition is met.

Growbig reported net income for the three years of £300,000, £475,000 and £350,000 respectively.

Growbig opened one new retail outlet on 1 April 2000 and another on 1 February 2002.

Computation of basic e.p.s.

	2000	2001	2002
Numerator	£300,000	£475,000	£350,000
Denominator			
Ordinary shares	1m	1.020m^c	1.020m
Retail outlet contingency	0.015m^a		0.018m^e
Earnings contingency	^{b}	^{d}	^{d}
Total shares	1.015m	1.020m	1.038m
Basic e.p.s.	29.6p	46.6p	33.7p

Computation of diluted e.p.s.

	2000	2001	2002
Numerator	£300,000	£475,000	£350,000
Denominator			
Ordinary shares in basic e.p.s.	1.015m	1.020m	1.038m
Additional shares for:			
Retail outlet contingency	0.005m^f		0.002m^f
Earnings contingency	^{g}	0.150m^h	0.850m^i
Total shares	1.020m	1.170m	1.890m
Diluted e.p.s.	29.4p	40.6p	18.5p

Notes:

a   20,000 × 9/12

b   In 2000, the earnings contingency has no effect on basic e.p.s. because the condition is not satisfied. (See also ^{d} below.)

c   In 2001, shares relating to the retail outlet opened on 1 April 2000 are included in basic e.p.s. from their date of issue.

d   In 2001 and 2002, the earnings contingency has no effect on basic e.p.s. because it is not certain that the condition is met until the last day of the three-year period. (See also ^{i} below.)

e   11/12 × 20,000

f   Additional shares included in diluted e.p.s., which includes contingently issuable shares from the beginning of the period.

g   Growbig did not have £700,000 net income at 31 December 2000.

h   (£775,000 − £700,000)/1,000 × 2,000.

i   (£1,125,000 − £700,000)/1,000 × 2,000. The shares will be included in basic e.p.s. as from 1 January 2003, their date of issue.

Presentation

In the past the information presented on earnings has been somewhat scrappy. Under FRS 14 explanatory notes seem destined to become much more complete and much more complex.

Companies are required to:
(a) present basic and diluted earnings per share on the face of the profit and loss account for each class of ordinary share that has a different right to share in the net profit for the period;
(b) present basic and diluted earnings per share with equal prominence for all periods presented;
(c) present basic and diluted earnings per share, even if the amounts disclosed are negative, i.e. a loss per share);
(d) disclose the amounts used as the numerators in calculating basic and diluted earnings per share, and a reconciliation of those amounts to the net profit or loss for the period;
(e) disclose the weighted average number of

ordinary shares used as the denominator in calculating basic and diluted earnings per share, and, excepting figures given in respect of different classes of ordinary share, a reconciliation of the denominators to each other.

(f) disclose the number of ordinary shares used as the denominator in calculating basic and diluted earnings per share, and, excepting figures given in respect of different classes of ordinary share, a reconciliation of these denominators to each other.

If any additional earnings per share computations are produced they should be presented on a consistent basis over time and, wherever disclosed, reconciled to the amount required by the FRS.

SEC GROUP *Extract from notes to the accounts at 30 September 1998*

[Page 150 shows how this was presented in the profit and loss account.]

11. (Loss)/earnings per share

The (loss)/earnings per share of £(4.41)p (1997: 12.79p) is calculated by dividing the loss attributable to ordinary shareholders of £800,000 (1997: £2,200,000 earnings) by the weighted average number of ordinary shares in issue during the year of 18,144,470 (1997: 17,227,186).

The fully diluted (loss)/earnings is calculated as follows:

	1998 £m	1997 £m
Basic (loss)/earnings	(0.8)	2.2
Add: Interest saved if shares converted	0.3	–
Fully diluted earnings	(0.5)	2.2
Weighted average number of ordinary shares in issue	18,144,470	17,227,186
Add: maximum dilution re: share options	102,500	82,500
Add: maximum dilution re: convertibles	2,586,957	–
Fully diluted weighted average number of ordinary shares in issue	20,833,927	17,309,686

The Institute of Investment Management and Research IIMR have defined an alternative calculation of earnings per share which excludes profit and losses on the sale of fixed assets or businesses and exceptional items. The directors feel that this IIMR earnings per share figure is a valuable guide as to maintainable earnings and has been disclosed as, in the opinion of the Directors, it provides additional information to shareholders on the results of the Group's activities. The IIMR earnings per share can be reconciled to the basic loss per share as follows:

	1998 £m	1997 £m
Basic (loss)/earnings	(0.8)	2.2
Exceptional items after tax	1.5	–
IIMR earnings	0.7	2.2
IIMR earnings per share	4.08p	12.79p

STATEMENT OF TOTAL RECOGNISED GAINS AND LOSSES

The Statement of total recognised gains and losses (STRGL) is a primary financial statement introduced by FRS 3. Its purpose is to highlight any items which even if they were very significant would otherwise only appear in a note to the accounts. For example, POLLY PECK took an adverse Exchange rate variance of £170.3m on net investment overseas direct to reserves in 1988, a year in which it only made an operating profit of £156.9m. The exchange variance was due largely to borrowing in Deutschmarks and Swiss francs, where interest rates were low, while keeping money on deposit in very soft Turkish lira. The very high interest received on the soft currency deposits was credited to the profit and loss account, while the capital loss was taken straight to reserves, together with the increase in the sterling value of Dm and SFr borrowings. This portent of disaster was missed by some analysts and by most shareholders, but would have been obvious from an STRGL.

The Statement of total recognised gains and losses shows the extent to which shareholders' funds have increased or decreased from all gains and losses recognised in the period. It normally appears either immediately after the profit and loss account or after the cash flow statement.

EMI GROUP (see next page) shows it between the balance sheet and the cash flow statement.

As shown by EMI Group such statements normally begin with the profit for the financial year (or 'period').

Other items commonly found include:

- Surpluses (deficits) on the revaluation of fixed assets;
- Currency translation differences (see Chapter 23);
- Prior period adjustments.

EMI GROUP *Interim statement 1998*
Statement of total recognised gains and losses for the six months ended 30 September 1998 (unaudited)

	Notes	Six months ended 30 Sep 1998 £m	£m	Six months ended 30 Sep 1997 (restated) £m	£m
Profit for the period:					
As reported			31.4		51.1
Prior period adjustments	9		–		(50.4)
			31.4		0.7
Currency retranslation – as reported		(32.6)		5.3	
Currency retranslation – prior period adjustments	9	–		(1.7)	
Gains (losses) on foreign currency borrowings		1.0		(0.6)	
Other recognised (losses) gains			(31.6)		3.0
Total recognised gains and losses relating to the period			(0.2)		3.7

Prior period adjustments

As explained on page 122, under FRS 3, para. 7, material prior period items which are the result of:

(a) changes in accounting policies, or

(b) the correction of fundamental errors,

are treated as 'prior period adjustments'.

It is a fundamental accounting concept that there is consistency of accounting treatment within each accounting period and from one period to the next. A change in accounting policy may therefore be made only if it can be justified on the grounds that the new policy is preferable to the one it replaces because it will give a fairer presentation of the result and of the financial position of a reporting entity (Explanation to FRS 3, para. 62).

Following a change in accounting policy, the amounts for the current and corresponding periods should be restated on the basis of the new policies. The cumulative adjustments should also be noted at the foot of the statement of total recognised gains and losses of the current period and included in the reconciliation of movements in shareholders' funds of the corresponding period in order to highlight for users the effect of the adjustments.

EMI GROUP *Note to Interim statement 1998*
9. Prior period adjustments. As explained in Note 1 Basis of preparation, FRS 9 *Associates and Joint Ventures,* FRS 10 *Goodwill and Intangible Assets* and FRS 12 *Provisions, Contingent Assets and Contingent Liabilities* were adopted with effect from 1 April 1998. In addition, the accounting treatment for our 50% holding in Jobete was changed from an associate to a subsidiary.

To reflect these changes in accounting policies and accounting treatment, the comparatives for the six months ended 30 September 1997 and the opening balances for the current reporting period have been restated as follows:

Copyrights:

	Six months ended 30 Sept 1997 £m	£m	Year ended 31 Mar 1998 £m	£m
As reported		399.6		529.1
Jobete restatement		151.0		–
Prior period adjustments:				
Amortisation for the period from acquisition to 31 Mar 1997	(134.1)		(134.1)	
Amortisation charge for the period	(13.6)		(27.0)	
Currency retranslation	(1.5)		4.2	
		(149.2)		(156.9)
As restated		401.4		372.2

Investments: associates

	£m	£m
As reported	94.8	13.7
Jobete restatement	(87.5)	–
Prior period adjustment (FRS 9: HW Media Group joint venture)		(8.4)
As restated	7.3	5.3

	Six months ended 30 Sept 1997		Year ended 31 Mar 1998	
	£m	£m	£m	£m
Provisions:				
As reported		(206.0)		(210.7)
Prior period adjustments (FRS 12):				
Balance at 31 Mar 1997	115.3		115.3	
Operating exceptional charge for the period	(38.7)		(92.6)	
Non-operating exceptional credit for the period	–		19.4	
		76.6		42.1
As restated		(129.4)		(168.6)

Financial statistics in historical summaries

FRS 3 does not refer to historical summaries, but where prior period adjustments are made, good accounting requires that information given in such summaries be restated, and many, but not all, companies do this.

FRS 14 does have regard to such summaries. In order to give a fair comparison over the period of any historical summary presented, the basic and diluted earnings per share figures need to be restated for subsequent changes in capital not involving full consideration at fair value (i.e. bonus issues, bonus elements in other issues or repurchases, share splits and share consolidations). The resultant earnings per share figures are described as restated and under FRS 14 are to be clearly distinguished from other non-adjusted data.

Equity dividends set out in the form of pence per share are to be adjusted similarly.

Movements in shareholders' funds

FRS 3 also requires (para. 28) companies to provide a note reconciling the opening and closing totals of shareholders' funds for the period. Often this follows the Statement of total recognised gains and losses but sometimes it is found in the note on reserves.

Typically the change in shareholders' funds which it discloses represents:

(a) Transfer from profit and loss account, i.e.
   (i) Profit attributable to shareholders; less
   (ii) Dividends;
(b) Unrealised profit (deficit) on revaluation of fixed assets (normally properties);
(c) Currency translation differences;
(d) New share capital subscribed (net);
(e) Scrip dividends;
(f) Goodwill on acquisitions written off;
(g) Goodwill on disposals written back;
(h) Purchase of own shares;
(i) Prior year adjustments.

EMI GROUP *Interim statement 1998*

Reconciliation of movements in shareholders' funds

		Six months ended 30 Sep 1998	Six months ended 30 Sep 1997 (restated)
		£m	£m
Opening shareholders' funds:			
As reported		(652.6)	3.5
Prior period adjustments	9	(115.1)	(22.7)
		(767.7)	(19.2)
Profit for the period		31.4	0.7
Dividends (preference)		–	(0.2)
Dividends (equity)		(33.4)	(33.3)
Other recognised (losses) gains		(31.6)	3.0
Goodwill on acquisitions		–	(35.4)
Goodwill – disposals and adjustments		1.9	–
Shares issued		1.8	3.7
Share capital reorganisation		–	(484.0)
Net decrease in shareholders' funds		(29.9)	(545.5)
Closing shareholders' funds		(797.6)	(564.7)

Where advantage is taken of CA 1985 s.130 (2) and the expenses of, or the commission paid, or discount allowed on an issue of shares or debentures of the company, or the premium payable on redemption of debentures of the company, is charged against share premium account rather than to profit and loss account, this will appear in the statement.

INVESTMENT RATIOS

These are the ratios used by investors when deciding whether a share should be bought, sold or held. Most of them relate to the current price of the share, and therefore vary from day to day. The two most popular ones are the Price Earnings Ratio (PER), already mentioned, and the dividend yield.

Price earnings ratio (PER)

$$\text{Price earnings ratio} = \frac{\text{Market price per ordinary share}}{\text{Basic earnings per share}}$$

where market price = the middle market price, which is the average of the prices at which shares can be sold or bought on an investor's behalf (the marketmaker's bid and offer prices respectively).

The analyst will normally calculate two price earnings ratios: the 'historical PER', using last year's e.p.s., and the 'prospective PER', using his estimate of e.p.s for the current year; he may also project his earnings estimates to produce a PER based on possible earnings for the following year.

What the PER represents

One way of looking at the PER is to regard it as the number of years' earnings per share represented by the share price, i.e. x years' purchase of e.p.s., but this assumes static e.p.s., while in practice the PER reflects the market's view of the company's growth potential, the business risks involved and the dividend policy. For example, a company recovering from a break-even situation, with zero e.p.s. last year, will have a historical PER of infinity but may have a prospective PER of 12 based on expectations of modest profits for the current year, falling to 6 next year if a full recovery is achieved.

The PER of a company also depends not only on the company itself, but on the industry in which it operates and, of course, on the level of the stock market, which tends to rise more than reported profits when the business cycle swings up and to fall more than profits in a downturn. The level of the PER of the *Financial Times* 500 Index shows this very clearly:

	500 PER
Top of the bull market, 19 May 1972	19.88
Bottom of the bear market, 13 December 1974	3.71
Top of the bull market, 16 July 1987	21.03

The Actuaries Share Indices table published in the *Financial Times* every day except Mondays also gives the PER for each industry group and subsection, so any historical PER calculated for a company can be compared with its sector and with the market as a whole. The result of comparing it with the market as a whole (usually with the FTSE All-Share PER) is called the PER Relative:

$$\text{PER Relative} = \frac{\text{PER of Company}}{\text{PER of Market}}$$

Example 18.16 Historical and prospective PER

Suppose the fully taxed normalised e.p.s. calculated from a company's latest report and accounts, published two to three months after the year has ended, are 8.0p. The analyst is expecting profits to rise by about 27% in the current year, and for there to be a disproportionately higher charge for minorities (because one partly owned subsidiary is making a hefty contribution to the improved profits). He therefore estimates that e.p.s. will rise a little less than profits, to about 10.0p.

The current share price is 120p, so last year's e.p.s. = 8p; current year e.p.s. = 10p; historical PER = 15.0; prospective PER = 12.0.

This provides a quick indication of whether a company is highly or lowly rated, although differences in the treatment of tax by individual companies do cause some distortion here, so most analysts use e.p.s. calculated on a full tax charge to compare PERs within a sector.

In general a high historic PER compared with the industry group suggests either that the company is a leader in its sector or that the share is overvalued, while a low PER suggests a poor company or an undervalued share. In each case check to see if the prospective PER is moving back into line with the sector, as a historic PER that is out of line may be due to expectations of an above average rise in profits for the current year (in which case the historic PER will be higher than average), or to poor results being expected (which would be consistent with a low PER). In addition, if Datastream is available (see Chapter 28), it is worth checking the company's PER history to see where it lies in relation to its historical range and to the sector PER.

Another useful rule of thumb is to be wary when a PER goes much above 20. The company may well be a glamour stock due for a tumble or, if it is the PER of a very sound high-quality company, the market itself may be in for a fall. One exception here is the property sector, where PERs are normally very high because property companies tend to be highly geared and use most of their rental income to service their debt, leaving tiny e.p.s.; investors normally buy property company shares more for their prospects of capital appreciation than for their current earnings.

Price earnings growth factor (PEG)

The Price earnings growth factor (PEG) is a yardstick introduced by Jim Slater in his very readable book *The Zulu Principle*, which is full of useful advice for the private investor. The PEG is a measure of whether a share looks overrated or underrated:

$$PEG = \frac{Price\ earnings\ ratio}{Prospective\ growth\ in\ e.p.s.}$$

Where the PER is appreciably higher than the prospective growth rate (i.e. PEG well over 1.0), the shares are likely to be expensive. Conversely a PEG of between 0.5 and 0.75 means that the prospective growth rate isn't fully reflected in the PER, and the shares look attractive.

Dividend policy and the P/E Ratio

As the price of a share is influenced both by the e.p.s. and the dividend, a company's dividend policy affects the P/E Ratio.

Some companies pay tiny dividends and plough back most of their profits to finance further growth. Shares in these companies may enjoy a glamour rating while everything is going well, but the rating is vulnerable to any serious setback in profits, as there is little yield to support the price.

Blue chip companies like to pay a reasonable dividend and to increase it each year to counteract the effects of inflation and reflect long-term growth; and that is what the shareholders expect, particularly those who are retired and need income from their investments. This means that major companies usually pay out between 30% and 40% of attributable profits, retaining a substantial amount to reinvest for future growth and to avoid having to cut the dividend in lean years. For example BRITISH AIRWAYS maintained its dividend in 1991, when profits had more than halved, but the dividend was still covered.

If a company pays out much more than 50% in dividends it suggests it has gone ex-growth; it also runs a higher risk of having to cut its dividend in hard times (which tends to be very unpopular with investors) and, in times of high inflation, a company distributing a large proportion of its reported profits (calculated on a historical cost basis) will tend to lose credibility.

Dividend yield

As described in Chapter 17, dividends still carry an associated tax credit. Traditionally, dividend yields were based on gross dividends per share, that is, on the dividends actually paid plus the associated tax credit; but since April 1999 the tax credit varies with the type of taxpayer, and dividend yields are now generally based on the net amount received,

i.e. the tax credit is now ignored.

Dividend yield (%) =

$$\frac{Net\ dividend\ in\ pence\ per\ share \times 100}{Ordinary\ share\ price\ in\ pence}$$

Dividend cover

$$Cover = \frac{e.p.s.}{Net\ dividends\ per\ share}$$

Example 18.17 Calculation of dividend cover

In year 2000 Cover plc had profits attributable to ordinary of £1.240m. 20m ordinary shares of £1 each were in issue throughout the year. The company paid total ordinary dividends of 23p per share net.
Basic earnings per share will be £1.240m ÷ 20m = 62p.
Cover = 62 ÷ 23 = 2.70.

Payout ratio

The payout ratio is the reciprocal of the dividend cover. It indicates the extent to which the attributable profits are distributed to ordinary shareholders. An equally valid measure is the amount retained by the company as a percentage of the attributable profit.

Example 18.18 Calculation of payout ratio

In year 2000 Cover plc had profits attributable to ordinary of £1.240m. 20m ordinary shares of £1 each were in issue throughout the year. The company paid total ordinary dividends of 23p per share net.
Basic earnings per share will be £1.240m ÷ 20m = 62p.
Cover = 62 ÷ 23 = 2.70.
Payout ratio = 1 ÷ Cover = 1 ÷ 2.70 = 0.37 or 37%.
The payout ratio could equally well be computed:
(20m × 23p) ÷ 1.240 = 0.37 or 37%.

Problem 18.1

The basic earnings per share of a listed company, PG, in 1999 are stated to be 71.4p.

1. How would you expect this figure to have been calculated?
2. How might you use the figure of earnings per share, i.e. with what might you compare it?
3. What other types of e.p.s. are likely to be found in published accounts, and why?

Chapter 19

CASH FLOW STATEMENTS

Background

Traditionally, published accounts comprised a balance sheet and a profit and loss account. In 1975 a third statement was introduced in the UK with the publication of SSAP 10 *Statement of source and application of funds*.

Although this statement helped to bridge the gap between each item in successive balance sheets, it centred on the increase/decrease in working capital, in which it included cash and short-term investments, rather than on whether the company's operations were generating or consuming cash.

SSAP 10 was criticised because it did not define 'funds' adequately, and failed to lay down specific formats. This gave considerable flexibility to the preparers of accounts, and made comparison between companies difficult.

Dissatisfaction with SSAP 10, coupled with the adoption of a cash flow statement in the United States (SFAS 95, published in 1987) and the increasing realisation of the importance of cash, led to the introduction of the cash flow statement in the UK with the publication in September 1991 of FRS 1 *Cash flow statements*.

The requirements of FRS 1 (revised)

FRS 1 requires companies to produce a cash flow statement instead of a source and application of funds. The requirement does not apply to 'small companies' as defined by the Companies Act 1989, see page 17; to mutual life assurance companies, open-ended investment funds or pension funds. Nor does it apply to subsidiary undertakings where 90% or more of voting rights are controlled within the group provided consolidated accounts are prepared for the group. This is a serious limitation to analysts who would like to make a detailed analysis of cash flows within a group, especially those within a complex international group.

FRS 1 lays down a clearly defined overall format: the cash flow statement should list cash flows for the period, classified under eight standard headings in the following order:

(a) operating activities (using either the direct or indirect method, as explained on page 166);
(b) returns on investments and servicing of finance;
(c) taxation;
(d) capital expenditure and financial investment;
(e) acquisitions and disposals;
(f) equity dividends paid;
(g) management of liquid resources;
(h) financing.

The last two headings can be shown in a single section provided a separate subtotal is given for each heading.

Individual categories of inflows and outflows under the standard headings should be disclosed separately either in the cash flow statement or in a note to it unless they are allowed to be shown net. Cash inflows and outflows may be shown net if they relate to the management of liquid resources or financing and the inflows and outflows either:

(a) relate in substance to a single financing transaction (which is one that fulfils conditions in para. 35 of FRS 4 *Capital instruments*); or
(b) are due to short maturities and high turnover occurring from rollover or reissue (for example, short-term deposits or a commercial paper programme).

The requirement to show cash inflows and outflows separately does not apply to cash flows relating to operating activities.

The cash flows that fall under each of the eight standard headings are described in some detail (FRS 1, paras 11–32) and illustrative examples of cash flow statements are provided in an Appendix to FRS 1 for:

- An individual company
- A group
- A bank
- An insurance group.

FRS 1, in fact, was the first time that an accounting standard attempted to identify the special needs of companies in different sectors.

Whereas the original FRS 1 adopted a fairly broad brush approach to cash, including cash equivalents, the revised standard adopts a strict cash approach (for definitions see the terminology box in the next column). It also introduced a section for cash flows relating to the management of liquid resources. This avoids an arbitrary cut-off point (three months) in the definition of cash equivalents; it distinguishes cash flows arising from accumulating or using liquid resources from those for other investing activities; and it provides information about a group's treasury activities that was not previously available because the instruments dealt in generally fell within the definition of cash equivalents.

According to the FRS, the cash flow statement serves two purposes:

(a) it reports the cash generation and cash absorption of a business; and
(b) it provides information to assist users to assess its liquidity, its solvency and its financial adaptability.

Reconciliation to operating profit

Either adjacent to the cash flow statement or in the notes the company must provide a reconciliation between operating profit reported in the profit and loss account and the net cash flow from operating activities (see ABBEYCREST Note 21 on page 165).

This reconciliation should disclose separately the movements in stocks, debtors and creditors related to operating activities and other differences between cash flows and profits. The reconciliation should show separately the difference between dividends received and results taken into account for associates and other equity accounted entities (see Chapter 23).

Reconciliation to net debt

A note reconciling the movement of cash in the period with the movement in net debt should be given either adjoining the cash flow statement or in a note. But the reconciliation is not part of the cash flow statement: even when it adjoins the cash flow statement, FRS 1 requires it to be clearly labelled and kept separate (see ABBEYCREST on page 165).

The changes in net debt should be analysed from the opening to the closing component amounts showing separately, where material, changes resulting from:

(a) the cash flows of the entity;
(b) the acquisition or disposal of subsidiary undertakings;
(c) other non-cash changes; and
(d) the recognition of changes in market value and exchange rate movements.

Where several balance sheet amounts or parts of them have to be combined to form the components of opening and closing net debt, sufficient detail should be shown to enable the cash and other components of net debt to be respectively traced back to the amounts shown under the equivalent captions in the balance sheet. A possible format for the analysis of net debt is provided in the examples in Appendix 1.

TERMINOLOGY
Cash flow statements

Cash is cash in hand and deposits repayable on demand with any qualifying financial institution less overdrafts from any qualifying financial institution repayable on demand; i.e. they can be withdrawn at any time without notice and without penalty or if a maturity or period of notice of not more than 24 hours or one working day has been agreed. Cash includes cash in hand and deposits denominated in foreign currencies.

A **qualifying financial institution** is an entity that as part of its business receives deposits or other repayable funds and grants credits for its own account.

A **cashflow** is an increase or decrease in an amount of cash.

Liquid resources are current asset investments held as readily disposable stores of value.

To be **readily disposable** an investment must be one that:

(a) is disposable by the reporting entity without curtailing or disrupting its business; and is
(b) either:
(i) readily convertible into known amounts of cash at or close to its carrying amount, or
(ii) traded in an active market.

Acquisitions and disposals

A note to the cash flow statement should show a summary of the effects of acquisitions and disposals of subsidiary undertakings indicating how much of the consideration comprised cash (see TARSUS GROUP on page 199 for an illustration). Material effects on amounts reported under each of the standard headings reflecting the cash flows of a subsidiary undertaking acquired or disposed of in the period should be disclosed, as far as practicable. This information can be given by dividing cash flows between continuing and discontinued operations and acquisitions.

This note provides useful background when studying the effects of an acquisition, merger or disposal.

Non-cash items and restrictions on transfer

Material transactions which do not result in movements of cash of the reporting entity should be disclosed in the notes to the cash flow statement if disclosure is necessary for an understanding of the underlying transactions (see Example 19.1 on page 167 for an illustration).

ABBEYCREST *Extracts from the 1998 account*

Consolidated Cash Flow Statement and notes for the year ended 28 February 1998

		1998 £000	1997 £000
Net cash inflow from operating activities	21	5,483	1,796
Returns on investments and servicing of finance	22	(1,224)	(1,309)
Taxation		(1,052)	(1,004)
Capital expenditure and financial investment	22	(1,056)	(1,786)
Acquisitions and disposals	22	(83)	(1,259)
Equity dividends paid		(945)	(874)
Cash inflow (outflow) before financing		1,123	(4,436)
Financing – issue of shares	22	25	109
(Decrease) increase in debt	22	(695)	1,464
Increase (decrease) in cash in the year		453	(2,863)

21. Reconciliation of operating profit to net cash inflow from operating activities

	Group	
	1998 £000	1997 £000
Operating profit	5,441	4,823
Depreciation	1,045	935
Profit on sale of tangible fixed assets	(104)	(71)
Decrease in stocks	2,832	515
Increase in debtors	(2,230)	(2,938)
Decrease in creditors	(1,501)	(1,468)
Net cash inflow from operating activities	5,483	1,796

22. Analysis of cash flows for headings netted in the Cash Flow Statement

Returns on investments and servicing of finance

	1998	1997
Interest received	30	35
Interest paid	(1,240)	(1,321)
Interest element of finance lease rental payments	(14)	(23)
Net cash outflow for returns on investments and servicing of finance	(1,224)	(1,309)

Capital expenditure and financial investment

Purchase of tangible fixed assets	(1,189)	(1,914)
Sale of tangible fixed assets	200	196
Purchase of own shares in Employee Benefit Trust	(67)	(166)
Proceeds of sale of own shares by Employee Benefit Trust	–	98
Net cash outflow for capital expenditure and financial investment	(1,056)	(1,786)

Acquisitions and disposals

Purchase of business	(83)	(1,259)
Net cash outflow for acquisitions and disposals	(83)	(1,259)

Financing

Issue of ordinary share capital	25	109
Debt due within one year:		
increase in secured loan	–	400
repayment of ECSC loans	(188)	(187)
repayment of secured loan	(400)	–
Debt due after one year:		
new secured loan repayable by quarterly instalments within five years	–	1,500
Capital element of finance lease rental payments	(107)	(249)
Net cash (outflow) inflow from financing	(670)	1,573

23. Analysis of net debt

	At 1 March 1997 £000	Cashflow £000	Other non-cash changes £000	At 28 Feb 1998 £000
Cash at bank and in hand	1,688	(1,683)	–	5
Overdrafts	(9,141)	2,136	–	(7,005)
	(7,453)	453	–	(7,000)
Debt due after one year	(1,500)	–	400	(1,100)
Debt due within one year	(588)	588	(400)	(400)
Finance leases	(161)	107	–	(54)
	(2,249)	695	–	(1,554)
Total	(9,702)	1,148	–	(8,554)

24. Reconciliation of net cash flow to movement in net debt

	1998 £000
Increase in cash in the year	453
Cash outflow from decrease in debt and lease financing	695
	1,148
Net debt at beginning of year	(9,702)
Net debt at end of year	(8,554)

25. Purchase of business

	1998 £000
Net assets acquired:	
Goodwill	83
Satisfied by cash	83

During the year the company acquired certain tooling assets and other intangible assets from the receivers of Excalibur Jewellery Ltd.

Exceptional and extraordinary items

Where cash flows relate to items that are treated as exceptional or extraordinary in the profit and loss account they are shown under the appropriate standard headings, according to the nature of each item but identified separately. The relationship between the cash flows and the originating exceptional or extraordinary item should be explained as shown in Example 19.1 on page 167.

Value Added Tax and other taxes

Cash flows are shown net of any attributable Value Added Tax or other sales tax unless the tax is irrecoverable.

Restrictions on remittability

Where restrictions prevent the transfer of cash from one part of the business or group to another a note to the cash flow statement should specify the amounts and explain the circumstances. Had POLLY PECK (see page 158) done that, a number of people might not have had their fingers burnt.

The direct and indirect methods

There are two methods for reporting net cash flow from operating activities:

1. The direct method, which shows operating cash receipts and payments (including, in particular, cash receipts from customers, cash payments to suppliers and cash payments to and on behalf of employees), aggregating to the net cash flow from operating activities.
2. The indirect method, which starts with operating profit and adjusts it for non-cash charges and credits to reconcile it to the net cash flow from operating activities.

FRS 1 encourages companies to use the direct method if they consider that the benefits of doing so outweigh the costs, but few companies do provide this extra information, perhaps because FRS 1 still requires companies to produce a reconciliation between the operating profit and the net cash flow from operations (i.e. to show figures using the indirect method).

Reconciliation of operating profit to net cash inflow from operating activities

It is important to recognise that, while a cash flow statement, whether of a single company or group, begins with 'Net cash inflow from operating activities', that figure appears nowhere in the accounting records. Its source is the supporting note 'Reconciliation of operating profit to net cash inflow from operating activities', which in the indirect method is not so much a reconciliation as an explanation of how the figure was arrived at. In other words, despite its relegation by FRS 1 to a note, it is a primary document and should be studied as such.

In effect, the 'reconciliation' takes as its starting point the concept that in a cash business with no depreciable assets, cash flow from operations equals operating profit; and the statement is largely devoted to timing differences caused by the business trading on credit and employing depreciable assets.

It is sometimes suggested that the reconciliation reflects those operating items which do not give rise to cash flows, which is true so far as it goes, but it is necessary to add 'in the period of account'. Thus credit given to trade debtors (i.e. the increase in trade debtors for the period) is deducted because the cash has yet to be received. Similarly, credit taken from trade and operating expense creditors (in the widest sense, e.g. including accrued wages) is added back since the cash has yet to be paid.

Note the emphasis on 'trade debtors' and 'trade and operating expense creditors'. A line is effectively drawn across the profit and loss account at 'Operating profit'. Under the indirect method all cash flows down to that point are lumped into one figure: 'Net cash inflow from operating activities'. Those below that line are stated directly as cash flows on the face of the statement, i.e. any debtors and creditors in relation to these items are ignored by the cash flow statement.

Depreciation and amortisation of operating assets are added back in the reconciliation because the cash flow took place in the past and the cost is simply being spread over the asset's effective life.

It is important to understand the full implications of any timing differences appearing in the reconciliation. Consider Example 19.1. The fact that the exceptional item appears in the reconciliation and is positive tells us that the expenditure, while charged in the profit and loss account of the year, represents expenditure the payment for which has yet to be made, i.e. which is a threat to future cash flows.

Example 19.1 Extract from reconciliation of operating profit to net cash flow from operating activities

	£000
Operating profit	1,230
Exceptional item: Fundamental restructuring of brickmaking operations	23,000
Net cash flow from operating activities	24,230

This shows the danger of taking at face value a cash flow statement, which shows a healthy 'Net cash flow from operations' without studying the reconciliation.

Although most items in the reconciliation reflect timing differences, there is one important exception. When an asset is sold, the sale proceeds appear not as an operating cash inflow but under 'Capital expenditure and financial investment'. If a profit (or loss) on sale occurred and was included (deducted) in arriving at operating profit, it has to be taken out of the 'Cash flow from operating activities' to avoid being counted twice.

Studying a cash flow statement

So far as the analyst is concerned cash flow statements serve two principal purposes:

1. They provide a historical explanation of the change in cash balances which occurred during an accounting period.
2. They provide the starting point for projections of future cash flows.

It is advisable to keep these two separate.

The statement as a historical explanation

Our method of working is:

1. To focus on the reconciliation of operating profit to net cash inflow from operating activities, which as we remarked earlier is not so much a reconciliation as an explanation of how the figure was arrived at. It is as we said earlier a primary document and should be studied as such.

    Sharply rising stocks and/or debtors; associates which while highly profitable hold on to the money rather than remitting it; and timing differences on amounts provided for, say, restructuring, will all stand out – but be missed if this reconciliation is passed over lightly.

2. To study the overall picture presented by the cash flow statement and then turn to study each section of the cash flow statement in order; in particular:

    (a) *Capital expenditure and financial investment*: To discover what major changes have taken place in fixed assets

    (b) *Acquisitions and disposals*: To discover the net cash cost of acquisitions (which if acquisitions are made for paper can be quite small or even negative) and the benefit derived from sales of businesses (which often involve deferred consideration). We also study any notes on this.

    (c) *Financing:* To discover what new money has been raised and what has been repaid.

3. To look with care at the cash effects of exceptional items.

4. To seek out any suggestion of restrictions on remittability which prevent the transfer of cash from one part of the business or group to another.

5. To focus on any non-cash transactions. Although uncommon, it is possible for two groups to exchange assets, considerably changing the focus of each, without any cash passing.

6. To study the reconciliation of net debt. The liquid and debt positions are really back to back; and neither can be viewed in isolation.

Projecting future cash flows

In projecting future cash flows it is necessary to distinguish changes which are one off from those likely to continue. Thus, a sharp fall in debtors with no corresponding fall in turnover may represent improved debt collection. The improved debt collection may be maintainable, but the *fall* in debtors is unlikely to be repeated the following year. On the other hand, rises in stocks and debtors roughly in line with turnover tend to be a feature from year to year.

Acquisitions and disposals, and any form of restructuring or reposition are likely to have a significant effect on future cash flows, making it difficult even for the group itself to make accurate projections. The analyst is not usually in a position to.

The direct method illustrated

Comparatively few (and growing fewer) listed companies employ the direct method, probably more on grounds of cost (because their computer systems are not designed to collect operating cash flows by their nature and it would be expensive to change) than from conviction. One which did, but does not now, is MANGANESE BRONZE HOLDINGS whose 1993 accounts illustrate the differences.

MANGANESE BRONZE HOLDINGS *1993 accounts*

Group cash flow statement for the year ended 31 July 1993

	1993 £000	1993 £000	1992 £000	1992 £000
Operating activities				
Continuing operations				
Cash received from customers	71,903		66,940	
Cash paid to suppliers	(53,370)		(48,037)	
Cash paid in respect of staff costs	(18,104)		(18,595)	
Other receipts	3,307		2,288	
See Note 24(a)		3,738		2,596
Discontinued operations				
Cash received from customers	14		3,140	
Cash paid to suppliers	(298)		(2,438)	
Cash paid in respect of staff costs	(5)		(1,568)	
Other receipts	23		(37)	
See Note 24(a)		(312)		(903)
Net cash inflow from operating activities		3,426		1,683

Note 24(a) Reconciliation of operating profit/(loss) to net cash inflow from operating activities

	1993 £000	1992 £000
Continuing operations:		
Operating profit	1,850	498
Depreciation	1,937	1,648
Profit/(Loss) on sale of fixed assets	(92)	88
(Increase) in stocks	(264)	(350)
(Increase) in debtors	(171)	(1,419)
Increase in creditors	444	1,912
Increase in provisions	34	219
	3,738	2,596
Discontinued operations		
Operating loss	–	(2,623)
Depreciation	–	220
Plant and machinery written off	–	1,054
Decrease in stocks	–	196
Decrease in debtors	14	358
(Decrease) in creditors	(326)	(108)
	(312)	(903)

Note the distinction under both methods between the cash flows of 'continuing' and 'discontinued' which is desirable though, surprisingly, not required by FRS 1.

It will be seen that the two forms of presentation are entirely different in scale; the direct method giving a much better feel for the overall size of cash flows than the indirect, which nets off inflows and outflows. The overall totals apart, not one figure in either of the two presentations bears the remotest resemblance to that in the other.

It is a pity that the direct method is not compulsory, as it can be very informative. In 1991, before TYNE-TEES TELEVISION became part of YORKSHIRE TYNE-TEES TELEVISION HOLDINGS, it presented its cash flow statement by the direct method. This made it clear just how receipts-sensitive the company was. Net cash flow from continuing operations was £3.235m. But the direct method made it clear that: receipts were £61.013m and that payments were largely fixed: employment costs, transmitter rents and programme costs, which could not be cut overnight. All that was before £6.431m of extraordinary items, shown separately, fighting to retain their franchise.

Limitations of cash flow statements

A cash flow statement is a record of historical facts. It will record expenditure upon additional plant and machinery, but can express no opinion upon whether the expenditure was necessary, or will be profitable.

Similarly it may show an expansion of stocks (or debtors), but it does not tell us whether this was due to:

- poor stock or production control;
- inability to sell the finished product; or
- a deliberate act of policy, because of a feared shortage of supply, a potential price rise, or the need to build up stocks of a new model (or product) before it is launched.

Furthermore, in the case of increased debtors, it will not tell us whether it is:

- the debtors who are slow to pay; or
- the credit policy which has changed, or
- the accounts department that has fallen behind with invoicing; or because
- they merely represent the expansion of turnover.

It will show how new capital was raised, but not whether it was raised in the best way, nor indeed whether it really needed to be raised at all or if the need could have been avoided by better asset control.

When companies have large amounts of cash, the cash flow statement does not tell us where the cash is. Only if it is locked up in an overseas subsidiary, perhaps deposited in an obscure currency in an obscure country (like Turkish Cyprus as was the case with POLLY PECK), where it cannot be remitted to the UK, can we expect to be told. By that time it may well be too late.

Where there are large amounts of both cash and borrowings, the cash flow statement does not tell us why the company does not use the cash to reduce its debts. There may be several reasons:

1. It may be better to borrow in the US, where corporation tax is higher than in the UK, and to keep deposits in the UK.
2. The cash may not have been remitted, to avoid having to pay tax on remitting it.
3. The company may have borrowed cheaply longer term or have favourable facilities and be 'round tripping' – borrowing at a lower rate and taking advantage of higher current interest rates to lend money back at a profit.

Few companies tell you how much is available to them by way of further bank facilities, though where this is stated it provides useful background to the making of cash projections. One company which does is SAFEWAY:

SAFEWAY *Extract from note 17.2 to the 1998 accounts*

Borrowing facilities:

The group has the following undrawn committed borrowing facilities available:

	1998 £m	1997 £m
Expiring within one year	40.0	50.0
Expiring after one year	53.0	205.0
	93.0	255.0

A cash flow statement may highlight a deteriorating situation, but does not tell the reader:

- just how close a company is to the limit of its facilities;
- whether it is in danger of breaching any of its borrowing covenants;
- whether the company's bankers are getting nervous, or are still confident of its recovery.

And, of course, it only shows the cash flows for the year which ended some months ago and, as we saw in the recession in the early 1990s, liquidity problems can and do arise very quickly.

 **Key point**

> A company which descends into loss making often succeeds in making a comeback; one which runs out of cash (and friends) rarely has a second chance.

Doubts about liquidity

If there is any doubt about the company's liquidity, the 'cash flow' should be examined (in as much detail as possible). There are two common definitions of cash flow:

Gross cash flow = depreciation plus profit after tax plus increase (less decrease) in deferred tax

Net cash flow = gross cash flow minus dividends

The question we need to ask is whether current year cash flow will cover cash requirements.

Cash requirements

There are three main areas to look at in identifying cash requirements:

1. *Repayment of existing loans* due in the next year or two, including convertible loans whose conversion rights are unlikely to be exercised.

2. *Increase in working capital*. Working capital tends, in an inflationary period and/or when a business expands, to rise roughly in line with turnover. It is useful therefore to use the Working capital/Sales ratio to establish the relationship between working capital and sales.

Working capital to sales =

$$\frac{(\text{Stock} + \text{Trade debtors}) - \text{Trade creditors}}{\text{Sales}}$$

3. *Capital expenditure requirements*.

Cash shortfall

If the net cash flow looks like falling short of the cash requirements we have identified, then the company may have to:

(a) increase its overdraft (but is it at the limit of its facilities? – we probably don't know);

(b) borrow longer term (can it do so within its borrowing limits?);

(c) make a rights issue (is its share price at least 20% above par, is it at least a year and preferably two years since its last rights issue, and are market conditions suitable?);

(d) acquire a more liquid and/or less highly geared company for paper (i.e. bid for another company using shares);

(e) sell some assets (has it any listed investments which could be sold, or has it any activities which could be sold off without seriously affecting the business?);

(f) sell and lease back some of the properties used in the business (has it any unmortgaged properties?);

(g) cut back on capital expenditure that has not already been put out to contract;

(h) tighten credit and stock control;

(i) reduce or omit the ordinary dividend, and possibly even the preference dividend too.

If the company takes none of these steps it will run into an overtrading situation, which is likely to precipitate a cash crisis unless, as a last resort, it:

(j) reduces its level of trading.

Cash flow ratios

It is possible to express cash flow in per share terms:

Cash flow per share = (Attributable profits plus depreciation) ÷ Number of ordinary shares in issue.

The definition used by REFS (see page 249) is:

Cash flow per share = (Cash flow from operating activities + Returns on investments and servicing of finance – Taxation paid) ÷ Weighted average number of ordinary shares in issue during the period.

The latter version recognises that, as explained in 2, alongside, cash is only available for other purposes once working capital requirements, tax and dividends have been met.

A closely related ratio is:

Capital expenditure per share ('Capex per share') = (The net cash outflow attributable to investment in fixed assets other than amounts attributable to property – Asset sales (other than property)) ÷ weighted average number of ordinary shares in issue during the period.

It is then possible to compare: Cash flow per share, with Capital expenditure per share. This will provide a broad indication of whether the business is a net generator of cash or is cash hungry.

Problem 19.1

Given these extracts from the 1995 accounts of CORDI-ANT, explain in simple terms why the cash generated by operations was so much less in 1995 than in 1994:

Consolidated statement of cash flows:

Year ended	Note	31 Dec 1995 £m	31 Dec 1994 £m
Net cash inflow from operating activities	16	16.6	58.9

Note 16

16. Reconciliation of operating profit to net cash inflow from operating activities

	Year ended 31 Dec 1995 £m	Year ended 31 Dec 1994 £m
Operating profit	28.3	44.5
Depreciation	25.7	25.7
(Profit) loss on sale of tangible fixed assets	(1.5)	0.2
Increase in work in progress	(9.4)	(8 0)
Increase in debtors	(54.8)	(77.8)
Increase in creditors	38.6	86.1
Utilisation of property provisions	(10.3)	(11.8)
Net cash inflow from operating activities	16.6	58.9

Chapter 20

SUBSIDIARIES AND GROUP ACCOUNTS

Interests in another company

If a company, A, wishes to obtain an interest in the activities of another company, B, it may do so in three ways:

- by buying some or all of the *assets* of B;
- by buying *shares* in B;
- by *making a bid* for B.

Buying assets of company B

If company A only wishes to acquire some or all of the assets of company B, it may do so either by paying cash or by paying in shares of company A; the latter is an example of a vendor consideration issue of shares described in Chapter 18.

Example 20.1 below illustrates acquiring all the assets of a company, rather than the company itself. Note that, in the example, company B remains an independent company.

Example 20.1 Acquisition of assets by share issue

Let us suppose that, at 31 December 1999, the balance sheets of A and B were:

	A	B
	£000	£000
Ordinary share capital	800	80
Reserves	280	340
	1,080	420
Net assets	1,080	420

Suppose A purchases the net assets of B by the issue to company B of 600,000 £1 ordinary shares (valued at par at the time).

Company A's balance sheet at that date would become:

	£000
Ordinary share capital	1,400
Reserves	280
	1,680
Net assets (£1,080,000 + £420,000)	1,500
Goodwill (£600,000 − £420,000)	180
	1,680

Company B's balance sheet after A's purchase would show:

	£000
Ordinary share capital	80
Reserves (£340,000 + £180,000 profit on realisation of net assets)	520
	600
Investment at cost	600

Company B would not cease to exist; it would become an investment holding company.

Had A's shares been listed and had they been standing at, say, 300p at the time, A might have issued 200,000 £1 ordinary shares, and A's balance sheet after the purchase would then have been:

	£000
Ordinary share capital	1,000
Share premium account	400
Other reserves	280
	1,680
Net assets	1,500
Goodwill	180
	1,680

Buying some shares in company B

There are four possibilities:

1. If A acquires less than 3% of the equity of B, A's balance sheet would show the purchase as an investment (see Chapter 9).

2. If A acquires 3% or more of the equity of B, the purchaser would still show the purchase as an investment, but would be obliged by Section 134 of the Companies Act 1989 to declare its interest.

3. If A acquires 20% or more of the equity of B, and is allowed by B to participate in the major policy decisions of B, usually by holding a seat on B's board, then A should treat B as an associated undertaking (see Chapter 22).

4. If A acquires 30% or more of the voting rights of B, or if A in any period of 12 months adds more than 2% to an existing holding of between 30% and 50% in B, then Rules 9.1 and 9.5 of the Takeover Code oblige A to make a bid for the remainder of the equity of B at a price not less than the highest price A paid for any B shares within the preceding 12 months.

Making a takeover bid for company B

Company A may offer the shareholders of B either cash or 'paper' (i.e. shares and/or loan stock and/or warrants of A). If A has already gone over the 30% limit or has added more than 2% in 12 months to a holding of 30–50%, the offer must be in cash or be accompanied by a cash alternative. If the bid results in A acquiring 90% or more of the shares of B that it did not already own, A may force the remaining B shareholders to accept the bid using the procedure laid down in Section 428 of the Companies Act 1985.

The remainder of this chapter is concerned with cases where company A acquires control of company B.

Two ways of accounting

There are two ways of accounting for an acquisition:

1. Acquisition accounting, and
2. Merger accounting.

The two methods are entirely different and give quite different results in the group accounts.

FRS 6 *Acquisitions and mergers* is standard as regards business combinations first accounted for in financial statements for accounting periods commencing on or after 23 December 1994. Previously, under SSAP 23, *Accounting for acquisitions and mergers*, providing the consideration paid for an acquisition was mostly 'paper' (shares of the acquirer), companies were allowed to choose which method to apply in each acquisition.

FRS 6 restricts the use of merger accounting to those business combinations where the use of acquisition accounting would not properly reflect the true nature of the combination. Acquisition accounting is to be used for all business combinations where a party can be identified as having the role of an acquirer. Because acquisition accounting is the usual method, and by far the more common method, we assume acquisition accounting in this chapter, leaving a detailed discussion of the two methods, acquisition accounting and merger accounting, to Chapter 21.

First the reader needs to understand:

(a) what holding companies, subsidiaries and groups are;

(b) how group accounts (or consolidated accounts) work.

HOLDING COMPANIES, SUBSIDIARIES AND GROUPS

Some definitions

Under CA 1985 as amended by CA 1989, s. 258–260), an undertaking is the *parent undertaking* of another undertaking (a *subsidiary undertaking*) if any of the following apply:

(i) it holds a majority of the voting rights in the undertaking;

(ii) it is a member of the undertaking and has the right to appoint or remove directors holding a majority of the voting rights at meetings of the board on all, or substantially all, matters;

(iii) it has the right to exercise a dominant influence over the undertaking:

    (a) by virtue of provisions contained in the undertaking's memorandum or articles; or

    (b) by virtue of a control contract in writing and of a kind authorised by the memorandum or articles and permitted by the law under which the undertaking is established;

(c) it is a member of the undertaking and controls alone, pursuant to an agreement with other shareholders, a majority of the voting rights in the undertaking;

(d) it has a participating interest in the undertaking and it actually exercises a dominant influence over the undertaking; or it and the undertaking are managed on a unified basis.

A *wholly owned subsidiary* is one in which all the share capital is held either by the holding company or by other wholly owned subsidiaries.

A *partially owned subsidiary* is one in which some of the share capital is owned outside the group. For an illustration of these terms, see Example 20.2. A parent undertaking is also often termed the *holding company*, and, as we have seen, a holding company and its subsidiaries are referred to as a *group*.

In the past, all these relationships depended on voting control, but over the years the ingenuity of companies and their financial advisors to facilitate operation overseas, or in an attempt to keep companies off balance sheet (to hide either their liabilities or true profitability or their tendency to be loss-making), or simply to avoid tax, led to numerous devices which kept companies outside the group for purposes of the consolidated accounts. The Companies Act 1985 (as amended) and FRS 2 *Accounting for subsidiary undertakings* have done much to prevent this.

Example 20.2 Partially and wholly owned subsidiaries

H is the holding company of a group of companies, and is incorporated in Great Britain.

H holds   100,000 of the 100,000 ordinary shares of S
H holds   7,500 of the 10,000 ordinary shares of T
S holds   5,100 of the 10,000 ordinary shares of U
T holds   1,000 of the 1,000 ordinary shares of V

The H group may be depicted thus:

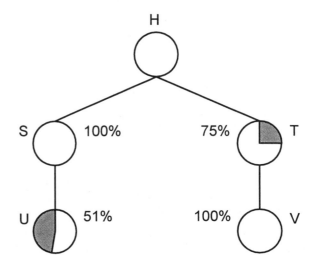

In law, the parent of a subsidiary is the parent of its subsidiary.

The H group consists of:

- H's wholly owned subsidiary S
- H's partially owned listed subsidiary T (in which there is a 25% minority)
- T's wholly owned subsidiary V (which in law is also a subsidiary of H, but colloquially a partially owned subsubsidiary of H)
- S's partially owned subsidiary U (in which there is a 49% minority).

Example 20.3 A more complex situation
Imagine that:

- Company U in Example 20.2 (itself the 51% subsidiary of S, and thus of H) holds:

  600,000 of the 1,000,000 ordinary shares of W
  800,000 of the 2,000,000 ordinary shares of X
  2,400,000 of the 4,000,000 ordinary shares of Y

  and has invested £3,000,000 in a convertible which gives it the right (a) to acquire in due course 80% of the shares of Z and, (b) in the mean time, to exercise control over Z.

- X is a UK company set up jointly with A, a US company. Under the terms of a written control contract, U has the right to appoint the majority of the board of X and thus to exercise control.

- By a reciprocal arrangement, Y, a US company, has a written control contract under which A has the right to appoint the majority of the board and to exercise control.

  U's holdings are depicted below.

W is the subsidiary of H because it is the subsidiary of U which is the subsidiary of S which is the subsidiary of H, despite the fact that H's interest in W is only 51% of 60% = 30.6%.

X is the subsidiary of U and thus of H because U is in a position to control the majority of the board, despite its being only owned 40% by U.

On the other hand, Y is not the subsidiary of U or of H because U is not in a position to control the majority of the board, despite owning 60% of the shares.

Although U holds no shares in Z, Z is a participating interest of U, and in so far as U is in a position to exercise a influence over Z, U is its parent, and it is a subsidiary of H.

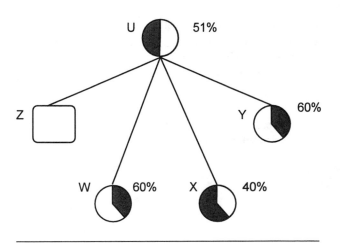

Group accounts

If, at the end of a financial year, a company is a parent company, group accounts have to be prepared as well as individual accounts for the parent company (CA 1985, s. 227), although small and medium-sized private groups are exempt from this (CA 1985, s. 248). Group accounts comprise:

- a consolidated balance sheet; and
- a profit and loss account dealing with the parent company and its subsidiary undertakings.

However, as we shall discuss, subsidiary undertakings may be excluded in certain circumstances (see page 181).

Additional information

If the matters required to be included in group or individual company accounts would not be sufficient to give a true and fair view, the Act requires that 'the necessary additional information shall be given'.

Merger relief

The merger relief provisions contained in Sections 131–134 of the Companies Act 1985, allow companies, subject to specified conditions, to show shares issued *either in a merger or in an acquisition* at their nominal value, i.e. excluding any share premium. Any surplus of net assets acquired over the consideration then becomes a merger reserve and any goodwill arising on consolidation is written off against this reserve.

CONSOLIDATED ACCOUNTS

The consolidated balance sheet

In simple terms a consolidated balance sheet shows all the assets and all the liabilities of all group companies whether wholly owned or partially owned. Where a partially owned subsidiary exists, its shareholders' funds are provided partly by the holding company and partly by the minority.

To illustrate the basic principles of consolidated accounts let us take the case of a holding company, H, with a partially owned subsidiary, S, and imagine that we wish to prepare the consolidated balance sheet for the H GROUP at 31 December 1998. H paid £340,000 cash for 200,000 of the 250,000 £1 ordinary shares of S on 1 January 1996.

The balance sheet of S at acquisition was:

S *Balance sheet at 1 January 1996*

		£000
Fixed assets:	1	
Freehold land and buildings		120
Plant and machinery		146
		266
Net current assets		169
		435
Ordinary share capital		250
Reserves		85
Ordinary shareholders' funds		335
7% Debenture		100
		435

H *and* S *Balance sheets at 31 December 1998*

	H £000	S £000
Fixed assets:		
Freehold land and buildings	150	120
Plant and machinery	250	180
	400	300
Shares in S	340	–
Net current assets	360	200
	1,100	500
Ordinary share capital	500	250
Reserve	480	150
Ordinary shareholders' funds	980	400
10% Unsecured loan stock	120	–
7% Debenture	–	100
	1,100	500

There are six steps to consolidating the two companies' balance sheets at 31 December 1998:

1. *Ascertain the goodwill cost of control* by comparing the cost to H of its investment in S with H's share of the equity shareholders' funds of S at the date of acquisition. The goodwill cost of control will be:

	£000	£000
Purchase consideration		340
Holding company's share of ordinary shareholders' funds at date of acquisition:		
4/5ths of Ordinary share capital	200	
4/5ths of Reserves	68	268
Goodwill cost of control		72

Note that:

(a) Any preacquisition profits of S which have not already been distributed will form part of that company's reserves, and are thus represented by equity shareholders' funds taken into account in computing goodwill cost of control.

(b) Any distribution by S after it is acquired by H which is made out of pre-acquisition profits (i.e. reserves existing at acquisition) must be credited not to the profit and loss account of H as income, but to the asset account 'Investment in S' as a reduction of the purchase price of that investment. The goodwill cost of control does not change.

2. *Compute the holding company's share* of the undistributed post-acquisition profits of the subsidiary.

This equals the holding company's proportion of the change in reserves since the date of acquisition:

$$\frac{200,000}{250,000} \times (£150,000 - £85,000) = £52,000$$

This, added to the holding company's own reserves, represents the reserves of the group which will appear in the consolidated balance sheet:

$$£52,000 + £480,000 = £532,000$$

3. *Compute minority interests* in the net assets of S:

Minority interests =

Minority proportion $\times$ Equity shareholders' funds of S at 31 December 1998

The minority interest in the equity shareholders' funds of S is:

$$\frac{50,000}{250,000} \times £400,000 = £80,000$$

4. *Draw up the consolidated balance sheet:*

 (i) insert as share capital the share capital of the holding company;
(ii) insert the figures already computed for

- goodwill (cost of control) (see 1 above) and
- minority interests (see 3 above);

(iii) show as 'reserves' the total of the reserves of the holding company and the post-acquisition reserves of the subsidiary applicable to the holding company (see 2 on page 175).

5. *Cancel out any inter-company balances*: the aim of the consolidated balance sheet is to show a true and fair view of the state of affairs of the group as a whole. Inter-company balances (where an item represents an asset of one group company and a liability of another) must be cancelled out since they do not concern outsiders. Thus, if S owes H on current account £10,000, this £10,000 will appear as an asset in H's own balance sheet, and as a liability in that of S, but it will not appear at all in the consolidated balance sheet.

6. *Consolidate*: add together like items (e.g. add freehold land and buildings of the holding company and freehold land and buildings of the subsidiary) and show the group totals in the consolidated balance sheet. Omit, in so doing, the share capital of the subsidiary, reserves, and the investment in the subsidiary, which have already been taken into account in steps 1 to 3.

It will be seen (Example 20.4 alongside) that only the share capital of the holding company appears in the consolidated balance sheet. The share capital of the subsidiary has disappeared, one-fifth of it becoming part of 'minority interests' while the other four-fifths (£200,000), together with H's share of S's reserves on acquisition (£68,000) and the 'goodwill-cost of control' (£72,000) balance out the removal of H's balance sheet item 'shares in S' (£340,000).

Example 20.4 H GROUP *Consolidated balance sheet at 31 December 1998: Goodwill treated as a fixed asset*

	£000
Fixed assets:	
Goodwill – cost of control, at cost	72
Freehold land and buildings	270
Plant and machinery	430
	772
Net current assets	560
	1,332

Ordinary share capital	500	
Reserves		532
Ordinary shareholders' funds	1,032	
Minority interests		80
H's 10% ULS		120
S's 7% Debenture		100
		1,332

Goodwill on consolidation in the past

Until about 40 years ago, that is where the 'Goodwill-cost of control' would have remained: in the consolidated balance sheet as a fixed asset at cost, unamortised, in perpetuity, without consideration for whether it continued to exist (i.e. whether acquired business had been closed down, had been sold or, to use the modern term, had become impaired). In their calculations analysts normally netted any goodwill – cost of control against reserves.

The practice grew up of companies doing the same: instead of carrying goodwill forward as a fixed asset, either actually writing it off against reserves (so that the balance no longer existed) or setting the balance off against the total of reserves.

SSAP 22 indeed recommended that: 'Purchased goodwill should normally be eliminated from the accounts immediately on acquisition against reserves ('immediate write-off')' (see Example 20.5 on page 177).

Example 20.5 H GROUP *Consolidated balance sheet at 31 December 1998: Goodwill written off against reserves*

	£000
Fixed assets:	
Freehold land and buildings	270
Plant and machinery	430
	700
Net current assets	560
	1,260
Ordinary share capital	500
Reserves (£532,000 – £72,000)	460
Ordinary shareholders' funds	960
Minority interests	80
H's 10% ULS	120
S's 7% Debenture	100
	1,260

An alternative treatment allowed by SSAP 22 was to amortise purchased goodwill through the profit and loss account over its useful economic life. This method, which is the only method allowed in the United States (see Chapter 30), was used by only a small number of companies in the UK because it reduces profits in future years, which immediate write-off does not (see Example 20.6).

Example 20.6 H GROUP *Consolidated balance sheet at 31 December 1998: Goodwill amortised*

		£000
Fixed assets:		
Goodwill-cost of control, at cost less depreciation		61
Freehold land and buildings		270
Plant and machinery		430
		761
Net current assets		560
		1,321
Ordinary share capital		500
Reserves		521
Ordinary shareholders' funds	1,021	
Minority interests		80
H's 10% ULS		120
S's 7% Debenture		100
		1,321

Note:

On the basis that S was acquired on 1 January 1996, and assuming write-off over 20 years, depreciation on a straight line basis would be £72,000 ÷ 20 = £3,600 per annum, and by 1998 aggregate depreciation would amount to £10,800 (rounded up to £11,000 in the accounts). Each year profits before tax would be £3,600 less than they would have been in either Example 20.4 or 20.5.

Few companies chose to amortise goodwill. One which decided to change *in some cases* to that method was BARCLAYS:

BARCLAYS *Accounting policies 1995*

Change in accounting policy

Up to 31 December 1994, all goodwill arising on the acquisition of subsidiary or associated undertakings was charged directly against reserves in the year of acquisition. Since that date, goodwill arising on acquisition may either be charged directly against reserves or capitalised and amortised against profit over its expected life. The revised policy reflects the view that, for certain strategic acquisitions, it may be more appropriate to capitalise goodwill. Goodwill of £229m arising on the acquisition of Wells Fargo Nikko Investment Advisors, together with the MasterWorks division of Wells Fargo Bank, has been capitalised and will be amortised over 20 years from 1 January 1996. No goodwill has been amortised against profit in 1995. ...

On the other hand, immediate write-off distorted key financial ratios; and some companies, either innocently or deliberately, ignored that fact. For example in 1987 UNILEVER with the acquisition of Chesebrough-Pond's wrote off £1.288 billion of purchased goodwill; then, as a 'key ratio' in its annual report's financial highlights, showed the return on shareholders' equity (ordinary share capital plus reserves) as having increased from 17.8% in 1986 to 25.4% in 1987. If the purchased goodwill had not been written off against reserves, the return in 1987 would have been 17.7%, marginally *down* on the previous year.

Traditionally, when a subsidiary was sold, any goodwill which arose on its purchase was ignored in computing the profit/loss on sale. For some years, that has been no longer the case.

Para. 14 Sch. 2 of the Companies Act 1989 requires companies to show the cumulative amount of goodwill resulting from acquisitions in the current and earlier years which has been written off. The figure is to be the net amount of goodwill attributable to subsidiary undertakings or businesses prior to the balance sheet date. In some cases (like BM GROUP at the top of page 178) the effect of writing off goodwill direct to reserve is spectacular, in others, as with our H GROUP, quite insignificant:

BM GROUP *Extract from Note 24 to 1993 accounts*

Reserves

	£000
At 30 June 1993	43,146
...	

Goodwill

Gross amount written off post 23 December 1989	80,714
Less: Disposals in year to June 1991	(5,924)
Disposals in year to June 1992	(307)
Disposals in year to June 1993	(10,064)
	64,329

The amounts written off in the case of major acquisitive groups could be massive as GRAND METROPOLITAN (now part of DIAGEO) showed:

GRAND METROPOLITAN *Extract from Note 24 to 1995 accounts*

Reserves

...

	£m
At 30 September 1995	2,568
...	

Aggregate goodwill written off, net of disposals, is £4,067m (1994 – £3,298m).

The amounts written off were sufficient in some cases to wipe out the equity shareholders' funds of a group altogether.

Goodwill on consolidation today

Under FRS 10 *Goodwill and intangible assets and* FRS 11 *Impairment of fixed assets and goodwill,* purchased goodwill must be capitalised and either:

(a) amortised over its useful economic life; or
(b) where useful economic life exceeds 20 years, or it is not amortised, its value must be reviewed annually for impairment.

KINGFISHER *Extract from the 1999 accounts*

Note 1. Accounting policies

...

Goodwill and intangible assets

Following the introduction of FRS 10, the Group has changed its accounting policy for goodwill and intangible assets.

Intangible assets, which comprise goodwill arising on acquisitions and acquired licences and copyrights, are stated at cost less amortisation.

Goodwill arising on all acquisitions prior to 31 January 1998 remains eliminated against reserves. This goodwill will be charged in the profit and loss account on subsequent disposal of the business to which it relates. Purchased goodwill arising on acquisitions after 31 January 1998 is treated as an asset on the balance sheet. Where goodwill is regarded as having a limited estimated useful economic life it is amortised on a systematic basis over its life. Where goodwill is regarded as having an indefinite life it is not amortised. The estimated useful economic life is regarded as indefinite where goodwill is capable of continued measurement and the durability of the acquired business can be demonstrated. Where goodwill is not amortised an annual impairment review will be performed and any impairment will be charged to the profit and loss account.

In estimating the useful economic life of goodwill arising, account has been taken of the nature of the business acquired, the stability of the industry, the extent of continuing barriers to market entry and expected future impact of competition. With the exception of BUT S.A. all acquisitions since 31 January 1998 are considered by the directors to have an estimated useful economic life of 20 years.

The Group's acquisition of additional shares in BUT S.A. gave rise to goodwill of £132.8m. The directors consider that BUT S.A. has a proven ability to maintain its market leadership over a long period and will adapt successfully to any foreseeable technological or customer-led changes and that barriers to entry into its market place exist, such that the business will prove to be durable. BUT S.A.'s record since 1972, when it commenced trading, has been one of consistent growth in both turnover and operating profits. Accordingly the goodwill is not amortised and, in order to give a true and fair view, the financial statements depart from the requirement of amortising goodwill over a finite period, as required by the Companies Act. Instead an annual impairment test is undertaken and any impairment that is identified will be charged to the profit and loss account. It is not possible to quantify the effect of the departure from the Companies Act, because no finite life for goodwill can be identified.

Goodwill arising on purchase of pharmacy businesses is amortised over a useful economic life of 20 years. ...

Note 31. Reserves

The cumulative amount of goodwill written off directly to reserves in respect of undertakings still within the Group is £ 1,541.2m (1998: £1,541.2m).

Balance sheet as at 30 January 1999

Group

	Notes	1999	£m 1998
Fixed assets			
Goodwill		264.5	–
Other intangible assets		2.8	–
Total intangible assets	13	267.3	–
Tangible assets	14	2,885.4	1,816.9
...			

REED ELSEVIER *Annual review 1998*

Accounting policies
Goodwill and intangible assets

On the acquisition of a subsidiary, associate, joint venture or business, the purchase consideration is allocated between the underlying net tangible and intangible assets on a fair value basis, with any excess purchase consideration representing goodwill.

In accordance with the new financial reporting standard FRS 10 *Goodwill and intangible assets*, acquired goodwill and intangible assets are now capitalised and amortised systematically over their estimated useful lives up to a maximum period of 20 years. In prior years goodwill was written off directly to reserves on acquisition, whereas intangible assets were capitalised and not amortised, subject to impairment review. This new policy has been applied retrospectively and prior year figures have been restated accordingly...

Under transitional arrangements, any goodwill which had previously been written off to reserves could remain there, until such time as the related business is disposed of (the policy adopted by KINGFISHER).

Companies have, however, the option to reinstate as an asset old goodwill previously written off to reserves. If they do this, either all 'old goodwill' or all 'post-FRS 7 goodwill' should be reinstated. REED ELSEVIER (shown alongside and below) reinstated all old goodwill, amortised as it would have been had the new accounting policy always applied.

REED ELSEVIER *Annual review 1998*

Note 14. Fixed assets – intangible assets and tangible assets

£m		Goodwill and intangible assets			Tangible assets		
Cost	Note	Goodwill	Intangible assets	Total	Land & buildings	Plant, equipment & computer systems	Total
At 1 January 1998 as originally reported		–	2,751	2,751	148	623	771
Prior year adjustment (adoption of FRS 10)	1	1,980	–	1,980	–	–	–
At 1 January 1998 as restated		1,980	2,751	4,731	148	623	771
Acquisitions	13	866	362	1,228	14	11	25
Capital expenditure		–	–	–	8	153	161
Transfer from investments in joint ventures		82	68	150	–	–	–
Disposals of businesses	12	(113)	(220)	(333)	–	(66)	(66)
Disposals		–	–	–	(4)	(48)	(52)
Exchange translation differences		12	12	24	–	6	6
At 31 December 1998		2,827	2,973	5,800	166	679	845
Accumulated amortisation and depreciation							
At 1 January 1998 as originally reported		–	250	250	40	383	423
Prior year adjustment (adoption of FRS 10)	1	909	900	1,809	–	–	–
At 1 January 1998 as restated		909	1,150	2,059	40	383	423
Transfer from investments in joint ventures		7	5	12	–	–	–
Disposals of businesses	12	(71)	(130)	(201)	–	(36)	(36)
Disposals		–	–	–	(3)	(38)	(41)
Amortisation of goodwill and intangible assets		157	166	323	–	–	–
Depreciation		–	–	–	5	92	97
Exchange translation differences		6	3	9	–	3	3
At 31 December 1998		1,008	1,194	2,202	42	404	446
Net book amount							
At 1 January 1998 as restated		1,071	1,601	2,672	108	240	348
At 31 December 1998		1,819	1,779	3,598	124	275	399

The net book amount of tangible fixed assets includes £15m (1997 £9m) in respect of assets held under finance leases.

As can be seen the effect on the balance sheet is significant. But so is that on profits:

REED ELSEVIER *Extract from combined profit and loss statement for the year ended 31 December 1998*

£m	1998 Before exceptional items and amortisation	Exceptional items and amortisation	Total
Gross profit	2,099	–	2.099
Net operating expenses before exceptional items and amortisation ...	(1,304)	–	(1,304)
Exceptional items ...	–	(79)	(79)
Amortisation of goodwill and intangible assets	–	(323)	(323)
Operating profit before joint ventures	795	(402)	393

As a consequence, few companies are likely to reinstate pre-FRS 10 goodwill. As a result, UK GAAP remain out of step with US GAAP (see Chapter 30); and ratios based on either earnings (which are after *some* amortisation of goodwill) or net asset values (which may include all goodwill amortised) or some goodwill (and the cut off date will vary from company to company) or no goodwill (if it is all prior to FRS 10), are distorted.

The consolidated profit and loss account

Consolidated profit and loss accounts follow the same pattern as described for single companies at the beginning of Chapter 16, except that if the group contains partially owned subsidiaries, the minority interests in the profits of those subsidiaries have to be deducted at the after-tax level. Continuing with our example (see page 176) of H owning four-fifths of the £250,000 ordinary share capital of S, let us suppose that at the beginning of 1997, S issued 30,000 £1 7% preference shares to a third party as part payment for a fixed asset, and that the pre-tax profits and tax charges of H and S for that year were as shown here:

	H £	S £	Total £
Profit before tax	72,000	51,200	123,200
Corporation Tax at 25%	18,000	12,800	30,800
Profit after tax	54,000	38,400	92,400

The combined pre-tax profit, tax and profit after tax will be shown in the group's consolidated profit and loss account.

Calculation of minority interests

The minority interests in the profits after tax of S will then be computed as follows:

	S £	Minority interests £
Profit before tax	51,200	
less Corporation Tax	12,800	
Profit after tax	38,400	
less Preference dividends	2,100	2,100
Attributable to ordinary		
	36,300 × ¹/₅ =	7,260
Minority interests total		9,360

It is this sum of £9,360 which will be deducted as 'minority interests' from the profit after tax in the consolidated profit and loss account.

Appropriations of the subsidiary

Suppose, for instance, that S proposed a single ordinary dividend of 4p for 1997. Then the profit attributable to S's ordinary shareholders would be appropriated as follows:

	Total	Minorities	H
Attributable	36,300	7,260	29,040
Proposed dividend of 4.0p per share	10,000	2,000	8,000
Retentions	26,300	5,260	21,040

H's share of the proposed dividend (£8,000) would also appear, as dividends receivable, in the holding company's accounts, and the two figures would cancel out on consolidation. The dividends payable to minority shareholders (£2,000) would be charged (behind the scenes) against the minority interests deducted on consolidation, and the minorities' share of the retentions (£9,360 – £2,100 preference dividends – £2,000 ordinary dividends = £5,260) added to the consolidated balance sheet item 'minority interests'.

The group profit and loss account

Suppose H Group declared dividends of £25,000 for the year. The group profit and loss account would then show:

	£
Profit before tax	123,200
Taxation	(30,800)
Profit after tax	92,400
Minority interests	(9,360)
	83,040
Dividends	(25,000)
Retentions	58,040

Retained profit

The group's retained profit of £58,040 would be carried forward partly in the holding company's accounts:

	£
H's profit after tax	54,000
H's dividends from S	8,000
less Dividends paid by H	25,000
	37,000

The remainder, £21,040, would be carried forward in S's accounts, being H's share of S's retentions.

Some companies show where the retained profits of the group are being carried forward either in the profit and loss account or in a note to the accounts.

Unrealised profits on stocks

It frequently happens that one group company supplies another company within the group with goods in the ordinary course of trade; indeed, this sort of trading link may often be at the very heart of the existence of the group in the first place. But where one group company has made a profit on the supply of goods to another group company and those goods, or some of them, remain in stock at the end of the accounting year, a problem arises and, although nothing can normally be gleaned from the accounts, the procedure for consolidation is designed to prevent a group's profits being artificially inflated by sales within the group.

Exceptions to consolidation of subsidiaries

Group accounts are not required where the company is, at the end of its financial year, the wholly owned subsidiary of a parent undertaking itself required to produce consolidated accounts (CA 1985, s. 228). In Example 20.2, S would not need to produce consolidated accounts, but T would.

Under Section 229 (3) and (4) of the Companies Act 1985 (as amended by Section 5 of the Companies Act 1989) subsidiaries *may* be excluded from consolidation in certain specific circumstances.

FRS 2 *Accounting for subsidiary undertakings*, specifically *requires* that a subsidiary be excluded from consolidation where:

(i) severe long-term restrictions substantially hinder the exercise of the rights of the parent undertaking over the assets or management of the subsidiary undertaking.

(ii) the interest in the subsidiary is held exclusively with a view to subsequent sale and the subsidiary undertaking has not previously been consolidated in group accounts prepared by the parent undertaking.

(iii) the subsidiary undertaking's activities are so different from those of other undertakings to be included in the consolidation that its inclusion would be incompatible with the obligation to give a true and fair view. As FRS 2 makes clear: 'It is exceptional for such circumstances to arise and it is not possible to identify any particular contrast of activities where necessary incompatibility with the true and fair view generally occurs.'

Where subsidiaries are not consolidated for any of these reasons FRS 2 describes the accounting treatment that should be used in each case (FRS 2, paras. 27 to 32).

RIO TINTO *Note to 1997 accounts*

Bouganville Copper Ltd (BCL) The Panguna mine remains shut down. Access to the mine has not been possible.

Accounting treatment of BCL The directors do not have access to reliable, verifiable or objective information on BCL and have therefore decided to exclude BCL information from the financial statements.

Investment in BCL The Group owns 53.6 per cent of the issued share capital ... at 31st December 1997, the market value of the shareholding in BCL was US$66m.

Parent company's own balance sheet

Subsidiaries are normally shown in the parent company's own balance sheet at cost less any amounts written off, but some companies show them at their underlying net asset value, i.e. they use the equity method of accounting (see page 191), which includes them at cost plus the parent company's share of the post-acquisition retained profits and reserves.

Parent company's own profit and loss account

Under Section 230 (3) of the Companies Act 1985, the parent company's profit and loss account may be omitted from the consolidated accounts providing the parent company's balance sheet shows the parent company's profit or loss for the year, as is shown by TT GROUP below. In practice one seldom if ever sees the parent company's own profit and loss account.

TT GROUP *Extract from note 21 to the 1998 accounts*

In accordance with the exemption allowed by Section 230 of the Companies Act 1985, the Company has not presented its own profit and loss account. Of the profit available for appropriation, the sum of £24.4m (1997 – £19.3m) has been dealt with in the financial statements of the Company.

Accounting periods and dates

The financial statements of all subsidiary undertakings to be used in preparing the consolidated financial statements should, wherever practicable, be prepared to the same financial year end and for the same accounting period as those of the parent undertaking of the group (FRS 2, para. 42, reflecting Companies Act 1989, s. 3).

Where the financial year of a subsidiary undertaking differs from that of the parent of the group, interim financial statements should be prepared to the date of the parent's year end. If it is not practicable to use such interim financial statements, the financial statements of the subsidiary for its last financial year should be used, providing that year ended not more than three months before the relevant year end of the parent undertaking of the group.

Further statutory requirements

Emoluments of directors

Chairman's and directors' emoluments, pensions and other details required by Schedule 4 of the Companies Act 1989 and described on page 113, only have to be shown in respect of directors of the parent company, but all their remuneration from the group has to be included (e.g. fees they receive for being directors of subsidiaries).

These requirements have to be met by each subsidiary in its own accounts, which are not normally published but do have to be filed at Companies House.

Information on subsidiaries

Schedule 3 of the Companies Act 1989 requires that where a company has a subsidiary, its accounts must show:

(a) the subsidiary's name;
(b) if incorporated in Great Britain, the subsidiary's country of registration (England or Scotland) if different from that of the holding company; if incorporated outside Great Britain, the subsidiary's country of incorporation;
(c) the proportion of the nominal value of each class of the subsidiary's share capital held by the holding company.

But information about a subsidiary either incorporated, or carrying on business, outside the United Kingdom, which would be harmful to the business of the company or any of its subsidiaries if made public, need not be disclosed if the Department of Trade and Industry agrees.

Where the required information would be of excessive length, details need be given only of subsidiaries principally affecting the profits or losses and the assets of the group, but in this case full particulars must be annexed to the annual return.

Holdings in subsidiaries held directly by the holding company must be distinguished from those held indirectly, i.e. by another subsidiary.

Investment in holding company's shares

With certain minor exceptions a subsidiary cannot be a member of its holding company (i.e. cannot hold shares in its holding company, either directly or through a nominee), and any allotment or transfer of shares in a company to its subsidiary is void (CA 1989, s. 129).

Where a group acquires a subsidiary that holds shares in the group, the group may cancel or retain them. If it retains them, it may not exercise any voting rights on them (CA 1989, s. 129).

Alternatively the shares can be offered to existing shareholders; this is what FEEDEX AGRICULTURAL INDUSTRIES did back in 1987 in a reverse takeover by USBORNE, when Usborne held a 28% stake in Feedex:

FEEDEX AGRICULTURAL INDUSTRIES *Circular to shareholders*

The 5,172,000 Feedex Ordinary shares presently owned by Usborne are being sold to raise additional capital for the Enlarged Group. Hambros, as agents for Usborne, is offering these shares at 45p per share to Qualifying shareholders by way of rights, on the basis of 38 Rights shares for every 100 Feedex Ordinary shares held on 30 October 1987 . . . The Rights Offer is being underwritten by Hambros.

Problem 20.1

Throughout 1999, the Bear Bones Group had three subsidiaries:

- Brown Bear, a 75% owned Canadian company;
- Bear Huggs, a Scottish company 50% owned by Bear Bones which is in a position to direct the financial and operating policies of Bear Huggs;
- Bear Pitts, a wholly owned subsidiary company registered in England.

No shares other than ordinary shares were in issue.

1. Explain clearly what the components of the Sales figure in the group accounts will be.
2. The group profit and loss account shows an operating profit of £13.456m. What proportion of Bear Huggs' operating profit will this include?
3. In the note on the group profit and loss account item Taxation appears 'Foreign Tax £0.123'. What will this represent?
4. In the group profit and loss account is deducted 'Minority interests £0.321m'. Explain what the figure represents.
5. Bear Huggs proposed dividends of £3m in 1999. How much of this will appear under the heading 'Dividends proposed' in the group profit and loss account?
6. In the balance sheet appears, 'Minority interest £34,190,000'. What does that represent?

Chapter 21

ACQUISITIONS AND MERGERS

References: FRS 2 *Accounting for subsidiary undertakings* (as amended by FRS 10); FRS 6 *Acquisitions and mergers*;

FRS 7 *Fair values in acquisition accounting*; FRS 10 *Goodwill and intangible assets*; *City code on takeovers and mergers*.

PREFACE

As we explained in Chapter 20, there are two ways of accounting for an acquisition:

1. Acquisition accounting, and
2. Merger accounting.

The rules for acquisition and merger accounting are contained in FRS 6 *Acquisitions and mergers*, published in September 1994, which restricts the use of merger accounting to those business combinations where the use of acquisition accounting would not properly reflect the true nature of the combination. Acquisition accounting is to be used for all business combinations where a party can be identified as having the role of an acquirer. Five criteria have to be met (see page 187) before merger accounting may be used.

ACQUISITION ACCOUNTING

In Chapter 20 we considered the principles of acquisition accounting. We look now at some of the detailed requirements of financial reporting standards.

Year of acquisition or disposal

In acquisition accounting, when a subsidiary is acquired (or disposed of) during the accounting period, the results of the subsidiary are included from the effective date of acquisition (or to the effective date of disposal), e.g. RMC GROUP.

RMC GROUP *Extract from accounting policies 1998*

Group accounts
The Group accounts comprise the audited accounts of the parent company and all its subsidiary undertakings made up to 31st December, together with the Group's share of the results of its principal joint ventures and associated undertakings. Where necessary, the accounts of subsidiary undertakings, joint ventures and associated undertakings are adjusted to reflect Group accounting policies. Where subsidiary undertakings, joint ventures and associated undertakings are acquired or disposed of during the year, the Group profit and loss account reflects their results from the date of acquisition or to the date of disposal.

The date for accounting for an undertaking becoming a subsidiary undertaking is the date on which control of that undertaking passes to its new parent undertaking (CA 1985, Sch. 4A, para. 9).

At one time unscrupulous companies sometimes backdated an acquisition made towards the end of an accounting period (or excluded the pre-disposal losses of a subsidiary sold during the year), so as to increase the apparent profits in the consolidated accounts, but this is no longer permissible in acquisition accounting.

The date for accounting for an undertaking ceasing to be a subsidiary undertaking is the date on which its former parent relinquishes its control over that undertaking (FRS 2 *Accounting for subsidiary undertakings*, para. 45). The gain or loss directly arising for the group on an undertaking ceasing to be its subsidiary undertaking is calculated by comparing the carrying amount of the net assets, including any related goodwill not previously written off through the profit and loss account, with any proceeds received. Related goodwill that has been written off direct to reserves must be included, i.e. companies are no longer allowed to acquire a subsidiary for, say, £500m, write off £350m of goodwill against reserves to reduce the book cost to £150m, and subsequently sell off the subsidiary for £400m and record a £250m profit on disposal. This was a device that several companies, including TRAFALGAR HOUSE, had used in the past. The requirement (UITF No. 3) that goodwill previously written off against reserves be charged on disposal to revenue did not find universal approval, however.

GOODHEAD GROUP 1993 Accounts

Acquisition goodwill previously written off to reserve was, as required by FRS 3, charged on disposal of discontinued operations to profit and loss account.

Extract from Chairman's Statement 1993
'... of the losses, £10,257,000 is a technical adjustment relating to goodwill previously written off against reserves.'

That is not the view of the ASB.

Scope for enhancing profits

In acquisition accounting, the lack of rules on attributing 'fair values' to assets acquired tempted some companies to attribute the lowest possible values, so that future depreciation charges on fixed assets were minimised and undervalued stock reduced future cost of sales, both of which enhanced profits. Excessive advantage was often taken in assessing fair values of provisions for anticipated future losses or costs of reorganisation of an acquisition. Any provision subsequently found to be excessive was then released to the profit and loss account. Some companies even went so far as to provide for rationalisation and restructuring costs of existing group companies. Indeed it was not unknown for a group to pay a substantial sum for a subsidiary the fair value of which was reported to be negative. A stop has been put to this.

FRS 7 *Fair values in acquisition accounting* (published in September 1994) requires that the

identifiable assets and liabilities acquired should be those of the acquired entity that existed at the date of acquisition, and in particular:

- should not reflect increases or decreases resulting from the acquirer's intentions or future actions;
- impairments, or other changes resulting from events subsequent to the acquisition; are to be treated as post-acquisition;
- provisions should not include provisions for future operating losses; or for reorganisation and integration costs to be incurred as a result of the acquisition, whether they relate to the acquired entity or to the acquiring group.

Except where the FRS lays down otherwise, the acquirer's accounting policies should be used. This can have a significant effect, as TOMKINS showed.

TOMKINS *Extract from Financial Review 1993*

Ranks Hovis McDougall
The harmonisation of RHM's accounting with Tomkins' more prudent policies and the fair valuation of assets would require reductions in the book value of assets acquired. ... As it is not Tomkins' policy to ascribe values to brands, we have written off RHM's brand valuation of £459m.

The fair value of a tangible fixed asset should be based on:

(a) market value, if assets similar in type and condition are bought and sold on a open market; or
(b) depreciated replacement cost, reflecting the acquired business's normal buying process and the sources of supply and prices available to it.

The fair value should not exceed the recoverable amount of the asset.

Where an intangible asset is recognised, its fair value should be based on its replacement cost, which is normally its estimated market value.

Stocks, including commodity stocks, that the acquired entity trades on a market in which it participates as both a buyer and a seller should be valued at current market prices. Other stocks, and work-in-progress, should be valued at the lower of replacement cost and net realisable value.

Quoted investments are to be valued at market price, adjusted if necessary for unusual price fluctuations or for the size of the holding.

The fair values of monetary assets and liabilities, including accruals and provisions, should take into account the amounts expected to be received or paid, and their timing. Values are to be discounted, if appropriate, to present value.

Special rules apply to businesses sold or held exclusively with a view to sale; and there are rules for determining the cost of acquisition.

The identification and valuation of assets and liabilities acquired should be completed, if possible, FRS 7 suggests, by the date on which the first post-acquisition financial statements of the acquirer are approved by the directors. If that is not possible, provisional valuations should be made, and these should if necessary be amended in the next financial statements, with a corresponding adjustment to goodwill. Thereafter, any adjustments, except for the correction of fundamental errors (which give rise to prior year adjustments), should be recognised as gains or losses when identified.

Disclosure requirements

FRS 6 distinguishes between acquisitions which are (a) material; and (b) substantial. Most disclosures are required in respect of all material acquisitions, but there are additional requirements which apply only to substantial acquisitions.

In the case of material acquisitions, it is necessary to show:

1. The composition and fair value of the consideration given, including the nature of any deferred or contingent purchase consideration, and where it is contingent the range of possible outcomes and the principal factors affecting it.
2. A table showing for each class of assets and liabilities of the acquired entity:

   (a) The book values as recorded in the acquired entity's books immediately before the acquisition and before any fair value adjustments;
   (b) The fair value adjustments analysed into:

      (i) revaluations;
      (ii) adjustments to achieve consistency of accounting policies, and
      (iii) any other significant adjustments; and

   (c) The fair values at the date of acquisition.

   The table should include a statement of the amount of purchased goodwill or negative goodwill arising on the acquisition. Provi-sions for reorganisation and restructuring costs that are included in the liabilities of the acquired entity, and related to asset write-downs, made in the twelve months up to the date of acquisition, should be identified separately. See TARSUS GROUP, on page 199.

3. As required by FRS 3 *Reporting financial performance*, in the period of acquisition the post-acquisition results of the acquired entity should be shown, normally as a component of continuing operations. If it has a material impact on a business segment, this should be disclosed and explained (see BTP alongside).

4. Any exceptional profit or loss in periods following the acquisition that is determined using the fair values recognised in the acquisition should be disclosed and identified as relating to the acquisition.
5. Costs incurred in reorganising, restructuring and integrating the acquisition which (i) would not have been incurred had the acquisition not taken place; or (ii) relate to a project identified and controlled by management as part of a reorganisation or integration programme or as a direct consequence of post-acquisition review, are to be disclosed.
6. Movements on provisions or accruals for costs related to an acquisition should be disclosed and analysed between amounts used for the specific purpose for which they were created and the amounts released unused.
7. Cash flow information is required in accordance with FRS 1 (see Chapter 19).
8. Information is required (a) for the period from the beginning of the acquired entity's financial year to the date of acquisition, and (b) for the previous financial year, on the profit after taxation and minority interests of the acquired entity (see BTP below).

BTP *Extracts from Note 25 to the 1998 accounts*
During the year, PCR Inc. contributed turnover of £30.3m and operating profit of £5.7m to the results of the Biocides & Fine Chemicals Division. The net assets of PCR Inc. at 31 March 1998 were £11.0m.

In the previous year, the company reported US $48m (£29.2m) turnover and US $10.2m (£6.2m) operating profit before US $1.8m (£1.1m) HQ charges. Net assets were US $26m (£15.8m).

...

On 6 October 1997, the Group acquired the leather and speciality chemical businesses of Yorkshire Group plc ('Yorkshire'), whose principal operations were in the UK, USA, Italy, Australia and Spain.

During the year the Yorkshire businesses contributed turnover of £14.3m and operating profit of £1.5m to the results of the Performance Chemicals Division. The net assets of the Yorkshire businesses at 31 March 1998 were £15.1m.

Because of the integrated manner in which the businesses of Yorkshire Group plc were historically managed it is not possible to determine historic operating profits. However, in the year ended 31 December 1996 the Yorkshire businesses had estimated operating profits, before allocation of central costs, of £5.7m on external turnover of £34.9m.

No comparable estimate is readily available for external turnover or operating profit for the period 1 January 1997 to 5 October 1997.

---

9. In the case of substantial acquisitions a summarised profit and loss account and statement of total recognised gains and losses of the acquired entity for the period from the beginning of its financial year to the effective date of acquisition is required.

10. Where an acquisition or disposal takes place shortly after the balance sheet date, it is likely to be a post balance sheet event requiring disclosure under SSAP 17 *Accounting for post balance sheet events* (see BLUE CIRCLE INDUSTRIES below and alongside).

BLUE CIRCLE INDUSTRIES *Extract from the notes to the 1998 accounts*

30. Post-balance sheet events

In early February 1999 the Group sold its Bathrooms Division, consisting of two main businesses, Armitage Shanks (UK) and Ceramica Dolomite (Italy), for a total consideration of £253.0m on a cash and debt free basis. The results of the Bathrooms Division are included within discontinued activities in the profit and loss account.

In late January 1999, the Group acquired convertible loan notes in Fortune Cement Corporation of the Philippines for a consideration of £52.0m and, if converted, the Group would raise its stake in the company from 20.0 per cent to 51.2 per cent.

In late October 1998, Malayan Cement Berhad (MCB), the Group's 57.83 per cent subsidiary, announced that it had signed a share purchase agreement to acquire 65.02 per cent of the equity of Kedah Cement Holdings Berhad, the Malaysian-based cement manufacturer. The acquisition will trigger a General Offer and it is intended that MCB will seek to purchase the remaining minority stakes. Total consideration for the 100 per cent stake is 1.079 billion Ringgit. In addition, MCB will assume 100 per cent of the net debt of the business, all denominated in local currency and estimated at 1.2 billion Ringgit at completion.

In February 1999, the Group signed a letter of intent for the sale of its German wholesaling business, Brotje Wholesalers, for an estimated cash consideration of DM 115 million, to be finalised at the date of closing. The transaction is expected to be completed by mid 1999, subject to clearance by the relevant authorities in Germany.

BTP *Extract from the 1998 accounts*

Group Profit and Loss Account for the year ended 31 March 1998

	Notes	1998 Before exceptional items £m	1998 Exceptional items £m	1998 Total £m	1997 £m
Turnover					
Continuing operations		299.7	–	299.7	285.4
Acquisitions		48.7	–	48.7	–
Discontinued operations		90.4	–	90.4	119.1
	1	438.8	–	438.8	404.5
Cost of sales	3	(309.0)	–	(309.0)	(294.0)
Gross profit		129.8	–	129.8	110.5
Distribution costs	3	(35.3)	–	(35.3)	(31.5)
Administration expenses	3	(37.0)	–	(37.0)	(29.0)
Share of losses of associate undertaking	12	(0.3)	–	(0.3)	(0.4)
Operating profit					
Continuing operations		46.3	–	46.3	44.3
Acquisitions		7.0	–	7.0	–
Discontinued operations		3.9	–	3.9	5.3
Operating profit	1,4	57.2	–	57.2	49.6
Loss on sale of discontinued businesses	2	–	(9.9)	(9.9)	–
Profit on ordinary activities before interest		57.2	(9.9)	47.3	49.6

...

MERGER ACCOUNTING

It was long argued that the acquisition method of accounting does not satisfactorily reflect a true amalgamation of interests because:

(a) any excess of consideration over net asset value gives rise to goodwill (and, normally, the need to amortise this);

(b) the formerly 'distributable' reserves of acquired companies become 'non-distributable';

(c) any excess of the market value of shares issued over their nominal value has to go into the share premium account.

To overcome these difficulties, the merger method of accounting was developed, and was used in several major mergers at the end of the 1960s, including CADBURY with SCHWEPPES and TRUST HOUSE with FORTE. Under merger accounting, aptly called 'pooling of interests' in the United States, the following occur:

1. The assets and liabilities of both companies are incorporated into the group accounts at book value. They are not required to be adjusted to fair value on consolidation, though appropriate adjustments are made to achieve uniformity of accounting policies.

2. The pre-acquisition reserves of the merging companies are not capitalised, but are available to the enlarged group.

3. The shares issued as consideration are recorded at their nominal value (so there is no share premium and no goodwill arises on consolidation).

4. If the total nominal value of the shares issued is more than the total nominal value of the shares of the merged company, the difference is deducted from group reserves. If the total value is less, the shortfall becomes a non-distributable reserve. The merger expenses are not included as part of this adjustment, but charged through profit and loss account.

5. At the subsequent year end, the consolidated profit and loss account takes in the turnover, costs and profits of all merging companies for a full year.

Although an early Exposure Draft (ED 3, issued in 1971) advocated merger accounting in certain limited circumstances (e.g. where the merging companies were not too dissimilar in size), the ruling in a subsequent test case, *Shearer* v. *Bercain Limited*, held that, because of Section 56 of the Companies Act 1948, the merger method of accounting was not lawful.

However, the situation was changed by the Companies Act 1981, which contained provisions allowing merger accounting where at least 90% of the cost of the acquisition is paid for by the issue of shares in the acquiring company (now CA 1989, Sch. 2, para. 10).

Under FRS 6 (September 1994) a business combination should be accounted for using merger accounting if (and only if):

(a) the use of merger accounting is not prohibited by the Companies Act; and

(b) the combination meets certain criteria:

   (i) no party to the combination is portrayed as either acquirer or acquired;

   (ii) all parties to the combination participate in establishing the management structure for the combined entity and in selecting the management personnel, and such decisions are made on the basis of a consensus;

   (iii) the relative sizes of the combining entities are not so disparate that one party effectively dominates the combined entity merely by virtue of its relative size;

   (iv) the consideration must be all or virtually all equity;

   (v) no equity shareholder of any of the combining entities must retain any material interest in only one part of the combined entity.

Example 21.1, at the top of the next page, shows how merger accounting works, and compares it with acquisition accounting.

Profits in the year of merger

The consolidated profit and loss account should include the profits (or losses) of all merged entities for the entire period, i.e. without adjustment for that part of the period prior to the merger. Corresponding amounts should be presented as if the companies had been combined throughout the previous period.

FRS 6 extends the Companies Act 1985, Sch. 4A, para. 13 (4) requirements somewhat. In particular, it requires:

1. An analyses of the principal components of the current year's profit and loss account and statement of recognised gains and losses into:

   (i) amounts relating to the merged entity for the period after the merger; and

   (ii) for each party to the merger, amounts relating to the period up to the merger.

Example 21.1 Merger accounting of an acquisition

At 31 December 1999 the balance sheets of companies A and B were:

	A	B
	£000	£000
Ordinary share capital	800	80
Reserves	280	340
	1,080	420
Net assets	1,080	420

A made a successful bid for B, acquiring the entire share capital of B by the issue of 200,000 new A £1 ordinary shares (standing at 300p each). The consolidated balance sheet of A would then show:

	Merger	Acquisition
	£000	£000
Ordinary share capital	1,000	1,000
Share premium account	–	400
Distributable reserves	500[1]	160
	1,500	1,560
Net assets	1,500	1,560[2]

[1] Computed as follows:

	£000
Distributable reserves of A	280
Distributable reserves of B	340
	620
Less the excess of the nominal value of the shares A issued (£200,000) over the nominal value of the shares in B (£80,000)	120
	500

[2] Under acquisition accounting, the net assets of B were taken at fair value £480,000, rather than at book value £420,000.

2. An analysis between the parties to the merger of the principal components of the profit and loss account and statement of total recognised gains and losses for the previous financial year.
3. The composition and fair value of the consideration given by the issuing company and its subsidiary undertakings.
4. The nature and amount of significant accounting adjustments made to the net assets of any party to the merger to achieve consistency of accounting policies, and an explanation of any other significant adjustments made to the net assets of any party to the merger as a consequence of the merger.
5. A statement of the adjustments to consolidated reserves resulting from the merger.

As a minimum the analyses in 1 and 2 should show turnover, operating profit, and exceptional items, split between continuing operations, discontinued operations and acquisitions; profit before taxation, taxation and minority interests; and extraordinary items.

Unfortunately, the term merger is used in at least three different senses:

1. To refer to a transaction which falls within the merger relief provisions in Sections 131–134 of the Companies Act 1985 (see page 174) which allow companies to show shares issued in a merger or in an acquisition at their nominal value, i.e. excluding any share premium. Any surplus of net assets acquired over the consideration then becomes a merger reserve and any goodwill arising on consolidation is written off against this reserve.
2. To refer to a transaction which is a merger as defined by FRS 6.
3. To refer to a transaction which management view as a merger. Which of these is this KINGFISHER transaction?

KINGFISHER *Extract from note 37 to the 1999 accounts*

37. Acquisitions
(a) Merger of B&Q and Castorama

On 18 December 1998, the effective date of acquisition, the Group completed the combination of B&Q plc with Castorama Dubois Investissements S.C.A. (Castorama). The transaction has been treated as an acquisition and was effected by the transfer by the Group of its 100% interest in B&Q in exchange for a 57.9% interest (54.6% on a fully diluted basis) in the consequently enlarged Castorama group. The transaction was effected by an exchange of shares, being new shares in Castorama for the Group's shares in B&Q, and the book value of the 42.1% of the assets of B&Q at the date of acquisition has been treated as the cost of that investment. The difference between the consideration and the fair value of the Castorama net assets received has been treated as a non-distributable reserve. Since the date of acquisition, Castorama contributed £140.8m to turnover, £3.4m to profit before interest and £2.3m to profit after interest. Castorama contributed £31.1m to the Group's net operating cash flows, paid £1.1m in respect of interest, utilised £3.7m for capital expenditure and incurred £6.5m in management of liquid resources.

A summarised profit and loss account for Castorama for the period from 1 January 1998 to completion of the merger is detailed in the table below:

	£m
Sales	2,102.1
Operating profit	98.8
Taxation	(42.4)
Profit after taxation	56.4
Minority interest	–
Profit after taxation and minority interest	56.4

The statement of total recognised gains and losses for the same period is:

	£m
Profit for the financial year	56.4
Unrealised surplus on revaluation of properties	–
Foreign exchange loss	(17.6)
Total recognised gains and losses relating to the year	38.8

In its last financial year to 31 December 1997, Castorama made a profit after tax and minority interests of £36.1m.

The above results have been translated at the exchange rates of £1: FF9.622 for the year ended 31 December 1998 and £1: FF9.656 for the year ended 31 December 1997.

The pre-acquisition figures quoted above are stated before any adjustments for Kingfisher accounting policies and were prepared under local accounting principles.

It falls under our category 3.

Problem 21.1

You are provided with this extract from the 1996 accounts of GIBBON GROUP.

Consolidated profit and loss account for the year ended 31 March 1996

	Continuing operations 1996 £000	Acqui-sitions 1996 £000	Total 1996 £000	1995 £000
Turnover	28,612	381	28,993	27,447
Cost of sales	(18,137)	(206)	(18,343)	(16,676)
Gross profit	10,475	175	10,650	10,771
Distribution costs	(3,839)	(12)	(3,851)	(4,090)
Administrative expenses	(4,006)	(99)	(4,105)	(4,281)
	2,630	64	2,694	2,400
Other operating income	91	–	91	102
Operating profit	2,721	64	2,785	2,502

During the year the group purchased two subsidiaries, the assets and liabilities of which were (in total) as follows:

	Book value £000	Fair value £000
Fixed assets	382	258
Stocks	295	255
Debtors	272	272
Cash at bank and in hand	153	153
Creditors	(911)	(911)
	191	27

The purchase consideration was satisfied by:

	£000
Cash	767
Issue of shares (10p ordinary shares with a nominal value of £22,000)	400
Deferred consideration – cash	251
Deferred consideration – shares to be issued	150
	1,568

The subsidiaries acquired had £153,000 in the bank. The share issues met the conditions in Sections 131–134 of the Companies Act 1985.

1. Did the transactions represent acquisitions or mergers in the terms of FRS 6?
2. Compute the goodwill which arose during the year.
3. What net outflow would appear in the group cash flow statement under the heading Purchase of subsidiaries?
4. What amount would be credited in respect of these transactions:
   (a) to share premium account;
   (b) to merger reserve?
5. You are asked whether the 'acquisitions' were successful. What important information, which the group was required to give, and in fact did, is not provided above but would be necessary to assess the companies' profitability?

Chapter 22

ASSOCIATES, JOINT VENTURES AND RELATED PARTIES

Companies Act requirements

The Companies Act 1989 abolished the term 're-lated company' and introduced two new terms: a *participating interest in an undertaking*, and an *associated undertaking*.

Undertakings include partnerships and unincorporated associations carrying on a trade or business as well as companies (CA 1989, s. 22) and an *interest* includes convertible securities and options as well as shares.

A *participating interest* is an interest held by the investing group or company on a long-term basis to secure a contribution to its activities by the exercise of control or influence. A holding by group companies of 20% or more of the shares of an undertaking is presumed to be a participating interest unless the contrary is shown.

An *associated undertaking* is an undertaking (other than a subsidiary or a proportionally consolidated joint venture) in which the investing group or company has a participating interest and over whose operating and financial policy it exercises a significant influence (CA 1989, Sch. 2, para. 20).

Accounting standards

SSAP 1 *Accounting for associated companies* seemed a strange subject with which to start accounting standards, but the ASC began there because this was an area which was perceived to be (and continued to be) troublesome. Published in January 1971, the standard was amended in August 1974, revised in April 1982, and amended again in December 1990. It now applies only to smaller entities. More generally, the rules on accounting for associates and joint ventures are now found in FRS 9 *Associates and joint ventures* published in

November 1997.

FRS 9 recognises five types of interest:

1. A subsidiary (which we considered in Chapters 20 and 21; see also FRS 2);
2. a joint arrangement that is not an entity;
3. a joint venture;
4. an associate;
5. a simple investment (which we considered in Chapters 9 and 12).

Of these 2, 3 and 4 fall under the heading associates and joint ventures, are the subject of this chapter and are covered by FRS 9.

Joint arrangement that is not an entity

Where two or more entities, e.g. companies, participate in an arrangement to carry on part of their trade, that arrangement falls under this heading unless it carries on a trade or business of its own. A joint arrangement will not be an entity if it is no more than a cost- or risk-sharing means of carrying out a process in the participants' trades or businesses – for example a joint marketing or distribution network or a shared production facility. A joint arrangement carrying out a single project (as, for example, occurs in the construction industry) tends to fall under this head, but the nature of such a joint arrangement may change over time – for example, a pipeline operated as a joint arrangement that initially provided a service only directly to the participants may develop into a pipeline business providing services to others.

Each party to a joint arrangement that is not an entity should account for its own share of the assets, liabilities and cash flows in the joint arrangement, measured according to the terms of that arrangement.

Associate

Where the investor holds a participating interest and exercises *significant influence* the entity is an associate. This covers cases where the investor:

- has a *long-term interest* and
- is actively involved, and influential, in the direction of its investee through its participation in policy decisions covering the aspects of policy relevant to the investor, including decisions on strategic issues such as:

(a) the expansion or contraction of the business, participation in other entities or changes in products, markets and activities of its investee;

(b) determining the balance between dividend and reinvestment.

The investor should include its associates in its consolidated financial statements using what is called *the equity method.*

The equity method

Under the equity method:

1. In the investor's consolidated profit and loss account the investor's share of its associates' operating result should be included immediately after group operating result [B] in the DI-AGEO illustration below.

2. Any amortisation or write-down of goodwill arising on acquiring associates should be charged at this point [None].

3. The investor's share of any exceptional items [I and Note 6] included after operating profit or of interest [C and Note 7] should be shown separately from amounts for the group.

4. From the level of profit before tax [D], the investor's share of the relevant amounts for associates should be included within the amounts for the group, though for items such as taxation [E and Note 8] the amounts relating

---

DIAGEO *Extract from 1998 accounts*
Consolidated profit and loss account

	Notes	18 months ended 30 June 1998 — Before exceptional items £m	Exceptional items £m	Total £m	12 months ended 31 December 1996 — Before exceptional items £m	Exceptional items £m	Total £m
Turnover [A]							
Continuing operations		17,592		17,592	12,753		12,753
Discontinued operations		106		106	687		687
Group turnover	...	17,698		17,698	13,440		13,440
Operating costs	...	(14,958)	(572)	(15,530)	(11,439)	–	(11,439)
Operating profit							
Continuing operations		2,740	(572)	2,168	1,965		1,965
Discontinued operations		–	–	–	36		36
Group operating profit	...	2,740	(572)	2,168	2,001	–	2,001
Share of profits of associates [B]	5	287	(15)	272	205	(24)	181
Trading profit		3,027	(587)	2,440	2,206	(24)	2,182
Continuing operations							
Disposal of fixed assets			(2)	(2)		(13)	(13)
Sale of businesses	6		523	523		(7)	(7)
Merger expenses	6		(85)	(85)		–	–
Discontinued operations							
Sale of businesses [I]	6		(272)	(272)		(292)	(292)
Utilisation/(set up) of provisions for losses on sale of businesses	6		250	250		(250)	(211)
			414	414		(562)	(562)
Interest payable (net) [C]	7	(428)	(58)	(486)	(288)	–	(288)
Profit on ordinary activities before taxation [D]		2,599	(231)	2,368	1,918	(586)	1,332
Taxation on profit on ordinary activities [E]	8	(710)	(199)	(909)	(523)	(23)	(546)
Profit on ordinary activities after taxation [F]		1,889	(430)	1,459	1,395	(609)	786

DIAGEO *Extract from 1998 accounts*
Consolidated balance sheet

	Notes	30 Jun 1998 £m	30 Jun 1998 £m	30 Jun 1997 (unaudited) £m	30 Jun 1997 (unaudited) £m	31 Dec 1996 £m	31 Dec 1996 £m
Fixed assets							
Intangible assets	...		4,727		4,976		4,925
Tangible assets	...		3,006		3,127		3,264
Investments [G]	14		1,244		1,522		1,598
			8,977		9,625		9,787
Current assets							
Stocks	...	2,236		2,374		2,349	
Debtors – due within one year	...	2,037		2,256		2,738	
Debtors – due after more than one year	...	999		950		920	
Debtors subject to financing arrangements (franchisee loans of £145m, less non-returnable proceeds of £127m.)	...	18		10		8	
Investments	...	484					
Cash at bank and in hand	...	2,503		1,255		1,448	
			8,277		7,763		8,068

...

---

to associates should be disclosed. In the consolidated statement of total recognised gains and losses the investor's share of the total recognised gains and losses of its associates should be included, shown separately under each heading, if material. It is rare to find any mention of associates here.

5. In the balance sheet the investor's share of the net assets of its associates should be included and separately disclosed [G and Note 14].

6. The cash flow statement should include the cash flows between the investor and its associates. Dividends received from associates now appear as the second line [K on page 193] immediately after *Net cash inflow from operating activities* and sales of associates [L] under *Acquisitions and disposals*. There were no *Loans to associates;* had there been they would have been disclosed.

7. Goodwill arising on the investor's acquisition of its associates, less any amortisation or write-down, should be included in the carrying amount for the associates but should be disclosed separately. In the profit and loss account the amortisation or write-down of such goodwill should be separately disclosed as part of the investor's share of its associates' results.

8. An indication may be given of the size of the business as a whole, by combining the investor's share of its associates' turnover with group turnover as a memorandum item

DIAGEO *Extract from notes to the 1998 accounts*
6. Exceptional items
(iii) Sale of businesses
(b) The sale of the group's interests in its pub estate associates, Inntrepreneur Pub Company Ltd and Spring Inns Ltd, for a consideration of £200m was completed on 28 March 1998. The loss on sale of £54m was after charging £37m of goodwill previously written off [I].

...

7. Interest payable (net)

	18m ended 30 Jun 1998 £m	12m ended 31 Dec 1996 £m
On bank loans and overdrafts	36	32
On all other loans	635	361
Share of net interest payable by Associates [J]	6	8
	677	401
	...	...
	486	288

8. Taxation

UK corporation tax payable at 31.3% (1996 – 33%)	465	319
Less: Double taxation relief	...	...
...		
Taxation on the group's share of profits of associates [H]	102	67

...

DIAGEO *Extract from 1998 accounts*
Consolidated cash flow statement

	18m ended 30 Jun 1998	12m ended 30 Jun 1998 (unaudited)	12m ended 31 Dec 1996
	£m	£m	£m
Net cash inflow from operating activities	3,069	1,866	2,2 15
Dividends received from associates [K]	162	120	50
...			
Returns on investments and servicing of finance	...	...	...
Taxation	(834)	(603)	(606)
...			
Capital expenditure and financial investment	(506)	(366)	(395)
Free cash flow	1,415	735	894
...	...	...	...
Sale of associates [L]	240	240	–
Acquisitions and disposals	1,405	1,368	114
...			

DIAGEO *Extract from Note 14 to the 1998 accounts*
14. Fixed assets – investments

	Investment in associates £m	...
Cost		
At 31 December 1996	1,451	
Exchange adjustments	(142)	
Additions	35	
Share of retained profits for the period	2	
Disposals	(254)	
At 30 June 1998	1,092	
Provisions		
At 31 December 1996	–	
Utilised	–	
At 30 June 1998	–	
Net book value		
At 30 June 1998	1,092	
At 31 December 1996	1,451	

Investment in associates of £1,092m (1996 – £1,451m) comprises the cost of shares, less goodwill written off on acquisition, of £900m (1996 -- £1,500m) plus the group's share of post-acquisition reserves of £192m (1996 – deficit of £49m). Investment in associates includes £825m (1996 – £902m) in respect of Moët Hennessy. The investment in Inntrepreneur Pub Company Ltd was sold during the period.

...

provided the investor's share of its associates' turnover is clearly distinguished. [A] on page 191 does not include associates.

Interest held on a long-term basis

For an interest to be an associate the investor must have a long-term interest, i.e. the interest must be held other than exclusively with a view to subsequent resale. An interest held exclusively with a view to subsequent resale is:

(a) an interest for which a purchaser has been identified or is being sought, and which is reasonably expected to be disposed of within approximately one year of its date of acquisition; or

(b) an interest that was acquired as a result of the enforcement of a security, unless the interest has become part of the continuing activities of the group or the holder acts as if it intends the interest to become so.

Significant influence

For an investment to be an associate, its investor must exercise, not simply *be in a position to*

exercise, significant influence over the investee's operating and financial policies. The investor needs an agreement or understanding, formal or informal, with its associate to provide the basis for its significant influence. An investor exercising significant influence will be directly involved in the operating and financial policies of its associate rather than passively awaiting the outcome of its investee's policies.

Over time, the associate will generally implement policies that are consistent with the strategy of the investor and avoid implementing policies that are contrary to the investor's interests. If an investee persistently implements policies that are inconsistent with its investor's strategy, that investor clearly does not exercise significant influence over its investee.

Active involvement in the operating and financial policies of an associate requires inter alia that the investor should have a voice in decisions on strategic issues such as determining the balance between dividend and reinvestment. The investor's involvement in its associate is usually achieved through nomination to the board of directors (or its equivalent) but may result from any arrangement that allows the investor to participate effectively in policy-making decisions. It is unlikely that an investor can exercise significant influence unless it has a substantial basis of voting power. A holding of 20 per cent or more of the voting rights in another entity *suggests, but does not ensure*, that the investor exercises significant influence over that entity (FRS 9 para. 16).

The decisive feature in identifying investments that are associates is the actual relationship between investor and investee. If the actual relationship develops differently from that assumed from the arrangements on acquisition, it may be necessary to modify the treatment originally adopted in the financial statements. But once the actual relationship has been established and the investor has qualified as exercising significant influence over an entity, it should be regarded as continuing to exercise such influence until an event or transaction removes the investor's ability to do so (para. 17).

The precise wording of the standard has changed over time particularly as regards the 20 per cent test. Many companies, like PHOTO-ME, consider that companies formerly treated as associates are not associates under the terms of FRS 9.

PHOTO-ME *Note on accounting policies 1998*

(b) Changes in accounting policy

...

(ii) Following the publication of FRS 9 *Associates and Joint Ventures*, the directors have decided that certain investments, previously accounted for as associated undertakings, no longer satisfy the definition of associated undertakings in FRS 9 as the Group is not able to exercise significant influence. As a result, such investments have been reclassified as other investments (Note 11). Debtor and creditor balances with associates are now included within trade debtors (Note 13) and trade creditors (Note 15), respectively, and the reserves have been restated (Note 19).

The comparative figures for the year to 30 April 1997 for debtors and creditors have been adjusted to reflect the new policy.

Joint venture

Where the investor holds a long-term interest and shares control under a contractual arrangement that arrangement is referred to as a joint venture.

The joint venture agreement can override the rights normally conferred by ownership interests with the effect that:

- acting together, the venturers can control the venture and there are procedures for such joint action;
- each venturer has (implicitly or explicitly) a veto over strategic policy decisions.

There is usually a procedure for settling disputes between venturers and, possibly, for terminating the joint venture.

The venturer should use the gross equity method to account for the joint venture.

Gross equity method

Under what is termed the gross equity method, all the amounts included under the equity method (see page 191) have to be shown and, in addition:

(a) *on the face of the balance sheet*, the venturer's share of:

- the gross assets [P in the GREAT UNIVERSAL STORES illustration on page 195] and
- the gross liabilities [Q]

of its joint ventures, and,

(b) *in the profit and loss account*, the venturer's share of their turnover [R] distinguished from that of the group.

Had it not been for the requirement to use the gross equity method, GREAT UNIVERSAL STORES would have shown the investment in BL UNIVERSAL in 1998 as £92.4m (1997 £30.2m), rather spelling out the very substantial gross assets and liabilities involved. This was often the case where there was a joint venture between the owners of land and builders/developers.

Where the venturer conducts a major part of its business through joint ventures, it may show fuller information provided all amounts are distinguished from those of the group [Note 16 on page 195–6].

The treatment of losses and interests in net liabilities

The investor should continue to record changes in the carrying amount for each associate and joint venture even if application of the equity method or gross equity method results in an interest in net liabilities rather than net assets i.e. if there are heavy losses. The only exception is where there is sufficient evidence that an event has irrevocably changed the relationship between the investor and its investee, marking its irreversible withdrawal from its investee as its associate or joint venture.

In the investor's own accounts

In the investor's own financial statements associates and joint ventures should be treated as fixed asset investments, at cost less any amounts written off, or at a valuation.

GREAT UNIVERSAL STORES *Consolidated profit and loss account*
Consolidated profit and loss account for the year ended 31 March 1998

	Notes	1998 *Before exceptional items* £m	1998 *Exceptional items (note ...)* £m	1998 *Total* £m	1997* *Before exceptional items* £m	1997* *Exceptional items (note ...)* £m	1997* *Total* £m
Turnover		3,362.7		3,362.7	2,893.8		2,893.8
Cost of sales	...	(1,879.4)	70.3	(1,809.1)	(1,611.9)	5.3	(1,606.6)
Gross profit		1,483.3	70.3	1,553.6	1,281.9	5.3	1,287.2
Net operating expenses	...	(996.0)		(996.0)	(851.5)		(851.5)
Group property income	5			–	68.5	2.9	71.4
Operating profit		487.3	70.3	557.6	498.9	8.2	507.1
Share of profit of BL Universal plc	5	41.3		41.3			–
Trading profit		528.6	70.3	598.9	498.9	8.2	507.1

* Restated – see note ...

Turnover and profit before taxation are derived from continuing operations. Turnover excludes the group's share of the turnover of BL Universal plc (joint venture) [R] of £31.2m (1997 nil).

Group balance sheet at 31 March 1998

	Notes	1998 £m	1998 £m	1997 £m	1997 (restated) (note 1) £m
Fixed assets					
Intangible assets	...		106.7		94.8
Tangible assets	...		549.6		473.7
Investment in joint venture	16				
Share of gross assets [P]		495.3		495.1	
Share of gross liabilities [Q]		(402.9)		(464.9)	
		92.4		30.2	
Loans to joint venture		215.0		670.0	
			307.4		700.2
Other fixed asset investments	...		23.7		5.0
			987.4		1,273.7

...

GREAT UNIVERSAL STORES *Note 5 to the 1998 accounts*

5. Share of profit of BL Universal plc and group property income

In accordance with the requirements of FRS 9, the share of profit of BL Universal plc is stated before the group's share of the interest expense of that company. The formation of this property joint venture gave rise to an exceptional profit after expenses of £2.9m in 1997. As a result of the formation of the joint venture, the group has also earned interest income of some £33m during the year on cash and loan balances outstanding.

GREAT UNIVERSAL STORES *Note 16 to 1998 accounts*

16. Investment in joint venture

	Shares in BL Universal £m	*Loans to BL Universal* £m	*Total* £m
The group			
Cost or valuation			
At 31 March 1997	30.2	670.0	700.2
Movements in year:			
Share of profit after tax	5.3		5.3
Revaluation of investment	56.9		56.9
Repayment of loans		(455.0)	(455.0)
At 31 March 1998	92.4	215.0	307.4

The group holds 50% of the ordinary share capital of BL Universal plc. The group's share of retained profits at 31 March 1998 is £5.3m (1997 nil).

The consolidated balance sheet of BL Universal plc is as follows:

	1998 £m	1997 £m
Investment properties	943.5	900.2
Other net (liabilities)/assets	(20.2)	30.6
	923.3	930.8
Less: Debt	(738.4)	(870.0)
Equity shareholders' funds	184.9	60.8
Attributable to the group	92.4	30.4
Debt is repayable as follows:		
in one year or less	90.0	530.0
in over five years	648.4	340.0
	738.4	870.0

Included within the debt are loans of £215.0m advanced by the company (1997 £670.0m).

Additional disclosures

FRS 9 requires the following disclosures separately for associates and joint ventures that exceed certain thresholds.

Where an investor's aggregate share in its *associates* exceeds 15 per cent of any of

1. the gross assets;
2. gross liabilities;
3. turnover; or
4. on a three-year average, operating result of the investing group;

then the investor's aggregate share of each of the following should be shown:

- turnover (unless it is already included as a memorandum item);
- fixed assets;
- current assets;
- liabilities due within one year; and
- liabilities due after one year or more.

Similarly, where an investor's aggregate share in its *joint ventures* exceeds 15 per cent of any of 1 to 4 above then the investor's aggregate share of each of fixed assets, current assets, liabilities due within one year and liabilities due after one year or more should be shown.

For any associate or joint venture where the investor's share *of that individual entity* exceeds 25 per cent of any of the gross assets, gross liabilities, turnover or, on a three-year average, operating result

of the investing group, the investor's share of the following items for that entity should be shown:

- turnover
- profit before tax
- taxation
- profit after tax
- fixed assets
- current assets
- liabilities due within one year
- liabilities due after one year or more.

DIAGEO *Extract from 1998 accounts*

5. Associates

	18m ended 30 Jun 1998 £m	12m ended 31 Dec 1996 £m
Share of operating profits before exceptional items	287	205
Share of interest payable (net)	(6)	(8)
Share of exceptional items	(15)	(24)
Share of taxation (note 8)	(102)	(67)
Share of profits after taxation	164	106
Dividends received by the group	(162)	(50)
Share of profits retained by associates	2	56

Group turnover includes sales to associates of £101m (1996 – £59m) and operating costs include purchases from associates of £225m (1996 – £156m). Dividends received include a dividend from Cantrell & Cochrane Group Ltd of £67m (1996 – £3m).

The group's profit and loss accounts for the 12 months and 18 months ended 30 June 1998 include its share of Moët Hennessy's operating profit of £114m (12 months to 30 June 1997 – £112m) and £150m (1996 – £119m, respectively. Moët Hennessy is a subsidiary of LVMH.

Information on associated undertakings

The Companies Act 1989 requires that the following information be given on associated undertakings:

(a) name;
(b) country of incorporation or address if unincorporated;
(c) identity of each class of share held and the proportion held (CA 1989, Sch. 3, para. 22).

Information also has to be given on other significant holdings, including participating interests in undertakings that are not associated undertakings, as described in Chapter 9.

Proportional consolidation

It has been a long-standing practice in certain industries (e.g. oil exploration, engineering and construction) to account for certain types of joint venture using proportional consolidation; and this is recognised by the Companies Act. Proportional consolidation involves adding the investor's share of the joint venture to each line of the consolidated profit and loss account and balance sheet. This is not the same as consolidation of, say, a minority interest in a subsidiary, where what is added line by line is the whole of the subsidiary's figure (the minority interest being taken out separately).

IAS 31 *Financial reporting of interests in joint ventures* does not recommend the use of the equity method, on the grounds that proportional consolidation better reflects the substance and economic reality of a venturer's interest in a jointly controlled entity. The ASB believes that it can be misleading to represent each venturer's joint control of a joint venture – which allows it to direct the operating and financial policies of the joint venture only with the consent of the other venturers – as being in substance equivalent to its having sole control of its

share of each of that entity's assets, liabilities and cash flows. FRS 9 abolishes proportional consolidation, but accounting treatment for joint arrangements which are not an entity is, arithmetically, virtually identical to proportional consolidation.

Keeping a grip on things

It is important to recognise that:

- The accounting treatment of subsidiaries (whether wholly or partly owned) and associates/joint ventures is entirely different.
- Information about associates and joint ventures tends to be scattered all over the accounts.
- Joint ventures are often a means of sharing risk where the risks are particularly high.
- The amounts involved can be considerable; and the effects of failure spectacular.
- In the past companies have used the rules on subsidiaries, associates and joint ventures as a means of concealing problems or failures, changing holdings and power to control (e.g. board representation).

RELATED PARTIES

'Related party transactions have been a feature of a number of financial scandals in recent years, many of which have had in common the dominance of the company by a powerful chief executive who was also involved with the related party' – ASB Press Notice on the publication of FRED 8, which became FRS 8 *Related party disclosures* (published October 1995).

Schedule 5 of the Companies Act 1985 contains requirements for the disclosure of related undertakings, and Chapters 11 and 12 of the London Stock Exchange's *Listing Rules* define related party transactions and lay down requirements on disclosure. FRS 8 extends the definition of related parties and increases the disclosure requirement.

FRS 8 requires a company to disclose all material transactions with related parties, i.e. parties having a relationship (control or influence) that affects the independence of either the reporting entity or the other party and could have a significant effect on the financial position and operating results of the reporting entity. There are a number of exceptions, e.g. pension contributions paid to a pension fund. Nor does the FRS require disclosure of the relationship and transactions between the reporting entity and providers of finance in the course of their business in that regard, even though

they may circumscribe the freedom of action of the entity or participate in its decision-making process.

Ultimate controlling party

Regardless of whether or not there have been transactions during the year, financial statements must disclose the name of the company's ultimate controlling party. For companies within widely-held public groups, this will be the holding company; for all others, the directors must look beyond the corporate structure to name the controlling interests. There may even be cases where the ultimate controlling party cannot be identified: if so, that fact must be disclosed.

Who is a related party?

The definition of related parties in the FRS is widely drawn. It includes, in addition to the more obvious relationships, such as ultimate and intermediate parent undertakings, subsidiaries and fellow subsidiaries, associates and joint ventures, directors of the reporting entity, pension funds, key management, members of the close family of any party in this list, and partnerships, companies, trusts and other entities in which any individual in the list or his close family has a controlling interest. Entities managed by the reporting entity under management contracts come within the definition of related parties. 'Close family' includes family members, or members of the same household, 'who may be expected to influence or be influenced ...' This clearly includes adult children as well as minors and would have made the late Robert Maxwell's children related parties.

Subject to certain exemptions, transactions with related parties have to be disclosed even if no consideration passes.

Related parties are considered in two groups:

- those that are deemed to be related; and
- those where a related party relationship is presumed.

The existence of 'deemed' related party relationships cannot be rebutted; all material transactions with directors, group members, associates and joint ventures must be disclosed apart from:

(a) transactions with subsidiaries, if the company accounts are presented with the corresponding group accounts;
(b) 90% subsidiaries: transactions with group members, providing that the relevant group accounts may be obtained by the public; and
(c) pension contributions need not be disclosed in the company or group accounts (except as required by SSAP 24); however, pension fund accounts should disclose company contributions received.

The existence of a 'presumed' relationship can be rebutted (and transactions need not therefore be disclosed) if it can be demonstrated that the relevant party does not exercise significant influence over the entity's financial and operating policies. If influence cannot be denied, the only disclosure exemption in the case of key management (but not, of course, directors) is emoluments paid in respect of employment.

Disclosures

Not only are related parties potentially numerous, the required disclosures are also lengthy:

(a) names of the transacting related parties;
(b) description of the relationship and the transactions;
(c) amounts involved;
(d) balances with the related parties at the balance sheet date, including provisions made and amounts written off such balances; and
(e) any other elements necessary for an understanding of the financial statements.

It will be necessary, for instance, to disclose substantial trading relationships where the basis of pricing has a material effect on the results for the period. The standard particularly notes that any statement made should not imply that the transactions were effected on terms equivalent to arm's length transactions unless they really were.

Just how useful disclosures regarding related parties are to the average investor remains to be seen:

1. They are often extremely complicated;
2. Their significance is difficult to assess;
3. Nevertheless, they largely remove the excuse: 'if only I had known, I would not have bought into the company'.

Consider, for example, TARSUS GROUP, the consolidated profit and loss account of which is shown on page 199. Start by trying to decide what happened to the group in 1997–98. We will comment and then gradually add further information.

TARSUS GROUP *Consolidated profit and loss account for 1998*

Consolidated profit and loss account for the year ended 31 December 1998

	Notes	Before Exceptional Items £000	Exceptional Items £000	1998 12 months Total £000	1997 8 months Total £000
TURNOVER					
– acquisitions		4,784	–	4,784	–
– discontinued operations		702	–	702	563
		5,486	–	5,486	563
Operating costs		(4,562)	(402)	(4,964)	(539)
OPERATING PROFIT	...				
– acquisitions		1,008	(402)	606	–
– discontinued operations		(84)	–	(84)	24
		924	(402)	522	24
Goodwill amortisation		(180)	–	(180)	–
		744	(402)	342	24
Loss on disposal of discontinued operation	...	–	(3,404)	(3,404)	–
Profit/(loss) on ordinary activities before interest		744	(3,806)	(3,062)	24
Net interest receivable/ (payable)	...	91	–	91	(15)
Profit/(loss) on ordinary activities before taxation		835	(3,806)	(2,971)	9
Taxation	...	(312)	121	(191)	–
Profit/(loss) on ordinary activities after taxation		523	(3,685)	(3,162)	9
Retained profit/(loss) for the financial period	...	523	(3,685)	(3,162)	9
Earnings/(loss) per share (pence)	...				
– adjusted				3.4	–
– basic				(19.6)	0.11
– diluted				(17.7)	0.11

The Company has no recognised gains or losses other than the profits and losses shown in the consolidated profit and loss account. Therefore no separate statement of total recognised gains and losses has been presented.

The first thing that strikes one is that 1997 represented an eight month accounting period. There is always a reason for an odd length period.

The second thing is that turnover in 1997 consisted entirely of discontinued activities; this means that the entire nature of the business changed between 1997 and 1998; something that prior to FRS 3 one would have been unlikely to discover from the accounts themselves. We looked at the directors' report for clues.

TARSUS GROUP *Extract from the directors' report 1998*
Principal activities etc
The principal activity of the Group since 25 June 1998 has been the ownership, organisation and management of exhibitions, conferences, related trade publications and new media.

Prior to 25 June 1998 the Group was principally engaged in design, publishing, marketing and computer related activities. These businesses were sold on 25 June 1998 to Glowdawn Ltd, a company controlled by Philip O'Donnell, a director of the company.

Since 25 June 1998 the Group has developed new and existing events and publications and has acquired business media companies with growth potential.

The related party mention led us to:

TARSUS GROUP *Extract from the directors' report 1998*
Close company status
The company is a close company within the meaning of the Income and Corporation Taxes Act 1988. There has been no change in this respect since the end of the financial year.

And that in turn led us to:

TARSUS GROUP *Extract from the directors' report 1998*

Substantial shareholdings
At 24 February 1999 the Company had been notified of the following discloseable interests in its issued ordinary share capital pursuant to section 198 Companies Act 1985:

	Number of Ordinary Shares	*Percentage*
N D Buch	6,229,171	26.7
C A Smith	5,000,000	21.4
P O'Donnell	3,828,159	16.4

We studied the note on related party transactions.

TARSUS GROUP *Note 23 to the 1998 accounts*

23. Related party transactions
During the year the Group disposed of the subsidiary BBB Design Ltd to Glowdawn Ltd, a company controlled by P. O'Donnell, a director of the Company. The consideration was £346,000 satisfied in cash. An adjustment may be made to the consideration depending upon the outcome of certain litigation claims as referred to in note ...

The Company acquired the Labelex Group of companies in June 1998. One of the Labelex vendors was C. Smith, a director of the Company. The initial combined consideration paid was £4.3m and an estimated deferred consideration of £850,000 in respect of the results for the two years ended 31 December 1998. A further deferred consideration payment may be made in 2000 based on the results of Tarsus Publishing Ltd for the year ended 31 December 1999 capped at £250,000.

Lease agreements were entered into, at the time of the Labelex acquisition, between Tarsus Exhibitions Ltd, The Labelex Ltd Retirement and Death Benefit Scheme (C. Smith's pension fund) and C. Smith, for the property situated at 129–131 Southlands Road, Bromley. The term of the lease is for five years with an option to break after three years for a combined annual rental of £34,000.

An acquisition search agreement was entered into between the Company and Mayfield Media Strategies Ltd, a company controlled by S. Monnington, a director of the Company. Under the agreement Mayfield Media Strategies Ltd is entitled to receive fees for acquisition search work and further fees for successful acquisitions introduced. The fees paid under this agreement to S. Monnington in 1998 amounted to £33,510.

The fees paid to N. D. Buch (£12,500), S. A. Monnington (£20,000) and B. T. R. Scruby (£3,750) as Directors of the Company are paid to companies controlled by these Directors namely Minevco Holdings Ltd, Mayfield Media Strategies Ltd and Data Financial Services Ltd respectively.

We are not criticising these accounts. Far from it: they provide a model of modern disclosure, leaving the individual investor to decide whether this is the right group for him.

The note on acquisitions is lengthy, so we reproduce only part of it (on page 201). We do so for two reasons:

- it shows just how much information is now available on related party transactions; and
- it demonstrates how acquisition accounting works including:

(i) the calculation of goodwill in a case where the net assets are negative;
(ii) the accounting adjustments made on an acquisition; and
(iii) a business purchase satisfied by a complex structure of consideration including deferred terms.

Problem 22.1
Given the extract from Note 18 to the 1998 accounts of TAY HOMES, reproduced at the bottom of page 201, explain:

1. Why the group item 'Investments in subsidiary undertakings' is zero, when that for the Company is £314,000 in both 1997 and 1998.
2. What a quasi-subsidiary is and the difference in treatment between Taygate Showhomes Ltd and Britannia New Homes (Scotland) Ltd.
3. Why the company item 'Investments in associated undertaking' is zero in both years.
4. What 'Deficiency in net assets of associated undertaking' represents and the significance of the increase between 1997 and 1998.
5. What the 'Loan to associated undertaking' represents.

Does this raise questions in your mind?

TARSUS GROUP *Extract from note 4 to the 1998 accounts*

4. Acquisitions

The Group made three acquisitions during the year for a total consideration of £7,761,000, of which £1,216,000 is deferred. These acquisitions resulted in goodwill of £9,413,000 before amortisation. From the date of acquisition to 31 December 1998 the acquisitions contributed £4,784,000 to turnover and £1,008,000 to operating profit before interest, goodwill amortisation, exceptional items and taxation. All of these purchases have been accounted for as acquisitions.

The fair value of the Group's identifiable assets and liabilities at the acquisition date (including goodwill) were:

Labelex Group

	Book value £000	*Consistency of accounting policies* £000	*Other* £000	*Total* £000
Net liabilities acquired:				
Goodwill	175	–	(175)	–
Tangible fixed assets	226	(36)	–	190
Cash	1,500	–	–	1,500
Debtors	2,702		28	2,730
Creditors	(5,501)	(20)	(20)	(5,541)
Provisions	–	–	(485)	(485)
	(898)	(28)	(680)	(1,606)
Goodwill on acquisition				7,247
				5,641
Satisfied by: Cash				1,450
Shares allotted				2,500
Deferred purchase consideration				1,100
Cost of acquisition				591
				5,641

TAY HOMES *Extract from note 18 to the 1998 accounts*

	Group		Company	
	1998 £000	1997 £000	1998 £000	1997 £000
18. Fixed Asset Investments				
Investments in subsidiary undertakings:				
Shareholdings at cost	–	–	314	314
Loans to subsidiary undertakings	–	–	40	40
	–	–	354	354
Investments in unlisted companies:				
Shareholdings at cost (see ...)	54	54	4	4
	54	54	358	358
Investments in associated undertaking:				
Loan to associated undertaking	2,332	2,096	--	–
Deficiency in net assets of associated undertaking	(272)	(181)	–	–
	2,060	1,915	–	–
	2,114	1,969	358	358

The Company has the following Ordinary share investments in subsidiary undertakings, all of which are included within the consolidated accounts using the acquisition method of accounting: ...Tay Homes (Scotland) Ltd (registered in Scotland) (Residential, Estate Developers and Builders) ...; Taygate Showhomes Ltd (50% owned quasi-subsidiary) (Showhouse Licensing) ... The directors consider that the Group participates substantially in the benefits and risks associated with Taygate Showhomes Ltd and hence the undertaking should be regarded as a quasi-subsidiary ...

The Group has the following joint venture associated undertaking which is 50% owned by Tay Homes (Scotland) Ltd: Britannia New Homes (Scotland) Ltd. (registered in Scotland) (Residential Estate Development).

Chapter 23

FOREIGN EXCHANGE

The problem of variable exchange rates

Floating exchange rates bring both accounting problems and operating problems. This chapter will deal first with the accounting problems, and then look at what companies do to mitigate the adverse effects that currency fluctuations may have on their operations.

The main accounting problem is the rate (or rates) of exchange to be used in translating the accounts of foreign subsidiaries, associates and branches, which are kept in foreign currencies, into sterling when producing the consolidated accounts of a group.

The choice lies between:

(a) the *closing rate*: the spot rate of exchange at the balance sheet date;
(b) the *average rate* of exchange during the period; and
(c) the *historical rate*: the spot rate of exchange at the date of the transaction.

Various methods of translation use different combinations of these rates.

The UK accounting standard

SSAP 20 *Foreign currency translation* is concerned with:

(a) *individual companies* which enter directly into business transactions denominated in foreign currencies, and
(b) *groups* which conduct foreign operations through subsidiaries, associated undertakings or branches whose operations are based in a country other than that of the investing company, and whose accounting records are maintained in a currency other than that of the investing company.

Individual companies

When a company enters into transactions denominated in a foreign currency (i.e. a currency other than that in which the company's accounts are kept), SSAP 20 requires that they should normally be translated at the rate ruling at the date of each transaction, i.e. at the spot rate.

In the accounts of the individual company:

(a) *non-monetary assets*, e.g. plant and machinery, will already be carried in the accounts in the company's reporting currency, having been translated at the time of acquisition;
(b) *foreign equity investments*, being non-monetary assets, are normally shown at the rate of exchange ruling at the time the investment was made but, where financed by foreign currency borrowings, they may be translated at the closing rate. Any exchange differences on the investments are then taken to reserves, where the exchange differences on the foreign borrowings may be offset against them (SSAP 20, para. 51).
(c) *monetary assets and liabilities denominated in foreign currencies* should be translated at the closing rate;
(d) all *exchange differences*, except those in (b) above, should be reported as part of the profit or loss for the year, e.g. differences arising from variations in exchange rates between the dates of invoicing in a foreign currency and the dates of payment. It is comparatively rare for such differences to be 'material' and nothing is normally disclosed .

Example 23.1 on the next page illustrates the treatment of four simple transactions involving foreign currency.

Example 23.1 Treatment of foreign transactions by an individual company

ABLE is a UK company whose accounting year ends on 31 December. During the year, ABLE:

		Rate of exchange
(i)	Purchases hock from a West German company, Weinburger GmbH, on 31 October for DM40,000	£1 = DM3.20
	Pays Weinburger GmbH on 30 November	£1 = DM3.04
	Goods remain in stock at 31 December	
(ii)	Sells cider to Pomme et cie, a French company, for FFr105,000.	£1 = FFr10.50
	Debt remains unpaid at 31 December	
(iii)	Borrows on long-term loan from a Swiss bank SFr750,000 on 1 April	£1 = SFr3.0
(iv)	Purchases plant and machinery from a US company for $480,000 on 15 August	£1 = US$1.50
	Pays on 30 September	£1 = US$1.60

On 31 December exchange rates are:

£1 = DM2.95
£1 = FFr10.00
£1 = SFr2.50
£1 = US$1.55

The company maintains its bank account in sterling and buys or sells foreign exchange as needed on the spot market.

Under SSAP 20 the transactions of Able will be treated as follows:

(i) The purchase will be recorded at the rate ruling on 31 October, £1 = DM3.20. The hock will appear in stock at a book cost of £12,500 and the eventual cost of sales will also be £12,500. When the account is paid, the rate has fallen to £1 = DM3.04, so it is necessary to pay £13,158 to buy the necessary currency.

An exchange loss of £658 (£13,158 − £12,500) will be charged to the profit and loss account for the year.

(ii) The sale is translated at the rate ruling at the date of the transaction, £1 = FFr10.50 = £10,000. At the end of the year, the debtor is a monetary item and translated at the closing rate, £1 = FFr10.00 = £10,500.

The resulting exchange gain of £500 (£10,500 − £10,000) will be credited to the profit and loss account for the year.

(iii) The loan will initially be translated at the transaction rate of £1 = SFr3.00, i.e. as £250,000. At the year end the loan will be translated at the closing rate £1 = SFr2.50, i.e. as £300,000.

The exchange loss of £50,000 (£300,000 − £250,000) may be treated as 'financing' and *may be* disclosed separately as part of 'other interest receivable/payable and similar income/expense'.

(iv) The fixed asset will be translated at the transaction rate of £1 = $1.50, i.e. as £320,000. The asset will continue to appear at this cost unless it is revalued. Depreciation will be charged on £320,000. Payment for the machine will take (at £1 = $1.60) £300,000.

The gain of £20,000 (£320,000 − £300,000) will be credited to the profit and loss account for the year and will appear separately if considered material.

In Able's statement of accounting policies, the treatment of these purchases and sales would be explained in a note similar to that in ML LABORATORIES accounts, illustrated below.

ML LABORATORIES *Extract from accounting policies 1998*

Foreign currency translation
Foreign currency transactions are translated into sterling at the rate prevailing at the date or the transaction. Assets held at the year end are translated into sterling at the rate prevailing at the balance sheet date. The resulting exchange differences are dealt with in the profit and loss account.

Group accounts

Where a company has foreign subsidiaries, associates, joint ventures or branches, the '*closing rate net investment method*' is normally used in translating local currency financial statements (SSAP 20, para. 52). Under this method:

(a) *Balance sheet* items should be translated into the currency of the holding company at the 'closing rate' (the spot rate on the balance sheet date). Where this year's closing rate differs from the previous year's closing rate, the differences arising from the retranslation of the opening *net investment* at this year's closing rate should be taken to reserves and will appear in both the Statement of recognised gains and losses and the Movements in shareholders' funds (see page 158).

The *net investment* is the holding company's proportion of the subsidiary or associates' share capital and reserves. Long-term indebtedness between members of the group should be treated as part of the net investment. The translation process is illustrated in Example 23.2 on the next page.

(b) *Profit and loss account* items should be translated using either the average rate for the accounting period or the closing rate and the method chosen should be applied consistently.

Example 23.2 Translation of an overseas subsidiary's accounts

On 31 December 2000, Injection Moulders PLC acquired a small foreign manufacturing company, Ruritania Plastics, to expand its operations into Ruritania, and paid asset value, 60m Ruritanian dollars (R$), for it. At the time the exchange rate was R$10 = £1, so the sterling cost was £6m.

During the first year of operation as a subsidiary Ruritanian Plastics made a profit after tax of R$10m, and the R$ fell to R$12.5 = £1. Ruritanian Plastics' actual and translated balance sheets for 2000 (R$10 = £1) and 2001 (R$12.5 = £1) were:

Year ended 31 December	2000		2001	
	R$m	£000	R$m	£000
Fixed assets	100	10,000	100	8,000
Current assets	20	2,000	32	2,560
	120	12,000	132	10,560
5 year State loan	50	5,000	50	4,000
Current liabilities	10	1,000	12	960
	60	6,000	62	4,960
Shareholders' funds	60	6,000	70	5,600

The difference between the opening net equity of R$60m translated at R$10 = £1 (the closing rate in the 2000 accounts) and at R$12.5 = £1 (the 2001 closing rate) is £6m – £4.8m = £1.2m, which would be taken from group reserves at 31 December 2001 as an exchange translation difference.

The profit of R$10m (represented in the absence of any capital input or dividends by the difference between opening and closing shareholders' funds) has been translated in the group accounts at the closing rate of R$12.5 = £1 to produce £0.8m.

The fall in sterling terms in the net equity of Ruritanian Plastics from £6m to £5.6m is made up of the exchange translation loss of £1.2m less the £0.8m profit for 2001, i.e. £0.4m.

Any difference between translation at the average rate and the closing rate should be taken to reserves.

The rate used can make a considerable difference to the reported profit; for example, if a West German subsidiary made a profit of DM27m during a year in which the rate of exchange fell from DM3.10 = £1 at the beginning of the year to DM2.70 = £1 at the end of the year, averaging DM3.00 = £1 because most of the fall occurred in the last three months, on an average basis the group accounts would include West German profits of £9m; on a closing rate basis they would include £10m.

If the closing rate method is used, no difference will arise between the profit or loss in sterling terms used for profit and loss account purposes, and the result of translation for balance sheet purposes. If the average rate is used there will be a difference, which should be recorded as a movement on reserves (SSAP 20, para. 54). The method used should be stated in the accounts. The advantage of using the average rate is that the translated results correspond more nearly to those given by management accounts prepared (say) on a monthly basis. Indeed, to reflect those results even better, GRAND METROPOLITAN used to say it employed the *weighted* average rate of exchange (on the basis that it takes account of seasonal fluctuations in profitability).

GRAND METROPOLITAN *Accounting policies 1995*

Foreign Currencies

...

Profits and losses of overseas subsidiaries and associates are translated into sterling at weighted average rates of exchange during the year other than material exceptional items which are translated at the rate on the date of the transaction. The adjustment to financial year end rates is taken to reserves.

(c) *Foreign exchange borrowings*: where borrowings have been used to finance equity investment in foreign subsidiaries or associates, differences arising on their translation (at the closing rate) due to currency movements during the period may be offset against differences arising from the retranslation of the opening net investment, as is explained by PIC INTERNATIONAL (see the next page).

PIC INTERNATIONAL *Extract from accounting policies 1998*

(i) Foreign currencies
The results of overseas subsidiaries are translated into sterling at average exchange rates and assets and liabilities are translated at the rates on 30 June. Exchange differences which arise from the translation of the net assets and results of overseas subsidiaries at rates different from the average rate during the year and the rate used at 30 June in the prior year are dealt with through reserves.

Differences arising on the translation of foreign currency borrowings which hedge group equity investments in foreign enterprises are taken directly to reserves to the extent of corresponding exchange differences on translation of the related net assets. The tax on those exchange differences which are taken directly to reserves is also recorded as a direct movement on reserves.

...

Hyperinflation

Urgent Issues Task Force (UITF) Abstract 9 is concerned with accounting for operations in hyperinflationary economies. The Abstract requires adjustments to be made when incorporating operations in hyperinflationary economies into consolidated accounts where the distortions caused by hyperinflation are such as to affect the true and fair view given by the accounts. In any event, adjustments are required where the cumulative inflation rate over three years is approaching or exceeds 100% (a level widely accepted internationally as an appropriate criterion). The Abstract discusses acceptable methods of handling the problem, one of which is to translate the results of operations in hyperinflationary economies using a relatively stable currency as the functional currency.

One group which operates in countries suffering very high rates of inflation, even hyperinflation, is LONMIN (formerly LONRHO), see page 207.

Where restrictions prevent the transfer of cash from one part of the business or group to another, a note to the cash flow statement should specify the amounts involved and explain the circumstances (see page 165).

The temporal method

Where, and only where, the trade of a subsidiary is a direct extension of the trade of a holding company, e.g. a subsidiary acting purely as a selling agency in a foreign country, the temporal method of translation should be used in consolidation:

(a) all transactions should be translated at the rate ruling on the transaction date or at an average rate for a period if this is not materially different;

(b) non-monetary assets should not normally be retranslated at the balance sheet date;

(c) monetary assets and liabilities should be retranslated at the closing rate; and

(d) all exchange gains and losses should be taken to the profit and loss account as part of the profit and loss from ordinary activities.

Current UK practice

A growing number, now about 60%, of companies use the average rate rather than the closing rate in translating overseas profits, and state which method is used in their accounting policies.

Taxation

The position with regard to overseas activities is complicated by the problems of taxation. Unless a profit or loss item falls within the scope of a tax schedule dealing with income subject to UK Corporation Tax, or arises from the disposal of an asset in such a way as to be within the computation of a capital gain, then the profit is not taxable, and no relief is available in respect of any loss. ICI explained back in 1993:

ICI *Extract from operating and financial review 1993*

Taxation
The total taxation charge for 1993 is £194m (1992 £183m). The charge in relation to continuing activities before exceptional items is £105m (1992 £124m), representing a rate of 36% (1992 76% [sic]).

Unrelieved tax losses arose in several countries where it was not possible to reflect the relief on a deferred basis.

However, as profitability returns in these countries, there should be opportunity to obtain relief for some of these losses.

The higher rate in 1992 reflected unrelieved losses in overseas subsidiaries together with a number of non-recurring items, in part related to the demerger [of Zeneca].

In particular, losses on repayment of foreign borrowings are not allowable for UK tax purposes. Some companies, including ICI, have overcome this difficulty by channelling foreign currency borrowings through a separate finance company subsidiary; there is no distinction between capital and revenue losses in a banking-type operation so foreign exchange losses show up as revenue losses and qualify for full tax relief.

Mitigating the effect of currency fluctuations

Exchange rate movements are difficult to predict. In the last two years the US dollar has fluctuated between a low of about US$1.50/£1 to $1.72/£1; see Example 23.3 (on page 206). The Deutschmark weakened steadily against sterling from 1995 to 1998, losing almost 40% between the beginning of 1996 and the beginning of 1998, but has pulled back since (see page 206).

The rise in the Yen has been even more marked. It gained about 25% between August 1998 and January 1999 (see Example 23.5).

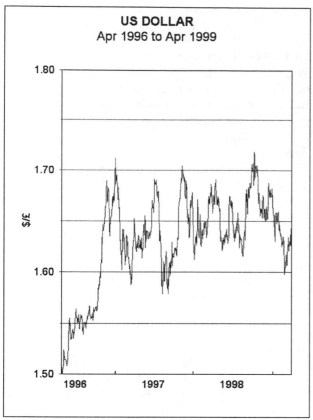

Example 23.3 US$/£ exchange rate

The way in which companies have sought to protect themselves against the effect of these and other currency fluctuations, both on their earnings and on their balance sheets, is explained in Chapter 14. But not all do this, e.g. BRENT INTERNATIONAL:

BRENT INTERNATIONAL *Extract from financial review 1997*

Brent does not hedge the translation of foreign currency profits earned by overseas subsidiaries. The balance sheets of overseas subsidiaries are only hedged to the extent that local currency denominated borrowing may offset overseas net assets.

Although selling currency forward does protect the sterling value of future foreign income, doing so can have adverse effects if the foreign currency then strengthens rather than weakens. For example, if a UK motor manufacturer covers the US dollar forward, when its European competitors do not, and the US dollar strengthens, they will have scope for cutting their prices in the United States, while UK manufacturers will not.

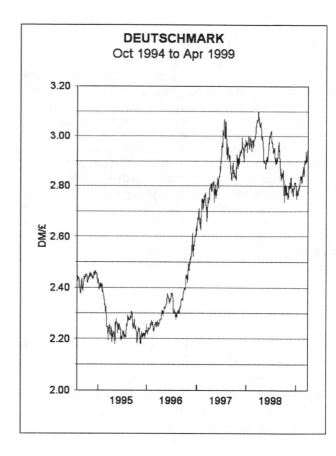

Example 23.4 The DM/£ exchange rate

Example 23.5 The Yen/£ exchange rate

Protecting the balance sheet can be done in a variety of ways, the most obvious one being to borrow in the foreign currency. If the foreign subsidiary does the borrowing, the net equity investment in the subsidiary will be reduced. If the parent company borrows in the foreign currency and switches it into sterling, it will have a gain (or loss) to offset against any loss (or gain) on translating the net equity investment of the foreign subsidiary. If interest rates in sterling are higher than those in the foreign currency the parent company will also make a profit on the differential.

What the analyst should study

As has been seen, information about foreign currency tends to be scattered around in reports and accounts. A suggested sequence for the analyst to follow is:

1. *Accounting policies on foreign currencies*
   Check that, as required by SSAP 20, differences on unmatched foreign borrowings are dealt with in the P & L account and not taken direct to reserves. Before SSAP 20, some companies borrowed in a hard currency, e.g. Deutschmarks or Swiss francs, to reduce their cost of borrowing for investment in the UK. The lower interest rates (broadly reflecting the lower expectations of inflation) increased the companies' profits and, when the foreign currency inevitably strengthened, they debited the increase in the sterling value of their borrowings direct to reserves. This method of enhancing the profits was short-sighted and often very costly. For example the WEIR Group managed to lose £3.6m on a DM denominated loan originally worth £6.3m, and the loss would have been even greater if the company hadn't arranged early repayment.

   Note also if there has been any change in accounting policy, as this can be a way of enhancing the year's results.

   There seems nothing strange or changed about LONMIN's accounting policies, but the rate changes during 1997–98 could have given more cause for worry.

LONMIN *Accounting policies 1998*

Exchange rates

Foreign currency assets and liabilities and the results for the year are translated into sterling at the rates ruling at 30 September. Exchange differences arising from the retranslation of the opening net investment in overseas companies are disclosed as movements on reserves. Exchange adjustments relating to borrowings which have been used to finance or provide a hedge against foreign equity investments are taken to reserves to the extent that they are matched by exchange movements on those

---

investments. All other adjustments due to fluctuations arising in the normal course of trade are included in profit before taxation. The principal sterling exchange rates used to translate foreign currency assets and liabilities and the results for the year are:

	1998	1997
South Africa rand	9.9171	7.5160
United States dollar	1.7025	1.6058
Zimbabwe dollar	54.0550	20.2411

But information is not always all in one place even in accounting policies.

LONMIN *Extract from the statement of accounting policies 1998*

Consolidation of Group companies

...

Results of subsidiaries and associates operating in hyper-inflationary economics are adjusted to reflect current price levels in those countries concerned.

---

2. *Note analysing operating profit*
   It is here that differences arising from variations in exchange rates between the dates of invoicing in a foreign currency and the dates of payment, and on monetary items should be (but are not always) shown where material. Most companies, including LONMIN show nothing.

3. *Statement of recognised gains and losses and Movements in shareholders' funds*
   Check whether the adjustments for currency fluctuations are material in relation to (i) the profit for the financial year and (ii) the transfer (from profit and loss account) to reserves.

LONMIN *Statement of total consolidated recognised gains and losses 1998*

Statement of total consolidated recognised gains and losses for the year ended 30 September

		1998 £m	1997 £m
Profit for the year	– Group	30	139
	– Associates	9	3
Dilution of the Group's interest in Ashanti		1	22
Unrealised net surplus on revaluation of assets			66
Exchange adjustments	– Group	(116)	(46)
	– Associates	(7)	(3)
Total recognised (losses)/gains relating to the year		(83)	181

£123m (in total) against a total profit for the year of £39m is certainly material!

LONMIN *Reconciliation of movement in equity interests*

Reconciliation of movement in equity interests for the year ended 30 September

	1998 £m	1997 £m
Total recognised (losses)/gains relating to the year	(83)	181
Dividends	(27)	(41)
Shares issued in lieu of cash dividends	5	9
Shares issued		3
Share buyback	(196)	
Demerger of Lonrho Africa	(221)	
Net surplus/(goodwill) on acquisition of subsidiaries and associates	8	(9)
Net goodwill on acquisition of subsidiaries by Ashanti	(19)	(37)
Share buyback in Ashanti	(4)	
Net (surplus)/goodwill realised on sale of subsidiaries	(56)	75
Movement of the Group's interest in Dulker Mining	(2)	
Other items	(3)	(5)
Net (reduction)/increase in equity interests in the year	(598)	176
Equity interests at 1 October	975	799
Equity interests at 30 September	377	975

In May 1998 shareholders received shares in Lonrho Africa following its demerger.

The £123m of exchange adjustments, incorporated in the figure for Total recognised (losses)/gains relating to the year (£83m), is certainly also material in relation to, say, closing equity interests of £377m.

4. *If the exchange adjustments thus found are large*
   Look for further information elsewhere. Wherever a balance sheet or cash flow statement note explains the change in an accounting item over the year, e.g. fixed assets, provisions or cash, if foreign currency is involved there may be a 'Currency translation difference'. It is here that depositing money in a soft depreciating currency (like POLLY PECK did) or borrowing (at a low rate of interest) in appreciating currency (like WEIR, mentioned above, did) would come to light.

5. *The reconciliation of group operating profit to net cash flow from operations*
   The reconciliation of group operating profit to net cash flow from operations does not usually show any exchange translation differences, but it may. This is likely to happen where a group translates 'profits, losses and cash flows' from overseas subsidiaries at average rate rather than closing rate (as TT GROUP did in its 1998 accounts).

TT GROUP *Extract from reconciliation of group operating profit to net cash flow from operations*

	1998 £m	1997 £m
...		
Exchange translation differences	(1.7)	(2.1)
...		

---

6. *Again, if the figures seem significant ....*
   Look for comments in the Financial Review, if there is one, or in the chairman's statement or possibly in the directors' report, or even elsewhere in the notes. Where exchange rates have a significant effect, further information may include tables of exchange rates.

7. *Study the note on contingent liabilities*
   Most companies do not in the past consider the potential liability in relation to swaps. But the note on contingent liabilities may today provide interesting information.

8. *Study any note on Derivative financial instruments*
   FRS 13 *Derivatives and other financial instruments* (see page 93) calls for a good deal of information on the use being made of derivatives and similar financial instruments. BP AMOCO includes more than a page on the matter its 1998 accounts.

9. *Look for any indication of significant exchange rate changes having an effect on profitability*
   Look also for any indication of the risks/costs/benefits of using financial instruments.

LONMIN *Extract from financial review 1998*

Financial risk management
Fluctuations in exchange rates can have significant effects on BP Amoco's operating results. The effects of most exchange rate fluctuations are subsumed within business operating results through changing cost competitiveness, lags in market adjustment to movements in rates, and conversion differences accounted on specific transactions. For this reason the total effect of exchange rate fluctuations

is not identifiable separately in the group's reported results.

Activities on a global scale inevitably involve many types risk. Few companies spell this out quite so clearly or at such length as BP AMOCO.

BP AMOCO *Extract from the financial review 1998*

The underlying economic currency of the group's cash flows is mainly the US dollar. Our foreign exchange management policy is to minimise economic and material transactional exposures from currency movements against the US dollar. Wherever possible, BP Amoco nets exposures using natural offsets to reduce foreign exchange risk. Significant residual non-dollar exposures are managed using a range of derivatives. In addition, most of the group's borrowings are in US dollars, are hedged with respect to the US dollar, or are swapped into dollars where this achieves a lower cost of financing.

BP Amoco is exposed to market risks arising from the group's normal business activities. Market risk is the possibility that changes in interest rates, currency exchange rates or commodity prices will adversely affect the value of the group's financial assets, liabilities or expected future cash flows. These risks are managed using a range of financial and commodity instruments including derivatives. We also trade derivatives in conjunction with these risk management activities.

BP Amoco is exposed to interest rate risk on short- and long-term floating rate instruments and as a result of the refinancing of fixed rate instruments included in the group's finance debt. Consequently, as well as managing the currency and the maturity of debt, BP Amoco manages interest costs through the balance between lower-cost floating rate debt, which has inherently higher risk, and more expensive, but lower-risk, fixed rate debt. The group is exposed predominantly to US dollar LIBOR (London Inter-Bank Offer Rate) interest rates as borrowings are mainly denominated in, or are swapped into, US dollars.

Historically BP has used derivatives to achieve the required mix between fixed and floating rate debt. Although Amoco was authorised to use derivative financial instruments as an additional tool in this regard, no derivatives have been used. During 1998 BP's upper limit for the proportion of floating rate debt was 65% of total net debt while Amoco's upper limit was 60% of total debt outstanding. An appropriate strategy for managing the interest rate risk of the new group is currently being formulated.

The group's oil trading division uses financial and commodity derivatives as part of the overall optimisation of the value of the group's equity oil production and as part of the associated trading of crude oil, products and related instruments. The group also uses financial and commodity derivatives to manage certain of its exposures to price fluctuations on natural gas transactions.

In risk management and trading, only well-understood conventional derivative instruments are used. These include futures and options traded on regulated exchanges, and 'over-the-counter' swaps, options and forward contracts.

Where derivatives constitute a hedge, the group's exposure to market risk created by the derivative is offset by the opposite exposure arising from the asset, liability or transaction being hedged. By contrast, where derivatives are held for trading purposes, changes in market risk factors give rise to realised and unrealised gains and losses, which are recognised in the current period.

BP AMOCO *Extract from notes to the 1998 accounts*

26. Derivative financial instruments

The following table shows the trading income arising from derivatives and other financial instruments. For oil price contract trading, this also includes income or losses arising on trading of derivative commodity instruments and physical oil trades, representing the net result of the oil-trading portfolio.

	1998	$m 1997
	Net gain (loss)	*Net gain*
Interest rate contracts	(26)	2
Foreign exchange contracts	38	23
Oil price contracts	215	144

9. *Consider the state of any overseas economies*
Probably equally if not more important for the profitability of foreign operations than a weak exchange rate is the state of the economy in the foreign countries concerned. If the weak exchange rate reflects a weak economy, then adverse trading conditions may be more damaging for profits than translation.

LONMIN *Extract from chief operating officer's review 1998*

Factors which have had a significant impact on the trading environment included the ever deepening Asian financial crisis, the devaluation of the Rand, the increase in interest rates to unprecedented levels and the abnormally warm 1998 winter in South Africa, which resulted in poor inland sales.

Remedial steps taken in the face of these developments include:

- actively seeking alternative markets in order to limit our exposure to the Far East
- using the export capacity of the Group to the full so as to maximise the benefits of the weaker exchange rate and so benefit from the higher margins on export sales
- focusing inland sales on a higher value, more stable customer base
- continuously pursuing cost saving and productivity measures
- curtailing cash outflows, working capital requirements and capital expenditure in order to reduce net borrowings and minimise financing costs.

...

Problem 23.1

Pie in the Sky plc is a UK listed company. Its accounting policies include:

Exchange rates

Exchange rates used to translate overseas profits and currency assets and liabilities (other than shares held by the parent company in overseas companies) are the rates ruling at the balance sheet date.

Currency gains and losses

Currency gains and losses are included in operating profit or investment income as appropriate except that the difference arising on the retranslation of the group's share, at the beginning of the year, of the net assets of overseas subsidiaries, associated companies and branches is treated as a movement in reserves.

In fact it has just one subsidiary, and no associated companies or branches. That subsidiary is Beyond (1994), a wholly owned subsidiary operating in a remote island group, the Beyond Islands, the currency of which is the Bac.

The Beyond Islands are largely undiscovered as a tourist destination and Beyond (1994) trades entirely within the islands. Pie in the Sky plc invested 10m Bacs in ordinary shares in Beyond (1994) at the time of its formation on 1 January 1994. No dividends have been paid; and no cash has been remitted in either direction.

The Bac is a somewhat unstable currency. Rates of exchange have been:

1 January 1994	1.00 Bac = £1.
31 December 1998	2.00 Bacs = £1.
31 December 1999	2.40 Bacs = £1.
31 December 2000	3.00 Bacs = £1.

You are provided with the balance sheet for Beyond (1994) as at 31 December 2000 shown alongside.

1. What amount would be included in Pie in the Sky's group accounts to represent the contribution to group profit of Beyond (1994) (a) in 1999; and (b) in 2000?
2. What currency translation difference would appear in the statement of total gains and losses of the group for 2000, and what would be the comparative figure in respect of 1999?

Ignore taxation.

BEYOND (1994) *Balance sheet as at 31 December 2000*

	Note	2000 Bacs m	1999 Bacs m
Fixed assets			
Freehold land and buildings		6.0	6.0
Plant and machinery, fixtures and fittings		12.0	10.0
		18.0	16.0
Current assets			
Stocks		13.5	11.1
Debtors		23.3	21.0
Cash at Bank		11.0	0.7
		47.8	32.8
Less: Current liabilities:			
Creditors: due within 1 year		15.0	11.0
Net current assets		32.8	22.8
Net assets		50.8	38.8
Ordinary share capital		10.0	10.0
Reserves:			
Profit and loss account	1	40.8	28.8
		50.8	38.8

NOTE 1:

Profit and loss account:

	2000	1999
Balance at 1 January	28.8	21.6
Profit for the year	12.0	7.2
Balance at 31 December	40.8	28.8

Chapter 24

HISTORICAL SUMMARIES, RATIOS AND TRENDS

HISTORICAL SUMMARIES

Variations in form and content

In 1964 the Chairman of The Stock Exchange wrote to the chairmen of all listed companies asking for various items of information to be included in their reports and accounts. One of the items which 'might be included' was 'Tables of relevant comparative figures for the past ten years'.

Apart from this request, listed companies are under no obligation to provide any form of historical summary: there is no FRS or SSAP, and no uniformity of content, layout, or period covered.

The majority of companies give a five-year summary; most of the remainder show ten years, although a few choose a different period, usually for a specific reason; e.g. LONRHO's 'Financial Record' for many years went right back to 1961, the year their then chief executive, Tiny Rowland, joined the company. Renamed LONMIN, the group now shows only five years.

Because there is, as yet, no standard on historical summaries, the content varies enormously. BULGIN, for example, show only five basic items in their 'Group five year record', illustrated below. Readers may recall BULGIN from Chapter 5, and will note the pain of 1997 and marked improvement in profits, earnings and dividends in 1998). Many companies give much more information than this. GLAXOWELLCOME, for instance, devotes four pages to its financial record, going back 11 years, and showing half-year figures. Some companies include information of particular relevance to their type of business; e.g. TESCO, in their five-year record (see pages 215–6), show the number of stores, sales area opened during the year and total sales area, and a number of other statistics which provide the reader with growth ratios some of which are not available from the accounts. BP AMOCO is among a number of oil companies giving useful statistics.

BULGIN *5-year statement 1998*

					£000
	1998	1997	1996	1995	1994
Turnover	19,496	19,155	20,273	18,155	15,666
Profit before taxation	760	238	1,027	903	507
Shareholders' net assets	4,760	4,600	4,653	4,071	3,349
Earnings per share	1.82p	0.53p	2.46p	2.27p	1.56p
Dividends per share	1.25p	0.50p	0.45p	0.40p	0.25p

BP AMOCO includes statistics on refinery throughput, crude oil and natural gas reserves, capital expenditure and acquisition in eight pages of historical information, and is among companies which now provide historical cash flow data.

There is a growing tendency for companies either to omit the normal table of historical information altogether in favour of often colourful diagrams of a few salient items (TAY HOMES does this); or to provide such information additionally (GKN supplies pie-charts and bar diagrams alongside the current year).

A Financial Reporting Standard would be welcome on historical summaries, but because they fall outside the statutory accounts, there appear to be no plans for one.

The main difficulty facing the shareholder or analyst who tries to interpret a five- or ten-year summary is lack of consistency. We will consider this under six heads:

1. Inflation;
2. Changes in accounting practices;
3. Changes in accounting policies;
4. Changes in accounting standards;
5. Changes in the business environment;
6. Changes in the composition of the group.

Inflation

Whereas pre-war it was reasonable in the UK to suppose that a pound today was the same as a pound last year and would be the same as a pound next year, rapid inflation made this concept of a stable currency (referred to in the US as the 'uniform dollar concept') unsustainable. A pound in 1999 was not the same as a pound in 1998, 1997, 1996, or 1995 let alone 1989 (or, for that matter, 1979). To read a ten-year record as though it was is to obtain a false picture, and would be just as misleading as the company chairman who makes much of yet another year of record profits when they have advanced a mere 2% compared with a 3% or 4% rate of inflation. We consider in Chapter 29 how the effects of inflation might be stripped out.

Changes in accounting practices

Most companies change their accounting ideas, either expressly or unknowingly, over a period. They might, for instance, decide that bills for main board directors' travelling and hotel accommodation expenses should be paid by the subsidiary visited, whereas previously they had been borne by group. Generally the amounts involved are not significant. But where they are, unless the figures for earlier years are revised, or a note drawing attention to the change in basis is included in the five- or ten-year summary, readers may be misled.

Changes in accounting policies

Changes in accounting policies can make a significant difference to the figures a company publishes; see, for instance, ML LABORATORIES (page 48). In 1998 the group's accounting policy in respect of research and development expenditure was changed from a policy of capitalisation of such expenditure as intangible fixed assets and subsequent amortisation, to a policy of immediate write off in the period in which such expenditure is incurred. The change was made in order to bring the group's accounting policy for such expenditure in line with that more commonly adopted by the UK pharmaceutical sector. The effect of the change in accounting policy was that intangible assets previously reported at 30 September 1997 for the Group of £22,135,293 were written off, with a consequent restatement of minority interests.

The comparative figures for the year to 30 September 1997 were adjusted as follows:

	£
Profit for year as originally reported	683,810
Change in treatment of research and development expenditure	(5,671,095)
Consequent restatement or minority interests	437,427
Loss as restated	(4,549,858)

Changes in accounting standards

The last decade has seen significant changes in accounting standards in a number of areas. In some cases, a succession of changes has proved necessary before agreement was reached.

Take, for instance, goodwill. Until UITF 3 *Treatment of goodwill on disposal of a business* (December 1991), there was no adjustment to goodwill on disposal of a business. Prior to FRS 10 *Goodwill and intangible assets* (December 1997) purchased goodwill was normally written off immediately against reserves; this reduced shareholders' funds (and in particular distributable reserves) of some companies to such an extent that they felt compelled to apply to the court for permission to raid their share premium account (as MEDEVA did). Others, like TESCO, were scarcely affected at all. FRS 10 requires goodwill arising after 31 March 1997 to be capitalised and amortised (see page 50). This change will affect most groups, since few chose the alternative of capitalisation and amortisation prior to FRS 10. Companies are, we believe, unlikely to adjust figures for previous years, so five- or ten-year summaries may not apply consistent accounting principles throughout in this regard.

Companies may under FRS 10 choose to reinstate goodwill previously written off as though it had been capitalised, amortised etc throughout. In this case, a five- or ten-year summary could, and probably would, reflect the new accounting policy all through the statement. FRS 2, 3, 4, 6, 14 and 15 have also had a significant effect on comparability; and many companies adjust figures for earlier years in line with the FRS.

BLUE CIRCLE *Group five year statement 1995*

Notes:
1. Prior year figures have been restated where appropriate to be in line with the provisions of Financial Reporting Standard No 2 (FRS 2), Financial Reporting Standard No 3 (FRS 3) and Financial Reporting Standard No 4 (FRS 4).
2. Issued ordinary shares, earnings per share, dividends per share and net assets per share have been adjusted for the rights issue in 1992.

But not all groups adjust *all* back figures. The information then becomes difficult, indeed almost impossible, to disentangle/interpret.

REUTERS *Notes to the 11 year consolidated financial summary 1998*

- 1995 and 1996 have been restated to reflect the effect of FRS 10 issued in 1997 which required purchased goodwill and intangible assets to be capitalised and amortised through the profit and loss account.
- 1988 to 1994 have not been restated for FRS 10.
- 1988 has not been restated to reflect the effects of the prior year adjustment for pensions made in 1989.
- 1988 to 1991 have not been restated to reflect the effects of the prior year adjustment for post-retirement medical benefits made in 1992.
- 1988 to 1991 have not been restated to reflect the change to reporting user accesses in 1994.
- 1988 to 1993 have been restated for the subdivision of every ordinary share of 10 pence each into four new ordinary shares of 2.5 pence each in April 1994.
- 1988 has been restated to reflect the cost of discontinuing operations at IDR Inc. as an exceptional item rather than an extraordinary item.
- 1990 to 1994 fixed assets have been restated to reflect the effect of UITF abstract 13 issued in 1995.

The point is: whether we like it or not, whether companies tell us or not, and whether we understand the effects or not, inconsistencies are present in historic figures, whether they form part of a group historical summary, come from our own past data or come from an Extel Card.

Changes in the business environment
Changes in basis may arise without any positive decision having to be made on the part of the company. For instance, the abolition of 100% first year allowances in 1991 made the year-on-year comparisons of after tax items very difficult for a number of years. Changes in ACT in 1993–99 have produced similar problems.

Changes in the composition of the group
Where a group either grows or contracts, comparability is bound to be affected. There are a number of possibilities:

1. New activities developed internally.
2. Acquisitions.
3. Termination of activities.
4. Disposals.

New activities developed internally
New products may be mentioned in the chief executive's or finance director's report, but figures in respect of them are unlikely to appear separately either in a five- or ten-year summary, or, unless they represent a very substantial investment, even in a segmental analysis, until they are relatively mature.

Acquisitions
FRS 3 *Reporting financial performance* requires profit and loss account figures down to the operating profit level to be split *inter alia* into (a) continuing activities and (b) acquisitions. Few companies do this in any five- or ten-year summary, simply lumping the figures together as continuing activities. You can safely assume that data represent total sales from all activities including new activities developed internally and acquisitions and that the operating profits include such activities. We discuss the rules on new acquisitions on page 183.

Mergers are treated differently (see page 187). Under FRS 6, in the year of the merger, corresponding figures for the preceding year have to be shown *somewhere* on the same basis as the current year figures (i.e. a straight addition of the figures for all the companies which merged) showing the figures for the individual merging companies separately, but these do not *have* to form the comparatives. If they do, the five- or ten-year summary may follow the same rationale and simply add the figures together (as do BP AMOCO's from 1994 to 1998 in 1998, the year in which those two companies merged); but it may not (see MITIE GROUP on page 222).

Termination of activities
In the past, most groups did not strip out companies no longer part of the group either in their profit and loss account or in a five- or ten-year summary. FRS 3 *Reporting financial performance* requires profit and loss account figures down to the operating

profit level to be split *inter alia* into a continuing activities and discontinued activities.

An element of subjectivity is inevitably involved when a decision is made to discontinue activities, but this is especially the case where the activities terminated were not previously a separate accounting unit.

To take a very simple illustration:

Example 24.1 Termination of activity

Clodhoppers is a small shop in a shopping precinct in York. The profit and loss account for the year to 31 December 2000 may be summarised:

	£000
Turnover	180
Cost of sales	(177)
Profit before tax	3

Disappointed, the owner goes through the results making the following analysis:

	Shoe sales £000	Shoe repairs £000
Turnover	120	60
Cost of shoes sold/Materials used	(80)	(30)
Gross profit	40	30
Employment costs:		
Staff	(12)	(15)
Manager	(10)	(10)
Rent and rates	(10)	(10)
Profit /(Loss) before tax	8	(5)

The shop has a manager and two assistants. One assistant is a specialist shoe repairer, the other a sales assistant. The manager supervises both and can fill in for either where necessary.

The shop lease has 6 years to run and it would be difficult to sublet part of the premises.

In assessing the profitability of operations, the manager's salary is apportioned half to shoe sales and half to shoe repairs; as are rent and rates. On this basis, shoe repairs are unprofitable.

It is decided on the last day of the year to cease repairing shoes and to make the shoe repairer redundant immediately at a cost of £2,500 (which, for simplicity, we will treat as a cost of the shoe repair department). The results might then be summarised:

	£
Profit from continuing operations	8,000
Loss on discontinued activity	(7,500)
Profit before tax	£500

Two points arise:

1. What will people make of the figures?
2. Was the decision the right one?

People will be tempted to look at these figures and say 'they have cut out an activity which was losing them £7,500 a year [it was not; £2,500 of the £7,500 represents redundancy pay which would not have been necessary apart from closure]; this has improved profitability; and the best estimate we can make is that next year's profit might be around £8,000.'

To believe that would be to delude oneself. For management to have argued that way would have been for them to have deluded themselves. Historical costing is inappropriate for making 'what if?' decisions. One needs to examine separately each item of cost and each item of revenue and ask what will happen to it if the proposal is effected.

For a start: half the manager's time was devoted to shoe repairs; and, not unreasonably, half his salary was apportioned to that activity. Are we going to replace him (paying yet more compensation), put him on half time, or what? If we don't do something, his costs will fall elsewhere, say, on shoe sales (and shoe sales are then likely to be loss-making).

Will his newly found spare time improve shoe sales? It might. Equally, the lack of a shoe repair facility might drive previous shoe customers elsewhere. We just do not know.

Equally, spare space may be a good thing. It may improve the shop's ability to display shoes, and attract custom. On the other hand, empty space, a 'dead' facility, may signal to customers a lack of profitability. But whatever is done: the rent and rates previously borne by shoe repairs must be borne somewhere. In the example, management split the rent and rates 50% to shoe sales and 50% to shoe repairs; but that is not the only way the cost might have been apportioned. It would not have been wrong to apportion the cost on the basis of:

- the number of square feet occupied by each of the activities;
- the 'site value' of the space occupied by each activity, e.g. putting twice the value per square foot on the shoe sales area at the front of the shop as on the area of shoe repairs at the back.
- labour cost, i.e. 12/17ths and 15/17ths.

The results would then have been different.

Oversimplified this example may be, but similar considerations arise in connection with closures whether the business involved is large or small.

TESCO *Five year record 1998*

Year ended February	1994	1995	1996	1997	1998[1]
Financial statistics £m					
Turnover excluding VAT					
UK	8,347	9,655	11,560	13,118	14,640
Northern Ireland and Republic of Ireland	–	–	–	–	1,028
Rest of Europe	253	446	534	769	784
	8,600	10,101	12,094	13,887	16,452
Operating profit – pre-integration costs					
UK	513	600	713	760	866
Northern Ireland and Republic of Ireland	–	–	–	–	49
Rest of Europe	8	17	11	14	(3)
	521	617	724	774	912
Operating margin [2]					
UK	6.1%	6.2%	6.2%	5.8%	5.9%
Northern Ireland and Republic of Ireland	–	–	–	–	4.8%
Rest of Europe	3.2%	3.8%	2.1%	1.8%	–
Total Group	6.1%	6.1%	6.0%	5.6%	5.5%
Share of loss from associated undertakings	–	–	–	–	(15)
Net interest (payable) /receivable	7	(22)	(43)	(24)	(65)
Underlying profit [3]	528	595	681	750	832
Wm Low/Ireland integration costs	–	(39)	–	–	(95)
Loss on disposal of discontinued activities	–	–	–	–	(8)
Net loss on disposal of fixed assets [4]	(93)	(5)	(6)	–	(1)
Profit before taxation	435	551	675	750	728
Taxation	(136)	(170)	(209)	(230)	(223)
Profit after taxation	299	381	466	520	505
Underlying fully diluted earnings per share [3]	18.8p	20.1p	21.9p	23.5p	26.6p
Earnings per share	15.2p	18.9p	22.2p	24.1p	23.1p
Dividend per share	7.75p	8.60p	9.60p	10.35p	11.60p
Net worth – £m [5]	2,749	3,104	3,588	3,890	3,876
Return on shareholders' funds [6]	19.4%	20.3%	20.4%	20.1%	21.4%
Return on capital employed [7]	15.7%	16.2%	16.9%	17.1%	18.4%
Net assets per share [8]	140p	151p	167p	179p	176p
UK food retail productivity £					
Turnover per employee [9]	138,658	140,842	143,335	146,326	146,404
Profit per employee [9]	8,522	8,752	8,841	8,478	8,660
Wages per employee [9]	13,922	13,941	13,948	14,222	14,500
Weekly sales per sq ft [10, 11]	16.37	17.00	18.31	19.74	21.12
UK food retail statistics					
Market share in food and drink shops [12]	10.7%	12.0%	13.7%	14.6%	15.2%
Number of stores	430	519	545	568	586
Total sales area – 000 sq ft [11]	11,006	12,641	13,397	14,036	14,585
Sales area opened in year – 000 sq ft	790	830	685	603	680
Average store size (sales area) – 000 sq ft [13]	25,700	24,900	25,600	26,300	26,600
Average sales area of stores opened in year – 000 sq ft [13]	33,100	28,200	30,700	25,800	26,700
Full-time equivalent employees [14]	60,199	68,552	80,650	89,649	99,997
Share price – pence Highest	260	255	338	370	539
Lowest	179	202	245	263	339
Year end	223.5	252	271	349	517

TESCO *Five year record 1998 continued*

Notes

1. 53 week period.
2. Based upon turnover exclusive of VAT.
3. Underlying profit and fully diluted earnings per share excludes net loss on disposal of fixed assets, loss on disposal of discontinued activities and Wm Low and Ireland integration costs.
4. Net loss on the disposal of fixed assets for 1994 includes £85m in respect of the write down of surplus development sites to their estimated net realisable value.
5. Total shareholders' funds at the year end.
6. Underlying profit divided by weighted shareholders' funds.
7. Operating profit divided by average capital employed.
8. Based on number of shares at year end.
9. Based on turnover exclusive of VAT, operating profit and total staff cost per full-time equivalent employee.
10. Based on weighted average sales area and turnover inclusive of VAT excluding property development.
11. Store sizes exclude lobby and restaurant areas.
12. Based on Tesco food, grocery, nonfood and drink sales and Institute of Grocery Distribution/Central Statistical Office data for the year to the previous December. The figures have all been restated following a change in the IGD market definition. The figure for 1998 is estimated.
13. Average store sizes exclude Metro and Express stores.
14. Based on average number of fulltime equivalent employees in the UK.

Continuing and discontinued operations

As explained on page 123, FRS 3 requires the subdivision in the profit and loss account of results down to operating profit level into continuing operations, acquisitions and discontinued operations. It also requires separate disclosure, after operating profit and before interest, of:

- profits or losses on the sale or termination of an operation;
- costs of a fundamental reorganisation or restructuring having a material effect on the nature and focus of the reporting entity's operations; and
- profits or losses on the disposal of fixed assets.

The FRS does not mention five- or ten-year summaries, which therefore do not *have* to do this. Most but not all do divide turnover and operating profit into those from continuing operations and those from discontinued operations. Most do not show profits or losses on the disposal of fixed assets.

In a simple case (like BENSONS CRISPS below) one has little difficulty seeing what happened and when. Here, in 1994, the entire business was unprofitable at the operating profit level; and operations with a turnover of £5.501m discontinued in that year are said to have lost £880,000.

In more complex cases (like ALLDAYS on page 217) it may be difficult to tell whether there has been one disposal or several over a period of years.

BENSONS CRISPS *Extract from five year record 1998*

Summarised profit and loss accounts

	1998 £000	1997 £000	1996 £000	1995 £000	1994 £000
Turnover					
Continuing operations	38,011	34,514	32,797	31,184	30,182
Discontinued operation	–	–	–	–	5,501
	38,011	34,514	32,797	31,184	35,683
Operating profit/(loss)					
Continuing operations	3,332	2,875	2,544	928	(2,690)
Discontinued operation	–	–	–	–	(880)
	3,332	2,875	2,544	928	(3,570)

...

ALLDAYS *Extract from five year record 1998*

Five year record

	1998	1997	1996	1995	1994
	£000	£000	£000	£000	£000
Turnover:					
Continuing operations	493,826	455,801	410,427	378,925	348,894
Discontinued operations	203,832	181,705	166,175	118,911	91,676
Total turnover	697,658	637,506	576,602	497,836	440,570
Operating profit before exceptional items:					
Continuing operations					
Alldays	14,720	19,492	15,064	12,086	7,949
Trademarket	590	1,518	1,650	1,602	1,940
Total – continuing operations	15,310	21,010	16,714	13,688	9,889
Discontinued operations					
W&P Foodservice	3,434	4,582	4,031	3,389	2,281
Wholesaling activity	–	–	2,754	3,261	3,840
Other	–	–	427	427	427
Total – discontinued operations	3,434	4,582	7,212	7,077	6,548
Total operating profit before exceptional items	18,744	25,592	23,926	20,765	16,437

BRUNEL HOLDINGS *Extract from five year record 1998*

Five Year Record 1998

	1994	1995	1996	1997	1998
Turnover (£m)					
Continuing operations	63.1	61.9	88.9	91.8	92.4
Discontinued operations	339.9	110.8	99.4	50.4	7.3
Total	403.0	172.7	188.3	142.2	99.7
Operating profit (£m)					
Continuing operations	3.6	3.5	5.1	5.0	2.9
Discontinued operations	3.1	4.7	1.9	2.4	–
Total	6.7	8.2	7.0	7.4	2.9

ALLDAYS' turnover figures would be consistent with there having been just one discontinuance of activities (in 1998). The analysis of operating profit makes it clear that there was an earlier discontinuance; and that the figures for 1996 and earlier represent both sets of activities since discontinued.

Just as there is little consistency in *what* is disclosed in a historical summary, there is no one order of *columns* which may, as in the ALLDAYS example, run in reverse chronological order from left to right (showing the most recent figures first) or they may run in the other direction (see BRUNEL HOLDINGS above). Brunel has seen a gradual whittling away of operations (in the chief executive's words 'after years of painful restructuring') such that it is impossible to interpret the figures without reference to earlier reports and accounts, e.g. figures for 1995–96 alongside look quite different.

BRUNEL HOLDINGS *Extract from 1996 accounts*

Group Profit and Loss Account	1996	1995
Note	£000	£000
Turnover		
Continuing operations	150,702	117,039
Discontinued operations	37,629	55,676
Total turnover ...	188,331	172,715
Cost of sales	(142,329)	(124,409)
Gross profit	46,002	48,306
Operating profit		
Continuing operations	8,331	8,794
Discontinued operations	(1,307)	(576)
Total operating profit ...	7,024	8,218

If the situation gets really complex companies simply give up, and, like NATIONAL POWER show 'Turnover: continuing operations' and 'Operating profit: continuing operations', stripping out discontinued activities entirely from the summary. Unfortunately, not every company makes it clear what it is doing. Most, but not all, which do not mention discontinued activities seem to leave turnover and profits from any discontinued activities in the figures in the summary.

The important thing to remember is that figures in a historical summary may not be what they seem: check before relying on them!

ANALYSIS

Earlier chapters have:

- dealt with the calculation of trends and ratios, describing each ratio in turn; and
- given an indication of the size of ratio one would expect.

Chapter 25 considers the sequence in which one might study a report and accounts.

Chapter 31 puts it all together by looking at BODY SHOP.

In this chapter we take an overall look at comparisons, that is to say, at the calculation of basic trends and ratios – most of which we have already met.

A word of warning

Do not allow yourself to get mesmerised by number-crunching. Ratios are not an end in themselves. They are merely a means of helping the analyst assimilate what is happening in the company, providing him with pointers to the reasons behind good or poor performance, and they will often give warning of increasing risk or even of impending disaster.

Throughout your study of a report and accounts be on qui vive for interesting points and if ratios help to pin-point or firm up your impression of what is happening, so much the better.

One of the final stages of any analysis is to interpret the trends and ratios, and assess likely current profits and future prospects. Here the analyst should:

(a) compare the company's performance with that in previous years;
(b) compare performance with that of similar companies (allowing for any differences in accounting policies) and/or with the industry's averages (using ratios); and
(c) consult other sources of information on the company and on the industry or industries in which the company operates (see Chapter 28).

The remainder of this chapter seeks to bring together, as aide memoir, everything about ratios and trends discussed earlier in the book.

Methods of relating items of information

There are four basic ways in which one item of financial information can be related to another numerically:

1. *A line-by-line comparison* can be made of the current year's accounts with those of the previous year. This is sometimes called *horizontal analysis*.
2. *The horizontal analysis* can be extended over several years, usually by giving the figure for an item in the first year of the series a value of 100 and relating subsequent years' figures to base 100. This is sometimes termed *trend analysis*.
3. *'Common size'* balance sheets or income statements can be prepared, each balance sheet item being expressed as a percentage of the balance sheet total and each profit and loss account item as a percentage of sales or earnings. This is sometimes called *vertical analysis*.
4. *Ratios* can be produced by comparing one item in a balance sheet or profit and loss account with another for the same period, or with the current price of the company's shares. This is sometimes termed *ratio analysis*.

Graphical presentation

It is also possible to present information in the form of graphs or charts. Properly designed and fairly presented, graphs or charts can present information quickly and vividly; and they are particularly useful where one's audience is not used to handling a mass of figures.

Examples of graphic presentation are to be found throughout the book. Readers might care to turn to pages 25, 47 and 57, and Chapters 29 and 31, to see a variety of presentations.

USING RATIOS AND STUDYING TRENDS

Choice of ratios

With the profit and loss account, balance sheet and cash flow statement each containing a minimum of 10 to 20 items, the scope for comparing one item with another is enormous, so it is important to be selective, both to limit the calculations required and, more importantly, to make the presentation of the selected ratios simple and readily understandable. No decision-maker wants a jungle of figures, so the ratios chosen should be the key ones, logically grouped.

Ratios can conveniently be divided into:

- *Operating ratios*, which are concerned with how the company is trading, and take no account of how the company is financed.

- *Financial ratios*, which measure the financial structure of the company and show how it relates to the trading activities.

- *Investment ratios*, which relate the number of ordinary shares and their market price to the profits, dividends and assets of the company.

In describing these ratios we give what we regard as the most useful and practical definition of each component. Although there is an increasing trend towards standardisation, individual analysts do not always agree on definitions, while companies do not all define ratio components in the same way.

Some companies include a table of key ratios in their report and accounts, and a few like REUTERS (at the bottom of the page) explain their definitions. This sort of table can be useful for looking at trends within the company concerned, but it is preferable to work out one's own ratios by a standard method, so that they form a fair basis for inter-company comparisons.

Main operating ratios

We explained in Chapter 16:

(i) Profit margin (page 126);
(ii) Return on capital employed (page 127);
(iii) Sales to capital employed (page 128);
and how they are related (page 128).

REUTERS *Extract from 11 year consolidated financial summary 1998*

	1998	1997	1996	1995	1994	1993	1992
Ratios							
Basic earnings per ordinary share	26.7p	24.0p	27.3p	23.2p	21.7p	18.0p	14.0p
Adjusted earnings per ordinary share (1)	30.3p	29.1p	30.4p	25.8p	21.7p	18.0p	14.0p
Dividends per ordinary share	14.4p	13.0p	11.75p	9.8p	8.0p	6.5p	5.3p
Cash flow per ordinary share (2)	67.9p	61.0p	60.7p	52.7p	45.6p	40.3p	33.6p
Book value per ordinary share (3)	23.3p	99.9p	88.3p	73.7p	44.7p	40.6p	51.2p
Cash flow/book value (4)	292.0%	61.0%	68.8%	71.5%	102.0%	99.2%	65.7%
Profit before tax as a percentage of revenue	19.1%	21.7%	22.4%	20.6%	22.1%	23.5%	24.4%
Return on tangible fixed assets (5)	48.2%	49.0%	60.0%	55.2%	57.6%	57.2%	53.2%
Return on equity (6)	78.5%	25.6%	33.7%	34.8%	50.8%	39.5%	29.9%
UK corporation tax rate	31.0%	31.5%	33.0%	33.0%	33.0%	33.0%	33.0%

Ratios:

1. Adjusted earnings per share are based on profit attributable to ordinary shareholders excluding capital reorganisation costs and goodwill amortisation.
2. Cash flow per ordinary share represents profit before taxation, goodwill amortisation and depreciation divided by the number of shares in issue after deducting shares held by employee share ownership trusts. In 1988 to 1997 shares in Reuters Holdings PLC held by group companies are also deducted.
3. Book value per ordinary share represents adjusted shareholders' equity divided by the number of shares in issue after deducting shares held by employee share ownership trusts. In 1988 to 1997 shares in Reuters Holdings PLC held by group companies are also deducted from shares in issue.
4. Cash flow/book value represents profit before taxation, goodwill amortisation and depreciation as a percentage of adjusted shareholders' equity.
5. Return on tangible fixed assets represents profit after taxation as a percentage of average tangible fixed assets. The average is calculated by adding tangible fixed assets at the start and the end of each year and dividing by two.
6. Return on equity represents profit attributable to ordinary shareholders divided by the average adjusted shareholders' equity. The average is calculated by adding adjusted shareholders' equity at the start and the end of each year and dividing by two. In 1998 a weighted average has been used to reflect the capital reorganisation.

Other operating ratios

Fixed assets:

In connection with fixed assets, Chapter 8 explained:

(i) Sales/Tangible assets (page 61);
(ii) Tangible fixed assets/Equity shareholders' funds (page 61);
(iii) Depreciation/Tangible fixed assets (page 62);
(iv) Additions to plant and machinery/Depreciation of plant and machinery (page 62)

Stocks:

In Chapter 10 we looked at ratios connected with stocks:

(i) Stocks/Turnover ratio (page 74);
(ii) the Stockturn ratio (page 75);
(iii) Stock in months or days (page 75); and
(iv) Cost of sales/Stock (page 75).

Debtors and creditors:

In Chapter 11, we considered (page 77):

(i) the debt collection period (in days and months); and
(ii) Trade debtors/Sales (%);

and factors which affect these.

Related ratios which we have not met before are:

(i) Trade creditors/Sales which gives some indication of the amount of credit a company is allowed by its suppliers, and quite a good indication, provided stock levels and profit margins are reasonably steady and the business is not highly seasonal;
(ii) Trade creditors/Cost of goods purchased is a better measure (but the cost of goods purchased during the year is seldom disclosed);
(iii) Trade creditors/Stocks, to see what proportion of the stocks is financed by the company's suppliers. This is of particular interest in retailing businesses, where 150% is a normal figure for an efficient food retailer like SAINSBURY.
(iv) Debtors/Trade creditors, a ratio watched by bankers. When things are normal this tends to be stable. Violent change in either direction is a warning signal.

Working capital:

In Chapter 15 (see page 101) we described the Working Capital/Sales ratio, which shows how much capital is required to finance operations in addition to capital invested in fixed assets. It can vary from a tiny 1% or even negative for a food retailer, to 30% or more for a heavy engineering company, and gives some indication of the likely additional cash needed with increased turnover.

Also useful are:

(i) Trading profit/Wages, which in a period of inflation gives a direct indication of the effect of wage increases on profits. For example, a company whose trading profit is only 15% of wages is likely to be much more adversely affected by a wage increase of 10% than a company with a ratio of 50%.
(ii) Sales per employee; and
(iii) Trading profit per employee.

The latter two give some indication of changing productivity.

Financial ratios

Financial ratios fall into two broad groups:

(i) Gearing ratios; and
(ii) Liquidity ratios.

Gearing is concerned with the proportion of capital employed that is borrowed, the proportion provided by shareholders' funds and the relationship between the two, while liquidity ratios are concerned with the company's cash position.

Gearing ratios

Financial gearing can be defined in a multiplicity of ways. As explained in Chapter 6 (page 45), the two most common are:

(i) the Debt/Equity ratio, shown as Borrowings/Shareholders' funds in the *Investors Chronicle*, and called 'Leverage' in the United States and elsewhere; and
(ii) the percentage of Capital employed represented by Borrowings.

Closely connected is:

(iii) Leverage effect: percentage change in earnings available to ordinary shareholders brought about by a 1% change in earnings before interest and tax (EBIT) (page 45).

Operational gearing

In Chapter 6 (page 46) we explained that operational gearing is the ratio of the percentage change of trading profit which results from 1% change in turnover, and depends on the relationship between fixed costs, variable costs and net profit, where fixed costs are costs that are incurred regardless of turnover, and variable costs are directly proportional to turnover:

(i) (Turnover − Variable costs) ÷ Trading profit;
(ii) (Trading profit + Fixed costs) ÷ Trading profit.

A related concept is:
(iii) Break-even turnover

$$= \text{Fixed costs} \times \frac{\text{Turnover}}{\text{Turnover} - \text{Variable costs}}$$

Liquidity ratios

The two ratios most commonly used in assessing a company's liquidity are, as explained in Chapter 15 (page 102):

(i) Current ratio;
(ii) Quick ratio.

In Chapter 19 (page 170) we looked at:

(i) Cash flow per share;
(ii) Capital expenditure per share.

A related ratio we have not met before is Contingent liabilities/Ordinary shareholders' funds. This gives an indication of how dire the effects of contingent liabilities actually materialising would be.

Investment ratios

Investment ratios are the ratios used by investors when deciding whether a share should be bought, sold or held. Most of them relate to the current price of the share, and therefore vary from day to day. The two most popular investment ratios are described in Chapter 18:

(i) the Price Earnings Ratio (PER) (page 161); and
(ii) the Dividend yield (page 162).

The Price earnings growth factor (PEG) is a yardstick introduced by Jim Slater (see page 162) and is a measure of whether a share looks overrated or underrated.

Ratios concerned with dividends are:
(i) Gross equivalent of a net dividend paid (but see page 162);
(ii) Dividend yield (%) (see page 162);
(iii) Dividend cover (see page 162);
(iv) Payout ratio (see page 162).

Net tangible assets per share (n.t.a.)

This shows the book value of tangible assets attributable to each ordinary share:

$$n.t.a. = \frac{\text{Ordinary shareholders' funds}}{\text{Number of ordinary shares in issue}}$$

The n.t.a. figure is very dependent on the balance sheet values of assets being realistic, and for a variety of reasons, most importantly:

(i) Inflation (see Chapter 29); and
(ii) The immediate write off in the past of purchased goodwill (see Chapter 16);

they are not realistic.

In an ideal world, n.t.a. does give some indication of how much the price of a share depends on the ability of the company to generate profits and how much is backed by assets.

The n.t.a. (sometimes called 'net asset value') is one reference point used in deciding on terms for an acquisition, assuming the potential biddee's assets are fairly valued or are adjusted for the purpose of the calculation.

Typical ratio values

Useful general guidance on the ratio values one might expect to find in various sectors of UK industry is contained in a book called *Industrial Performance Analysis* published by ICC (Inter Company Comparisons), 72 Oldfield Road, Hampton, Middlesex TW12 2HQ (phone 0181 783 1122). It shows aggregated balance sheet and profit and loss account data, together with key ratios calculated from the data. Analysts using this book should be careful to note the definitions of each ratio component, and in particular that 'total assets' include intangible assets and that 'capital employed' does not include short-term borrowings or overdraft. The ICC Information Group also publishes *Business Ratio Plus* (phone 0181 481 8720) on each of more than 160 sectors, giving detailed information on companies in the sector, and provides a variety of on-line services. Another source of information on ratios is the book *Key Business Ratios*, published by Dun & Bradstreet, Holmers Farm Way, High Wycombe, Bucks HP12 3BR.

Market capitalisation

The market capitalisation of a company is the market price of a company's ordinary shares multiplied by the number of shares in issue. 'Market cap' is a useful measure of the relative size of companies:

Market capitalisation: Food retailing 14 May 1999:

	£m
TESCO	12,187
SAINSBURY	7,736
ASDA	5,791
BUDGENS	104
PARK GROUP	43

Investigating trends

It is frequently a worthwhile, even profitable, exercise to set alongside one another, growth in:

(a) turnover;
(b) profit before tax;
(c) earnings per share;
(d) dividend per share.

If they are wildly different, the cause should be investigated. In the sixth edition we looked at MITIE GROUP, a relatively small cleaning and maintenance contractor, saying that it was 'taking advantage of the trend towards out-sourcing such services' while at the same time expanding by making a series of small acquisitions.

As we said on page 151, and as is shown in the 1995 extract below (not adjusted for the share sub-division in 1997), growth was spectacular:

- turnover was up almost 703% in 5 years;
- profits had almost, but not quite, kept pace (up 604%); but
- because of acquisitions for paper, e.p.s had grown only 165%;
- from a very low base (and covered nine times) dividends had increased 500% so shareholders certainly did not complain.

One can consider growth taking one year against the preceding year, or over a period. Here we look, as further practice, at 1998 against 1994:

- the very rapid growth in turnover was replaced by somewhat more moderate growth (turnover up just 132% in 4 years!);

- Profit before tax grew faster than sales (it was up 230%);
- Earnings rose almost 203% (nearly as fast as profits before tax);
- Dividends grew, but less fast than previously, up *only* 178% in the period!
- Cover remained high (at about 4 times) which enabled MITIE GROUP to make most acquisitions for cash.

In other words the group was exhibiting ratios typical of a highly profitable, but more mature group.

You can follow the history of MITIE GROUP, and study in depth research into it, in *Analyst* (see page 248).

Analyst originally recommended the shares in March 1994 when, adjusted for subsequent sub-divisions, they were 22p. On 14 May 1999 they were 185p, representing a gain of 741%.

MITIE GROUP *Group statistical record 1995 (extract)*

	1995 £000	1994 £000	1993 £000	1992 £000	1991 £000	1990 £000	Increase 1990–95
Turnover	125,183	101,732	72,994	52,276	32,699	15,594	702.8%
Profit on ordinary activities before taxation	4,571	3,361	2,402	1,808	1,231	649	604.3%
Earnings per share	12.2p	8.5p	6.6p	5.8p	5.5p	4.6p	165.2%
Dividend per share	3.0p	2.25p	1.75p	1.375p	1.0p	0.5p	500.0%

Earnings and Dividend per share figures have been re-stated to reflect the sub-division of shares referred to in Note … The results of merger accounted acquisitions are reflected in full in the year of acquisition and subsequent years but only the year prior to acquisition has been re-stated on a comparable basis.

MITIE GROUP *Group statistical record 1998 (extract)*

	1998 £000	1997 £000	1996 £000	1995 £000	1994 £000	Increase 1994–98
Turnover	236,293	209,425	161,149	125,183	101,732	132.3%
Profit on ordinary activities before taxation	11,100	8,210	6,302	4,571	3,361	230.3%
Earnings per share	10.3p	8.1p	6.5p	4.9p	3.4p	202.9%
Dividend per share	2.5p	2.0p	1.6p	1.2p	0.9p	177.8%

Earnings and Dividend per share figures have been restated to reflect the sub-division of shares in 1994 and in 1997. The results of merger accounted acquisitions are reflected in full in the year of acquisition and subsequent years but only the year prior to acquisition has been restated on a comparable basis.

Problem 24.1

Given the following extracts from the five year summary of a group, provide a short commentary.

Extracts from 5 year summary	1996 £m	1995 £m	1994 £m	1993 £m	1992 £m
Turnover	1,083.6	1,079.1	1,045.5	1,139.3	1,179.8
Profit from retail operations	102.0	87.2	65.2	43.0	10.0
Exceptional items	1.2	–	(6 4)	(31.4)	–
Profit for the financial year	74.6	61.6	38.9	0.4	10 8
Earnings per share	17.8p	14.8p	9.4p	0.1p	2.6p
Dividend per share	7.2p	6.3p	5.5p	5.0p	5.0p
Total net assets	532.0	484.2	447.3	423.9	438.3
Number of stores	435	433	431	425	736
Net selling space (000 sq ft)	5,268	5,005	4,815	4,704	6,452

Chapter 25

CHAIRMAN'S STATEMENT, OPERATING AND FINANCIAL REVIEWS AND DIRECTORS' REPORT

In this chapter we look at what can be learned from those parts of the report of a company which are not strictly part of the accounts. The directors' report has long been part of the reporting system and is required by the Companies Acts. The other documents covered in this chapter, for example, the chairman's statement, the operating (or operational) review, and financial review, are relatively new and not required by the Companies Acts.

Sequence of study of a report and accounts

It is difficult to lay down a set of rules as to the best order in which to study a report and accounts, and each individual will – indeed should – develop his own method. The important thing is not to miss information regardless of where it is presented.

One stockbroker tells us he always goes straight to the directors' holdings to see if they are reducing their holdings! – indeed, one co-author maintains on file details of all directors' share transactions in their own company and spends a few minutes each week studying them.

That the directors have sharply reduced their holdings in the company certainly tends to be a warning sign – but it is unwise for a director (or any other investor) to have too many eggs in one basket – so reductions are not necessarily a warning signal – an individual director may have special, personal, financial needs at a particular time.

Similarly, an increase in directors' holdings tends to be encouraging particularly where a company's shares seem undervalued or under pressure, but directors can and do get it wrong, personally as well as commercially, pouring good money after bad even when it is their own.

Major own-share activity on the part of one or more directors does, however, focus attention: something seems to be happening. One needs to find out what.

It is certainly helpful to start by glancing at the chairman's statement and the directors' report simply to see whether anything has occurred which would invalidate a straightforward comparison between one year and another. If, for instance, a major acquisition took place early in the year under review, almost all operating and financial ratios are likely to have been affected. This does not mean that the ratios are useless: simply that the analyst must bear in mind that change in composition every time he compares one ratio with another.

Having then studied the accounts (a process we will discuss in detail in Chapter 31) and having examined any segmental analysis of turnover and pre-tax profits between classes of business and any geographical analysis of turnover and trading results outside the United Kingdom, the reader will have a good idea of how the company has fared in the past year, but little idea why (except in the context of happening to know that it was a good, average or bad year for the industry or industries in which the company operates), and little idea of how the company is likely to do in the current year and beyond. It is to the chairman's statement and the operating review, if there is one, that we should look for this information.

The chairman's statement

Companies are not required to publish a chairman's statement, but listed companies invariably do. In the case of companies which believe in keeping shareholders well informed, the chairman's statement will usually contain comment on:

(a) overall trading conditions during the period, current climate and general outlook;

(b) the performance achieved by each activity, current trading and future prospects;

(c) items of special interest (e.g. closures and new ventures);

(d) changes in the board;

(e) company strategy and plans for the future.

Study the chairman's statement, not only for what it says, but also for what it does not, where one is left to read between the lines. We find it's useful to read through the whole statement highlighting with a marking pen key phrases and points of interest as we go, before getting down to any detailed analysis.

Review of operations

A growing number of companies produce, sometimes instead of a Chairman's Statement but more commonly in addition to one, either a Chief Executive's Review or Operational Review. BTP has all three.

Where these documents exist, and even the more enlightened and/or investment hungry smaller companies publish them too, they provide a vital part of the information package, often avoiding the stilted form and language of the directors' report and shedding additional light on information in the accounts.

Typically, where one or more of these documents exist in addition to a Chairman's Statement, that document is devoted largely to overall performance, plans and strategy, while the detailed review of operations, usually division by division, is left to the Chief Executive's Review and/or Operational Review. It is here that one learns in detail what the various parts of the group do, where, and how, the group's various markets are shaping, and where the focus of management attention lies. Statistics and graphs often present useful information on this and on trends over the years.

Financial Review

Discussions during the preparation of the Cadbury Report, during which it was suggested that a Financial Review should form part of the reporting package (as it does with some US companies), and publication of an ASB Statement *Operating and financial review* (July 1993), have led to a number of UK groups adopting this practice. CADBURY SCHWEPPES, for instance, includes eight pages of commentary on its 1998 accounts in its Financial Review.

The main purpose of the Financial Review tends to be to explain the accounts and to shed light on financial performance and strategy:

- Why did interest payable rise (or fall) so much year on year?
- What exactly do the exceptional items represent?
- Why does the effective tax rate differ from the rate of UK corporation tax?
- Where does the group keep its main cash reserves – the UK? If not, why there?
- What has happened to gearing, and why?
- What was the capital expenditure during the year actually used for? How much more is needed to complete the group's plans, and where is it coming from? (Is it in place?)?
- How was (is) the group affected by exchange rates and interest rates?
- Risk management, with comment on:
  (a) treasury risk management;
  (b) liquidity risk;
  (c) finance and interest rate risk;
  (d) currency risk;
  (e) commodity risk;
  (f) credit risk.
- Which recent accounting standards have been adopted for the first time in the accounts?
- What has the group done about the Year 2000 problem?

Where a financial review is included, it should be regarded by analysts as being, to all intents and purposes, part of the accounts; and studied as such.

Environmental reports

In recent years there has been a growth in environmental reporting in the UK. More and more companies now include information on environmental issues in their annual reports and accounts and there are now over 50 dedicated environmental reports available.

The scope of environmental matters covered is wide; perhaps 20 separate issues are discussed. Some of these are obvious and covered by most of the reports, e.g. waste, emissions, use of natural resources, energy usage and recycling. Others, like the decommissioning of oil rigs, are problems specific to particular industry groups.

Until such time as environmental reporting has matured to the stage where there is a substantial amount of historical information and a free flow of information on environmental matters, the usefulness of any information to shareholders and analysts is limited. Nevertheless, environmental issues cannot be ignored. The costs of (i) a major environmental disaster; (ii) decommissioning, could mortally wound all but the largest groups.

Legal claims, particularly in the US, may run back many years; may be covered by insurance or uncovered; and the courts seem unpredictable, not to say wild, in their assessment of damages. Any note on contingent liabilities in this area needs to be studied with care (see page 106).

Estimating current year profits

A rough estimate of profits for the current year can be constructed (for each activity which is separately reported on) by quantifying the chairman's comments (and those by the chief executive and finance director in related reports – for simplicity we will refer to the chairman), bearing in mind prevailing conditions and prospects for the industry concerned; for example, POLYGON HOLDING PLC (Example 25.1 below).

The chairman may also give an overall indication, e.g. Polygon Holding's turnover in the first three months of the current year has been 22% higher than the same period last year, the paper division's order-book is now four months, compared with one month last year, and, despite constant pressure on margins and the increasing ineptitude of government, the outlook for the group is encouraging. 'Outlook encouraging' sounds to us like a 20–25% increase in pre-tax profits, i.e. to £4.3–£4.5m, pointing to the middle of the range we constructed division by division.

Other points to bear in mind in making a profits estimate are these:

1. Loss-makers discontinued will not only eliminate the loss but should, in addition, improve liquidity (and thus reduce interest charges, assuming there is an overdraft). But have all terminal losses been provided for?

2. What is the chairman's previous record? Has he been accurate, cautious, unduly optimistic – erratic? Have past assurances of better times ahead remained unfulfilled?

3. Remember, too, that one of the chairman's most important jobs is to maintain general confidence in the company, so he is likely to concentrate on the good points and only touch briefly or remain silent on the weaker aspects of the company. Here it is a good idea to jot down questions one would like the answer to, even if the analyst or shareholder is unlikely to have the opportunity of putting them to the company, because it focuses the mind and helps to establish what the chairman hasn't revealed and whether any unexplained area is likely to be significant. Good questions to ask oneself are: (i) 'what are the company's main problems, and (ii) what is being done about them?'

4. Beware of vague statements, such as:

   (a) 'Turnover in the first ten weeks of the current year has exceeded the corresponding figure for last year.' It could be 1% ahead in value because inflation more than covered the 4% drop which occurred in volume.

   (b) 'Unforeseen difficulties have occurred in ... and a provision of £1.3m has been made.' Unless there is some indication of the likely overall cost of overcoming these difficulties, or of abandoning the activity altogether, the company should be assumed to have an open-ended loss-maker on its hands.

Example 25.1 Estimating current year profits: POLYGON HOLDINGS PLC

Activity	Industrial climate	Chairman's remarks	Previous year £m	Reported year £m	Estimate of current year £m
Building	Continued recession	'Further decline inevitable'	1.0	0.8	0.5–0.6
Paper	Cyclical upturn	'Marked improvement'	2.2	1.8	2.4–2.8
Bookmaking	One of the UK's few growth industries	'Continued progress'	1.0	1.2	1.4–1.5
Plastic extrusions	Demand flat	'Market share increasing but lower margins'	0.6	0.75	0.6–0.8
Interest charges	Rates down 2%	'Improvement in liquidity likely'	–0.8	–1.0	–0.8
		Pre-tax total	4.0	3.55	4.1–4.9

Longer-term prospects

The chairman of a company should be continually looking to the future and, unless he and his board have good sound ideas on where the future growth in profits is likely to come from, and are steering the company in that direction, then above-average profits growth is unlikely. Although there must, of course, be some restrictions on what a chairman discloses about plans for the future, because of competition, he will usually include some indication of where he thinks the company is going in his annual statement.

A good past growth record is clearly encouraging (a no-growth company is likely to stay a no-growth company unless the management or the management's attitude changes), but what indications are there of future growth? Possibilities to look for are the following:

1. *Better margins on existing business.* This is an unreliable source of growth unless the company has *either*

   (a) some very strong competitive advantage, such as patents or lucrative long-term contracts, or

   (b) spent large sums of money building up brand images and carving out market share, and is now beginning to reap the benefits, and even then the profits growth will only last until the patents expire, the long-term contracts run out or the brand images tarnish.

2. *Further expansion of existing activities within the United Kingdom.* Is there any scope for this, or is the company in a position like BOOTS or W. H. SMITH, with a store in every town of any size, or like PILKINGTON, with 90% of the UK glass market?

3. *Diversification within the United Kingdom.* This was BOOTS' answer to its saturation problem with chemist shops: it widened the range of goods sold to include records and tapes, hi-fi, cameras, binoculars, even sandwiches. BOOTS was using its retailing expertise in wider product ranges, rather than going into some totally unrelated activity, and there does need to be some logic in diversifications or they can come very badly unstuck.

4. *Acquisition within the United Kingdom.* Has the company got a successful record of acquisitions, or would this method of growth be new to it (and therefore more risky)? This was part of W. H. SMITH'S solution for further growth: in 1986 it took over the recorded music chain OUR PRICE, with 130 outlets, added 40 music outlets it already had and by 1990, with further acquisitions, built the chain up to around 300 outlets.

5. *Exports.* Is the product suitable for export, or would transport costs make competitiveness overseas unlikely or impossible (e.g. bricks)? Does the company export already, is it a significant amount, and is it growing? The chairman may report that 'exports are 80% up on last year', but if this is an increase from 0.1% to 0.18% of turnover, it is hardly thrilling, and one should be wary of the chairman whose efforts to paint a rosy picture involve misleading statements like that, which should in honesty be qualified by some phrase like 'albeit from a very low base'.

6. *Are there opportunities for overseas growth* like W.H. SMITH's acquisition of the US news and gifts chain ELSON specialising in shops in hotels and airports, or PILKINGTON putting down float-glass plants overseas, either on its own or in joint ventures, or by licensing the process to foreign glass manufacturers? There are, however, a good many hazards in opening up operations abroad, apart from the initial expense: different business ethics and practices, language, law, accounting and tax systems, and so on. For manufacturing abroad, cost levels and exchange rates may change over time, so that what today looks a good investment may prove otherwise in years to come if the cost of living rises faster in that country than elsewhere.

7. *Is the company spending money on, and attaching importance to, developing new products?* This is particularly important for pharmaceutical companies; GLAXOWELLCOME, for instance, in 1998 reported £1,163m spent on research and development, representing 14.6% of the group's turnover.

   Although any manufacturing company that isn't developing new products is almost certainly going downhill, it is also bad news if the chairman is always eulogising about new products that never come to anything: the company's track record on product development should be checked.

8. *Is the company ploughing profits back?* Profits in most industries cannot expand beyond a given point unless the asset base (needed to support the trading needed to generate the profits) is also expanded. There is a limit to gearing up, while acquisitions and rights issues don't necessarily enhance e.p.s.: only steady ploughback gives scope for steady growth in e.p.s.

In the context of future growth, it is also worth checking press cuttings for stories on the company, which often contain glimpses of the company's thoughts on the future (many people use the FT McCarthy press cutting service).

Information on the quality of management

Returning to the business of assessing the strength of the management, perhaps the most encouraging facet is when the chairman admits to a mistake or to being caught wrong-footed, and reports what is being or has been done about it. A classic example comes from the 'rag trade': the chairman's statement for WEARWELL in 1976, a year in which trading results had fallen from £1m profit to £28,000 loss on turnover down from £7.1m to £6.2m and with over £½m in terminal losses, contained the following comments:

WEARWELL *Extracts from chairman's report 1976*

... in 1973 we operated what was basically a cash and carry operation. [In 1974 and 1975 the company made two acquisitions for cash and we] found ourselves in the business of building up stock and financing customers for considerable periods ... sales not as buoyant as expected ... liquidity difficulties in the opening weeks of 1976 instituted immediate measures, namely:

1. Closure of the mail order supply business which has required the financing of substantial stocks.
2. Cutting out much of the credit business with chain stores.
3. The waiver by directors of a substantial part of their salary entitlement together with a waiver of between 94.0% and 99.9% of their total entitlement to the interim dividend.
4. Strenuous efforts were made to liquidate stocks.

... your company operates now only in the cash and carry type business which is where your management has proved its expertise.

Wearwell's drastic action paid off. The company just managed to get out of the red in 1977, and from then on pre-tax profits grew steadily; five years later the chairman, Asil Nadir (of POLLY PECK fame, the group which Wearwell subsequently joined) was able to report pre-tax profits in excess of £4m.

Wearwell's shareholders had a bumpy ride: from an Offer for Sale price of 30p (adjusted for subsequent scrip and rights issues) in July 1973

they saw the ordinary share price fall to a low of 8p in November 1976, and received no dividends at all in 1977 and 1978. But if they got out in time (i.e. before Polly Peck bit the dust) they were amply rewarded: in 1984 Wearwell merged with Polly Peck, whose chairman was also Mr Asil Nadir. The deal gave Wearwell shareholders 53 Polly Peck shares for every 100 Wearwell, valuing Wearwell's ordinary shares at 164p each: twenty times the 1976 level.

In contrast, the chairman of a housebuilding company reported proudly in 1974 that 'notwithstanding all these problems [the three-day week, the shortage of mortgage funds, rising interest rates and increases in building costs] your company increased its turnover to a new record level'. The turnover had risen from £25.4m to almost £44m on an equity base of less than £2m net of goodwill and after writing £8.7m off the value of the land bank, by then in the books at a mere £24.4m plus £23.4m work in progress. Apart from the feeling that the chairman was steering his company straight for the eye of a financial typhoon, and his failure to even mention the year's pre-tax loss of £6.3m in his statement, there were a number of fairly conspicuous danger signals scattered around the report:

(a) the notice of the AGM included a resolution to appoint a top London firm of accountants to be joint auditors with the existing provincial firm of auditors;
(b) the directors' report contained a little paragraph on 'financial arrangements', which revealed that the group's bankers had agreed to 'roll up' interest on group borrowings.

But perhaps the most telling fact was an omission: the group's habit of including a historical summary (which in the previous year's accounts had shown a seven-year progression in pre-tax profits from £142,000 to over £7m) had been discontinued! The fall into loss was too painful to face. Liquidation followed quite shortly afterwards.

THE DIRECTORS' REPORT

Contents

The contents of the directors' report fall broadly into three categories:

- *Information required by law* – the statutory requirements – a mass of information some of which is obvious from the accounts anyway, some of which is of comparatively little interest to the analyst (but appears to have been motivated by political considerations, e.g. contributions for political purposes), but some of which may be of vital interest and importance to anyone interpreting the accounts, e.g. the review of the year and likely future developments.
- *Information required by The Stock Exchange* which we described in Chapter 4, some of which overlaps the statutory requirements.
- *Voluntary information* – additional information and commentary which the company wants to include: this is usually concerned with the events of the past year, current trading and future plans and prospects.

Voluntary information is, these days, normally contained mainly or wholly in the chairman's statement or the operating review or similar reports, leaving the directors' report to be largely a catalogue of compulsory details. But if there is no chairman's statement and, as we said earlier, there is no compulsion for a chairman to report separately from the board of directors, any voluntary information will be included in the directors' report.

Statutory requirements

Under the Companies Acts as amended by the Miscellaneous Accounting Amendments Regulations 1996, a directors' report must give the following information:

(i) a fair review of the development of the business during the year, together with an indication of likely future developments and of research and development activities (CA 1989, s. 8 and CA 1985, Sch. 7, paras 6(b) and (c));

(ii) the names of the directors and details of their interests (shareholdings) (CA 1989, Sch. 5);

(iii) details of company's own shares acquired by the company during the year (CA 1985, Sch. 7, Part 11);

(iv) important events affecting the company which have occurred since the end of the year (CA 1985, Sch. 7, para. 6(a); see also post balance sheet events, page 230);

(v) details of political or charitable contributions, if over £200 in the year (CA 1985, Sch. 7, para. 3).

During a recent slump, it was suggested that some companies, often leading companies, were bringing problems to their suppliers by delaying payment. As a consequence, from March 1996 directors of public companies and their large subsidiaries are required to give details of policies for the payment of suppliers in the following year.

Such statements often refer to the CBI's Prompt Payment Code but tend to be bland and of little use to the analyst. SAFEWAY doesn't and its note is slightly more interesting than most.

SAFEWAY *Extract from the 1998 directors' report*

Suppliers' Payment Policy

A strategic objective of the group is to have mutually beneficial long-term relationships with our suppliers and we seek to settle, in advance, the terms of payment with suppliers and abide by those terms. The average number of days credit taken by the group for trade purchases at 28 March 1998 was 46 days (1997 – 43 days), whereas the average during the year was 39 days (1997 38 days).

This makes the point, and it is worth remembering: figures (e.g. bank balances and ratios) at balance sheet date are not necessarily typical of those the rest of the year.

An analyst would certainly find more revealing a report by a junior member of the accounts department of a food company whose products are on every supermarkets' shelves that instructions are frequently given by the managing director to 'call for a copy invoice – that will keep them happy for another couple of weeks'.

Control of the company

It is always worth checking whether a company is a 'bid prospect'. If an acquisition-minded company has a substantial holding, this can explain why the company's shares are looking overrated or expensive in comparison with other similar companies.

On the other hand, if the company is a close company (i.e. under the control of its directors or of five or fewer persons – see Chapter 3), or if the directors' interests are substantial although not controlling, the dividend policy is likely to be conservative. In addition, growth will probably be limited to ploughing back profits, because directors or the controlling shareholders are unlikely to be in a position to take up their entitlement in a rights issue, and because acquisitions for paper would dilute their control.

However, if the principal director shareholder is nearing retirement, with no obvious successor (check list of shareholders for family names of the next generation, and remember that new issue prospectuses give directors' ages), then an agreed bid could well be in store.

The board of directors

This is, perhaps, an opportune time to discuss the board. Although many companies are built up primarily through the efforts of a single person, a one-man band is a potentially dangerous situation. He's going to present a succession problem in due course, and what would happen if he had a heart attack tomorrow? And, if he's egocentric, he may surround himself with yes-men and come an awful cropper with 'his' company.

Investors prefer a top management *team*: it is, for example, preferable not to combine the posts of chairman and managing director, and to have a separate finance director, and to have at least five board members. We were (and probably, today, the market would be) unhappy with the statement of one chairman/MD: 'Apart from overall control of the Group's affairs, I shall have particular responsibility for financial control, and investigating possible acquisitions by the company.'

Non-executive directors

We have long liked the inclusion of a few non-executive directors. This is now a recommendation of the Cadbury Committee – one which most companies accept though a few loudly proclaim their disagreement.

Non-executive directors are valuable provided, and only provided, they:

(a) are of a healthily independent disposition;
(b) devote sufficient time to the company to have a good grasp of its affairs (i.e. to know what's going on);
(c) are prepared to make a stand/resign if they disagree on important issues; and
(d) bring relevant experience to the boardroom.

Even so, history suggests that non-executive directors provide little protection from a dominant chairman/chief executive.

Where a company has been in difficulties or has become complacent, the effects of a change in the top management should be followed closely. It often marks the beginning of an upturn in a company's fortunes; for example the appointment of Eugene Anderson as chief executive of JOHNSON MATTHEY after a disastrous foray into banking and the appointment of Derek Birkin as chief executive of RTZ after several years of little or no real growth in e.p.s.

It is well worth checking on the track record of new management and, if you can, going to the AGM to meet them.

Internal controls and looking to the future

Terms which often figure in accounts, director's reports and chairmen's statements are: estimates, forecasts and budgets. Not only do business decisions depend upon estimates, forecasts and budgets, so do interim statements and annual accounts. The future cannot be foretold with certainty, but managers have to try.

But it is not just the future that has to be estimated. Some information about the past (e.g. a detailed breakdown of a competitor's local sales; or a detailed analysis of a potential acquisition's cost and revenue structure) may not be available at all. Even where information about the past was potentially available, it may not have been collected. Or it may have been collected, e.g. as part of a computerised sales system, but never analysed.

In all such cases resort is frequently had to estimation. Sometimes this may be based on a limited sample; often it is largely or entirely unsupported.

Management can be criticised:

- for not using information which was obtainable;
- for failing to undertake research;
- for conducting it sloppily; or
- for drawing incorrect or unwise conclusions.

TERMINOLOGY

Estimates, forecasts and budgets

An **estimate** is a judgement (i.e. an opinion) as to the amount, or quantity, of something, e.g. sales, expenses or profit, often, but not necessarily, made before the event. It is of necessity approximate. The accuracy of an estimate depends upon (i) the skill of the estimator; and (ii) the accuracy with which the facts upon which it is based are known or can be forecast.

A **forecast** is simply a prediction. But the term **profit forecast** has a special meaning. A profit forecast is a formal statement drawn up in connection with a bid (see Chapter 28).

A **budget** is a formal **plan**, i.e. a statement of intentions. Most companies budget as a regular annual exercise; but where one or more factors change significantly, a **revised budget** is prepared. More usually, a system of continually **reforecasting** the current year is employed. This terminology is clearer: the budget remains the budget; the forecast represents current expectations.

It is often necessary to look forward, i.e. to make forecasts, e.g. when acquiring new plant, entering a new line of business, or expanding in a particular direction. It is fair to criticise managers if they have clearly been over-optimistic, or have failed to do their homework. But it is wrong to criticise managers for *trying* to forecast the future.

No manager can expect, or be expected, to be right 100% of the time.

A budget is a formal plan. Logically, it too needs to be based on forecasts: indeed, on a mutually consistent group of forecasts and plans. Too often, in an attempt to meet market expectations, budgets are imposed from above without proper regard to consistency.

Combined Code of Best Practice

Another factor influencing reports and accounts is the Combined Code of Best Practice, published in June 1998 (see Chapter 26).

Statements published in compliance with that Code are supposedly designed to shed light on internal controls and systems, and refer to the forecasting, budgeting, reporting and control structure which lies behind the annual accounts and has a marked influence upon them.

Consider ICELAND:

ICELAND *Extract from directors' report 1998*
The board is responsible for establishing and maintaining the Group's system of internal financial controls and has formally adopted a schedule of matters which must be brought to it for approval. Such controls are designed to address the key business and financial risks, to ensure that the financial position of the Group is disclosed with reasonable accuracy and to ensure that the board maintains full and effective control over key financial, operational, compliance and strategic matters. They are not designed to give absolute assurance against material misstatement or loss as this would be impractical and

not cost effective.

Annual budgets and other key performance targets and objectives are approved for the Group and for each operating and cost unit. Performance against these targets is monitored weekly with detailed reviews held quarterly.

Clear lines of management responsibility and levels of delegated authority have been established to enable management to operate effectively within both their authority limits and approved budgets. Approval, reporting and monitoring procedures ensure compliance with these limits.

As mentioned above, an audit committee meets regularly ...

That looks like a good system. But in the recent past (if not still today) many organisations:

(i) reported to management cumulative, year-to-date, 'actuals' and compared these with the budget to date (thus failing to focus specifically on the results of each individual month or quarter);
(ii) tried to hold to the budget even when it was patently outdated (i.e. no longer achievable);
(iii) failed to reforecast the expected annual results;
(iv) lacked a continuous inventory system;
(v) often prepared no balance sheet at the end of the month or quarter (and, if they did, fell back upon estimates, budgets and forecasts rather than used 'hard' accounting data);
(vi) failed even to consider cash flows in the succeeding period.

We are not convinced that the Combined Code has done much to prevent this.

Under the Combined Code of Best Practice directors are also called upon to report that the business is a going concern. We cover this in Chapter 26.

POST BALANCE SHEET EVENTS

It might be thought that, since a company's report and accounts reflect the state of affairs at the balance sheet date, events arising after that date would be excluded, but this is not entirely the case: post balance sheet events (events occurring between the balance sheet date and the date the accounts are approved by the board) should be

reflected or disclosed if they are important (CA 1985, Sch. 7, para. 6).

SSAP 17 *Accounting for post balance sheet events* distinguishes between two types of post balance sheet event: (i) Adjusting events; (ii) Non-adjusting events.

Adjusting events

Adjusting events are post-balance sheet events, which provide additional evidence of conditions existing at the balance sheet date. The accounts should be adjusted accordingly, but separate disclosure is not normally required.

Typical adjusting events include:

- the subsequent determination of the purchase price of a fixed asset purchased or sold before the year end;
- a property valuation which provides evidence of a permanent diminution in value;
- receipt of the financial statements or other information regarding an unlisted company which provides evidence of a permanent diminution of value of a long-term investment;
- The receipt of evidence that the previous estimate of accrued profit on a long-term contract was materially inaccurate.

Where any subsequent events indicate that the 'going concern' concept should not have been applied to the company or to a material part of it, the accounts should also be adjusted accordingly.

Non-adjusting events

Non-adjusting events are post-balance sheet events which concern conditions which did not exist at the balance sheet date. The events should be disclosed together, if practicable, with an estimate of the financial effect, e.g. MEDEVA:

MEDEVA *Note 27 to 1998 accounts*

27. Post balance sheet events

...

On 4 February 1999 Medeva signed an agreement to dispose of the Group's Swiss manufacturing operations to RSP Pharma AG ('RSP'), a company owned by the local management team. Details of this transaction are set out in the Operating and Financial Review on page

...

Although SSAP 17 calls for the disclosure of post balance sheet events in the financial statements:

(i) There is normally no 'pointer' to any such note in the accounts, i.e. it is 'stand alone', so it is necessary to read the notes in their entirety and not rely on references to them elsewhere in the accounts;
(ii) Non-adjusting events tend also to be mentioned or further detail given in the Chairman's Statement, Financial Review or Review of Operations. For example MEDEVA told more about the RSP deal in its Operating and Financial Review.

MEDEVA *Extract from the operating and financial review 1998*

On 5 February 1999 the conditional disposal of the Swiss manufacturing operations to RSP Pharma AG ('RSP'), a company owned by the local management team, was announced. The transaction is expected to be effective by 23 April 1999. The assets being disposed consist of the manufacturing facility and products and certain development projects. In 1998 these assets generated sales of £6.7m (1997: £5.9m) and an operating loss of £0.2m (1997: loss £0.3m). These assets are being sold to RSP at their net asset value of £3.9m and thus no gain or loss will be generated on this disposal. Medeva will receive an initial payment of £1.7m, with the balance payable over a maximum period of 12 years, depending on the profitability of RSP. As part of the deal Medeva will also retain the rights to earn royalties on certain products RSP plan to develop, mainly Purepa, a concentrated, modified fish oil product. Medeva has also entered into an agreement to acquire a 20% investment in RSP at a cost of £0.7m.

Window dressing

One method of improving the appearance of a company's accounts was to borrow short-term money, perhaps just overnight, in order to bump up liquidity at the balance sheet date, a trick that was particularly popular amongst fringe bankers in the early 1970s.

SSAP 17 endeavours to preclude this and similar types of cosmetic operation by requiring the disclosure of 'the reversal or maturity after the year end of transactions entered into before the year end, the substance of which was primarily to alter the appearance of the company's balance sheet'.

This requirement does not prevent this type of window dressing, but it certainly discourages auditors from being party to deliberate deception.

Problem 25.1

A company which is the holding company of a group involved in a diverse range of activities from computer services to foundries, and door manufacture to motor dealerships, reported in 1995 as a result of Cadbury:

Corporate governance

...

Formal procedures in respect of matters reserved to the Board and authorisation levels have been established during the year. Guidelines for Directors' access to independent professional advice, and for the appointment of non-executive Directors have not yet been formalised.

What purpose is served by such a statement?

Chapter 26

CORPORATE GOVERNANCE AND THE AUDITORS' REPORT

CORPORATE GOVERNANCE

Corporate governance, the system by which companies are managed and controlled, is a topic of increasing importance to the directors of a company. Over the last few years, guidelines and codes have been developed by the Cadbury, Greenbury and Hampel Committees. This process culminated in (a) the publication in June 1998 of the *Combined Code – Principles of Good Governance and Code of Best Practice*, which brought together the work of those committees, and in due time (b) changes in the Stock Exchange rules requiring its adoption.

The rules on corporate governance seek to ensure that companies are managed and controlled in such a way that management is competent and honest.

Corporate governance has, of course, existed since the creation of the first company, but attention only focused on it with the publication of a *Code of Best Practice* in December 1992 by the Committee on the Financial Aspects of Corporate Governance ('Cadbury') – or perhaps more accurately with a series of incompetencies and scandals which had made it clear that assumptions on the part of investors of the competence and honesty of boards of directors were, in some cases, misplaced.

Cadbury laid down 19 specific requirements compliance with which would serve to reassure shareholders. Although it provided a flood of additional information, most of it was little more than a bland reassurance that the board was on top of its job.

Provided that directors actually do what they claim to do (and before the *Code* was published too many did not), one can say that the new disclosures are a good thing.

The *Combined Code* is even more detailed, containing 14 principles of good governance and 45 code provisions which are applicable to listed companies. It is in four parts:

Part A: Directors;
Part B: Directors' remuneration;
Part C: Relations with shareholders;
Part D: Accountability and audit.

The directors are required in their report to state how the principles of the code have been applied. But the required information, which we will not list in detail, may be found almost anywhere in the report and accounts.

SWAN HILL *Extract from the directors' report 1998*
Corporate Governance
The Combined Code and amended Stock Exchange Listing rules were only published during 1998 and formal guidance is still awaited from the Accounting Standards Board regarding internal controls. The Directors' review of internal controls may not, therefore, constitute a review for the purposes of the Combined Code as ultimately interpreted. However the Directors are satisfied that Swan Hill has complied with the provisions of the Combined Code throughout the year for internal financial controls.

A complete review of all other corporate governance requirements specified in the Combined Code has been undertaken. The Directors' believe the Company complies materially with the principles and provisions of the Code. The only exceptions relate to provision A6.2 (Rotation of Directors) where directors retire by rotation at least every three years and to recommendation A2.1 which requires that there should be a senior independent non-executive director, other than the chairman. The current articles provide that no more than one third of directors can retire by rotation annually. Whilst this may result in some directors continuing for a fourth year before rotation, the Board believes this is satisfactory. The Board considers that having an equality of executive and independent non-executive directors on the board, including an independent non-executive chairman, provides an appropriate balance of power and authority and consequently it is not planning to appoint a senior non-executive director. As regards provision B1.7 (Term of Service Contracts), the Board has adopted this provision with the exception of Service Contracts for the Group Chief Executive and Group Finance Director. It believes as part of its remuneration policy and in accordance with current industry practice that these periods are not exceptional.

There are other provisions which are now part of the Combined Code and which, whilst applying for the year under review, could not be implemented. They relate to practices which are dependent upon the AGM and in the case of your company this was held in 1998 prior to the publication of the Combined Code, specifically provisions C2.1 (Declaration of proxy votes) and C2.4 (20 working days notice for AGM), which will be adopted this year.

Much of the information required is of background interest only and does not assist one in interpreting the accounts proper. For example:

SWAN HILL *Extract from the directors' report 1998*

The board

The Board comprises four executive and four non-executive directors. It is responsible for all elements of corporate governance and ensures compliance with these by receiving and reviewing regular reports from Board Committees or individual directors on internal financial controls. It meets regularly throughout the year to determine overall Group strategy, to review management reports and to approve major new projects and capital expenditure as well as significant financing matters. It approves annual profit and loss and cash flow budgets and monitors these, in conjunction with revised forecasts, at regular intervals against actual performance. It also sets limits for working capital and capital expenditure as part of the budgeting process and authorises major new projects or contractual obligations under the reserved powers procedures. The Board also considers and, if appropriate, approves external appointments of the executive directors and the terms of these.

One gains some reassurance from descriptions of internal financial controls, while at the same time recalling banks, merchant banks, local authorities and major listed companies which firmly believed that they had appropriate controls in place only to find, to their cost, that they had not worked.

SWAN HILL *Extract from the directors' report 1998*

Internal financial controls

The directors are responsible for the Group's systems of internal financial control. These have been developed over a number of years and are in place to provide reasonable but not absolute assurance against material mis-statement or loss. The control framework may be summarised as follows:

Financial Reporting – There is a comprehensive budgeting system with the annual budget approved by the board of directors. The results of each business are reported monthly and compared with the budget. Revised forecasts are prepared regularly through the year encompassing both profit and loss and cash flow reporting.

Organisation and Accountability – The organisational structure is clearly defined with a formal process in place to review operating business performance on a monthly basis.

Operating Business Controls – There are numerous business controls and procedures in place including those of a financial and insurance nature. These are monitored continuously and enhanced as appropriate. Group accounting policies for each of the business units are set down in a manual. The Group's external auditors review internal financial controls as part of their audit and provide recommendations for improvements.

Project Appraisal – The Group has clearly defined guidelines for approving new contracts or projects. These are subject to detailed appraisal and review within the context of the group reserved powers procedures. Actual performance is measured against the original appraisal.

The Audit Committee has reviewed the operation and effectiveness of these internal financial controls during 1998.

Investors expect, indeed are entitled to expect, the directors of companies in which they invest to conduct the companies' affairs properly, efficiently and honestly. Cadbury was set up because some boards failed to meet those expectations. What the reports the Combined Code requires tell investors, if anything, is less important than what they tell directors. By focusing their attention on their own performance and methods of working, and compelling them to state in writing their procedures, directors cannot avoid being made conscious of what is expected of them.

Going concern

As explained in Chapter 2, one of the four fundamental accounting concepts laid down by the ASC in SSAP2, *Disclosure of accounting policies* was the going concern concept: 'the accounts are compiled on the assumption that there is no intention or need to go into liquidation or to curtail the current level of operations significantly.'

Under the listing rules the report must include a statement by the directors that the company is a going concern. The statement normally appears in the report on corporate governance where there is one, or in the directors' report if there is not, but it can be in the financial review or statement of directors' responsibilities.

That the company is a going concern is of obvious importance to all who deal with it; but any suggestion that it might not be could result in its early demise. Once again what matters is that the directors should give thought to the morrow. The statement tends to be a simple formal statement. BRUNEL HOLDINGS is more explicit than most:

BRUNEL HOLDINGS *Extract from the 1998 directors' report*

Going concern

It should be recognised that any consideration about the foreseeable future involves making a judgement, at a particular point in time, about future events that are inherently uncertain. After making enquiries, the Directors have a reasonable expectation that the Company and the Group have adequate resources to continue in operational existence for the foreseeable future. For this reason, the Directors continue to adopt the going concern basis in preparing the accounts.

Auditors' review

In addition to their audit of a listed company's financial statements, auditors are required by the Code to review the directors' statements concerning the company's compliance with the Combined Code.

SWAN HILL *Extract from the auditors' report 1998*

Respective responsibilities of directors and auditors

We report to you our opinion as to whether the financial statements give a true and fair view and are properly prepared in accordance with the Companies Act. We also report to you if, in our opinion, the directors' report is not consistent with the financial statements, if the company has not kept proper accounting records, if we have not received all the information and explanations we require for our audit, or if information specified by law or the Listing Rules regarding directors' remuneration and transactions is not disclosed.

We read the other information contained in the Annual Report and consider the implications for our report if we become aware of any apparent misstatements or material inconsistencies with the financial statements.

We review whether the statement on page ... reflects the company's compliance with those provisions of the Combined Code specified for our review by the London Stock Exchange, and we report if it does not. We are not required to form an opinion on the effectiveness of the company's or group's corporate governance procedures or its internal controls.

Report of the Remuneration Committee

In the light of public concern at the levels of remuneration of certain directors, notably those of some privatised former nationalised industries, the Study Group on Directors' Remuneration (the 'Greenbury Committee') produced a *Code of Best Practice*, which took effect fully for accounting periods beginning on or after 31 December 1995. The code has been incorporated in the *Combined Code*.

The resultant report tends to be long and detailed – that of CADBURY SCHWEPPES in its 1998 report running to 10 pages. Typically the report details:

- Composition of the Remuneration Committee
- Remuneration policy
- Annual incentive awards
- Share option schemes
- Long term incentive plan
- Retirement benefits
- Share schemes
- Service agreements
- External appointments policy
- Non-executive directors
- Directors' emoluments.

There is an obvious overlap with information required in the directors' report. This tends to be overcome by a cross reference in the directors' report. The information provided is often interesting, but it is doubtful if it sheds much light on the accounts and their interpretation. One paragraph of Cadbury Schweppes' report does perhaps deserve comment:

CADBURY SCHWEPPES *Extract from the 1998 report*
Report on Directors' Remuneration ...
Executive directors - outside appointments
The Company recognises the benefits to the individual and to the Company of involvement by Executive Directors of the Company as Non-Executive Directors in companies not associated with the Company. Subject to certain conditions, each Executive Director is permitted to accept an appointment as a Non-Executive Director in another company. The Executive Director is permitted to retain any fees paid for such service. Unless otherwise determined by the Board, Executive Directors may not accept more than one such Non-Executive Directorship.

When, in other groups, one reads that the chief executive, X, is president of the Institute of ..., a member of the ... Committee, and of the Council of ..., and a non-executive director of A, B and C, one does somehow wonder about his time commitments; or even his commitment to the group. On the other hand, the man or woman who joins a group at 20 and never works anywhere else can scarcely be said to have the breadth of experience necessary to direct a public company.

THE AUDITORS' REPORT

Appointment of auditors

Every company is required to appoint at each annual general meeting an auditor or auditors to hold office from the conclusion of that meeting until the conclusion of the next AGM.

Auditors' access to information

Under the Companies Act 1985 it is an offence for a director or company secretary to give false or misleading information to auditors, and auditors of holding companies have the right to obtain information about subsidiary companies which they themselves do not audit.

The auditor has a right of access at all times to the books and accounts and vouchers of the company and to require from the officers of the company such information and explanations as he thinks necessary for the performance of his duty. He has the right to attend any general meeting, and to be heard thereat on any part of the business of the meeting which concerns him as auditor.

Scope of the report

The auditors are required to report to the members (i.e. to the shareholders) whether in their opinion the profit and loss account and the balance sheet, and any group accounts, have been properly prepared in accordance with the Companies Acts and all relevant accounting standards, and give a true and fair view of the profit and state of affairs of the company or group.

If they are of the opinion that proper accounting records have not been kept, or that the accounts are not in agreement with the books, or if they are unable to obtain all the information and explanations necessary for their audit, they must state the fact in their report; i.e. they must qualify their report.

The Auditing Practices Board

The Auditing Practices Board (APB) was established in 1991 by the Consultative Committee of Accountancy Bodies (CCAB) – the six principal accountancy bodies – 'to advance standards of auditing and associated review activities in the UK and Republic of Ireland and to provide a framework of practice for the exercise of the auditors' role.'

The pronouncements of the APB fall into three principal categories:

1. Statements of Auditing Standards (SASs).
2. Practice notes.
3. Bulletins.

Auditors who do not comply with Auditing Standards when performing company or other audits in Great Britain make themselves liable to regulatory action by the recognised supervisory body (RSB) with whom they are registered. Practice notes and Bulletins are persuasive rather than prescriptive. However, they indicate what is regarded as good practice.

Statement of Auditing Standards 600

Statement of Auditing Standards 600, Auditors' reports on financial statements, published in May 1993, requires that auditors' reports on financial statements contain:

- a title identifying the person or persons to whom the report is addressed;
- an introductory paragraph identifying the financial statements audited;
- separate sections, appropriately headed, dealing with

    (a) respective responsibilities of directors (or equivalent persons) and auditors;
    (b) the basis of the auditors' opinion;
    (c) the auditors' opinion on the financial statements;

- the manuscript or printed signature of the auditors; and
- the date of the auditors' report.

The Cadbury Report recommended that 'the directors should explain their responsibility for preparing the accounts' and 'auditors' reports should state clearly the auditors' responsibilities.'

It seems reasonable to set these statements adjacent to one another, as CADBURY SCHWEPPES does.

CADBURY SCHWEPPES *Extract from the financial statements in the 1998 report*

Statement of Directors' responsibilities in relation to Financial Statements

The following statement, which should be read in conjunction with the auditors' statement of auditors' responsibilities set out in their report, is made with a view to distinguishing for shareholders the respective responsibilities of the Directors and of the auditors in relation to the financial statements.

The Directors are required by the Companies Act 1985 to prepare financial statements for each financial year which give a true and fair view of the state of affairs of the Company and of the Group as at the end of the financial year and of the Group's profit or loss and cash flows for the financial year.

The Directors consider that in preparing the financial statements the Company has used appropriate accounting policies, consistently applied and supported by rea-

235

sonable and prudent judgements and estimates, and that all accounting standards which they consider to be applicable have been followed. The Directors have responsibility for ensuring that the Company keeps accounting records which disclose with reasonable accuracy the financial position of the Company and which enable them to ensure that the financial statements comply with the Companies Act 1985.

The Directors have general responsibilities for taking such steps as are reasonably open to them to safeguard the assets of the Group and to prevent and detect fraud and other irregularities.

Immediately following this below comes the auditors' report:

CADBURY SCHWEPPES *Extract from the financial statements in the 1998 report*

Auditors' Report

To the Shareholders of Cadbury Schweppes plc

We have audited the financial statements on pages 86 to 134 which have been prepared under the historical cost convention as modified by the revaluation of certain fixed assets and the accounting policies set out on pages 92 to 96. We have also examined the amounts disclosed relating to the emoluments, share options, long-term incentive scheme interests and pension benefits of the directors which form part of the Report of the Directors on pages ... to ....

Respective responsibilities of directors and auditors

The Directors are responsible for preparing the Annual Report including, as described above, the financial statements. Our responsibilities, as independent auditors, are established by statute, the Auditing Practices Board, the Listing Rules of the London Stock Exchange, and by our profession's ethical guidance.

We report to you our opinion as to whether the financial statements give a true and fair view and are properly prepared in accordance with the Companies Act. We also report to you if, in our opinion, the directors' report is not consistent with the financial statements, if the Company has not kept proper accounting records, if we have not received all the information and explanations we require for our audit, or if information specified by law or the Listing Rules regarding directors' remuneration and transactions with the Company and the Group is not disclosed.

We review whether the statement on pages 62 to 67 reflects the Company's compliance with those provisions of the Combined Code specified for our review by the Stock Exchange, and we report if it does not. We are not required to form an opinion on the effectiveness of the Company's corporate governance procedures or its internal controls.

We read the other information contained in the Annual Report, including the corporate governance statement, and consider whether it is consistent with the audited financial statements. We consider the implications for our report if we become aware of any apparent misstatements or material inconsistencies with the financial statements.

Basis of audit opinion

We conducted our audit in accordance with auditing standards issued by the Auditing Practices Board in the UK which are substantially the same as those generally accepted in the US. An audit includes examination, on a test basis, of evidence relevant to the amounts and disclosures in the financial statements. It also includes an assessment of the significant estimates and judgements made by the directors in the preparation of the financial statements and of whether the accounting policies are appropriate to the circumstances of the Company and of the Group, consistently applied and adequately disclosed.

We planned and performed our audit so as to obtain all the information and explanations which we considered necessary in order to provide us with sufficient evidence to give reasonable assurance that the financial statements are free from material misstatement, whether caused by fraud or other irregularity or error. In forming our opinion we also evaluated the overall adequacy of the presentation of information in the financial statements.

Opinion

In our opinion the financial statements (a) give a true and fair view of the state of affairs of the Company and of the Group at 2 January 1999 and of the Group's profit and cash flows for the year then ended and have been properly prepared in accordance with the Companies Act 1985; (b) present fairly in all material respects, the consolidated financial position of the Group at 2 January 1999 and 3 January 1998 and the consolidated results of its operations and cash flows for each of the three years in the period ended 2 January 1999 and in conformity with generally accepted UK accounting principles.

Accounting practices used by the Company in preparing the accompanying financial statements conform with generally accepted principles in the UK but do not conform with accounting principles generally accepted in the United States. A description of these differences and a complete reconciliation of consolidated net income and shareholders' equity to United States generally accepted accounting principles is set forth in Note 31 to the financial statements.

Arthur Andersen
Chartered Accountants and Registered Auditors
London
24 February 1999

Cadbury Schweppes is one of a growing number of UK companies listed in the US which combine their annual report and Form 20-F (see page 246) in a single document. Hence the reference to UK GAAP and US GAAP (see Chapter 30). Some groups now go so far as to have their report signed by both the UK and US offices of their auditors. BARCLAYS (in 1998) includes separate audit reports in the UK and US form on the same accounts.

This is all a great deal longer than a report would have been even in, say, 1992, but it does not change anything. It does spell out clearly quite clearly, however, that:

- directors have a responsibility as regards accounts and internal control which they cannot avoid;
- audit fees are not such as would permit the auditor to verify every transaction, so the new form of report makes it quite clear that reliance is placed upon audit 'tests', i.e. samples.

The auditors' opinion

An auditors' report 'should contain a clear expression of opinion on the financial statements' (SAS 600.5).

That opinion may be unqualified (as was the report to shareholders of CADBURY SCHWEPPES illustrated above) or qualified.

A *qualified* opinion is issued when either:

(a) there is a limitation on the scope of the auditors' examination; or

(b) the auditor disagrees with the treatment or disclosure of a matter in the financial statements.

Example 26.1 A qualified opinion where there is limitation of scope

... However, the evidence available to us was limited because £... of the company's turnover comprises cash sales, over which there was no system of control on which we could rely for the purposes of our audit. There were no other satisfactory audit procedures that we could adopt to confirm that cash sales were properly recorded.

In respect alone of the limitation of our work relating to cash sales, we have not obtained all the information necessary for the purposes of our audit; and we were unable to determine whether proper accounting records had been maintained.

Example 26.2 A qualified opinion where there is disagreement

Qualified opinion arising from disagreement about accounting treatment

Included in the debtors shown on the balance sheet is an amount of £y due from a company which has ceased trading. XYZ plc has no security for this debt. In our opinion the company is unlikely to receive any payment and a provision of £y should have been made, reducing the profit before tax and net assets by that amount.

Except for the absence of this provision ... give a true and fair view ...

Adverse opinion

An adverse opinion is issued when the effect of disagreement is so material or pervasive that the auditors conclude that the financial statements are seriously misleading, i.e. that they did not give a true and fair view.

Example 26.3 An adverse opinion

Adverse opinion

As more fully explained in Note ... no provision has been made for losses expected to arise on certain long-term contracts currently in progress, as the directors consider that such losses should be off-set against amounts receivable on other long-term contracts. In our opinion, provision should be made for foreseeable losses on individual contracts as required by SSAP 9. If losses had been so recognised, the effect would have been to reduce the profit before and after tax for the year ... and the contract work in progress at 31 December 19.. by £x.

In view of the effect of the failure to provide for the losses, in our opinion the financial statements do not give a true and fair view ...

Disclaimer of opinion

A disclaimer of opinion is expressed when the possible effect of a limitation on scope is so material or pervasive that the auditors have been unable to obtain sufficient evidence to support, and accordingly are unable to express, an opinion on the financial statements.

Example 26.4 An adverse opinion with disclaimer

... However, the evidence available to us was limited because we were appointed auditors on ... and in consequence we were unable to carry out auditing procedures necessary to obtain adequate assurance regarding the quantities and condition of stock and work in progress appearing in the balance sheet at £z. Any adjustment to this figure would have a consequential effect on the profit for the year.

Disclaimer on view given by financial statements

Because of the possible effect of the limitation in evidence available to us, we are unable to form an opinion as to whether the financial statements give a true and fair view ...

Fundamental uncertainty

Where an inherent uncertainty exists which in the auditors' opinion is fundamental and is adequately accounted for and disclosed in the accounts, auditors include an explanatory paragraph in their report, making it clear that their opinion is not qualified. Such opinions are comparatively rare, so we look back for an example (see the next page) to REGALIAN PROPERTIES 1994 accounts. This is emphasis: the auditors are simply drawing attention to something already fully covered in the accounts.

REGALIAN PROPERTIES *1994 Accounts: an unqualified opinion with fundamental uncertainty*

Fundamental uncertainty

In forming our opinion, we have considered the adequacy of the disclosures made in the accounts concerning the carrying value of the Group's investment in its associated undertaking. Uncertainty exists as to whether the Group's associated undertaking will be able to develop with financial success a site at Bishopsbridge, Paddington. In view of this we are unable to determine whether any further write down of the Group's investment in that undertaking is required.

Details of the circumstances relating to this fundamental uncertainly are described in note 14. Our opinion is not qualified in respect of the above matter.

But the degree of uncertainty about the outcome of a future event and its potential impact on the view given by the financial statements may be very great. In such a case a disclaimer of opinion is appropriate.

Going concern assumption

The Combined Code of Best Practice calls upon directors to report that the business is a going concern. Take HUNTERPRINT GROUP: in 1993 the group suffered its fifth consecutive year of loss-making. In 1992, there had been a capital reduction scheme.

HUNTERPRINT GROUP *Extract from financial review 1993*

Going concern

The directors have considered the adequacy of the group's banking facilities and cashflow forecasts as outlined in Note 1 to the financial statements and have concluded that the preparation of financial statements on the going concern basis is appropriate.

The auditors have also concluded that it is appropriate to draw up the financial statements on the going concern basis and accordingly have issued an unqualified audit opinion. However, under the circumstances of the group's funding, and in accordance with Auditing Standards, the auditors have included reference to going concern in their report, under the heading of 'fundamental uncertainty'.

HUNTERPRINT GROUP *Extract from Notes to the 1993 accounts*

1. Group funding

The group's bankers have recently confirmed their agreement to extend the group's loan and overdraft facilities which remain payable on demand, through to 30 September 1994. The group meets its day to day working capital requirements through its overdraft facility, which at the year end was substantially utilised.

The nature of the group's business is such that there can be considerable variations in the timing of cash inflows and continued tight financial management is required for the group to remain within its available facilities. The directors have prepared projected cashflow forecasts covering the period through to September 1995. On the basis of:

- this cashflow information;
- the confirmed availability of borrowing facilities through to 30 September 1994; and
- the group's demonstrated ability to control its cash requirements tightly,

the directors consider it appropriate to prepare financial statements on the going concern basis.

But they were proved wrong. The ordinary shares, which stood at around 25p in June 1994, fell sharply in the second half of 1994, and shareholders received about 2p a share when the group was taken over by a major Canadian printer.

Problem 26.1

1. What do you understand by 'a going concern'?
2. What responsibilities do:

   (a) directors;
   (b) auditors;

   have in relation to this?
3. Why does it matter to investors?

Chapter 27

INTERIM STATEMENTS

The EEC directive on Interim Reports requires each listed company to prepare a report on its activities and profit and loss for the first six months of each financial year. This report must *either* be sent to shareholders *or* be inserted in at least one national newspaper not later than four months after the end of the period (see The Stock Exchange's *The Listing Rules*, Chapter 12, para. 49). The Stock Exchange requires interim reports to include 'an explanatory statement including any significant information enabling investors to make an informed assessment of the trend of the group's activities and profit or loss' (*The Listing Rules*, Chapter 12, para. 56).

Among the recommendations of the Cadbury Committee were that:

1. Interim reports should be extended to include balance sheet information.
2. They should be reviewed (rather than audited) by the company's auditors, and their findings discussed with the audit committee.

The review process is described in a Bulletin *Review of Interim Financial Information*, issued by the Auditing Practices Board. Where an auditor reviews interim information his report is along the following lines:

DIAGEO *Extract from interim statement 1999*

Review report by the auditor to Diageo plc

We have reviewed the interim financial information for the six months ended 31 December 1998 set out on pages 6 to 12 of this interim statement which is the responsibility of, and has been approved by, the directors. Our responsibility is to report on the results of our review.

Our review was carried out having regard to the bulletin Review of Interim Financial Information issued by the Auditing Practices Board. The review consisted principally of applying analytical procedures to the underlying financial data, assessing whether accounting policies have been consistently applied, and making enquiries of management responsible for financial and accounting matters. The review was substantially less in scope than an audit performed in accordance with Auditing Standards and accordingly we do not express an audit opinion on the interim financial information.

On the basis of our review:

- in our opinion the interim financial information has been prepared using the accounting policies consistent with those adopted by Diageo plc in its financial statements for the 18 months ended 30 June 1998, except as set out in note 10; and
- we are not aware of any material modifications that should be made to the interim financial information as presented.

KPMG Audit Plc
Chartered Accountants
London, 10 March 1999

ASB Statement on *Interim reports*

The ASB issued in September 1997 a Statement *Interim reports* setting out best practice. Like the *Statement on the operating and financial review*, this Statement is intended for voluntary use, having persuasive rather than mandatory force.

The statement suggests that interim reports should:

(a) be drawn up using the same measurement bases, principles and practices as those used for annual reporting; and

(b) include:

    (i)   a narrative commentary;

    (ii) summarised profit and loss account;

    (iii) balance sheet;

    (iv) cash flow statement; and

    (v) a statement of total recognised gains and losses where relevant.

(c) provide:

    (i)   details of acquisitions and discontinued operations;

    (ii) segmental information;

    (iii) details of exceptional items;

    (iv) comparative figures for the corresponding interim period and the previous full financial year.

Companies are encouraged to make their interim reports available within 60 days of the interim period end.

Discrete v. integral approach

Traditionally, there are two fundamental approaches to the preparation of interim accounts: the 'integral approach' and the 'discrete approach'.

The integral approach views the interim period as a part of the larger annual reporting cycle; its function largely being to predict and explain the financial information for the full financial year. Items are therefore recognised in interim periods on the basis of estimating the total annual revenue and expenses and allocating accordingly.

Under the discrete approach, the interim period is treated as an accounting period distinct from the annual cycle. Incomplete transactions are treated according to the same principles as are applied at the year-end. This has the advantage that the elements of financial statements are defined in the same way as for the annual financial statements.

With the specific exception of taxation, the ASB recommends the discrete approach.

Although *Interim Reports* is an ASB Statement representing best practice, and not a Standard, most listed companies have adopted its proposals. Some, like DIAGEO, go further and include both a chairman's statement and an operating and financial review, as well as the recommended: (a) half-year cash flow statement; and (b) segmental analyses for the half year. DIXONS even include statistics showing the change in the number of stores and sales area.

Accounting policies

The Statement expects interim statements to be drawn up using the same measurement bases, principles and practices as those used for annual reporting;

Where a group recognises that its next annual accounts will adopt different policies, best practice is to spell this out:

DIAGEO *Extract from notes to the interim statement 1999*

9. Basis of preparation

The interim financial information has been prepared on the basis of accounting policies consistent with those applied in the 1998 financial statements, except for the accounting policy changes set out in the note below. The information is unaudited but has been reviewed by the auditor, KPMG Audit Plc, and the review report is set out below. The information does not comprise the statutory accounts of the group. The statutory accounts of Diageo plc for the 18 months ended 30 June 1998 have been filed with the registrar of companies. KPMG Audit Plc and PricewaterhouseCoopers, the previous joint auditors, have reported on these accounts; their report was unqualified and did not contain any statement under section 237 of the Companies Act 1985.

10. Accounting policy changes

The group has revised its accounting policies, where necessary, to comply with the following Financial Reporting Standards issued by the Accounting Standards Board.

FRS 10 – *Goodwill and Intangible Assets* and FRS 11 – *Impairment of Fixed Assets and Goodwill*. FRS 10 requires that purchased goodwill and intangible assets should be capitalised as assets on the balance sheet. Where goodwill and intangible assets are regarded as having limited useful economic lives, they should be amortised over those lives. In other cases, they should not be amortised but an annual impairment test, under the rules set out in FRS 11, is required to demonstrate that the current market value of the goodwill or intangible is not below its carrying value. The standard does not require reinstatement of goodwill previously eliminated against reserves and Diageo has not reinstated such goodwill. Diageo's brands are regarded as having indefinite useful economic lives and will be reviewed for impairment at the end of each reporting period. Intangible assets capitalised in the six month period amounted to £84m.

FRS 12 – *Provisions, Contingent Liabilities and Contingent Assets*. This standard requires that a provision should only be recognised when there is a legal or constructive obligation arising from past events, that it is probable that there will be an outflow of benefits and that the amount can be reliably estimated. A constructive obligation arises where other parties have a valid expectation that an action will be carried out because of past practice or sufficiently detailed public statements. In addition, obligations should not be recognised unless they exist independently of the entity's future actions. FRS 12 also mandates that, where material, provisions should be discounted to net present value and should not be net of any anticipated recoveries or expected gains on asset sales. Compliance with FRS 12 has not given rise to any restatement of Diageo's consolidated balance sheets at 30 June 1998 or 31 December 1996.

FRS 14 – Earnings per Share. This requires entities to present both basic and diluted earnings per share with equal prominence on the face of the profit and loss account and also introduces certain changes to the method by which earnings per share is calculated. Compliance with FRS 14 has not changed the published basic earnings per share figures for the six months ended 31 December 1997, the year ended 30 June 1998, or the 18 months ended 30 June 1998.

Using the interim report

It is often helpful to compute the year on year change at the interim stage, since this enables one to focus on areas of interest e.g. problem areas. We show below part of the interim report of TAY HOMES. We have added a column comparing the first half (H1) figures for 1998 and 1997.

Note how easy it is to see that, half-year on half-year:

- Turnover increased by £4.035m (about 6%);
- Profit on ordinary activities fell by £3.114m (about 75%);
- The associated undertaking was unprofitable (the loss of £64,000 being nearly 21% up on the comparable period);
- The tax charge fell by 75%;
- There is no ordinary dividend for the half year in 1998;
- The number of dwellings sold increased.

In addition to providing information on the first six months, interim figures can and should be used subsequently in conjunction with the full year's figures to detect changes in trends in the second half. For example VIBROPLANT's annual report to 31 March 1993 made no mention that the group had slipped into loss in the second half, but this can easily be deduced:

VIBROPLANT *Second-half results*

Pre-tax profit reported

	£000
Six months to 30 September 1992	2,032
Year ended 31 March 1993	1,900
Pre-tax loss in second half, deduced	(132)

Spotting change

Many management accounting systems report cumulatively against budget (or against the previous year) rather than each month against budget. Because of this, where there is an abrupt swing from a strong market to a weak one, favourable variances early in the year may obscure unfavourable ones in later months, leading management to be:

- slow to react;
- slower even than they might otherwise have been to publicise the downturn.

TAY HOMES *Interim report 1998–99*

Group profit & loss account for the six months ended 31 December 1998	*Half Year Ended 31 Dec 1998*	*Half Year Ended 31 Dec 1997*	*Year Ended 30 Jun 1998*	*Change 1998 H1– 1997 H1*
	£000	£000	£000	£000
Turnover: Continuing operations (excluding BES resales)	67,875	63,840	120,496	4,035
Operating Profit: Continuing operations	3,035	5,668	6,753	(2,633)
Share of net loss from associated undertaking	(64)	(53)	(144)	(11)
Profit on ordinary activities before interest	2,971	5,615	6,609	(2,644)
Interest payable (net)	1,915	1,445	3,163	470
Profit on ordinary activities before taxation	1,056	4,170	3,446	(3,114)
Taxation	330	1,313	1,097	(983)
Profit on ordinary activities after taxation	726	2,857	2,349	(2,131)
Minority interests	(18)	(18)	(29)	–
Profit for the period	708	2,839	2,320	(2,131)
Ordinary dividends		526	2,281	(526)
Retained profit for the period	708	2,313	39	(1,605)
Dwellings sold (excluding BES resales)	746	743	1,408	3
Sales from joint ventures	25	20	24	5

TAY HOMES *Interim report 1998–99 used to compute second half results*

Group profit & loss accounts for the six months ended 30 June 1998 and 31 December 1998

	Half year ended 31 Dec 1998 £000	Half year ended 31 Dec 1997 £000	Year ended 30 Jun 1998 £000	Half year ended 30 Jun 1998 £000
Turnover: Continuing operations (excluding BES resales)	67,875	63,840	120,496	56,656
Operating Profit: Continuing operations	3,035	5,668	6,753	1,085
Share of net loss from associated undertaking	(64)	(53)	(144)	(91)
Profit on ordinary activities before interest	2,971	5,615	6,609	994
Interest payable (net)	1,915	1,445	3,163	1,718
Profit on ordinary activities before taxation	1,056	4,170	3,446	(724)
Taxation	330	1,313	1,097	(216)
Profit on ordinary activities after taxation	726	2,857	2,349	(508)
Minority interests	(18)	(18)	(29)	(11)
Profit for the period	708	2,839	2,320	(519)
Ordinary dividend	–	526	2,281	1,755
Retained profit for the period	708	2,313	39	(2,274)
Dwellings sold (excluding BES resales)	746	743	1,408	665
Sales from joint ventures	25	20	24	4

Second half-year results

Unless readers of accounts take time to compute, and focus on, second half-year results, they too may miss the early warning signs. But this tends to be something of a chore: it is not British practice to include interim figures in the annual accounts, so it is normally necessary to turn them up. An exception is BAT INDUSTRIES, which follows the US practice of reporting quarterly, and shows quarter by quarter results in its annual accounts, including the final quarter.

If one had focused on the second half results of TAY HOMES for 1997–98, as we do above, one would have searched thoroughly in the 1998 report and accounts for comment and explanations on:

- Apparently poor turnover in the half year to 30 June 1998;
- Apparently falling sales by the associated company;
- An unsatisfactory operating profit (only 19% of the first half year!);
- A loss for the period of £508,000 (including £91,000 from the associated undertaking);
- A dividend which was barely covered.

Then the first half of 1998–99 would not have not come as a surprise.

Exceptional items

As explained earlier, interim statements are not audited, and in the past, when they were not reviewed either, it is possible that the stringent look which is given to the balance sheet at the end of the year, and the consequent making of adequate provisions, did not occur at the half-year. It perhaps still does not, and this tends to mean that adverse exceptional items are somewhat more likely to be included in the second half of a year than in the first half. But where they are found in first half year figures they may be material as is demonstrated by DIAGEO (at the top of page 243).

Major transactions

Although not specifically mentioned, it is clearly desirable that interim statements should report other major transactions such as the redemption or conversion of share or the purchase of a company's own shares and their subsequent cancellation. See the second DIAGEO example on page 243.

DIAGEO *Extract from notes to the interim statement 1999*

2. Exceptional items

	Six months ended 31 Dec 1998		Six months ended 31 Dec 1997	
Charged to:	£m	£m	£m	£m
Operating profit				
Merger integration costs	(156)		(44)	
Haagen-Dazs plant closure	(35)		–	
Foodservice integration costs	(7)		–	
Agreement with LVMH	–		(250)	
		(198)		(294)
Associates				
Share of MH re-organisation costs	–		–	(17)
Disposal of fixed assets				
(Loss)/ gain-on sales		(8)		12
Sale of businesses				
Cantrell & Cochrane	142			
Laurent Perrier	(18)			
Inntrepreneur Pub Company:	–		(54)	
European national food businesses	–		(22)	
Gonzalez Byass	–		(23)	
Other	3		(2)	
		127		(101)
Merger expenses				
Transaction costs		–		(85)
		(79)		(485)

DIAGEO *Note to the interim statement 1999*

8. Repurchase of shares

In July 1998, 3m B shares were redeemed at a cost of £15m. On 1 August 1998, the company converted the remaining B shares into 12m ordinary shares at a price of 725 pence per share. In October 1998, the company purchased, and subsequently cancelled, 10.5m ordinary shares at an average price of 555 pence per share for an aggregate consideration of £59m.

Seasonal businesses

According to the ASB 'Fluctuating revenues of seasonal businesses are generally understood by the marketplace and it is appropriate to report them as they arise.' What, in the past, may have been less well known, is the effect on the balance sheet and cash flow statement (which traditionally were not disclosed).

Problem 27.1

Given the extract alongside from Note 10 to the 1996/97 interim statement of DIXONS GROUP, compute (a) the operating profit and (b) net cash (outflow)/inflow from operating activities for the 24 weeks to 27 April 1996. Comment on what you find.

10. Net cash (outflow)/inflow from operating activities

	28 weeks to 9 Nov 1996 £m	28 weeks to 11 Nov 1995 £m	52 weeks to 27 Apr 1996 £m
Operating profit	53.5	34.7	128.1
Share of profit of related companies	(0.3)	–	(3.0)
Utilisation of store closure provision	(1.3)	(2.8)	(2.6)
Utilisation of provision for rationalisation of the Group's administrative offices	–	(1.0)	(1.2)
Depreciation	25.0	19.7	38.7
Amortisation of own shares	0.5	0.3	0.6
Increase in stocks	(191.7)	(187.7)	(75.9)
Increase in debtors	(47.9)	(78.7)	(17.4)
Increase in creditors	73.1	101.1	52.0
	(89.1)	(114.4)	119.3

Chapter 28

OTHER SOURCES OF INFORMATION

![key icon] **Keep your eyes open!**

Investors and analysts should recognise that the annual report and accounts of a company represent only a part, albeit a key part, of the total information available to them, and they should not neglect other sources. For convenience the other sources can be divided into:

(a) information the company provides;
(b) external information;
(c) personal computer based systems;
(d) on-line dealing services.

INFORMATION PROVIDED BY THE COMPANY

The main sources of information from the company itself, apart from the annual report and accounts, are:

(a) half-yearly (and in a few cases quarterly) reports, considered in Chapter 27;
(b) prospectuses;
(c) circulars;
(d) form 20-F (if listed in the US);
(e) company newsletters and magazines;
(f) catalogues and sales information literature;
(g) annual meetings;
(h) company visits.

Prospectuses and listing particulars
When a company offers shares or debentures for sale to the general public it is obliged in law to issue a prospectus; the Third Schedule to the Companies Act 1985 lays down the items which a prospectus must contain.

When a company 'goes public' – that is, when its shares gain a listing on The Stock Exchange (see Chapter 4) – its prospectus has to include all the information required for listing (see The Stock Exchange's *The Listing Rules*, Chapter 6: 'Contents of Listing Particulars'), and so the prospectus is about the most comprehensive document a company ever produces about itself. The normal layout used is as follows:

1. Details of the offer, share capital and indebtedness.
2. Details of the company's directors, secretary, auditors, financial advisers, solicitors, bankers and stockbrokers.
3. Description of the company, giving:

   - an introduction and a brief history;
   - a comprehensive description of its business;
   - information on the management and staff;
   - details of the company's premises;
   - the use to be made of the proceeds of the issue (where any new shares are being issued);
   - the earnings record, with a forecast for the current year's profits and intended dividends;
   - the company's plans and prospects for the future.

4. The accountants' report, containing a table of the last three years' profit and loss accounts and cash flow statements and the latest balance sheet.

5. Various statutory and general information on share capital and options, on the Articles of Association, on subsidiary and associated companies, directors' interests and service agreements, taxation clearances, material contracts, and any pending litigation.

On other occasions of shares being offered to the general public either directly, as in a secondary offer for sale of existing shares already listed, or indirectly, as in a rights issue of new shares of a company whose existing securities are already listed, much less information is required; nevertheless, the prospectus of a secondary offer or the circular letter to shareholders produced for a rights issue can be a useful source of up-to-date information on a company.

Circulars on acquisitions and disposals
Chapter 10 of the Yellow Book divides transactions into classes, as shown in Example 28.1 below.

When a listed company makes a Super Class 1 transaction (i.e. equivalent to 25% or more of the existing company), shareholders have to be sent a circular giving full details; alternatively, if the company is making a takeover bid, they can be sent a copy of the offer document, provided the offer document includes all the information required for circulars on acquisitions (as contained in Chapter 10 of the Yellow Book). In either case the information provides the analyst with useful details of any major additions to or realisations of the com-

pany's assets.

Where there is a Super Class 1 transaction or reverse takeover, it must be subject to shareholders' approval, and the acquiring company will normally be treated as a new applicant for listing.

Circulars also have to be sent to shareholders for transactions with related parties (those involving a director or substantial shareholder, past or present); these can be of considerable interest if the transactions are large and/or if there is any question of sharp practice, but the majority are fairly mundane, produced mainly to ensure that shareholders' interests are scrupulously protected (see Chapter 11 of the Yellow Book).

Documents issued in a contested bid
When the management of a company defends a bid, it has to make the best possible case for the company's continued independence and, in doing so, it will often be rather more forthcoming about the company's future plans and prospects than it normally is in the annual report. Analysts should therefore find it worth reading any documents that a company has issued in successfully contesting a bid. It is also interesting to see whether a company subsequently lives up to any rosy picture it may have painted of its future at the time of the bid.

The detail provided often far exceeds that in published accounts. ENTERPRISE OIL's offer to purchase/prospectus in respect of LASMO in April 1994 ran to 259 pages.

Example 28.1 Criteria for classification of transactions

Class	Size of acquisition or disposal (A) Value of net assets or Net profit before tax before tax or Consideration given or Equity capital issued	Ratios in relation to acquiring or disposing company (B) to company's assets to company's net profit to company's assets to equity capital prior to issue	Stock Exchange requirements
Super Class 1		Transaction is Super Class 1 if any of the four ratios (A)/(B) is 25% or over	Company must inform the Company Announcements (CAO) and send circular to shareholders. Shareholders' approval required.
(Class 1 has been abolished)			
Class 2	as above	Class 2 if any ratio is 5% or more but none if 25% or more	Company must notify CAO
Class 3	as above	Class 3 if all ratios less than 5%	Company must notify CAO if listing is being sought for securities in consideration

Related party transactions (formerly Class 4)

Where transactions involve, or involve an associate of, a director, past director, substantial shareholder or past substantial shareholder, The Stock Exchange should be consulted beforehand. A circular to shareholders and their consent in general meeting is required unless the transaction is 'small' (all ratios less than 0.25%). See page 197 regarding FRS 8 *Related party disclosures.*

Company newsletters and magazines

An increasing number of companies now produce a house magazine or newsletter for employees, and many produce a 'report to employees' summarising the company's results for the year, often presenting the information in charts or diagrams.

These publications can be very helpful in giving the analyst (as well as the employee) a better feel for the company, and they may contain information that is not included in the accounts.

Companies producing an annual newsletter or report to employees may also send copies to shareholders to ensure that information given to employees is also made available to the shareholders, but where newsletters are published more frequently or where a large group has several subsidiaries, each of which has its own separate newsletter, they are unlikely to be distributed to investors. If the analyst can lay his hands on them he may gain a better insight into the various activities of the company and pick up facts that are not generally available.

Company websites

A growing number of companies have websites and these can be useful source of recent news and may provide information not available, or not easily available, elsewhere, e.g. the text of press releases, preliminary announcements, new product details etc. Some sites are more obviously investor-orientated than others; and many larger groups are currently conspicuous by their absence, but a number offer a free newsletter, or provide their employee newsletter on Internet request. Others offer a free company news service via the Internet.

Companies with websites, and hot links to them, are listed in –

http://www.ukbusinessnet.com/cdb/home.html

Form 20-F

This is the annual report that UK and other 'foreign' companies have to file with the Securities and Exchange Commission (SEC) if their shares are listed in the United States. Most companies supply copies to shareholders on request. BP used to offer to do so in their annual report but their accounts now include Form 20-F information.

Companies which are listed in the US normally provide additional information in their accounts on the differences between their accounts, following UK GAAP, with similar accounts prepared under US GAAP. The differences can be quite startling as shown in Chapter 30.

Catalogues and sales information literature

The shareholder or analyst who really wants know a company should study its catalogues and sales literature for evidence of pricing policy, marketing ability, and changes in product range, quality or design.

Failure to adapt to changing circumstances is an early sign of sleepy management. Innovation may be essential if the company is to keep moving – but not every management is capable of thinking up new ideas and of putting them into practice. Promotional literature on new products can sometimes indicate the potential for success.

Annual general meeting

When all is going well, annual meetings tend to be sparsely attended. This is a pity, because they provide an opportunity for investors and analysts to seek and obtain further information about the company.

The routine business of an AGM is:

(a) to receive the report and accounts;
(b) to declare a dividend;
(c) to elect directors;
(d) to appoint auditors;
(e) to transact any other ordinary business.

The chairman will often take the opportunity to make a statement on current trading and/or to amplify the statement he made in the annual report. This is usually done before the routine business, sometimes to pre-empt hostile questions.

Any ordinary shareholder may attend the AGM and speak. Normally his best opportunity to obtain information is upon the motion considering the accounts. If the information he seeks is reasonable (e.g. not of a confidential nature or likely to be of more value to the competition than to members) and he does not obtain a satisfactory answer, he should press the point and state publicly his dissatisfaction. He may find he has more support than he expects.

Generally, directors are prepared to answer all reasonable questions when times are good, but become guarded when the situation is unsatisfactory. If this occurs, the individual shareholder may find that he can obtain the information during informal discussion after the meeting.

Company visits

Companies differ widely in their attitude to company visits by analysts and/or shareholders. Most major companies welcome the interest of both and arrange from time to time group visits at which plans and prospects are discussed in depth, and those interested are able to seek further information.

When making a visit ask yourself:

- Is there any evidence of cut-back, of falling sales and growing stocks or of maintenance delayed to save cash?
- Is the workforce contented – or are labour relations uneasy?
- Do they look efficient – or is there a general atmosphere of chaos?
- Do people appear forthcoming, or are they hiding something?
- Do management appear enthusiastic? …
  the sort of people you could trust?

It is also worth asking management whether it is experiencing any difficulties. Good management is usually prepared to talk about the problems facing the company, and to explain the action being taken to overcome them. But companies have to be careful not to provide those visiting with price-sensitive information which has not first been released to the market.

Always ask about the competition
The replies will help to show whether the management has a practical and realistic attitude to the business environment in which it operates, and may well provide useful information about other companies in the industry. We well remember on one company visit, in reply to a question about a competitor, the chairman simply remarked 'that company is structured for disaster'. It did indeed go bust a year later.

EXTERNAL INFORMATION

There is a vast range of external information useful to the analyst who wishes to make a study in depth of a particular company, group or industrial sector.

We list sources which we personally find useful and, where we find it helpful, their Internet website. In some cases we quote prices in order to put products into perspective. Where we do, they are those current in April 1999.

The Registrar of Companies

The Registration Department of the Department of Trade and Industry has offices at Companies House, 55–71 City Road, London EC1Y 1BB, at Crown Way, Cardiff CF4 3UZ (phone 01222 380801) and in Birmingham, Leeds, Manchester, Edinburgh and Glasgow.

Rules for filing accounts
Section 11 of the Companies Act 1989 requires a company to lay its annual report and accounts before its members in general meeting and to deliver them to the Registrar within certain time limits fixed by reference to its accounting year end. The limit for a UK public company is seven months, which can be extended by three months if the company has interests outside the United Kingdom.

The Stock Exchange requires listed companies to issue an annual report and accounts within six months of the end of the financial year being reported on (the Yellow Book, Chapter 12, para. 42), but this may be extended for companies with significant overseas interests.

Other information to be filed
Companies are also required to file with the Registrar:

(a) copies of their Memorandum and Articles of Association, and details of any changes;
(b) the address of the registered office, and the place at which the company's registers are kept, if not at the registered office;
(c) details of the company's share capital and debentures;
(d) details of each mortgage and charge on the assets of the company;
(e) a list of the directors and secretary and any changes.

In addition, Section 363 of the Companies Act 1985 requires a company to file an *annual return,* which contains a summary of (b) to (e) above and a list of past and present members. Every third year the list must be a complete list of persons holding shares or stock in the company; in the intervening years only changes need be given, but in each year the return must show anyone whose name has appeared on the register as holding shares or stock in the company at any time since the last return. It is therefore possible to find out if anyone has been a registered shareholder at any time, however short the period of ownership, although nominee names may hide the beneficial owner.

Microfiche records
Companies House holds the public records of more than one million companies. Members of the public

making a standard search of a company record are provided with a microfiche copy of information held. There are up to three different types of microfiche for each record:

- The 'W' fiche contains the annual returns and accounts of the company for the last three years, and, since 1 January 1991, any documents which may update the information contained on the annual return.
- The 'M' fiche contains details of any charges or mortgages the company may have created or satisfied, together with a copy of the register of these charges. Not all companies have an 'V' fiche.
- The 'G' fiche contains all other documents of the company, and includes such things as the incorporation and capital documents.
- If the company has an 'M' fiche, this will be indicated by a letter 'M' at the top of the first 'G' fiche.

A standard search costs £3.50. The microfiche belongs to and may be taken away by the searcher, so anyone with suitable microfiche equipment can consult the file at leisure in his or her own office. Hard copy can also be obtained at an additional 10p per page.

A search can also be made by post or telephone to the Cardiff office. The fee for a microfiche by post is £5.00, and hard copy is £6.00 per document. There are also a number of search agents who will provide the service on payment of a suitable fee.

The microfiche facilities available at City Road, London and at Cardiff are virtually identical, and there is no significant time difference in the recording of information at the two offices.

Fax searches

Copies of individual documents can be supplied by fax for people who are paying by credit card or who have an account. Orders can be placed by telephoning (01222 380801) or faxing (01222 380517).

Courier services

A courier service is available from the London office for delivery of searches (phone 0171 254 2000).

Companies House Direct

Companies House Direct provides on-line information direct to your PC and is a fast, accurate and inexpensive way of obtaining up-to-date information from Companies House.

Available to subscribers, it brings the Companies House database directly to one's personal computer. It gives direct access to the names and addresses of company directors and secretaries, with their appointments history since 1991; lists of documents filed by companies; dates of accounts and annual returns filed, and details of disqualified directors since 1986. You can also select images of accounts (registered since March 1995) for on-line viewing, printing or downloading to your PC. Microfiche ordering facilities are provided, including the option to order up to 20 microfiches at a time.

Counter staff at any of the offices can answer any general enquiries about Companies House Direct. For more specific queries and for demonstration and subscription details, contact the Companies House Direct Help Desk (phone 0345 573991).

Analysing a group

Most group accounts contain a general breakdown of their activities, but much more detail can sometimes be obtained by examining the accounts which each subsidiary and associated company has to file at Companies House.

Further information

Companies House publishes a large number of helpful information leaflets on its services and on company law and practice. A good starting point is CHN32 *Products and services information and price list* (free from any of their offices) – *http://www.companies-house.gov.uk/*

Newspapers and journals

The *Financial Times*, daily, and the *Investors Chronicle*, weekly, are required reading for any investor or analyst who wants to keep abreast of the market and of news about individual companies.

There are numerous journals, newsletters and tip sheets which vary greatly in quality but which may point one in the direction of a company worth investigating further.

We will mention just one: *Analyst* from Analyst Subscriptions, Garrard House, 2–6 Homesdale Road, Bromley, BR2 9WL (phone 0181 289 7966). Analyst focuses on growth stocks, which almost by definition tend to be small or medium sized companies.

At the time of first recommending a share, it produces a Company Profile of perhaps six A4 pages. This contains very much the sort of information, and the detail, we feel is right if one is to know a company. Profiles are regularly updated. As these profiles make clear, annual and half-yearly accounts are not enough: it is important not merely to watch the news but, where possible, to talk to management.

Extel Cards

Extel (Extel Financial Ltd (phone 0171 825 8000), 13–17 Epworth Street, London EC2A 4DL, formerly part of the Financial Times group) has long been regarded as one of the world's leading providers of specialist and business information. They produce a range of printed and electronic company information and news services, including handbooks, Extel Card Services, and 4 PC services namely Company Research, Equity Research, Precedents Deal Tracker and Company Analysis.

They are currently part of the US information group Primark – *http://www.primark.com.*

Hemmington Scott

Hemmington Scott Publishing Ltd (phone 0171 278 7769), 26–31 Whiskin Street, is one of the leading suppliers of business information and investment data on UK registered quoted companies. A team of analysts collect, collate and analyse data from primary sources to maintain the Hemmington Scott Corporate Information Database. From this database a number of equity products are generated.

Jointly devised by Jim Slater and Hemmington Scott Publishing, *REFS* (Really Essential Financial Statistics) draws upon his experience as a successful private investor, putting together all the key statistics and ratios needed by investors seeking growth and value.

In a single source one can find:

- Individual brokers' estimates from over 50 contributing research houses plus the consensus estimate;
- Detailed five-year financials plus two years' estimates;
- Listing of all directors and their shareholdings;
- Company contact details;
- Activities;
- Concise coverage of events, announcements and changes affecting the company in the last 12 months;
- All the usual key performance statistics and value indicators and many more, such as:

  - Price earnings growth rate
  - Price to book value
  - Price to cash flow
  - Price to sales
  - Price to research
  - Net cash per share.

Definitions of all the ratios and terms used in REFS are supplied and are available from their website which also provides enlightening information on Jim Slater's investment philosophy and strategy –
http://www.hemscott.com/indman.htm

From the August 1999, REFS includes a comprehensive listing of companies added or removed, or whose name has been changed. Initially this will cover the previous three months.

Also new from August 1999 is a table which features current values of the main FT-SE indices, and their recent percentage growth.

REFS costs £675 per annum for 12 monthly editions or £275 for four issues (February, May, August, November).

It is also available on CD-ROM. *CD REFS* allows one to:

- View or print the full set of essential financial statistics available on each company;
- Search through all 2000+ UK equities to find those that meet any particular set of criteria in seconds;
- Monitor the performance of your portfolio and to see at a glance exactly what profit/loss you've made.

CD REFS costs £675 per annum + VAT for 12 monthly editions or £275 + VAT for four issues (February, May, August, November). Demo disks are available.

REFS is also available on a pay to view basis on the Internet.

The *Hemscott Company Guide* is a useful source of information on all 2,300 UK stockmarket companies. It provides: 5 year profit and loss and balance sheet history, 5 year share price performance relative to the All-share Index, brokers' consensus earnings estimates, FRS3 and 'normalised' earnings per share figures, who's behind each company and how to contact them, capital structure and major shareholders, return on capital employed and gearing, company address, telephone number, activity, sector and status and the financial calendar. It also lists professional advisers and their client companies. Published: February, May, August, November it costs (in the UK) £149.50.

The *PricewaterhouseCoopers Corporate Register* enables one to find 'key decision makers' fast. It includes full contact details for 20,000 directors, senior executives and professional advisers, including for each director and executive: a list of all the companies, professional bodies or institutes with which they are connected, together with their career history, current job title and secretary's name. Published: March, June, September, December it costs (in the UK) £195.

HS Abacus is a monthly service which provides spreadsheet analysis of UK quoted companies on CD–ROM.

Financial Times Electronic Publishing

Financial Times Electronic Publishing, 13–17 Fitzroy House, London EC2A 4DL (phone 0171 970 0100), one of the world's most respected suppliers of online information, provides authoritative business news and information to business professionals around the globe. Financial Times Electronic Publishing comprises FT.com, FT Profile, FT Discovery, Asia Intelligence Wire (AIW), China Intelligence Wire (CIW), Broadcast Monitoring Company and Business Research Centre, each of which we consider separately in the paragraphs which follow. Financial Times Electronic Publishing is part of the Financial Times Group, a division of Pearson plc, the international media group – *http://www.ftep.ft.com*
http://www.financialtimes.co.uk
http://www.ft.com (in the US).

FT.com

FT.com delivers global business and financial news, comment and analysis to more than a million registered users in some 160 countries. Combining the editorial values of the *Financial Times* with the immediacy, depth and interactivity of the web, *FT.com* is updated 11 or more times daily. Its offerings include a comprehensive archive, discussion groups and company briefing reports.

FT Discovery

Accessible via the world wide web, *FT Discovery* is a powerful desktop briefing tool designed for business professionals. For a fixed monthly cost, you can gain immediate access to over 4,000 key business sources, including the full text of the *Financial Times*.

FT Profile

Useful for in-depth business research, *FT Profile* is an online business information service with over 6,000 sources including newspapers, newswires, industry reports, market research, financial data and company information.

Asia Intelligence Wire

Asia Intelligence Wire is a comprehensive online collection of English-language Asian business information sources. Over 200 sources are included from the region's leading newspapers, trade journals and government documents.

China Intelligence Wire

China Intelligence Wire is a comprehensive online source of Chinese language business intelligence, providing business news and information from over 350 key business sources within mainland China and overseas.

Broadcast Monitoring Company

The *Broadcast Monitoring Company* provides leading broadcast and print media monitoring services. Highly skilled analysts carefully select news items relevant to your needs and work day and night to alert you the moment a story breaks. Verbatim transcripts, summaries of broadcasts, video tapes and audio tapes can also be provided.

Business Research Centre

The *Business Research Centre* offers one-to-one research services, on a subscription or ad-hoc basis. Experienced staff will discuss your particular needs, then use an extensive range of information services to provide the solution, whether you require data on a single exchange rate or a full market report.

Datastream Research Services

Datastream Services consist of a computer based system which provides detailed information on 140,000 securities and instruments from markets world-wide. Analysis of individual company accounts can be obtained on a five-year basis, covering profit and loss account, balance sheet and financing table, together with key accounting ratios, while the same information for a single year can be displayed on up to five companies at a time. Much of the data has 20 years or more history.

Services are provided online to PCs (networked or stand alone), in Windows or DOS environments and, once the initial program has been selected, a series of questions is displayed on the VDU to enable the user to specify exactly what he requires. The information is then displayed on the VDU and can be printed out on a Datastream printer if hard copy is required.

Datastream Research Services also include a chart plotting facility, macro-economic data, price monitoring and performance measurement, a portfolio performance program and a news channel.

Pioneered by stockbrokers Hoare & Co. Govett, *Datastream Services* are now run by Datastream /ICV (phone 0171 250 3000), 58–64 City Road, London EC1Y 2AL, part of Primark Corporation, the US-based information services company.

Datastream Services are used by over 1,500 financial and investment institutions in 40 countries across four continents. The full service is available for an annual charge or one can take company accounts data only. Alternatively, for a small monthly subscription, access to the Datastream system can be obtained on a metered dial-up basis –

http://www.datastream.co.uk/

Key Notes

Key Note Ltd, Field House, 72 Oldfield Road, Hampton, Middlesex TW12 2HQ (phone 0181 481 8750) produces the following types of market information:

1. Key Note Market Reports;
2. Key Note Plus Market Reports;
3. Key Note Market Reviews;
4. The Guide.

Each *Key Note Market Report* provides a concise introduction to a sector of British industry. The series covers more than 220 sectors, and each one includes:

- A summary and interpretation of the latest production and trade statistics from Government, industry and market sources;
- An appraisal of the market background, highlighting recent developments and future prospects;
- A SWOT analysis of the market, detailing Strengths, Weaknesses, Opportunities and Threats;
- Financial data of the major companies in the sector;
- Sources of information: a list of trade associations, trade publications, Government sources and statistical studies.

Some companies quote from Key Notes to help give investors an overview of the sector, e.g. :

COUNTRY GARDENS *Extract from 1988 report*
The Market Place
The garden retail market is served by a variety of outlets as shown below:

Garden centres	35
DIY multiples	28
Mail order	12
Independent specialists	8
Grocery multiples	6
Variety stores	3
Others	8
	100

+ Includes department stores
++ Includes forecourt stores, market stalls and mobile shops
(Source: Key Note Report, Horticultural retailing)

Key Note Plus titles are expanded versions of the standard Market Reports, and contain additional features:

- A brands chapter, listing the major players and the brands owned;
- Hot Points – a selection of comments on the state of the market, made by industry insiders;

- Company Financial – a list of the latest financial results of the top companies in the industry;
- Market Growth – a graphical representation of market trends over the last decade.

Key Note Market Reviews give an up to date perspective across an entire market sector. They provide a comprehensive analysis of the industry drawing together all the relevant segment information under one cover.

The Guide is a comprehensive directory of western European marketing research sources, from trade associations, chambers of commerce and embassies, to primary research companies. *http://www.keynote.co.uk.*

The Estimate Directory

Published by Barra UK (phone 0131 473 7070),10–12 Young Street, Edinburgh EH24JB, *The Estimate Directory* provides a useful profile of over 1,400 UK stocks, giving a short statement outlining what the group does (often clearer than its own statement of principal activities); a share price graph; market capitalisation; 12 month price highs and lows; a table of price relative movements for 1 month, 3 months and 12 months; and a list of major shareholders. Its main interest lies in its table of broker forecasts which shows: the recommendation (e.g. 'buy on weakness'), the date of the forecast, forecast sales, profit, e.p.s., and d.p.s. for the current year, one year and two years ahead. That of the company's own broker is highlighted; and there are consensus figures in absolute terms and relative to the previous forecast, including prospective price earnings ratio and dividend yield. A separate section highlights upgradings and downgradings and there is also a table showing percentage movement in sector forecasts. Brokers often differ wildly in their expectations, making it desirable, where possible, to have several sources of research. For example, in April 1999, three brokers upgraded or downgraded their forecast in respect of NEXT.

NEXT *Extract from Estimate Directory April 1999*
Change in EPS for year to January 2000

	New forecast	Old forecast	Change %
Salomon Smith Barney	36.8	34.8	6
Teather & Greenwood	36.0	38.4	-6
Williams de Broe	40.0	34.5	16

The directory is published monthly, mid-month, and costs £565 per year; £180 quarterly; or £665 a year including weekly revisions. Also available are The Estimate Directory: Continental Europe; Pacific Basin and Japan. Global data are also available via Internet.

The Economist Intelligence Unit (EIU)

The EIU produces a wide range of business as well as economic publications, including special reports (e.g. *World Outlook 1999*, a guide to the year's political and economic prospects country by country, quarterly *Country Reports* on doing business in each of 180 countries and periodic reviews covering particular industries. The EIU's London headquarters are at 15 Regent Street, London SW1Y 4LR (phone 0171 830 1000) – *http://eiu.com.*

Government statistical publications

The best overall presentation of the huge range of statistics prepared by government departments is given in the *Monthly Digest of Statistics*, published by the Central Statistical Office (CSO).

Other statistical publications include:

Financial Statistics (monthly) – gives the key financial and monetary statistics of the United Kingdom.

Economic Trends (monthly) – commentary and a selection of tables and charts providing a broad background to trends in the UK economy.

Annual Abstract of Statistics – contains many more series than the monthly digest and provides a longer run of years.

United Kingdom National Accounts, known as the 'Blue Book', which is published annually and gives detailed estimates of the national accounts including consumers' expenditure over the previous ten years.

United Kingdom Balance of Payments – known as the 'Pink Book'.

Business Monitors – monthly, quarterly and annual publications produced by the CSO, giving statistical information from various government departments on a wide range of subjects, e.g. motor vehicle production, published quarterly, and the monthly overseas trade figures.

The Source, a catalogue of all Government Statistical Service publications, is available free from the Public Inquiry Unit, Central Statistical Office, Great George Street, London SW1P 3AQ – *http://www.statistics.gov.uk*
http://www.statistics.gov.uk/statbase/

Specialist and trade publications

Trade magazines published by trade associations may contain useful statistical information compiled from the association's own members, as well as general news about the industry, while independent specialist magazines provide useful background information in their particular sphere. Periodicals are published on a private subscription-only basis, for example the market intelligence reports on consumer goods, retailing, leisure and personal finance in the United Kingdom; published by Mintel International, 18–19 Long Lane, London EC1A 2HE (phone 0171 606 4533). Reports are also available on CD–ROM and on-line –

http://www.mintel.co.uk/

Other sources of information

Finally, on a broader note, an independent view and forecasts on the UK and world economy are contained in the *National Institute Economic Review*, published quarterly by the National Institute of Economic and Social Research, NIESR. The NIESR, 2 Dean Trench Street, Smith Square, London SW1P 3HE (phone 0171 654 1923) is an independent non-profit-making body, which conducts research by its own staff and in co-operation with the universities and other academic bodies on a wide range of broadly economic subjects –

http://www.enquiries@niesr.ac.uk.

PERSONAL COMPUTER BASED SYSTEMS

A number of PC-based computer systems are available to suit all types of investor and analyst; and all pockets.

FairShares

FairShares Software Ltd, New Forest Enterprise Centre, Rushington Business Park, Totton, Hampshire SO40 9LA (phone 01703 660111) market a variety of systems tailored to particular groups of users. *The Private Investor Monitoring and Selection System* costs £99 + VAT and is intended to provide private investors with full portfolio management, together with share selection tools and a choice of updating methods. The system can handle up to 12 portfolios with up to 200 shares in each and there is database storage for up to 5,000 shares.

A free link is provided to both Teletext and Fairshares E-mail service, for daily or weekly price updates. The option is provided of log and linear scaling for your charts, plus automatic date scaling. Graphical valuation of whole portfolio over time is provided with moving average capabilities, weighted or simple, for faster trend identification Fast, easy performance comparisons are possible. with relative strength graphs and the ability to display multiple graphs on the screen. Select any number of items from Company Results, Dividends and/or Hemmington Scott data – and analyse them against a comprehensive set of investment criteria to identify the shares you want to invest in.

As regards tax, the system provides comprehensive and detailed Capital Gains Tax calculation, annual income reports and tax reports.

The Private Investor Advanced Analysis System which costs £499 + VAT provides a range of analysis tools for private and professional investors. It includes all software in the Private Investor Monitoring, Selection and Analysis systems but can handle unlimited portfolios with up to 400 shares in each. Teletext Day Graphs add a 'real time' mode to your system, allowing you to display prices several times a day.

This system provides, in addition to the usual graphics capabilities, further technical indicators enabling the forecasting of trend changes, the identification of price breakouts, comprehensive moving average indicators and envelopes, Bollinger bands, MACD, ADX, Stochastics and the like.

The Professional Portfolio Manager which costs £2,000 + VAT is designed to meet the needs of professional investors and tax houses, having the capability to provide up-to-the-minute analysis on an unlimited number of portfolios. Shares from any Stock Exchange in the world can be included as the Multi-Currency system allows securities in up to 40 different currencies to be managed in the same portfolio. The system allows unlimited portfolios with up to 2,000 shares in each and there is database storage for up to 5,000 shares.

The use of a Market-Eye link brings second-by-second trading prices into your system with charts changing in 'real-time'. Data Pack Three £55 per month, £640 per year (excluding VAT).

Data are available in a series of 4 packages, can be paid for either monthly or annually and are delivered by e-mail or floppy disk – *www.fairshares.com.*

The Analyst

Another system allowing one to capture, store and analyse share price data, manage a portfolio and produce portfolio valuations is *The Analyst* (from £79.95 + VAT) from WinStock Software, 10 Jewry Street, Winchester, Hants, SO23 8RZ (phone 01962 715557).

It is possible to draw as many overlays as you like on any chart: moving averages (simple, exponential, centred, lagged), Bollinger bands; stop-loss; comparisons with other shares or indices (relative, rebased and absolute); multiple regression and freeform trend lines; confidence bands and rate of change displays. Indicators available include: moving average convergence/divergence (MACD); overbought/oversold (OBOS); stochastic; relative strength; momentum; and Fibonacci fan lines – used by chartists.

A price imaging module provides an alternative method of displaying share price histories. This shows price movement as bands of colour (blue for up; red for down, green for steady – the more intense the colour, the greater the speed of change). By this means one can quickly gain an overview of market trends. One could, for example, display in a single window six months of share price movements for all shares in a sector; scroll through the image and see trends at a glance; and then click on any company that interested you to see its price chart.

To start off your archives, WinStock provides over 2,000 data sets covering most of the UK stockmarket as well as currencies, indices, gilts, commodities etc. The data sets range in size from 2 to 12 years and all are included free of charge.

Data may be updated in various ways: using a Teletext adapter card and updating module, The Analyst will automatically capture prices for over 2,000 shares, options, commodities, indexes, gilts and currencies. Any new instruments are added to the archives automatically. WinStock provides end of day updates free of charge on the Internet (you need a modem and access to the Internet.) The Analyst also accepts data from other vendors. Alternatively, their Data Service Diskettes provide daily data surprisingly economically.

Chartistics

Pangsway Ltd, PO Box 11463, London SW1V 4ZL (phone 0171 872 5473) markets two programs under the name Chartistics.

Chartistics Technical Analysis (£135 + VAT to the single private user) is designed to analyse an investment security's price trend, volatility and performance profile across time in many different ways. The software is equipped with more than 30 chart study tools, which fall into 3 groups: line series study, risk and return and momentum indicators, and work for stocks, funds, forex and commodities.

Chartistics Trade Alert (£75 + VAT) is a system dedicated to the study of price movements, volatility, moving average cross-over and the relative strength index (RSI). It is designed to alert the investor to possible buy/sell signals more readily and allows users to back-test the performance of their portfolio allocation and stock selections, based on the signals generated in the past.

Sharetracker

Sharetracker from Dolphin Software, 30 Golden Cross Road, Ashington, Essex, SS4 3DG (phone 01702 545984) is another package with extensive analysis tools. It comes supplied with up to 12 years' daily closing data for approximately 2,000 prices, indices and currencies. It displays up to six Teletext pages simultaneously with the optional Microtext or Optimum Technology card, early WinTV decoders or external unit.

Prices for new companies and for companies whose Teletext or SEAQ name has changed are saved automatically (which anyone using a more primitive system will see as a real plus).

Sharetracker for Windows (£95 inclusive) produces clear, easy to read log or linear graphs quickly and easily. They have optional grids and adjustable timescales for months or years. There are three optional true moving averages which use all the data available and may be normal, centred or offset. Bollinger Bands and Dealing Bands may be overlaid on the main graph. The moving averages and bands have user selectable periods and colours. The scaling is automatic and sensible with the option of zero start values. Automatic buy/sell indicators may be displayed. A scanning facility enables all share graphs in a sector, the whole database or a portfolio to be viewed sequentially.

Secondary graphs may be produced with a choice of short-term indicators. These indicators include Rate of Change (Relative Strength Indicator), OBOS (Over Bought and Over Sold), MACD and Momentum. Daily prices as supplied with Sharetracker give accurate results with these short-term indicators. Weekly prices are not sufficiently fast for these indicators.

A feature not always found in similar programs is that Sharetracker for Windows exports data in ASCII text to many share analysis programs and spreadsheets. These include Metastock, Fairshares, Synergy, Indexia, Stockwatcher, Chartist, Supercharts, Lotus 123, Excel, Quattro Pro, Quicken and others.

Updata

Updata Software, Updata House, Old York Road, London SW18 1TG (phone 0171 328 1989) market two systems: *Updata Trader* and *Updata Invest 4.5* aimed at two rather different markets.

Updata Invest costs £49 + VAT and you get free 'club' membership for 60 days. *Club Updata* is an exclusive area with live market information for use with Updata products, on-line resources and Updata services. You can download price files from *Updata Internet*. Club members can obtain +20 (minutes) real-time from the Club area. This is useful to someone (like one of us) who deals occasionally and wants to keep an eye on the market from time to time but is not prepared to pay £400 a year or more for live data. Others can run Updata Invest indefinitely with no ongoing fee using Updata's free end of day data service. A 14 day trial is available via the Internet.

Updata Trader costs for the first year £1,160.13 including software, Stock Exchange fees and a Prestel decoder box; and £410.07 in later years, for the basic Stock Exchange system without LIFFE. The free price histories (over three years on all UK shares and up to 10 years on the top 100 companies) allow one to create meaningful graphs right away. There are hot links to Hemmington Scott, *The Investors Chronicle* (i.e. to an index of every mention of a particular company in recent months), Charles Schwab and other on-line dealers.

Features of *Updata Trader* include:

- *Quotescreen*, which shows each trade in detail for any chosen company on the screen as it happens.
- You can have intra-day candlestick charts breaking up trading into periods of your choice – hour on hour, or for the really active trader 5 minute bars.
- *Newstore* makes possible a news archive search using keywords for any period of time. This is great for building up background knowledge on a company quickly.
- Using *Updata Analytics:* if you are using trend channels the trend channel actually changes slope and width as you move it with your mouse over a chosen section.
- Trader now has currencies fully integrated to include the euro –

http://www.updata.co.uk

Indexia

INDEXIA Intro (£125 + VAT), *INDEXIA II* (£349 + VAT) and *INDEXIA II Plus* (£775 + VAT) from Indexia Research, 121 High Street, Berkhamsted, Herts, HP4 3DJ (phone 01442 878015) are designed with the particular needs of chartists in mind, and have advanced trend analysis features.

For example, designed for the serious investor trading in the equity, foreign exchange or futures markets, who already understands, or wants to delve into, technical analysis, the top of the range program, *INDEXIA II Plus*, handles over 30 different chart types (including candlesticks, wave charts, CCI, equivolume, volatility); four types of moving average including *INDEXIA* 'filters' (proprietary forms of moving average); least squares regression lines and channels; beta analysis with lead and lag periods; and more.

With *INDEXIA* you are not forced to use any one particular updating method or service. *INDEXIA* does not run its own data service, users have a choice between a number of UK and overseas feeds: CitiFeed Plus, Investor Ease, ESI on Internet, RegisData, Market-Eye on Internet, PC Market-Eye End-of-Day, CSI, Stock Data Corp,

CEEFAX, Teletext 2000, FINSTAT, InvestorData, Weblink ASX and JustData. There is an *INDEXIA* Smart Auto Update program available for all these listed data services.

Smart Auto Update not only updates the *IN-DEXIA* system, it also maintains your database, by automatically adding new issues when they are listed, removing those that have been delisted, correcting historical data, and recalculating for splits and rights issues. Not all data services yet incorporate these features.

Also available from *INDEXIA* are *INDEXIA Real time technical analysis systems*; and *Option Trader*, a traded options valuation and strategy analysis system. 30 Day Trial Programs are available of any program for £25 + VAT. A deposit of £75 + VAT is required. Even if you decide not to go ahead, the deposit is refunded – *http://www.indexia.co.uk*.

PC Sharewatch

PC Sharewatch comes from Dividend Associates Ltd, 2 The Dell, Vernham Dean, Andover, SP11 0LF (phone 01264 737 642) and costs £59.95 including VAT. The package is complete with a database covering 2,300 shares; with 5 years' weekly share price data where available, hi, lo and close; annual and half-year results; dividends; sector indices, and the FT-SE 100, 250 and 350, and the FT-A All Share indices.

The package provides an excellent introduction to share watching. It is inexpensive, intuitive and surprisingly flexible. It is extremely easy, for instance, to focus on the big movers, to graph a share price, possibly against appropriate FT-SE index or sector index; to focus on a sector to see how it is behaving: the weekly gain, the gain over a defined period, the average PE; to list companies in the sector by market capitalisation, PE, dividend yield; and to experiment with moving averages, stop losses, PEGs and so on. There is a teletext version; and weekly updates are available very economically (£3.25 a week including VAT).

ShareScope

ShareScope is an inexpensive but fast and flexible analysis and portfolio management system marketed by Ionic Information Ltd, Unit 1, The Business Centre, 19–23 Wedmore Street, London, N19 4RU (phone 0500 321 456). Lifetime membership, which covers any upgrades, costs £79.95 and there is a monthly fee of £9.95 (both including VAT).

This covers five years' historic daily prices, three years' forecast results, six years' historic results, information on analysts' buy/hold/sell recommendations; directors' and major shareholders' dealings and major shareholders. Daily updates are

via the Internet or by direct dial-up from a single key press, and take as little as 10 seconds. Results, forecasts and fundamental data are updated weekly. The system provides for rolling, projected and historic P/Es, PEGs, EPS and Yield.

Up to 1,000 portfolios can be handled and compared against indexes (90 FT and other indexes are maintained) or other portfolios.

MetaStock

MetaStock is a US-based company supplying real-time trading software. There are a variety of systems for direct connection to Reuters etc. and specialist chart analysis programs. Top of the range, and aimed at the professional trader, is *MetaStock Professional*, a powerful 32-bit program that works with Windows 95, Windows 98, and Windows NT.

MetaStock Professional's Object Oriented Interface means that all of the commands for every object on your screen, such as price plots, toolbars and indicators are built into the object itself. Instead of hunting through menus to figure out how to modify your charts, you can simply Click and Pick, and Drag and Drop, in the best Windows tradition.

For the technical, *MetaStock Pro* takes advantage of another technology advance, 'threading'. Threading allows *MetaStock Pro* to split up all the things you want it to do into separate tasks for your computer to work on apparently simultaneously.

The best way to determine whether or not a trading system will work for you is by back-testing on the markets you'll actually be trading. You can learn a great deal about a trading system by letting *MetaStock Pro* test it. For each test, an extensive report that shows:

- Total net profit/loss and Percent gain/loss
- Total number of trades
- Number of winning/losing trades
- Information on each individual trade.

In addition, *MetaStock Pro* clearly labels all entry and exit points on the chart of the security you're testing. You can also view the equity line for your trading system that shows your equity position each day of the entire test period. With this kind of information, hopefully you'll be able to decide which systems seem to consistently bring you profits, and avoid those that don't work before committing real money – *http://www.metastock.com*

Prestel

Prestel On-line offer a wide range of end-of-day data for the private and corporate investor. These services can be downloaded in seconds and used with virtually every investment package available in the UK and beyond.

Metastock, Supercharts, Indexia, Updata, Meridian, Fairshares all recommend Prestel's CitiFeed data. Services include:

1. UK Equity Prices – All 3,000 closing prices from the London Stock Exchange direct to your PC every evening: £35 pa. For those who want them, they supply the Open, High, Low, Close and Volume (also known as OCHLV) for all 3,000 UK stocks for just £90 pa. A limited free service is available.
2. Futures/Options – Direct from LIFFE, they can supply the settlement prices for all LIFFE financial futures and options for £60 pa. OCHLV data for LIFFE financial futures and options cost £115 pa.
3. Indices/Currencies/Commodities – a wide range of key indicators from around the globe cost £50 pa. UK sector indices, world indices, currencies against both dollar and sterling and key commodity prices are all included.
4. Historical data for all the above are available at a low cost.
5. Unit Trusts for the private investor as a weekly download for £49 pa. The same service for IFAs starts from £475 pa and includes offshore and onshore Life and pension funds too –

http://www.prestel.co.uk/one.htm

Market-Eye

Market-Eye Internet utilises the display conventions that dealers and traders see on their office screens. Not only are the display conventions the same; but the news and market reports come from Datastream/ICV's news service which is the most commonly found system in most City offices.

The *Investor service* is free, provides 20 minutes delayed data, limited historical data and a limited news facility.

The basic *Premium service* costs £23.50 a month (including VAT), and provides OHLCV historical data, complete news magazines, a portfolio management facility and optional real-time data – *http://www.market-eye.co.uk/default.htm*

Accounting information

One obvious way of obtaining a copy of a company's report and accounts is to write to the Secretary, expressing interest in (in investing in) the company. Several websites carry accounts on-line, but the number of companies covered in each case is still fairly small. Try:

http://www.hemscott.com/equities/index.htm
http://www.corpreports.co.uk/
http://www.carol.co.uk/

ON THE INTERNET

A number of City institutions and services have web pages; and a great deal of helpful information is readily available free. The number of sites grows daily but among the more useful at the time of writing are:

Accounting standards and financial reporting

Accountancy, the journal of the Institute of Chartered Accountants in England and Wales, which provides, on its UK edition pages, a progress update on new and forthcoming UK standards, and on its overseas edition pages, international standards –
http://www.accountancymag.co.uk.
The Accounting Standards Board website is –
http://www.asb.org.uk/

The accounting firm KPMG provides useful update material on tax and financial reporting –
http://www.kpmg.co.uk.

For those interested in standards internationally, the home page of the US Financial Accounting Standards Board is –
http://www.rutgers.edu:80/Accounting/raw/fasb/

City and general news

The *Financial Times* provides news, prices and an excellent information service. You can obtain the current annual/interim report of any company annotated with ♣ in the newspaper or the London Share Price Service (on Internet) by ringing 0181 770 0770 (open 24 hours including weekends) or faxing 0181 770 3822 and quoting the code stated on the web page. Reports will be posted the next working day subject to availability. An instant snapshot of key financial and fundamental information on more than 11,000 listed companies world-wide is available, free. There is also a useful glossary and set of ratio definitions –

http://www.financialtimes.co.uk.

NewsPage Direct is a US-based world-wide news service with good coverage of UK business news, including the major dailies, Sundays, the FT and *Investors Chronicle*. There are three service levels: *BASIC* which gives you your own issue of NewsPage, unlimited access to headlines and briefs from over 2,500 topics and unlimited access to full-text versions of all stories from basic sources; *PREMIUM* ($3.95 per month) with unlimited access to full-text versions of all stories from Premium sources and access to Pay-Pcr-View sources, which carry additional charges; and NEWSPAGE DIRECT – Daily e-mail Delivery ($6.95 per month) to your e-mail every weekday morning – *http://www.newspage.com/NEWSPAGE/newspageh ome.html*

A more UK-oriented news source is the Press Association, which provides news 24 hours a day – *http://www.pa.press.net/news/*

Useful information on AIM including rules and statistics is to be found on – *http://www.worldserver.pipex.com:80/aim/market/i ndex.htm.*

Teletext services

The cheapest way to start with real-time data collection is to use Teletext. BBC2 Ceefax (currently start at page 200) carries the FTSE 100 index delayed by 20 minutes; prices of 400 Equities updated every 20 minutes, and other indices, Gilts and Forex information.

BBC1 Ceefax (start at page 200) has 2,000 Equities several times a day. Channel 4 (start at page 500) carries a similar service to BBC2 and prices of 3,000 shares updated several times daily.

Sky Text provides the cheapest way to obtain real-time LIFFE Futures and FTSE Cash Index. Data available include:

- Real-time Futures – FTSE, Bund, Italian Bond, Short Sterling, Long Gilt, bid, ask, last trade, near & far contract;

- Real-time FTSE 100 cash index, Reuters 150 index, Gold, Brent Crude, US T Bonds, Gilts & Libor;

- Real-time exchange rates against sterling and the dollar, world indices from UK, Asia, USA, and Europe;

- Real-time top 100 shares every 15 minutes, additional 250 shares updated 3 times a day.

Sky Text is on the free Sky News channel on both satellite or cable.

N-TV Text currently provides the best free real-time service for world futures, indices and foreign exchange. NTV is a free German financial channel available in the UK and Europe on Satellite.

Electronic Share Information

Founded in 1993, Electronic Share Information Ltd (ESI) was the first website outside the US to provide real-time equity prices and share dealing facilities. ESI's aim is to offer private investors convenience and control of their financial investments.

ESI offers three levels of service, ranging from free 20 minute delayed prices to continuous real-time quotes plus comprehensive financial information and access to dealing services. This fully comprehensive range of services is available 24 hours a day – seven days a week, from anywhere in the world. ESI has over 200,000 registered users.

The *ESI Investor service* costs £5 per month; the *ESI News service* an additional £11 per month and *ESI Data* an extra £150 a year. *http://www.esi.co.uk/public/brochure/*

Hemmington Scott Publishing Ltd, publishers of *The Hemscott Company Guide, Company REFS, CD REFS* and *The PricewaterhouseCoopers Corporate Register*, offer *UK Equities Direct*, a free service providing details of companies, industry sectors, corporate advisers, companies removed, mergers and acquisitions, name changes, new issues, press releases and the latest updated figures e.g. prelims – *http://www.hemscott.com/equities/*.

DataStream does not provide much for nothing on the web but is useful for information on the largest UK share-price changes (updated at 9:30, 11:00, 13:00, 15:00, 16:30, 17:30 & 18:15); major world stock indices (updated throughout the day); exchange rates (updated daily) and key economic indicators world-wide (updated monthly). *http://www.datastream.com/services.htm.*

CompuServe

A number of services are available on CompuServe. The UK Company Research Centre, for instance, makes information available from a number of UK databases. This provides a simple way of obtaining access to these services without the need for direct access to, and an account with, them. But they are not free services. In addition to CompuServe base connect charges, there is usually a search fee (sometimes a charge for not finding an item), and a charge for supplying the record.

UK Historical Pricing is a CompuServe service which provides pricing information on over 5,000 UK equity issues and about 350 market indices, mostly going back to 1 July 1990.

ON-LINE DEALING SERVICES

United States

It is estimated that Internet share trading currently accounts for around 20% of all trades in the United States and that 12 brokers handle 90% of Internet accounts. They are:

- Ameritrade – *http://www.ameritrade.com/*
- Charles Schwab – *http://www.schwab.com/*
- Datek Online – *http://www.datek.com/*
- Discover Brokerage Direct – *http://www.discoverbrokerage.com/*
- DLJ Direct – *http://www.dljdirect.com/*
- E Trade – *http://www.etrade.com/*
- Fidelity – *http://www.fidelity.com/*
- National Discount Brokers – *http://www.ndb.com/*
- Quick & Reilly – *http://www.quickwaynet.com/*
- SureTrade – *http://www.suretrade.com/*
- Waterhouse – *http://www.waterhouse.com/*
- Web Street Securities – *http://www.webstreetsecurities.com/*

Most offer service either by Internet, touch tone telephone or live broker. *Chas Schwab*, *Discover Direct* and *Waterhouse* all currently operate 24 hours a day, 7 days a week.

US brokers vary quite widely in charges. *Ameritrade, Datek Online* and *SureTrade* all charge less than $10 per trade. At the other end of the market, but a market leader, is *Charles Schwab* which charges $29.95.

All provide real-time quotes (usually free), news (often personalised news pages for the individual investor), company reports and earnings estimates.

The Street provides regular helpful research on the performance of US on-line brokers – *http://www.thestreet.com/index.html.*

To give some idea of what US investors have come to expect, *Datek* offer all Internet deals at $9.99 up to a maximum of 5,000 shares; undertake to deal free if (market conditions apart) your trade takes more than 60 seconds to execute, and claim an average execution time of less than 10 seconds. On the basis that nominal values, and so share prices, are much higher in the US than in the UK, 5,000 shares can represent a substantial investment. Let us say that Microsoft shares stand at 93, then one could buy 5,000 ($465,000 of shares) for commission of $9.99!

For non-professional clients of *Datek* on-line quotes are free and unlimited. A great deal of useful information is available, including earnings estimates and summaries of brokers' opinions for major companies.

It is estimated that investors dealing on-line deal far more frequently than those using traditional methods – perhaps 6 or 7 times more frequently, and number around 5m in the US, a growing number of them 'day trading', i.e. going in and out of a stock the same day. We report this as a fact; we do not encourage it. When prices fall as they did in 1929 and again in 1973–74, getting out may be difficult – rather like trying to board a lift at an intermediate floor in a bomb alert: lifts will tend to be full and they will not stop at every floor! Even if the Internet and the electronics hold fast, the market itself may not be able to cope.

United Kingdom

Currently seven firms offer Internet share dealing in the UK but the market is developing rapidly with each broker claiming to have the best technology.

Service varies from live on-line execution to sending your broker an e-mail order to trade.

In on-line dealing the shares are actually traded with the brokers' systems linking straight to the market. Transaction details are then confirmed seconds later on your screen. This level of sophistication is standard in the US and is rapidly becoming so in the UK. A number of smaller brokers came on the scene early with less sophisticated systems.

On-line dealing is super competitive. A broker's success depends upon (and competing services should be judged by):

- speed of execution (seconds count);
- the price at which shares are traded; and
- the dealing commission (which in the US is a fraction of that in the UK);
- provision of accurate account statements;
- overall reliability (service disruption is frequently a problem on the Internet; and lack of capacity in an active market caused difficulties in the US in October 1997 but any repetition would not be tolerated).

Investors are likely to opt for a broker who provides the ability for one to look at one's portfolio on-line (as *Charles Schwab* already does) – *http://www.schwab-worldwide.com/europe*

While larger brokers seem willing to deploy substantial resources to develop live transaction services, some smaller ones have already developed unsophisticated e-mail based systems.

Brewin Dolphin, which has for some time offered an Internet share dealing service called Stocktrade, recently launched what it claims to be the first real-time paperless service with next day settlement – *http://www.stocktrade.co.uk/*

Charles Stanley, with its *Xest* system, has hundreds of investors already dealing on-line via a simple email service. It works and customers appear satisfied – *http://www.xest.co.uk/*

Torrie & Co, with *Fastrade*, demonstrate that smaller regional brokers can offer their clients Internet dealing with a personal service – *http://www.fastrade.co.uk/*

James Brearley of Blackpool offers a similar service; and Cave & Sons in Ferndown, Dorset have developed a system –

http://www.jbrearly.co.uk/
http://www.caves.co.uk/

Barclays

Barclays.net is an Internet service offering free unlimited Internet access, online banking and stockbroking services. It is offered free to all Barclays 14m personal and small business customers, through all Barclays 2,000 branches, via the telephone on 0345 776 776 and from the Barclays website. Barclays.net is powered by BT. Registration for the broking service is free using the link alongside.

Barclays Stockbrokers Price Improver is a service exclusive to Barclays Stockbrokers. Through automatic direct links with major market makers, it instantaneously identifies the most competitive price available, guaranteeing the optimum price for buying and selling your shares.

An independent audit conducted during September and October 1998 is said to have confirmed that over 50% of deals handled through Price Improver were executed at a better price than the 'best' price displayed on the London Stock Exchange.

Commission on Internet deals in UK equities is:
- First £5,000   1.5%
- Next £10,000   0.85%
- Thereafter   0.5%

There is a minimum charge is £17.50 ($28.50) per transaction.

The cost of purchases is normally taken from one's bank by direct debit ten business days from the date of the deal – *http://www.barclays-stockbrokers.co.uk/*

Problem 28.1

Share prices are used by investors and analysts for a variety of purposes.

1. Name four widely used ratios based on the market price(s) of equity shares.
2. Suggest four other ways in which an investor or analyst might use the price history of a share.
3. Explain four ways of obtaining share prices and suggest the advantages of each.

Chapter 29

INFLATION ACCOUNTING

INTRODUCTION

Some people, some of the time, think that company accounts should make allowance for the effects of inflation, while others think it's too difficult: 'don't let's bother'. The latter tend to predominate unless the rate of inflation is high.

In the 1970s and early 1980s, when inflation in the UK was running in double figures, efforts were made to introduce inflation accounting, but the accountancy profession was split between two methods: Current Purchasing Power (CPP), which simply adjusts figures for the rise in the Retail Price Index (RPI), and Current Cost Accounting (CCA), which allows for changes in relative prices.

Because both these methods have been tried and abandoned, there is a temptation to treat the subject as irrelevant. This attitude is like the ostrich burying its head in the sand: even a single figure rate of inflation has an insidious effect on reported profits. For example, if a company reports steady earnings per share in a period when inflation is

running at 3% per annum, and the reported e.p.s. are adjusted for inflation, the result is:

Year	0	5	10	25
Reported e.p.s.	10p	10p	10p	10p
E.p.s. in constant £s	10p	8.58p	7.37p	4.67

This adjustment only allows for the effect of inflation on reported e.p.s. If inflation was allowed for in the accounts themselves, i.e. in calculating the e.p.s., then the earnings per share by Year 10 or Year 25 would probably be much less for the majority of companies.

If the Chancellor fails to keep the lid on inflation, or some future government resorts to Harold Wilson's old trick of promising the earth, and paying for it by printing money, then the whole subject will be back at the top of the agenda.

We first examine the shortcomings of historical cost accounts in some detail, and then give a brief history and description of CPP and CCA.

THE SHORTCOMINGS OF HISTORICAL COST ACCOUNTING

In attempting to present a true and fair view of a company's affairs, accounting systems have two principal enemies: inflation and subjective judgement.

Historical cost (HC) accounting

In a time of stable prices, the historical cost system works well. What an asset cost is seldom in dispute, and although the directors have to assess the expected useful lives of fixed assets, and their

likely disposal values, there is limited scope for subjective judgement. Furthermore, the quality of historical cost accounts has steadily improved over the years, largely thanks to the efforts of the ASC and, more recently, the ASB have considerably reduced the number of options available.

Though problems do still remain, few other than accounting theorists would seriously suggest that historical cost be abandoned as the basis of accounting in a period of zero inflation.

HC accounting and inflation

In a period of substantial price rises (which, for simplicity, we will term 'inflation'), historical cost accounting has five main weaknesses:

1. *Depreciation is inadequate for the replacement of fixed assets.*

    Historical cost accounting seeks to write off the cost of fixed assets over their effective lives. It does not set out to provide a fund from which the fixed assets can be replaced at the end of their lives. Nevertheless, in a period of stable prices, sufficient cash could be set aside over the life of an asset to replace it at its original cost. In times of inflation, insufficient is provided in this way to enable the business to replace its assets. For example, where an asset is written off on a straight line basis over ten years, the total provisions for depreciation as a percentage of cost (in constant pounds) are:

Inflation rate	Depreciation as % of cost
5%	79.1%
10%	64.4%
15%	53.8%

2. *Cost of sales is understated.*

    In historical cost accounts, stock consumed and sold is charged against sales at its original cost, rather than at the cost of replacing it. But, in order to retain the same stock level, the company has to finance the difference and, since the abolition of stock relief, has to do so entirely out of profits after tax. This is perhaps most easily understood if we add a few figures. Assume that the company has in stock items which cost £4,000. It sells them for £6,000, incurring overheads of £1,600, and replaces them at a cost of £4,400. Corporation tax is payable at, say, 30%.

    HC accounts will say that the company has made a profit of £400 (£6,000 – £4,000 – £1,600) on which it will pay corporation tax of £120, leaving a net profit after tax of £280. But out of this the company has to meet the additional cost of replacement (£400), so it will be left with minus £120.

3. *Need for increase in other working capital not recognised.*

    In most companies, debtors are greater than creditors, so, on an unchanged volume of business, 'debtors minus creditors' increases with inflation, requiring extra money to be provided for working capital. Historical cost accounts fail to recognise that this extra working capital is necessary to maintain the operating capacity of a business and that it has to be provided (again out of after tax profits) for the business to remain a going concern.

4. *Borrowing benefits are not shown.*

    Borrowings are shown in monetary terms, and if nothing is repaid, and nothing further is borrowed, borrowings appear stable. This is a distortion of the picture, because a gain has been made at the expense of the lender (since in real terms the value of the loan has declined): some people feel that this gain ought to be reflected in the accounts.

5. *Year-on-year figures are not comparable.*

    In addition to being overstated due to:

    (a) inadequate provision for depreciation,

    (b) understated cost of sales, and

    (c) no provision for increase in other working capital,

    profits are stated in terms of money which has itself declined in value. Similarly, sales and dividends are not comparable with those of other years, because they are expressed in pounds of different purchasing power.

Although inflation has moderated, it has not disappeared; and memories are short. Before studying Examples 29.1 and 29.2, try this test: sketch out approximately the trend in year-on-year inflation:

- over the past 16 years;
- over the past two years.

If your estimates bear any real resemblance to the graphs on page 262, we shall be surprised.

So how good is the average investor or analyst likely to be at stripping out inflation accurately off the top of his head?

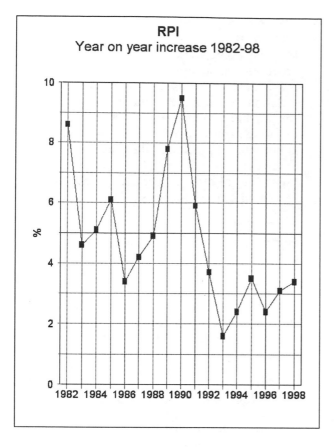

Example 29.1 Sixteen years of inflation

Key point
The reporting of profits in inflated pounds gives a far too rosy impression of growth in profitability:

- This lulls both managers and shareholders into thinking that their company is doing much better than it really is;
- It encourages unions and employees to expect wage increases that are unmatched by real (as opposed to reported) profit growth; and
- It encourages government measures that are harmful to the long-term prosperity of companies, e.g. price controls or excess profits tax made on a completely false impression of profitability.

It is somewhat difficult, without making proper adjustment, even in times of modest inflation, to estimate profits, earnings and dividends, and their trend in real terms, as is shown on page 263 by building and construction group JOHN LAING.

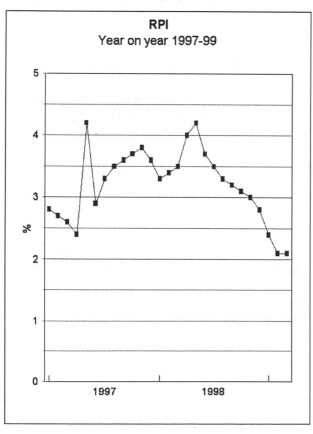

Example 29.2 A downward trend? But can it be sustained? That is always the question.

JOHN LAING *Five year review 1998*

	1998	1997*	1996	1995	1994
Turnover £m	1,606.6	1,461.4	1,254.9	1,206.4	1,171.7
Profit before taxation £m	20.1	32.2	24.5	20.1	23.8
Profit attributable to shareholders £m	15.5	26.1	18.7	14.8	17.9
Shareholders' funds £m	219.0	214.3	198.5	192.3	185.4
Cash net of borrowings £m	43.8	19.7	64.6	53.1	65.1
Profit before taxation as % of					
– turnover %	1.3	2.2	2.0	1.7	2.0
– shareholders' funds %	9.2	15.0	12.3	10.5	12.8
Earnings per share pence	14.0	25.7	17.7	13.5	17.0
Dividends per share pence	10.75	10.50	9.50	9.00	9.00
Dividend cover times	1.3	2.4	1.9	1.5	1.9

*Restated to comply with Financial Reporting Standard 9, *Associates and joint ventures* (see Accounting Policies).

Looking at these figures in terms of year-on-year percentage change we get:

JOHN LAING *Year on year percentage change: actual prices*

	1998/ 1997	1997*/ 1996	1996/ 1995	1995/ 1994
Turnover	9.9	16.5	4.0	3.0
Profit before taxation	(37.6)	31.4	21.9	(15.5)
Profit attributable to shareholders	(40.6)	39.6	26.4	(17.3)
Shareholders' funds	2.2	8.0	3.2	3.7
Cash net of borrowings	122.3	(69.5)	21.7	(18.4)
Profit before taxation as % of				
– turnover %	(40.9)	10.0	17.6	(15.0)
– shareholders' funds %	(38.7)	22.0	17.1	(18.0)
Earnings per share	(45.5)	45.2	31.1	(20.6)
Dividends per share	2.4	10.5	5.6	0.0

To allow for inflation it is necessary to restate these figures at the price levels ruling at a particular point in time. Two obvious points are 1994 (the beginning of the five years) or 1998 (the end). We have chosen to convert everything to 1994 prices, using the average index for each year:

Example 29.3 Computation of adjustment factor to convert to 1994 prices

	1998	1997	1996	1995	1994
Average RPI for year	162.9	157.5	152.7	149.1	144.1
Factor to bring to average 1994 prices*	0.885	0.915	0.944	0.966	1.000

* Index for current year/Index for 1994

JOHN LAING *Five year summary 1998: adjusted for inflation to 1994 prices using factors in Example 29.3*

	1998	1997	1996	1995	1994
Turnover £m	1,421.2	1,337.1	1,184.2	1,165.9	1,171.7
Profit before taxation £m	17.8	29.5	23.1	19.4	23.8
Profit attributable to shareholders £m	13.7	23.9	17.6	14.3	17.9
Shareholders' funds £m	193.7	196.1	187.3	185.9	185.4
Cash net of borrowings £m	38.7	18.0	61.0	51.3	65.1
Profit before taxation as % of					
– turnover %	1.3	2.2	2	1.7	2
– shareholders' funds %	9.2	15	12.3	10.5	12.8
Earnings per share pence	12.4	23.5	16.7	13.0	17.0
Dividends per share pence	9.5	9.6	9.0	8.7	9.0

JOHN LAING *Year on year percentage change: at 1994 prices*

	1998/ 1997	1997*/ 1996	1996/ 1995	1995/ 1994
Turnover	6.3	12.9	1.6	(0.5)
Profit before taxation	(39.6)	27.4	19.0	(18.4)
Profit attributable to shareholders	(42.6)	35.3	23.4	(20.1)
Shareholders' funds	(1.2)	4.7	0.8	0.2
Cash net of borrowings	115.0	(70.4)	18.8	(21.2)
Profit before taxation as % of				
– turnover %	(40.9)	10.0	17.6	(15.0)
– shareholders' funds %	(38.7)	22.0	17.1	(18.0)
Earnings per share pence	(47.3)	40.8	28.0	(23.3)
Dividends per share pence	(1.0)	7.2	3.1	(3.4)

Not only do the adjusted figures look less promising, the year-on-year change looks much less happy. We see, for instance, that in real terms:

- shareholders' funds fell in 1998 and grew very little in either 1995 or 1996;
- dividends failed to keep pace in two years out of four.

But unlike many companies, JOHN LAING made no attempt to hide this.

JOHN LAING *Extract from the chairman's statement 1998*

Although 1998 did not meet the Board's expectations, this was entirely due to the Millennium Stadium project in Cardiff and the consequent acceleration of the reorganisation in our Construction activities. Profit before taxation was £20.1m in comparison with the £32.2m achieved in the previous year. The Board is, as indicated in October, recommending a maintained final dividend of 7.0 pence (1997 – 7.0 pence) making a total of 10.75 pence (1997 – 10.5 pence) for the year.

This disappointing result includes a provision of £26.1m on the Millennium Stadium due to costs exceeding the guaranteed maximum price quoted to the client. There is still much work to be done but we believe that the provision is sufficient to complete the contract ....

A comprehensive programme of reorganisation is being accelerated within our Construction activities, for which a charge of £5.1m is included in the results, and which involves new management appointments.

Now we are not suggesting that all this was due to inflation; cost over-runs are often due to inefficiency and JOHN LAING clearly blame management. But fixed price contracts, and contracts with limited price protection, do present problems in a period of rising prices – and not merely to on site management.

The staggering impact of inflation

Before going on to discuss how inflation accounting developed, it is worth looking in more detail at the impact that even quite modest rates of inflation have on the value of money if they persist for several years.

Example 29.4 Effect of inflation on the value of £1

Annual rate of inflation	After 5 years	After 10 years	After 20 years
2½%	88.3p	78.1p	61.0p
5%	78.3p	61.3p	37.6p
7½%	69.6p	48.5p	29.5p
10%	62.0p	38.5p	14.8p
15%	49.7p	24.7p	6.1p
20%	40.1p	16.1p	2.6p

Between 1960 and 1996 inflation averaged a touch over 7.2% compound; but it was extremely variable in rate (from a low of 1.3% p.a. to a peak of over 25%); and it was throughout that period very difficult to predict what the rate of inflation would be a year later.

It wasn't always like this. Prior to the Second Word War prices had changed surprisingly little in a hundred years. By 1940, prices were a shade over twice their 1840 level.

But, as Example 29.5 on page 265 shows, the effect of inflation on the value of money since 1940 and, in particular, since 1970, has been staggering.

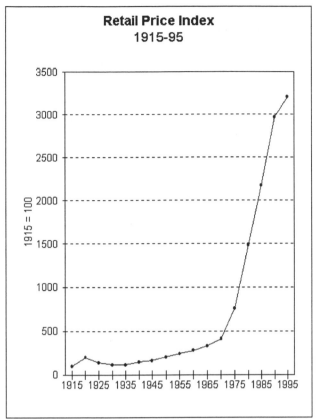

Retail Price Index
1915-95

Example 29.5 The RPI at 5 year intervals (1915 = 100)

The effect of inflation on the investor in fixed interest stocks

Anyone who bought £100 of Government, irredeemable, 3½% War Loan when it stood at par in the 1940s by 1996 saw it standing at about 45, which reflected interest rates and inflationary expectations at that time. If one adjusted the original £100 by the subsequent movement in the RPI (which was about 24 times its 1940 level), and expressed £100 in 1996 pounds, you got about £2,400. In real terms the investor had lost over 98% of his capital: horrifying! Since then, interest rates have fallen and inflationary expectations are much less.

The years 1996 to 1999 have seen a gain in real terms on stocks like War Loan – but nothing will ever make up for the inroads of 60 years' inflation.

In 1940 the RPI was 6.6 (taking 1987 = 100) and that in March 1999 was 164.1, which represents a rise of 76.4 times.

Appendix 3 provides tables showing the effect of inflation in the United Kingdom on the Retail Price Index.

THE DEVELOPMENT OF INFLATION ACCOUNTING SYSTEMS

Current purchasing power accounting (CPP)

An Exposure Draft, ED 8 – *Accounting for changes in the purchasing power of money* – was issued in 1973 recommending that companies adopt what came to be known as current purchasing power accounting (CPP). The main features of ED 8 were that, in addition to HC accounts, listed companies would show a *supplementary statement* in terms of the value of the pound at the end of the period being reported on, and that the RPI should be used in making the adjustments.

CPP accounting was concerned solely with removing the distorting effects of changes in the general purchasing power of money on accounts prepared in accordance with established practice (i.e. on a historical cost basis). It did not deal with changes in the *relative* values of non-monetary items such as raw materials of various types (which can and do occur in the absence of inflation).

CPP accounts were criticised on a number of grounds. Among these were the following:

- Shareholders were faced with a choice between two sets of figures which frequently gave very different results. Both could not be correct.
- CPP accounting enhanced the profits of companies which were heavily borrowed, particu-

larly those showing low profits on a historical cost basis, and could even turn a loss into a profit. This was because assets on which perhaps little or no profit was being made (e.g. land held for use and not for re-sale) were shown by CPP to be increasing in value in line with inflation (i.e. maintaining their real value), while money borrowed to acquire them was treated as declining in real value. The more heavily borrowed the company, the more the profits became boosted by CPP:

GRAND METROPOLITAN *Extracts from 1974 accounts*

	£000
Ordinary shareholders' funds	429,436
less Goodwill	295,361
OSF net of goodwill	134,075
10% CULS 1991/96	121,114
Other loan capital	281,219
Bank overdrafts and short-term borrowings	130,396
Total debt	532,729
Earnings per share (historical)	7.3p
Earnings per share (CPP basis)	35.2p

- The Retail Price Index is not a true index of general purchasing power: it may quite badly represent the effects of inflation upon some groups of individuals, and it is not *designed* to reflect the effects of inflation on companies.

In spite of being adopted by quite a large number of public companies, CPP accounting was overtaken by the appointment of the Sandilands Committee, which was set up by government in 1974 under the chairmanship of Mr (later Sir) Francis Sandilands.

Current cost accounting (CCA)

The Sandilands Report

The Sandilands Committee reported to the Chancellor of the Exchequer and the Secretary for Trade in June 1975: the Committee rejected the proposals contained in PSSAP 7 (a provisional SSAP on CPP, which had been issued as a follow up to ED 8 pending the Sandilands findings), and recommended instead the development of a system to be known as current cost accounting (CCA), in which:

- no adjustment is made for inflation (i.e. for changes in the purchasing power of money);

- assets and liabilities are shown in the balance sheet at their 'value to the business'; unfortunately, this can be very much a matter of subjective judgement;

- 'operating profit' is struck after charging the value to the business of assets consumed during the period, thus excluding holding gains from profit and showing them separately.

The Sandilands report also recommended that current cost accounting should become the basic published accounts of companies 'as soon as practicable'.

Opposition

In response to the Sandilands recommendations there followed much debate and a special committee, which produced an Exposure Draft (ED 18) in November 1976. ED 18 met with considerable opposition – the members of the Institute of Chartered Accountants in England and Wales actually voted at an extraordinary general meeting that current cost accounting should not be made compulsory – so a new committee was appointed, leading to the eventual publication of a Standard on CCA (SSAP 16) in March 1980.

SSAP 16

SSAP 16 required larger companies to produce a separate current cost P & L account and balance sheet, to recognise two basic concepts, that:

- The profitability of a company should be assessed after deducting the amount of money it needs in order to stand still in real terms.

- The assets of a company should be shown at their value to the business.

The SSAP 16 system of CCA calculates the profit of a business by making adjustments to the HC profit and loss account.

Three *operating adjustments* are made to the HC trading profit to allow for the impact of price changes:

1. The *depreciation adjustment.*
2. The *cost of sales adjustment.*
3. The *monetary working capital adjustment.*

A fourth adjustment, the *gearing adjustment*, is then made to allow for the proportion of assets financed by borrowings.

Specific price indices are used in CCA in calculating the operating adjustments, to reflect relative price changes and, for a time, the Government Statistical Service produced a special book annually, *Price Index Numbers for Current Cost Accounting* containing a myriad of industry-specific and asset-specific indices, updating it by a monthly supplement.

But, in spite of the enormous effort put into developing CCA, the system had major shortcomings:

- It was very complicated: even the Accounting Standards Committee's step-by-step guide *CCA the Easy Way* ran to 145 pages of A4.
- There was much scope for discretion, so that similar companies produced wildly different figures for individual adjustments.
- The figures produced each year were not comparable with figures for the previous year.
- The system was irrelevant for tax purposes.

Attempts were made to modify the system (by ED 35), but CCA failed to gain sufficient acceptance to become the basis of published accounts of companies, as Sandilands had recommended. When inflation eased, SSAP 16 was gradually abandoned.

SSAP 16 was suspended in June 1985, and formally withdrawn in April 1988.

WHAT ARE WE TRYING TO ACHIEVE?

The nub of the matter is whether we are trying to achieve:

- a system that allows for the general effect of inflation, or
- what the Sandilands Committee was asked to produce, a system to 'allow for changes (including relative changes) in costs and prices'.

Measuring inflation

The Sandilands Committee took the view that inflation was 'not a phenomenon capable of independent and objective measurement' and, in line with government thinking at the time, rejected the concept of using the Retail Price Index (RPI) to index accounts. As the RPI has since been used satisfactorily by government to index personal tax allowances, for index-linked gilt-edged securities and SAYE schemes and, most recently, for the indexation of acquisition cost in CGT calculations, the Sandilands view is scarcely tenable. The RPI *is* the generally accepted measure of inflation in the United Kingdom.

What we believe inflation accounts should achieve

Let us consider the problem under five heads:

1. If the cost of a fixed asset is written off in pounds of falling value, the provision for depreciation is inadequate. In order that the total amount written off over the useful life of a fixed asset should be its cost (less residual value) expressed in *pounds at the date of purchase*, each annual depreciation charge needs to be adjusted by the movement in the RPI since the asset was acquired. Fixed assets should therefore appear in the balance sheet at cost less accumulated depreciation, adjusted for inflation into balance sheet date pounds.
2. In calculating the cost of goods sold, the opening stock should be adjusted for the RPI movement during the year so as to eliminate stock profits due to general inflation; and profits so computed should provide the basis for taxation.
3. The amount of additional working capital required by a company due to the effects of inflation should be deducted in calculating distributable profits.
4. The benefit of inflation in reducing the real value of borrowings and the adverse effect of inflation on holdings of cash should be taken into account.
5. Figures for previous years should be adjusted

to balance sheet date pounds, so that like can be compared with like, a point well recognised by the Central Statistical Office (imagine how misleading their financial statistics would be if they weren't expressed in constant pounds).

Because inflation accounting would allow for the general effect of inflation but not for any relative change in price levels, inflation accounts would, in a long period of zero inflation, produce the same figures as historical cost accounts. But there is nothing wrong with that.

The future

Until the purpose of inflation accounting is agreed no system of inflation accounting is likely to be introduced.

Consequently, HC accounts will continue:

(i) to lull many managers and shareholders into thinking that their companies are doing better (sometimes considerably better) than they really are, and
(ii) to encourage unions and employees to seek wage increases that are not justified by real (as opposed to reported) profits.

Furthermore, unless the system so developed produces accounts acceptable to the Inland Revenue for tax purposes and which become the *only* accounts a company produces, there will continue to be a problem. The production of *two* sets of accounts will always pose the question 'Which one is to be believed?'

Problem 29.1

1. Compare current purchasing power accounting and current cost accounting, bringing out:

   (a) their similarities; and
   (b) their differences.

2. Why do you think the attempt to introduce:

   (a) CPP,
   (b) CCA,

   failed?

Chapter 30

GENERALLY ACCEPTED ACCOUNTING PRINCIPLES: UK V. US GAAP

Companies incorporated in the UK, securities of which are listed in the US, prepare their accounts in accordance with UK Generally Accepted Accounting Principles (GAAP), but, for the benefit of US shareholders, show the effect of using US GAAP. As we shall see, the effect of using different accounting principles can be startling.

The matter is important for four reasons:

1. Shareholders resident in the UK are accustomed to UK GAAP; whereas those in the US are used to US GAAP. Where there is a marked difference between the results using one set of GAAP and the other there will be a tendency for performance to he viewed differently in the two countries, and for shareholders to react in different ways. This may well cause management to look over its shoulder, and in an attempt to please both markets, make compromises.

2. It is clearly unsatisfactory for two major accounting countries to account for key items in different ways: both cannot be right.

3. As increased emphasis is placed on international trade, there is likely to be pressure:

    (a) on countries to develop an agreed fundamental accounting theory;

    (b) to harmonise standards world wide.

4. A study of the differences between UK GAAP and US GAAP highlights areas of disagreement and helps one focus both on the likely areas for change and the effect of that change if and when it comes.

Two key differences between UK and US GAAP have already been noted (see pages 135 and 180). International practice, and in particular US and UK practice is moving closer but remain a host. of

other differences, some of which we discuss in the rest of this chapter.

Goodwill

Under UK GAAP prior to FRS 10, goodwill arising on the acquisition of a subsidiary was charged against reserves in the year in which the subsidiary was acquired. Under US GAAP such goodwill is capitalised and is amortised through the profit and loss account over its estimated useful life, not exceeding 40 years. FRS 10 (see page 178) changed things, but does not remove the differences as regards goodwill, as is explained by GLAXOWELLCOME (see below and on page 269).

GLAXOWELLCOME *Extract from note 29 to the 1998 accounts*

Goodwill and intangible fixed assets

As from the 1998 financial year, the company has changed its accounting policy for goodwill and intangible assets under UK GAAP in respect of acquisitions from 1998, such that no material difference will exist between UK and US GAAP. A difference continues to exist in respect of prior years' goodwill and intangible assets until fully amortised under US GAAP. Goodwill arising on acquisitions before 1 January 1998 was set against shareholders' funds under UK GAAP. Under US GAAP, this goodwill is capitalised and amortised over its expected useful economic life and charged against income. Intangible assets recognised before 1 January 1998 under US purchase accounting requirements are amortised over their estimated revenue earning life, which is taken to be patent life plus five years. The carrying value of these intangible assets is reviewed annually for any impairment in value.

Under UK GAAP, costs to be incurred in integrating and restructuring the Glaxo and Wellcome businesses into a single business, following the acquisition in 1995, are charged to the profit and loss account post acquisition. Under US GAAP, certain of such costs are considered in the allocation of purchase consideration thereby affecting the goodwill arising on acquisition.

Companies like GLAXOWELLCOME which pride themselves on good reporting not only explain changes of accounting policy in their half-year report but show their effect as regards comparative GAAPs. As will be seen from the upper illustration, profits under US GAAP were roughly half those under UK GAAP.

The effect on the balance sheet is even more striking. Under UK GAAP equity shareholders' funds at the year end were £2,702m. According to US GAAP they were £8,112, three times as much.

Deferred taxation

Under UK GAAP, no provision is made for deferred taxation if there is reasonable evidence that such deferred taxation will not be payable in the foreseeable future. Under US GAAP, deferred taxation is provided for all differences between the book and tax bases of assets and liabilities.

BP AMOCO *Extract from US GAAP in the 1998 accounts*

Under UK GAAP, provision for deferred taxation is made where timing differences are expected to reverse in the foreseeable future. Under US GAAP, deferred taxation is provided on a full liability basis on all temporary differences as defined in US Statement of Financial Accounting Standard No.109. As required by this standard assets and liabilities of acquired businesses have been adjusted from a net-of-tax to a pre-tax basis.

One American depositary share is equivalent to six 50 cent ordinary shares.

Ordinary dividends

Under UK GAAP, final ordinary dividends are provided in the financial statements on the basis of the recommendation by the Directors which requires subsequent approval by the shareholders to become a legal obligation of the Company. Under US GAAP, dividends are only provided when the legal obligation to pay arises – see page 270.

GLAXOWELLCOME *Extract from note 16 to the half-year report and accounts 1998*
As from the 1998 financial year, the company has changed its accounting policy for goodwill and intangible assets under UK GAAP in respect of acquisitions from 1998, such that no material difference will exist between UK and US GAAP; a difference will continue to exist in respect of prior years' goodwill until fully amortised under US GAAP.

Profit	6 months to 30.6.98 £m	6 months to 30.6.98 US$m	6 months to 30.6.97 £m	6 months to 30.6.97 US$m	Year to 31.12.97 £m	Year to 31.12.97 US$m
Profit attributable to shareholders under UK GAAP	827	1,364	1,045	1,703	1,850	3,034
US GAAP adjustments:						
Amortisation of goodwill	(276)	(455)	(280)	(456)	(554)	(909)
Amortisation of intangible assets	(135)	(223)	(247)	(403)	(326)	(534)
Deferred taxation	(41)	(68)	–	–	(31)	(51)
Other	7	12	21	35	13	21
Net income under US GAAP	382	630	539	879	952	1,561

GLAXOWELLCOME *Extract from note 29 to the 1998 accounts*

	£m	US$m	£m	US$m
Equity shareholders' funds under UK GAAP	2,702	4,485	1,843	3,041
US GAAP adjustments:				
Capitalised interest	16	26	10	16
Computer software	(29)	(48)	–	–
Goodwill	3,517	5,838	4,040	6,666
Intangible assets	995	1,652	1,264	2,085
Unrealised gains on equity investments	277	460	218	360
Unrealised gains on liquid investments	10	17	7	12
Pensions	133	221	89	147
Ordinary dividends	760	1.261	715	1,180
Deferred taxation	(258)	(428)	(304)	(502)
Employee Share Ownership Plan	(11)	(18)	(9)	(15)
Shareholders' equity under US GAAP	8,112	13,466	7,873	12,990

BARCLAYS *Extract from note 60 to the 1998 accounts*

60. Differences between UK and US accounting principles

...

Dividend payable

UK GAAP

Dividends declared after the period end are recorded in the period to which they relate.

US GAAP

Dividends are recorded in the period in which they are declared.

Pension costs

Under UK GAAP, the costs of providing pension benefits may be calculated by the use of any recognised actuarial method which is appropriate and whose assumptions reflect the long term nature of the assets and liabilities involved. Under US GAAP, the costs of providing these benefits are calculated using the projected unit credit method and a discount rate (being the rate of interest at which pension liabilities could be effectively settled) which reflects current market rates.

The disclosures are complex and, as shown by GLAXOWELLCOME, the difference can be staggering.

GLAXOWELLCOME *Extract from note 29 to the 1998 accounts*

Pensions

The key differences between UK and US GAAP in relation to defined benefit pension plans are:

- under UK GAAP the plan assets are valued using a discounted income valuation. US GAAP requires plan assets to be measured at market-related value.

- under UK GAAP the effect of variations in cost can be accumulated at successive valuations and amortised on an aggregate basis. Under US GAAP the amortisation of the transition asset and the costs of past service benefit improvements are separately tracked: experience gains/losses are dealt with on an aggregate basis but amortised only if outside a 10 per cent corridor.

- UK GAAP allows measurements of plan assets and liabilities to be based on the result of the latest actuarial valuation. US GAAP requires measurement of plan assets and liabilities to be made at the date of the financial statements or up to three months prior to that date.

The disclosures required by FAS132 are included in Note ...

GLAXOWELLCOME *Extract from note 24 to the 1998 accounts*

24. Employee costs

...

Pension and other post-retirement costs

	1998 £m	1997 £m	1996 £m
UK pension schemes	7	7	21
US pension schemes	47	49	50
Other overseas pensions schemes	22	32	40
Unfunded post-retirement healthcare schemes	14	17	14
Post-employment costs	8	–	–
	98	105	125

elsewhere we read:

Net periodic pension (income)/cost under US GAAP	(17)	(16)	28

Restructuring costs

Under UK GAAP provisions are made for restructuring costs once a detailed formal plan is in place and valid expectations have been raised in those affected that the restructuring will be carried out. US GAAP requires a number of specific criteria to be met before such costs can be recognised as an expense. Among these is the requirement that all the significant actions arising from a restructuring and their completion dates must be identified by the balance sheet date.

BARCLAYS *Extract from note 60 to the 1998 accounts*
60. Differences between UK and US accounting principles

Restructuring of business provisions

UK GAAP

In accordance with FRS 3, provisions have been made for any direct costs and net future operating losses arising from a business that management is committed to terminate.

US GAAP

The application of Emerging Issues Task Force (EITF) 94-3 has created recognition timing differences in respect of certain of the termination provisions. EITF 94-3 sets out specific conditions which must be met to enable liabilities relating to involuntary terminations to be recognised in the period management approve the termination plan. In respect of costs other than employee termination benefits, the basic requirement for recognition at the date of commitment to the plan to terminate is that they are not associated with, or do not benefit, activities that will be continued.

There are differences too in the treatment of severance costs.

(2) Severance costs

Under UK GAAP, voluntary severance costs for employees leaving as part of the Group's restructuring programme are charged to expense when both the decision to reduce staff numbers is taken and the amounts involved can be estimated with reasonable accuracy. Voluntary severance costs include severance payments and costs resulting from augmentation of existing pension benefits and these are dealt with in the pension cost adjustment referred to in note (1) above.

Under US GAAP, such severance costs are charged to expense in the year in which employees accept the terms of the severance programme.

Fixed assets

Under UK GAAP, fixed assets and, in particular, properties may be restated on the basis of appraised values in financial statements prepared in all other respects in accordance with the historical cost convention. Such re-statements are not permitted under US GAAP.

BARCLAYS Extract from note 60 to the 1998 accounts

60. Differences between UK and US accounting principles

Revaluation of property
UK GAAP

Property is carried either at original cost or at subsequent valuation less related depreciation (as described in Accounting policies), calculated on the revalued amount where applicable. Revaluation surpluses are taken directly to shareholders' funds, while deficits below cost, less any related depreciation, are included in attributable profit.

US GAAP

Revaluations of property are not permitted in the accounts under US GAAP. As a result, when a property is disposed of, a greater profit or lower loss is generally recorded under US GAAP than under UK GAAP.

Under UK GAAP, major plant repair costs are charged to the profit and loss account by companies like NATIONAL POWER on the basis of the long-term trend underlying the actual incidence of major repairs. The difference between the amount charged to expense and the actual expenditure is then dealt with through a major plant repair provision in the balance sheet.

Under US GAAP, repair costs are charged to expense in the period that such costs are incurred, without consideration of the long-term trend of such costs.

Software

Under UK GAAP revenue and related direct costs from contracts for the outright sale of software systems are recognised at the time of client acceptance. Under US GAAP, specific rules were introduced from January 1998 for the determination of client acceptance in cases where future significant modifications or upgrades to the software are considered to be part of the client's overall acceptance of the product. Under these rules, an amount of revenue is required to be deferred until these software upgrades have been delivered and accepted by the client. Under UK GAAP, costs of developing computer software products are expensed in the year in which they are incurred. Warranties provided in connection with the delivery of millennium versions of software fall within these rules and an element of revenue and related direct cost will have to be deferred under US GAAP. Differences also arise with regard to software development costs:

REUTERS Extract from the 1998 accounts

Software development costs

Under UK GAAP, costs of developing computer software products are expensed in the year in which they are incurred. Under US GAAP, the costs of developing computer software products subsequent to establishing technical feasibility are capitalised. The amortisation of the capitalised costs is based on the estimated future revenues or remaining estimated useful economic lives of the products involved.

Capitalised interest

Traditionally, British companies have under UK GAAP been allowed in certain circumstances to capitalise interest but have not been required to.

GLAXOWELLCOME Extract from note 29 of 1998 accounts

Capitalised interest

Under UK GAAP, the Group does not capitalise interest. US GAAP requires interest incurred as part of the cost of constructing fixed assets to be capitalised and amortised over the life of the asset.

Foreign exchange

Under UK GAAP unrealised gains and losses on foreign currency transactions to hedge anticipated, but not firmly committed, foreign currency transactions may be deferred and accounted for at the same time as the anticipated transactions. Under US GAAP such deferral is not permitted except in certain defined circumstances. See, for example, CADBURY SCHWEPPES at the top of page 272.

CADBURY SCHWEPPES *Extract from note 31 to the 1998 accounts*

(d) Foreign currency hedges

Under US GAAP, hedging of foreign currency transactions is only allowable for transactions which are firm commitments. Some of the Group's foreign currency contracts hedge forecast or budgeted transactions which do not meet the definition of a firm commitment; gains or losses on these contracts cannot be deferred but must be recognised in net income.

Under UK GAAP, these gains or losses can be deferred until the hedged transaction actually occurs.

Stocks

Even something as simple as stock can be treated differently under the two GAAPs. Consider for instance the difference that the choice of GAAP made to the figures for AMOCO at the time it merged with BP:

BP AMOCO *Extract from note 45 to the 1998 accounts*

(b) Stock accounting

Amoco carried stocks at the lower of current market values or cost. Cost is determined under the last-in, first-out (LIFO) method for the majority of stocks of crude oil, petroleum products and chemical products. The costs of remaining stocks are determined on the first-in, first-out (FIFO) or average cost methods. BP carried stocks at the lower of cost or net realisable value. Cost to BP is determined using the FIFO method. Cost of sales determined on a FIFO basis is adjusted to a replacement cost basis, i.e. to reflect the average cost of supplies incurred during the year, by excluding stock holding gains and losses.

As a result of this adjustment replacement cost of sales is reduced by $7m (increased by $130m); there are stockholding losses of $415m ($419m); profit for the year is reduced by $408m ($549m). The carrying value of stock is increased by $549m.

Exceptional items

Although the UK and the US have grown much closer in recent years in accounting for exceptional items, important differences of presentation remain.

BP AMOCO *Extract from note 45 to the 1998 accounts*

(e) Exceptional items

Under UK GAAP, certain exceptional items should be shown separately on the face of the income statement after operating profit. Under US GAAP these items would be classified as operating income or expenses.

For 1998 there were profits on the sale of businesses of $8m ($117m) and on the sale of fixed assets of $312m ($495m) and merger expenses of $119m.

Equity accounting

Although the differences in GAAP have no overall effect on either profit for the year or net assets, the detailed figures for equity accounted investments look rather different.

BP AMOCO *Extract from note 45 to the 1998 accounts*

(f) Equity accounting

UK GAAP requires the operating profit or loss, exceptional items, interest expense and taxation of associated undertakings and joint ventures to be shown separately from those of the group. For US GAAP, the after-tax profits or losses (i.e. operating results after exceptional items, interest expense and taxation) should be included in the income statement as a single line item.

UK GAAP requires the investor's share of the gross assets and gross liabilities of the joint venture to be shown on the face of the balance sheet, whereas under US GAAP the net investment should be included as a single line item.

This adjustment has no overall effect on profit for the year or net assets.

Sale and leaseback

A sale and leaseback is a sale under UK GAAP whereas under US GAAP it is not.

BP AMOCO *Extract from note 45 to the 1998 accounts*

(g) Sale and leaseback

The sale and leaseback of the Amoco building in Chicago is treated as a sale for UK GAAP whereas for US GAAP it is treated as a financing transaction. The effect of this adjustment is to increase exceptional items and profit for the year by $211m. Net assets are increased by $211m.

Fixed asset investments

Under UK GAAP, fixed asset investments are held in the balance sheet at the lower of cost or net realisable value. Under US GAAP, fixed asset investments which are available for sale are stated at fair value with unrealised gains or losses included in shareholders' equity.

Acceptances and similar transactions

Most banks conduct business involving acceptances, guarantees, performance bonds and indemnities. The majority of these facilities are offset by corresponding obligations of third parties. In addition, there are other off-balance sheet financial instruments, including swaps, futures, forwards and option contracts or combinations thereof (all commonly known as derivatives) the nominal amounts for which are not under UK GAAP reflected in the consolidated balance sheet.

An acceptance is an undertaking by a bank to pay a bill of exchange drawn on a customer. Most acceptances are presented, and reimbursement by the customer is normally immediate. Endorsements are residual liabilities of the Group in respect of bills of exchange which have been paid and subsequently rediscounted.

US GAAP requires a different treatment from UK GAAP.

BARCLAYS *Extract from note 60 to the 1998 accounts*

60. Differences between UK and US accounting principles

Acceptances
UK GAAP
Acceptances are not recorded within the balance sheet.
US GAAP
Acceptances and the related customer liabilities are recorded within the balance sheet.

In its accounts according to UK GAAP BARCLAYS recorded acceptances and endorsements as a contingent liability of £1,384m. Under US GAAP they would be both an asset (i.e. the customers' obligations) and a liability (the bank's obligation).

Losses and gains on discontinued operations
Under UK GAAP a loss or gain on discontinuance of operations appears in the profit and loss account between 'Total group operating profit including associates' and 'Profit on ordinary activities before taxation'.

CADBURY SCHWEPPES *Extract from 1998 accounts*

Group profit and loss account for the 52 weeks ended 2 January 1999 (Note ...1)

	1998 £m	1997 £m	1996 £m
Total operating profit including associates	598	639	702
Profit on sale of subsidiaries and investments	38	412	–
Profit on ordinary activities before interest	636	1,051	702

Under US GAAP any gain on discontinued operations is shown below the 'Profit for the financial year'. The figures are also computed somewhat differently (as shown in the next column).

Cash flow statements
The principal differences between cash flow statements prepared in accordance with FRS 1 (revised) and cash flow statements in accordance with US FAS are shown alongside.

CADBURY SCHWEPPES *Extract from note 31 to the 1998 accounts*

31 Summary of differences between UK and US generally accepted accounting principles

Approximate effects on profit of differences between UK and US generally accepted accounting principles

	1998 £m	1997 £m	1996 £m
Profit for the financial year from continuing operations, net of tax, as adjusted for US GAAP	257	260	208
Profit from discontinued operations, net of tax, as adjusted for US GAAP	–	1	39
Gain on disposal of discontinued operations, net of tax, as adjusted for US GAAP	–	356	–
Profit for the financial year adjusted for US GAAP	257	617	247

Differences in treatment of cash flows:

1. Under UK GAAP net cash flow from operating activities is determined before considering cash flows from (a) returns on investments and servicing of finance and (b) taxes paid. Under US GAAP, net cash flow from operating activities is determined after these items.
2. Under UK GAAP, capital expenditure is classified separately while under US GAAP, it is classified as an investing activity.
3. Under UK GAAP, dividends are classified separately while under US GAAP, dividends are classified as financing activities.
4. Under UK GAAP movements in short-term investments are not included in cash but classified as management of liquid resources. Under US GAAP, short-term investments with a maturity of three months or less at the date of acquisition are included in cash.
5. Under UK GAAP movements in bank overdrafts are movements in cash while under US GAAP they are classified as financing.

So even cash flow statements look very different.

Problem 30.1
Where a company is listed both in the UK and in the US, why might the note explaining differences in GAAP between the two countries be of interest:

(a) to an analyst;
(b) to a US investor;
(c) to a student of accounting theory?

Chapter 31

PUTTING IT ALL TOGETHER

Chosen Company: THE BODY SHOP.

Reasons for choice: Started from scratch by Anita Roddick, whose enormous panache enabled her to become the UK's only truly world-wide retailer, with 1,663 outlets in 47 countries. The share price has behaved spectacularly, reflecting investor sentiment: euphoria followed, after two profit warnings in four months, by disenchantment. See the share price graph on page 277. The share price has recently bounced, but is it a 'dead cat' bounce, or is there scope for further and sustained recovery?

We are told that at the time Anita formed the company her flatmate had a friend, a Littlehampton garage owner, who put in £4,000 for a 50% stake. He is still the principal shareholder:

THE BODY SHOP *Extracts: 1998 report and accounts*

Directors' report

Substantial shareholdings

At 12 May 1998 the Company had been notified of the following interests of 3% or more in its ordinary shares (excluding Directors' share interests which are disclosed in Note 6 to the Accounts): Mr I.B. McGlinn had a beneficial interest in 45,666,768 ordinary shares, amounting to 23.5%; Prudential Corporation had an interest in 6,911,146 ordinary shares, amounting to 3.6%; and ...

Note to the accounts

Directors' share interests

The beneficial interests of directors in the ordinary shares of the Company are shown below as at the beginning of the year and at the end of the year.

	At 28 Feb 1998	At 2 Mar 1987
A.L. Roddick OBE	24,010,456	24,010,456
T.G. Roddick	24,226,680	24,226,680

[The other 9 directors hold 29,085 shares between them, with options on 5,028,365 shares.]

From this we deduce that:

1. Mr McGlinn has done well with his £4,000 investment – we don't know whether he has done any profit taking, but his stake at the financial year end was worth £55m (1997: £106m).

2. Between them Anita Roddick., her husband Gordon Roddick and Mr McGlinn hold around 48.5% of the equity. In practice this amounts to control, assuming the Roddicks still have Mr McGlinn's support, in spite of the value of his holding declining by £51m during the last financial year. We checked the 1997 accounts and his holding was unchanged.

Ground rules

Let's start with a couple of ground rules:

1. Always make a list of questions you would like to ask, firstly to make clear to yourself what you do know and what you don't about the company, and secondly because you may get a chance to ask them. Here's our first question:

Q1.   Have the Roddicks still got Mr McGlinn's support?

2. Always make a note too of anything you notice, and may want to follow up later, but haven't got the time to do so now.

In checking Mr McGlinn's holding at the end of FY 1997 (FY = Financial Year), we noticed that the 1997 report and accounts felt a lot thinner than 1998.

To be precise, it was 40 pages compared with about 68 pages in 1998. We say 'about' because page numbering in 1998 didn't start until page 25.

The 1998 report – a 'New Look'

The reason for the increased thickness was the inclusion, as the first 20 pages, of a series of large illustrations of varying relevance:

Unnumbered

Page	Contents
1	A message from Anita Roddick, which began 'Another year – and if anyone has managed to sort out the difference between stress and enthusiasm, they haven't told me. But at least we are now in a very interesting place, a place where the competition won't easily follow.' [*Our reaction:* 'She's in overdrive this year!']
2	Colour photo of a marijuana plant.
3	A tube of cream labelled '*Hemp Hand Protector* Dry to very dry skin 100ml'.
4 & 5	A*romatherapy.* Top half of a 'port quarter' view of a naked lady, arms outstretched.
6 & 7	*Bergamot* a small and inedibly bitter fruit.
8 & 9	Double spread photo of a Body Shop.
10 & 11	The Body Shop Direct at home shopping.
12 & 13	Human rights.
14 & 15	Our model children's home in Romania.
16 & 17	*The Big Issue* magazine about the homeless, set up in the UK by Gordon Roddick in 1992.
18 & 19	*Self-esteem.* Photo of a very fat Barbie-type doll, lying on a sofa. Caption: 'The dawn of a new consciousness in the beauty business: Love your body – just the way it is.'
And, eventually	The Chairman's statement, printed on tomato red paper:

THE BODY SHOP *Extract from chairman's statement 1998*

We have recently carried out a comprehensive strategic review of all of our activities which has highlighted the need for some fundamental changes in order to develop the business going forward ... The proposed joint venture in the USA and the senior management changes ... signal the first stages of a plan that will define the future of The Body Shop.

[*Our first reaction:* Are they in trouble?]
Let's have a quick look at earnings per share and cash flow.

THE BODY SHOP *Extract from the 1998 accounts*

Profit and loss account

	1998	1997
...		
Eps including exceptional item	11.8p	9.2p
Eps excluding exceptional item	11.8p	11.4p

Note 3 on Operating expenses

Administrative expenses – exceptional item	£6.5m

This was a provision against the amounts advanced and facilities extended to the former head franchisee in France prior to the acquisition of the French business [by The Body Shop] in November 1997.

Cash flow statement	1998	1997
Net cash inflow from operating activities	41.5	51.7
[We also noticed a £20.3m Loan Repayment]		

Group balance sheet

	1998	1997
	£m	£m
Current assets		
Cash at bank and in hand	29.6	47.1

Nothing obvious to worry about there, though we did notice the tax charge was rather high; something to which we will return.

Before we continue we would like to make one important point:

 A warning sign

In our experience, when a company's report and accounts are hyped, it raises questions. Excessive hype or a marked increase in hype (as in the case of THE BODY SHOP) are often a strong warning signal.

For example, SPRING RAM's 1991 report and accounts, which was plastered with colour photographs or drawings of sporting events: stylised drawing of relay race runners crossing the line on the front cover and, inside, mountaineers reaching a peak, with snow covered mountain tops in the background – white water rafting – show jumping – boat race – cycle track racing – boxing – bobsleighing – polo – sky diving. You name it, they had it, and all to reinforce the chairman's message:

SPRING RAM *Extracts from preface and chairman's statement*

Successful enterprises must employ able motivated and effective people in order to progress profitably.

When those people operate as focused teams, not only within the company but in partnership with suppliers, with advisers and with customers, then synergistic benefits are quite remarkable. This synergy at Spring Ram multiplies rather than merely adds value and produces impressive results.

Profitable growth will continue to be a major corner-stone in Spring Ram's future strategy and will be achieved through teamwork.

Operating profit slipped the following year from £32.9m to £18.7m, and into a £33.2m operating loss in 1993.

Now we are not suggesting that The Body Shop is in any way comparable to Spring Ram (where the combined chairman/chief executive was expanding the bathroom and kitchen manufacturer in the teeth of a looming recession), but we do get a bit anxious when management begins to believe its own PR.

OK Back to Square 1.

Assumptions about our readers

For this chapter we will assume you are working from home, with no ready access to a business library, a stockbroker's office or other financial institution.

Getting a first feel

One book we always have to hand at home and in the office is the *Hemscott* (formerly *Hambro*) *Company Guide*. Each UK Listed and AIM company gets a one-sixth of a page entry, or a larger entry for companies prepared to pay for the extra space. For further details, see page 249.

In the right hand column are the 1989 and 1998 entries for The Body Shop:

They present quite a record:

	1984 £m	1998 £m	Compound growth per annum
Turnover	4.91	293	34%
Pre-tax profit	1.04	38	29%
Earnings per share	1.50p	11.8p	16%
Dividend per share	0.18p	5.60p	26%

Three points to make before we move on:

1. Notice how the payout ratio (d.p.s./e.p.s.) has gone from 12% in 1984 to 47% in 1998. A high retention rate (i.e. very low payout ratio) is a good sign in a small company: retentions help to fuel expansion.
2. Calculations based on e.p.s. and d.p.s. growth can't be relied on unless you have details of rights and scrip issues.
3. The Guide entry gives the telephone number of the Registrars, Lloyds, Worthing. We can phone them for a copy of the latest report and accounts, and any subsequent interim report.

While we wait for the report and accounts – and Lloyds are particularly good at posting them promptly – let us look at The Body Shop's share price graph (see Example 31.1, next page).

BODY SHOP INTERNATIONAL PLC (THE)

ACTIVITIES Produces and sells natural skin and hair care products.
STATUS: Full. FT LIST: Drapery & stores.

HEAD & REG OFF: Hawthorn Road, Wick, Littlehampton, West Sussex BN17 7LR Tel: (O903) 717107. Tlx: 877055 Fax: (0903) 726250. REGISTRARS: Lloyds, Worthing Tel: (0903) 726250

ANNCMNTS: Int - mid Nov Final - mid Jun, AGM late Jul.

GEARING: 15.7 (8 10%). ROCE: 39.3% (83.5%).
NOTES: Period to Feb 89, 517 days (17 months)

year ended 30 September		1984	1985	1986	1987	1989
turnover	£m	4.91	9.36	17.4	28.5	73.0
pre tax profit	£m	1.04	1.93	3.45	6.00	15.2
retained profit	£m	0.41	0.87	1.76	3.13	7.11
earn per share	p	1.50	2.55	5.15	9.30	20.4
div per share	p	0.18	0.38	1.50	1.50	3.38
intangibles	£m	–	–	–	–	–
fixed assets	£m	0.61	0.68	1.74	4.09	15.6
fixed investments	£m	0.03	–	–	–	–
stocks	£m	0.87	2.20	4.23	4.61	15.7
debtors	£m	1.32	1.95	3.13	5.67	8.98
cash, securities	£m	0.25	0.01	1.06	0.83	0.20
creditors short	£m	1.93	1.89	6.47	5.34	16.2
creditors long	£m	0.32	0.26	0.23	0.12	0.24
prefs, minorities	£m	–	–	0.02	0.16	0.52
ord cap. reserves	£m	0.81	1.68	3.45	6.59	23.5

Extracts from the Hambro Company Guide (above for 1989; below for 1998)

BODY SHOP INTERNATIONAL PLC (THE)

ACTIVITIES: Produces and sells naturally based skin and hair care products and related items STATUS: Full INDEX: FTSE Small Cap. SECTOR: Retailers, general

HEAD & REG OFF: Watersmead, Littlehampton, West Sussex BN17 6LS Tel: (01903) 731500 Fax: (01903) 726250 REGISTRARS: Lloyds, Worthing. Tel: (01903) 502 541

ANNCMNTS: Int – late Oct, Final - mid May, AGM mid Jun

INTERIM: (29 Oct 97) 1/2 yr to 30 Aug 97. T/O £123m (£117m) Pre tax profit £12.3m (£11.8m). EPS: 3.80p (3.60p) int div 1.80p (1.50p). NOTES: Figures from 28 Feb 92 in accordance with FRS 3.

year ended 25 February		1994	1995	1996	1997	1998
turnover	£m	195	220	257	271	293
pre tax profit	£m	29.7	33.5	32.7	31.7	38.0
norm earn per share	p	10.3	11.8	10.0	11.7	12.0
FRS 3 earn per share	p	10.3	11.5	9.80	9.30	11.8
div per share	p	2.00	2.40	3.40	4.70	5.60
intangibles	£m	3.70	2.20	0.70	–	–
fixed assets	£m	67.9	73.6	78.2	74.9	78.4
fixed investments	£m0	0.50	0.50	0.50	2.00	
stocks	£m	34.6	38.6	37.6	34.5	47.7
debtors	£m	37.2	44.3	44.0	45.0	47.0
cash, securities	£m	24.9	29.0	30.1	47.1	29.6
creditors short	£m	35.6	51.2	49.1	59.0	70.4
creditors long	£m	35.8	26.6	19.4	13.2	4.00
prefs, minorities	£m	–	–	–	–	–
ord capital, reserves	£m	96.9	111	123	130	130

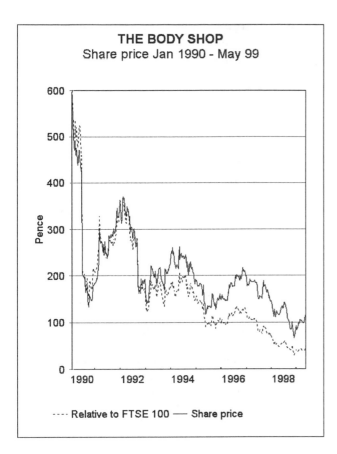

THE BODY SHOP
Share price Jan 1990 - May 99

Example 31.1 The Body Shop: A bumpy ride! But a potential recovery situation?

We also like to look at a Lin/Log graph of Sales growth. If a company's turnover goes up by a given percentage year after year, a Lin/Log graph will show a straight line. On a linear scale, the growth will appear to be exponential.

We show The Body Shop's turnover since 1984 both ways:

- on a linear scaled graph (Example 31.2);
- as a Lin/Log graph (Example 31.3);

which make it very clear why we prefer a Lin/Log presentation.

Historical background from the *Investors Chronicle*

Unless you've kept them year by year, it's not easy to lay your hands on the last 5 or 10 years' reports and accounts of any company. With or without them, a good place to get some history is the *Investors Chronicle*, which we take and keep for six or seven years. With the excellent Quarterly Index and the Hemmington Scott hot-link (see page 254) it is quite easy, as we have done, to devil back several years (we went back to 1993). On the next page are some of the more interesting extracts from the *Investors Chronicle* (*IC*) together with our comments and questions (**Q2** etc.).

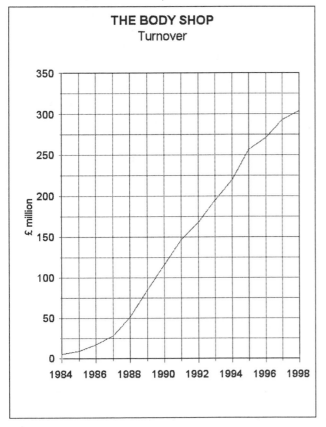

THE BODY SHOP
Turnover

Example 31.2 Body Shop's ever-increasing turnover on a linear scale

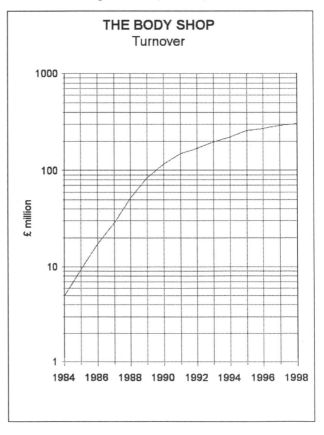

THE BODY SHOP
Turnover

Example 31.3 The same turnover as a Lin/Log graph

THE BODY SHOP *Extracts from the Investors Chronicle and the questions they raise*

IC 15/01/93

[After profits warning] At 158p ... less than half what they were a year ago, when they were trading at 350p. ... while discount competition nibbles at volumes in some of its low cost standard items, like bubble baths, Body Shop is slow to expand its presence in other areas, such as cosmetics.

Questions about the group's management and financial controls have never disappeared. There has been concern that the marketing and buying functions have minds of their own. And there have been worries as to whether Body Shop is wise to be tying up so much working capital by making its own bottles.

In Chapter 15 we looked at Body Shop's working capital (see page 101) and noticed an alarming jump in stocks in 1998. We may be on to something there, so another question for our list:

Q2. Are stock levels a problem and, if so, what is the company doing about it?

After we'd finished reading the *IC* cuttings, we phoned the company and asked to speak to Angela Bawtree, Head of Investor Relations – we had spotted her name in a couple of the *IC* articles. Introducing ourselves as prospective investors – quite true; we are always on the qui vive for interesting investments – we asked her some of our questions.

On stocks, Angela told us:

- Bottle making had been sold to PLYSU a couple of years ago.
- Stocks were receiving the attention of the new Chief Executive, with a target to cut by 20%.
- EPOS (Electronic Point of Sale) was being put in more stores, to improve stock control.

IC 14/05/93

Body Shop has just come through the most difficult year in its remarkable history. Two profits warnings in four months left investors bruised and brought to an end the company's long romance with the market ... its first ever fall in full-year profits ... Thanks to aggressive overseas expansion, Body Shop now generates only about half of sales and profits in the UK.

IC 28/05/93

... the group has more enthusiasm and commitment than most of its competitors

IC 22/10/93

Competition is intensifying, particularly from BOOTS.

Q3. How is morale standing up in adversity?

Q4. Are margins being squeezed? Let's do an analysis.

Q5. Is there any independent market research data on UK market shares in the sector?

Q6. And in the US?

Q7. How serious is BOOTS as a competitor?

Q8. How much of a premium are Body Shop customers prepared to pay?

IC 15/07/94

For the first time since March 1988 two Body Shop International founders sold a sizeable stake in the company. A week ago MD Anita Roddick and chairman Gordon Roddick sold 3.5m shares at 240p, taking their joint holding down two percentage points to 25.4%. The shares fell just 3p to 240p.

In 1988 the MD and Mr McGlinn sold 5% of the equity as part of a placing of shares to raise £9.6m to build a new warehouse. The shares fell 8 per cent immediately after the cash call.

News that the £8.4m raised this time will be used to fund several philanthropic ventures including a Healthcare Foundation project and a film, is apparently more acceptable to the markets. [We think the writer here may be jumping to conclusions. If the 1988 placing was done at. say, a 10% discount, a fall of 8% could easily have been due to market makers marking the price down to discourage placees from making a quick turn.]

IC 26/08/94

BODY SHOP CRITICS MAKE A VICE OUT OF A VIRTUE. The cuddly image of Anita and Gordon's retail empire has taken a series of knocks. However insubstantial the allegations the loss of goodwill can't avoid hammering the value of the company. ... The US Federal Trade Commission is understood to have requested information concerning a dispute between the company and disgruntled franchisees.

Q9. How have turnover and profits in the US been affected? We need a segmental analysis.

IC 02/09/94

Just why Body Shop is panicking over its green image may become apparent in a critical report to be published in the US ... Mr Entine's report is expected to call Body Shop to account ... over the terms under which the company operates its 'Trade, Not Aid' links with developing countries [and] the use of non-renewable resources. Body Shop has expended more effort on discrediting the author than on rebutting his charges. Mr Entine, an award winner several times over for TV documentaries, has been engaged in 'a single-minded campaign of vilification against the Body Shop', according to this week's communiqué from Chairman Gordon Roddick.

... Instead of improving its lot, the Body Shop has come over as an overbearing tyrant.

Q10. Who handles the company's PR now?

The Body Shop has already said that it will soon appoint two non-executive directors. The latest flap highlights the need for an independent boardroom voice in a company which is no stranger to the charges of autocratic management.

Q11. How many non-executive directors (NEDs) are there on the Board now?
Q12. Who are they? and
Q13. Are the Roddicks likely to listen to them?

IC 21/10/94
Competition is hotting up with US chain Bath and Body Works launching in the UK.

Q14. How has Bath and Body Works fared in the UK since launch?

Body Shop's head of investor relations told us that Bath and Body Works still have only five UK stores.

IC 27/10/95
Last time's £1.5m operating profit evaporated into a £2.4m loss and concerns are growing about Body Shop's US strategy. It now has 262 US shops, up from 199, a large proportion company owned rather than franchised out. It's thus responsible for a large chunk of US sales, whereas the strength of franchising ... only has to worry about manufacturing the product.

Q15. How many shops are there now, and what proportion are franchised in each geographical area?

IC 03/11/95
It's official: Anita and Gordon Roddick have discussed taking Body Shop International private, but said this week that they had no plans formally to propose such a move 'in the near future, if at all.' There is no love lost between Anita and the City gents she has so often accused of 'short-termism.'

IC 10/05/96
Anita and Gordon Roddick abandoned their attempts to buy back the 75% of Body Shop they don't already own, fearing that the burden of debt would restrict expansion opportunities. Chairman Gordon Roddick said he would prefer to maximise returns to shareholders in the longer term than offer them cash today.

IC 08/11/96
First the good news: Body Shop is doing well in Asia. Now the bad news: Body Shop is still losing money in the US. The loss was £3.4m – £1m more than last time. The recently appointed head of US operations, Steen Kanter, has plenty of retailing experience. He spent 22 years with Swedish retailer IKEA and was chief executive with US houseware retailer Lechters. [Leading retail analyst] John Richards regards the US problem as insoluble: 'the point is that they are trying to be a retailer, but they are not.'

IC 16/05/97
Body Shop ... shocked the market by making a £6.5m provision to cover loans made to its French franchisee.

Q16. What's happening in France now?

The company told us they needed to take it under their direct control to sort it out, and may perhaps refranchise it later.

IC 31/10/97
Only 261 of 1530 stores in 47 countries are directly owned. The downside is that franchised stores need hefty handouts when profits fail.

Q17. What *are* the normal terms of contracts with franchisees?

IC 31/10/97
An old concept called the Green Room, where customers could pay for beauty treatments and massages, has been revamped as The Doorway. It has been rolled out in five stores so far and will be expanding in the second half.

Q18. Not a very inspiring name. How is it going?

IC 23/01/98 [in a leading article on the woes of Laura Ashley and The Body Shop].
One [Ann Iverson] played the City to the letter, pocketing £3m in two years. The other [Anita Roddick] has railed against such excess, lambasting the City and admitting 'finance bores the pants off me.'

Q19. What are Gordon and Anita's salaries?

We subsequently checked the Notes to the 1998 accounts and this is what we found:

THE BODY SHOP Extract from the 1998 accounts

6. Directors: Total Directors' emoluments

Name	Position	SALARY 1998 £000	1997 £000	BENEFITS 1998 £000	1997 £000
A.L. Roddick OBE	Chief Executive	140	135	22	12
T.G. Roddick	Chairman	140	135	22	14
S.A. Rose	Managing	250	240	–	1

The Remuneration Committee recommended that the salary of both A.L. Roddick and T.G. Roddick should be at a rate of £300,000 per annum, but the Roddicks have chosen to be remunerated at the rate set out in the table above.

IC 23/01/98 [in a leading article on the woes of Laura Ashley and The Body Shop] continued.

... Body Shop's added Asian flu to its woes in the US and its mature UK market.

...

'Companies with entrenched family shareholdings tend not to be so responsive to the market', says one institutional shareholder in both companies. 'They tend to wait until there in a crisis before they start reacting.'

...

Gordon Roddick said: 'We are taking a conservative view with regard to trade in South East Asia.' That translates as: our big growth market, worth over a third of operating profits, has just collapsed.

...

Neither is there any sign of a pick-up in the US. Despite buying back many of its franchised stores to improve operational controls – it now owns 203 of its 291 US shops – Body Shop is still heading for the same-again losses. Mr Roddick complains of 'aggressive discounting' by copycat US competitors, such as Garden Botanica.

One problem is that US consumers do not rate Body Shop as a premium brand. 'It's a completely different market to the UK,' says Matthew Siebert, retail analyst at the company's house broker ABN Amro Hoare Govett. 'The consumer is much more price-driven.'

IC 12/02/98

US HEADACHE AS BOSS QUITS. This week's sudden resignation of Steen Kanter, head of US Operations, has rekindled speculation over Body Shop's strategy for the US.

[Leading retail analyst] John Richards said; 'To move heavily into direct retail (owning the stores) was both high risk and a mistake. Especially in the US, which is the most difficult retail market in the world.'

IC 15/05/98

... the hope is that new chief Patrick Gourney from Danone will cope with Body Shop's problems... Running the troubled US operation as a joint venture may cure its woes. Rejuvenating an increasingly tired-looking format looks as big a challenge.

IC 29/01/99

A shake-up is planned at cosmetics retailer Body Shop. Chief executive Patrick Gournay plans to take it out of manufacturing and decentralise. All manufacturing will now be outsourced and managements will be divided into regions: UK, US, Europe and Asia.

Mr Gournay's appointment and other new appointments were given in the interim report, published in October 1998:

THE BODY SHOP *Interim report to 29 August 1998*

Statement from the Co-Chairs

Our new chief executive, Patrick Gournay, joined us in July and is already working on the fundamental changes needed to develop the business ... In the USA, our joint venture with Adrian Bellamy has been put in place and is already delivering positive results ... we are set on the path of radical change. We fully recognise the importance of developing our people in order to achieve this, and this is reflected in our recent appointment of a Director of Human Resources, Rick Corcoran.

IC 14/05/99

Pre-exceptionals operating profit fell 35 per cent after a truly lousy Christmas and declines in profits in every single geographical area ... Making a loss in the booming US – despite selling over £100m worth of goods – took some doing.

Top management

Our first meeting. We first met Anita and her husband at a Body Shop AGM in the eighties. It was held in their warehouse at Littlehampton on a Friday afternoon.

After the formal proceedings, tea was laid out on a long double line of trestle tables down the centre of the warehouse, and Anita came round with a smile and a tray of sticky buns. A really friendly person and a wonderful personality, unspoilt by her meteoric success. We thought she was terrific, but didn't buy any shares, because they were on an astronomical P/E.

Our second meeting. Two or three years later, in 1991, we went again to the AGM, this time held at the Beach Hotel, Marine Parade, Worthing.

We felt short changed! Anita Roddick wasn't even there, but a taped message from her was played at the start of the proceedings. The gist of her message was that she was out scouring the world for new products. But the message we got was that she didn't care about shareholders, and why should she? She effectively had control:

THE BODY SHOP *Note to the 1991 accounts*

25. Close company

The close company provisions of the Taxes Act 1988 applied to the Company at 28 February 1991 [the year end] and have continued to apply since that date.

Hadn't anyone told her that it is bad manners for an MD to duck her own AGM deliberately? We also noted that there were no non-executive directors, but we struck up a conversation with one of the executive directors, who told us that she had been with Body Shop's PR agents, but that Anita had brought her on to the Board full time. We groaned inwardly. Any GCSE business studies student knows that PR people are in the flattery business.

 Key point

It is the duty of non-executive directors (NEDS) to tell management what management *needs* to hear, not what management *wants* to hear, and to do this effectively they should be completely independent (see page 229).

Including as an NED anyone connected with the company's solicitors, auditor, financial adviser, stockbroker or PR agency is not to be recommended. It is too cosy, and tends to preclude any criticism of the professional adviser concerned.

TO UNDERSTAND A COMPANY dominated by a *star*, you need to understand that star. Anita's picture appeared on the cover of the *Investors Chronicle* of 22 December 1989, to accompany a lead story 'Secrets of Body Shop's success' and a few quotes from that two-pager may help the reader understand Anita and, hence, the company and some of the investment community's reservations:

INVESTORS CHRONICLE *Extracts from an article on The Body Shop*

Body Shop is that great contradiction, caring capitalism. Roddick admits that it is 'very much a benign dictatorship.'

In 1984, when Greens were still too weird to take, Body Shop came to the market, with 7 of its own shops and 92 franchises ... Valued at £4.75m, a prospective rating of 25 times was thought demanding ... Less than six years on, and the Body Shop share price stands at more than 520p ... now valued at over £440m.

Awards have been showered on her like acid rain: Business Woman of the Year (1985), Company of the Year (1987), Order of the British Empire (1988), Communicator of the Year (1988), Retailer of the Year (1989), United Nations 'Global 500' award, for her work in the rainforests (1989).

On the business side, Body Shop is essentially a franchising and wholesaling operation. This has helped to keep down capital and staff needs.

The Body Shop ethos includes a determination to cut out hype, packaging and (wherever possible) company cars. Using natural products, it aims to promote health rather than glamour ('Our concept of beauty is Mother Teresa, not some bimbo' is a throwaway line from the past). However, the priority is the company. 'I'm not responsible for those people who come in for monetary gain.' The company's holistic view places the interests of shareholders a poor fourth, behind those of the staff, the community and the planet. 'Nobody asks the shareholders what they think,' Roddick once said. 'So far they can only be grateful.'

But not any more they can't. In the year ending February 1999 the share price (over 500p in 1990) ranged between a high of 143 pence and a low of 66.5 pence. We will leave it there for the time being, but will come back later to discuss the new management. Meanwhile we must have a quick look at the 1999 Report and Accounts, which has just arrived.

1999 Report and Accounts

Earlier on we said we must consider margins, and the segmental analysis of turnover and profit. And we know from the high tax charge that the United States was making significant losses (see page 138).

We always try to work systematically, with a highlighter pen to hand to mark anything interesting that we spot.

Inside front cover. This makes a good place to start. We recalled that in 1998 it included a personable young man saying to Anita 'what's a nice girl like you doing in a place like this', and Anita's reply 'I own it'. This attitude, and the reminder that one is involved with a close company, tends to jar both shareholders and the market. And in 1998 her one pager on page one ended: 'We're doing it our way, which demands a huge amount of reflection, dialogue and consideration. To me, that feels like the only way to run a socially responsive company, especially one that is on course for the future.' This is not the thing to do if your profits have just fallen out of bed and your share price is down to 20% of its all time high.

In 1999 she's on the inside cover again, celebrating the 50th Anniversary of the Universal Declaration of Human Rights, with the caption: 'I want to work for a company that contributes to and is part of the community. I want something not just to invest in. I want something to believe in.'

Now we are not unsupportive of good causes, though some potential investors are, and reject THE BODY SHOP for two reasons: they don't want *their* money, shareholders' money, spent on someone else's good causes; and they prefer managers who manage rather than become involved in countless good works. Others welcome this 'kind faced capitalism'.

That kind face is understandable in view of Anita's background:

THE BODY SHOP *Extract from 1997 Directors Report*

Board of Directors

Anita L Roddick OBE (Age 54) Chief Executive
Anita Roddick is responsible for the Company's style and image. She opened the first branch of The Body Shop in Brighton in 1976. Before opening a restaurant

and hotel with her husband Gordon in 1970, Anita was a member of staff in the Women's Rights Department of the International Labour Organisation based at the United Nations in Geneva.

But it inevitably has its effect on the share price.

In this year's report, we noticed that shareholders still come last in her list of stakeholders, after employees, franchisees, customers and suppliers.

Anita Roddick is photographed on page four with husband Gordon. A 'Letter from the Co-Chairs' on page 5 tells us: 'We are happy to report that the direction we devised for The Body Shop is taking shape under the leadership of Patrick Gournay. Patrick has brought with him a culture of strong leadership, vision and accountability which has been unanimously welcomed by the Company.'

In the authors' view, there are four stages involved in management putting things right:

1. Realise you have got it wrong;
2. Admit you've got it wrong;
3. Take action; we call it *'grasping the nettle'*;
4. Get it right.

Well, THE BODY SHOP appears to have got to Stage 3, even if Stage 2 was a bit fudged. Before we put any money into THE BODY SHOP, we will need to be satisfied that they have reached Stage 4.

Chief Executive's Review. Four pages. First of all a talk through the 1999 Trading Results (see consolidated profit and loss account opposite) which we read in conjunction with the Notes:

[A] Group turnover was 4% higher at £303.7m but

[B] operating profit fell [by 19%] from £38.1m to £24.6m [not shown in the profit and loss account] excluding exceptional and restructuring costs ... disappointing retail sales, reduced wholesale prices in certain markets, lower wholesale volumes and the impact of higher stock write-offs. The last two factors were due in part to initiatives to lower inventory. Note 15 shows stocks down from £47.7m to £38.6m, mainly due to lower Finished goods. [*Grasping the nettle.*]

[C] Note 3: The 1998 figure of (4.5) is the cost associated with closing unprofitable shops and an impairment review of the remaining shops in the USA. [*More grasping the nettle.*]

[D] Note 4 showed an analysis of the Restructuring Costs: £10.2m in the UK, including £6.8m redundancy costs, and £6.4m in the US, including £2.0m redundancy. [*Grasping the nettle again.*]
Pre-tax profit fell from £38.0m to £3.4m.

[E] Note 5 showed £1.4m interest paid, and £1.3m received.

The Chief Executive didn't actually mention:

[F] the abnormally high tax charge (see Note 7);
[G] the loss after tax of £4.6m, or the retained loss of £15.5m [H].

THE BODY SHOP *Note to the 1999 accounts*

7. Tax on profit on ordinary activities

	1999 £m	1998 £m
The charge is based on the profit before taxation and consists of:		
UK corporation tax at 31%	8.9	12.4
Deferred taxation	(1.2)	2.3
Overseas taxation	0.3	0.5
	8.0	15.2

The effective tax rate has increased as a result of the losses of the US subsidiary, after exceptional and restructuring costs, of approximately £27.0m (1998: £11.5m) which are not available for relief in the year.

Instead, he went on to more cheerful topics:

- Our cash flow from operations remained strong and we ended the year with net cash of £5.1m after acquisition expenditure of £16.1m.
- We are maintaining our final dividend ... reflecting our confidence in the benefits arising from our reorganisation programme and in the future prospects for The Body Shop brand ... this makes a total of 5.7 pence net per share, an increase of 2%.

'We ended the financial year with 1,663 shops, a net increase of 69 on the previous year, with most of these openings taking place in the Asia Pacific and European regions ... our Christmas offering was not strong enough. This had a significant impact on performance in the second half.' Ah! Let's have a look at that second half, which we can deduce by subtracting the interim results from the full year, and compare them with the previous year's H2, similarly deduced:

THE BODY SHOP *Six months to 28 February 1999 (deduced)*

	Full year £m	— Interims — H1/99 £m	H2/99 £m
Operating profit	24.6	8.9	15.7

Six months to 28 February 1998 (deduced)

	Full year £m	— Interims — H1/98 £m	H2/98 £m
Operating profit	38.1	12.2	25.9

Operating profit in H2/99 was £15.9m, down a thumping 39% from H2/98's figure of £25.9m. A little devilling is often very rewarding.

THE BODY SHOP *Consolidated profit and loss account, 1999*

Consolidated profit and loss account

	Comment	Note	1999 £m	1998 £m
Turnover	[A]		303.7	293.1
Cost of sales			(127.7)	(115.9)
Gross profit			176.0	177.2
Operating expenses – excluding exceptional costs	[B]		(151.4)	(139.1)
– exceptional costs	[C]	3	(4.5)	–
Operating profit			20.1	38.1
Restructuring costs	[D]	4	(16.6)	–
	[G]		3.5	38.1
Interest payable (net)	[E]	5	(0.1)	(0.1)
Profit on ordinary activities before taxation			3.4	38.0
Taxation on profit on ordinary activities	[F]	7	(8.0)	(15.2)
(Loss)/profit for the financial year	[G]		(4.6)	22.8
Dividends paid and proposed			(10.9)	(10.8)
Retained (loss)/profit	[H]	21	(15.5)	12.0

Basic earnings per ordinary share ...

The United States

It's apparent that the US has been a thorn in The Body Shop's side, but for how long? We look back over the last 10 years.

THE BODY SHOP *Extracts from Segmental analyses*

Year	Turnover £m	USA Operating profit £m	USA Operating margin %	Group Operating margin %
1990	5.8	(1.9)	(33.2)	20.0
1991	13.3	(0.6)	(4.7)	19.0
1992	23.4	1.5	6.4	18.9
1993	37.8	2.1	5.5	14.4
1994	50.4	6.2	12.3	15.4
1995	58.8	4.9	8.3	15.7
1996	70.8	(1.3)	(1.8)	13.1
1997	73.1	(3.0)	(4.1)	11.8
1998	78.0	(1.7)	(2.2)	13.0
1999*	97.8	0.8	0.8	6.6

* The Americas, as opposed to USA

Answer: from the start. But interestingly, between 1990 and 1998 the segmental analysis showed 'USA' and 'Americas (excluding USA)' separately. In 1999 they were reported together as 'Americas'.

We look below at 1998 as reported, separately, and at what the figures would have been had they been reported together:

THE BODY SHOP *Extracts from segmental analyses*

As reported, separately

Year	USA Turnover £m	USA Operating profit £m	USA Operating margin %	Group Operating margin %
1998	78.0	(1.7)	(2.2)	13.0

Year	Americas (excluding USA) Turnover £m	Americas (excluding USA) Operating profit £m	Americas (excluding USA) Operating margin %	Group Operating margin %
1998	12.8	3.4	26.5	13.0

If they had been reported together

Year	Americas Turnover £m	Americas Operating profit £m	Americas Operating margin %	Group Operating margin %
1998	90.8	1.7	1.9	13.0

Our immediate reaction to the combining of 'USA' and 'Americas (excluding USA)', with their very different margins, was 'naughty naughty!'

Key point

Always be highly suspicious when a company reports *less* information than it did last year. Ask yourself: is there a good reason, or is this a cover-up?

Q20. In the 1999 segmental analysis, why are 'USA and 'Americas (excluding USA)' now reported together?

The reason may be the current reorganisation into four new regional businesses, which Patrick Gournay describes later in his report: UK, The Americas, Europe & Middle East and Asia Pacific.

BODY SHOP *Extract from the chief executive's review 1999*

Our strategy is to operate as a retailer in a select number of markets within all four regions through company-owned stores while partnering in other markets with a group of strong and forward-looking head franchisees. We will continue to work with those of our franchisees who are keen to invest and develop their businesses going forward. With others, we will look at different ways to reorganise our arrangements.

Now there is the first glimmer of what we are looking for: a tough, not to say ruthless approach. In effect: 'those who won't toe our new line will go'.

Tough? ... Hang on a minute: in the Directors' report it says:

THE BODY SHOP *Extract from 1999 Directors' Report*

Board of Directors
Adrian Bellamy (Age 57) Executive Director
... appointed to the Board on 6 January 1997 as Executive Director. On 19 June 1998, Adrian entered into a joint venture arrangement with the Company which granted him management rights over the US subsidiary and an option to acquire up to a 51% interest in the US business between the years 2000 and 2002, subject to the achievement of performance targets.

Doesn't that mean that they have solved the problems in the USA effectively by giving them away? That certainly does not appear to be their planned route, which, like that in the UK, is much tougher.

BODY SHOP *Extract from the chief executive's review*

In the USA, a number of actions have been taken under the management of Adrian Bellamy following the joint venture arrangement which took effect last June.

These include reorganisation of the central office and the creation of a product and marketing team now located in San Francisco, 28 store buy-backs from franchisees, the closure of 11 under-performing stores, the closure of three warehouses to consolidate the distribution system, a reduction in inventory levels of over 30%, the transfer of bottle filling to a third party and the closure of our filling plant. In the USA, we are close to achieving our targeted mix of stores for that market, with some three quarters of the stores now company-owned.

Q21. But what happens if the US operation falls back into serious losses. Would The Body Shop have to pick up 49% of the losses, and be powerless to do anything about it?

Q22. What went wrong with Steen Canter, highly experienced as a chief executive in US retailing, who was brought in as head of US operations towards the end of 1996, and resigned suddenly in February 1998?

Angela Bawtree, Head of Investor Relations, told us that they had deliberately head-hunted a Chief Executive in the United States, as they wanted someone with wide international experience. They certainly found one:

THE BODY SHOP *Extract from 1999 Directors' report*

Board of Directors
Patrick P Gournay (Age 51) Chief Executive Officer
... appointed on 14 July 1998, having previously worked for 26 years with Groupe Danone in a number of key roles in Europe and the USA. More recently, Patrick was Executive Vice President of Danone's North and South American Division, with strategic responsibilities for eight companies in five countries.

In Patrick Gournay have they got the right man, then? We are willing to believe they have, despite revealing press comment at the time of his appointment:

THE SUNDAY TELEGRAPH *'Body Shop's Mr Makeover City Profile' by Amanda Hall 31 January 1999*

When Patrick Gournay first met Anita Roddick, the founder of The Body Shop International, last year, she took him to her Oxford Street store and booked him in for a massage. Hardly your everyday interviewing technique, but this is mode Body Shop after all.
... 'She had me have a massage,' he says early last Friday morning sitting in his London office a few minutes from Oxford Circus. 'Then we looked at the store and she told me her thoughts on what needed to be done. And that was it – then she left!'
... Gordon Roddick says he hired Gournay because 'he had the kind of integrity and international experience Body Shop really needed. As a person I felt he was the best possible fit, given the ethics and philosophy of the company.'
Anita was reported at the time as saying she hired him because she liked the way he treats his wife.
The Roddicks had spent a long time looking for a chief executive who could marry profit with ethics.

While increased profits are a medium term goal, Gournay shows no signs of believing that the company should as one newspaper suggested last week, 'spend more money promoting its products and less time getting its customers to save the whale.'

A strange sort of interview. But our instincts tell us that Gordon Roddick was right. Patrick Gournay is a man who makes things happen.

To continue that quote:

THE SUNDAY TELEGRAPH *31 January 1999*

'We sat for two hours and talked,' says Gournay. 'It was an instant fit. It is hard to explain but I knew from that moment we could work together. Obviously we have our fights, our discussions, but what is good about working with entrepreneurs is that at the end of the day what matters to them is the business.'

Last week Gournay went public on probably the most radical reshape Body Shop has seen since Roddick founded the business in 1974. Manufacturing operations in Littlehampton, employing 550 people, will be sold; franchising operations will be reappraised; a new structure will organise the business into four regions – UK, Europe, America and Asia; and a loyalty programme is to be introduced in the UK.

In its statement, the company said these changes would be completed by the end of this year, but Gournay wants them done before then. Most of it will be done by June, he says.

'We'll do it. And we'll do it quick,' he says when I ask him why shareholders should be any more excited by these pronouncements than all the other reviews and alterations that have come out of Body Shop over the past few years.

Of all the changes announced last week, the plan to outsource manufacture strikes most keenly at the heart of what Body Shop is all about. Does this mean, I ask, that Anita will no longer go scouring the world for Brazil nuts to bring home to Littlehampton to make shampoo? And how can Gournay be sure that whoever lands his manufacturing contract will do it to Body Shop standards?

SUMMARY

The key questions

Whether one should consider investing in The Body Shop depends on:

- Who is doing the investing?
- And what else do they have in their portfolio?

For the private investor with a relatively small portfolio upon which he or she is dependent for income, The Body Shop would be an unwise choice. But an investor with a significant and relatively secure basic portfolio who has funds beyond this which he is prepared to risk, or the investment manager of a recovery fund might well think The Body Shop worth considering, subject to convincing answers to a number of key questions:

1. *Brand image:* Is The Body Shop brand image in decline, with its customers wearied by Anita Roddick's endless good causes, and its margins squeezed by strong competition? Under Patrick Gournay can it be revitalised?
2. *How is Mr Bellamy getting on?* In our view, everything in the US depends upon him, and he faces no easy task. Mr Bellamy has the US experience, but The Body Shop is not alone in finding the US a difficult market.
3. *What is the scope for expansion* elsewhere in the world, both in existing territory and in new territory, e.g. South America, bearing in mind Mr Gournay's background?
4. *Policy on franchising* seems to have changed from time to time. Have they got it right now?
5. *Is Patrick Gournay being helped, or hampered, by the co-chairs?*
6. *What other nettles are still on his list?*

Our experience is that face to face discussion with the management at (but not during) the AGM is the way for a private investor not to just:

- Get answers to specific questions; but
- Get *the feel of a company*, which we believe is extremely important. By that we mean: its people, its products, its aspirations, its problems, its strengths and its weaknesses.

➤ If you come away cheerful, BUY.
➤ If you come away feeling depressed, SELL.

The Body Shop AGM is coming up soon; we plan to attend.

A back-of-the-envelope calculation

The Body Shop has a very healthy cash flow, and virtually no debt. With competent management and a turnover of £300m it should easily be able to make margins of 10% to 12%. Operating profit £30 to £36m, with Pre-tax the same. Taxed at 30% = £21 to £25m after tax. 194 million shares in issue, e.p.s. 11 to 13 pence. Taking the lower figure and a boring ex-growth PER of 10 justifies the present share price of around 110 to 115 pence.

If our general impression at the AGM is, as we expect, that prospects are better than 'boring, ex-growth', then The Body Shop is a BUY; and if they are *much better*, a STRONG BUY.

Chapter 32

FUTURE DEVELOPMENTS IN ACCOUNTING

This chapter seeks to do three things:

- to provide an overview;
- to consider ASB proposals that are at the Exposure Draft and Discussion Paper stage, and Financial Reporting Standards which have not yet come into effect.
- to discuss subjects that the ASB is currently working on.

Overview

Over the past ten years the ASB has done much to make accounts more informative and to close loopholes. There is more to be done, there always will be. But we are reaching the stage of stability.

In the past it was sometimes suggested that ASB was going too far, too fast. But if earlier standards regimes had an overwhelming fault it was that progress was slowed to the pace of the slowest – and that in some areas, like fundamental principles of accounting and accounting theory, not only was nothing achieved, nothing much was even attempted.

The degree to which ASB pronouncements, despite the speed of change, have met with acceptance, among the accounting and auditing professions, the City and private investors, is quite remarkable. Indeed, there is little to suggest any degree of overkill on the part of financial reporting standards.

But the overall position of company reporting is less satisfactory; and there is overkill. Not only are too many cooks involved; but they do not always work in harmony, and occasionally the product appears half-cooked.

The EU, Parliament, the Stock Exchange, Cadbury, Greenbury, Hampel, the ASB and the Auditing Standards Committee all today impinge on reports and accounts. Forty years ago, only two of them did and the real power remains with those two: UK statutes and, as regards listed companies, The Stock Exchange. But they are by no means at the forefront of improvements in reporting.

Company law is a mess. Statute law is to be found today largely in the Companies Act 1985, but a major part consists of amendments placed in that Act by the Companies Act 1989, and there are at least ten statutory instruments, setting out the details. Company legislation is long overdue not just for consolidation but for a fundamental rethink.

The lack of enthusiasm for improvement on the part of those closest to the problem means that it is left to the other bodies we list to improve reporting piecemeal. But those bodies merely have influence, without responsibility. Even ASB has to work within limits laid down by statute.

Fifty years or so ago a set of accounts of a major listed company like MARKS & SPENCER consisted of four pages (quarto pages, that is, smaller than A4). We are certainly not suggesting that we go back to that, but we do question the increase in verbiage – for instance whether the many pages of additional information required by the Combined Code (14 pages in the BARCLAYS report for 1998) serve an essential purpose. Who reads them?

Back in 1964 the Chairman of The Stock Exchange wrote to the chairmen of all listed companies asking for various items of information to be included in their reports and accounts. One which 'might be included' was 'Tables of relevant comparative figures for the past ten years'. Apart from this request more than 30 years ago, listed companies are under no obligation to provide any form of historical summary: there is no FRS or SSAP, so little uniformity of content, layout or period covered has emerged. The majority of larger companies provide a five-year summary; most of the remainder show ten years, although a few choose a different period (for many years LONRHO's 'Financial Record' went right back to 1961).

Convenient, even valuable, though the information is, The Stock Exchange did not progress the idea; and it has yet to become part of company law; and so is outside the influence of ASB. But a historical summary is a very useful document, and not merely to shareholders of listed companies.

An EC directive on *Interim Reports* requires each listed company to prepare a report on its activities and profit and loss for the first six months of each financial year. The Stock Exchange requires interim reports, largely focusing on profit and loss account information, to include 'an explanatory statement including any significant information enabling investors to make an informed

assessment of the trend of the group's activities and profit or loss'. Greenbury suggested that interim reports should be extended to include balance sheet information.

The Stock Exchange has not updated its requirement. Directives take years to be adopted; and that section of Greenbury has not been implemented. Since UK company law is still silent, the ASB was able to produce only a non-mandatory Statement, not a standard because standards can, in effect, only reinforce an existing legal requirement; and there is none to produce interim statements.

Unless legislators, and accountants involved in Parliamentary drafting, see the need for improvements in reporting, and do something about it, because ASB's powers are limited, other people will inevitably come into the kitchen. We must not then be surprised if the result proves an indigestible broth.

ON THE WAY IN

Provisions, contingent liabilities and contingent assets

Issued in September 1998, and amended in December 1998 (surely a record), FRS 12 *Provisions, contingent liabilities and contingent assets* seeks to ensure that a provision (a liability that is of uncertain timing or amount) is recognised only when it actually exists at the balance sheet date. A provision should be recognised therefore only when:

- there is a present obligation (legal or constructive) as a result of a past event;
- it is probable that a transfer of 'economic benefits' will be required to settle the obligation; and
- a reliable estimate can be made of the amount of the obligation.

Then the amount recognised should be the best estimate of the expenditure required to settle the present obligation at the balance sheet date.

Contingent liabilities and contingent assets are not recognised as liabilities or assets. However, a contingent liability should be disclosed if the possibility of an outflow of economic benefit to settle the obligation is more than remote. A contingent asset should be disclosed if an inflow of economic benefit is probable.

Provisions often have a substantial effect on a business' financial position and performance, but earlier published guidance tended to concentrate on

particular forms of provision rather than the general principles underlying all provisions.

More disturbing, the practice grew up of providing not just for liabilities but for expected liabilities of future years, including sometimes items related to ongoing operations, making one large provision which was then often reported as an exceptional item. The effect of such 'big bath' provisions was not only to report excessive 'liabilities' at the outset but also to boost profitability during the subsequent years, at the very time when the liabilities were being incurred.

FRS 12 superseded SSAP 18 *Accounting for contingencies*. It was developed as a joint project with IASC.

Derivatives and other financial instruments

FRS 13 *Derivatives and other financial instruments* was issued in September 1998 and amended in December 1998.

Many financial instruments, such as cash, debtors and creditors, arise as part of an entity's operating and financing activities and tend to be highly visible in the financial statements. Others (such as swaps, forwards, caps and collars, and other derivatives) are entered into in order to manage the risks arising from the operating and financing activities of the entity and are generally less visible. FRS 13 seeks to improve the disclosures provided in respect of all financial instruments. It does so by focusing on the way in which they are used by the reporting entity. The objective is to provide information about:

- the impact of the instruments on the entity's risk profile;
- how the risks arising from financial instruments might affect the entity's performance and financial condition; and
- how these risks are being managed.

FRS 13 applies to all entities (other than insurance companies and groups) that have one or more of their capital instruments listed or publicly traded on a stock exchange or market and all banks and similar institutions.

The FRS requires:

(i) Narrative disclosures: including an explanation of the role that financial instruments play in creating or changing the risks that the business faces in its activities. The directors' approach to managing each of those risks should also be explained, and this should include a description of the objectives, policies and strategies for holding and issuing financial instruments.

(ii) Numerical disclosures: intended primarily to show how these objectives and policies were implemented in the period but focusing on:

    (a) interest rate risk;
    (b) currency risk;
    (c) liquidity risk (except for banks and similar institutions, which are covered by existing requirements);
    (d) fair values; and
    (e) hedging activities.

All entities falling within the scope of FRS 13 are required to provide the same type of narrative disclosures, but different numerical disclosures for entities that are not financial institutions; banks and similar institutions; and other types of financial institution.

FRS 13 is concerned with reporting; the measurement of derivatives and financial instruments is the subject of a separate project.

Earnings per share

FRS 14 *Earnings per share* was issued in October 1998 and is effective for accounting periods ending on or after 23 December 1998. It is largely based on the International Accounting Standard, IAS 33, which was developed concurrently with the US standard-setting body, the FASB, as it progressed its own standard on the topic (FAS 128).

There are few changes in substance to SSAP 3 *Earnings per share*, which FRS 14 superseded. The FRS does, however, make changes to the calculation of diluted earnings per share and it sets out additional disclosures to be given where companies choose to publish additionally their own figures of earnings per share.

Tangible fixed assets

FRS 15 *Tangible fixed assets* was issued in February 1999 and is effective for accounting periods ending on or after 23 March 2000. It permits a choice as to whether tangible fixed assets are stated at cost or at revalued amount. However, where a company chooses to revalue some assets, all assets of the same class (that is, those with a similar nature, function or use) must be revalued. The FRS also contains requirements that ensure that the valuations are kept up to date.

FRS 15 incorporates many of the requirements of SSAP 12 *Accounting for depreciation* which it will supersede in due course. It accepts that in a limited number of cases, no depreciation charge may be made on the grounds that it is immaterial. Where this is the case, or where depreciation is calculated on a basis that assumes that the useful economic life of an asset is longer than 50 years, the standard requires annual impairment reviews.

EXPOSURE DRAFT

Statement of Principles

Way back in 1988, the Review Committee under the Chairmanship of Sir Ron Dearing, which recommended the setting up of the Accounting Standards Board in its report *The making of accounting standards,* observed that the:

'lack of a conceptual framework is a handicap to those involved in setting standards as well as to those applying them. Work on its development should, therefore, be pursued at a higher rate than hitherto ... We believe that work in this area will

assist standard-setters in formulating their thinking on particular accounting issues, facilitate judgements on the sufficiency of the disclosures required to give a true and fair view, and assist preparers and auditors in interpreting accounting standards and in resolving accounting issues not dealt with by specific standards.'

Not that the idea was exactly new: the Financial Accounting Standards Board (FASB) had by that time published six *Statements of Financial Accounting Concepts* and the International Accounting Standards Committee (IASC) was working on its *Framework for the Preparation and Presentation of Financial Statements* (which was published in 1989).

The first draft of the ASB's Statement was published in the early 1990s as a series of discussion drafts, and a revised complete draft was published in 1995 as an Exposure Draft.

That Exposure Draft attracted more letters of comment than any other document published by the Board; most of them were critical. Some highlighted fundamental differences of opinion over key issues dealt with in the draft Statement. Others 'suggested that debate over the Exposure Draft had become obscured by misunderstandings and confusion'. The ASB therefore decided that, rather than proceeding directly to the development of a final Statement, it would prepare a revised draft. This was published in March 1999 and takes the form of a pack with an Introductory Booklet and a Technical Supplement. The Introductory Booklet tries to clear up the misconceptions that arose in respect of the previous draft and provides an overview of the draft Statement itself. The Technical Supplement explains the rationale underlying the draft Statement, seeking at the same time to address some of the most common criticisms of the ASB's approach.

The purpose of a conceptual framework or statement of principles is 'to describe the accounting model that the financial reporting standard-setters use as the conceptual underpinning for their work.' So, the final Statement of Principles will be neither an accounting standard nor any other form of mandatory document. It will therefore not be necessary to adopt the principles in the Statement in order to prepare financial statements that show a true and fair view. It is, as we said earlier, a conceptual framework.

The comment period for the Exposure Draft ended on 11 June 1999.

ASB'S WORKLIST

At 15 May 1999 the ASB had projects in hand relating to:

- Business combinations
- Derivatives and other financial instruments;
- Leasing;
- Pensions;
- Reporting financial performance;
- Accounting for tax;
- Year-end financial reporting structure.

Business combinations

In December 1998 the ASB published a Discussion Paper *Business Combinations*. This was, in effect, a Position Paper it had prepared for the international group known as the G4+1 – a group which includes accounting standard-setters for five countries: the UK, Australia, Canada, New Zealand and the USA; with the International Accounting Standards Committee (IASC) as an observer.

The Paper's main recommendation is that only one method of accounting for business combinations should be used: acquisition accounting. Merger accounting should be banned. The ASB has not itself debated the Position Paper, but international harmonisation would provide an excellent excuse for getting rid of what to many seems a rather uncomfortable anomaly: that provided five criteria are met merger accounting has to be used, which gives an entirely different balance sheet and results not just in the first year but permanently.

The idea is that a standard will in time supersede FRS 6 *Acquisitions and mergers*.

Derivatives and other financial instruments

Financial instruments can rapidly transform the risk profile of a group in a way that is not made apparent under present reporting practices. For example, a derivative, acquired for nil cost (and so not recognised in the balance sheet) can be used to convert a dollar floating rate liability into a sterling fixed rate one. Or a derivative may be used to 'hedge' the risk that sales expected to occur next year in a foreign currency may be worth less when converted into sterling because sterling may strengthen in the meantime. In both cases, the value of the derivative can change very significantly so that it represents a substantial asset or liability by the year-end. This probably will not be apparent to the reader under present accounting standards.

In some cases derivatives and other financial instruments have been used unwisely, exposing entities (not just companies but local authorities) to potentially large losses. Under the present system of reporting, such gains and losses are often not reported as they arise but are deferred until realised. This gives rise to the abuse of 'cherry picking' (in a bad year selling instruments with an otherwise unrealised gain so as to boost reported profits).

These concerns and proposals to meet them were set out in a Discussion Paper issued in July 1996. That Paper proposed that a standard on disclosure should be developed as fast as possible, that being a relatively uncontentious area. The result was FRS 13 *Derivatives and other financial instruments*.

That left the more difficult question of how financial instruments should be measured (i.e. cost or fair value) and whether hedge accounting should be used. The 1996 Discussion Paper proposed that the best approach would be for all financial instruments – both derivatives and non-derivatives and both assets and liabilities – to be measured at fair value. But that would represent a significant change from present practices. Nevertheless, the same conclusion has been reached by other standard-setters including the FASB and IASC. Over 90% of respondents to the Discussion Paper supported some form of hedge accounting, despite the conceptual difficulties and opportunities for abuse that this presents. The ASB has therefore focused its efforts on developing a method of hedge accounting and criteria for its use that it believes will give the best information to the user of the accounts and will avoid the worst abuses. It recognises that the chance of successfully implementing an effective standard in this controversial area will be greatly improved if it can move in tandem with other major standard-setters. So, in November 1997 the ASB joined an international group of other national standard-setters and IASC, with the aim of developing a common standard. This group has adopted the working premise that all financial instruments – both derivatives and non-derivatives and both assets and liabilities – should be measured at fair value and that some form of hedge accounting should be used. But that leaves the problem of:

- how to present the various gains and losses that arise in a fair value system;
- how to value loan assets for which there is no market;
- whether changes in an entity's own credit rating should affect the reported fair value of its debt liabilities;
- how to value instruments that can be settled immediately for one amount but that yield a different amount if held to maturity; and
- the detailed working of hedge accounting.

An Exposure Draft is planned early in 2000. Meanwhile, there are other cooks in the kitchen:

- The IASC has developed an 'interim' standard on the recognition and measurement of financial instruments designed to fill the gap until the international group concludes its work. The ASB has no plans to adopt this interim standard (or to devise its own variant of it) before the outcome of the work of the international group is clear.
- The European Commission has begun the process of revising the Fourth Directive. Its aim is to allow more financial instruments to be measured at fair value, thus enabling the international proposals outlined above to be implemented within the EU.

Leasing

The ASB and other standard-setters regard present leasing standards as deficient because they omit material assets and liabilities arising from operating lease contracts. Furthermore, the 'all or nothing' approach of SSAP 21 to capitalisation of leased assets does not, the ASB believes, adequately reflect modern complex transactions.

A report *Accounting for leases: A new approach – recognition by lessees of assets and liabilities arising under lease contracts*, was prepared by the G4+1 and published in 1996. The suggestion was that new standards should be developed removing the distinction between finance leases and operating leases. All material rights and obligations arising under lease contracts would then be capitalised.

The ASB hopes to publish a Discussion Paper in the third quarter of 1999.

Pensions

SSAP 24 *Accounting for pension costs* is criticised for (i) allowing too many options and (ii) inadequate disclosure. The ASB issued a Discussion Paper *Pension Costs in the Employer's Financial Statements* in April 1995 which examined the major issues involved in accounting for pension costs. It sought views on two approaches to pension cost accounting: (i) an actuarial approach that retains the basic principles of SSAP 24 and (ii) a market value approach. The responses to that Paper expressed strong support for an actuarial approach.

However, in the meantime, IASC had issued an Exposure Draft of a revision to its standard on pension cost accounting which proposed a market value approach. IASC then proceeded with this approach, resulting in IAS 19 (revised), which was issued in February 1998. The ASB considered it necessary to await the outcome of IASC's deliberations on this matter before proceeding with development of a UK standard.

In July 1998, the ASB issued a second Discussion Paper *Aspects of Accounting for Pension Costs* which set out its reaction to IAS 19 (revised) and sought views on four specific issues:

- the use of market values;
- the discount rate;
- the treatment of actuarial gains and losses; and
- the treatment of past service costs.

The ASB is considering the responses and intends to publish a FRED later in 1999.

Taxation

The key UK requirements on tax are both found in Standards of the old ASC: SSAP 8 (dealing mainly with corporation tax and, in particular, ACT) and SSAP 15 (dealing with deferred tax).

For 10 years the ASB has intended 'to review SSAP 15 as soon as was feasible'. Quite right too: since the SSAP was introduced in 1978, there have been substantial changes both in the tax system and in general economic conditions. Furthermore, SSAP 15 has been widely criticised:

- it is inconsistent with international practice and other UK standards;
- it takes account of future transactions; and
- it is subjective.

SSAP 15 was amended in May 1985 and December 1992. But the criticisms are so wide-ranging that the ASB does not believe that SSAP 15 is capable of further amendment. It will be replaced in due course by a new standard.

As a first stage, the ASB in March 1995 issued a Discussion Paper *Accounting for tax*. That Paper looked at the whole question of accounting for tax from first principles; including:

(a) the circumstances in which deferred tax arises;
(b) the different views people have of deferred tax; and
(c) the alternative methods that have been proposed of accounting for deferred tax.

The ASB's main initial proposals as laid out in the Discussion Paper were:

(a) SSAP 15 should be withdrawn and replaced with a new FRS requiring that tax should be accounted for using the full provision method. The ASB has not yet reached a consensus as to whether tax effects should be recognised in respect of fair value adjustments in acquisition accounting or revaluations.
(b) In principle, deferred tax should be discounted. Any future FRS will certainly either require or prohibit discounting, not simply permit it.
(c) Disclosures relating to tax should aim to give the reader more insight into the reporting entity's tax affairs than is the case at present. In particular, there should be a reconciliation between the actual and expected tax charge.

Since the Discussion Paper was published, IASC has developed a revision to its standard on tax, IAS 12. IAS 12 (revised) was published in October 1996.

A FRED on deferred tax is planned during the second quarter of 1999.

A separate project is considering the revision of SSAP 8 *The treatment of taxation under the imputation system in the accounts of companies* in the light of recent changes in the UK system. Again, the ASB intends to publish an Exposure Draft in the second quarter of 1999.

Reporting financial performance

FRS 3 *Reporting financial performance* is the current UK standard. But this is another area where international discussion is afoot.

In January 1998 the G4+1 published a special report *Reporting financial performance: current developments and future directions*. This may well lead to the revision of FRS 3 in the UK.

FRS 3, it may be recalled, introduced a new primary statement of financial performance, the Statement of total recognised gains and losses (STRGL). The idea was not new: the FRS 3 approach was modelled on a US FASB draft standard of ten years earlier. But other countries have since moved in a similar direction.

At present the G4+1 favours the introduction of a single performance statement split into three sections:

- Operating/trading activities;
- Financing/treasury activities;
- Other gains and losses.

But the debate is continuing on how items should be allocated between these categories.

A Discussion Paper is expected, probably during the second quarter of 1999, proposing a revision of FRS 3.

Year-end financial reporting structure

Growing concern is expressed that the financial statements as a whole are increasingly lengthy and complex. Not only are they costly and time-consuming to produce but much of the information is not read or understood by many shareholders. The ASB has established a working party consisting of representatives from industry, the auditing profession and the investment community. It has asked the working party to explore these issues further and in particular whether there is greater scope to build on and further develop the statutory summary financial statements and preliminary announcements. The aim is a Discussion Paper for the ASB's consideration to be developed into a non-mandatory statement of best practice.

Problem 33.1

1. What (and who) influences ASB (a) in planning its work programme; and (b) in its standards-setting operations?
2. Is it appropriate for UK standard-setters continually to look over their shoulder at what other standard-setters are doing elsewhere in the world?

APPENDICES

APPENDIX 1 - CURRENT FINANCIAL REPORTING STANDARDS AND EXPOSURE DRAFTS

The following Standards, UITF Abstracts and Exposure Drafts were current in April 1999:

Date of Issue

Standards

ASB	Foreword to accounting standards	Jun 1993
FRS 1	Cash flow statements (Revised Oct 1996)	Sep 1991
FRS 2	Accounting for subsidiary undertakings	Jul 1992
FRS 3	Reporting financial performance (Amended Jun 1993 regarding insurance companies)	Oct 1992
FRS 4	Capital instruments	Dec 1993
FRS 5	Reporting the substance of transactions (Amended re insurance broking transactions Dec 1994 and regarding private finance initiative and similar contracts Sep 1998)	Apr 1994
FRS 6	Acquisitions and mergers (amended Nov 1997 and Dec 1998)	Sep 1994
FRS 7	Fair values in acquisition accounting	Sep 1994
FRS 8	Related party disclosures	Oct 1995
FRS 9	Associates and joint ventures	Nov 1997
FRS 10	Goodwill and intangible assets	Dec 1997
FRS 11	Impairment of fixed assets and goodwill	Jul 1998
FRS 12	Provisions, contingent liabilities and contingent assets	Sep 1998
FRS 13	Derivatives and other financial instruments	Sep 1998
FRS 14	Earnings per share	Oct 1998
FRS 15	Tangible fixed assets	Feb 1999
FRSSE	Financial reporting standard for smaller entities (amended Jul 1998)	Nov 1997

Urgent Issues Task Force (UITF)

ASB *Abstract No.:*	Foreword to UITF Abstracts	Feb 1994
4	Presentation of long-term debtors in current assets	Jul 1992
5	Transfers from current assets to fixed assets	Jul 1992
6	Accounting for post-retirement benefits other than pensions	Nov 1992
7	True and fair view override disclosures	Dec 1992
9	Accounting for operations in hyper-inflationary economies	Jun 1993
10	Disclosure of directors' share options	Sep 1994
11	Capital instruments: issuer call options	Sep 1994
12	Lessee accounting for reverse premiums and similar incentives	Dec 1994
13	Accounting for ESOP trusts	Jun 1995
14	Disclosure of changes in accounting policy	Nov 1995
15	Disclosure of substantial acquisitions (revised Feb 1999)	Jan 1996
16	Income and expenses subject to non-standard rates of tax	Feb 1997
17	Employee share schemes	May 1997
18	Pension costs following the 1997 tax changes in respect of dividend income	May 1997
19	Tax on gains and losses that hedge an investment in a foreign enterprise	Feb 1998
20	Year 2000 issues: accounting and disclosures	Mar 1998
21	Accounting issues arising from the proposed introduction of the euro	Mar 1998
22	Accounting for acquisition of a Lloyd's business	Jun 1998

Exposure Drafts

None

Discussion Papers

The role of valuation in financial reporting	Mar 1993
Accounting for tax	Mar 1995
Pension costs in the employer's financial statements	Jun 1995
Provisions	Nov 1995
Impairment of tangible fixed assets	Apr 1996
Derivatives and other financial instruments	Jul 1996
Measurement of tangible fixed assets	Oct 1996
Aspects of accounting for pension costs	Jul 1998
Business combinations	Dec 1998

Non-mandatory statement

Preliminary announcements	Jul 1998

ASB Statement of Principles

Statement of principles for financial reporting (Exposure Draft) (Revised Mar 1999)	Nov 1995
Progress Paper Statement of principles for financial reporting – the way ahead	Jul 1996

Other ASB Statements

Operating and financial review	Jul 1993
Accounting for goodwill	Dec 1993

Accounting Standards Committee

The following standards issued by the ASC continue in force:

SSAP 2	Disclosure of accounting policies	Nov 1971
SSAP 4	Accounting for government grants (Revised July 1990)	Apr 1974
SSAP 5	Accounting for value added tax	Apr 1974
SSAP 8	The treatment of taxation under the imputation system in the accounts of companies (Appendix 3 added Dec 1977)	Aug 1974
SSAP 9	Stocks and long-term contracts (Part 6 added Aug 1980, revised Sept 1988)	May 1975
SSAP 12	Accounting for depreciation (amended Nov 1981 and revised Jan 1987)	Dec 1977
SSAP 13	Accounting for research and development (Revised Jan 1989)	Dec 1977
SSAP 15	Accounting for deferred tax (Revised May 1985, amended Dec 1992)	Oct 1978
SSAP 17	Accounting for post balance sheet events	Aug 1980
SSAP 19	Accounting for investment properties (Amended Jul 1994)	Nov 1981
SSAP 20	Foreign currency translation	Apr 1983
SSAP 21	Accounting for leases and hire purchase contracts (amended Feb 1997)	Aug 1984
SSAP 24	Accounting for pension costs	May 1988
SSAP 25	Segmental reporting	Jun 1990

APPENDIX 2 - PRESENT VALUE

£1 received in a year's time is worth less than £1 received today, because £1 available today could be invested to earn interest for the next 12 months. If £1 now could be invested at a rate of interest i (expressed as a decimal), it would be worth $£(1 + i)$ in a year's time. If the $£(1 + i)$ at the end of the year was left invested, it would be worth:

$£(1 + i) \times (1 + i) = £(1 + i)^2$ at the end of the second year, and $£(1 + i)^3$ at the end of the third year, and so on; in other words, it would earn compound interest at the rate of i per annum.

Present value is like compound interest in reverse: the value of £1 received in a year's time is worth $£1 \div (1 + i)$ now, and £1 in two years' time is worth $£1 \div (1 + i)^2$ now, and so on. For example, if i (known as the discount rate) is 10% p.a., then the present value of £1 received in a year's time is $£1 \div (1 \div 0.10) = £0.9091$. Similarly the present value of receiving £1 in two years' time is:

$£1 \div (1 + 0.10)^2 = £0.8264$

and £1 in three years' time is:

$£1 \div (1.10)^3 = £0.7513$,

and £1 in n years' time is $£1 \div (1.10)^n$.

Tables *of present values* are available for various rates of interest and periods of years. The table below is a very simplified and abbreviated version.

Present value of 1 in n years' time

n	1%	2%	3%	4%	5%	10%	15%
1	0.990	0.980	0.971	0.962	0.952	0.909	0.870
2	0.980	0.961	0.943	0.925	0.907	0.826	0.756
3	0.971	0.942	0.915	0.889	0.864	0.751	0.658
4	0.961	0.924	0.889	0.855	0.822	0.683	0.572
5	0.951	0.906	0.863	0.822	0.784	0.621	0.497
10	0.905	0.820	0.744	0.676	0.614	0.386	0.247
20	0.820	0.673	0.554	0.456	0.377	0.149	0.061

Present value tables refer to the value of 1, rather than the value of £1, because they can be used for any currency: the 1 may be $1, €1, DM1, 1 peseta or 1 of any other currency you care to name.

The present value concept (which is also the basis of discounted cash flow, DCF) can be applied to any streams of future income and to repayments of capital. For example, £20 nominal of 5% loan stock redeemable in three years would be worth the interest payments of £1 at the end of each year plus the £20 in three years' time, all discounted at 10% per annum, to give a present value of:

$$\frac{£1}{(1.1)^1} + \frac{£1}{(1.1)^2} + \frac{£1}{(1.1)^3} + \frac{£20}{(1.1)^7}$$

$= £(0.909 + 0.826 + 0.751 + 15.026) = £17.512$

The calculation of the present value of a steady stream of income can be assisted by the use of annuity tables, an annuity of 1 for n years simply being an annual payment of 1 for n years; such a table is set out below.

In our previous example, the present value of £1 per annum for three years, discounted at 10%, could have been obtained from the annuity table: three years at 10% = 2.487.

In practice, interest on fixed-interest securities is usually paid half-yearly in arrears (i.e. at the end of each half-year), and so the half-yearly discount rate, which is the square root $(1 + i)$, is used to discount each half-yearly interest payment. For example, £100 of 5% Loan Stock with three years to redemption, discounted at 10% per annum, would have a present value of:

$$\frac{250}{(\sqrt{1.10})} + \frac{250}{(\sqrt{1.10})^2} + ... + \frac{250}{(\sqrt{1.10})^6} + \frac{10}{(1.10)^3}$$

$= 2.3837 + 2.2728 + ... + 1.8784 + 75.1315 = £87.8734$.

Annuity table: present value of an annuity of 1 for n years

Rate of interest (the discount rate)

n	1%	2%	3%	4%	5%	10%	15%
1	0.990	0.980	0.971	0.962	0.952	0.909	0.870
2	1.970	1.942	1.913	1.886	1.860	1.736	1.626
3	2.941	2.884	2.829	2.775	2.723	2.487	2.283
4	3.902	3.808	3.717	3.630	3.546	3.170	2.855
5	4.853	4.713	4.580	4.452	4.329	3.791	3.352
10	9.471	8.983	8.530	8.111	7.722	6.145	5.019
15	13.865	12.849	11.938	11.118	10.380	7.606	5.847

APPENDIX 3 - RETAIL PRICE INDICES SINCE 1950

The Retail Price Index (RPI) as published in the Government Statistical Service's *Monthly Digest of Statistics.*

Space has been left for the reader to insert RPIs month by month in the future as they are announced in the press.

Accountancy, the monthly journal of the Institute of Chartered Accountants in England and Wales, publishes each year a long-range table, currently from 1915 (the latest in March 1999 issue) and the *Investors Chronicle* includes figures for the last three months under Economic Indicators.

Year	Jan	Feb	Mar	Apr	May	Jun	Jul	Aug	Sep	Oct	Nov	Dec	Average for year
1950	8.3	8.3	8.3	8.3	8.4	8.3	8.3	8.3	8.3	8.4	8.5	8.5	8.4
1955	10.7	10.7	10.7	10.8	10.7	11.0	11.0	10.9	11.0	11.1	11.3	11.3	10.9
1960	12.4	12.4	12.3	12.4	12.4	12.5	12.5	12.4	12.4	12.5	12.6	12.6	12.5
1965	14.5	14.5	14.5	14.8	14.9	14.9	14.9	14.9	14.9	14.9	15.0	15.1	14.8
1970	17.9	18.0	18.1	18.4	18.4	18.5	18.6	18.6	18.7	18.9	19.0	19.2	18.5
1975	30.4	30.9	31.5	32.7	34.1	34.8	35.1	35.3	35.6	36.1	36.6	37.0	34.2
1976	37.5	38.0	38.2	38.9	39.3	39.5	39.6	40.2	40.7	41.4	42.0	42.6	39.8
1977	43.7	44.1	44.6	45.7	46.1	46.5	46.6	46.8	47.1	47.3	47.5	47.8	46.1
1978	48.0	48.3	48.6	49.3	49.6	50.0	50.2	50.5	50.7	51.0	51.3	51.8	50.0
1979	52.5	53.0	53.4	54.3	54.7	55.7	58.1	58.5	59.1	59.7	60.3	60.7	56.7
1980	62.2	63.1	63.9	66.1	66.7	67.4	67.9	68.1	68.5	68.9	69.5	69.9	66.8
1981	70.3	70.9	72.0	74.1	74.6	75.0	75.3	75.9	76.3	77.0	77.8	78.3	74.8
1982	78.7	78.8	79.4	81.0	81.6	81.9	81.9	81.9	81.9	82.3	82.7	82.5	81.2
1983	82.6	83.0	83.1	84.3	84.6	84.8	85.3	85.7	86.1	86.4	86.7	86.9	84.9
1984	86.8	87.2	87.5	88.6	89.0	89.2	89.1	89.9	90.1	90.7	91.0	90.9	89.2
1985	91.2	91.9	92.8	94.8	95.2	95.4	95.2	95.5	95.5	95.6	95.9	96.1	94.6
1986	96.2	96.6	96.7	97.6	97.9	97.8	97.5	97.9	98.3	98.5	99.3	99.6	97.8
1987	100.0	100.4	100.6	101.8	101.9	101.9	101.8	102.1	102.4	102.9	103.4	103.3	101.9
1988	103.3	103.7	104.1	105.8	106.2	106.6	106.7	107.9	108.4	109.5	110.0	110.3	106.9
1989	111.0	111.8	112.3	114.3	115.0	115.4	115.5	115.8	116.6	117.5	118.5	118.8	115.2
1990	119.5	120.2	121.4	125.1	126.2	126.7	126.8	128.2	129.3	130.3	130.0	129.9	126.1
1991	130.2	130.9	131.4	133.1	133.5	134.1	133.8	134.1	134.6	135.1	135.6	135.7	133.5
1992	135.6	136.3	136.7	138.8	139.3	139.3	138.8	138.9	139.4	139.9	139.7	139.2	138.5
1993	137.9	138.8	139.3	140.6	141.1	141.0	140.7	141.3	141.9	141.8	141.6	141.9	140.7
1994	141.3	142.1	142.5	144.2	144.7	144.7	144.0	144.7	145.0	145.2	145.3	146.0	144.1
1995	146.0	146.9	147.5	149.0	149.6	149.8	149.1	149.9	150.6	149.8	149.8	150.7	149.1
1996	150.2	150.9	151.5	152.6	152.9	153.0	152.4	153.1	153.8	153.8	153.9	154l4	152.7
1997	154.4	155.0	155.4	156.3	156.9	157.5	157.5	158.5	159.3	159.5	159.6	160.0	157.5
1998	159.5	160.3	160.8	162.6	163.5	163.4	163.0	163.7	164.4	164.5	164.4	164.4	162.9
1999	163.4	163.7	164.1										
2000													
2001													
2002													

APPENDIX 4 - YEAR ON YEAR CHANGE IN RPI

Month by month 1990 onwards

Percentage increase on a year earlier

	1990	1991	1992	1993	1994	1995	1996	1997	1998	1999	2000	2001	2002
Jan	7.7	9.0	4.1	1.7	2.5	3.3	2.9	2.8	3.3	2.4			
Feb	7.5	8.9	4.1	1.8	2.4	3.4	2.7	2.7	3.4	2.1			
Mar	8.1	8.2	4.0	1.9	2.3	3.5	2.7	2.6	3.5	2.1			
Apr	9.4	6.4	4.3	1.3	2.6	3.3	2.4	2.4	4.0				
May	9.7	5.8	4.3	1.3	2.6	3.4	2.2	2.6	4.2				
Jun	9.8	5.8	3.9	1.2	2.6	3.5	2.1	2.9	3.7				
Jul	9.8	5.5	3.7	1.4	2.3	3.5	2.2	3.3	3.5				
Aug	10.6	4.7	3.6	1.7	2.4	3.6	2.1	3.5	3.3				
Sep	10.9	4.1	3.6	1.8	2.2	3.9	2.1	3.6	3.2				
Oct	10.9	3.7	3.6	1.4	2.4	3.2	2.7	3.7	3.1				
Nov	9.7	4.3	3.0	1.4	2.6	3.1	2.7	3.8	3.0				
Dec	9.3	4.5	2.6	1.9	2.9	3.2	2.5	3.6	2.8				

Annually from 1976

Year	Annual average	% increase on previous year
1976	39.8	16.4
1977	46.1	15.8
1978	50.0	8.5
1979	56.7	13.4
1980	66.8	17.8
1981	74.8	12.0
1982	81.2	8.6
1983	84.9	4.6
1984	89.2	5.1
1985	94.6	6.1
1986	97.8	3.4
1987	101.9	4.2
1988	106.9	4.9
1989	115.2	7.8
1990	126.1	9.5
1991	133.5	5.9
1992	138.5	3.7
1993	140.7	1.6
1994	144.1	2.4
1995	149.1	3.5
1996	152.7	2.4
1997	157.5	3.1
1998	162.9	3.4
1999		
2000		
2001		
2002		

APPENDIX 5 - SOLUTIONS TO PROBLEMS IN THE TEXT

Solution 1.1 Elcho (Mossdale).

Three reasons why the bank might reject Farnesbarn's request:

1. An extra £60,000 is not enough.

The bank manager is likely to say to himself: 'They are asking for £60,000. Let us see how much they really need.'

	£	£
A. New machine		60,000
B. Current overdraft limit	50,000	
Overdraft at balance sheet date	48,150	
This must bring difficulties; to be safe, they really need another, say,		10,000
C. Working capital: Additional raw material stock, say,	5,000	
Finished goods, say	12,000	
Debtors, say 2 months	100,000	
	127,000	
Less: Additional creditors, say,	40,000	
That looks like		87,000
A total of		£157,000

These figures certainly won't be accurate, but one thing one can say for certain is that: £60,000 is not enough.

Trawling for information (and watching carefully his customer's reaction), the bank manager might well ask:

- How is the present limit working?
- What are delivery arrangements … are you going to be holding much stock for them?
- What about payment terms? How long credit have they asked for?

On the other hand, he might simply say to himself: 'Either they haven't done their homework; or they know full well that they need more and they plan to break the news as a nasty shock later.'

Neither scenario is likely to commend the proposition to him.

2. Farnesbarn's profit estimate seems to be based on simplistic logic:

'On turnover of £600,000 per annum we make £15,785 after tax', he seems to suggest. 'If we double sales we should make twice that.'

But that ignores:

(i) the price to be paid by JQB (which is likely to be less (possibly much less) than that paid by smaller customers for the same items). If the price paid is substantially less than other people pay, sales *volume* (hence the total material and labour costs) is going to be more than double with a doubling of turnover;

(ii) the cost structure of the business, i.e the variability of cost (see Chapter 10); Hence:

(iii) the profit margin (or profit) likely to be achieved (almost certainly different from that on existing business);

(iv) the additional interest which would be payable at 15%.

Either (i) Farnesbarn has not got the necessary information; or (ii) he does not see its significance; or (iii) both.

And that certainly will not have impressed the bank.

3. JQB:

- Undue dependence on one customer is risky. There is no sign that Farnesbarn recognises this.
- Has Farnesbarn investigated JQB?
  He does not say so; but he would earn a black mark if he had not.
- The bank will almost certainly know more (or be in a position to find out more) about JQB's credit standing than Farnesbarn. They may also know things about JQB's trading methods which Farnesbarn may not, e.g. that after the first couple of years the contract price is likely to be driven down so hard that the business becomes unprofitable.
- Can JQB break the contract for any reason, e.g. late delivery, poor workmanship?
  i.e. what are the risks involved? Is Farnesbarn aware of them?

Other possible reasons:

- **The bank manager may himself be under pressure.**
  He may be limited in what he can lend in certain business areas; and he will have a limit to his discretion beyond which he must seek head office approval.

- **The history of Elcho's past dealings** with the bank may not make the proposal one which he should be seen to endorse, e.g. the overdraft was nearly at limit at balance sheet date. Is there a history of bounced cheques; or requests to bend the limit to pay wages etc?

- **Elcho's assets** do not provide very convincing security. In any case, lending to the company will be based less on its assets than on its forecast future trading. And Farnesbarn does not appear to have done his homework. His forecast is therefore unlikely to be accurate, and that would worry any banker.

- **What happens at the end of two years?**
  How likely is it that the contract will continue at a similar level of profitability?
  If not, can the output from the new plant and machinery be sold elsewhere at a profit?
  Or is it special purpose plant? Might it be necessary to sell it (at well below book value?), to write it down sharply or even write it off all together?

Solution 2.1

The fundamental accounting concepts are those broad basic assumptions which underlie the periodic financial accounts of business enterprises. Under SSAP 2 the four following fundamental concepts (the relative importance of which varies according to the circumstances of the particular case) are seen as having general acceptability:

(a) the '*going concern*' concept: the enterprise will continue in operational existence for the foreseeable future. This means in particular that the profit and loss account and balance sheet assume no intention or necessity to liquidate or curtail significantly the scale of operation;

(b) the '*accruals*' concept: revenue and costs are accrued (that is, recognised as they are earned or incurred, not as money is received or paid), matched with one another so far as their relationship can be established or justifiably assumed, and dealt with in the profit and loss account of the period to which they relate; provided that where the accruals concept is inconsistent with the 'prudence' concept (paragraph (d) below), the latter prevails. The accruals concept implies that the profit and loss account reflects changes in the amount of net assets that arise out of the transactions of the relevant period (other than distributions or subscriptions of capital and unrealised surpluses arising on revaluation of fixed assets). Revenue and profits dealt with in the profit and loss account are matched with associated costs and expenses by including in the same account the costs incurred in earning them (so far as these are material and identifiable);

(c) the '*consistency*' concept: there is consistency of accounting treatment of like items within each accounting period and from one period to the next;

(d) the concept of '*prudence*': revenue and profits are not anticipated, but are recognised by inclusion in the profit and loss account only when realised in the form either of cash or of other assets, the ultimate cash realisation of which can be assessed with reasonable certainty; provision is made for all known liabilities.

To look at each in turn:

(a) If an enterprise may not continue in operational existence for the foreseeable future, the profit and loss account and balance sheet must assume the likelihood, or intention, that the business will be placed in liquidation or its scale of operation significantly reduced. This will have a major effect on the values placed on stocks and fixed assets, in particular plant and machinery, fixtures and fittings, trade marks and brands. Debtors may prove difficult to collect and it is likely to be difficult to operate efficiently as the business is closing,

(b) It would clearly be wrong for a year's accounts to include, say, only 11 months' salaries; or 15 months' rent, because that was what was paid in the year.

(c) For a business paying rent of £12,000 a month to charge it entirely against administration costs in the past and in January to July of the current year, but (without any change) split it £5,000 to administration costs and £7,000 as selling and distribution for the remainder of the year would clearly distort things.

(d) Revenue and profits clearly ought not to be recognised by inclusion in the profit and loss account until they are realised in the form either of cash or of other assets (like debtors), the ultimate cash realisation of which can be assessed with reasonable certainty; on the other hand if provision is not made for all known liabilities the accounts present an unfairly rosy picture.

Solution 3.1

1. One can tell whether a company is (a) a public or (b) a private limited company from its name. A company whose name ends 'plc' or 'PLC' or Public Limited Company is a public company; one whose name ends with 'Ltd' or 'Limited' is a private company.

   One cannot tell from its name alone whether a company is limited by shares or limited by guarantee, it is necessary to study the company's memorandum of association.

   And it is quite difficult to tell whether a business with a name like 'Home Wreckers' is a business name of an individual or a partnership or an unlimited company. If it is an unlimited company it will be possible to inspect its file at Companies House and study its memorandum. Such companies are quite rare.

2. If XY plc is a close company and is listed on The Stock Exchange, and the directors are aware the company is a close company, it must include, in its annual report, a statement to that effect. While at one time the tax consequences of being a close company were important, today they have largely lost their significance.

   But a close company is one which is under the control of five or fewer persons together with their associates or is under the control of its directors, and in the case of a listed company is one where less than 35% of the voting power is unconditionally and beneficially held by the public. Directors may be tempted to treat it as their personal property, their company, and have less regard than might be proper (or seem fair) to the outside shareholders.

Solution 4.1

In a bid driven market there are market makers, who have to quote bid and offer prices during the trading day in all the shares in which they deal. They are then obliged to buy at the bid price and to sell at the offer price in the size (amount of shares) they have indicated, or any lesser amount. For less actively traded shares the size may only be a nominal amount, say 1,000 shares.

The market maker makes a profit by buying at the bid price and selling at the offer price; the difference between the two is known as the spread.

In an order driven market there are no market makers: buyers and sellers are matched at the same price.

To an investor the advantage of a quote driven market is that there should always be a market in which he can deal, although the size may be limited. In an order driven market the investor avoids the cost of the spread, but he can only buy if there are sellers, and vice versa.

Solution 5.1

Preference shares carry a fixed rate of dividend, but unlike the holders of loan capital, who can take action against a company in default of interest payments, preference shareholders have no legal redress if the board of directors decides to recommend that no preference dividends should be paid.

However, if no preference dividend is declared for an accounting period, no dividend can be declared on any other type of share for the period concerned, so the subsidiary cannot pay an ordinary dividend to its holding company.

Cases have arisen where, though the subsidiary is very profitable, the holding company says it wishes to retain those profits, and no dividends, preference or ordinary, have been paid for a number of years. In these circumstances the preference shareholders may become entitled to vote at shareholders' general meetings. But this is little comfort, unless it gives them a majority of the votes, which is unlikely.

Solution 6.1

	£	£	£	£	£	£	£	£
(a) and (c) Profits before interest	750,000	800,000	900,000	1,000,000	1,100,000	1,200,000	1,300,000	1,4000,00
Scenario (i)								
Interest at 10% on £8m	800,000	800,000	800,000	800,000	800,000	800,000	800,000	800,000
Return earned by venture capital company (%)	10.00%	10.00%	10.00%	10.00%	10.00%	10.00%	10.00%	10.00%
Profits available to management	(50,000)	0	100,000	200,000	300,000	400,000	500,000	600,000
Return earned by management (%)	-2.50%	0.00%	5.00%	10.00%	15.00%	20.00%	25.00%	30.00%
Scenario (ii)								
Interest at 9% on £6m	540,000	540,000	540,000	540,000	540,000	540,000	540,000	540,000
Profits due to equity owned by venture capital company	105,000	130,000	180,000	230,000	280,000	330,000	380,000	430,000
Total to venture capital company	645,000	670,000	720,000	770,000	820,000	870,000	920,000	970,000
Return earned by venture capital company (%)	8.06%	8.38%	9.00%	9.63%	10.25%	10.88%	11.50%	12.13%
Profits available to management	105,000	130,000	180,000	230,000	280,000	330,000	380,000	430,000
Return earned by management (%)	5.25%	6.50%	9.00%	11.50%	14.00%	16.50%	19.00%	21.50%

(b)

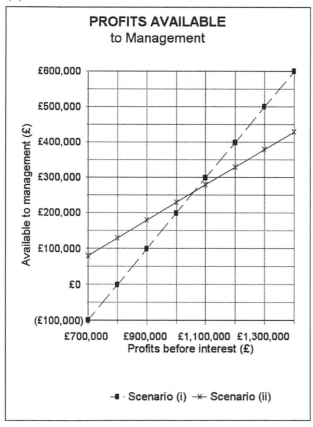

Solution 7.1

ML Laboratories appararently took a last opportunity to move *from* what was an FRS 10 basis *to* a treatment which would no longer be permitted under FRS 10. Whether that was a good idea we leave the reader to decide.

Solution 8.1

Fleetwood: Balance Sheet as at 31 December 1999

	Note	1999 £	1998 £
Fixed assets:			
...			
Motor vehicles	1	145,375	117,000

Notes:
1. Fixed assets

Motor vehicles	Cost £	Depreciation to date £	Net £
1999	227,500	82,125	145,375
1998	165,000	48,000	117,000

Solution 9.1

(i) Companies hold fixed asset investments for a variety of reasons, among them:

(a) as a consequence of acquiring control of other companies (i.e. subsidiaries) and 'running them';

(b) as a way of entering into some sort of joint operation (i.e. a joint venture or consortium);

(c) as an investment to generate income (as an investment trust does);

(d) for protection, e.g. life policies on senior employees;

(e) as a means of gaining a foothold (a prelude to a possible bid);

(f) for self-aggrandisment on the part of the directors, e.g. works of art.

(ii) It is important for the reader of accounts to have a clear idea of the reasons for any significant holding:

    (a) to understand how the holding and income from it will be treated in the accounts. As will be seen, the treatment of subsidiaries is quite different from that of associated companies;

    (b) to predict future actions on the part of the board (e.g. a bid);

    (c) to judge board behaviour (pictures, race-horses, yachts and aircraft may not be the most profitable use of funds).

Solution 10.1

(i) The items (a) land and (b) development and construction costs suggest these are the accounts of a group engaged in construction and residential property development; but there appears also to be activity in commercial, industrial and mixed development property.

(ii) The figures suggest that there was an expansion of the land bank; and that development costs in progress grew 35% either because of:

    (a) stock building to meet a perceived **improvement** in the market; or

    (b) stock was unsold because of a **deterioration** in the market for residential property.

It should be possible to identify which of these is the probable cause by studying:

- the directors' report;
- the chairman's statement;
- any financial review;
- notes to the accounts, in particular any analysis of turnover and profit;
- the cash flow statement.

The accounts are, in fact, those of TAYLOR WOODROW for 1995 (redated). Their financial review explained:

'The UK construction business suffered a cash outflow due to the lower turnover and the cash costs of restructuring the operations in the year. There was also an outflow due to the build up of the landbank and residential work in progress around the world, particularly in the UK and California. ...'

(iii) The issue of transfers from current assets to fixed assets was considered by the UITF which, in July 1992, issued Abstract 5, *Transfers from current assets to fixed assets.*

The UITF was concerned, in the then current economic climate, that 'companies might avoid charging the profit and loss account with

write-downs to net realisable value arising on unsold trading assets. This could be done by transferring the assets from current assets to fixed assets at above net realisable value, as a result of which any later write down might be debited to revaluation reserve.'

The UITF agreed that in respect of such transfers, the current asset accounting rules should be applied up to the effective date of transfer (the date of management's change of intent). The transfer should then be made at the lower of cost and net realisable value. Thus the land that cost £56m should be transferred to fixed assets at £27.6m, and the shortfall charged to the profit and loss account.

Solution 11.1

	1998	1997
	£m	£m
Turnover	293.1	270.8
Trade debtors	31.3	31.7
(i) Collection period (months)	1.28	1.40
(ii) Trade debtors/Sales	10.68%	11.71%

These two ratios are closely related. Indeed (i) is 12/100ths of (ii), so they inevitably move in the same way. Some people may find one easier to understand than the other. It is correct to say that 'At the balance sheet date in 1998, debtors equalled 1.28 months average sales' but not that 'Debtors consisted of the last 1.28 months' sales'. and not that 'customers take 1.28 months to pay'.

Whichever yardstick one takes, debt collection appears to have improved by roughly 10%.

In the case of THE BODY SHOP, the figures are somewhat more difficult to interpret than is usually the case because the business is partly a normal retail operation and partly a franchise one; and trade debtors are mostly, if not entirely, franchisees whereas turnover is the sum of sales to franchisees and the sales from own shops. The figures provided do not show whether there was a change in the make-up of turnover, i.e. whether there were more sales via franchisees, the same, or less.

Solution 12.1

(a) Possible reasons why companies hold current asset investments include:

    (i) to set aside (and earn interest on) money later required to pay taxation;

    (ii) to save towards a planned expansion, refurbishment, or reorganisation;

    (iii) to cover contingencies (e.g. a short-fall in receipts);

    (iv) to assure potential joint venture partners that the company, while not in the same league in size terms as they are, can fund its share of future operations (found for example in oil exploration and development);

(v) as a more general store of value;

(vi) to earn income (there being no better use of funds in the short term);

(vii) where required under the terms of a contract, or by statute, as with insurance funds;

(viii) where the group acts as its own insurer (because cover is impossible to obtain or prohibitively expensive, e.g. certain types of disaster cover), as large sums could be needed urgently.

(b) It is important for the reader of accounts to have a clear idea of the reasons for any significant holding of current asset investments because:

- Money which is tied up (under, say, (vii) or (viii) above) is not available to support general operations.
- Money set aside for a purpose (e.g. taxation) is earmarked.
- If money currently earning income is used for non-income generating activities, income will fall.
- If large sums of money are invested:

  (a) has management clear plans as to their use? or

  (b) has the business become a 'cash cow', a generator of cash which it cannot itself usefully employ?

  (c) is management simply sitting on money that it does not know what to do with (black mark!)?

Solution 13.1

1.

	£000
Reduction in lease finance	(372)
Finance leases disposed off	(1,454)
New finance leases	465
Net change (reduction)	(1,361)

2. The clue is there: by disposing of subsidiaries. See pages 125 and 217 for confirmation.

3. Bills of exchange discounted per 1998

balance sheet	2,794
less increase during 1998	(1,193)
Bills of exchange discounted which would have appeared in the 1997 balance sheet	1,601
less increase during 1997	(613)
Bills of exchange discounted which would have appeared in the 1996 balance sheet	988

Solution 14.1

(a) The initial outlay is:

(250 × 100 × £10).

(b) That is also the maximum amount risked.

(c) If the index rises to 4,155, the fund manager can sell the option back to the market realising a profit of £137,500 (55 × 250 × £10). With over a month left to expiry there would also be some time value left, say 25 index points. In this case the manager would sell the options back to the market for 180 index points, an overall profit of:

£200,000 (80 × 250 × £10).

Solution 15.1

(a)

(i) An accrual is a known liability the amount of which has been calculated; whereas a provision is an amount provided for any liability or loss which is either likely to be incurred, or certain to be incurred but uncertain as to amount or as to the date on which it will arise.

(ii) Income in advance represents income received which at the date of the balance sheet had not been earned; whereas a deposit either represents money paid by a customer/client as an earnest (or a sign) of good faith; or in the case of a financial institution, customers' money which earns interest for them.

(iii) A commitment is a financial obligation which a company has already contracted or which the directors have approved but which does not yet constitute a contractual obligation. A contingent liability is one which may or may not arise.

(b) Examples:

(i) Of an accrual: rent of £24,000 per annum payable quarterly in arrear on 31 March, 30 June etc. Company makes up its accounts to 30 April 1999, having paid rent up to 31 March. Rent of £2,000 (i.e. one month) will be accrued.

(ii) Of a provision: A major customer goes into liquidation owing £54,000. It is estimated that around 20p in the £ will be received. Provision is therefore made for a bad debt of £43,200.

(iii) Of income in advance: a magazine publisher receives prepayment in respect of annual subscriptions to journals. At the end of the year £213,000 represents journals to be supplied in future years.

(c) In seeking to estimate the effect on a company's future cash flows and its viability in the medium term:

  (i) Accruals are rarely of much significance. As to provisions, their background and adequacy should be considered, as well as their size, what calls they will bring on the company and when.

  (ii) There is a tendency for companies hard-pressed for cash to spend what is in effect other people's money. In an ideal world deposits would be banked separately in a 'client/customer account', and never used for purposes of the company until such times as they were earned. This is not an ideal world. Solicitors and travel agents may work like that; other businesses tend not to. For example, a magazine publisher selling discounted three year subscriptions would be in trouble if he spent receipts in the year they were received; he would then be relying on future receipts to provide copies to people who had already paid for them, in much the same way governments were able, in the early years of schemes, to treat pensions on a pay as you go basis; but once a large pensioner population built up, the costs escalated and there were no funds to fall back on.

  (iii) Capital commitments require financing. The wise finance director ensures that this is planned and negotiated in advance. Some even explain what has been done in the financial review.

Solution 16.1
QUEENS BOROUGH

(a) Year-on-year change overall and for each segment

	Growth in turnover including acquisitions	Growth in profit before taxation including acquisitions	Growth in turnover excluding acquisitions	Growth in profit before taxation excluding acquisitions	Growth in net assets 1998/1997
Class of business					
Day visitor attractions – UK	7.27	-0.74	7.27	-0.74	8.17
Caravan parks – UK	28.09	38.33	23.42	27.44	7.71
Caravan parks – France	120.45	-62.38	10.23	-109.90	224.57
Hotel – UK	4.80	15.80	4.80	15.80	0.31
Restaurants – UK					Infinite
Overall	20.58	15.98	15.59	13.46	16.14

(b) Vertical analysis of turnover, profit before tax and net assets in 1997 and 1998.

	Including acquisitions			Excluding acquisitions			Net assets 1998	Net assets 1997
	Turnover	*Turnover*	*Profit before tax*	*Profit before tax*	*Turnover*	*Profit before tax*		
	1998	1997	1998	1997	1998	1998		
Class of business								
Day visitor attractions – UK	22.07	24.81	26.79	31.30	23.02	27.39	21.42	23.00
Caravan parks – UK	57.42	54.05	52.15	43.73	57.72	49.11	48.37	52.15
Caravan parks – France	3.71	2.03	0.58	1.80	1.94	-0.16	10.58	3.79
Hotel – UK	16.61	19.11	23.14	23.18	17.32	23.66	18.19	21.06
Restaurants – UK	0.19		-2.67				1.44	
	100.00	100.00	100.00	100.00	100.00	100.00	100.00	100.00

(c) Brief summary describing the company's activities, and the changes which occurred in 1998.

QUEENSBOROUGH is a relatively small company in the leisure and hotels sector. At the time of writing there were.61 listed companies in the sector, and it was 47th in terms of market capitalisation. That being the case, market for its shares is narrow and its share price behaves erratically, halving or doubling in the course of a day or so.

Prior to 1998 its business consisted of caravan parks in the UK and to a much lesser extent in France; day visitor attractions in the UK, and a hotel in the UK. During 1998 the company made a least two acquisitions:

- some UK restaurants which have still to prove profitable and
- more caravan parks in both the UK and France (the scale of the French operations trebled in 1998).

In other words it is a company expanding in an area in which it has experience.

Although net assets only grew 16% overall, the big expansion was in caravan parks – France (225%) and restaurants – UK which did not exist before.

In considering growth in turnover and growth in profit before tax one can either include or exclude the effect of the acquisitions. Including them, turnover increased by about 21%, and profit before tax a little less (16%). Excluding them, turnover would have increased 16% and the profit before tax, 13%.

More than half the turnover in each year came from caravan parks – UK and that is where over 50% of the profits before tax are earned. Almost 11% of the assets are tied up in caravan parks – France, but less than 4% of the turnover came from there; but we have to ask how much of the holiday season in France was post-acquisition?

(d) Is ROCE a valid indicator of its progress?

On the basis that the profit after tax in 1998 was £3.595m (1997 £3.586m) and that capital employed is represented by net assets of £32.150m in 1998 (1997 £26.848), the return on capital employed appears to have fallen from 13.4% in 1997 to 11.2% in 1998. But that fails to recognise: (i) goodwill written off during this and previous years, just under £3m; (ii) that only part of a year's profit/loss was included as regards the businesses acquired. Note 20 reveals that the two companies acquired *lost* £415,000 in the part year before they were acquired.

Solution 17.1

The effective rate of tax (i.e. taxation as a percentage of pre-tax profits) might be: (a) much less, or (b) much greater, than the normal rate of UK corporation tax because of:

Cause	*Effect*
Adjustments to previous years	(a) or (b)
Disallowed expenses	(b)
Franked income	(a)
Capital gains	(a)
Loans (see page …)	(b)
Losses and loss relief	(a) or (b)
Overseas income	(a) or (b)
Exceptional items	(a) or (b)

If an abnormal tax charge is not explained in the note on taxation, it may be referred to by the chairman, or in the directors' report, operating or financial review.

An abnormal tax charge is important because it directly affects after tax profits, and hence earnings per share, the p-e ratio and cover. And, less obviously, the effect is not proportionate. For example, take a company with pre-tax profits of £100m which has 1000m 10p ordinary shares. If the effective tax rate is 30%, tax is £30m and the after tax profit £70m. Were that rate to increase (because, say, a greater proportion was earned overseas and subject to higher rates of tax) to 35%, the after tax profits would fall (on the same income) to £65m, i.e. by 5/70ths = 7.14%.

Solution 18.1

1. Earnings per share (e.p.s.) are the amount of profit on ordinary activities, after tax and all other charges, that has been earned for each ordinary share

$$\text{e.p.s} = \frac{\text{Profit attributable to ordinary shareholders}}{\text{Number of ordinary shares in issue}}$$

   Adjustments are necessary where there is:

   - a scrip (bonus) issue or share split;
   - an issue of shares in an acquisition;
   - a rights issue;

   during the period. These adjustments are explained on page 151.

2. One might use the e.p.s. figure:

   - in computing a price earnings ratio;
   - to compute cover or dividend payout ratio;
   - in assessing earnings growth;
   - as a basis in estimating future earnings.

   Where dilution may arise (because of, say, convertibles, warrants or options) it may be necessary to show the fully diluted earnings.

3. Some companies compute their own preferred versions (as well) because they feel their

method of calculating earnings provides better comparability (or because they do not like hefty charges for exceptional items reducing their apparent earnings) or show earnings on an IIMR basis (for much the same reasons).

Solution 19.1

The 1995 net cash inflow from operating activities of CORDIANT was less than that in 1994 because:

* The two principal components of cash inflow from operations tend to be:

  1. Operating profit: which was only £28.3m, against £44.5m in 1994; and
  2. Depreciation: unchanged at £25.7m.

* But cash flow is also affected by increased working capital demands:

  1. Increase in work in progress (£9.4m in 1995; £8.0m in 1994);
  2. Increase in debtors (£54.8m in 1995, £77.8m in 1994); and while the increase in creditors £38.6m operated in the reverse direction, it was far less than the increase of £86.1m the previous year. Had the increase in creditors been only £38.6m in 1994, the working capital requirement would have been £47.5m greater, and the cash generated from operations not £58.9m but £12.4m.

* In each year property provisions were utilised (£10.3m in 1995 and £11.8m in 1994). These had already been charged against the profits of earlier years, but the cash was not spent until 1995 and 1994 respectively.

Solution 20.1
BEAR BONES GROUP

1. Sales in the group profit and loss account will consist of the entire sales of all four companies added together.
2. The operating profit appearing in the group profit and loss account will consist of the entire operating profit of all four companies added together.
3. Since only Brown Bear is a foreign company it is likely that the foreign tax represents Canadian tax on Brown Bear's profits; but attempts have been made by foreign countries (like India) to tax profits deemed to have been made by companies exporting to the country concerned; so it could represent a tax on any of the companies.
4. Minority interests £321,000 will represent 25% of the after tax profits of Brown Bear translated into £; plus 50% of the after tax profits of Bear Huggs.

5. The item 'Dividends proposed', appearing in the group profit and loss account, will represent the dividends proposed by Bear Bones Group. It will not include any dividends paid by Bear Huggs.
6. The item 'Minority interests £34,190,000' appearing in the group balance sheet will consist of 50% of the net assets of Bear Huggs plus 25% of the net assets of Brown Bear.

Solution 21.1
GIBBON GROUP

1. The transactions represented acquisitions under the terms of FRS 6, otherwise the whole of the profits of all companies involved would appear as continuing operations, there would have been no Acquisitions column, and the figures for 1995 would have been shown as 'restated'.
2. Consideration was:

	£000
Cash	767
Issue of shares	400
Deferred consideration – cash	251
Deferred consideration – shares to be issued	150
Total	1,568

Total consideration	1,568

Assets acquired were:

	Fair value £000	
Fixed assets	258	
Stocks	255	
Debtors	272	
Cash at bank and in hand	153	
Creditors	(911)	
		27
Goodwill		1,541

3. Analysis of the net outflow of cash in respect of the acquisition of …

	£000
Cash consideration	767
Cash acquired	(153)
Net outflow	614

4. The amount credited in respect of these transactions:

   * to share premium account would be nil because the share issues met the conditions in Sections 131–134 of the Companies Act 1985;

- to merger reserve would be £400,000, less £22,000 credited to share capital = £378,000.

5. To assess the companies' profitability we would need to know when the acquisitions took place. One of the two companies involved was acquired on 2 January 1996 and the other on 9 February 1996; so they contributed nearly 3 months, and nearly 2 months, profits, respectively. So, in a full year one is looking not at £64,000, but at perhaps 5 × £64,000 = £320,000. Looks like a bargain.

Solution 22.1

1. The company column is always zero in the case of subsidiaries. As explained in step 6 on page 176, the process of consolidation requires one to omit the share capital of the subsidiary, reserves, and the investment in the subsidiary, which have already been taken into account in steps 1 to 3.
2. A quasi-subsidiary is 'a company, trust, partnership or other vehicle that, though not fulfilling the definition of a subsidiary, is directly or indirectly controlled by the reporting entity and gives benefits for that entity that are in substance no different from those that would arise were the vehicle a subsidiary'.

   A 50% owned quasi-subsidiary is treated in the group accounts just as though it were a subsidiary, i.e. 100% of the value of its assets and liabilities is included and 100% of its operating profit appears in group operating profit, whereas a 50% associate (like Britannia New Homes (Scotland) Ltd) is not consolidated. The group's share of its operating profit does not appear in group operating profit but on a line immediately below; and it is the share of the profit not the whole profit.
3. The company item 'Investments in associated undertaking' is zero in both years because the investment is held not by the holding company but by Tay Homes (Scotland) Ltd.
4. 'Deficiency in net assets of associated undertaking' represents Tay Homes' share of the excess of liabilities over assets of Britannia New Homes (Scotland) Ltd. The change between 1997 and 1998 represents the group's share of the loss of Britannia New Homes (Scotland) Ltd in 1998.
5. The item 'Loan to associated undertaking' represents the entire amount of a loan made by the Group to its associate (not just the group share).

The 'Deficiency in net assets of associated undertaking' (£272,000 in 1998; £181,000 in 1997) represents the cost of the shares in the associate less the group's share of losses of the associated company. That is to say, losses have wiped out not only its share of earlier profits (if any) but its investment too.

One is left asking:

- How long has this been going on?
- Is there a liability to other joint venturers or the bank?
- How secure is the loan to the joint venture?

Solution 23.1

1. (a) Beyond (1994) made profit for the year 1999 of 7.200m Bacs. This would be translated in the 1999 accounts at the closing rate of 2.400 Bacs = £1, that is as £3.000m.

   (b) Beyond (1994) made profit for the year 2000 of 12.000m Bacs. In the 2000 accounts, this would be translated at the closing rate of 3.00 Bacs = £1, that is as £4.000m.
2. At 31 December 1999 Pie in the Sky plc had a net investment in Beyond (1994) of 38.800m Bacs. In the 1999 accounts this would have been translated at 2.4 Bacs = £1, i.e. as £16.167m. Retranslated at the 2000 rate of 3.00 Bacs = £1 this becomes £12.933m. The difference between £16.167m and £12.333m represents an unfavourable translation difference in 2000 of £3.833m (allowing for rounding).

   At 31 December 1998 Pie in the Sky plc had a net investment in Beyond (1994) of 31.600m Bacs. In the 1998 accounts this would have been translated at 2.0 Bacs = £1 i.e. as £15.800m. Retranslated at the 1999 rate of 2.400 Bacs = £1 this becomes £13.167m. The difference between £15.800m and £13.167m represents an unfavourable translation difference in 1999 of £2.633m.

   So the entry in the statement of total gains and losses for 2000 would be:

	2000	1999
	£m	£m
Currency translation differences	(3.833)	(2.633)

Solution 24.1

- The first clue is the reference to 'stores'. This is a fairly substantial store company with just over 400 stores (averaging 12,350 sq ft). It is in fact STOREHOUSE which at the time of writing ranked 10th in the Retailers – General sector and owns BHS and Mothercare.
- A major change occurred in 1993:

  (a) The number of stores fell from 736 to 425.
  (b) There were exceptional items in both 1993 and 1994 (£31.4m and £6.4m respec-

tively). This looks like the closure or sale of stores.

(c) The dividend of 5p against earnings of 2.6p in 1992 suggests there was a marked drop in profitability around that time.

- Turnover was drifting sideways (it increased in the last two years from £1,045.5m to £1,083.6m, i.e. by 3.6%, and in the last year by 0.4%, which did not keep up with inflation.
- That was despite adding two news stores in each year and 263,000 sq ft of selling space.
- Profit margins, however, improved markedly, year by year:

	%
1992	0.85
1993	3.77
1994	6.24
1995	8.08
1996	9.41

Solution 25.1

The statements required by Cadbury (and more recently by the Combined Code) probably are not very useful to readers of accounts. Their principal purposes seems to be to educate boards of directors in their responsibilities. It is for instance difficult to believe that a group with a diverse range of activities (almost certainly spread over a number of separate locations) could operate efficiently without managers knowing what they alone could decide and what needed board approval; and what their spending approval limits were.

Solution 26.1

1. A going concern is a company or other enterprise which does not intend or need either:
   - to go into liquidation or
   - to curtail the current level of operations significantly.

2.
   (a) The directors are responsible for making appropriate enquiries to satisfy themselves that company and group have adequate resource to continue in operation existence for the foreseeable future before continuing to adopt the going concern basis of accounting;
   (b) It is the auditors' responsibility to form an independent opinion on the financial statements. Were they to consider the company was not a going concern the accounts would present a true and fair view only if they were prepared on a 'gone concern' basis and provided adequate explanations – otherwise the auditors would qualify their report.

3. The matter is important to investors because the value of shares in a break-up is only a fraction of that as a going concern. Typically the yield on an equity investment is far less than that on fixed interest securities for the simple reason that equities are expected to grown in value (to provide a hedge against inflation). A business which ceases to be a going concern is certainly not a hedge against inflation. It is a dead duck.

Solution 27.1

DIXONS GROUP

Workings:

Net cash (outflow)/inflow from operating activities

	28 weeks to 9 Nov 1996 £m	28 weeks to 11 Nov 1995 £m	52 weeks to 27 April 1996 £m	24 weeks to 27 April 1996 £m
Operating profit	53.5	34.7	128.1	93.4
Share of profit of related companies	(0.3)	–	3.0	3.0
Utilisation of store closure provision	(1.3)	(2.8)	(2.6)	0.2
Utilisation of provision for rationalisation of the Group's administrative offices	–	1.0	(1.2)	(2.2)
Depreciation	25.0	19.7	38.7	19.0
Amortisation of own shares	0.5	0.3	0.6	0.3
(Increase)/decrease in stocks	(191.7)	(187.7)	(75.9)	111.8
(Increase)/decrease in debtors	(47.9)	(78.7)	(17.4)	61.3
(Increase)/decrease in creditors	73.1	101.1	52.0	(49.1)
	(89.1)	(114.4)	119.3	233.7

Solution:

	28 weeks to 9 Nov 1996 £m	28 weeks to 11 Nov 1995 £m	52 weeks to 27 April 1996 £m	24 weeks to 27 April 1996 £m
(a) Operating profit	53.5	34.7	128.1	93.4
(b) Net cash (outflow)/inflow from operating activities	(89.1)	(114.4)	119.3	233.7

Comment:

It seems that in cash flow terms Dixons is highly seasonal. From May to early November the net cash flow from operating activities was negative (taking the average of the two years, around £100m outflow); whereas from November to April (which of course includes Christmas) it was highly positive (in 1995/96 the cash inflow was £233.7m net).

In part this is because operating profits are seasonal (£34.7m in the first half of 1995/96 against £93.4m in the second half). But it is the stocks, debtors and creditors which create much of the cash flow seasonality: increasing sharply in the first half and falling back again in the second.

Solution 28.1

1. Four widely used ratios based on the market price(s) of equity shares are:

(a) Gross dividend yield (%) =
    (Net dividend in pence per share ÷ (1 − ACT rate, if any) ÷ Ordinary share price in pence) × 100.

(b) Price/Earnings Ratio (P/E ratio or PER), which is the market price of the ordinary share divided by the earnings per share
    i.e. PER = Share price ÷ e.p.s.

(c) Price earnings growth factor (PEG) is a yardstick introduced by Jim Slater in *The Zulu Principle*. The PEG is a measure of whether a share looks overrated or underrated:

    PEG = Price/Earnings ratio ÷ Prospective growth rate of e.p.s.

(d) Increase (decrease) in price (normally the closing price) on the day, week, month or year:

    (Share price at end of period ÷ Share price at end of previous period × 100) − 100%

2. Four other ways in which an investor or analyst might use the price history of a share are:

   - to draw a chart depicting the share's price behaviour;
   - to compare the behaviour of an individual share against (a) the FT-SE 100 or (b) the All-Share Index;
   - to compare the behaviour of an individual share with that of its sector index or of another share in the same sector;
   - to value the portfolio for any purpose, e.g. inheritance tax purposes or to project the capital gains tax that would be payable on the sale of a holding.

3. Four ways of obtaining share prices are:

   - Look up the price in the City pages of the *FT* or of any good daily paper. Where a daily paper is already purchased or is available in a library, this involves no additional cost; but it is tiresome to keep track of a large number of prices.
   - Look the price up on teletext (this again involves no additional cost assuming one has a TV with teletext) or use a teletext board in a PC (once purchased, with appropriate software this will update prices automatically at a stated time daily, free; and it is possible to watch prices during the day updated every couple of hours).
   - Download prices from a modem-based service like Prestel or watch them live using that service.
   - Purchase data from a data source, say, weekly on disk or CD-ROM.

Solution 29.1

This question is answerable directly from the text.

Solution 30.1

Where a company is listed both in the UK and in the US, the note explaining differences in GAAP between the two countries will be of interest:

(a) to an analyst because: it sheds futher light on certain types of transaction; it enables him to use actual figures rather make his own estimates of, say, full provision for deferred tax; information in respect of goodwill written off in past periods direct to reserve may enable him to compute a reliable return on capital employed; he may well prefer the US treatment of pension costs to the UK.

(b) **to a US investor** because he is familiar with US GAAP but not with UK GAAP.

(c) **to a student of accounting theory** because: where US GAAP and UK GAAP differ it is questionable whether both can be 'right'; as international trade and cooperation increase, there is a tendency for the GAAPs of industrialised and major trading nations in particular to move ever closer, i.e. 'it is likely to happen here too'.

INDEX